CIMA

Paper P1

Performance Operations

Study Text

Published by: Kaplan Publishing UK

Unit 2 The Business Centre, Molly Millars Lane, Wokingham, Berkshire RG41 2QZ

Acknowledgements

The CIMA Publishing trade mark is reproduced with kind permission of CIMA

British Library Cataloguing in Publication Data
A catalogue record for this book is available from the British Library

ISBN: 978-0-85732-975-2

Printed and bound in Great Britain

Contents

		Page
Chapter 1	CIMA verb hierarchy – Operational level exams	1
Chapter 2	Traditional costing	9
Chapter 3	Techniques for modern environments	59
Chapter 4	Modern costing – throughput accounting	95
Chapter 5	Modern costing – activity-based and environmental costing	121
Chapter 6	Variance analysis: calculations	169
Chapter 7	Variance analysis: discussion elements	243
Chapter 8	Advanced variances	271
Chapter 9	The budgeting framework	333
Chapter 10	Forecasting techniques	381
Chapter 11	The treatment of uncertainty and risk in decision making	417
Chapter 12	Investment appraisal techniques	475
Chapter 13	Further aspects of investment appraisal	541
Chapter 14	Working capital management	619
Chapter 15	Working capital management – inventory control	663
Chapter 16	Working capital management – cash control	691
Chapter 17	Working capital management – accounts receivable and payable	731
Chapter 18	Short-term finance and investments	771

Contents

Paper Introduction

Acknowledgements

Every effort has been made to contact the holders of copyright material, but if any here have been inadvertently overlooked the publishers will be pleased to make the necessary arrangements at the first opportunity.

How to Use the Materials

These Official CIMA learning materials brought to you by CIMA Publishing and Kaplan Publishing have been carefully designed to make your learning experience as easy as possible and to give you the best chances of success in your *Performance Operations'* examination.

The product range contains a number of features to help you in the study process. They include:

- a detailed explanation of all syllabus areas;

- extensive 'practical' materials, including readings from relevant journals;

- generous question practice, together with full solutions.

This Study Text has been designed with the needs of homestudy and distance learning candidates in mind. Such students require very full coverage of the syllabus topics, and also the facility to undertake extensive question practice. However, the Study Text is also ideal for fully taught courses.

The main body of the text is divided into a number of chapters, each of which is organised on the following pattern:

- *Detailed learning outcomes.* You should assimilate these before beginning detailed work on the chapter, so that you can appreciate where your studies are leading.

- *Step-by-step topic coverage.* This is the heart of each chapter, containing detailed explanatory text supported where appropriate by worked examples and exercises. You should work carefully through this section, ensuring that you understand the material being explained and can tackle the examples and exercises successfully. Remember that in many cases knowledge is cumulative; if you fail to digest earlier material thoroughly, you may struggle to understand later chapters.

- *Question practice.* The test of how well you have learned the material is your ability to tackle computer based standard questions. Make a serious attempt at producing your own answers, but at this stage don't be too concerned about attempting the questions in exam conditions. In particular, it is more important to absorb the material thoroughly by completing a full solution than to observe the time limits that would apply in the actual exam.

- *Solutions.* Avoid the temptation merely to 'audit' the solutions provided. It is an illusion to think that this provides the same benefits as you would gain from a serious attempt of your own. However, if you are struggling to get started on a question you should read the introductory guidance provided at the beginning of the solution, and then make your own attempt before referring back to the full solution.

Icon Explanations

Definition – these sections explain important areas of knowledge which must be understood and reproduced in an exam environment.

Key Point – identifies topics which are key to success and are often examined.

Supplementary reading – indentifies a more detailed explanation of key terms, these sections will help to provide a deeper understanding of core areas. Reference to this text is vital when self studying.

Test Your Understanding – following key points and definitions are exercises which give the opportunity to assess the understanding of these core areas.

Illustration – to help develop an understanding of topics and the test your understanding exercises the illustrative examples can be used.

Exclamation Mark – this symbol signifies a topic which can be more difficult to understand, when reviewing these areas care should be taken.

Study technique

Passing exams is partly a matter of intellectual ability, but however accomplished you are in that respect you can improve your chances significantly by the use of appropriate study and revision techniques. In this section we briefly outline some tips for effective study during the earlier stages of your approach to the exam.

Planning

To begin with, formal planning is essential to get the best return from the time you spend studying. Estimate how much time in total you are going to need for each subject you are studying for the Operational Level. Remember that you need to allow time for revision as well as for initial study of the material. You may find it helpful to read 'Pass First Time!' second edition by David R. Harris, ISBN 9781856177986. This book will provide you with proven study techniques. Chapter by chapter it covers the building blocks of successful learning and examination techniques. This is the ultimate guide to passing your CIMA exams, written by a past CIMA examiner and shows you how to earn all the marks you deserve, and explains how to avoid the most common pitfalls. You may also find "The E Word: Kaplan's Guide to Passing Exams" by Stuart PedleySmith ISBN: 9780857322050 helpful. Stuart PedleySmith is a senior lecturer at Kaplan Financial and a qualified accountant specialising in financial management. His natural curiosity and wider interests have led him to look beyond the technical content of financial management to the processes and journey that we call education. He has become fascinated by the whole process of learning and the exam skills and techniques that contribute towards success in the classroom. This book is for anyone who has to sit an exam and wants to give themselves a better chance of passing. It is easy to read, written in a common sense style and full of anecdotes, facts, and practical tips. It also contains synopses of interviews with people involved in the learning and examining process.

With your study material before you, decide which chapters you are going to study in each week, and which weeks you will devote to revision and final question practice.

Prepare a written schedule summarising the above and stick to it!

It is essential to know your syllabus. As your studies progress, you will become more familiar with how long it takes to cover topics in sufficient depth. Your timetable may need to be adapted to allocate enough time for the whole syllabus.

Students are advised to refer to the notice of examinable legislation published regularly in CIMA's magazine (Financial Management), the students newsletter (Velocity) and on the CIMA website, to ensure they are up-to-date.

Tips for effective studying

(1) Aim to find a quiet and undisturbed location for your study, and plan as far as possible to use the same period of time each day. Getting into a routine helps to avoid wasting time. Make sure that you have all the materials you need before you begin so as to minimise interruptions.

(2) Store all your materials in one place, so that you do not waste time searching for items around the house. If you have to pack everything away after each study period, keep them in a box, or even a suitcase, which will not be disturbed until the next time.

(3) Limit distractions. To make the most effective use of your study periods you should be able to apply total concentration, so turn off the TV, set your phones to message mode, and put up your 'do not disturb' sign.

(4) Your timetable will tell you which topic to study. However, before diving in and becoming engrossed in the finer points, make sure you have an overall picture of all the areas that need to be covered by the end of that session. After an hour, allow yourself a short break and move away from your books. With experience, you will learn to assess the pace you need to work at. You should also allow enough time to read relevant articles from newspapers and journals, which will supplement your knowledge and demonstrate a wider perspective.

(5) Work carefully through a chapter, making notes as you go. When you have covered a suitable amount of material, vary the pattern by attempting a practice question. Preparing an answer plan is a good habit to get into, while you are both studying and revising, and also in the examination room. It helps to impose a structure on your solutions, and avoids rambling. When you have finished your attempt, make notes of any mistakes you made, or any areas that you failed to cover or covered more briefly.

(6) Make notes as you study, and discover the techniques that work best for you. Your notes may be in the form of lists, bullet points, diagrams, summaries, 'mind maps' or the written word, but remember that you will need to refer back to them at a later date, so they must be intelligible. If you are on a taught course, make sure you highlight any issues you would like to follow up with your lecturer.

(7) Organise your notes. Make sure that all your notes, calculations etc., can be effectively filed and easily retrieved later.

Structure of subjects and learning outcomes

Each subject within the syllabus is divided into a number of broad syllabus topics. The topics contain one or more lead learning outcomes, related component learning outcomes and indicative knowledge content.

A learning outcome has two main purposes:

(a) To define the skill or ability that a well prepared candidate should be able to exhibit in the examination

(b) To demonstrate the approach likely to be taken in examination questions

The learning outcomes are part of a hierarchy of learning objectives. The verbs used at the beginning of each learning outcome relate to a specific learning objective and they are explored further in chapter 1.

PAPER P1
PERFORMANCE OPERATIONS

Syllabus overview

This paper primarily deals with the tools and techniques that generate information needed to evaluate and control present and projected performance. Thus, forecasting key variables, recognising uncertainties attached to future events, is a basis for budget construction; the budget is then used with costing systems to evaluate actual performance. Project appraisal relies similarly on future financial projections to provide the information on which managers can evaluate expected performance and actual outcomes. Both budgeting and project appraisal emphasise the critical importance of optimising cash flow and the final section of the paper continues this theme from the perspective of managing working capital.

Syllabus structure

The syllabus comprises the following topics and study weightings:

A	Cost Accounting Systems	30%
B	Forecasting and Budgeting Techniques	10%
C	Project Appraisal	25%
D	Dealing with Uncertainty in Analysis	15%
E	Managing Short Term Finance	20%

Assessment strategy

There will be a written examination paper of three hours, plus 20 minutes of pre-examination question paper reading time. The examination paper will have the following sections:

Section A – 20 marks
A variety of compulsory objective test questions, each worth between two and four marks. Mini scenarios may be given, to which a group of questions relate.

Section B – 30 marks
Six compulsory short answer questions, each worth five marks. A short scenario may be given, to which some or all questions relate.

Section C – 50 marks
One or two compulsory questions. Short scenarios may be given, to which questions relate.

P1 – A. COST ACCOUNTING SYSTEMS (30%)

Learning outcomes
On completion of their studies students should be able to:

Lead	Component	Indicative syllabus content
1. discuss costing methods and their results.	(a) compare and contrast marginal (or variable), throughput and absorption accounting methods in respect of profit reporting and stock valuation;	• Marginal (or variable), throughput and absorption accounting systems of profit reporting and stock valuation. [2], [4]
	(b) discuss a report which reconciles budget and actual profit using absorption and/or marginal costing principles;	• Activity-based costing as a system of profit reporting and stock valuation. [5]
	(c) discuss activity-based costing as compared with traditional marginal and absorption costing methods, including its relative advantages and disadvantages as a system of cost accounting;	• Criticisms of standard costing in general and in advanced manufacturing environments in particular. [3], [7]
		• Integration of standard costing with marginal cost accounting, absorption cost accounting and throughput accounting. [2], [4]
	(d) apply standard costing methods, within costing systems, including the reconciliation of budgeted and actual profit margins;	• Manufacturing standards for material, labour, variable overhead and fixed overhead. [6]
		• Price/rate and usage/efficiency variances for materials, labour and variable overhead. [6]
	(e) explain why and how standards are set in manufacturing and in service industries with particular reference to the maximisation of efficiency and minimisation of waste;	• Further subdivision of total usage/efficiency variances into mix and yield components. (*Note:* The calculation of mix variances on both individual and average valuation bases is required). [8]
	(f) interpret material, labour, variable overhead, fixed overhead and sales variances, distinguishing between planning and operational variances;	• Fixed overhead expenditure and volume variances. (*Note:* the subdivision of fixed overhead volume variance into capacity and efficiency elements will not be examined). [6]
		• Planning and operational variances. [8]
	(g) prepare reports using a range of internal and external benchmarks and interpret the results;	• Standards and variances in service industries (including the phenomenon of 'McDonaldization'), public services (e.g. Health), (including the use of 'diagnostic related' or 'reference' groups), and the professions (e.g. labour mix variances in audit work). [7]
		• Sales price and sales revenue/margin volume variances (calculation of the latter on a unit basis related to revenue, gross margin and contribution margin). Application of these variances to all sectors, including professional services and retail analysis. [6]
	(h) explain the impact of just-in-time manufacturing methods on cost accounting and the use of 'back-flush accounting' when work-in-progress stock is minimal.	• Interpretation of variances: interrelationship, significance. [7]
		• Benchmarking. [7]
		• Back-flush accounting in just-in-time production environments. The benefits of just-in-time production, total quality management and theory of constraints and the possible impacts of these methods on cost accounting and performance measurement. [3]

Learning outcomes On completion of their studies students should be able to:		Indicative syllabus content
Lead	Component	
2. explain the role of MRP and ERP systems.	(a) explain the role of MRP and ERP systems in supporting standard costing systems, calculating variances and facilitating the posting of ledger entries.	• MRP and ERP systems for resource planning and the integration of accounting functions with other systems, such as purchase ordering and production planning. [3]
3. apply principles of environmental costing.	(a) apply principles of environmental costing in identifying relevant internalised costs and externalised environmental impacts of the organisation's activities.	• Types of internalised costs relating to the environment (e.g. emissions permits, taxes, waste disposal costs) and key externalised environmental impacts, especially carbon, energy and water usage. Principles for associating such costs and impacts with activities and output. [5]

P1 – B. FORECASTING AND BUDGETING TECHNIQUES (10%)

Learning outcomes On completion of their studies students should be able to:		Indicative syllabus content
Lead	Component	
1. explain the purposes of forecasts, plans and budgets.	(a) explain why organisations prepare forecasts and plans; (b) explain the purposes of budgets, including planning, communication, co-ordination, motivation, authorisation, control and evaluation, and how these may conflict.	• The role of forecasts and plans in resource allocation, performance evaluation and control. [9] • The purposes of budgets and the budgeting process, and conflicts that can arise (e.g. between budgets for realistic planning and budgets based on 'hard to achieve' targets for motivation). [9]
2. prepare forecasts of financial results.	(a) calculate projected product/service volumes employing appropriate forecasting techniques; (b) calculate projected revenues and costs based on product/service volumes, pricing strategies and cost structures.	• Time series analysis including moving totals and averages, treatment of seasonality, trend analysis using regression analysis and the application of these techniques in forecasting product and service volumes. [10] • Fixed, variable, semi-variable and activity-based categorisations of cost and their application in projecting financial results. [2]. [5]
3. prepare budgets based on forecasts.	(a) prepare a budget for any account in the master budget, based on projections/ forecasts and managerial targets; (b) apply alternative approaches to budgeting.	• Mechanics of budget construction: limiting factors, component budgets and the master budget, and their interaction. [10] • Alternative approaches to budget creation, including incremental approaches, zero-based budgeting and activity-based budgets. [10]

P1 – C. PROJECT APPRAISAL (25%)

Learning outcomes
On completion of their studies students should be able to:

Lead	Component	Indicative syllabus content
1. prepare information to support project appraisal.	(a) explain the processes involved in making long-term decisions; (b) apply the principles of relevant cash flow analysis to long-run projects that continue for several years; (c) calculate project cash flows, accounting for tax and inflation, and apply perpetuities to derive 'end of project' value where appropriate; (d) apply activity-based costing techniques to derive approximate 'long-run' product or service costs appropriate for use in strategic decision making; (e) explain the financial consequences of dealing with long-run projects, in particular the importance of accounting for the 'time value of money'; (f) apply sensitivity analysis to cash flow parameters to identify those to which net present value is particularly sensitive; (g) prepare decision support information for management, integrating financial and non-financial considerations.	• The process of investment decision making, including origination of proposals, creation of capital budgets, go/no go decisions on individual projects (where judgements on qualitative issues interact with financial analysis), and post audit of completed projects. [13] • Identification and calculation of relevant project cash flows taking account of inflation, tax, and 'final' project value where appropriate. [13] • Activity-based costing to derive approximate 'long-run' costs appropriate for use in strategic decision making. [13] • Need for and method of discounting. [12] • Sensitivity analysis to identify the input variables that most affect the chosen measure of project worth (payback, ARR, NPV or IRR). [13] • Identifying and integrating non-financial factors in long-term decisions. [13] • Methods of dealing with particular problems: the use of annuities in comparing projects with unequal lives and the profitability index in capital rationing situations. [12], [13]
2. evaluate project proposals.	(a) evaluate project proposals using the techniques of investment appraisal; (b) compare and contrast the alternative techniques of investment appraisal; (c) prioritise projects that are mutually exclusive, involve unequal lives and/or are subject to capital rationing.	• The techniques of investment appraisal: payback, discounted payback, accounting rate of return, net present value and internal rate of return. [12] • Application of the techniques of investment appraisal to project cash flows and evaluation of the strengths and weaknesses of the techniques. [12]

P1 – D. DEALING WITH UNCERTAINTY IN ANALYSIS (15%)

Learning outcomes
On completion of their studies students should be able to:

Lead	Component	Indicative syllabus content
1. analyse information to assess the impact on decisions of variables with uncertain values.	(a) analyse the impact of uncertainty and risk on decision models that may be based on relevant cash flows, learning curves, discounting techniques etc; (b) apply sensitivity analysis to both short and long-run decision models to identify variables that might have significant impacts on project outcomes; (c) analyse risk and uncertainty by calculating expected values and standard deviations together with probability tables and histograms; (d) prepare expected value tables; (e) calculate the value of information; (f) apply decision trees.	• The nature of risk and uncertainty. [11] • Sensitivity analysis in decision modelling and the use of computer software for "what if" analysis. [11] • Assignment of probabilities to key variables in decision models. [11] • Analysis of probabilistic models and interpretation of distributions of project outcomes. [11] • Expected value tables and the value of information. [11] • Decision trees for multi-stage decision problems. [11]

P1 – E. MANAGING SHORT TERM FINANCE (20%)

Learning outcomes
On completion of their studies students should be able to:

Lead	Component	Indicative syllabus content
1. analyse the working capital position and identify areas for improvement.	(a) explain the importance of cash flow and working capital management; (b) interpret working capital ratios for business sectors; (c) analyse cash-flow forecasts over a twelve-month period; (d) discuss measures to improve a cash forecast situation; (e) analyse trade debtor and creditor information; (f) analyse the impacts of alternative debtor and creditor policies; (g) analyse the impacts of alternative policies for stock management.	• The link between cash, profit and the balance sheet. [14] • The credit cycle from receipt of customer order to cash receipt and the payment cycle from agreeing the order to making payment. [14] • Working capital ratios (e.g. debtor days, stock days, creditor days, current ratio, quick ratio) and the working capital cycle. [14] • Working capital characteristics of different businesses (e.g. supermarkets being heavily funded by creditors) and the importance of industry comparisons. [14] • Cash-flow forecasts, use of spreadsheets to assist in this in terms of changing variables (e.g. interest rates, inflation) and in consolidating forecasts. [16] • Variables that are most easily changed, delayed or brought forward in a forecast. [16] • Methods for evaluating payment terms and settlement discounts. [17] • Preparation and interpretation of age analyses of debtors and creditors. [17] • Establishing collection targets on an appropriate basis (e.g. motivational issues in managing credit control). [17] • Centralised versus decentralised purchasing. [16] • The relationship between purchasing and stock control. [15] • Principles of the economic order quantity (EOQ) model and criticisms thereof. [15]
2. identify short-term funding and investment opportunities.	(a) identify sources of short-term funding; (b) identify alternatives for investment of short-term cash surpluses; (c) identify appropriate methods of finance for trading internationally; (d) illustrate numerically the financial impact of short-term funding and investment methods.	• Use and abuse of trade creditors as a source of finance. [17] • Types and features of short-term finance: trade creditors, overdrafts, short-term loans and debt factoring. [17] • The principles of investing short term (i.e. maturity, return, security, liquidity and diversification). [18] • Types of investments (e.g. interest-bearing bank accounts, negotiable instruments including certificates of deposit, short-term treasury bills, and securities). [18] • The difference between the coupon on debt and the yield to maturity. [18] • Export finance (e.g. documentary credits, bills of exchange, export factoring, forfeiting). [18]

PRESENT VALUE TABLE

Present value of $1, that is $(1+r)^{-n}$ where r = interest rate; n = number of periods until payment or receipt.

Periods (n)	Interest rates (r)									
	1%	2%	3%	4%	5%	6%	7%	8%	9%	10%
1	0.990	0.980	0.971	0.962	0.952	0.943	0.935	0.926	0.917	0.909
2	0.980	0.961	0.943	0.925	0.907	0.890	0.873	0.857	0.842	0.826
3	0.971	0.942	0.915	0.889	0.864	0.840	0.816	0.794	0.772	0.751
4	0.961	0.924	0.888	0.855	0.823	0.792	0.763	0.735	0.708	0.683
5	0.951	0.906	0.863	0.822	0.784	0.747	0.713	0.681	0.650	0.621
6	0.942	0.888	0.837	0.790	0.746	0705	0.666	0.630	0.596	0.564
7	0.933	0.871	0.813	0.760	0.711	0.665	0.623	0.583	0.547	0.513
8	0.923	0.853	0.789	0.731	0.677	0.627	0.582	0.540	0.502	0.467
9	0.914	0.837	0.766	0.703	0.645	0.592	0.544	0.500	0.460	0.424
10	0.905	0.820	0.744	0.676	0.614	0.558	0.508	0.463	0.422	0.386
11	0.896	0.804	0.722	0.650	0.585	0.527	0.475	0.429	0.388	0.350
12	0.887	0.788	0.701	0.625	0.557	0.497	0.444	0.397	0.356	0.319
13	0.879	0.773	0.681	0.601	0.530	0.469	0.415	0.368	0.326	0.290
14	0.870	0.758	0.661	0.577	0.505	0.442	0.388	0.340	0.299	0.263
15	0.861	0.743	0.642	0.555	0.481	0.417	0.362	0.315	0.275	0.239
16	0.853	0.728	0.623	0.534	0.458	0.394	0.339	0.292	0.252	0.218
17	0.844	0.714	0.605	0.513	0.436	0.371	0.317	0.270	0.231	0.198
18	0.836	0.700	0.587	0.494	0.416	0.350	0.296	0.250	0.212	0.180
19	0.828	0.686	0.570	0.475	0.396	0.331	0.277	0.232	0.194	0.164
20	0.820	0.673	0.554	0.456	0.377	0.312	0.258	0.215	0.178	0.149

Periods (n)	Interest rates (r)									
	11%	12%	13%	14%	15%	16%	17%	18%	19%	20%
1	0.901	0.893	0.885	0.877	0.870	0.862	0.855	0.847	0.840	0.833
2	0.812	0.797	0.783	0.769	0.756	0.743	0.731	0.718	0.706	0.694
3	0.731	0.712	0.693	0.675	0.658	0.641	0.624	0.609	0.593	0.579
4	0.659	0.636	0.613	0.592	0.572	0.552	0.534	0.516	0.499	0.482
5	0.593	0.567	0.543	0.519	0.497	0.476	0.456	0.437	0.419	0.402
6	0.535	0.507	0.480	0.456	0.432	0.410	0.390	0.370	0.352	0.335
7	0.482	0.452	0.425	0.400	0.376	0.354	0.333	0.314	0.296	0.279
8	0.434	0.404	0.376	0.351	0.327	0.305	0.285	0.266	0.249	0.233
9	0.391	0.361	0.333	0.308	0.284	0.263	0.243	0.225	0.209	0.194
10	0.352	0.322	0.295	0.270	0.247	0.227	0.208	0.191	0.176	0.162
11	0.317	0.287	0.261	0.237	0.215	0.195	0.178	0.162	0.148	0.135
12	0.286	0.257	0.231	0.208	0.187	0.168	0.152	0.137	0.124	0.112
13	0.258	0.229	0.204	0.182	0.163	0.145	0.130	0.116	0.104	0.093
14	0.232	0.205	0.181	0.160	0.141	0.125	0.111	0.099	0.088	0.078
15	0.209	0.183	0.160	0.140	0.123	0.108	0.095	0.084	0.079	0.065
16	0.188	0.163	0.141	0.123	0.107	0.093	0.081	0.071	0.062	0.054
17	0.170	0.146	0.125	0.108	0.093	0.080	0.069	0.060	0.052	0.045
18	0.153	0.130	0.111	0.095	0.081	0.069	0.059	0.051	0.044	0.038
19	0.138	0.116	0.098	0.083	0.070	0.060	0.051	0.043	0.037	0.031
20	0.124	0.104	0.087	0.073	0.061	0.051	0.043	0.037	0.031	0.026

Cumulative present value of $1 per annum, Receivable or Payable at the end of each year for n years $\frac{1-(1+r)^{-n}}{r}$

Periods (n)	Interest rates (r)									
	1%	2%	3%	4%	5%	6%	7%	8%	9%	10%
1	0.990	0.980	0.971	0.962	0.952	0.943	0.935	0.926	0.917	0.909
2	1.970	1.942	1.913	1.886	1.859	1.833	1.808	1.783	1.759	1.736
3	2.941	2.884	2.829	2.775	2.723	2.673	2.624	2.577	2.531	2.487
4	3.902	3.808	3.717	3.630	3.546	3.465	3.387	3.312	3.240	3.170
5	4.853	4.713	4.580	4.452	4.329	4.212	4.100	3.993	3.890	3.791
6	5.795	5.601	5.417	5.242	5.076	4.917	4.767	4.623	4.486	4.355
7	6.728	6.472	6.230	6.002	5.786	5.582	5.389	5.206	5.033	4.868
8	7.652	7.325	7.020	6.733	6.463	6.210	5.971	5.747	5.535	5.335
9	8.566	8.162	7.786	7.435	7.108	6.802	6.515	6.247	5.995	5.759
10	9.471	8.983	8.530	8.111	7.722	7.360	7.024	6.710	6.418	6.145
11	10.368	9.787	9.253	8.760	8.306	7.887	7.499	7.139	6.805	6.495
12	11.255	10.575	9.954	9.385	8.863	8.384	7.943	7.536	7.161	6.814
13	12.134	11.348	10.635	9.986	9.394	8.853	8.358	7.904	7.487	7.103
14	13.004	12.106	11.296	10.563	9.899	9.295	8.745	8.244	7.786	7.367
15	13.865	12.849	11.938	11.118	10.380	9.712	9.108	8.559	8.061	7.606
16	14.718	13.578	12.561	11.652	10.838	10.106	9.447	8.851	8.313	7.824
17	15.562	14.292	13.166	12.166	11.274	10.477	9.763	9.122	8.544	8.022
18	16.398	14.992	13.754	12.659	11.690	10.828	10.059	9.372	8.756	8.201
19	17.226	15.679	14.324	13.134	12.085	11.158	10.336	9.604	8.950	8.365
20	18.046	16.351	14.878	13.590	12.462	11.470	10.594	9.818	9.129	8.514

Periods (n)	Interest rates (r)									
	11%	12%	13%	14%	15%	16%	17%	18%	19%	20%
1	0.901	0.893	0.885	0.877	0.870	0.862	0.855	0.847	0.840	0.833
2	1.713	1.690	1.668	1.647	1.626	1.605	1.585	1.566	1.547	1.528
3	2.444	2.402	2.361	2.322	2.283	2.246	2.210	2.174	2.140	2.106
4	3.102	3.037	2.974	2.914	2.855	2.798	2.743	2.690	2.639	2.589
5	3.696	3.605	3.517	3.433	3.352	3.274	3.199	3.127	3.058	2.991
6	4.231	4.111	3.998	3.889	3.784	3.685	3.589	3.498	3.410	3.326
7	4.712	4.564	4.423	4.288	4.160	4.039	3.922	3.812	3.706	3.605
8	5.146	4.968	4.799	4.639	4.487	4.344	4.207	4.078	3.954	3.837
9	5.537	5.328	5.132	4.946	4.772	4.607	4.451	4.303	4.163	4.031
10	5.889	5.650	5.426	5.216	5.019	4.833	4.659	4.494	4.339	4.192
11	6.207	5.938	5.687	5.453	5.234	5.029	4.836	4.656	4.486	4.327
12	6.492	6.194	5.918	5.660	5.421	5.197	4.988	7.793	4.611	4.439
13	6.750	6.424	6.122	5.842	5.583	5.342	5.118	4.910	4.715	4.533
14	6.982	6.628	6.302	6.002	5.724	5.468	5.229	5.008	4.802	4.611
15	7.191	6.811	6.462	6.142	5.847	5.575	5.324	5.092	4.876	4.675
16	7.379	6.974	6.604	6.265	5.954	5.668	5.405	5.162	4.938	4.730
17	7.549	7.120	6.729	6.373	6.047	5.749	5.475	5.222	4.990	4.775
18	7.702	7.250	6.840	6.467	6.128	5.818	5.534	5.273	5.033	4.812
19	7.839	7.366	6.938	6.550	6.198	5.877	5.584	5.316	5.070	4.843
20	7.963	7.469	7.025	6.623	6.259	5.929	5.628	5.353	5.101	4.870

FORMULAE

PROBABILITY

$A \cup B = $ **A or B**. $A \cap B = $ **A and B** (overlap).

$P(B \mid A) = $ probability of B, **given** A.

Rules of Addition

If A and B are mutually exclusive: $P(A \cup B) = P(A) + P(B)$

If A and B are not mutually exclusive: $P(A \cup B) = P(A) + P(B) - P(A \cap B)$

Rules of Multiplication

If A and B are *independent*:: $P(A \cap B) = P(A) * P(B)$

If A and B are **not** *independent*: $P(A \cap B) = P(A) * P(B \mid A)$

$E(X) = \sum (\text{probability} * \text{payoff})$

DESCRIPTIVE STATISTICS

Arithmetic Mean

$$\bar{x} = \frac{\sum x}{n} \quad \bar{x} = \frac{\sum fx}{\sum f} \quad \text{(frequency distribution)}$$

Standard Deviation

$$SD = \sqrt{\frac{\sum (x - \bar{x})^2}{n}} \quad SD = \sqrt{\frac{\sum fx^2}{\sum f} - \bar{x}^2} \quad \text{(frequency distribution)}$$

INDEX NUMBERS

Price relative = $100 * P_1/P_0$ Quantity relative = $100 * Q_1/Q_0$

Price: $$\frac{\sum w * \left(\dfrac{P_1}{P_0} \right)}{\sum w} \times 100$$

Quantity: $$\frac{\sum w * \left(\dfrac{Q_1}{Q_0} \right)}{\sum w} \times 100$$

TIME SERIES

Additive Model

Series = Trend + Seasonal + Random

Multiplicative Model

Series = Trend * Seasonal * Random

FINANCIAL MATHEMATICS

Compound Interest (Values and Sums)
Future Value S, of a sum of X, invested for n periods, compounded at $r\%$ interest

$$S = X[1 + r]^n$$

Annuity
Present value of an annuity of £1 per annum receivable or payable for n years, commencing in one year, discounted at $r\%$ per annum:

$$PV = \frac{1}{r}\left[1 - \frac{1}{[1+r]^n}\right]$$

Perpetuity
Present value of £1 per annum, payable or receivable in perpetuity, commencing in one year, discounted at $r\%$ per annum:

$$PV = \frac{1}{r}$$

LEARNING CURVE

$$Y_x = aX^b$$

where:
Y_x = the cumulative average time per unit to produce X units;
a = the time required to produce the first unit of output;
X = the cumulative number of units;
b = the index of learning.

The exponent b is defined as the log of the learning curve improvement rate divided by log 2.

INVENTORY MANAGEMENT

Economic Order Quantity

$$EOQ = \sqrt{\frac{2C_oD}{C_h}}$$

where: C_o =   cost of placing an order
            C_h =   cost of holding one unit in inventory for one year
            D =   annual demand

CIMA verb hierarchy – Operational level exams

Chapter learning objectives

CIMA VERB HIERARCHY

CIMA place great importance on the choice of verbs in exam question requirements. It is therefore critical that you answer the question according to the definition of the verb used.

The P1 syllabus contains 43 learning outcomes using the following verbs that you need to understand:

Level 2 verbs

- "Explain" – occurs 7 times
- "Identify" – occurs 3 times
- "Illustrate" – occurs once

Level 3 verbs

- "Apply" – occurs 9 times
- "Prepare" – occurs 4 times
- "Calculate" – occurs 4 times

Level 4 verbs

- "Discuss" – occurs 3 times
- "Analyse" – occurs 6 times
- "Prioritise" – occurs once
- "Interpret" – occurs 2 times
- "Compare" – occurs 2 times

Level 5 verbs

* "Evaluate" – occurs once

The verbs given in the syllabus limit the scope of the question requirements that the examiners can ask. For example, syllabus learning outcome A2(a) is "**explain** the role of MRP". "Explain" is a level 2 verb, so the examiner would not ask you a level 3 or 4 verb here, such as to "**compare**" or "**discuss**" a firms MRP approach.

It can be seen above that level 2 and 3 verbs occur most often in the syllabus.. For example, the number of occurrences of level 3 verbs is 17, compared to only 15 occurrences for levels 4 and 5 combined. The average verb weighting in exams is just under level 3. But in some questions, particularly in section C of the exam, some level 4 and 5 verbs will be used. It is therefore important that students are comfortable with the verbs at all levels.

This chapter looks at the verbs and the differences between them.

1 Operational Level Verbs

It is vital that you identify which verb is used in an exam question requirement and answer accordingly. The examiner has repeatedly said that students in the exam are generally good at the knowledge aspects of questions but poor when discussion and/or application to a scenario is required.

Level 1: KNOWLEDGE

What you are expected to know

VERBS USED	DEFINITION
List	Make a list of.
State	Express, fully or clearly, the details / facts of.
Define	Give the exact meaning of.

Level 2: COMPREHENSION

What you are expected to understand

VERBS USED	DEFINITION
Describe	Communicate the key features of.
Distinguish	Highlight the differences between.
Explain	Make clear or intelligible/state the meaning or purpose of.
Identify	Recognise, establish or select after consideration.
Illustrate	Use an example to describe or explain something.

Level 3: APPLICATION

How you are expected to apply your knowledge

VERBS USED	DEFINITION
Apply	Put to practical use.
Calculate	Ascertain or reckon mathematically.
Demonstrate	Prove with certainty or exhibit by practical means.
Prepare	Make or get ready for use.
Reconcile	Make or prove consistent/compatible.
Solve	Find an answer to.
Tabulate	Arrange in a table.

Level 4: ANALYSIS

How you are expected to analyse the detail of what you have learned.

VERBS USED	DEFINITION
Analyse	Examine in detail the structure of.
Categorise	Place into a defined class or division.
Compare and contrast	Show the similarities and/or differences between.
Construct	Build up or compile.
Discuss	Examine in detail by argument.
Interpret	Translate into intelligible or familiar terms.
Prioritise	Place in order of priority or sequence for action.
Produce	Create or bring into existence.

Level 5: EVALUATION

How you are expected to use your learning to evaluate, make decisions or recommendations

VERBS USED	DEFINITION
Advise	Counsel, inform or notify.
Evaluate	Appraise or assess the value of.
Recommend	Propose a course of action.

2 Further guidance on operational level verbs that cause confusion

Verbs that cause students confusion at this level are as follows:

Level 2 verbs

- **The difference between "describe" and "explain".**

  An explanation is a set of statements constructed to describe a set of facts which clarifies the **causes**, **context**, and **consequences** of those facts.

  For example, if asked to **describe** the features of a budgeting process, you could talk, among other things, about understanding the principal budget factor, the budgets that need to be produced, the link between the budgets, the other information provided to senior management etc. This tells us what the budgeting system looks like.

  However if asked to **explain** the budgeting process, then you might include the descriptions above. But you would also have to talk about why firms may choose a particular processing method, why they would budget at all, the principles of good budgeting etc..

  More simply, to describe something is to answer "what" type questions whereas to explain looks at "what" and "why" aspects.

- **The verb "to identify"**

  This area is most commonly used in chapters 17 and 18 where students will have to "identify" appropriate sources of finance and investment opportunities for an organisation. This means that you need to be aware of the sources available and when they may be most suitable to an organisation. For example, forfaiting will only be applicable to an organisation with overseas transactions.

Level 3 verbs

- **The verb "to apply"**

  Given that all level 3 verbs involve application, the verb "apply" is rare in the exam. Instead one of the other more specific verbs is used.

- **The verb "to calculate"**

  The verb "to calculate" is one of the most commonly used verbs in the exam. Students must come to a numerical answer or choose a numerical option.

- **The verb "to prepare"**

  This will also involve performing calculations, but now students must provide those calculations in a standard format such as a cash forecast or operating statement.

Level 4 verbs

- **The verb "to analyse"**

  To analyse something is to examine it in detail in order to discover its meaning or essential features. This will usually involve breaking the scenario down and looking at the fine detail, possibly with additional calculations, and then stepping back to see the bigger picture to identify any themes to support conclusions.

  The main error students make is that they fail to draw out any themes and conclusions and simply present the marker with a collection of uninterpreted, unexplained facts and figures.

- **The verb "to discuss"**

  To discuss something is very similar to analysing it, except that discussion usually involves two or more different viewpoints or arguments as the context, rather than a set of figures. To discuss viewpoints will involve looking at their underlying arguments, examining them critically, trying to assess whether one argument is more persuasive than the other and then seeking to reach a conclusion.

  For example, if asked to discuss whether a particular technique could be used by a company, you would examine the arguments for and against, making reference to the specific circumstances in the question, and seek to conclude.

- **The verb "to prioritise"**

  To prioritise is to place objects in an order. The key issue here is to decide upon the criteria to use to perform the ordering. For example, prioritising projects for investment will depend on the method of project appraisal used. An IRR ranking might be very different to a NPV ranking for example.

  The main mistake students make is that they fail to justify their prioritisation – why is this the most important issue?

- **The verb "to interpret"**

  In these questions it is likely that either some results are provided for students or perhaps it may be a follow on requirement based on numbers that the student has calculated for themselves. "Interpret" means that students will be expected to explain the meaning of the numbers and how they should influence the decisions of the decision makers.

  For example, students may be asked to interpret the meaning of an adverse materials usage variance. So students would need to understand the difference between an adverse and a favourable variance, consider the possible causes of the variance and suggest whether decision makers should take any further action.

- **The verb "to compare"**

  Students must look for areas of similarities in the sets of processes/outcomes provided or calculated, as well as identify where the results are different and would lead to different decisions. The key to success in these areas will therefore be to have an awareness of the advantages and disadvantages of different techniques. Students, for example, could be asked to compare Activity Based Costing (ABC) to Absorption Costing.

Level 5 verbs

- **The verb "to evaluate"**

  This verb will mean a combination of other verbs. Students are likely to have to make a **calculation**(s) as well as then **prioritising** or **discussing** it in order to provide an overall opinion.

  For example, a student might be asked to "evaluate" a new project proposal. They would therefore have to calculate its NPV and then give an opinion on whether the new project should proceed.

Traditional costing

Chapter learning objectives

Lead	Component
A1. Discuss costing methods and their results.	(a) Compare and contrast marginal (or variable), throughput and absorption accounting methods in respect of profit reporting and stock valuation.
	(b) Discuss a report which reconciles budget and actual profit using absorption and/or marginal costing principles.

1 Chapter overview diagram

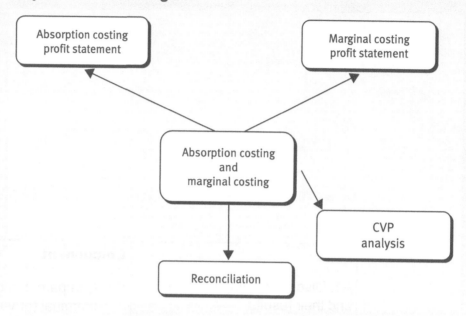

2 The purpose of costing

In the first few chapters of the syllabus we examine different techniques for determining the production cost of products. It's therefore useful to remind ourselves why we might need to know this cost.

- Inventory valuation – the cost per unit can be used to value inventory in the statement of financial position (balance sheet).

- To record costs – the costs associated with the product need to be recorded in the income statement.

- To price products – the business may use the cost per unit to assist in pricing the product. For example, if the cost per unit is $0.30, the business may decide to price the product at $0.50 per unit in order to make the required profit of $0.20 per unit.

- Decision making – the business may use the cost information to make important decisions regarding which products should be made and in what quantities.

How can we calculate the cost per unit?

So we know why it's so important for the business to determine the cost of its products. We now need to consider how we can calculate this cost.

Revision of cost behaviour

Many factors affect the level of costs incurred; for instance, inflation will cause costs to increase over a period of time. In management accounting, when we talk about cost behaviour we are referring to the way in which costs are affected by fluctuations in the level of activity. The level of activity can be measured in many different ways. For example, we can record the number of units produced, miles travelled, hours worked, percentage of capacity utilised and so on.

An understanding of cost behaviour patterns is essential for many management tasks, particularly in the areas of planning, decision-making and control. It would be impossible for managers to forecast and control costs without at least a basic knowledge of the way in which costs behave in relation to the level of activity.

In this section, we will look at the most common cost behaviour patterns and we will consider some examples of each.

Fixed cost

The CIMA Terminology defines a fixed cost as *'a cost which is incurred for an accounting period that, within certain output or turnover limits, tends to be unaffected by fluctuations in the levels of activity (output or turnover)'.*

Another term which can be used to refer to a fixed cost is 'period cost'. This highlights the fact that a fixed cost is incurred according to the time elapsed, rather than according to the level of activity.

Examples of fixed costs are rent, rates, insurance and executive salaries.

However, it is important to note that this is only true for the relevant range of activity. Consider, for example, the behaviour of the rent cost. Within the relevant range it is possible to expand activity without needing extra premises and therefore the rent cost remains constant. However, if activity is expanded to the critical point where further premises are needed, then the rent cost will increase to a new, higher level. This cost behaviour pattern can be described as a *stepped fixed cost*. The cost is constant within the relevant range for each activity level but when a critical level of activity is reached, the total cost incurred increases to the next step.

This warning does not only apply to fixed costs: it is never wise to attempt to predict costs for activity levels outside the range for which cost behaviour patterns have been established.

Also, whilst the fixed cost total may stay the same within a relevant activity range, the fixed cost per unit reduces as the activity level is increased. This is because the same amount of fixed cost is being spread over an increasing number of units.

Variable cost

The CIMA Terminology defines a variable cost as a 'cost that varies with a measure of activity'.

Examples of variable costs are direct material, direct labour and variable overheads. In most examination situations, and very often in practice, variable costs are assumed to be linear.

Although many variable costs do approximate to a linear function, this assumption may not always be realistic. Non-linear variable costs are sometimes called curvilinear variable costs. There may be what are known as economies of scale whereby each successive unit of activity adds less to total variable cost than the previous unit. An example of a variable cost which follows this pattern could be the cost of direct material where quantity discounts are available.

On the other hand, there may be what are known as diseconomies of scale which indicates that each successive unit of activity is adding more to the total variable cost than the previous unit. An example of a variable cost which follows this pattern could be the cost of direct labour where employees are paid an accelerating bonus for achieving higher levels of output.

The important point is that managers should be aware of any assumptions that have been made in estimating cost behaviour patterns. They can then use the information which is based on these assumptions with a full awareness of its possible limitations.

Semi-variable cost

A semi-variable cost is also referred to as a semi-fixed, hybrid, or mixed cost. The CIMA Terminology defines it as 'a cost containing both fixed and variable components and thus partly affected by a change in the level of activity'.

Examples of semi-variable costs are gas and electricity. Both of these expenditures consist of a fixed amount payable for the period, with a further variable amount which is related to the consumption of gas or electricity.

Alternatively, The cost might remain constant up to a certain level of activity and then increase as the variable cost element is incurred. An example of such a cost might be the rental cost of a photocopier where a fixed rental is paid and no extra charge is made for copies up to a certain number. Once this number of copies is exceeded, a constant charge is levied for each copy taken.

3 Absorption costing

The aim of traditional absorption costing is to determine the full production cost per unit.

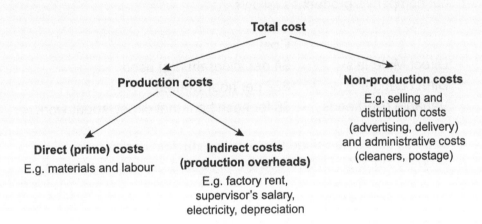

When we use absorption costing to determine the cost per unit, we focus on the production costs only. We can summarise these costs into a cost card:

	$
Direct materials per unit	X
Direct labour per unit	X
Production overhead per unit (Note 1)	X
	—
Full production cost per unit	X
	—

Note 1:

All production overheads must be absorbed into units of production, using a suitable basis, e.g. units produced, labour hours or machine hours. The assumption underlying this method of absorption is that overhead expenditure is connected to the volume produced.

If, for example, units produced are used as the basis, the absorption rate is calculated as:

$$\frac{\text{Total overhead cost (allocated and apportioned)}}{\text{Budgeted production volume}}$$

Example 1

A company accountant has gathered together some cost information for her company's product as follows:

	Cost
Direct Materials	$4 per kilogram (kg) used
Direct Labour	$22 per hour worked
Variable overheads	$6 for each hour that direct labour work

She has also determined that fixed production overheads will be $400,000 in total. Overheads are absorbed on a per unit basis.

Investigation has shown that each unit of the product uses 3 kilograms of material and needs 2 hours of direct labour work.

Sales and production were budgeted at 20,000 units, but only 16,000 were actually produced and 14,000 actually sold.

There was no opening stock.

Required:

Produce a standard cost card using absorption costing and value the company's closing stock on that basis.

More on calculating absorption rates

It is relatively easy to estimate the cost per unit for direct materials and labour. In doing so we can complete the first two lines of the cost card. However, it is much more difficult to estimate the production overhead per unit. This is an indirect cost and so, by its very nature, we do not know how much is contained in each unit. Therefore, we need a method of attributing the production overheads to each unit.

Review of overhead absorption procedure

Accounting for overhead costs in an absorption costing system can be quite complex, and production overhead costs are first allocated, then apportioned and finally absorbed into production costs (or service costs).

- **Overhead allocation**. Indirect production costs are initially allocated to cost centres or cost codes. Allocation is the process of charging a cost directly and in full to the source of the expenditure. For example, the salary of a maintenance engineer would be allocated to the engineering maintenance department.

- **Overhead apportionment**. The overhead costs that have been allocated to cost centres and cost codes other than direct production departments must next be apportioned to direct production departments. Apportionment is the process of sharing on a fair basis. For example, factory rental costs might be apportioned between the production departments on the basis of the floor area occupied by each department. Similarly, the costs of the engineering maintenance department might be apportioned between production departments on the basis of the operating machine hours in each department. At the end of the apportionment process, all the production overheads have been allocated or apportioned to the direct production departments.

- **Overhead absorption**. An absorption rate is calculated for each production department. This is the rate at which production overheads will be added to the cost of production going through the department.

When the department produces a single product, production volume can be measured as the number of units produced, and the absorption rate would be a rate per unit produced.

More usually, organisations produce different products or carry out non-standard jobs for customers, and production volume is commonly measured as one of the following:

- direct labour hours worked in the department, and the absorption rate is a rate per direct labour hour worked

- machine hours worked in the department, and the absorption rate is a rate per machine hour operated

- sometimes the cost of direct labour might be used as a measure of production volume, and the absorption rate is then calculated as a percentage of direct labour cost.

Predetermined absorption rates

Although it is possible to calculate absorption rates using actual overhead costs and actual production volume, this is not the usual practice. This is because:

- It is usually inconvenient to wait until the end of an accounting period to work out what the absorption rates should be. In absorption costing systems, overhead costs are added to the cost of production as it passes through each stage in the production process, and overhead costs are absorbed when the production happens.

- A predetermined rate is required to enable a price to be estimated.

- Overhead costs may vary throughout the year. The overhead absorption rate smoothes variations in overheads by applying an average overhead cost to each unit of product throughout the year.

The normal practice is therefore to absorb production overhead costs at a predetermined rate, based on budgeted overhead expenditure and budgeted production volume.

This however can lead to an over-or under-absorption of the overheads when compared to the actual overheads incurred.

This **over-or under-absorption** can be calculated as follows:

= (Budgeted overhead rate per unit × actual units) − Actual overheads incurred

Absorption advantages/disadvantages

Advantages of absorption costing

The arguments used in favour of absorption costing are as follows:

- Fixed production costs can be a large proportion of the total production costs incurred. Unless production overheads are absorbed into product costs, a large proportion of cost would be excluded from the measurement of product costs.

- Absorption costing follows the matching concept (accruals concept) by carrying forward a proportion of the production cost in the inventory valuation to be matched against the sales value when the items are sold.

- It is necessary to include fixed production overhead in inventory values for financial statements; absorption costing produces inventory values which include a share of fixed production overhead.

- Analysis of under-/over-absorbed overhead may be useful for identifying inefficient utilisation of production resources.

- There is an argument that in the longer term, all costs are variable, and it is appropriate to try to identify overhead costs with the products or services that cause them. This argument is used as a reason for activity-based costing (ABC). ABC is a form of absorption costing, and is described in a later chapter.

Disadvantages of absorption costing

There are serious disadvantages with using absorption costing to measure costs and profits.

- **The apportionment and absorption of overhead costs is arbitrary**

  The way in which overhead costs are apportioned between cost centres and absorbed into production costs is subjective and many methods of cost allocation may be deemed appropriate. Although the process attempts to be 'fair', it is arbitrary.

For example, suppose that a factory rental cost is apportioned between production departments on the basis of the floor area for each department. This might seem a fair way of sharing out the costs, but it is still subjective. Why not apportion the costs on the basis of the number of employees in each department? Or why not allow for the fact that some of the accommodation might be more pleasant to work in than others? In a manufacturing environment, production overheads might be absorbed on the basis of either direct labour hours or machine hours. However, choosing one instead of the other can have a significant effect on job costs or product costs, and yet it still relies on a subjective choice.

It may be easier in some departments than others. If a department is labour intensive then allocations can be made on the basis of labour hours worked. Or if the department is machine intensive then allocations can be made on the basis of machine hours. But not every department will have this clear distinction.

- **Profits vary with changes in production volume**

  A second criticism of absorption costing is that profits can be increased or reduced by changes in inventory levels. For example, by increasing output, more fixed overhead is absorbed into production costs, and if the extra output is not sold, the fixed overhead costs are carried forward in the closing inventory value. This can encourage managers to over-produce in order to inflate profits.

4 Marginal costing

Marginal costing is a costing method which charges products with variable costs alone. The fixed costs are treated as period costs and are written off in total against the contribution of the period.

Marginal cost

Marginal cost is the extra cost arising as a result of producing one more unit, or the cost saved as a result of producing one less unit. It comprises:

- Direct material
- Direct labour
- Variable overheads

Example 2

Use the same data as that provided in Example 1.

Required:

Produce a standard cost card using marginal costing and value the company's closing stock on that basis.

Marginal costing advantages/disadvantages

Advantages of marginal costing

- It is a simpler costing system, because there is no requirement to apportion and absorb overhead costs.

- Marginal costing reflects the behaviour of costs in relation to activity. When sales increase, the cost of sales rise only by the additional variable costs. Since most decision-making problems involve changes to activity, marginal costing information is more relevant and appropriate for short-run decision-making than absorption costing.

- Marginal costing avoids the disadvantages of absorption costing, described above.

Disadvantages of marginal costing

- When fixed costs are high relative to variable costs, and when overheads are high relative to direct costs, the marginal cost of production and sales is only a small proportion of total costs. A costing system that focuses on marginal cost and contribution might therefore provide insufficient and inadequate information about costs and product profitability. Marginal costing is useful for short-term decision-making, but not for measuring product costs and profitability over the longer term.

- It could also be argued that the treatment of direct labour costs as a variable cost item is often unrealistic. When direct labour employees are paid a fixed wage or salary, their cost is fixed, not variable.

5 Absorption and marginal costing profit statements

Absorption costing format

	$	$
Sales		X
Less Cost of Sales		
Opening stock	X	
+ Production costs	X	
	—	
	X	
Less: Closing stock	(X)	
	—	(X)
		—
		X
(Under)/over absorption		±X
		—
Gross Profit		X
Less: Selling, distribution and admin. costs,		
Variable	X	
Fixed	X	
	—	
		(X)
		—
Net profit/ (loss)		X
		—

Marginal costing format

	$	$
Sales		X
Less: **Variable** Cost of Sales		
Opening stock	X	
+ **Variable** production costs	X	
	—	
	X	
Less: Closing stock	(X)	
	—	(X)
		—
		X
Less: **Variable** Selling, distribution and admin. costs		(X)
		—
Contribution		X
Less: Fixed costs		
Production	X	
Selling, distribution and admin.	X	
	—	
		(X)
		—
Net profit/ (loss)		X
		—

Example 3

Perry Ltd makes and sells a single product with the following information:

	$/unit
Selling price	50
Direct material	15
Direct labour	10
Variable overhead	5

Fixed overheads are $5,000. Budgeted and actual output and sales are 1,000 units.

(a) Using absorption costing:
   (i) Calculate the profit for the period.

   (ii) Calculate the profit per unit.

(b) Using marginal costing:
   (i) Calculate the contribution per unit?

   (ii) Calculate the total contribution?

   (iii) Calculate the profit for the period?

6 Reconciling the profits

The differences between the two profits can be reconciled as follows:

	$
Absorption costing profit	X
(Increase) / decrease in stock × fixed overheads per unit	(X) / X
Marginal costing profit	X

Justification

The profit differences are caused by the different valuations given to the closing stocks in each period. With absorption costing, an amount of fixed production overhead is carried forward in stock to be charged against sales of later periods.

If stocks increase, then absorption costing profits will be higher than marginal costing profits. This is because some of the fixed overhead is carried forward in stock instead of being written off against sales for the period.

If stocks reduce, then marginal costing profits will be higher than absorption costing profits. This is because the fixed overhead which had been carried forward in stock with absorption costing is now being released to be charged against the sales for the period.

Marginal costing and absorption costing systems give the same profit when there is no change in stocks.

Profit differences in the long term

In the long term the total reported profit will be the same whichever method is used. This is because all of the costs incurred will eventually be charged against sales; it is merely the timing of the sales that causes the profit differences from period to period.

Example 4

The details are exactly the same as for Example 3, but output and sales are now 3,000 units instead of 1,000.

Calculate the profit for the period using both absorption and marginal costing? Answer the question in any way that you want.

Example 5

Z Limited manufactures a single product, the budgeted selling price and variable cost details of which are as follows:

	$
Selling price	15.00
Variable costs per unit:	
Direct materials	3.50
Direct labour	4.00
Variable overhead	2.00

Budgeted fixed overhead costs are $60,000 per annum charged at a constant rate each month.

Budgeted production is 30,000 units per annum.

In a month when actual production was 2,400 units and exceeded sales by 180 units, identify the profit reported under absorption costing:

A $6,660

B $7,570

C $7,770

D $8,200

E $8,400

Profits from one period to the next can be reconciled in a similar way. For example, the difference between periods can be explained as the change in unit sales multiplied by the contribution per unit if using marginal costing.

Further explanation on reconciling profits between periods

Just like reconciling profits between the two accounting systems can be achieved via a proforma, similar proformas can be used for reconciling profits between one period and the next using the same accounting system as follows:

Marginal costing reconciliation

	$
Profit for period 1	X
Increase / (decrease) in sales × contribution per unit	X / (X)
Profit for period 2	X

Absorption costing reconciliation

This is a little trickier as the reconciliation needs to be adjusted for any over/under-absorptions that may have occurred of fixed overheads.

	$
Profit for period 1	X
Increase / (decrease) in sales × profit per unit	X / (X)
(Over–) / under-absorption in period 1	(X) / X
Over× / (under)-absorption in period 2	X / (X)
Profit for period 2	X

Note:

You must be careful with the direction of the absorption. For example, an over-absorption in period 1 makes profit for that month higher, therefore it must be deducted to arrive at period 2's profit. On the other hand, an over-absorption in period 2 makes period 2's profit higher than period 1's, therefore it must be added in the reconciliation.

Reconciling profits when there has been a change in costs

When reconciling profits between periods, care needs to be taken if the standard cost card has changed between these periods. In the reconciliation, the difference in the inventory valuation should be split between the difference in the opening inventory valuation and the difference in the closing inventory valuation. This is not as complicated as it sounds and is best illustrated in the following example:

Example

In the previous financial year, a company had the following standard cost card for one of its products:

	$
Direct materials per unit	4
Direct labour per unit	2
Fixed production overhead per unit (Note 1)	4
Full production cost per unit	10

In the current financial year, due to some cost changes the standard cost card for this product had to change as follows:

	$
Direct materials per unit	5
Direct labour per unit	3
Fixed production overhead per unit (Note 1)	6
Full production cost per unit	14

Note 1: Fixed overheads are absorbed on a per unit basis.

During the current year, budgeted and actual production was 8,000 units. The company budgets to sell 10,000 units at $20 per unit. Opening inventory of finished goods was 4,000 units.

Requirement

(a) Calculate the marginal costing profit for the current year.

(b) Calculate the absorption costing profit for the current year.

(c) Prepare a statement which reconciles the profit from the marginal costing system to the profit from absorption costing system.

Solution

(a) Marginal costing profit

		$	$
Sales	(10,000 units × $20/unit)		200,000
Less: cost of sales			
Opening inventory	(4,000 units × $6/unit)	24,000	
Direct materials	(8,000 units × $5/unit)	40,000	
Direct labour	(8,000 units × $3/unit)	24,000	
Fixed production overhead	(8,000 units × $6/unit)	48,000	
Less: closing inventory	(2,000 units × $8/unit)	(16,000)	
			(120,000)
Marginal costing budgeted profit			80,000

(b) Absorption costing profit

		$	$
Sales	(10,000 units × $20/unit)		200,000
Less: cost of sales			
Opening inventory	(4,000 units × $10/unit)	40,000	
Direct materials	(8,000 units × $5/unit)	40,000	
Direct labour	(8,000 units × $3/unit)	24,000	
Fixed production overhead	(8,000 units × $6/unit)	48,000	
Less: closing inventory	(2,000 units × $14/unit)	(28,000)	
			(124,000)
Absoprtion costing budgeted profit			76,000

(c) Reconciliation of profits

When reconciling the marginal costing profit to the absorption costing profit we should deduct in the difference in opening inventory valuation and add the difference in the closing inventory valuation.

		$
Marginal costing profit		80,000
Difference in opening inventory valuation	(4,000 units × $4/unit)	(16,000)
Difference in closing inventory valuation	(2,000 units × $6/unit)	12,000
Absoprtion costing budgeted profit		76,000

7 Contribution to sales ratios and breakeven points

Cost-Volume-Profit (CVP) analysis

CVP analysis makes use of the contribution concept in order to assess the following measures for a single product:

- contribution to sales (C/S) ratio
- breakeven point
- margin of safety

C/S ratio

The C/S ratio of a product is the proportion of the selling price that contributes to fixed overheads and profits. It is comparable to the gross profit margin. The formula for calculating the C/S ratio of a product is as follows:

$$\text{C/S ratio} = \frac{\text{Contribution per unit}}{\text{Selling price per unit}} \quad \text{or} \quad \frac{\text{Total contribution}}{\text{Total sales revenue}}$$

The C/S ratio is sometimes referred to as the P/V (Profit/Volume) ratio.

Breakeven point

The breakeven point is the point at which neither a profit nor a loss is made.

*   At the breakeven point the following situations occur.

    Total sales revenue = Total costs, i.e. Profit = 0
    or
    Total contribution = Fixed costs, i.e. Profit = 0

*   The following formula is used to calculate the breakeven point in terms of numbers of units sold.

    $$\text{Breakeven point (in terms of numbers of units sold)} = \frac{\text{Fixed costs}}{\text{Contribution per unit}}$$

*   It is also possible to calculate the breakeven point in terms of sales revenue using the C/S ratio. The equation is as follows:

    $$\text{Breakeven point (in terms of sales revenue)} = \frac{\text{Fixed costs}}{\text{C/S ratio}}$$

Margin of safety

The margin of safety is the amount by which anticipated sales (in units) can fall below budget before a business makes a loss. It can be calculated in terms of numbers of units or as a percentage of budgeted sales.

The following formulae are used to calculate the margin of safety:

$$\text{Margin of safety (in terms of units)} = \text{Budgeted sales} - \text{Breakeven point sales}$$

$$\text{Margin of safety (as a \% of budgeted sales)} = \frac{\text{Budgeted sales} - \text{Breakeven sales}}{\text{Budgeted sales}} \times 100\%$$

Example 6

A company manufactures and sells a single product that has the following cost and selling price structure:

	$/unit
Selling price	120
Direct material	(22)
Direct labour	(36)
Variable overhead	(14)
Fixed overhead	(12)
Profit per unit	36

The fixed overhead absorption rate is based on the normal capacity of 2,000 units per month.

Assume that the same amount is spent each month on fixed overheads.

Budgeted sales for next month are 2,200 units.

Required:

(i)   the breakeven point, in sales units per month;

(ii) the margin of safety for next month;

(iii) the budgeted profit for next month;

(iv) the sales required to achieve a profit of $96,000 in a month.

8 Chapter summary

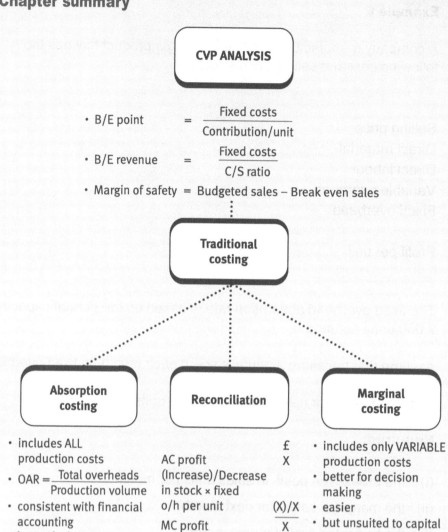

CVP ANALYSIS

- B/E point $= \dfrac{\text{Fixed costs}}{\text{Contribution/unit}}$

- B/E revenue $= \dfrac{\text{Fixed costs}}{\text{C/S ratio}}$

- Margin of safety = Budgeted sales – Break even sales

Traditional costing

Absorption costing

- includes ALL production costs
- OAR $= \dfrac{\text{Total overheads}}{\text{Production volume}}$
- consistent with financial accounting
- better for long-term pricing

Reconciliation

	£
AC profit	X
(Increase)/Decrease in stock × fixed o/h per unit	(X)/X
MC profit	X

Marginal costing

- includes only VARIABLE production costs
- better for decision making
- easier
- but unsuited to capital intensive environments

9 Practice questions

Test your understanding 1

Saturn, a chocolate manufacturer, produces three products:

- The Sky Bar, a bar of solid milk chocolate.
- The Moon Egg, a fondant filled milk chocolate egg.
- The Sun Bar, a biscuit and nougat based chocolate bar.

Information relating to each of the products is as follows:

	Sky Bar	Moon Egg	Sun Bar
Direct labour cost per unit ($)	0.07	0.14	0.12
Direct material cost per unit ($)	0.17	0.19	0.16
Actual production/ sales (units)	500,000	150,000	250,000
Direct labour hours per unit	0.001	0.01	0.005
Direct machine hours per unit	0.01	0.04	0.02
Selling price per unit ($)	0.50	0.45	0.43

Annual production overhead = $80,000

Required:

Using traditional absorption costing, calculate the full production cost per unit and the profit per unit for each product. Explain the implications of the figures calculated.

(10 marks)

Test your understanding 2

E plc operates a marginal costing system. For the forthcoming year, variable costs are budgeted to be 60% of sales value and fixed costs are budgeted to be 10% of sales value.

If E plc increases its selling prices by 10%, but if fixed costs, variable costs per unit and sales volume remain unchanged, identify the effect on E plc's contribution:

A   a decrease of 2%

B   an increase of 5%

C   an increase of 10%

D   an increase of 25%

Test your understanding 3

When comparing the profits reported under marginal and absorption costing during a period when the level of stocks increased, identify which of the following statements would be true:

A   absorption costing profits will be higher and closing stock valuations lower than those under marginal costing

B   absorption costing profits will be higher and closing stock valuations higher than those under marginal costing

C   marginal costing profits will be higher and closing stock valuations lower than those under absorption costing

D   marginal costing profits will be lower and closing stock valuations higher than those under absorption costing

Test your understanding 4

Exe Limited makes a single product whose total cost per unit is budgeted to be $45. This includes fixed cost of $8 per unit based on a volume of 10,000 units per period. In a period, sales volume was 9,000 units, and production volume was 11,500 units. The actual profit for the same period, calculated using absorption costing, was $42,000.

If the profit statement were prepared using marginal costing, identify the profit for the period:

A $10,000

B $22,000

C $50,000

D $62,000

Test your understanding 5

Keats plc commenced business on 1 March making one product only, the standard cost of which is as follows:

	$
Direct labour	5
Direct material	8
Variable production overhead	2
Fixed production overhead	5
Standard production cost	20

The fixed production overhead figure has been calculated on the basis of a budgeted normal output of 36,000 units per annum.

You are to assume that actual fixed overheads were as expected and that all the budgeted fixed expenses are incurred evenly over the year. March and April are to be taken as equal period months.

Selling, distribution and administration expenses are:

Fixed	$120,000 per annum
Variable	15% of the sales value

The selling price per unit is $35 and the number of units produced and sold were:

	March (units)	April (units)
Production	2,000	3,200
Sales	1,500	3,000

Required:

(a) prepare profit statements for each of the months of March and April using:

   (i) absorption costing, and

   (ii) marginal costing

(7 marks)

(b) prepare a reconciliation of the profit or loss figures given in your answers to (a)(i) and (a)(ii) accompanied by a brief explanation.

(3 marks)

(Total: 10 marks)

Test your understanding 6

If inventory levels have increased during the period, identify which of the following options would be correct for the profit calculated using marginal costing when compared with that calculated using absorption costing:

A   higher

B   lower

C   equal

D   impossible to answer without further information

(2 marks)

Test your understanding 7

Identify which of the following statements would be true: fixed production overheads will always be under-absorbed when:

A   actual output is lower than budgeted output

B   actual overheads incurred are lower than budgeted overheads

C   overheads absorbed are lower than those budgeted

D   overheads absorbed are lower than those incurred

(2 marks)

Test your understanding 8

A company uses a standard absorption costing system. The fixed overhead absorption rate is based on labour hours.

Extracts from the company's records for last year were as follows:

	Budget	Actual
Fixed production overhead	$450,000	$475,000
Output	50,000 units	60,000 units
Labour hours	900,000	930,000

The under- or over-absorbed fixed production overheads for the year were:

A $10,000 under-absorbed

B $10,000 over-absorbed

C $15,000 over-absorbed

D $65,000 over-absorbed

(2 marks)

Test your understanding 9

A company's summary budgeted operating statement is as follows:

	$000
Revenue	400
Variable costs	240
Fixed costs	100
Profit	60

Assuming that the sales mix does not change, identify the percentage increase in sales volume that would be needed to increase the profit to $100,000:

A   10%

B   15%

C   25%

D   40%

(2 marks)

Test your understanding 10

The following information relates to Product Alpha.

Selling price per unit	$100
Variable cost per unit	$56
Fixed costs	$220,000

Budgeted sales are 7,500 units.

Required:

(a) Calculate the breakeven point in terms of units sold and overall sales revenue

(2 marks)

(b) Calculate the margin of safety (expressed as a percentage of budgeted sales).

(3 marks)
(Total: 5 marks)

Test your understanding 11

A break down of KP's profit in the last accounting period showed the following:

	$000
Sales	450
Variable costs	(220)
Fixed costs	(160)
Profit	70

Due to a downturn in market conditions the company is worried that next year may result in losses and would like to know the change in sales that would make this happen.

Required:

Calculate the break-even sales revenue for the business based on its current cost structure. Use this information to determine the percentage fall in sales that would be necessary before the company would begin to incur losses.

(5 marks)

Test your understanding 12

A summary of a manufacturing company's budgeted profit statement for its next financial year, when it expects to be operating at 75% capacity, is given below.

	$	$
Sales 9,000 units at $32		288,000
Less:		
direct materials	54,000	
direct wages	72,000	
production overhead – fixed	42,000	
– variable	18,000	
		186,000
Gross profit		102,000
Less: admin., selling and dist'n costs:		
– fixed	36,000	
– varying with sales volume	27,000	
		63,000
Net profit		39,000

It has been estimated that:

(i) if the selling price per unit were reduced to $28, the increased demand would utilise 90 per cent of the company's capacity without any additional advertising expenditure;

(ii) to attract sufficient demand to utilise full capacity would require a 15 per cent reduction in the current selling price and a $5,000 special advertising campaign.

Required:

(a) Calculate the breakeven point in units, based on the original budget;

(4 marks)

(b) Calculate the profits and breakeven points which would result from each of the two alternatives and compare them with the original budget.

(8 marks)

(c) The manufacturing company decided to proceed with the original budget and has asked you to calculate how many units must be sold to achieve a profit of $45,500.

(4 marks)

Test your understanding answers

Example 1

Standard cost card

		$
Direct materials per unit	3kgs × $4/kg	12
Direct labour per unit	2hrs × $22/hr	44
Variable overheads	2hrs × $6/hr	12
Production overhead per unit (note)		20
		—
Full / absorption cost per unit		88
		—

Note:

Production overhead per unit in the standard cost card should be based on *budgeted* production. Therefore in this example they will be ($400,000 / 20,000 units=) $20 per unit.

Stock valuation

If 16,000 units were produced and 14,000 units sold then there will be 2,000 units in closing stock.

Valuing that stock at the absorption cost will give a value of

= 2,000 × $88

= $176,000

Example 2

Standard cost card

		$
Direct materials per unit	3kgs × $4/kg	12
Direct labour per unit	2hrs × $22/hr	44
Variable overheads	2hrs × $6/hr	12
Marginal cost per unit		68

Note:

Fixed production overhead is not included in a marginal costing standard cost card.

Stock valuation

Valuing that stock at the marginal cost will give a value of

= 2,000 × $68

= $136,000

Example 3

(a)

(i)

		$	$
Sales	1,000 units × $50		50,000
Direct materials	1,000 units × $15	15,000	
Direct labour	1,000 units × $10	10,000	
Variable Overheads	1,000 units × $5	5,000	
Fixed Overheads		5,000	
			35,000
Profit			15,000

(ii)

$$\text{Profit per unit} = \frac{\$15000}{1,000 \text{ units}} = 15/\text{unit}$$

(b)

   (i) Contribution per unit = \$50 − (\$15 + \$10 + \$5) =   \$20

   (ii) Total contribution = \$20/unit × 1,000 units =   \$20,000

   (iii)   \$

Contribution	
\$20/unit × 1,000 units	20,000
Fixed cost	5,000
Profit	15,000

The two systems give the same profit provided there is no change in stock.

Example 4

Either marginal costing or absorption costing principles can be used. The two systems will give the same profit as there is no change in stock (production = sales). Marginal costing will be simpler and is illustrated first.

           \$

Contribution	
\$20 per unit × 3,000 units	60,000
Fixed cost	5,000
Profit	55,000

Alternatively:

		$	$
Sales	3,000 units × $50		150,000
Direct materials	3,000 units × $15	45,000	
Direct labour	3,000 units × $10	30,000	
Variable Overheads	3,000 units × $5	15,000	
Fixed Overheads	3,000 units × $5	15,000	
		——	
			(105,000)
Over-absorption of fixed overheads	($15,000 – $5,000)		10,000
			——
			55,000
			——

Notice that we did not use the $15 per unit profit figure. Unlike contribution per unit, profit per unit is not constant.

Example 5

B

A common short-cut in multiple choice questions is to calculate the marginal costing profit and then use the reconciliation of profits to get to the absorption costing profit.

First of all – the profit under marginal costing:

Contribution per unit = $15 – (3.50 + 4.00 + 2.00) = $5.50

No of units sold = 2,400 – 180 = 2,220

	$
Contribution	
$5.50/unit × 2,220 units	12,210
Fixed cost	
$60,000 p.a./12 months	5,000
	——
	7,210
	——

As production is greater than sales, absorption costing will show the higher profit.

Difference in profit = change in stock x fixed production overhead per unit.

Difference in profit = 180 units × $2/unit = $360.

Therefore, profit reported under absorption costing = $7,210 + 360 = $7,570.

$$\text{The FOAR was worked out as} \quad \frac{\text{Budgeted Overheads}}{\text{Budgeted Level of Activity}} = \frac{\$60,000}{30,000 \text{ units}} = \$2 \text{ per unit}$$

Example 6

(i) **Break even point**

The key to calculating the breakeven point is to determine the contribution per unit.

Contribution per unit = 120 − 22 − 36 − 14 = $48

$$\text{Breakeven point (in terms of number of units sold)} = \frac{\text{Fixed costs}}{\text{Contribution per unit}}$$

$$\text{Breakeven point} = \frac{\$12 \times 2,000 \text{ units}}{\$48}$$

Breakeven point =   500 units

(ii) **Margin of safety**

Margin of safety   = Budgeted sales − Breakeven point sales
Margin of safety   = 2,200 − 500
Margin of safety   = 1,700 units (or 77% of budgeted sales)

(iii) **Budgeted profit**

Once breakeven point has been reached, all of the contribution goes towards profits because all of the fixed costs have been covered.

Budgeted profit   =   1,700 units (margin of safety) × $48
Budgeted profit   = $81,600

(iv) **Target profit**

To achieve the desired level of profit, sufficient units must be sold to earn a contribution that covers the fixed costs and leaves the desired profit for the month.

$$\text{Unit sales required} = \frac{\text{Fixed overhead} + \text{desired profit}}{\text{Contribution per unit}}$$

$$\text{Unit sales required} = \frac{\$24,000 + \$96,000}{\$48}$$

$$\text{Unit sales required} = 2,500 \text{ units}$$

Test your understanding 1

As mentioned, it is relatively easy to complete the first two lines of the cost card. The difficult part is calculating the production overhead per unit, so let's start by considering this. We need to absorb the overheads into units of production. To do this, we will first need to calculate an overhead absorption rate (OAR):

$$\text{OAR} = \frac{\text{Production overhead} \quad \text{(this is \$80,000, as per the question)}}{\text{Activity level} \quad \text{(this must be chosen)}}$$

The activity level must be appropriate for the business. Saturn must choose between three activity levels:

- Units of production – This would not be appropriate since Saturn produces more than one type of product. It would not be fair to absorb the same amount of overhead into each product.

- Machine hours or labour hours – It is fair to absorb production overheads into the products based on the labour or machine hours taken to produce each unit. We must decide if the most appropriate activity level is machine or labour hours. To do this we can look at the nature of the process. Production appears to be more machine intensive than labour intensive because each unit takes more machine hours to produce than it does labour hours. Therefore, the most appropriate activity level is machine hours.

Working – OAR

$$OAR = \frac{\$80{,}000 \text{ production overhead}}{(0.01 \times 500k) + (0.04 \times 150k) + (0.02 \times 250k) \text{ hours}}$$

$$= \frac{\$80{,}000}{16{,}000 \text{ hours}}$$

$$= \$5 \text{ per machine hour}$$

We can now absorb these into the units of production:

	Sky Bar	Moon Egg	Sun Bar
Production overheads ($) = machine hours per unit × $5	0.05	0.20	0.10

This is the difficult part done. We can now quickly complete the cost card and answer the question:

	Sky Bar	Moon Egg	Sun Bar
	$	$	$
Direct labour cost per unit	0.07	0.14	0.12
Direct material cost per unit	0.17	0.19	0.16
Production overhead per unit	0.05	0.20	0.10
Full production cost per unit	**0.29**	**0.53**	**0.38**
Selling price per unit	0.50	0.45	0.43
Profit/ (loss) per unit	**0.21**	**(0.08)**	**0.05**

Outcome of absorption costing

Based on absorption costing, the Sky Bar and the Sun Bar are both profitable. However, the Moon Egg is loss making. Managers would need to consider the future of the Moon Egg. They may look at the possibility of increasing the selling price and/ or reducing costs. If this is not possible, they may make the decision to stop selling the product. However, this may prove to be the wrong decision because absorption costing does not always result in an accurate calculation of the full production cost per unit. ABC can be a more accurate method of calculating the full production cost per unit and as a result should lead to better decisions.

Test your understanding 2

D

The easiest way to answer this question is to make up a number for sales, say $1,000, then the relationships will be much easier to visualise.

If sales = $1,000, then:

Variable cost = 60% × $1,000 = $600

Current situation

	$
Sales	1,000
Variable cost	600
Contribution	400

New situation

	$
Sales (10% higher)	1,100
Variable cost	600
Contribution	500

Contribution increases by $100, which is an increase of 25% on its original value.

Fixed cost should be ignored as it does not affect contribution.

Test your understanding 3

B

Test your understanding 4

B

Production is greater than sales, so absorption costing will have the higher profit.

Difference in profit = change in stock × fixed production overhead per unit.

Difference in profit = 2,500 units × $8/unit = $20,000.

Therefore, profit reported under marginal costing = $42,000 – 20,000 = $22,000.

Test your understanding 5

(a) (i)

	March $	March $	April $	April $
Sales		52,500		105,000
Cost of Sales				
Op. stock (W1)		0		10,000
Production costs (@$20/unit)	40,000		64,000	
		40,000		74,000
Less cl. stock (@$20/unit) (W2)		10,000		14,000
		30,000		60,000
		22,500		45,000
(Under)/over-absorption (W3)		(5,000)		1,000
Gross profit		17,500		46,000
Selling etc costs				
Fixed (W4)		10,000		10,000
Variable		7,875		15,750
		17,875		25,750
Net Profit/Loss		(375)		20,250

(ii)

	March		April	
	$	$	$	$
Sales		52,500		105,000
Variable cost of Sales				
Op. stock (W1)	0		7,500	
Variable production costs (@$15/unit)	30,000		48,000	
	30,000		55,500	
Less cl. stock (@$15/unit) (W2)	7,500		10,500	
		22,500		45,000
		30,000		60,000
Variable selling etc costs		7,875		15,750
Contribution		22,125		44,250
Fixed costs				
Production	15,000		15,000	
Selling etc	10,000		10,000	
		25,000		25,000
Profit/Loss		(2,875)		19,250

Workings

(W1) The closing stock for March becomes the opening stock for April.

(W2)

	March	April
	Units	Units
Op. stock	0	500
Production	2,000	3,200
	2,000	3,700
Less sales	1,500	3,000
Cl. stock	500	700

(W3) Under-/over-absorption is the difference between overheads incurred and overheads absorbed.

"Overheads incurred" means actual overheads and we are told that the actual fixed overheads were as expected. Therefore the actual fixed overheads incurred are the same as the budgeted fixed overheads.

Budgeted fixed overhead = $5 per unit × 36,000 units

= $180,000 per annum

÷ 12

= 15,000 per month

March

Overheads incurred	15,000
Overheads absorbed	
$5/unit × 2,000 units	10,000
Under-absorption	(5,000)

April

Overheads incurred	15,000
Overheads absorbed	
$5/unit × 3,200 units	16,000
Over-absorption	1,000

(W4) Selling, etc fixed overhead = $120,000/12 = $10,000 per month.

(b) If there is no change in stock, the 2 systems give the same profit. If production is greater than sales then absorption costing shows the higher profit.

Difference in profit = change in stock × fixed production overhead cost per unit

In both March and April, production is greater than sales and thus absorption costing will show the higher profit (the smaller loss in March).

	March	April
Marginal costing profit/loss	(2,875)	19,250
Difference in profit		
(2,000 – 1,500) × $5 per unit	2,500	
(3,200 – 3,000) × $5 per unit		1,000
Absorption costing profit/loss	(375)	20,250

This difference occurs because marginal costing writes off the entire fixed overhead in the period incurred, whereas absorption costing carries forward some fixed production overhead into the next period in the valuation of closing stock.

Test your understanding 6

B

Marginal costing values inventory at a lower amount because it does not include fixed overheads in the valuation. Therefore as inventory levels increase the value of closing inventory under marginal costing will be lower. This will give a higher cost of sales and a lower and profit.

Test your understanding 7

D

Under-absorption occurs when the amount absorbed is less than the actual overheads incurred.

Test your understanding 8

D

$$\text{Absorption rate} \quad = \quad \frac{\$450{,}000}{900{,}000} \quad = \$0.50/\text{hour}$$

$$\text{Absorbed overheads} \quad = \quad \begin{array}{c} 60{,}000 \text{ units} \times 18 \text{ hrs/unit} \times \\ \$0.50/\text{hour} \end{array} \quad = \$540{,}000$$

$$\text{Actual overheads} \quad = \quad \$475{,}000$$

$$\text{Over-absorption} \quad = \quad \$65{,}000$$

Test your understanding 9

C

$$\text{Contribution margin} \quad = \quad \frac{160}{400} \quad = 40\%$$

$$\text{Target revenue} \quad = \quad \frac{100 + 100}{40\%} \quad = 500$$

$$\% \text{ Increase in revenue} \quad = \quad \frac{500}{400} \quad = 25\%$$

Test your understanding 10

(a) **Break Even Point**

Contribution per unit = $(100 – 56) = $44

$$\text{C/S ratio} = \frac{\text{Contribution per unit}}{\text{Selling price per unit}} = \frac{\$44}{\$100} = 0.44$$

Breakeven point in terms numbers of units sold

$$= \frac{\text{Fixed costs}}{\text{Contribution per unit}}$$

$$= \frac{\$220{,}000}{\$44} = 5{,}000 \text{ units}$$

Breakeven point in terms of sales revenue

$$= \frac{\text{Fixed costs}}{\text{C/S ratio}}$$

$$= \frac{\$220{,}000}{0.44} = \$500{,}000 \text{ units}$$

(Proof: breakeven units × selling price per unit = 5,000 × $100 = $500,000)

(b) **Margin of safety**

(as a % of Budgeted sales)

$$= \frac{\text{Budgeted sales} - \text{Break-even sales}}{\text{Budgeted sales}} \times 100\%$$

$$= \frac{7{,}500 - 5{,}000}{7{,}500} \times 100\%$$

= 33.33%

Test your understanding 11

Firstly we need to calculate the breakeven sales revenue.

Because we haven't been given any information on units, we must have to use the contribution sales revenue technique:

$$\text{C/S ratio} = \frac{\text{Total contribution}}{\text{Total sales revenue}} = \frac{(450 - 220)}{450}$$

= 0.511 (or 51.1%)

$$\text{Breakeven point (in terms of sales revenue)} = \frac{\text{Fixed costs}}{\text{C/S ratio}}$$

$$\text{Breakeven point (in terms of sales revenue)} = \frac{\$160,000}{0.511}$$

$$\text{Breakeven point (in terms of sales revenue)} = \$313,000$$

Now that we know the break-even position we can calculate the margin of safety (this is what is required in the second element of the question).

$$\text{Margin of safety (as a \% of budgeted sales)} = \frac{\text{Budgeted sales} - \text{Breakeven sales}}{\text{Budgeted sales}} \times 100\%$$

$$\text{Margin of safety (as a \% of budgeted sales)} = \frac{450 - 313}{450} \times 100\%$$

$$= 0.3044 \text{ (or 30.44\%)}$$

This tells us that for the company to fall into a loss making position its sales next year would have to fall by over 30.44% from their current position.

Test your understanding 12

(a) First calculate the current contribution per unit.

	$000	$000
Sales revenue		288
Direct materials	54	
Direct wages	72	
Variable production overhead	18	
Variable administration etc.	27	
	—	
		171
		——
Contribution		117
		——
Contribution per unit ($117,000/9,000 units)		$13
		——

Now you can use the formula to calculate the breakeven point.

Breakeven point =

$$\frac{\text{Fixed costs}}{\text{Contribution per unit}} = \frac{\$42,000 + \$36,000}{\$13} = 6,000 \text{ units}$$

(b) *Alternative (i)*

Budgeted contribution per unit	$13
Reduction in selling price ($32 – $28)	$4
	—
Revised contribution per unit	$9
	—
Revised breakeven point = $78,000/$9	8,667 units
Revised sales volume = 9,000 × (90/75)	10,800 units
Revised contribution = 10,800 × $9	$97,200
Less fixed costs	$78,000
	——
Revised profit	$19,200
	——

Alternative (ii)

Budgeted contribution per unit	$13.00
Reduction in selling price (15% × $32)	$4.80
	———
Revised contribution per unit	$8.20
	———

$$\text{Revised breakeven point} \quad = \quad \frac{\$78,000 + \$5,000}{\$8.20} \qquad 10,122 \text{ Units}$$

Revised sales volume = 9,000 units × (100/75)	12,000 Units
Revised contribution = 12,000 × $8.20	$98,400
Less fixed costs	$83,000
	———
Revised profit	$15,400
	———

Neither of the two alternative proposals is worthwhile. They both result in lower forecast profits. In addition, they will both increase the breakeven point and will therefore increase the risk associated with the company's operations.

(c) This exercise has shown you how an understanding of cost behaviour patterns and the manipulation of contribution can enable the rapid evaluation of the financial effects of a proposal. We can now expand it to demonstrate another aspect of the application of CVP analysis to short-term decision-making.

Once again, the key is the required contribution. This time the contribution must be sufficient to cover both the fixed costs and the required profit. If we then divide this amount by the contribution earned from each unit, we can determine the required sales volume.

$$\text{Required sales} \quad = \quad \frac{\text{Fixed costs + required profit}}{\text{Contribution per unit}}$$

$$= \quad \frac{(\$42,000 + \$36,000 + \$45,500)}{\$13} \quad = \underline{\textbf{9,500 units}}$$

Techniques for modern environments

Chapter learning objectives

Lead	Component
A1. Discuss costing methods and their results.	(h) Explain the impact of just-in-time manufacturing methods on cost accounting and the use of 'back-flush accounting' when work-in-progress stock is minimal.
A2. Explain the role of MRP and ERP systems.	(a) Explain the role of MRP and ERP systems in supporting standard costing systems, calculating variances and facilitating the posting of ledger entries.

1 Chapter overview diagram

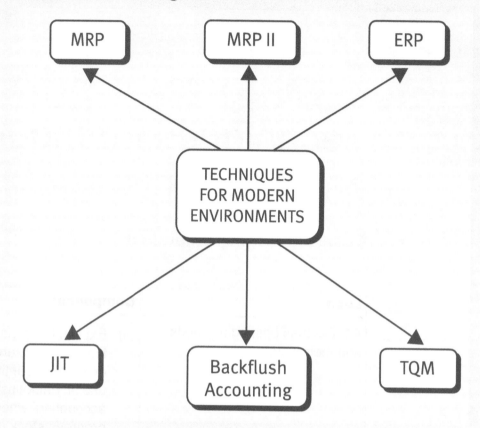

2 Modern manufacturing environment

'To compete successfully in today's highly competitive global environment companies are making customer satisfaction an overriding priority, adopting new management approaches, changing their manufacturing systems and investing in new technologies. These changes are having a significant influence on management accounting systems.

' Colin Drury in ' Management and Cost Accounting'.

The modern manufacturing environment is very different from the traditional production environment. It means that traditional costing methods covered in the previous chapter are becoming less relevant.

In this chapter we explore how the modern production system has changed. We then need to consider how costing has adapted to this and created new ways to calculate a product's production cost. This final element is explored in more detail in the following two chapters.

The background to change

Cost is an important competitive weapon. Low-cost producers will have an advantage in the marketplace over those whose cost base is higher. However, cost is only one competitive weapon and it is one that has become of declining importance in recent years. Other dimensions of competition have become increasingly important: product reliability, product innovation, shortened time to market, and flexibility of response to customer demands – these last three being features of time-based competition.

It is obvious that a manufacturer would gain competitive advantage if it were able to produce the diversity of output seen in a jobbing system (where each product is almost unique) at a cost associated with mass production (so that economies of scale make the cost per unit much smaller). In recent years, some manufacturers, most notably the Japanese, have been successful in moving towards this. Furthermore, the products of these manufacturers have an enviable reputation for reliability. These suppliers have clearly gained competitive advantage in the marketplace, forcing competitors to follow or exit the market. Consumers, given the opportunity to enjoy diversity and reliability at a mass-produced cost, have reacted not unexpectedly by requiring all manufacturers to offer these features. Further, a corollary of the requirement for greater diversity has been a shortening of product life cycles.

This fundamental shift in demand patterns dictates a need for companies to constantly review and redesign existing products, and to shorten the time to market of each new line in order to ensure satisfactory returns from it. Against this new background, companies will find it increasingly difficult to gain economic returns from an expensive, dedicated mass-production line operated in traditional way. Means must be found whereby manufacturing facilities cannot only accommodate the production of existing lines and their inevitable redesigned successors, but also facilitate the rapid introduction of new products at minimum cost. The challenge of the modern, globally competitive market is to offer an increased and increasing choice of high-quality products at a cost traditionally associated with mass production; to enjoy economies of scale, along with the economies of scope that result from the increased manufacturing flexibility. This challenge can be met by investment in new technology, and the adoption of alternative production management strategies. Those who successfully meet this challenge are the 'world-class manufacturers' that provide the benchmark against which other manufacturers are measured.

'World class' organisations make products using the latest manufacturing technologies and techniques. Those products are typically sold around the world and are generally viewed as being first rate in terms of quality, design, performance and reliability. Companies such as Toyota, BMW and Boeing have been described at various times as being world-class manufacturers. The world-class manufacturer will probably invest heavily in research, product design, CAD/CAM technology. It will also make extensive use of modern management concepts such as Total quality management (TQM), flexible manufacturing systems and customer relationship management. These concepts variously known as advanced manufacturing technologies (AMTs) or the new manufacturing are discussed in detail below.

3 Characteristics of the modern manufacturing environment

The key changes in a modern production environment are as follows:

- greater use of Advanced Manufacturing Technology (**AMT**)
- a much more **global environment**
- a greater focus on **cost reduction**
- better **customer focus**
- a need for more **flexible** production systems
- more **employee participation**
- **shorter product life cycles**
- a greater emphasis on **quality**

More details

Advanced manufacturing technology (AMT)

AMT is a collective term for a wide variety of modern practices and techniques based on computer systems. You do not need to know these in detail, just the effect they have on companies today – for instance the vast reduction in labour costs.

It includes systems such as MRP, ERP and JIT for controlling inventories and other resources and these systems are explored in more detail in this chapter.

Global environment

- Companies operate in a world economy
- Customers and competitors come from all over the world
- Products are made from components from around the world
- Firms have to be world class to compete.

Cost reduction

Clearly an important factor to the customer, a key part of World Class Manufacturing can be to be the lowest cost supplier. This means that during a price war the business has the opportunity to quote lower than its competitors, but also more importantly, in less severe circumstances similar pricing to competitors will lead to greater profitability.

Customer focus

In the past the linking of product to consumer was relatively hazy in many instances. A product would be produced within a large production run and then a customer would be 'sold' that unit. As competition increases, customers are demanding ever-improving levels of service in cost, quality, reliability, delivery and the choice of innovative new products. Companies need to be able to react quickly to changes in the environment to survive these days. They must be able to meet these customer requirements.

Flexibility

The move away from standardised units of production towards individual customised units means that mass production techniques are redundant, instead, it is of greatest importance to take an order from placement to completion in the shortest time possible. This means that production processes will be designed differently to accommodate flexibility of production rather than just throughput.

Employee participation

To ensure this flexibility, managers need to empower their employees to make decisions quickly, without reference to more senior managers. By empowering employees and giving them relevant information they will be able to respond faster to customers, increase process flexibility, reduce cycle times and improve morale.

The changes required in the way that the workforce is managed are frequently the most difficult aspects of World Class Manufacturing to implement. The changes often require a considerable amount of time and education so that trust, mutual respect and a common purpose can be established between the company's managers and production personnel. The employees are given a great deal more responsibility for production quality and scheduling. The operators are cross-trained so that they can perform a wide variety of tasks and therefore provide more production flexibility. A team approach is established which is designed to encourage all company employees to work co-operatively, eradicating the traditional job demarcation and incentive pay plans

Management Accounting Systems are moving from **providing information to managers** to monitor employees to **providing information to employees** to empower them to focus on continuous improvement.

Shorter product life cycles

Companies need to be continually developing new products in order to survive.

Quality

The World Class Manufacturing approach to quality is quite different from the traditional approach because the primary emphasis is placed on the resolution of the problems that cause poor quality, rather than merely detecting it. These systems are more proactive and try to prevent problems from occurring in the first place rather than waiting for them to occur and then fixing them.

The system might be developed formally under Total Quality Management.

Cost reduction

Cost reduction in a loose sense is simply any action which results in a reduction in costs for an organisation. Used incorrectly, it is often just a reaction to a crisis, whereby for instance budgets for all activities of the company are cut by 5%, whether or not the activity is being run efficiently at present. More correctly: Cost reduction is a management technique concerned with reducing the unit cost of a product or a service on a permanent basis without affecting the perceived quality.

Value analysis

Value analysis is one example of a cost reduction technique. It is also known as value engineering. The CIMA definition of value analysis is 'A systematic inter-disciplinary examination of factors affecting the cost of a product or service, in order to devise means of achieving the specified purpose most economically at the required standard of quality and reliability'.

The purpose of value analysis is to identify any unnecessary cost elements within the components of goods and services. It is more comprehensive than simple cost reduction in that it examines the purposes or functions of the product and is concerned with establishing the means whereby these are achieved. Any cost data that does not add value to the product or service should be eliminated.

Value analysis will often lead to the reduction of components used in a product, the use of alternative, cheaper components and the standardisation of parts across several product lines.

As a consequence of this:

- many companies now have very diverse product ranges, with a high level of tailormade products and services;

- product life cycles have dramatically reduced, often from several years to just a few months;

- standard costing techniques are becoming less relevant to businesses and new techniques such as backflush accounting and throughput accounting are becoming more widespread. These techniques are explained and discussed further over the coming chapters.

Other AMT abbreviations

Your syllabus specifically mentions MRP and ERP systems, but there are other three-letter acronyms that you will need to be aware of, particularly if the examiner describes them briefly in objective test questions, include the following:

- Computer Aided Manufacturing **(CAM)** uses computer-based technology to program and control the production process.

- Computer Aided Design **(CAD)** is computer-based technology which allows products to be designed, modified and tested interactively on a computer screen.

- Flexible Manufacturing System **(FMS)** is a highly automated, integrated, computer controlled production system. An FMS is capable of producing a wide range of parts and can switch rapidly and economically from one production run to another, while maintaining the quality of output.

- Computer Integrated Manufacturing **(CIM)** is a feature of a Flexible Manufacturing System which enables an organisation to link all its functions, from the offices to the factory floor, to a system of total automation using computers. It brings together AMT, quality control activities and so on into a single coherent computerised system.

- Electronic Data Interchange **(EDI)** is a computer-to-computer system that facilitates the transmission of business data electronically, enabling an organisation to communicate directly and immediately with its customers and suppliers.

- Supply Chain Management **(SCM)** is the coordination and integration of the flow of information between all of the various organisations in a supply chain, from the supplier to the manufacturer and right through to the retailer and the final customer.

- Optimised Production Technology **(OPT)** is a technique that has developed from MRP systems and which requires similar operational and resource information. It seeks to identify and make optimum use of the bottleneck resources within a process, which prevent throughput from being higher. Non-bottleneck resources are scheduled around these and are utilised at an appropriate capacity to avoid the build up of excessive inventory.

4 Total quality management (TQM)

Total quality management (TQM) is a philosophy of quality management that has a number of important features.

- Total – means that everyone in the value chain is involved in the process, including employees, customers and suppliers.

- Quality – products and services must meet the customers' requirements.

- Management – quality is actively managed rather than controlled so that problems are prevented from occurring.

There are three basic principles of TQM:

(1) 'Get it right, first time'

(2) Continuous improvement

(3) Customer focus

The key impacts of TQM are often that problems are avoided rather than solved, and inventory levels can be greatly reduced.

Further details

There are three basic principles of TQM:

(1) **'Get it right, first time'**

TQM considers that the costs of prevention are less than the costs of correction. One of the main aims of TQM is to achieve *zero* rejects or defects and to ensure that all customer needs or expectations are satisfied.

(2) **Continuous improvement**

The second basic principle of TQM is dissatisfaction with the status-quo. Realistically a zero-defect goal may not be obtainable. It does however provide a target to ensure that a company should never be satisfied with its present level of rejects. The management and staff should believe that it is always possible to improve and to be able to get it more right next time!

The system is based on a 'kaizen' approach which is a costing technique to reflect continuous efforts to reduce product costs, improve product quality, and/or improve the production process after manufacturing activities have begun.

(3) **Customer focus**

Quality is examined from a customer perspective and the system is aimed at meeting customer needs and expectations.

TQM will often involve the use of Just-In-Time stock control in order to eliminate any waste in stock.

TQM and standard costing

TQM is often seen as being at odds with traditional standard costing methods for the following reasons:

- TQM expects continuous improvement rather than standard performance

- TQM expects everyone to take responsibility for failures in the system

- TQM systems do not accept waste as being acceptable.

- TQM is concerned with quality related costs rather than production costs

- TQM often incorporates JIT inventory control (explained later) so that material variances are less likely

More details

TQM is often seen as being at odds with traditional standard costing methods for the following reasons:

- In the pursuit of continuous improvement, standard costs become out of date and irrelevant. In TQM environments managers are expected to find better ways to perform tasks, eliminate waste etc. The business itself is likely to be operating in a changing environment and therefore the idea of a 'standard' or repetitive cost is unlikely.

- Standard costing techniques attempt to allocate responsibility for each cost to an individual manager. With TQM There is an expectation that everyone takes responsibility for failures in the system.

- Traditional standard costing techniques allow for elements of waste and scrap in product costs. The cost of materials in the standard cost card, for example, will be altered if some materials experience 'normal' wastage levels. TQM systems accept no waste as being acceptable.

- TQM is concerned with quality related costs rather than financial costs solely concerned with cost control and efficiency. For example, traditional costing might be concerned with how quickly a product is produced (e.g. the labour efficiency variance, whereas TQM would be most interested in how well it has been produced (e.g. whether there has been a significant number of returns from customers – known as external failure costs).

- TQM often incorporates JIT inventory control (explained later) so that material variances are less likely and less significant. Close relationships with suppliers mean that material price variances are unlikely and a focus on quality means that adverse materials usage variances become less likely.

As a result, in TQM environments, **benchmarking** is preferred to standard costing as a performance measurement technique because TQM emphasises continuous improvement and reference to a predetermined internal standard gives no incentive to improve.

These ideas are explored again in chapter 7 after variances have been considered in more detail.

Quality related costs

Failing to satisfy customers' needs and expectations, or failing to get it right first time, costs the average company between 15 and 30 per cent of sales revenue.

A quality-related cost is the 'cost of ensuring and assuring quality, as well as the cost incurred when quality is not achieved. Quality costs are classified as prevention costs, appraisal cost, internal failure cost and external failure cost' (BS6143).

(1) **Prevention cost**

Prevention costs represent the cost of any action taken to prevent or reduce defects and failures. It includes the design and development of quality control equipment and the maintenance of the equipment.

(2) **Appraisal costs**

Appraisal costs are the costs incurred, such as inspection and testing, in initially ascertaining the conformance of the product to quality requirements. They include the costs of goods inwards inspection, and the monitoring of the production output.

(3) Internal failure cost

Internal failure costs are the costs arising from inadequate quality where the problem is discovered before the transfer of ownership from supplier to purchaser. They include the cost of reworking or rectifying the product, the net cost of scrap, downtime of machinery due to quality problems, etc.

(4) External failure cost

The cost arising from inadequate quality discovered after the transfer of ownership from supplier to purchaser such as complaints, warranty claims, recall cost, costs of repairing or replacing returned faulty goods, etc.

Conformance costs and non-conformance costs

Appraisal costs and prevention costs may also be referred to as conformance costs, whilst internal failure costs and external failure costs may be referred to as non-conformance costs.

Example 1

E plc provides a computer upgrading, servicing and repair facility to a variety of business and personal computer users.

An issue which concerns the management of E plc is the quality of the service provided for clients. The Operations Manager has suggested that the company should introduce Total Quality Management (TQM) but the management team is unsure how to do this and of the likely costs and benefits of its introduction.

Required:

(a) Explain Total Quality Management in the context of E plc.

(8 marks)

(b) Describe the likely costs and benefits that would arise if E plc introduced a TQM policy.

(8 marks)

(Total: 16 marks)

5 Just In Time

Just-in-time (JIT) is a method of inventory control based on two principles

- goods and services should be **produced only when they are needed**.

- products (or services) must be **delivered to the customer at the time the customer wants them** ('just in time').

This in turn requires that suppliers deliver raw materials to production just as they are needed so that **purchasing happens just-in-time for production**.

JIT sees inventory as a cost burden and in its extreme form, a JIT system seeks to have **zero inventories**.

Further details

Just-in-time (JIT) is an approach to operations management based on the idea that goods and services should be **produced only when they are needed**.

At the same time, products (or services) must be **delivered to the customer at the time the customer wants them** ('just in time'). To be able to do this with no inventory, the production cycle must be short, and there can be no hold-ups in production due to defective items, bottlenecks or inefficiency.

JIT sees inventory as a cost burden and in its extreme form, a JIT system seeks to have **zero inventories**. When there are no inventories of raw materials, part-finished work-in-progress or finished goods, a break-down or disruption in one stage of the production chain will have an immediate impact on all the other stages of the chain. In practice, it might be impossible to have no inventory at all, but management should be trying continually to reduce and minimise inventory levels.

- JIT can be described as a 'pull through' system. This is a system that responds to customer demand: components are drawn through the system as required, so that items are manufactured only when ordered by a customer. Similarly, raw materials are obtained from suppliers only when they are needed for production.

- This contrasts with a 'push' system, in which items are produced, and if there is no immediate demand, inventories build up.

Another aspect of the JIT philosophy is **high quality**, and JIT is consistent with Total Quality Management or **TQM**.

The JIT philosophy is based on:

- continuous improvement ('kaizen') – doing things well and gradually doing them better, and
- the elimination of waste.

Examples of waste

Waste is defined as any activity that does not add value. Examples of waste are:

- **Overproduction**. Producing more than is needed immediately creates unnecessary inventory.

- **Waiting time**. Waiting time is evidence of a hold-up in the flow of production through the system. Set-up time is also non-productive time. ('Set-up' is the work needed at the end of one job or batch of work to get the production process ready for the next job or batch.) The aim is to achieve quick set-up times and low-cost set-up.

- **Unnecessary movement** of materials or people. Moving items around a production area does not add value.

- **Waste in the process**, caused by design defects in the product, or poor maintenance work. Work flow is an important element in JIT. Work needs to flow without interruption in order to avoid a build-up of inventory or unnecessary waiting times. The movement of materials and part-finished work is wasteful, and this waste can be reduced by laying out the work floor and designing the work flow so as to minimise movements. JIT production is associated with the use of work cells: a work cell is a small area on the factory floor that is given responsibility for the production of an entire product or part. The employees in the work cell do all the work on the product from the beginning to the end of the process, and so the work cell manager or supervisor is entirely responsible for the work flow and the product quality.

- **Inventory** is wasteful. The target should be to eliminate all inventory by removing the reasons why it builds up.

- **Complexity in work processes**. Simplification of work gets rid of waste in the system (the 'waste of motion') by eliminating unnecessary actions.

- **Defective goods** are a significant cause of waste in many operations.

- **Inspection time** is wasteful because it adds nothing to value. Inspection time can be eliminated by making the process free from errors and defects.

Pre-requisites for JIT

The operational requirements for the successful implementation of JIT production are as follows:

- **High quality.** Without high quality there will be disruptions in production, reducing throughput. Production must be reliable and not subject to hold-ups.

- **Speed.** Throughput in the operation must be fast, so that customer orders can be met by production. Without fast throughput, it will be necessary to hold some inventory to meet customer orders.

- **Flexibility.** The production system must be able to respond immediately to customer orders. Production must therefore be flexible, and in small batch sizes. The ideal batch size is 1.

- **Lower costs.** Fewer errors, less waste, greater reliability and flexibility and faster throughput should all help to reduce costs.

The most suitable conditions for applying JIT management are where:

- there are short set-up times and low set-up costs

- there are short lead times and low ordering costs for buying raw materials from suppliers

- work flow is fairly constant over time, and customer demand is not uneven and unpredictable

- production throughput time is very short

- there are no downtimes due to poor quality or stock-outs.

Benefits and problems of JIT

Benefits	Problems
• less cash tied up in inventory	• relies on predictable demand, flexible supplier and a flexible workforce
• less storage space needed	
• better quality	• there will be initial set-up costs (e.g. in FMS)
• more flexible production	
• fewer bottlenecks	• it is very difficult for businesses with a wide geographical spread
• better co-ordination	
• more reliable and supportive suppliers	• there is no fallback position if disruptions occur in the supply chain
	• it may be harder to switch suppliers

More details

Benefits from JIT

Successful adopters of JIT production have enjoyed tremendous savings. The most obvious saving arises from the much lower investment required to hold inventory. When inventory levels are reduced from three months to one month of sales (increasing the stock turnover from 4 times to 12 times) financing costs are reduced by two-thirds. In fact, stock turnover can be increased to 30 or 60 once production problems, made visible by inventory reductions are solved

Beyond these obvious financing savings, companies also discovered large space savings. They found that up to 50% of factory space had previously been used to store in-process inventory. Having eliminated WIP, companies found another factory inside their old factory. Such savings permitted planned expansions to be curtailed, and previously dispersed operations could be consolidated inside a single location.

But even the carrying cost and floor space savings were smaller than the savings from improved JIT operations as companies attempted to reduce inventories, many problems emerged in the factory that had formerly been hidden by inventory buffers: quality problems, bottlenecks, co-ordination problems, inadequate documentation, and supplier unreliability, among others. Without the discipline to achieve JIT operations, these problems would remain unsolved. The rationalisation of production processes, the elimination of waste, and the more visible display of production problems that were achieved under successful JIT operations led to great reductions in material losses and great improvement in overall factory productivity.

6 Production management strategies – MRP and MRP II

Material requirements planning (MRP)

MRP can be defined as a computerised planning system that first determines the quantity and timing of the finished goods demanded, and then uses this to determine the requirements for raw materials, components and subassemblies at each of the prior stages of production.

Output from an MRP system

The output from an MRP system is an overall production schedule, and in addition it produces purchase orders and works orders that will initiate the purchasing of raw materials and the manufacture of parts and sub-assemblies.

Benefits of the MRP system

A significant benefit of MRP systems is that if any change is necessary to the manufacturing schedule, for example due to an unexpected change in customer demand patterns, a new production schedule can be prepared in a very short time, together with new purchase orders and works orders.

A benefit claimed for MRP I is that it should reduce inventory levels. Through reliable scheduling of production requirements, it should be possible to avoid producing items that are not required in the foreseeable future, and so are held as inventory.

More details

Material requirements planning (MRP I)

Traditionally material requirements were planned by continuously reviewing stock levels, and a predetermined quantity was ordered each time stocks fell below a predetermined level. This stock control approach was based on the assumption that replenishment of stocks could be planned *independently* of each other. However, the demand for materials is *dependent* on the demand for the assemblies of which they are part.

MRP I originated in the early 1960s as a computerised approach for co-ordinating the planning of materials acquisition and production. MRP I is a flow control system in the sense that it orders only what components are required to maintain the manufacturing flow. The orders can be for purchased parts or manufactured parts, and MRP I thus provides the basis for production scheduling and materials purchasing. MRP I can be defined as a computerised planning system that first determines the quantity and timing of the finished goods demanded, and then uses this to determine the requirements for raw materials, components and subassemblies at each of the prior stages of production.

Core data requirements

The core data requirements for operating an MRP system are:

(1) The **Master Production Schedule** (MPS). This specifies the quantity of each finished unit to be produced, and the time at which the unit will be required.

(2) The **Bill of Materials** file (BOM). This file sets out a detailed specification for each finished product in terms of subassemblies, components and materials. It distinguishes between those items which are purchased from outside the company and those which are internally manufactured.

(3) The **Inventory File.** This maintains details of current stock levels for each subassembly, component and part. It distinguishes between stock items that are already allocated to orders but which have not yet been released from stock, and those items which have not yet been allocated. It also records scheduled receipts of items.

Master production schedule

A master production schedule is a plan summarising the volume and timing of end-products required. The schedule is constructed from known customer orders (not yet fulfilled) and forecasts of future orders. It sets out how many units of each product will be required from production, and by when.

Having established the quantities and completion times for end products, the system works back to earlier stages of the production process, and prepares a schedule of the quantities of sub-assemblies, components and raw materials required, and the time by which these need to be available.

'The master production schedule (MPS) is the most important planning and control schedule in a business, and forms the main input to materials requirements planning…. In manufacturing, the MPS contains a statement of the volume and timing of the end products to be made; this schedule drives the whole operation in terms of what is assembled, what is manufactured and what is bought. It is the basis of planning the utilisation of labour and equipment and it determines the provisioning of materials and cash' (Operations Management, Slack, Chambers and Johnston).

Bills of materials

For every product manufactured by the business, there is a bill of materials. A bill of materials lists in detail the parts that make up the product and their production lead time. It also shows the relationship between the parts in the end-product.

Using the bills of materials for each product, the master production schedule is 'exploded' to work out:

- the number of sub-assemblies that are needed, and the quantities of raw materials and parts
- the time by which they are needed, and therefore
- the time by which their manufacture must begin or the purchase orders must be placed.

The scheduling is based on an assumption that lead times for purchasing and manufacture are constant and predictable, which might not be realistic in practice.

Inventory file

The MRP I system must have access to inventory records, so that current availability of inventories can be checked. The inventory records should relate to all raw material items, components and sub-assemblies as well as finished goods items.

The manufacturing schedule is prepared with allowances made for current inventory levels.

The data in the system are then analysed to produce a **materials requirements plan** for purchasing and manufacturing. This is a time phased schedule (usually in 'buckets' of one week) detailing when the orders are to be placed for subassemblies and components.

Manufacturing resources planning (MRP II)

When MRP is extended beyond the planning of raw materials, components and subassemblies to encompass other input resources, such as machine capacity and labour, so that the system provides a fully integrated planning approach to the management of all the company's resources it is known as Manufacturing Resources Planning. To produce MRP II schedules the database is extended to include labour resource data and machine availability data.

MRP and accounting

MRP I and accounting

An MRP I system is not integrated with other related systems within the organisation. From an accounting perspective, an MRP I system cannot produce a production cost budget or a materials purchases budget.

However, the system does provide information that can be used by accountants.

- The master production schedule provides the basis for drawing up a production cost budget.

- The schedule of materials purchase requirements can be used to prepare a materials purchases budget, by applying expected purchase prices to the quantities of purchases required.

- A bill of materials for each product can be used to construct a standard or budgeted material cost for products, by applying a cost to each of the component parts of the end-product.

MRP II and accounting

MRP II systems offer integration between the production planning, inventory control and purchasing systems and the accounting system. The accounting function has access to bills of materials and production schedules through the common database. The system also holds data on prices for materials and labour.

It is therefore possible for the system to produce:

- a production cost budget from the master production schedule

- a materials purchases budget

- elements of a cash budget

- a standard material and labour cost for each unit produced.

In addition, when changes are made to production specifications, the bill of materials is amended, and this should work through to the accounting function, where a new, updated standard cost can be calculated for the product.

7 ERP: Enterprise resource planning

An enterprise resource system is a powerful computer system that integrates information from all parts of the organisation. It is an extension of the MRP philosophy, but provides more integration between different parts of the organisation.

An ERP system is expensive to acquire and install, given the size and complexity of many global businesses. However, the elements of an ERP system should include modules for:

- **manufacturing**: production planning and control, materials purchasing, plant maintenance, quality management

- **sales and distribution**: sales order management, customer management, distribution, transportation and shipping

- **accounting**: accounts receivable, accounts payable, budgeting, standard costing

- **human resources**: recruitment and workforce scheduling, payroll, training and development.

The system should also offer some decision support facilities, by giving decision-makers access to up-to-date company information.

8 Backflush accounting

Backflush accounting is a method of accounting that is **typically used with JIT inventory control systems**. Costs are not tracked sequentially to production, but are instead calculated and charged when the product is sold.

It means **there are much fewer accounting entries** and administration as costs are not added to products at each stage of production – records of **materials used and work-in-progress values are usually not required**.

Backflush accounting does not account for individual transactions such as when materials are issued to production, overheads are absorbed into products, etc. Instead block entries are made at the end of the month and inventory values are based on **budget/standard** cost.

A comparison with traditional systems

Review of a traditional system

In traditional accounting systems inventory is a key item. Traditional manufacturing firms hold high levels of inventory and much of the work of the management accountant is to put a value on this inventory.

The traditional approach is to track the cost of products through the sequential stages of production, building up costing records for the direct material consumed, the direct labour cost and the overhead expense for each product. This involves a number of 'double entries' in the accounting system, such as:

- raw materials purchased are recorded in a raw materials account

- as each individual transfer is made to work-in-progress (WIP) a double entry is made out of the raw materials account and into a WIP account. This means that **there are entries for every nut, bolt and screw transferred in system**

- further entries are made into this account to record wages and absorbed overheads (conversion costs)

- when the units are finished entries are made to transfer the total cost out of the WIP account into a finished goods account

- when the finished goods are sold an entry is made to transfer the goods out of a finished goods account and into a cost of sales account.

With hundreds or thousands of movements in inventories between raw materials, WIP and finished goods, **the accounting and administration of this system is complex and expensive to operate**.

A backflush accounting system

Backflush accounting offers a simplified approach to costing by getting rid of unnecessary costing records.

It is suitable for use in a just-in-time (JIT) environment. A JIT company holds minimal amounts of inventory; raw materials are only ordered when they are required, production is fast and efficient keeping work-in-progress to a minimum and once production is complete goods are delivered straight to the customer which minimises the amount of finished goods held.

Instead of building up product costs sequentially from the start to the finish of production, back-flush accounting calculates product costs retrospectively, at the end of the accounting period.

There are much fewer double entries:

- the cost of raw materials is allocated to a 'raw materials and in progress' (RIP) account

- labour and production overheads are allocated straight to the cost of goods sold account

- at the end of the accounting period an inventory stock-take is carried out to determine closing balances for raw materials, WIP and finished goods. This is quick as there are few inventories. Inventory values are based on budget/standard cost.

- the closing inventory values for raw materials and WIP are then 'backflushed' from the cost of goods sold account into the RIP account. Similarly the closing inventory value for finished goods is 'backflushed' into a finished goods account.

Effectively, rather than record every movement of inventory, a **block entry is made at the end of the accounting period** – typically when the item is sold (see the discussion on 'trigger points' later). The only accounts in the double entry system with respect to inventory can be raw materials purchases and cost of sales.

Thus with back-flush accounting **there will be a significant reduction in accounting costs**. Instead of making potentially hundreds of thousands of entries each month (if there are that many transfers of inventory), this system can reduce the double entries to dozens, regardless of how often materials and inventory is transferred across the business.

Note: In the exam you will NOT be required to perform the double entry for backflush accounting.

Link to external reporting

This runs counter to the accounting principles laid out in IAS 2, however as inventory in JIT systems is largely immaterial, this may not cause issues for external reporting. For internal reporting and management accounts, IAS 2 does not apply and the sequential valuation of inventory in a JIT system is seen as being unnecessarily time consuming.

Advantages and disadvantages of backflush accounting

Advantages	Disadvantages
• simple	• not appropriate if inventories are high
• less administration	
• gives the same results as traditional costing when inventories are low	• not appropriate for long production cycles
	• provides less detailed information
	• losses may be over-valued

More details

Advantages of backflush accounting

The advantages of using backflush accounting are:

- It is a simple costing system.

- It avoids the need to record production costs sequentially as items move through step-by-step operations in the production process.

- When inventory levels are low or constant, it yields the same results as traditional costing methods would.

It is therefore appropriate in a mature JIT environment where there is a short production cycle and low inventories.

Disadvantages of backflush accounting

The main disadvantages of backflush accounting are:

- It is not appropriate for manufacturing environments where inventory levels are high, due to the problems of counting and valuing the inventory at the end of each period.

- It is probably inappropriate for production systems with a long production cycle. In such an environment, it is probably preferable to record the production costs as the work passes sequentially through each stage of the production system.

- It provides less detailed management information than traditional costing systems.

- Losses in a backflush accounting system will be valued at full standard cost. That is, they will be assumed to be completed units. In reality, the losses are unlikely to have been of fully complete units and therefore the full cost of production will not be attributable to them.

Variants of backflush accounting

Different companies might use different variations of backflush accounting – often determined by how much inventory they hold and whether they use a 'true' JIT in time system that delivers to customers just as they need the product.

Trigger points

The key differences between the systems relates to the differing 'trigger points' at which costs are recognised within the cost accounts and thus associated with products. **Trigger points determine when entries are made in the accounting system**, and effectively relate to how many elements of inventory the system wants to reflect at the end of the period. Therefore, the most common variants of backflush accounting are:

	Number of trigger points	Trigger point (s)	Inventory balances at the year end
Variant 1	1	Inventory transactions are only recorded when a product is sold	None
Variant 2	1	Inventory transactions are only recorded when production is complete	Finished goods
Variant 3	2	Inventory transactions are recorded at two points: • when materials are received • When materials production is complete	• Raw materials • Finished goods

Variant 1 is often used to motivate staff to focus on sales. Transactions are only recorded when a sale is made (rather than when a product is produced) and this could be linked to staff rewards. Variant 2 might be needed if there is some unpredictability in demand or where some inventory needs to be stockpiled before delivery to customers. In that case, finished goods might be seen to be significant enough to be recorded on the statement of financial position. Variant 3 may have to be used if suppliers deliveries are unpredictable so that some buffer stock (covered later in the syllabus) needs to be held of raw materials. It also makes managers aware of the cost of not using stock and having it stored and idle.

Commonalities between variants

Most variants have the following common features:

- the focus is on output – costs are first associated with output (measured as either sales or completed production and valued at standard cost) and then allocated between inventories and costs of goods sold by working back.

- conversion costs (labour and overheads) are never attached to products until they are complete (or even sold) – thus the traditional WIP account doesn't exist. Materials are recognised at different points according to the variant used, but only to the extent of being either inventories of raw materials or part of the cost of inventories of finished goods. Again, materials are not attached to WIP.

It should be seen that as stock of raw materials, WIP and finished goods are decreased to minimal levels, as **in a 'true' JIT system, these variants will give the same basic results**.

9 Chapter summary

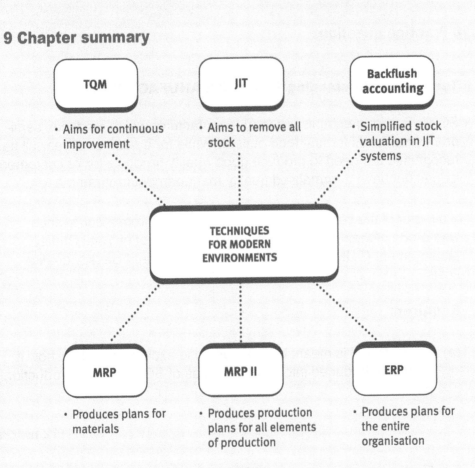

10 Practice questions

Test your understanding 1 – FOOD MANUFACTURER

SG plc is a long-established food manufacturer which produces semi-processed foods for fast food outlets. While for a number of years it has recognised the need to produce good quality products for its customers, it does not have a formalised quality management programme.

A director of the company has recently returned from a conference, where one of the speakers introduced the concept of Total Quality Management (TQM) and the need to recognise and classify quality costs.

Required:

(a) Explain what is meant by TQM and use examples to show how it may be introduced into different areas of SG plc's food production business.

(12 marks)

(b) Explain why the adoption of TQM is particularly important within a Just-in-Time (JIT) production environment.

(5 marks)

(c) Explain four quality cost classifications, using examples relevant to the business of SG plc.

(8 marks)

(Total: 25 marks)

Test your understanding 2

Explain whether back-flush accounting would be suitable for a major construction firm (which makes bridges, roads, buildings, etc.).

(5 marks)

Test your understanding 3 – QUALITY COST

Explain how quality cost can be measured in a programme of Total Quality Management (TQM).

(5 marks)

Test your understanding 4

Identify which of the following statements are true:

(i) Enterprise Resource Planning (ERP) systems are accounting oriented information systems which aid in identifying and planning the enterprise wide resources needed to resource, make, account for and deliver customer orders.

(ii) Flexible Manufacturing Systems (FMS) are integrated, computer-controlled production systems, capable of producing any of a range of parts and of switching quickly and economically between them.

(iii) Just-In-Time (JIT) is a system whose objective is to produce, or to procure, products or components as they are required.

    A   (i) and (ii) only

    B   (i) and (iii) only

    C   (ii) and (iii) only

    D   (i), (ii) and (iii)

(2 marks)

Test your understanding answers

Example 1

(a) Total quality management (TQM) has two main concepts:

(1) **Get it right first time**

TQM considers that the costs of prevention are less than the costs of correction. One of the main aims of TQM is to achieve *zero* rejects or defects and to ensure that all customer needs or expectations are satisfied.

(2) **Continuous improvement**

The second basic principle of TQM is dissatisfaction with the status quo. Realistically a zero-defect goal may not be obtainable. It does however provide a target to ensure that a company should never be satisfied with its present level of rejects. The management and staff should believe that it is always possible to improve and to be able to get it more right next time!

There must be a focus on the customer and what they require and there must be a constant review of costs and performance to ensure that the aims of the TQM programme are being met.

The aim is to build good quality in rather than inspect poor quality out. The aim in the end is to design such good products and processes and obtain such good materials that inspection is no longer necessary.

E plc should focus on the whole of its operation from start to finish if it wishes the TQM programme to be a success.

It must ensure that the input to its processes is defect-free. It must choose first-class suppliers who will guarantee the quality of their components. It must communicate with the suppliers to let them know what is expected of them. E plc is likely to have to pay a premium price to obtain these premium quality components.

It must also examine its own processes to ensure that there are as few quality problems as possible. Where there are known quality problems efforts should be directed at improving the processes by whatever means are appropriate, e.g. training, preventative maintenance, newer more reliable machines, etc.

The output process must also be controlled, i.e. the relationship with the customer. Efforts must be made to ensure that no defective products reach the customer, perhaps by means of final inspection before the goods leave the business and that where problems do occur, they are corrected as soon as possible. Communication with the customer is very important to ensure that the customer's needs are being met.

It is not enough to decide that a TQM system should be introduced. The programme should be carefully considered and communication to the staff should be clear. They should be educated as to the ideas behind TQM and given the necessary training to accomplish its aims. TQM should permeate the whole of the organisation and must be continually assessed to ensure that its goals are still being achieved.

(b) The likely costs that would arise include:

(1) Extra prevention cost

These are any costs incurred in order to prevent quality problems from occurring. Examples would include training, preventative maintenance, the purchase or hire of new, more reliable machines, the sourcing of better quality components, etc.

(2) Extra appraisal costs

Appraisal costs are the costs incurred in checking the raw materials and the product against the quality standard. These would include the wages and salaries of the quality control staff and any capital expenditure on testing equipment.

We would expect appraisal costs to increase at first when a TQM programme is introduced but then decline as quality is 'built in' rather than inspected out.

The likely benefits for E plc would be:

(1) A reduction in internal failure costs. Internal failure costs are the costs incurred as a result of quality problems where the problem is discovered before the product leaves the business, e.g. less mistakes when upgrading, servicing or repairing which then have to be corrected involving more labour and possibly more components.

(2) A reduction in external failure costs. External failure costs are the costs incurred as a result of quality problems where the problem is only discovered after the product leaves the business, e.g. loss of customer through delivering poor quality work, the material cost and labour cost of repairing poor quality which has been returned by the customer.

(3) An improvement in the company's reputation as a result of its good quality work.

Test your understanding 1 – FOOD MANUFACTURER

(a) Total Quality Management (TQM) has two main concepts:

(1) **Get it right first time**

TQM considers that the costs of prevention are less than the costs of correction. One of the main aims of TQM is to achieve zero rejects and 100% quality.

(2) **Continuous improvement**

The second basic principle of TQM is dissatisfaction with the status quo. Realistically a zero-defect goal may not be obtainable. It does, however, provide a target to ensure that a company should never be satisfied with its present level of rejects. The management and staff should believe that it is always possible to improve and to be able to get it more right next time!

There must be a focus on the customer and what they require and there must be a constant review of costs and performance to ensure that the aims of the TQM programme are being met.

The aim is to build good quality in rather than inspect poor quality out. The aim in the end is to design such good products and processes and obtain such good materials that inspection is no longer necessary.

SG plc should focus on the whole of its operation from start to finish if it wishes the TQM programme to be a success.

It must ensure that the input to its processes is defect-free. It must choose first-class suppliers who will guarantee the quality of their ingredients. It must communicate with the suppliers to let them know what is expected of them. SG plc is likely to have to pay a premium price to obtain these premium quality ingredients.

It must also examine its own processes to ensure that there are as few quality problems as possible. Where there are known quality problems, efforts should be directed at improving the processes by whatever means are appropriate, e.g. training, preventative maintenance, newer more reliable machines, etc.

The output process must also be controlled, i.e. the relationship with the customer. Efforts must be made to ensure that no defective products reach the customer, perhaps by means of final inspection before the goods leave the business and that where problems do occur, they are corrected as soon as possible. Communication with the customer is very important to ensure that the customer's needs are being met.

It is not enough to decide that a TQM system should be introduced. The programme should be carefully considered and communication to the staff should be clear. They should be educated as to the ideas behind TQM and given the necessary training to accomplish its aims. TQM should permeate the whole of the organisation and must be continually assessed to ensure that its goals are still being achieved.

(b) With a Just-In-Time (JIT) situation there are negligible stocks. There is no buffer stock. If there is a problem in production there is nothing to fall back on. The company does not keep a stock of raw materials or finished goods just-in-case. Thus, in a JIT system any problems can be catastrophic and therefore the idea is not to have any problems, i.e. perfect quality with zero defects. A TQM system is therefore necessary. In a JIT system quality is the responsibility of each employee.

(c) **Prevention costs**

These are the costs of preventing quality problems from occurring. They would include training, preventative maintenance, the purchase or hire of new more reliable machines, the sourcing of better quality ingredients, etc.

Appraisal costs

Appraisal costs are the costs incurred in checking the raw materials and products against the quality standard expected. They would include inspecting the ingredients and the semi-processed food destined for SG's customers, etc.

Internal failure costs

There are the costs incurred as a result of quality problems, where the problem is discovered before the product leaves the business, e.g. the cost of any out-of-date food which has to be disposed of, the material cost and labour cost of replacing a batch of defective product, etc.

External failure cost

These are the costs incurred as a result of quality problems, where the problem is discovered after the product leaves the business, e.g. loss of customer through delivering poor quality products, the material cost and labour cost of replacing a defective batch, the cost of being sued because of food poisoning, etc.

Test your understanding 2

Backflush accounting is a system of accounting used to simplify accounting records when inventory levels are low and controlled. It does not sequentially record movements of inventory in the accounting record between raw materials stores, work in progress and finished goods. Instead, all inventory, wages and overheads costs are charged to the cost of sales account. Inventory is valued at the period end at standard cost and a single transfer is made out of the cost of sales account. It means that no detailed accounting records are maintained of material usage, work in progress or movements of inventory. It is commonly used in Just In Time inventory control environments where inventory levels are low or non-existent.

For a major construction company, inventory is likely to be significant. There are likely to be high level of raw materials of building equipment. There will also be high work in progress as projects could take weeks, months or years to complete. It will be important for the business to know the amount of costs invested in these inventories. In some projects, sales invoices may be based on cost incurred to date and therefore it will be even more vital that this information is known. Therefore the company will need to record sequentially all movements of inventory and have an up-to-date valuation of work in progress.

Back-flush accounting is therefore likely to be unsuitable for such a business as it will not provide the information or accuracy that the company would require. The company should resort to traditional cost accounting systems.

Test your understanding 3 – QUALITY COST

There are different philosophies about the cost of quality. Many businesses engineer quality into their processes while others set up systems to provide quality assurance.

The typical characteristics of quality cost are sometimes cited as follows:

Prevention cost

This would consist perhaps of the cost of the salaries of a quality control unit that carries out the sampling process to detect quality failures and prevents them from getting to the customer

Inspection/appraisal cost

This would include the cost of investigation into quality failures as well as the cost of consumable items used to carry out routine examinations.

Internal failure cost

This would cover the cost of scrapped items, reworking any defective output or undertaking any re-engineering process to improve quality.

External failure cost

This would cover the cost of warranties, free replacements, repairs and other efforts to repair the loss of customer goodwill.

Test your understanding 4

D

All of the statements are true.

Modern costing – throughput accounting

Chapter learning objectives

Lead	Component
A1. Discuss costing methods and their results.	(a) Compare and contrast marginal (or variable), throughput and absorption accounting methods in respect of profit reporting and stock valuation.

1 Chapter overview diagram

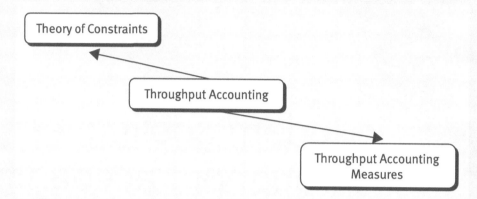

2 Introduction

Throughput accounting is very similar to marginal costing, but it can be used to make longer-term decisions about capacity/production equipment.

Throughput accounting is based on three concepts: throughput, inventory (or investment) and operating expenses. The basic premise is that managers should aim to increase throughput while simultaneously reducing inventory and operational expense.

 Throughput

In throughput accounting, the only cost that is deemed to relate to volume of output is the direct material cost. All other costs (including all labour costs) are deemed to be fixed. These fixed costs may be called Total Factory Costs (TFC).

Throughput contribution = Revenue – Totally variable costs

The aim of throughput accounting is to maximise this measure of throughput contribution.

Since totally variable costs are normally just raw materials and bought-in components, it is often convenient to define throughput contribution as:

Throughput contribution = Revenue – direct material costs

Investment

This is defined as all the money the business invests to buy the things that it intends to sell and all the money tied up in assets so that the business can make the throughput. Investment therefore includes unused raw materials, work-in-progress and unsold finished goods. It can also include non-current assets if these are used for buying or creating materials (such as equipment and buildings used to produce materials or research and development costs that can be attributed to its creation) .

Operating expenses

Operating expenses are defined as all the money a business spends to produce the throughput (i.e. to turn the inventory into throughput). It is not correct to think of operating expenses as fixed costs. They are costs that are not totally variable.

Origins and history

Throughput accounting emerged in the 1980s and 1990s as an alternative system of management accounting. It is associated with the work of Dr Eli Goldratt, who developed the Theory of Constraints (TOC) and the concept of throughput accounting comes from this theory.

Dr Goldratt described the approach of traditional accounting systems as 'Cost World', in which product cost is the main way to understand value. Costs are categorised as fixed and variable costs, and in absorption costing overheads are charged to products using many arbitrary assumptions that have no commercial relevance. Even in marginal costing, it is assumed that direct labour costs vary with the activity level, and that fixed costs are the same for a given time period, regardless of the activity level.

Throughput accounting challenges these assumptions.

- Direct labour costs are not wholly variable. Skilled workers are paid fixed salaries, and so their cost does not vary directly with output volume.

- Fixed costs are 'less fixed' than they might have been in the past.

- The only totally variable cost is the purchase cost of raw materials and components that are bought from external suppliers.

3 Profit reporting

Since a business makes its money from throughput, management accounting systems should focus on the value of throughput created. Profit should therefore be reported as follows (illustrative figures are included):

		$
Revenue		750,000
Raw material cost	(totally variable cost)	200,000
Throughput contribution		550,000
Operating expenses		400,000
Net profit		150,000

Super variable costing

Throughput accounting has been described as a form of 'super-variable costing' because the concept of throughput has similarities to the concept of contribution. It could therefore be seen as an alternative to marginal costing as a costing method. However, this is not an accurate description. This is because in throughput accounting, the concept of product cost is rejected. The throughput earned by individual products is calculated, but no attempt is made to charge operating expenses to products. This makes throughput accounting radically different from both traditional cost accounting systems such as absorption costing and marginal costing and also from activity based costing.

4 Inventory valuation

Inventory should be valued at the purchase cost of its raw materials and bought-in parts.

It should not include any other costs, not even labour costs. No value is added by the production process, not even by labour, until the item is sold.

Example 1

A company makes 1,000 units of an item during a period and sells 800 units for $8,000. Costs of production were as follows:

	$
Materials	3,000
Direct labour	2,000
Fixed production overhead	1,000
Other overhead	1,000

Actual production volume and production overhead expenditure were both the same as budgeted.

Required:

Calculate the profit for the period using:

(a) absorption costing

(b) marginal costing

(c) throughput accounting.

5 Maximising throughput

Using throughput accounting, the aim should be to maximise throughput, on the assumption that operating expenses are a fixed amount in each period.

- If the business has more capacity than there is customer demand, it should produce to meet the demand in full.

- If the business has a constraint that prevents it from meeting customer demand in full, it should make the most profitable use that it can of the constraining resource. **This means giving priority to those products earning the highest throughput for each unit of the constraining resource that it requires**.

This goal is achieved by determining what factors prevent the throughput being higher. This constraint is called a *bottleneck*. A bottleneck may be a machine whose capacity limits the output of the whole production process. **The aim is to identify the bottlenecks and remove them, or, if this is not possible, ensure that they are fully utilised at all times**. Non-bottleneck resources should be scheduled and operated based on the constraints within the system, and should not be used to produce more than the bottlenecks can absorb.

Calculation – multi-product decision making

The usual requirement in questions is to maximise contribution (given that fixed costs are unaffected by the production decision in the short run) per unit of the limiting factor. In throughput accounting the approach should be to maximise the *throughput* contribution earned.

Step 1: identify the bottleneck constraint.

Step 2: calculate the throughput contribution per unit for each product.

Step 3: calculate the throughput contribution per unit of the bottleneck resource for each product.

Step 4: rank the products in order of the throughout contribution per unit of the bottleneck resource.

Step 5: allocate resources using this ranking and answer the question.

Example 2

The following data relates to two products manufactured by DJ Ltd

	Product X	Product Y
Selling price per unit	$15	$20
Direct material cost per unit	$10	$11
Maximum demand (units)	25,000	30,000
Time required on the bottleneck (hours per unit)	2	6

The firm has 80,000 bottleneck hours available each period.

Total factory costs amount to $128,000 in the period.

Required:

Calculate the optimum product mix and the maximum profit.

Contrasting TA with the limiting factor approach

Illustration

A company produces two products, A and B, the production costs of which are shown below:

	A	B
	$	$
Direct materials	10	10
Direct labour	5	9
Variable overhead	5	9
Fixed overhead	5	9
	25	37

Fixed overhead is absorbed on the basis direct labour cost.

The products pass through two processes, Y and Z, with associated labour cost of $10 per direct labour hour in each. The direct labour time taken associated with the two products for these processes is shown below:

Process	Product A	Product B
Y	10 mins	39 mins
Z	20 mins	15 mins

Selling prices are set by the market. The current market price for A is $65 and that for B, $52. At these prices, the market will absorb as many units of A and B as the company can produce. The ability of the company to produce A and B is limited by the capacity to process the products through Y and Z. The company operates a two-shift system, giving 16 working hours per day. Process Z is a single-process line and 2 hours in each shift will be downtime. Process Y can process two units simultaneously, although this doubles the requirement for direct labour. Process Y can operate for the full 16 working hours each day.

Required:

What production plan should the company follow in order to maximise profits?

Solution

In order to find the profit maximising solution in any problem, the constraints which prevent the profit from being infinite must be identified; the greater the number of constraints, the more difficult the problem is to solve. In the simplest case, where there is only one binding constraint, the profit maximising solution is found by maximising the contribution per unit of the scarce resource, that is binding constraint. Linear programming may be used to solve the problem where more than one constraint is binding for some, but not all, feasible solutions.

Where the number of products is limited to two, and such constraints are relatively few in number, the problem can easily be expressed graphically to reveal the profit maximising solution, and/or the problem can be expressed in the form of a set of simultaneous equations. As the number of potentially binding constraints increases, the use of a computer becomes the only feasible way to solve the necessary number of simultaneous equations.

In this question, the only constraint is the company's ability to process the product. The total daily processing time for processes Y and Z are:

* Maximum process time Y = 2 × 16 hours × 60 minutes = 1,920 minutes

* Maximum process time Z = 12 hours × 60 minutes = 720 minutes

So the maximum number that could be produced of each of the two products is:

	Product A Maximum units	Product B Maximum units
Y	$\dfrac{1,920}{10}$ = 192	$\dfrac{1,920}{39}$ = 49.23
Z	$\dfrac{720}{20}$ = 36	$\dfrac{720}{15}$ = 48

In the case of both products, the maximum number of units which can be produced in Process Y exceeds the number that can be produced in Process Z, and thus the capacity of Process Y is not a binding constraint. The problem therefore becomes one of deciding how to allocate the scarce production capacity of Process Z in such a way as to maximise profit.

Traditional approach – maximising the contribution per minute in Process Z

Contribution of A = $65 (selling price) – $20 (variable cost) = $45
Contribution of B = $52 (selling price) – $28 (variable cost) = $24

Contribution of A per minute in process Z = $45 /20 = $2.25
Contribution of B per minute in process Z = $24/15 = $1.60

The profit maximising solution is therefore to produce the maximum possible number of units of A, 36, giving a contribution of $45 × 36 = $1,620.

Throughput approach – maximising throughput per minute in bottleneck resource Z

Throughput of A = $65 (selling price) – $10 (material cost) = $55
Throughput of B = $52 (selling price) – $10 (material cost) = $42

Throughput contribution of A per minute in process Z = $55/20 = $2.75
Throughput contribution of B per minute in process Z = $42/15 = $2.80

The profit maximising solution is therefore to produce the maximum number of units of B, 48, giving a throughput contribution of $42 × 48 = $2,016.

It is clear that, given the different solutions, the two approaches cannot both lead to profit maximisation. Which technique is correct depends on the variability or otherwise of labour and variable overheads, which in turn depends on the time horizon of the decision. This type of profit maximisation technique is a short-term one and in today's world labour is likely to be fixed in the short term and so it can be argued that TA provides the more correct solution. Variable overheads would need to be analysed to assess their variability.

Marginal costing rose to popularity in the 1930s when labour costs were usually variable as the workforce was usually paid on a piece-rate basis. Since then textbooks, at least, have always assumed that labour is a variable cost in the short term. All that has happened with TA is that it tends to recognise the present reality, which is that most cost excluding materials are now fixed in the short term.

The marginal costing approach should of course be modified to accommodate this, as it requires only variable costs to be used to calculate contribution. If only material costs are variable, then only those costs should be used in the calculation of contribution. Thus there should be no difference between the two systems in this respect.

The theory of constraints

Goldratt and Cox (1992) describe the process of identifying and taking steps to remove the constraints that restrict output as the **theory of constraints** (TOC). The process involves 5 steps:

(1) Identify the system's bottlenecks.

(2) Decide how to exploit the bottlenecks.

(3) Subordinate everything else to the decision in Step 2.

(4) Alleviate the system's bottlenecks.

(5) If, in the previous steps, a bottleneck has been broken, go back to Step 1.

The bottleneck is the focus of management's attention. Decisions regarding the optimum mix of products must be undertaken. Step 3 requires that the optimum production of the bottleneck activity determines the production schedule of the non-bottleneck activities. There is no point in a non-bottleneck activity supplying more than the bottleneck activity can consume. This would result in increased WIP inventories with no increased sales volume. The TOC is a process of continuous improvement to clear the throughput chain of all the constraints. Thus, step 4 involves taking action to remove, or elevate the constraint. This may involve replacing the bottleneck machine with a faster one, providing additional training for a slow worker or changing the design of the product to reduce the processing time required on the bottleneck activity. Once a bottleneck has been elevated it will generally be replaced by a new bottleneck elsewhere in the system. It then becomes necessary to return to step 1.

Constraints on throughput

The idea of constraints is central to the throughput approach. Examples of constraints on either production or sales may include:

- inadequately trained sales force

- poor reputation for meeting delivery dates

- poor physical distribution system

- unreliability of material supplies, delivery and/or quality

- inadequate production resources

- inappropriate management accounting system which cannot provide sufficient information to decision makers

6 Throughput accounting measures

Various performance measures have been devised to help measure throughput:

$$\text{Return per factory hour} = \frac{\text{Throughput contribution}}{\text{Product's time on the bottleneck resource}}$$

$$\text{Cost per factory hour} = \frac{\text{Total factory cost}}{\text{Total time on the bottleneck resource}}$$

$$\text{Throughput accounting ratio} = \frac{\text{Return per factory hour}}{\text{Cost per factory hour}}$$

Explanation of the ratios

The return per factory hour shows the value added by the organisation and managers are encouraged to maximise this (for example, by increasing throughput or reducing the time taken in the process).

The cost per factory hour shows the cost of operating the factory in terms of overheads, labour costs etc.

The throughput accounting ratio measures the return from a product against the cost of running the factory. Some people would argue that only products with a throughput accounting ratio greater than 1 are worthwhile. This is because the ratio is telling us that the return that is made at this point is less than the cost of producing that return. For example, if the return was $2 per hour but it was costing $4 per hour to operate the factory, then the throughput accounting ration would be 0.5. This could easily be benchmarked against the target of 1 to tell us that production is not worthwhile.

But notice that the return per factory hours and the throughput accounting ratios are for each individual product, whereas the cost per factory hour is for the company as a whole. So it could be argued that a throughput accounting ratio of less than 1 does not reveal the full story.

Example 3

Calculate the throughput accounting ratio for each product in the previous example.

Criticism of throughput accounting

A criticism of throughput accounting is that it concentrates on the short term, when a business has a fixed supply of resources and operating expenses are largely fixed.

It is more difficult to apply throughput accounting concepts to the longer term, when all costs are variable, and vary with the volume of production and sales or another cost driver.

This criticism suggests that although throughput accounting could be a suitable method of measuring profit and performance in the short term, an alternative management accounting method, such as activity based costing, might be more appropriate for measuring and controlling performance from a longer-term perspective.

7 Chapter summary

```
              ┌─────────────────┐
              │   Throughput    │
              │   accounting    │
              └─────────────────┘
             ·····      ······
         ····               ·····
     ┌──────────────┐   ┌──────────────┐
     │  Throughput  │   │  Maximising  │
     │ contribution │   │  throughput  │
     │              │   │ contribution │
     └──────────────┘   └──────────────┘
```

- • = Revenue – raw material costs
- • Inventory valued using material costs only
- • TAR = $\dfrac{\text{Return/hour}}{\text{Cost/hour}}$

1 Identify bottleneck
2 Calculate throughput contribution
3 Calculate throughput contribution per resources
4 Rank products
5 Allocate resources

8 Practice questions

Test your understanding 1

A business makes four products, W, X, Y and Z. Information relating to these products is as follows:

	W	**X**	**Y**	**Z**
Sales price / unit	$20	$25	$18	$40
Materials required / unit	$10	$15	$11	$22
Labour hours / unit	4	5	2	6
Monthly sales demand (units)	500	800	1,000	400

There is a limit to the availability of labour, and only 8,000 hours are available each month.

Required:

Identify which products the business should produce.

(5 marks)

Test your understanding 2

A company manufactures a product that requires machine time of 1.5 hours per unit. Machine time is a bottleneck resource, due to the limited number of machines available. There are 10 machines available and each machine can be used for up to 40 hours each week.

The product is sold for $85 per unit and the material cost per unit is $42.50. Total operating expenses are $8,000 each week.

Required:

Calculate the throughput accounting ratio.

(2 marks)

Test your understanding 3

Justin Thyme manufactures four products, A, B, C and D. Details of sales prices, costs and resource requirements for each of the products are as follows.

	Product A	Product B	Product C	Product D
	$	$	$	$
Sales price	1.40	0.80	1.20	2.80
Materials cost	0.60	0.30	0.60	1.00
Direct labour cost	0.40	0.20	0.40	1.00
	Minutes	Minutes	Minutes	Minutes
Machine time per unit	5	2	3	6
Labour time per unit	2	1	2	5
	Units	Units	Units	Units
Weekly sales demand	2,000	2,000	2,500	1,500

Machine time is a bottleneck resource and the maximum capacity is 400 machine hours each week. Operating costs, including direct labour costs, are $5,440 each week. Direct labour costs are $12 per hour, and direct labour workers are paid for a 38-hour week, with no overtime.

(a) Identify the quantities of each product that should be manufactured and sold each week to maximise profit and calculate the weekly profit.

(10 marks)

(b) Calculate the throughput accounting ratio at this profit-maximising level of output and sales.

(2 marks)

Test your understanding 4

The following data relate to the single product made by Squirrel Ltd:

Selling price per unit	$16
Direct material cost per unit	$10
Maximum demand (units) per period	40,000
Time required (hours) in Process X, per unit	1
Time required (hours) in Process Y, per unit	1.5

The capacities are 35,000 hours in Process X and 42,000 hours in Process Y.

The total factory costs are $105,000 in the period.

Required:

(a) Identify the process bottleneck.

(2 marks)

(b) Calculate the throughput accounting ratio.

(2 marks)

Test your understanding 5 – THROUGHPUT ACCOUNTING

Explain why throughput accounting has been described as a form of 'super variable costing' and how the concept of contribution in throughput accounting differs from that in marginal costing.

(5 marks)

Test your understanding 6

A company manufactures three products: W, X and Y. The products use a series of different machines, but there is a common machine that is a bottleneck. The standard selling price and standard cost per unit for each product for the next period are as follows:

	W $	X $	Y $
Selling price	180	150	150
Cost:			
Direct material	41	20	30
Direct labour	30	20	50
Variable production overheads	24	16	20
Fixed production overheads	36	24	30
Profit	49	70	20
Time (minutes) on bottleneck machine	7	10	7

The company is trying to plan the best use of its resources.

(a) **Using a traditional limiting factor approach, the rank order (best first) of the products would be:**

    A   W, X, Y

    B   W, Y, X

    C   X, W, Y

    D   Y, X, W

(2 marks)

(b) **Using a throughput accounting approach, the rank order (best first) of the products would be:**

    A   W, X, Y

    B   W, Y, X

    C   X, W, Y

    D   Y, X, W

(2 marks)

Test your understanding answers

Example 1

The valuation of closing inventory is:

- $1,200 ($6,000 × 200/1,000) in absorption costing
- $1,000 ($5,000 × 200/1,000) in marginal costing
- $600 ($3,000 × 200/1,000) in throughput accounting.

Profit statements

(a) **Absorption costing**

Value of closing inventory = $1,200

	$	$
Sales		8,000
Cost of production	6,000	
Less: closing inventory	1,200	
Cost of sales		4,800
Gross profit		3,200
Non-production overhead		1,000
Profit		2,200

(b) Marginal costing

Value of closing inventory = $1,000

	$	$
Sales		8,000
Cost of production	5,000	
Less: closing inventory	1,000	
Cost of sales		4,000
Contribution		4,000
Fixed overhead		1,000
Non-production overhead		1,000
Profit		2,000

(c) Throughput accounting

Value of closing inventory = $600

	$	$
Sales		8,000
Material costs	3,000	
Less: closing inventory	600	
Cost of sales		2,400
Throughput		5,600
Operating expenses		4,000
Profit		1,600

Example 2

	Product X	Y
	$	$
Selling price	15	20
Direct material	10	11
	—	—
Throughput	5	9
No. of bottleneck hours per unit	2	6
Return per factory hour	2.50	1.50
	1st	2nd

	Units	Bottleneck hrs per unit	Bottleneck hrs	Throughput $
Product X	25,000	2	50,000	125,000
Product Y	5,000[Bal]	6	30,000[Bal]	45,000
			80,000	170,000
Total factory cost				128,000
Gross profit				42,000

Example 3

					Product A	Product B

$$\text{Return per factory hour} = \frac{\text{Throughput per unit}}{\text{Bottleneck hrs per unit}}$$

	Product A	Product B
	$\dfrac{15-10}{2\text{ hrs}}$	$\dfrac{20-11}{6\text{ hrs}}$
	= $2.50	= $1.50

$$\text{Cost per factory hour} = \frac{\text{Total Factory Cost}}{\text{Total Bottleneck Hrs}}$$

$$= \frac{\$128{,}000}{80{,}000\text{ hrs}} = \$1.60$$

$$\text{Throughput Accounting Ratio} = \frac{\text{Return per factory hour}}{\text{Cost per factory hour}}$$

	Product A	Product B
	$\dfrac{\$2.50}{\$1.60}$	$\dfrac{\$1.50}{\$1.60}$
	= 1.56	= 0.94

Product X has the higher throughput accounting ratio and thus should be given priority over Product Y.

Test your understanding 1

The business should seek to maximise the total throughput.

	W	X	Y	Z
	$	$	$	$
Sales price / unit	20	25	18	40
Materials required / unit	10	15	11	22
Throughput / unit	10	10	7	18
Labour hours / unit	4	5	2	6
Throughput / labour hour	$2.50	$2.00	$3.50	$3.00
Priority	3rd	4th	1st	2nd

The production volumes that will maximise throughput and net profit are:

Product	Units	Labour hours	Throughput $
Y	1,000	2,000	7,000
Z	400	2,400	7,200
W	500	2,000	5,000
		6,400	
X (balance)	320	1,600	3,200
		8,000	22,400

Test your understanding 2

Throughput per bottleneck machine hour = ($85 – $42.50)/1.5 hours = $28.33

Operating expenses per bottleneck machine hour = $8,000/(10 × 40) = $20

Throughput accounting ratio = $28.33/$20 = 1.42

Test your understanding 3

(a) **Step 1:** Determine the bottleneck constraint

The bottleneck resource is machine time. 400 machine hours available each week = 24,000 machine minutes.

Step 2: Calculate the throughput per unit for each product

	A $	B $	C $	D $
Sales price	1.40	0.80	1.20	2.80
Materials cost	0.60	0.30	0.60	1.00
Throughput/ unit	0.80	0.50	0.60	1.80

Step 3: Calculate the throughput per machine minute

Machine time per unit	5 minutes	2 minutes	3 minutes	6 minutes
Throughput per minute	$0.16	$0.25	$0.20	$0.30

Step 4: Rank

Rank	4th	2nd	3rd	1st

Step 5: Allocate resources using this ranking and answer the question.

The profit-maximising weekly output and sales volumes are as follows.

Product	Units	Machine minutes	Throughput per unit $	Total throughout $
D	1,500	9,000	1.80	2,700
B	2,000	4,000	0.50	1,000
C	2,500	7,500	0.60	1,500
		20,500		
A (balance)	700	3,500	0.80	560
		24,000		5,760
Operating expenses				5,440
Profit				320

(b) Throughput per machine hour: $5,760/400 hours = $14.40

Cost (operating expenses) per machine hour: $5,440/400 hours = $13.60.

TPAR: $14.40/$13.60 = 1.059.

Test your understanding 4

(a) **Process bottleneck**

$$\text{Capacity in Process X} = \frac{35,000}{1} = 35,000 \text{ units per period}$$

$$\text{Capacity in Process Y} = \frac{42,000}{1.5} = 28,000 \text{ units per period}$$

Process Y has the lower capacity and therefore this is the bottleneck.

(b) **Throughput accounting ratio**

$$\text{Throughput per unit} = \$16 - \$10 = \$6$$

$$\text{Return per factory hour} = \frac{\$6}{1.5} = \$4$$

$$\text{Cost per factory hour} = \frac{\$105,000}{42,000 \text{ hours}} = \$2.50$$

$$\text{Throughput accounting ratio} = \frac{\$4}{\$2.50} = 1.60$$

As the throughput accounting ratio is greater than 1 it provides a satisfactory result.

Test your understanding 5 – THROUGHPUT ACCOUNTING

Throughput accounting has been described as a form of 'super variable costing' because the concept of throughput has similarities to the concept of contribution. However there is a major difference in the definition of contribution in the two systems or, more specifically, in what is described as a variable cost.

The traditional marginal costing approach assumes that direct labour is a variable cost. Although this may have been true in the past when labour was typically paid a piece rate, this is no longer the case. In the short term, throughput accounting treats labour as a fixed cost.

Marginal costing also tends to emphasise cost behaviour, especially overheads, and usually attempts to separate these into fixed and variable components. As with labour costs, throughput accounting treats all production overhead as fixed in the short term and aggregates these with labour into what is referred to as 'total factory cost'. Consequently, in throughput accounting the only cost that is treated as variable is the direct material cost.

Furthermore, throughput accounting uses the total of direct materials purchased in the period in the calculation of throughput, rather than the cost of material actually used, as is the case with marginal costing.

Test your understanding 6

(a) **A**

	W $	X $	Y $
Contribution	85	94	50
Time at bottle neck	7	10	7
Contribution per minute	12	9	7
Rank	1	2	3

(b) **B**

	W $	X $	Y $
Throughput*	139	130	120
Time at bottle neck	7	10	7
Throughput per minute	20	13	17
Rank	1	3	2

* throughput = sales less material costs

5

Modern costing – activity-based and environmental costing

Chapter learning objectives

Lead	Component
A1. Discuss costing methods and their results.	(c) Discuss activity-based costing as compared with traditional marginal and absorption costing methods, including its relative advantages and disadvantages as a system of cost accounting.
A3. Apply principles of environmental costing.	(a) Apply principles of environmental costing in identifying relevant internalised costs and externalised environmental impacts of the organisation's activities.

1 Chapter overview diagram

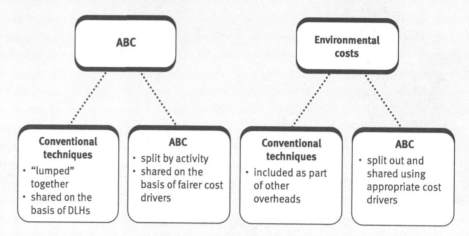

2 Modern production environments

Modern producers have changed the way that they produce so that they have:

- much more machinery and computerised manufacturing systems
- smaller batch sizes
- less use of 'direct' labour

This has had the following **impact on production costs:**

- more indirect overheads (for example, insurance and depreciation of the machines and computers)
- less direct labour costs

This means that the **traditional** methods of costing (marginal and absorption) produce **standard cost cards that are less useful** due to inaccurate product costs:

- the largest cost of production is indirect overheads but these are categorised together in one figure that lacks detail and is not useful to management
- because management does not know what the components are of the largest production cost (indirect overheads) they cannot implement proper cost control

- the costs are often allocated between products on the basis of direct labour hours – despite the fact that direct labour is becoming a smaller proportion of product costs and does not fairly reflect the relationship between the products and the indirect overheads

- because costs are inappropriately or inaccurately shared between products it means that the total production cost can be wrong which can lead to poor pricing and production decisions

Activity based costing **(ABC) has been developed to solve the problems** that traditional costing methods create in these modern environments.

Traditional costing problems

Problems with absorption costing

Traditional absorption costing charges overhead costs to products (or services) in an arbitrary way. In product costing, overheads are absorbed on the basis of the volume of production in each production department or centre. The basis for setting an absorption rate is volume-related, such as an overhead absorption rate per unit produced, a rate per direct labour hour or a rate per machine hour.

The assumption underlying this method of costing is that overhead expenditure is connected to the volume of production activity.

- This assumption was probably valid many years ago, when production systems were based on labour-intensive or machine-intensive mass production of fairly standard items. Overhead costs were also fairly small relative to direct materials and direct labour costs; therefore any inaccuracy in the charging of overheads to products costs was not significant.

- The assumption is not valid in a complex manufacturing environment, where production is based on smaller customised batches of products, indirect costs are high in relation to direct costs, and a high proportion of overhead activities – such as production scheduling, order handling and quality control – are not related to production volume.

- For similar reasons, traditional absorption costing is not well-suited to the costing of many services.

The criticism of absorption costing is that it cannot calculate a 'true' product cost that has any valid meaning. Overheads are charged to departments and products in an arbitrary way, and the assumption that overhead expenditure is related to direct labour hours or machine hours in the production departments is no longer realistic.

Problems with marginal costing

There are also major problems with marginal costing, but for different reasons. In marginal costing, products or services are valued at their marginal cost, and profitability is assessed by calculating the contribution earned from each product or service. Fixed costs are assumed to be time-related and are charged against profits as a cost for the period. This can be a useful costing method when variable costs are a large proportion of total costs.

The main criticisms of marginal costing as a method of measuring product costs and profitability are that:

- variable costs might be small in relation to fixed costs

- 'fixed' costs might be fixed in relation to production volume, but they might vary with other activities that are not production-related.

In many manufacturing and service environments, it is therefore inappropriate to treat overhead costs as fixed period costs, and they should be charged to products or services in a more meaningful way

3 Activity-based costing

Activity-based costing (ABC) is an alternative approach to product costing. It is a form of absorption costing, but , rather than absorbing overheads on a production volume basis it firstly allocates them to **cost pools** before absorbing them into units using **cost drivers**.

- A **cost pool** is an activity that consumes resources and for which overhead costs are identified and allocated. For each cost pool, there should be a cost driver.

- A **cost driver** is a unit of activity that consumes resources. An alternative definition of a cost driver is a factor influencing the level of cost.

Illustration 1

Imagine the machining department in a traditional absorption costing system. The OAR would be based on machine hours because many of the overheads in the machine department would relate to the machines, e.g. power, maintenance, machine depreciation, etc., so using a machine hour basis would seem fair, however, not only does the machine department have machine related costs, but also in an absorption costing system, it would also have picked up a share of rent and rates, heating, lighting, building depreciation, canteen costs, personnel cost, etc. These costs would also be absorbed on a machine hour basis, because everything in the machine department is absorbed on machine hours and whilst this is fair for power, maintenance and machine depreciation, it is inappropriate for the other costs.

ABC overcomes this problem by not using departments as gathering points for costs, but instead using activities, and there would for example be a machine-related activity to which power would be charged, machine depreciation would be charged, and machine maintenance would be charged. It would not pick up a share of personnel costs or rent or rates or indeed anything not machine related. ABC's flexibility thus reduces the incidence of arbitrary apportionments.

ABC vs absorption costing

Service Departments   Production Departments   Product Lines

Stage 1   Stage 2

Assigning costs using measures of service usage   Absorbing costs using a measure of volume

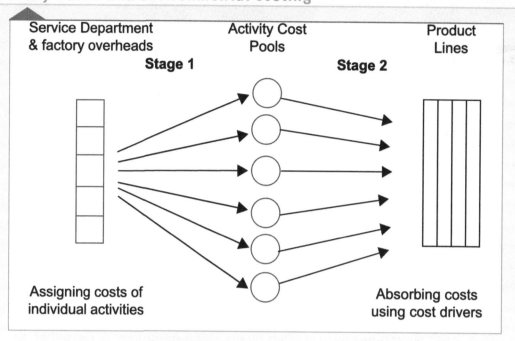

Service Department & factory overheads	Activity Cost Pools	Product Lines
Stage 1	Stage 2	
Assigning costs of individual activities		Absorbing costs using cost drivers

Identifying activities and drivers

If a business decides to adopt activity-based costing to measure the costs and profitability of its products or services, it must identify the key activities that consume resources and the cost driver for each of those activities.

- There might be a large number of different activities, but in an accounting system it is usually necessary to simplify the overhead cost analysis and select a fairly small number of activities. If a large number of activities are identified and used in ABC, the task of analysing costs becomes more complex and time-consuming, and the value of the additional accuracy might not justify the cost and effort.

- For any activity there might be just one cost driver or several different cost drivers. Where there are several cost drivers, it is necessary to select just one for the purpose of ABC analysis.

Identifying activities

The main activities that consume overhead resources differ from one type of business to another. A useful approach to identifying suitable activities within a business is to consider four different categories of activity or transaction:

- **Logistical transactions.** These are activities or transactions concerned with moving materials or people, and with tracking the progress of materials or work through the system.

- **Balancing transactions.** These are concerned with ensuring that the resources required for an operation are available. For example, the buying department has to make sure that raw materials are available to meet production requirements.

- **Quality transactions.** These are concerned with ensuring that output or service levels meet quality requirements and customer expectations. Inspections and handling customer complaints are both examples of quality transactions.

- **Change transactions.** These are activities required to respond to changes in customer demand, a change in design specifications, a scheduling change, a change in production or delivery methods, and so on.

For any business, there could be important resource-consuming activities in each of these categories.

Identifying cost drivers

For each selected activity, there should be a cost driver. The chosen cost driver must be:

- **Relevant.** In other words, there should be a connection between the cost driver and the consumption of resources for the activity.

- **Easy to measure.** Measuring the units of cost driver and identifying the products or services to which they relate needs to be a fairly easy and straightforward process.

Often, the cost driver is the number of transactions relating to the activity. For example:

- the cost of setting up machinery for a production run might be driven by the number of set-ups (jobs or batches produced)

- the cost of running machines might be driven by the number of machine hours for which the machines are running

- the cost of assembling the product may be based on the number of direct labour hours

- the cost of order processing might be related to the number of orders received

- the cost of despatch might be related to the number of orders despatched or to the weight of items despatched

- the costs of purchasing might be related to the number of purchase orders made

- the costs of quality control might be related to the number of inspections carried out, or to the incidence of rejected items.

Calculating the full production cost per unit using ABC

There are five basic steps to calculating an activity based cost:

Step 1: **Group production overheads into activities, according to how they are driven.**

A cost pool is the grouping of costs relating to a particular activity which consumes resources and for which overhead costs are identified and allocated. For each cost pool, there should be a cost driver.

Step 2: **Identify cost drivers for each activity, i.e. what causes these activity costs to be incurred.**

A cost driver is a factor that influences (or drives) the level of cost.

Step 3: **Calculate a cost driver rate for each activity.**

The cost driver rate is calculated in the same way as the absorption costing OAR. However, a separate cost driver rate will be calculated for each activity, by taking the activity cost and dividing by the cost driver information.

Step 4: **Absorb the activity costs into the product.**

The activity costs should be absorbed by applying the cost driver rate into the individual products.

Step 5: **Calculate the full production cost and/ or the profit or loss.**

Some questions ask for the production cost per unit and/ or the profit or loss per unit.

Other questions ask for the total production cost and/ or the total profit or loss.

Example 1

A manufacturing business makes a product in two models, model M1 and model M2. details of the two products are as follows.

	Model M1	Model M2
Annual sales	8,000 units	8,000 units
Number of sales orders	60	250
Sales price per unit	$54	$73
Direct material cost per unit	$11	$21
Direct labour hours per unit	2.0 hours	2.5 hours
Direct labour rate per hour	$8	$8
Special parts per unit	2	8
Production batch size	2,000 units	100 units
Setups per batch	1	3
Production batch size	1	1

	$	Cost driver
Setup costs	97,600	Number of setups
Material handling costs	42,000	Number of batches
Special part handling costs	50,000	Number of special parts
Invoicing	31,000	Number of sales orders
Other overheads	108,000	Direct labour hours
Total overheads	328,600	

A customer has indicated an interest in placing a large order for either model M1 or M2, and the sales manager wished to try to sell the higher-priced model M2.

Required:

(a) Calculate the profit per unit for each model, using ABC.

(12 marks)

(b) Using the information above identify which product the sales manager should try to sell on the basis of the information provided by your ABC analysis.

(3 marks)

4 When is ABC relevant?

ABC is a more expensive system to operate than traditional costing, so it should only be introduced when it is appropriate to do so. Activity-based costing could provide much more meaningful information about product costs and profits when:

- indirect costs are high relative to direct costs

- products or services are complex

- products or services are tailored to customer specifications

- some products or services are sold in large numbers but others are sold in small numbers.

In these situations, ABC will often result in significantly different product or service overhead costs, compared with traditional absorption costing.

Comparison to traditional costing

Any unit cost, no matter how it is derived, can be misinterpreted. There is temptation to adopt a simplistic approach, which would say, for example, that if it cost $1,000 to produce ten units, it will cost $10,000 to produce 100 units. As we know, this in incorrect in the short term, owing to the existence of short-term fixed costs. The ABC approach does not eliminate this problem anymore than the traditional approach. The alternative to presenting full absorption costing information in a traditional costing system has been to provide the user with a marginal costing statement which distinguishes clearly between the variable cost of production and the fixed cost of production. This carries an implication for the decision-maker that if the variable cost of production is $50 for 10 units, the additional cost of producing a further 40 units will be 40 × $5 = $200.

Activity-based costing, on the other hand, can provide the user with a more sophisticated breakdown of cost. This breakdown relates cost to the level of activities undertaken. The structure of reporting will vary from company to company, but Cooper (1992) has suggested that four levels of activity, which he terms a hierarchy of cost, will commonly be found in practice. These are shown below:

(i) *Unit-level activities*. These are activities where the consumption of resources is very strongly correlated with the number of units produced. Costs traditionally defined as direct costs would fall into this category, for example direct material and direct labour.

(ii) *Batch-level activities.* Some activities – for example, machine set-up, materials handling and batch inspection – consume resources in proportion to the number of batches produced, rather than in proportion to the number of units produced. By identifying the consumption of resources at a batch rather than a unit level, it is easier than in a traditional costing system for a user to visualise the changing cost that will come about in the long term by changing a product mix or production schedule.

(iii) *Product-level activities.* Consumption of resources by, for example, administration, product specification or purchasing may be related to the existence of particular products. If the activity is performed to sustain the existence of a particular product line, it is a product-level activity.

(iv) *Facility-level activities.* Even within an ABC system, it is accepted that there are some costs that relate simply to being in business and that therefore cannot be related in any way to the production of any particular product line. Grounds maintenance, plant security and property taxes would be examples of this type of cost.

Consideration of (i)–(iv) shows that the difference between traditional costing and ABC costing will be dependent on the proportion of overhead cost that falls into each of the four categories. If this overhead is made up primarily of (i) and (iv), it is obvious that the traditional approach and the ABC approach will lead to very similar product costs. However, if the bulk of overhead cost falls into category (ii) and/or category (iii), there will be a very significant difference between the two.

The debate as to whether ABC is actually a new technique, or whether it simply encourages a more accurate tracing of costs to products in a manner that is perfectly consistent with the traditional approach, is interesting but sterile – and misses the point of ABC, as is demonstrated in the rest of this chapter. Nevertheless, it is worth pointing out that ABC product costs are full absorption costs and, as such, suffer from the same type of deficiencies in a decision-making context as do traditional full absorption costs – they are historical, based on current methods of organisation and operation and, at the level of the product, contain allocations of joint/common costs, etc.

However, it can be strongly argued that ABC has an important 'attention-directing' role to play in both cost management and decision-making. ABC is defined in the CIMA Official Terminology as:

an approach to the costing and monitoring of activities which involves tracing resource consumption and costing final outputs. Resources are assigned to activities, and activities to cost objects based on consumption estimates. The latter utilise cost drivers to attach activity costs to outputs.

In decision-making, it is arguable that activity-based costs are much more helpful than traditional costs in determining the costs relevant for decision-making and, more particularly, in drawing attention to the likely impact on long-run variable costs of short-term decisions.

Advantages and disadvantages of ABC

Advantages	Disadvantages
• more accuracy	• not always relevant
• better cost understanding	• still need arbitrary cost allocations
• fairer allocation of costs	• need to choose appropriate drivers and activities
• better cost control	• complex
• can be used in complex situations	• expensive to operate
• can be applied beyond production	
• can be used in service industries	

Advantages and disadvantages of ABC

ABC has a number of advantages:

* It provides a more accurate cost per unit. As a result, pricing, sales strategy, performance management and decision making should be improved (see next section for detail).

* It provides much better insight into what drives overhead costs.

* ABC recognises that overhead costs are not all related to production and sales volume.

- In many businesses, overhead costs are a significant proportion of total costs, and management needs to understand the drivers of overhead costs in order to manage the business properly. Overhead costs can be controlled by managing cost drivers.

- It can be applied to derive realistic costs in a complex business environment.

- ABC can be applied to all overhead costs, not just production overheads.

- ABC can be used just as easily in service costing as in product costing.

Disadvantages of ABC:

- ABC will be of limited benefit if the overhead costs are primarily volume related or if the overhead is a small proportion of the overall cost.

- It is impossible to allocate all overhead costs to specific activities.

- The choice of both activities and cost drivers might be inappropriate.

- ABC can be more complex to explain to the stakeholders of the costing exercise.

- The benefits obtained from ABC might not justify the costs.

The implications of switching to ABC

The use of ABC has potentially significant commercial implications:

- Pricing can be based on more realistic cost data.
    - Pricing decisions will be improved because the price will be based on more accurate cost data

- Sales strategy can be more soundly based.
    - More realistic product costs as a result of the use of ABC may enable sales staff to:
        - target customers that appeared unprofitable using absorption costing but may be profitable under ABC
        - stop targeting customers or market segments that are now shown to offer low or negative sales margins.

- Decision making can be improved.
  - Research, production and sales effort can be directed towards those products and services which ABC has identified as offering the highest sales margins.

- Performance management can be improved.
  - Performance management should be enhanced due to the focus on selling the most profitable products and through the control of cost drivers.
  - ABC can be used as the basis of budgeting and longer term forward planning of overhead costs. The more realistic budgeted overhead cost should improve the system of performance management.

5 Environmental management accounting

Organisations are beginning to recognise that environmental awareness and management are not optional, but are important for long-term survival and profitability.

The importance of environmental management

All organisations:

- are faced with increasing legal and regulatory requirements relating to environmental management

- need to meet customers' needs and concerns relating to the environment

- need to demonstrate effective environmental management to maintain a good public image

- need to manage the risk and potential impact of environmental disasters

- can make cost savings by improved use of resources such as water and fuel

- are recognising the importance of sustainable development, which is the meeting of current needs without compromising the ability of future generations to meet their needs.

Illustration – Manchester United Football Club

Manchester United are one of the largest sporting organisations in the world. However, the club recognises that success as a company will not just be judged via sporting and financial success. Their environmental policy statement includes the following:

> We know that our performance as an internationally recognised institution will be measured not only by our success on the field of play or our profitability as a business but also by our impact on the quality of life in our communities and on the environment we share.

> We will continue to develop plans to improve the environmental performance of our suppliers and contractors where appropriate. We will look for opportunities to promote environmental best practice initiatives with our commercial partners.

Some of the environmental policies that the football club have introduced in recent years are:

- the club created a nature reserve at its training ground to provide a pond and grassland for wildlife which has become a haven for many species which may otherwise have been disturbed by the club's ongoing building improvements

- the club signed an agreement with Cheshire Wildlife Trust to enable the Trust to manage the land at the training ground for nature conservation purposes

- the training centre also features a lagoon with reed bed technology, where dirty water is cleaned and recycled in order to provide water for the training pitches

- a wide range of products are sent for re-use or are recycled including glass, plastics, cans, green waste from the pitches, wood, surplus event materials like carpets and signage boards, office stationery and marketing materials

- printed publications are now produced from sustainable sources.

- old IT equipment and printer cartridges are also recycled or re-used and donated for charitable purposes.

- stadium short distance vehicles (which used to run on carbon fuel) have been replaced with 'green' vehicles which are battery operated

- all incandescent light bulbs and strip lighting at the clubs stadium and training facilities have been replaced with energy efficient light bulbs

- the club promotes sustainability to suppliers and supporters – with senior players often becoming spokespeople for the cause.

Illustration – Manchester United Football Club

These are just some of the many policies that the club have introduced. They have won many awards through these schemes and in February 2012, the Manchester United stadium achieved ISO 14001 certification, becoming the first major stadium in the UK to achieve this international Environmental Management System standard.

Depletion of natural resources

One of the key elements is that natural resources such as carbon, energy and water may run out in the future. For example, it is predicted that by 2030, the global demand for fresh water will exceed supply by 40 percent. Also, fossil fuel consumption contributes to around 90% of all of the worlds energy consumption, but estimates suggest that current oil reserves, for example, will run out within the next 50 years. On top of this, since the beginning of the Industrial Revolution, the burning of fossil fuels has contributed to the increase in carbon dioxide in the atmosphere which is attributed to global warming and climate change which are creating more frequent natural disasters. This is forcing companies to consider

- reducing existing usage of carbon, energy and water
- finding future alternative sources of these resources
- reducing unnecessary detrimental impacts on these resources

Where organisations have avoided making these decisions voluntarily, governments are stepping in to enforce environmental standards in order to force organisations to do so. For example, 191 national states have signed up to what is known as the Kyoto accord which is an international agreement and plan to reduce worldwide carbon emissions and energy usage. Governments have created targets for the reduction of carbon in their environments and are using controls, limits and grants in order to encourage businesses and individuals help the country meet its targets set out in the Kyoto accord.

Organisations are also finding that stakeholders such as employees and customers are becoming increasingly aware of and concerned about environmental policies. Companies with a poor record on abusing natural resources might find that they lose customers and staff to rivals who are more environmentally 'friendly'.

The contribution of environmental management accounting (EMA)

EMA is concerned with the accounting information needs of managers in relation to corporate activities that affect the environment as well as environment-related impacts on the corporation. This includes:

- identifying and estimating the costs of environment-related activities

- identifying and separately monitoring the usage and cost of resources such as water, electricity and fuel and to enable costs to be reduced

- ensuring environmental considerations form a part of capital investment decisions

- assessing the likelihood and impact of environmental risks

- including environment-related indicators as part of routine performance monitoring

- benchmarking activities against environmental best practice.

EM and effect on financial performance

There are a number of ways in which environmental issues can have an impact on the financial performance of organisations.

Improving revenue

Producing new products or services which meet the environmental needs or concerns of customers can lead to increased sales.

It may also be possible to sell such products for a premium price. RecycleMatch is an online business-to-business (B2B) marketplace that allows companies to buy, sell or give away large volumes of waste including plastics, textiles, paper, chemicals, food, metals and building materials.

Improved sales may also be a consequence of improving the reputation of the business.

It is possible that in the future, rather than good environmental management resulting in improved sales, poor management will lead to losses. All businesses will be expected to meet a minimum standard related to environmental issues.

Cost reductions

Paying close attention to the use of resources can lead to reductions in cost. Often simple improvements in processes can lead to significant costs savings. For example, Manchester United have estimated that they have saved around US$790,000 since introducing its environmental policies (explained earlier).

Increases in costs

There may be increases in some costs, for example the cost of complying with legal and regulatory requirements, and additional costs to improve the environmental image of the organisation. A recent study of the Syrian olive oil industry suggested that compliance costs could run to as much as 2% of total revenue.

However some of these costs may be offset by government grants and this expenditure may save money in the long-term as measures taken may prevent future losses.

For example, in countries such as the United Kingdom, Germany and Australia grants are available for companies who install solar panels as alternative energy supply systems. There is a high initial cost for the company but typically around two thirds of this is funded by government grants. Users also report that the balance of the cost is recovered over around four or five years through savings in energy bills.

Costs of failure

Even if short-term increases in costs through compliance or environmental policies cannot be recovered via increased revenue or other cost savings, it may still be considered to be financially acceptable if it avoids potential longer-term failure costs.

Poor environmental management can result in significant costs, for example the cost of clean-up and fines following an environmental disaster.

In April 2010, oil company British Petroleum was responsible for an oil spill off the Gulf of Mexico. By 2012 the company had spent US$21bn on the clean up operation and for compensation payments, and it had also reserved $40bn for expected future costs concerned with this environmental issue.

EMA and TQM

Organisations should be striving to achieve an integrated environmental strategy underpinned by the same type of culture that is required for the successful operation of a programme of total quality management (TQM).

It is arguable that the two are inextricably linked insofar as good environmental management is increasingly recognised as an essential component of TQM. The focus is upon 'continuous improvement' and the pursuit of excellence. Such organisations pursue objectives that may include zero complaints, zero spills, zero pollution, zero waste and zero accidents. Information systems need to be able to support such environmental objectives via the provision of feedback – on the success or otherwise – of the organisational efforts in achieving such objectives. In this respect, the organisation becomes self-regulating and the undertaking of environmental audits on a regular basis provides the platform for organisations to adopt a self-critical and analytical posture as part of their routine organisational management processes.

This approach to environmental quality management requires the development of environmental performance measures and indicators that will enable a comprehensive review of environmental performance to be undertaken. Many – if not all – total quality management accounting techniques can be modified and used in EMA.

6 Identifying and accounting for environmental costs

Classification of environmental costs

Management are often unaware of the extent of environmental costs and cannot identify opportunities for cost savings. In order to determine the potential for costs savings it will be important to understand the nature of environmental costs that can be experienced by a firm.

Environmental costs can be categorised as quality related costs (covered in chapter 3 alongside TQM). This results in four cost categories:

- Environmental **prevention costs** – those costs associated with preventing adverse environmental impacts

- Environmental **appraisal costs** – the cost of activities executed to determine whether products, service and activities are in compliance with environmental standards and policies
- Environmental **internal failure costs** – costs incurred to eliminate environmental impacts that have been created by the firm
- Environmental **external failure costs** – costs incurred after environmental damage has been caused outside the organisation

Further details

Environmental prevention costs

The aim here is to prevent adverse environmental impacts occurring in the first place. Examples include:

- evaluating and selecting pollution control equipment
- selecting and evaluating suppliers
- training staff
- designing processes and products
- creating environmental policies
- environmentally driven research and development
- site and feasibility studies
- investment in protective equipment
- community relations and outreach programmes

Environmental appraisal costs

The aim in incurring these costs is to determine whether adverse impacts are being created and whether environmental standards and internal policies are being complied with. Examples include:

- monitoring, testing and inspection costs
- site survey costs
- reporting costs
- improved systems and checks in order to prevent fines/penalties
- permit costs
- certification costs
- developing performance measures
- monitoring supplier performance

Environmental internal failure costs

These costs are borne exclusively by the organisation. Examples include:

- the cost of recycling or disposing of waste or harmful materials

- product take back costs (i.e. in the EU, for example, companies must provide facilities for customers to return items such as batteries, printer cartridges etc. for recycling. The seller of such items must bear the cost of these "take backs")

- clean up costs (as in the case of British Petroleum discussed earlier)

- legal costs, insurance and fines

- site decontamination

- back-end costs such as decommissioning costs on project completion

- compensation payments to employees and customers

- off-set costs (for example, many paper manufacturers also plant trees in order to off-set the damage they may be creating to existing forestry)

Environmental external failure costs

These are the most significant costs: they are incurred after the hazardous materials have been introduced into the environment. Examples of such costs are:

- adverse impact on the organisation's reputation. This may lead to bans on or boycotts of the company's products.

- adverse impact on natural resources such as rivers, forests and rock formations

- carbon emissions and the adverse impact these have on the global climate

- medical costs for employees and local communities

Some external failure costs might be caused by the company but the 'cost' will be borne by society at large. However, governments are becoming increasingly aware of these external costs and are using taxes and regulations to convert them to internal costs. For example, companies might have to have a tree replacement programme if they cause forest degradation, or they receive lower tax allowances on vehicles that cause a high degree of harm to the environment. On top of this, some companies are voluntarily converting external costs to internal costs.

A study by accountants KPMG in 2012 estimated that if a company were to internalise all environmental external failure costs then, on average, this would reduce profits by around 41% per annum. This highlights the need for further investment in prevention and appraisal costs. There is often a trade-off here: investment in prevention and appraisal can often reduce the occurrence of failure costs.

Accounting for environmental costs

Conventional management accounting practices do not provide adequate information for managing the environment in a world where environmental concerns, as well as environment-related costs, revenues, and benefits, are on the rise. Environmental costs are not traced to particular processes or activities and are instead "lumped in" with general business overheads or other activity costs.

Environmental activity-based accounting

In ABC, environmental costs are removed from general overheads and traced to products and services. This means that cost drivers are determined for these costs and products are charged for the use for these environmental costs based on the amount of cost drivers that they contribute to the activity. This should give a good attribution of environmental costs to individual products.

Illustration

A consumer electronics manufacturing company has established the following cost driver rates for internal environmental costs:

Category	Cost	Total cost	Cost driver	Cost driver rate
Prevention cost	Staff environmental training costs	$8m	40,000 training hours	$200 per training hour
Appraisal cost	Power usage inspection costs	$5m	150m kw hours consumed in final output	$0.033 per kw hour consumption
Internal failure cost	Product take back costs	$25m	15m batteries used in products	$1.67 per battery used

By including these costs in standard cost cards the company hope to encourage managers to focus on reducing total costs as well as the associated drivers. So, for example, managers may try to reduce the amount of batteries used in the product in order to be able to reduce that cost and also the selling price of the product.

The company now also wants to incorporate external environmental failure costs into its standard costing system. It is estimated the total external failure costs to be $15m. This is made up of pollution and clean up costs associated with the company's CO_2 emissions. It has therefore determined that the cost driver will be based on the number of tons of resources to be produced. In total 600,000 tonnes of resources were consumed last year and this gives a cost driver rate of $25 per tonne of resources consumed. Again, the company is hoping that this will encourage more awareness and control by managers.

Advantages of environmental costing	Disadvantages
• better/fairer product costs	• time consuming
• improved pricing – so that products that have the biggest environmental impact reflect this by having higher selling prices	• expensive to implement
• better environmental cost control	• determining accurate costs and appropriate costs drivers is difficult
• facilitates the quantification of cost savings from "environmentally-friendly" measures	• external costs not experienced by the company (e.g. carbon footprint) may still be ignored/unmeasured
• should integrate environmental costing into the strategic management process	• some internal environmental costs are intangible (e.g. impact on employee health) and these are still ignored
• reduces the potential for cross-subsidisation of environmentally damaging products	• a company that incorporates external costs voluntarily may be at a competitive disadvantage to rivals who do not do this

Input/output analysis

An alternative technique which can be used to identify and allocate environmental costs is Input/output analysis.

This technique records material flows with the idea that 'what comes in must go out – or be stored' (Jasch, 2003).

The purchased input is regarded as 100% and is balanced against the outputs – which are the produced, sold and stored goods and the residual (regarded as waste). Materials are measured in physical units and include energy and water. At the end of the process, the material flows can be expressed in monetary units. Process flow charts can help to trace inputs and outputs, in particular waste. They demonstrate the details of the processes so that the relevant information can be allocated to main activities.

The United Nations Centre for Sustainable Development (UNDSD) provides the following example:

Input	Output	
	Product	60%
	Scrap for recycling	20%
	Disposed of as waste	15%
	Not accounted for	5%
100%		100%

Flow management involves not only material flows, but also the organisational structure. Classic material flows are recorded as well as material losses incurred at various stages of production.

EMA can benefit from flow cost accounting because it aims to reduce the quantities of materials, which leads to increased ecological efficiency.

7 Chapter summary

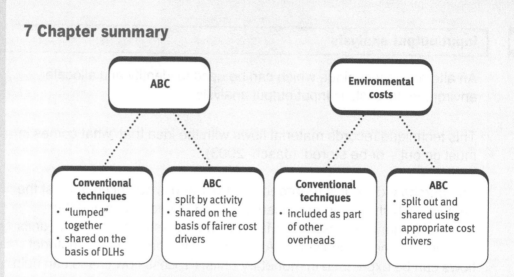

8 Practice questions

Test your understanding 1 – HENSAU LTD

Hensau Ltd has a single production process for which the following costs have been estimated for the period ending 31 December 20X1:

	$
Material receipt and inspection cost	15,600
Power cost	19,500
Material handling cost	13,650

Three products – X, Y and Z are produced by workers who perform a number of operations on material blanks using hand held electrically powered drills. The workers have a wage rate of $9 per hour.

The following budgeted information has been obtained for the period ending 31 December 20X1:

	Product X	Product Y	Product Z
Production quantity (units)	2,000	1,500	800
Batches of material	10	5	16
Data per product unit			
Direct material (sq. metres)	4	6	3
Direct material ($)	5	3	6
Direct labour (minutes)	24	40	60
Number of power drill operations	6	3	2

Overhead costs for material receipt and inspection, process power and material handling are presently each absorbed by product units using rates per direct labour hour.

An activity based costing investigation has revealed that the cost drivers for the overhead costs are as follows:

Material receipt and inspection: number of batches of material.

Process power: number of power drill operations.

Material handling: quantity of material (sq. metres) handled.

Required:

(a) to prepare a summary which calculates the budgeted product cost per unit for each of the products X, Y and Z for the period ending 31 December 20X1 detailing the unit costs for each cost element:

(i) using the existing method for the absorption of overhead costs and

(ii) using an approach which recognises the cost drivers revealed in the activity based costing investigation

(17 marks)

(b) to explain the relevance of cost drivers in activity based costing. Make use of figures from the summary statement prepared in (a) to illustrate your answer.

(8 marks)

(Total: 25 marks)

Test your understanding 2 – SAPU PLC

Sapu plc make and sell a number of products. Products A and B are products for which market prices are available at which Sapu plc can obtain a share of the market as detailed below. Estimated data for the forthcoming period is as follows:

(i) Product data

	Product A	Product B	Other products
Production/sales (units)	5,000	10,000	40,000
	$000	$000	$000
Total direct material cost	80	300	2,020
Total direct labour cost	40	100	660

(ii) Variable overhead cost is $1,500,000 of which 40% is related to the acquisition, storage and use of direct materials and 60% is related to the control and use of direct labour.

(iii) It is current practice in Sapu plc to absorb variable overhead cost into product units using companywide percentages on direct material cost and direct labour cost as the absorption bases.

(iv) Market prices for Products A and B are $75 and $95 per unit respectively.

(v) Sapu plc require a minimum estimated contribution:sales ratio of 40% before proceeding with the production/sale of any product.

Required:

(a) Calculate estimated unit product costs for Product A and Product B where variable overhead is charged to product units as follows:

(i) Using the existing absorption basis as detailed above.

(5 marks)

(ii) Using an activity based costing approach where cost drivers have been estimated for material and labour related overhead costs as follows:

	Product A	Product B	Other products
Direct material related overheads – cost driver is material bulk. The bulk proportions per unit are:	4	1	1.5
Direct labour related overheads – cost driver is number of labour operations (not directly time related). Labour operations per product unit	6	1	2

(10 marks)

(b) Illustrate the decision strategy which Sapu plc may implement with regard to the production and sale of Products A and B. Use unit costs as calculated in (a) (i) and (a) (ii) together with other information given in the question in your analysis. Your answer should include relevant calculations and discussion and be prepared in a form suitable for presentation to management.

(10 marks)

(Total: 25 marks)

Test your understanding 3

Fixed overhead absorption rates are often calculated using a single measure of activity. It is suggested that fixed overhead costs should be attributed to cost units using multiple measures of activity (Activity Based Costing).

Explain Activity Based Costing and how it may provide useful information to managers.

(Your answer should refer to both the setting of cost driver rates and subsequent overhead cost control.)

(5 marks)

Test your understanding 4

Explain the benefits of using multiple activity bases for variable overhead absorption.

(5 marks)

Test your understanding 5

A company produced three products, the standard costs of which are shown below:

	$	$	$
Direct material	50	40	30
Direct labour (@ $10 per hour)	30	40	50
Production overhead*	30	40	50
	110	120	130
Production units	10,000	20,000	30,000

* Absorbed on the basis of direct labour hours

Total production overheads are $2,600,000 giving rise to an overhead absorption rate of $10 per hour (being $2.6 m overheads / 260,000 total direct labour hours worked).

The company wishes to introduce ABC, and has identified two major cost pools for production overhead and their associated cost drivers.

Information on these activity cost pools and their drivers is given below:

Activity cost pool	Cost driver	Cost associated with activity cost pool
Receiving/ inspecting quality assurance	Purchase requisitions	$1,400,000
Production scheduling/machine set-ups	Number of bathes	$1,200,000

Further relevant information on the three products is also given below:

	P	R	S
Number of purchase requisitions	1,200	1,800	2,000
Number of set ups	240	260	300

Required:

(a) Calculate the activity-based production cost of products, P, R and S.

(8 marks)

(b) Comment on the differences between the original standard costs and the activity-based costs you calculate.

(5 marks)

Test your understanding 6

Cabal makes and sells two products, Plus and Doubleplus. The direct costs of production are $12 for one unit of Plus and $24 per unit of Doubleplus.

Information relating to annual production and sales is as follows:

	Plus	Doubleplus
Annual production and sales	24,000 units	24,000 units
Direct labour hours per unit	1.0	1.5
Number of orders	10	140
Number of batches	12	240
Number of setups per batch	1	3
Special parts per unit	1	4

Information relating to production overhead costs is as follows:

	Cost driver	Annual cost
		$
Setup costs	Number of setups	73,200
Special parts handling	Number of special parts	60,000
Other materials handling	Number of batches	63,000
Order handling	Number of orders	19,800
Other overheads	–	216,000
		432,000

Other overhead costs do not have an identifiable cost driver, and in an ABC system, these overheads would be recovered on a direct labour hours basis.

(a) Calculate the production cost per unit of Plus and of Doubleplus if the company uses traditional absorption costing and the overheads are recovered on a direct labour hours basis.

(5 marks)

(b) Calculate the production cost per unit of Plus and of Doubleplus if the company uses ABC.

(10 marks)

(c) Explain the reasons for the differences in the production cost per unit between the two methods.

(5 marks)

(d) Explain the implications for management of using an ABC system instead of an absorption costing system?

(5 marks)

(Total: 25 marks)

Test your understanding 7

A supermarket chain is considering building a new shop. There are two possible locations. Explain the environmental factors that the management accountant should consider when providing information to support the decision making.

(5 marks)

Test your understanding 8 – ABC COST DRIVERS

Explain the factors that should be considered when selecting cost drivers for an activity based costing system.

(5 marks)

Test your understanding 9

A table manufacturing company is considering introducing a new environmental policy and specialist control team as a reaction to some concerns that buyers are having over the company's potential adverse impact on natural resources. The company is concerned about how following an environmental policy might impact on its costs.

State what types of environmental costs the company might incur and explain how these might change in the future with the introduction of an environmental policy.

(5 marks)

Test your understanding answers

Example 1

Solution

(a)

Workings	M1	M2	Total
Number of batches	4	80	84
Number of setups	4	240	244
Special parts	16,000	64,000	80,000
Direct labour hours	16,000	20,000	36,000

Activity	Cost		M1	M2
	$		$	$
Setups	97,600	Cost per setup $400	1,600	96,000
Materials handling	42,000	Cost per batch $500	2,000	40,000
Special parts handling	50,000	Cost per part $0.625	10,000	40,000
Invoicing	31,000	Cost per order $100	6,000	25,000
Other overheads	108,000	Cost per hour $3	48,000	60,000
	328,600		67,600	261,000

	M1		M2	
	$	$	$	$
Sales		432,000		584,000
Direct materials	88,000		168,000	
Direct labour	128,000		160,000	
Overheads	67,600		261,000	
Total costs		283,600		589,000
Profit/(loss)		148,400		(5,000)
Profit/loss per unit		18.55		(0.625)

(b) The figures suggest that model M2 is less profitable than M1. The sales manager should try to persuade the customer to buy model M1. Note that the apparent loss on M2 does not necessarily mean that production should be ceased. To assess this management should consider the incremental relevant cash flows involved – e.g. is the product making positive contribution, how many overheads are avoidable? They could also consider ways to reduce the cost drivers for the product to reduce its share of the overheads and convert the product loss into a profit.

Test your understanding 1 – HENSAU LTD

(a)

(i) The existing overhead absorption rate is:

$$\frac{\$15,600 + \$19,500 + \$13,650}{(2,000 \times 24/60) + (1,500 \times 40/60) + (800 \times 60/60)} = \frac{\$48,750}{2,600 \text{ hours}}$$

$$= \$18.75 \text{ per hour.}$$

Unit cost

	Product X	Product Y	Product Z
Direct material	5.00	3.00	6.00
Direct labour	3.60	6.00	9.00
Production overhead	7.50	12.50	18.75
	$16.10	$21.50	$33.75

(ii) Cost driver rates

$$\text{Material receipt and inspection} = \frac{\$15,600}{10 + 5 + 16} = \$503.23 \text{ per batch}$$

$$\text{Process power} = \frac{\$19,500}{(2,000 \times 6) + (1,500 \times 3) + (800 \times 2)}$$

$$= \$1.0773 \text{ per power drill operation}$$

$$\text{Material handling} = \frac{\$13,650}{(2,000 \times 4) + (1,500 \times 6) + (800 \times 3)}$$

$$= \$0.70361 \text{ per sq. metre handled}$$

	Product		
	X	Y	Z
Direct material	5.00	3.00	6.00
Direct labour	3.60	6.00	9.00
Production overhead			
Material receipt/inspection (W1)	2.52	1.68	10.06
Process power (W2)	6.46	3.23	2.15
Material handling (W3)	2.81	4.22	2.11
Cost per unit	$20.39	$18.13	$29.32

Workings

(W1) **Material receipt/inspection**

Cost/unit

Product X   503.23/batch × 10 batches/2,000 units
= $2.52/unit

Product Y   503.23/batch × 5 batches/1,500 units
= $1.68/unit

Product Z   503.23/batch × 16 batches/800 units
= $10.06/unit

(W2) **Process power**

Cost/unit

Product X $1.0773/operation × 6 operations = $6.46
Product Y $1.0773/operation × 3 operations = $3.23
Product Z $1.0773/operation × 2 operations = $2.15

(W3) **Material handling**

Cost/unit

Product X $0.70361/m^2 of material × 4m^2 = $2.81
Product Y $0.70361/m^2 of material × 6m^2 = $4.22
Product Z $0.70361/m^2 of material × 3m^2 = $2.11

(b) A cost driver is that factor which is most closely related to the way in which the costs of an activity are incurred. It could be said to cause the costs. Under ABC we do not restrict ourselves to just six possible OARs. We choose whatever basis we consider suitable to charge overheads to the product.

A good example of the superiority of ABC over absorption costing is that of process power in part (a) above. Under traditional absorption costing Product Z was the dearest for process power merely because it used the most labour hours per unit – a fact completely and utterly unconnected with the way in which process power costs are incurred. Under ABC we investigate the business and actually take the time to find out what factor is most closely related to the cost and use that factor to charge overheads. Here we find that Product X should be the dearest because it uses the most power drill operations.

ABC supporters would argue that this cost/power drill operation is useful information. Costs are $1.0773 per power drill operation and thus product X costs $6.46. This cost is not insignificant and in fact is nearly as much as the direct material cost and direct labour cost combined. It would be inconceivable that the direct material costs and direct labour costs would not be very carefully controlled and yet under traditional absorption costing the process power costs would be included within the general overheads and would not be subject to such severe scrutiny.

Under ABC, once we realise that power drill operations cost $1.0773 each then when designing new products, we would have better cost information and thus would be able to make better informed decisions.

Test your understanding 2 – SAPU PLC

(a) (i) **Workings**

Material related overhead cost	= 40% × $ 1,500,000 = $600,000
Overhead absorption rate ($600,000/$2,400,000)	= 25% on direct material cost
Labour related overhead cost	= 60% × $1,500,000 = $900,000
Overhead absorption rate ($900,000/$800,000)	= 112.5% on direct labour cost

Using the overhead absorption rates calculated above and average direct material and direct labour costs from the data in the question we have:

	Unit costs	
	Product A	**Product B**
	$	$
Direct material cost	16	30
Direct labour cost	8	10
	—	—
	24	40
Variable overhead		
Material related at 25%	4	7.5
Labour related at 112.5%	9	11.25
	—	—
Total variable cost	37	58.75
	—	—

(ii) **Workings**

Material related overhead has bulk as the cost driver.

Total bulk factor = (5,000 × 4) + (10,000 × 1) + (40,000 × 1.5) = 90,000

Material related overhead per unit of bulk = $600,000/90,000 = $6.67

Hence overhead cost per product unit:

Product A = $6.67 × 4 = $26.67

Product B = $6.67 × 1 = $6.67

Labour related overhead has the number of labour operations as the cost driver.

Total labour operations = (5,000 × 6) + (10,000 × 1) + (40,000 × 2) = 120,000

Labour related overhead per labour operation = $900,000/120,000 = $7.50

Hence overhead cost per product unit:

Product A = $7.50 × 6 = $45

Product B = $7.50 × 1 = $7.50

The amended unit product costs may now be shown as:

	Unit costs	
	Product A	**Product B**
	$	$
Direct material cost	16	30
Direct labour cost	8	10
	24	40
Variable overhead		
Material related	26.67	6.67
Labour related	45.00	11.25
Total variable cost	95.67	54.17

(b)

From: Management accountant
To: Management team
Subject: Production strategy for Products A and B

The unit market prices for Products A and B are $75 and $95 respectively. At these prices we can obtain market share of 5,000 units of A and 10,000 units of B in the forthcoming period. The unit product cost and contribution information may be calculated using our existing basis for the absorption of variable overhead cost by product units or by using an ABC approach which recognises the cost drivers which cause costs to occur.

Unit product information is as follows:

	Product A		Product B	
	Existing approach	ABC approach	Existing approach	ABC approach
	$	$	$	$
Direct material cost	16	16	30	30
Direct labour cost	8	8	10	10
	—	—	—	—
	24	24	40	40
Variable overhead cost				
Material related	4	26.67	7.50	6.67
Labour related	9	45.00	11.25	7.50
	—	—	—	—
Total variable cost	37	95.67	58.75	54.17
Contribution	38	(20.67)	36.25	40.83
	—	—	—	—
Selling price	75	75.00	95.00	95.00
	—	—	—	—
Contribution: sales (%)	50.7%	negative	38.2%	43.0%

Based on the company policy of a minimum contribution: sales ratio of 40% before proceeding with the sale of any product, our current product costing procedure would confirm the production and sale of Product A with a CS ratio of 50.7%, but would reject Product B with a CS ratio of 38.2%.

The amended product costs using the ABC approach which recognises the cost drivers for overhead cost will reverse our decision. Product A would now be rejected with a negative CS ratio whereas Product B would be acceptable with a CS ratio of 43%. The ABC based calculations recognise the relatively high cost driver levels for Product A and 1 would recommend that we use the ABC calculations as the basis for our decision strategy and produce and sell Product B.

Test your understanding 3

Activity Based Costing (ABC) is a system of full costing which recognises that the more traditional method of absorption costing using cost centre absorption rates may not provide accurate product costs.

ABC identifies the activities of a production process and the extent to which individual products make use of those activities. Costs are then estimated for each of these activities which are referred to as cost pools. The number of times which the activity is expected to be carried out is also estimated and a cost driver rate calculated:

$$\frac{\text{Estimated cost of pool}}{\text{Estimated number of times activity is to be performed}}$$

An individual product will probably make use of a number of different activities, and a proportion of the cost of each activity will be attributed to the product using these predetermined cost driver rates.

The actual costs of each cost pool together with the number of times the activity is performed will be collected and a comparison made with the corresponding estimated values. This is similar to the comparison of actual and budgeted costs and volumes using the traditional absorption costing approach except that there are likely to be a greater number of cost driver rates using ABC than the one per cost centre absorption rate found in traditional absorption costing.

Test your understanding 4

Such an approach is beneficial because it identifies overhead costs with their cause, rather than assuming that they are all driven by a single cause.

This should enable management to control such costs more easily, the variances reported will be more meaningful and this will help management to control costs.

Test your understanding 5

(a) **Cost drivers**

Receiving/inspecting quality assurance (based on purchase requisitions) $= \dfrac{\$1,400,000}{5,000} = \$280$

Production scheduling/machine set-ups (based on number of set-ups) $= \dfrac{\$1,200,000}{800} = \$1,500$

Standard cost cards

	P	R	S
	$	$	$
Direct material	50.00	40.00	30.00
Direct labour	30.00	40.00	50.00
Production overhead			
Receiving/inspecting quality assurance			
$280 × 1,200/10,000	33.60		
$280 × 1,800/20,000		25.20	
$280 × 2,000/30,000			18.66
Production scheduling/machine set-ups			
$1,500 × 240/10,000	36.00		
$1,500 × 260/20,000		19.50	
$1,500 × 300/30,000			15.00
Total production cost	149.60	124.70	113.66

(b) Comparison of the ABC cost with the original traditionally calculated cost reveals that product S was significantly overcosted by the traditional system relative to the ABC system, while product P was seriously undercosted. Product S is high-volume product with a high direct labour content, while product P is a low-volume product with a low direct labour content; this result is therefore to be expected. Both the activities in this simple example are batch-related, not unit-related. ABC reflects this reality in its allocation of production overhead costs to the product. The traditional approach allocated all production overhead costs to products as if the overheads were driven by unit-level activities, that is the number of direct labour hours worked – with the inevitable costing consequence seen above.

You should note that this example, with only two activity cost pools, will almost certainly have necessitated some arbitrary cost allocations. All that is being claimed is that the resulting ABC costings give a better insight into the cost of producing the products than traditional costs.

Test your understanding 6

(a) **Traditional absorption costing**

Budgeted direct labour hours	60,000
(24,000 × 1.0) + (24,000 × 1.5)	
Budgeted overhead costs	$432,000
Recovery rate per direct labour hour	$7.20

	Plus	**Double plus**
	$	$
Direct costs	12.00	24.00
Production overhead	7.20	10.80
Full production cost	19.20	34.80

(b) ABC

Workings

	Plus	Double plus	Total
Batches	12	240	252
Setups	12	720	732
Special parts	24,000	96,000	120,000
Orders	10	140	150
Direct labour hours	24,000	36,000	60,000

Cost driver rates

Setup costs	$73,200/732	$100 per setup
Special parts handling	$60,000/120,000	$0.50 per part
Order handling	$19,800/150	$132 per order
Materials handling	$63,000/252	$250 per batch
Other overheads	$216,000/60,000	$3.60 per hour

	Plus	Double plus	Total
	$	$	$
Setup costs	1,200	72,000	73,200
Special parts handling costs	12,000	48,000	60,000
Order handling costs	1,320	18,480	19,800
Materials handling costs	3,000	60,000	63,000
Other overheads	86,400	129,600	216,000
	103,920	328,080	432,000

	Plus	Double plus
Number of units	24,000	24,000
	$	$
Direct cost	12.00	24.00
Overhead cost per unit	4.33	13.67
Full cost	16.33	37.67

Note: In the example above the full production costs were:

	Plus	Double plus
• Using traditional absorption costing	$19.20	$34.80
• Using ABC	$16.33	$37.67
• Assume the selling prices are	$25.00	$40.00
• Using absorption costing sales margins are	23.2%	13.0%
• ABC sales margins are	34.7%	5.8%

(c) The reasons for the difference in the production cost per unit between the two methods

- The allocation of overheads under absorption costing was unfair. This method assumed that all of the overheads were driven by labour hours and, as a result, the Double Plus received 1.5 times the production overhead of the Plus.

- However, this method of absorption is not appropriate. The overheads are in fact driven by a number of different factors. There are five activity costs, each one has its own cost driver. By taking this into account we end up with a much more accurate production overhead cost per unit.

- Using ABC, the cost per unit of a Double Plus is significantly higher. This is because the Double Plus is a much more complex product than the Plus. For example, there are 140 orders for the Double Plus but only 10 for the Plus and there are 4 special parts for the Double Plus compared to only one for the Plus. As a result of this complexity, the Double Plus has received more than three times the overhead of the Plus.

- This accurate allocation is important because the production overhead is a large proportion of the overall cost.

(d) **The implications of using ABC**

- Pricing – pricing decisions will be improved because the price will be based on more accurate cost data.

- Decision making – this should also be improved. For example, research, production and sales effort can be directed towards the most profitable products.

- – Performance management – should be improved. ABC can be used as the basis of budgeting and forward planning. The more realistic overhead should result in more accurate budgets and should improve the process of performance management. In addition, an improved understanding of what drives the overhead costs should result in steps being taken to reduce the overhead costs and hence an improvement in performance.

- – Sales strategy – this should be more soundly based. For example, target customers with products that appeared unprofitable under absorption costing but are actually profitable, and vice versa.

Test your understanding 7

Suggestions for issues to consider

- The design of the shop and its usage of utilities such as water and electricity.

- The costs of ensuring that the building and the operation comply with any local environmental regulations and requirements such as those of planning authorities.

- The environmental impact on the local area and the cost of any measures needed to minimise it – for example the potential increase in traffic and the provision of a free bus service as an alternative for customers.

- The locations and their position relative to the chain's distribution network and the fuel costs of supplying goods.

- The views and influence of local environmental pressure groups and the likely cost of public relations activities and modifications to plans to address their concerns.

- The product range to be offered and the market locally for higher-priced environmentally-friendly products such as organic fruit and vegetables.

Test your understanding 8 – ABC COST DRIVERS

The cost driver for a particular activity is the factor that causes a change in the cost of the activity. For the cost driver to be useful there must be an identifiable relationship between the cost and the cost driver, i.e. changes in the number of cost drivers must cause corresponding changes in the total cost incurred on the activity.

Another major consideration is the ease of accurately recording the number of cost drivers incurred. If the process of recording the cost drivers is very complex and time-consuming then the cost of the recording system might outweigh the benefits derived from the information obtained.

It is possible to identify three types of cost driver:

Transaction drivers

Here, the cost of an activity is affected by the number of times a particular action is undertaken. Examples would include number of set-ups, number of power drill operations, number of batches of material received, number of purchase orders, etc.

Duration drivers

In this case, the cost of the activity is not so much affected by the number of times the action is undertaken as by the length of time that it takes to perform the action, e.g. set-up costs may not be related to the number of set-ups so much as to the set-up time, because some products involve more complicated and time consuming set-ups than others

Intensity drivers

In this case, efforts would be directed at determining what resources were used in the making of a product or service, e.g. rather than charging all purchase orders with the same cost per order, we might determine that overseas orders involve more work than home orders and apply a weighting to the overseas orders to reflect the extra work.

Test your understanding 9

There are four main types of environmental costs:

- prevention costs – such as improvements in staff training and awareness,

- appraisal costs – such as measuring the adverse impact on natural resources,

- internal failure costs – such as fines that might be incurred for breaches of environmental standards, and

- external failure costs – such as a loss of sale from a damaged reputation and customer boycotts.

If the company was to focus more on its environmental policies and have a specialist team to do so then they are likely to experience changes in all of these costs. It is likely, for example, that prevention and appraisal costs will increase. Creating the specialist team and performing more monitoring are likely to increase the company's overall costs.

But these might be offset by savings in other environmental costs. Better staff awareness and preventative measures should reduce the occurrence of internal failures. For example, the company may be less likely to breach environmental standards and incur fines. They might also see less product boycotts and increased sales so that external failure costs also fall.

Many organisations have found that the savings in failure costs can often outweigh the investment in prevention and appraisal costs.

Variance analysis: calculations

Chapter learning objectives

Lead	Component
A1. discuss costing methods and their results.	(d) Apply standard costing methods, within costing systems, including the reconciliation of budgeted and actual profit margins.

1 Chapter overview diagram

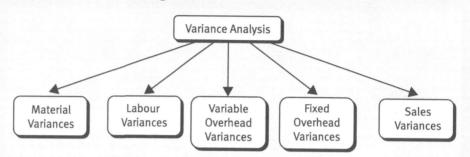

2 Standard costing and variance analysis

 Standard costing is a technique which establishes predetermined estimates of the costs of products and services and then compares these predetermined costs with actual costs as they are incurred. The predetermined costs are known as standard costs and the difference between the standard cost and actual cost is known as a variance.

The process by which the total difference between actual cost and standard is broken down into its different elements is known as **Variance Analysis**.

 A variance is the difference between actual results and the budget or standard.

Taken together, cost and sales variances can be used to explain the difference between the budgeted profit for a period and the actual profit.

When actual results are *better than* expected results, a **favourable (F)** variance occurs.

When actual results are *worse than* expected results, an **adverse variance (A)** occurs.

Variance groups

Variances can be divided into three main groups:

- sales variances
- variable cost variances
  - material variances
  - labour variances
  - variable overhead variances
- fixed overhead variances

Further explanation of standard costing

Whenever identical operations are performed or identical products are manufactured many times over, it should be possible to decide in advance not merely what they are *expected to cost*, but also what they *ought to cost*.

Similarly, when a standard service is provided many times over, it should be possible to establish in advance how the service should be provided, how long it should take and how much it should cost.

- A **standard** is 'a benchmark measurement of resource usage or revenue or profit generation, set in defined conditions' (CIMA *Official Terminology*).

- A **standard cost** for a product or service is a predetermined (planned) unit cost, based on a standard specification of the resources needed to supply it and the costs of those resources.

  A standard cost is based on technical specifications for the materials, labour time and other resources required and the prices and rates for the materials and labour.

  Standard costs can be prepared using either absorption costing or marginal costing.

- A **standard price** for a product or service is the expected price for selling the standard product or service. When there is a standard sales price and a standard cost per unit, there is also a **standard profit per unit** (absorption costing) or **standard contribution per unit** (marginal costing).

Variance analysis

Variances can be calculated for both costs and sales. Cost variances analyse the difference between actual costs and standard costs. Sales variances analyse the difference between actual and budgeted sales prices and sales volumes.

Where standard costing is used, variance analysis can be an important aspect of performance measurement and control. It is defined in the CIMA Official Terminology as 'the evaluation of performance by means of variances, whose timely reporting should maximise the opportunity for managerial action'.

Variance reports comparing actual results with the standards or budget are produced regularly, perhaps monthly.

3 Sales variances

The difference between a budgeted profit and the actual profit achieved in a period is explained by both cost variances and sales variances. Cost variances explain the differences between actual costs and budgeted or standard costs. Sales variances explain the effect of differences between:

- actual and standard sales prices, and
- budgeted and actual sales volumes.

Sales price variance

A sales price variance shows the effect on profit of a 'change in revenue caused by the actual selling price differing from that budgeted' *(CIMA Official Terminology)*. It is calculated as the difference between:

(a) Standard selling price multiplied by the actual number of units sold, and

(b) Actual selling price multiplied by the actual number of units sold.

Proforma		
Sales price variance		$
Units sold should have sold for	(actual sales units × standard sales price per unit)	X
They did sell for	(actual sales revenue)	Y
Sales price variance		X–Y

This variance is favourable if actual sales revenue is higher than sales at the standard selling price, and adverse if actual sales revenue is lower than standard.

Sales volume variance

The sales volume variance is a 'measure of the effect on contribution/profit of not achieving the budgeted volume of sales' *(CIMA Official Terminology)*. It is the difference between actual and budgeted sales volumes valued at either standard profit, in an absorption costing system, or standard contribution in a marginal costing system.

Proforma

A sales volume variance measured in units has to be calculated first. The variance is favourable if actual sales volume is higher than budgeted sales volume, and adverse if actual sales volume is lower than budget.

Sales volume variance	Units of sale
	Units
Actual sales volume	X
Budgeted sales volume	Y
Sales volume variance	X–Y

The variance in units can then be valued in one of three ways:

- at the **standard profit per unit** – if using absorption costing

- at the **standard contribution per unit** – if using marginal costing

- at the **standard revenue per unit** – this is rarely used and you should only do so if it was specifically asked for in an exam question

Example 1

Walter Dean Ltd has budgeted sales of 400 units at $25 each. The variable costs are expected to be $18 per unit, and there are no fixed costs.

The actual sales were 500 units at $20 each and costs were as expected.

Calculate the selling price variance and the sales volume contribution variance.

Example 2

The following data is available for the most recent month of sales:

	Budget	Actual
Sales units	320	380
Selling price per unit	$45	$42
Total cost per unit	$23	$22
Variable cost per unit	$17	$15

Calculate the sales variances, calculating the sales volume variance using absorption costing, marginal costing and standard revenue per unit.

4 Direct material cost variances

This section has three variances. The direct material total variance, which shows the total difference in the amount spent on materials, and this can also be split into two further components – the materials price and materials usage variances.

Direct material total variance

The difference between:

(a) the standard direct material cost of the actual production and

(b) the actual direct material cost.

Proforma

Direct material total variance		$
Actual quantity of output	should cost (standard)	X
	did cost	Y
Total cost variance		X–Y

Example 3

James Marshall Ltd makes a single product with the following budgeted material costs per unit:

> 2 kg of material A at $10/kg

Actual details:

> Output 1,000 units
> Material purchased and used 2,200 kg
> Material cost $20,900

Calculate the direct material total variance.

A total material variance actually conveys very little useful information. It needs to be analysed further. It can be analysed into two sub-variances:

(1) a Direct Material Price variance, i.e. paying more or less than expected for materials and

(2) a Direct Material Usage variance, i.e. using more or less material than expected.

CIMA definitions

The total direct material variance is defined as:

> *measurement of the difference between the standard material cost of the output produced and the material cost incurred.*
> *(CIMA Official Terminology).*

The material price variance is defined as:

> *the difference between the actual price paid for purchased materials and their standard cost.*
> *(CIMA Official Terminology).*

The material usage variance is defined as a variance which:

> *measures efficiency in the use of material, by comparing standard material usage for actual production with actual material used, the difference is valued at standard cost.*
> *(CIMA Official Terminology).*

Direct material price variance

It is calculated as the difference between:

(a) standard purchase price per kg (or per litre for liquids) and

(b) actual purchase price

multiplied by the actual quantity of material purchased or used.

Note that the material price variance can be calculated either at the time of purchase or at the time of usage.

Proforma		
Direct materials price variance		$
Actual quantity of materials	should cost (standard)	X
	did cost (actual)	Y
		___
Direct materials price variance		X–Y
		___

The impact of stock valuation
If stock is valued at standard cost, then the calculation should be performed using the quantity of materials *purchased*. This will ensure that all of the variance is eliminated as soon as purchases are made and the stock will be held at standard cost.
If stock is valued at actual cost, then the calculation should be performed using the quantity of materials *used*. This means that the variance is calculated and eliminated on each item of stock as it is used up. The remainder of the stock will then be held at actual price, with its price variance still 'attached', until it is used and the price variance is calculated.

Direct material usage variance

The difference between:

(a) the standard quantity of material specified for the actual production and

(b) the actual quantity used

multiplied by the standard purchase price.

Proforma

Direct materials usage variance

		$
Actual output produced	should use (standard quantity)	X
	did use (actual quantity)	Y
		—
Direct materials usage variance	(in material quantity)	X–Y
		—
× standard price	(per unit of material)	$P
Direct materials usage variance		$P × (X–Y)

Example 4

For example 3, calculate the price and usage variances for materials.

An alternative method

Using the data in Example 3, calculate the same variances for materials using the following format:

SQSP
} Usage variance
AQSP } } Total variance
} Price variance
AQAP

Where	SQ	means Standard Quantity
	SP	means Standard Price
	AQ	means Actual Quantity
and	AP	means Actual Price

Standard Quantity means the standard quantity of the actual output.

Note: This assumes purchases = issues and/or the price variance is calculated at the time of issue.

					$		
SQSP							
	2 kg/unit x 1,000 units	X	$10/kg	=	20,000	}	Usage $2,000 A
AQSP							
	2,200 kg	X	$10/kg	=	22,000	}	
AQAP							$1,100 F
		X		=	20,900	}	Price

5 Direct labour cost variances

This section has four variances. The direct labour total cost variance, which shows the impact of any overall change in the amount spent on labour, and this can also be split into two further components – the labour rate and labour efficiency variances. In some scenarios we might also see a labour idle time variance.

Direct labour total variance

The difference between:

(a) the standard direct labour cost of the actual production and

(b) the actual cost of direct labour.

Proforma		
Direct labour total variance		$
Actual quantity of output	should cost (standard)	X
	did cost	Y
Total cost variance		X–Y

A total labour variance can also be analysed further. It can be analysed into two sub-variances:

(1) a Direct Labour Rate variance, i.e. paying more or less than expected per hour for labour and

(2) a Direct Labour Efficiency variance, i.e. using more or less labour hours per unit than expected.

CIMA definitions

The total direct labour variance is defined as one which:

indicates the difference between the standard direct labour cost of the output which has been produced and the actual direct labour cost incurred.

(CIMA Official Terminology).

The direct labour rate variance is defined as one which:

indicates the actual cost of any change from the standard labour rate of remuneration.

(CIMA Official Terminology).

The direct labour efficiency variance is defined as:

standard labour cost of any change from the standard level of labour efficiency.

(CIMA Official Terminology).

Direct labour rate variance

The difference between:

(a) standard rate per hour and the

(b) actual rate per hour

multiplied by the actual hours that were paid for.

Proforma

Direct labour rate variance		$
Number of hours paid	should cost / hr (standard)	X
	did cost (actual)	Y
Direct labour rate variance		X–Y

Direct labour efficiency variance

The difference between:

(a) the standard hours specified for the actual production and

(b) the actual hours worked

multiplied by the standard hourly rate.

Proforma		
Direct labour efficiency variance:		**Hours**
Actual output produced	should take (standard hours)	X
	did take (actual hours)	Y
Direct labour efficiency variance	(in hours)	X–Y
x standard rate per hour		$P
Direct labour efficiency variance		$P × (X–Y)

Example 5		

Ivan Korshunov Ltd makes a single product and has the following budgeted/standard information:

Budgeted production	1,000 units
Labour hours per unit	3
Labour rate per hour	$8

Actual results:

Output	1,100 units
Hours paid for and worked	3,400 hours
Labour cost	$28,300

Calculate rate and efficiency variances for labour.

An alternative method

Using example 5, calculate appropriate variances for labour using the following format:

SHSR ⎫
⎬ Efficiency variance ⎫
AHSR ⎬ ⎬ Total variance
⎬ Rate variance ⎭
AHAR ⎭

Where SH means Standard Hours
SR means Standard Rate
AH means Actual Hours
and AR means Actual Rate

Standard Hours means the standard hours of the actual output.

(this assumes that there is no idle time)

					$		
SHSR							
	3 hrs/unit x 1,100 units	x	$8/hr	=	26,400	⎫	Efficiency
AHSR						⎬	$800 A
	3,400 hrs	x	$8/hr	=	27,200	⎬	
AHAR						⎬	$1,100 A
				=	28,300	⎭	Rate

Idle time and idle time variances

During a period, there might be idle time, when the work force is not doing any work at all.

When idle time occurs, and if it is recorded, the efficiency variance should be separated into two parts:

- an idle time variance
- an efficiency variance during active working hours.

If there is no standard idle time set, then **the idle time variance is always adverse**, because it represents money 'wasted'.

Idle time definition

The purpose of an efficiency variance should be to measure the efficiency of the work force in the time they are actively engaged in making products or delivering a service.

The direct labour idle time variance is defined as:

this variance occurs when the hours paid exceed the hours worked and there is an extra cost caused by this idle time. Its computation increases the accuracy of the labour efficiency variance.

(CIMA Official Terminology).

Illustration 1

A product has a standard direct labour cost of $15, consisting of 1.5 hours of work for each unit at a cost of $10 per hour. During April, 100 units were produced. The direct labour workers were paid $2,000 for 160 hours of attendance, but the idle time records show that 30 hours in the month were recorded as idle time.

(a) We can record an idle time variance of 30 hours (A). This is costed at the standard rate per hour, $10, to give an idle time variance of $300(A).

(b) The efficiency variance should then be calculated using the active hours worked, not the total hours paid for.

Direct labour efficiency variance

		Hours
Actual output produced 100 units	should take (standard hours) 1.5 hrs per unit	150
	did take (160hrs – 30hrs)	130
Direct labour efficiency variance (in hours)		20 F
× standard rate per hour		$10/ hr
Direct labour efficiency variance		$200 F

Example 6

Melanie Mitchell Ltd makes a single product with the following information:

Budget/Standard

Output	1,000 units
Hours	6,000
Labour cost	$42,000

Actual

Output	900 units
Hours paid	5,500
Hours worked	5,200
Labour cost	$39,100

Calculate appropriate variances for labour

Expected idle time

Some organisations may experience idle time on a regular basis. For example, if demand is seasonal or irregular, but the organisation wishes to maintain and pay a constant number of workers, they will experience a certain level of 'expected' or 'normal' idle time during less busy periods.

In this situation the standard labour rate may include an allowance for the cost of the expected idle time. Only the impact of any unexpected or abnormal idle time would be included in the idle time variance. If actual idle time is greater than standard then the variance is adverse; if it is less than standard then it would be favourable.

Example

IT plc experiences seasonal demand for its product. During the next period the company expects that there will be an average level of idle time equivalent to 20% of hours paid. The company's standard labour rate is $9 per hour before the adjustment for idle time payments.

The standard time to produce one unit of output is 3 active (productive) hours.

Actual results for the period were as follows:

Number of units produced	3,263
Actual hours paid for	14,000
Actual active (productive) hours	10,304

Required:

Calculate the following variances for the period:

(i)   the idle time variance;

(ii) the labour efficiency variance.

Solution

The basic standard rate per hour must be increased to allow for the impact of the idle time:

Standard rate per hour worked $= \dfrac{\$9.00}{0.8} = \$11.25$

The variances can now be evaluated at this increased hourly rate.

Idle time variance

	Hours
Expected idle time = 20% × 14,000 hours paid	2,800
Actual idle time = 14,000 – 10,304 hours	3,696
	———
Variance (hours)	896 A
Standard rate per hour worked	$11.25
	———
Idle time variance	$10,080 A

Labour efficiency variance

	Hours
3,263 units should have taken (×3)	9,789
But did take (productive hours)	10,304
	———
Variance (hours)	515 A
Standard rate per hour worked	$11.25
	———
Labour efficiency variance	$5,794 A

6 Variable overhead variances

Variable overhead variances are similar to direct materials and direct labour cost variances.

- In standard product costing, a variable production overhead total variance can be calculated, and this can be analysed into an expenditure variance and an efficiency variance.

- With service costing, a variable overhead total variance can be calculated, but this might not be analysed any further.

Since variable production overheads are normally assumed to vary with labour hours worked, **labour hours are used in calculations**. This means, for example, that the variable production overhead efficiency variance uses exactly the same hours as the direct labour efficiency variance.

Details on the variances

Variable production overhead total variance

The difference between:

(a) the standard variable overhead cost of the actual production and

(b) the actual cost of variable production overheads.

Variable production overhead total variance		$
Actual quantity of output	should cost (standard)	X
	did cost	Y
Total variance		X-Y

A total variable production overhead variance can also be analysed further. It can be analysed into two sub-variances:

(1) a variable production overhead expenditure variance, i.e. paying more or less than expected per hour for variable overheads and

(2) a variable production overhead efficiency variance, i.e. using more or less variable overheads per unit than expected.

The official CIMA definitions are as follows:

The variable production overhead total variance is defined as one which:

> *measures the difference between the variable overhead that should be used for actual output and variable production overhead actually used.*
>
> *(CIMA Official Terminology).*

The variable production overhead expenditure variance is defined as one which:

> *indicates the actual cost of any change from the standard rate per hour. Hours refer to either labour or machine hours depending on the recovery base chosen for variable production overhead.*
>
> *(CIMA Official Terminology).*

The variable production overhead efficiency variance is defined as the:

> *standard variable overhead cost of any change from the standard level of efficiency.*
>
> *(CIMA Official Terminology).*

Variable production overhead expenditure variance

		$
Number of hours worked	should cost/hr (standard)	X
	did cost (actual)	Y
Variable production overhead expenditure variance		X–Y

Variable production overhead efficiency variance

		Hours
Actual output produced	should take (standard hours)	X
	did take (actual hours)	Y
Efficiency variance	(in hours)	X–Y
x standard variable overhead rate per hour		$P
Variable production overhead efficiency variance		$P × (X–Y)

Example 7

The budgeted output for Kathryn Bennett Ltd for May was 1,000 units of product A. Each unit requires 2 direct labour hours. Variable overheads are budgeted at $3 per labour hour.

Actual results:

Output	900 units
Labour hours worked	1,980 hours
Variable overheads	$5,544

Calculate appropriate variances for variable overheads.

Alternative method

Using the same example, calculate appropriate variances for variable overhead using the following format:

```
SHSR
                Efficiency variance
AHSR          }                      }  Total variance
                Expenditure variance )
AHAR  )
```

Where	SH	means Standard Hours
	SR	means Standard Rate
	AH	means Actual Hours
and	AR	means Actual Rate

Standard Hours means the standard hours of the actual output.

```
                                              $
SHSR
     2 hrs/unit x 900 units   x   $3/hr   =   5,400  )  Efficiency
AHSR                                             }     $540 A
          1,980 hrs           x   $3/hr   =   5,940  {
AHAR                                                   $396 F
                                         =   5,544  )  Expenditure
```

Idle time variances and variable production overhead

The analysis of variable production overhead variances is affected by the existence of idle time. It is usually assumed that variable production overhead is incurred during active hours only.

The variable production overhead efficiency variance is calculated in the same way that the direct labour efficiency variance is calculated when there is idle time.

The variable production overhead expenditure variance, when there is idle time, is the difference between:

- the standard variable overhead cost of the active hours worked, and
- the actual variable overhead cost.

Example 8

Extracts from the standard cost card of a product are as follows:

		$/unit
Direct labour	2 hours × $ 15 per hour	30
Variable production overhead	2 hours × $ 4 per hour	8

During May, 200 units were produced. The direct labour workers were paid $6,600 for 440 hours of work, but the idle time records show that 20 hours in the month were recorded as idle time. Actual variable production overhead expenditure incurred was $1,530.

Calculate the labour and variable overhead variances.

7 Fixed production overhead cost variances

Fixed production overhead total variance

The amount of overhead absorbed for each unit of output is the standard fixed overhead cost per unit. The total cost variance is therefore calculated as follows:

The difference between:

(a) the standard fixed production overhead cost absorbed by the actual production (i.e. the amount of fixed overhead actually absorbed into production using the standard absorption rate), and

(b) the actual fixed production overheads incurred

Proforma	
Fixed production overhead total variance	**$**
Overheads absorbed (Actual output × standard fixed production overhead absorption rate)	X
Actual fixed overhead incurred	Y
	—
Fixed production overhead total cost variance	X
	Y
	—

Under/over-absorption
In standard absorption costing, the total cost variance for fixed production overhead variances is the amount of over-absorbed or under-absorbed overhead. Over-absorbed overhead is a favourable variance, and under-absorbed overhead is an adverse variance.
Under/over-absorption is the difference between the overheads incurred and the overheads absorbed.

The under/over-absorption occurs because the OAR is based upon two predictions – the budgeted fixed overhead and the budgeted level of activity. If either or both predictions are wrong there will be under/over-absorption and there will be a fixed overhead total variance.

- If the actual expenditure is different from the budgeted expenditure there is an expenditure variance and

- If the actual production is different from the budgeted production there is a volume variance. A fixed production overhead volume variance represents the amount of fixed overhead that has been under- or over-absorbed due to the fact that actual production volume differed from the budgeted production volume.

Fixed production overhead expenditure variance

The difference between:

(a) Budgeted Fixed Production Overhead and

(b) Actual Fixed Production Overhead

Proforma	
Fixed production overhead expenditure variance	$
Budgeted fixed overhead	X
Actual fixed production overhead incurred	Y
Fixed production overhead expenditure variance	X–Y

An expenditure variance can be calculated for fixed production overhead. A similar variance can be calculated (if required) for other fixed overhead costs:

- a fixed administration overhead expenditure variance

- a fixed sales and distribution overhead expenditure variance.

The volume variance is calculated as the difference between:

(a) Budgeted output in units and

(b) Actual output in units

multiplied by the Standard Fixed Overhead Cost per unit

The fixed overhead volume variance does not occur in a marginal costing system.

Proforma

Fixed production overhead volume variance

		Units
Actual output produced		X
Budgeted output		Y
		—
Volume variance	(in units)	X–Y
		—
x standard fixed overhead rate per hour		$F
Fixed production overhead volume variance		$F × (X–Y)

You may be aware that the fixed production overhead volume variance can be sub-divided into a fixed production overhead capacity and fixed production overhead efficiency. These variances are most definitely **NOT** in the syllabus.

Example 9

The following data relates to the fixed production overhead costs of producing widgets in March:

Budgeted fixed production overhead expenditure	$4,375
Budgeted production volume (widgets)	1,750 units
Standard fixed production overhead cost:	
(0.25 hours @ $10 per hour)	$2.50
Number of widgets produced in March	1,800 units
Actual fixed production overhead expenditure	$4,800

Required:

Calculate the fixed production overhead expenditure and volume variances in March.

Marginal costing fixed production overhead variances

In marginal costing, fixed production overheads are not absorbed into the cost of production. For this reason, there is no fixed production overhead volume variance.

The only fixed production overhead variance reported in standard marginal costing is a fixed production overhead expenditure variance. This is the difference between actual and budgeted fixed production overhead expenditure, as described above for absorption costing.

8 Operating statement

An operating statement is a top-level variance report, reconciling the budgeted and actual profit for the period.

An operating statement starts off with the expected figure, e.g. budgeted or standard profit or contribution or cost, etc. and ends up with the corresponding actual figure. In between we list all the appropriate variances in as much detail as possible.

The format will be similar to the following, the numbers have no significance. They are purely for illustration purposes.

Operating Statement for Period 12

	$	$	$
Budgeted gross profit			100,000
Sales volume profit variance			15,000F
			————
Budgeted profit from actual sales volume			115,000
Sales price variance			28,750F
			————
			143,750

		Adverse	Favourable	
Cost variances				
Direct material A	Price	3,100		
	Usage		10,000	
Direct material B	Price		3,050	
	Usage		7,500	
Direct labour	Efficiency		7,000	
	Rate		12,000	
	Idle time		3,000	
Variable overhead	Efficiency	4,000		
	Expenditure		3,500	
Fixed Prod overhead	Expenditure		11,500	
	Volume	30,400		
		_____	_____	
		37,500	57,550	20,050F
		_____	_____	_____
Actual gross profit				163,800
				_____

In some questions the usage variance will be sub-divided into mix and yield variances. This is covered in the chapter on 'Advanced Variances' later in the text.

Variance reporting

Variances should be reported to management at the end of each control period, for example at the end of each month. There might be a hierarchy of control reports:

- a top level report reconciling budgeted and actual profit should be prepared for senior management
- variance reports might be prepared for individual managers with responsibility for a particular aspect of operations.

For example, regional sales managers might be sent variance reports showing sales price and sales volume variances for their region. Production managers might be sent variance reports relating to materials usage, labour efficiency and other items of expenditure under their control. Similarly, detailed reports on overhead expenditure variances might be sent to the managers responsible for departmental spending.

Variance reports should be provided as soon as possible after the end of each control period, since there is a risk that variance information might be considered 'out of date' if it is received several weeks after the control period has ended.

Example 10 – SAM MENDES LTD

Sam Mendes Ltd is a manufacturing company which produces a variety of products. The following information relates to one of its products – Product W:

Standard cost data

		$	$
Selling Price			100
Direct Material X	5 kg	15	
Direct Material Y	4 kg	20	
Direct Labour	@ $8/hr	24	
Variable Overheads		18	
Fixed Overheads		6	
		—	
			83
			—
Profit per unit			17
			—

The budgeted production is 24,000 units per annum evenly spread throughout the year, with each calendar month assumed to be equal. March is a bad month in terms of sales revenue and it is expected that sales will only be 1,700 units during the month. Fixed overheads were expected to be $144,000 per year and are absorbed on a labour hour basis.

Actual results for the month of March were that sales were 2,200 units at a price of $90. There was no change in stock of finished goods or raw materials.

The purchases during the month were 11,300 kg of material X at $2.80 per kg and 8,300 kg of material Y at $5.30 per kg.

4,800 labour hours were worked at a rate of $8.10 per hour and 1,600 hours at $8.30

The actual variable overheads for the period were $33,000 and the fixed overheads were $12,500

The company uses an absorption costing system and values its raw materials at standard cost.

Required:

Calculate appropriate variances for the month of March in as much detail as possible and present an operating statement reconciling budgeted profit with actual profit.

You are not required to calculate mix or yield variances as Sam Mendes Ltd does not sub-analyse the material usage variance.

Variance analysis and other accounting methods

Variances and ABC

An ABC approach to the analysis of overhead costs is possible. This follows the ABC logic that all overheads are variable if one understands what they vary with. Let us illustrate the approach with a simple example.

Example

ABC Ltd produces the Unit and all overheads are associated with the delivery of Units to its customers. Budget details for the period include $8,000 overheads, 4,000 Units output and 40 customer deliveries. Actual results for the period are $7,800 overheads, 4,200 Units output and 38 customer deliveries.

The overhead cost variance for the period is

	$
Actual cost	7,800
Standard cost (4,200 units × $2 per unit)	8,400
Cost variance	600 F

Applying the traditional fixed overhead cost variance analysis gives the following result:

		$	
Volume variance	($8,400 standard – $8,000 budget)	400	F
Expenditure variance	($8,000 budget – $7,800 actual)	200	F
Cost variance		600	F

Adopting an ABC approach gives the following result:

		$	
Efficiency variance	(42 standard – 38 actual deliveries) × $200	800	F
Expenditure variance	[(38 deliveries × $200) – $7,800]	200	A
Cost variance		600	F

The ABC approach is based on an assumption that the overheads are essentially variable (but variable with the delivery numbers and not the Units output). The ABC cost variances are based on a standard delivery size of 100 Units and a standard cost per delivery of $200. Both of these figures are derived from the budget. The activity variance reports the cost impact of undertaking more or less activities than standard, and the expenditure variance reports the cost impact of paying more or less than standard for the actual activities undertaken.

Calculating actual data from standard cost details and variances

An excellent way of testing whether you really understand the reasons for and the calculation of operating variances is to 'work backwards' from standard cost data and variances to arrive at the actual results.

Example on working backwards

Q Limited operates a system of standard costing and in respect of one of its products, which is manufactured within a single cost centre, the following information is given.

For one unit of product the standard material input is 16 litres at a standard price of $2.50 per litre. The standard labour rate is $5 per hour and 6 hours are allowed to produce one unit. Fixed production overhead is absorbed at the rate of 120% of direct labour cost. During the last 4 weeks accounting period the following occurred.

- The material price variance was extracted on purchase and the actual price paid was $2.45 per litre.
- Total direct labour cost was $121,500.
- Fixed production overhead cost incurred was $150,000.

Variances included:

	Favourable $	Adverse $
Direct material price	8,000	
Direct material usage		6,000
Direct labour rate		4,500
Direct labour efficiency	3,600	
Fixed production overhead expenditure		6,000

Required:

Calculate the following for the 4-week period:

(a) budgeted output in units;

(b) number of litres purchased;

(c) number of litres used above standard allowed;

(d) actual units produced;

(e) actual hours worked;

(f) average actual direct labour rate per hour.

Solution

The best thing to do as a first step is to pull together all of the standard cost information to calculate a standard cost per unit.

	$
Direct material (16 litres × 2.5 per litre)	40
Direct labour (6 hours × $5 per hour)	30
Fixed production overhead ($30 × 120%)	36
Total	106

Calculating the required figures is now just a series of exercises in logic. These exercises can seem difficult to the novice – but the logic becomes simple and obvious with familiarity.

(a) If actual fixed production overhead was $150,000 and the fixed production overhead expenditure variance was $6,000 adverse, then it follows that the budget fixed overhead was $144,000. From this it follows that the budget must have been 4,000 units (that is, $144,000 budgeted overhead/$36 standard overhead cost per unit).

(b) If the standard material purchase price was $2.50 per litre and the actual purchase price was $2.45, then it follows that the material price variance is $0.05 per litre favourable. We are told that the material price variance was $8,000 favourable, so it follows that 160,000 litres must have been purchased (that is, $8,000 price variance/$0.05 price variance per litre).

(c) If the direct material usage variance was $6,000 adverse and the standard price of materials is $2.50 per litre, then it follows that the number of litres used above the standard allowance is 2,400 ($6000/$2.50 per litre).

(d) If the actual direct labour cost was $121,500 and labour cost variances totalling $900 adverse ($4,500 adverse rate plus $3,600 favourable efficiency) were experienced, then the standard labour cost for the output achieved was $120,600. It follows that the units produced were 4,020 (that is, $120,600 standard labour cost/$30 standard labour cost per unit).

(e) The total hours actually worked is 24,120 standard hours worked (that is, 4,020 units produced at 6 standard hours per unit) minus the 720-hour favourable labour efficiency variance (that is, $3,600 efficiency variance/$5 standard rate per hour). This gives a total of 23,400 actual hours worked.

(f) If the actual labour cost was $121,500 and the actual hours worked was 23,400, then it follows that the actual wage rate per hour was $5.1923.

9 Chapter summary

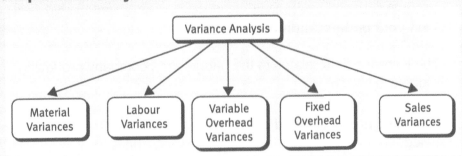

10 Practice questions

Test your understanding 1

The following data relates to the budget for a company producing widgets in March:

Budgeted production and sales (widgets)	1,750 units
Standard cost per unit:	$
Direct materials	6.00
Direct labour	3.00
Variable production overhead	0.75
Fixed production overhead	2.50
	12.25
Standard sales price	18.25
Standard profit per unit	6.00
Number of widgets produced and sold in March	1,800 units
Actual sales revenue	$32,300

Required:

Calculate the sales price and sales volume profit variance. What would be the sales volume contribution variance if standard marginal costing were used?

Test your understanding 2

Major Caldwell Ltd makes and sells a single product. Each unit of the product requires 3 kg of material at $4 per kg.

The actual details for last period were that 1,200 units of finished goods were produced, 3,600 kg of material were purchased for $14,800 and 3,520 kg were used.

Major Caldwell Ltd maintains its raw materials account at standard.

Calculate appropriate variances for materials.

Test your understanding 3

The standard direct material and labour costs for a product are:

		$
Direct material A	2 kg × $ 4/kg	8
Direct material B	0.5 litres × $6 / ltr	3
Direct labour	0.75 hours × $12 per hour	9
		—
		20
		—

During November, the company made 3,200 units and sold 2,900. Actual production costs were:

		$
Direct material A	6,100 kgs	25,000
Direct material B	1,750 litres	11,600
Direct labour	2,200 hours paid	28.000
	(only 2,000 hours worked)	

Required:

Calculate the following variances:

- direct materials price
- direct materials usage
- direct labour rate
- direct labour idle time
- direct labour efficiency

Test your understanding 4 – MAY LTD

May Ltd produces a single product for which the following data are given:

Standards per unit of product:

Direct material	4 kg at $3 per kg
Direct labour	2 hours at $6.40 per hour

Actual details for given financial period:

Output produced in units		38,000
Direct materials:		$
purchased	180,000 kg for	504,000
issued to production	154,000 kg	
Direct labour	78,000 hours worked for	546,000

There was no work in progress at the beginning or end of the period.

You are required to:

(a) Calculate the following variances:
  (i) direct labour efficiency
  (ii) direct labour rate
  (iii) direct materials usage
  (iv) direct materials price, based on issues to production.

(b) State whether in each of the following cases, the comment given and suggested as the possible reason for the variance, is consistent or inconsistent with the variance you have calculated in your answer to (a) above, supporting each of your conclusions with a brief explanatory comment.

Item in (a):

(i) Direct labour efficiency variance: the efficiency of labour was commendable

(ii) Direct labour rate variance: the union negotiated wage increase was $0.60 per hour lower than expected

(iii) Direct materials usage variance: material losses in production were less than had been allowed for in the standard.

(iv) Direct materials price variance: the procurement manager has ignored the economic order quantity and, by obtaining bulk quantities, has purchased material at less than the standard price

(Total: 10 marks)

Test your understanding 5

Jack Doherty Ltd makes a single product with the following standard cost details per unit.

				$
Direct materials	5 kg	@	$4/kg	20
Direct labour	4 hrs	@	$6/hr	24

Actual results were that 1,000 units were produced and sold. The actual hours paid for were 4,100 and the hours worked were 3,900. The actual labour cost was $27,060. The number of kg purchased in the month was 5,200 kg for $21,320 and the number of kg used was 4,900 kg. The company calculates the material price variance at the time of purchase.

Calculate appropriate variances for materials and labour.

Test your understanding 6

Col. Axelrod Ltd makes and sells a single product with the following information:

Std/Budget

Output	1,000 units
Material	3,000 kg @ $5/kg
Labour	5,000 hours @$6/hr

Actual

Output	1,100 units		
Material	Purchased	3,600 kg	for $18,720
	Used	3,400 kg	
Labour hrs	Paid for	5,200 hrs	for $32,760
	Worked	4,900 hrs	

Col. Axelrod Ltd maintains its raw material account at standard cost. Calculate the variances for materials and labour.

Test your understanding 7

Ivan Radek Ltd produces a single product which requires 3 standard hours. Fixed overheads are budgeted at $12,000 and are absorbed on a labour hour basis. Budgeted output is 1,000 units.

Actual results:

Output	1,100 units
Labour hours	3,080 hours
Overheads incurred	$13,000

Calculate appropriate variances for fixed overhead.

Test your understanding 8 – MALCOLM REYNOLDS LTD

Malcolm Reynolds Ltd makes and sells a single product, Product Q, with the following standard specification for materials:

	Quantity	Price per kg
	kg	$
Direct material X	12	40
Direct material Y	8	32

It takes 20 direct labour hours to produce one unit with a standard direct labour cost of $10 per hour.

The annual sales/production budget is 2,400 units evenly spread throughout the year. The standard selling price was $1,250 per unit.

The budgeted production overhead, all fixed, is $288,000 and expenditure is expected to occur evenly over the year, which the company divides into 12 calendar months. Absorption is based on direct labour hours.

For the month of October the following actual information is provided.

	$	$
Sales (220 units)		264,000
Cost of sales		
Direct materials used	159,000	
Direct wages	45,400	
Fixed production overhead	23,000	
		227,400
Gross profit		36,600
Administration costs	13,000	
Selling and distribution costs	8,000	
		21,000
Net profit		$15,600

Costs of opening stocks, for each material, were at the same price per kilogram as the purchases made during the month but there had been changes in the materials stock levels, viz.:

	1 October	30 October
	kg	kg
Material X	680	1,180
Material Y	450	350

Material X purchases were 3,000 kg at $42 each.

Material Y purchases were 1,700 kg at $30 each.

The number of direct labour hours worked was 4,600 and the total wages incurred $45,400.

Work-in-progress stocks and finished goods stocks may be assumed to be the same at the beginning and end of October.

Required:

(a) to prepare a standard product cost for one unit of product Q showing the standard selling price and standard gross profit per unit

(3 marks)

(b) to calculate appropriate variances for the materials, labour, fixed production overhead and sales, noting that it is company policy to calculate material price variances at time of issue to production and that RS Ltd does not calculate mix and yield variances

(12 marks)

(c) to prepare a statement for management reconciling the budgeted gross profit with the actual gross profit

(5 marks)

(Total: 20 marks)

Test your understanding 9 – GOOCH LTD

Gooch Ltd makes a single product and operates a standard costing system. The following variances, standard costs and actual results relate to period 6:

Variances

	Favourable	Adverse
Direct material price variance		1,012
Direct material usage variance		1,380
Direct labour rate variance		920
Direct labour efficiency variance	3,680	
Variable overhead expenditure variance		1,288
Variable overhead efficiency variance	920	

Standard cost data

		$/unit
Direct materials	2 kg @ $3/kg	6
Direct labour	3 hrs @ $8/hr	24
Variable overheads	3 hrs @ $2/hr	6
Fixed overheads	3 hrs @ $4/hr	12
		$48

Fixed overheads were budgeted at $24,000 and the budgeted profit per unit was 20% of the selling price. Budgeted sales were 1,900 units.

Actual results

Material purchased and used	$16,192
Labour cost	$52,440
Variable overhead cost	$14,168
Fixed overhead cost	$23,500

Selling price per unit was $3 lower than budget and there was no change in stock levels.

You are required to calculate the:

(a) actual output

(b) actual material price per kg

(c) labour hours worked

(d) fixed overhead volume variance

(e) fixed overhead expenditure variance

(f) sales volume profit variance

(g) selling price variance

(h) budgeted profit

(i) actual profit.

(25 marks)

Test your understanding 10 – RBF TRANSPORT

RBF Transport, a haulage contractor, operates a standard costing system and has prepared the following report for April 20X0:

Operating statement

			$	$	$
Budgeted profit					8,000
Sales volume profit variance					880 (A)
					7,120
Selling price variance					3,560 (F)
					10,680
Cost variances			A	F	
Direct labour	– rate			1,086	
	– efficiency		240		
Fuel	– price		420		
	– usage		1,280		
Variable overhead	– expenditure			280	
	– efficiency		180		
Fixed overhead	– expenditure			400	
	– volume		1,760		
			3,880	1,766	2,114 (A)
Actual profit					8,566

The company uses delivery miles as its cost unit, and the following details have been taken from the budget working papers for April 20X0:

(1) Expected activity   200,000 delivery miles

(2) Charge to customers $0.30 per delivery mile

(3) Expected variable cost per delivery mile:

     Direct labour (0.02 hours) $0.08

     Fuel (0.1 litres) $0.04

     Variable overhead (0.02 hours) $0.06

The following additional information has been determined from the actual accounting records for April 20X0.

- Fixed overhead cost $15,600

- Fuel price $0.42 per litre

- Direct labour hours   3,620

Required:

(a) Calculate for April 20X0:

     (i) the actual number of delivery miles;

     (ii) the actual direct labour rate per hour;

     (iii) the actual number of litres of fuel consumed;

     (iv) the actual variable overhead expenditure.

(16 marks)

(b) State TWO possible causes of the fuel usage variance.

(4 marks)

(c) Prepare a report, addressed to the transport operations manager, explaining the different types of standard which may be set, and the importance of keeping standards meaningful and relevant.

(10 marks)

(Total: 30 marks)

Test your understanding 11

Flexed budgets for the cost of medical supplies in a hospital, based on a percentage of maximum bed occupancy, are shown below:

Bed occupancy	82%	94%
Medical supplies cost	$410,000	$429,200

During the period, the actual bed occupancy was 87% and the total cost of the medical supplies was $430,000.

Identify the medical supplies expenditure variance:

A $5,000 adverse

B $12,000 adverse

C $5,000 favourable

D $12,000 favourable

(2 marks)

Test your understanding answers

Example 1

Selling price variance

	$
Standard selling price	25
Actual selling price	20
	5 A
× Actual no of units sold	× 500
	2,500 A

Sales volume contribution variance

	Units
Budgeted sales	400
Actual sales	500
	100 F
× Standard contribution per unit	× $7
	$700 F

In this scenario there are no fixed costs, so the answer is the same whether we are using marginal or absorption costing.

Example 2

		$
Sales price variance		
Units sold should have sold for	(380 units × $45 per unit)	17,100
They did sell for	(actual sales revenue)	15,960
		———
Sales price variance		1,140 (A)
		———

Absorption costing

	Units
Sales volume profit variance	
Actual sales volume	380
Budgeted sales volume	320
	———
Sales volume variance	60 (F)
	———
× standard profit per unit ($45 − $23)	× $22
	———
Sales volume profit variance	$1,320 (F)
	———

Marginal costing

	Units
Sales volume contribution variance	
Actual sales volume	380
Budgeted sales volume	320
	———
Sales volume variance	60 (F)
	———
× standard contribution per unit ($45 − $17)	× $28
	———
Sales volume contribution variance	$1,680 (F)
	———

Standard revenue per unit

Sales volume revenue variance	Units	
Actual sales volume	380	
Budgeted sales volume	320	
Sales volume variance	60	(F)
× standard selling price per unit	× $45	
Sales volume revenue variance	$2,700	(F)

Example 3

Direct material total variance

	$
Standard cost of actual output	
2kg × 1,000 units × $10/kg	20,000
Actual cost	20,900
	900 A

Example 4

Direct materials price variance:		$
Actual quantity of materials	should cost (standard)	
2,200kgs	$10 / kg	22,000
	did cost (actual)	20,900
Direct materials price variance		1,100 F

Direct materials usage variance:		$
Actual output produced	should use (standard quantity)	
1,000 units	2 ks / unit	2,000
	did use (actual quantity)	2,200
Direct materials usage variance	(in material quantity)	200 A
× standard price	(per unit of material)	$10
Direct materials usage variance		2,000 A

Example 5

Direct labour rate variance:		$
Number of hours worked	should cost / hr (standard)	
3,400 hours	$8 / hr	27,200
	did cost (actual)	28,300
Direct labour rate variance		1,100 A

Direct labour efficiency variance:		Hours
Actual output produced	should take (standard hours)	
1,100 units	3 hrs per unit	3,300
	did take (actual hours)	3,400
Direct labour efficiency variance	(in hours)	100 A
× standard rate per hour		$8/ hr
Direct labour efficiency variance		$800 A

Example 6

$$\begin{array}{lllll}
& & & \$ & \\
\text{SHSR} & & & & \\
& 6 \text{ hrs/unit x 900 units} \quad \times \quad \$7/\text{hr} \quad = \quad 37{,}800 & \} \text{Efficiency} \\
\text{AHSR} & & & & \$1{,}400 \text{ F} \\
& 5{,}200 \text{ hrs} \quad \times \quad \$7/\text{hr} \quad = \quad 36{,}400 &
\end{array}$$

The efficiency variance looks at whether people **WORK** fast or slow and looks at hours **WORKED**.

$$\begin{array}{lllll}
& & & \$ & \\
\text{AHSR} & & & & \\
& 5{,}500 \text{ hrs} \quad \times \quad \$7/\text{hr} \quad = \quad 38{,}500 & \} \$600 \text{ A} \\
\text{AHAR} & & & & \text{Rate} \\
& & = \quad 39{,}100 &
\end{array}$$

The rate variance looks at the rate of **PAY** so it looks at the hours **PAID**.

Idle time variance

(5,500 – 5,200) × $7 per hour $2,100 A

Or the idle time variance is simply the difference between the $38,500 and the $36,400 above = $2,100 A.

Example 7

Variable production overhead expenditure variance:		$
Number of hours worked	should cost / hr (standard)	
1,980 hours	$3 / hour	5,940
	did cost (actual)	5,544
Variable production overhead expenditure variance		396 F

Variable production overhead efficiency variance:		**Hours**
Actual output produced	should take (standard hours)	
900 units	2 hours / unit	1,800
	did take (actual hours)	1,980
Efficiency variance	(in hours)	180 A
× standard variable overhead rate per hour		$3
Variable production overhead efficiency variance		$540 A

Example 8

(a) The idle time variance is 20 hours × $15 = $300 (A).

(b) The efficiency variances are then calculated based on the active hours worked, not on the total hours paid for.

Efficiency variances:		**Hours**
Actual output produced 200 units	should take (standard hours) 2 hours / unit	400
	did take (440 – 20)	420
Efficiency variance	(in hours)	20 A
× standard direct labour rate per hour		$15
Direct labour efficiency variance		$300 A
× standard variable overhead rate per hour		$4
Variable production overhead efficiency variance		$80 A

(c) The variable production overhead expenditure variance is based on active hours only, since variable production overhead cost is not incurred during idle time.

Variable production overhead expenditure variance:		$
Number of hours worked 420 hours	should cost / hr (standard) $4 / hour	1,680
	did cost (actual)	1,530
Variable production overhead expenditure variance		150 F

Example 9

Fixed production overhead expenditure variance:	$
Budgeted fixed overhead	4,375
Actual fixed overhead incurred	4,800
Fixed production overhead expenditure variance	425 (A)

Fixed production overhead volume variance:	**Units**
Actual output produced	1,800
Budgeted output	1,750
Volume variance (in units)	50
× standard fixed overhead rate per unit	$2.50
Fixed production overhead volume variance	$125 (F)

Example 10 – SAM MENDES LTD

Standard product cost

		$	$
Standard selling price			100
Material X	5 kg @ $3/kg	15	
Material Y	4 kg @ $5/kg	20	
Direct labour	3 hrs @ $8/hr	24	
Variable overheads	3 hrs @ $6/hr	18	
Fixed overheads (W1)	3 hrs @ $2/hr	6	
			83
Standard profit per unit			17

Material X variances

			$	
SQSP				
5 kg/unit x 2,200 units	x	$3/kg	=	33,000
AQSP				
11,300 kg	x	$3/kg	=	33,900
AQAP				
11,300 kg	x	$2.8/kg	=	31,640

Usage $900 A

$2,260 F Price

Material Y variances

			$	
SQSP				
4 kg/unit x 2,200 units	x	$5/kg	=	44,000
AQSP				
8,300 kg	x	$5/kg	=	41,500
AQAP				
8,300 kg	x	$5.30/kg	=	43,990

Usage $2,500 F

$2,490 A Price

Labour variances

			$	
SHSR				
3 hrs/unit x 2,200 units	x	$8/hr	=	52,800
AHSR				
6,400 hrs	x	$8/hr	=	51,200
AHAR				
(4,800 hrs x $8.10) + (1,600 hrs x $8.30) =				52,160

Efficiency $1,600 F

$960 A Rate

Variable overhead variances

			$	
SHSR				
3 hrs/unit x 2,200 units	x	$6/hr	=	39,600
AHSR				
6,400 hrs	x	$6/hr	=	38,400
AHAR				
			=	33,000

Efficiency $1,200 F

$5,400 F Expenditure

Fixed overhead expenditure variance

	$
Budgeted Cost	12,000
Actual Cost	12,500
	500 A

Fixed overhead volume variance

	Units
Budgeted output	2,000
Actual output	2,200
	200 F
x Std Fixed Overhead Cost per unit	× $6
	$1,200 F

Sales volume profit variance

	Units
Budgeted sales	1,700
Actual sales	2,200
	500 F
× Std profit per unit	× $17
	$8,500 F

Sales price variance

	$
Std selling price	100
Actual selling price	90
	10 A
× Actual No of units sold	× 2,200
	$22,000 A

Operating statement

	$	$	$
Budgeted gross profit (W2)			28,900
Sales volume profit variance			8,500 F
Budgeted profit on actual sales			37,400
Selling price variance			22,000 A
			15,400

		Favourable	Adverse	
Cost variances				
Material X	Usage		900	
	Price	2,260		
Material Y	Usage	2,500		
	Price		2,490	
Direct labour	Efficiency	1,600		
	Rate		960	
Variable Overhead	Efficiency	1,200		
	Expenditure	5,400		
Fixed Prod Overhead	Expenditure		500	
	Volume	1,200		
		14,160	4,850	9,310 F
Actual profit (W3)				24,710

Workings

(W1) Budgeted fixed overheads are $144,000 per year and the budgeted output is 24,000 units for the year. Thus the budgeted/standard fixed cost per unit is $6.

The overheads are absorbed on direct labour hours and each unit takes 3 hours. Therefore the budgeted/standard fixed overhead is $2 per hour ($6 ÷ 3 hours).

(W2) Budgeted profit = $17 per unit × Budgeted **sales** of 1,700 units = $28,900

(W3)

		$	$
Sales	2,200 units x $90		198,000
Material X	11,300 kg × $2.80/kg	31,640	
Material Y	8,300 kg × $5.30/kg	43,990	
Direct labour	(4,800 hrs × $8.10) + (1,600 hrs × $8.30)	52,160	
Variable overhead		33,000	
Fixed overhead		12,500	
			173,290
Actual Profit			24,710

Test your understanding 1

Sales price variance: $

		$
Units sold should have sold for	(1.800 units × $18.25 per unit)	32,850
They did sell for	(actual sales revenue)	32,300
Sales price variance		550 (A)

Sales volume variance	**Units**
Actual sales volume	1,800
Budgeted sales volume	1,750
Sales volume variance	50
× standard profit per unit	× $6
Sales volume profit variance	$300 (F)

Marginal costing

The contribution per unit is $ 8.50 ($18.25 − 6.00 − 3.00 − 0.75)

Sales volume variance	**Units**
Actual sales volume	1,800
Budgeted sales volume	1,750
Sales volume variance	50
× standard contribution per unit	× $8.50
Sales volume contribution variance	$425 (F)

Test your understanding 2

SQSP

                                               $

3 kg/unit x 1,200 units   x $4/kg   =   14,400   } Usage

AQSP $320 F

3,520 kg   x $4/kg   =   14,080   }

For a **USAGE** variance the quantity must be the quantity **USED**

                                               $

AQSP

3,600 kg   x $4/kg   =   14,400   } $400 A

AQAP   Price

                                           =   14,800   }

As the price variance is calculated at the time of **PURCHASE** then the quantity must be the quantity **PURCHASED** and we had to use the more complicated format.

Test your understanding 3

Direct material A price variance:

		$
Actual quantity of materials	should cost (standard)	
6,100 kgs	$4 / kg	24,400
	did cost (actual)	25,000
Direct material A price variance		600 A

Direct material A usage variance:

		$
Actual output produced	should use (standard quantity)	
3,200 units	2 kgs / unit	6,400
	did cost (actual quantity)	6,100
Direct materials price variance	(in material quantity)	300 F
× standard price	(per unit of material)	$4
Direct material A usage variance		1,200 F

Direct material B price variance:

		$
Actual quantity of materials	should cost (standard)	
1,750 ltrs	$6 / ltr	10,500
	did cost (actual)	11,600
Direct material B price variance		1,100 A

Direct material B usage variance:

		$
Actual output produced	should use (standard quantity)	
3,200 units	0.5 ltrs / unit	1,600
	did cost (actual quantity)	1,750
Direct materials usage variance	(in material quantity)	150 A
× standard price	(per unit of material)	$6
Direct material B usage variance		900 A

Direct labour rate variance: $

Number of hours paid	should use / hr (standard)	
2,200 hours	$12 / hr	26,400
	did cost (actual)	28,000

Direct labour rate variance		1,600 A

Idle time variance:

There are 200 hours of idle time. At a standard cost of $12 per hour, this gives an idle time variance of

$$= \quad 200 \text{ hours} \times \$12 / \text{hour}$$
$$= \quad \$2,400 \text{ A}$$

Direct labour efficiency variance: $

Actual output produced	should use (standard hours)	
3,200 units	0.75 hrs per unit	2,400
	did take (actual hours)	2,000

Direct labour efficiency variance	(in hours)	400 F

× standard rate per hour	$12/hr
Direct labour efficiency variance	$4,800 F

Test your understanding 4 – MAY LTD

(a) **Direct labour variances**

					$		
SHSR	2 hrs/unit x 38,000 units	x	$6.40/hr	=	486,400	}	Efficiency $12,800 A
AHSR	78,000 hrs	x	$6.40/hr	=	499,200	{	
AHAR		x		=	546,000	}	$46,800 A Rate

(i) $12,800 A
(ii) $46,800 A

Direct material variances

					$		
SQSP	4 kg/unit x 38,000 units	x	$3/kg	=	456,000	}	Usage $6,000 A
AQSP	154,000 kg	x	$3/kg	=	462,000	{	
AQAP	154,000 kg	x	$2.80/kg	=	431,200	}	$30,800 F Price

The requirement in part (iv) asks for the price variance to be calculated at the time of issue, which is the same as at the time of usage, so the quantity must be the quantity issued/used.

The actual price of the material is $504,000/180,000 kg.

(iii) $6,000 A

(iv) $30,800 F

(b)

(i)   Inconsistent. The workforce were inefficient.

(ii)   Inconsistent. In fact the wage increase was $0.60 per hour higher than expected.

(iii) Inconsistent. If the losses had been less than expected then the usage variance would have been favourable.

(iv) Consistent. A bulk purchase discount should lead to cheaper materials and hence a favourable material price variance.

Test your understanding 5

Material variances

$

SQSP

    5 kg/unit x 1,000 units   x $4/kg   =   20,000   } Usage

AQSP $400 F

          4,900 kg   x $4/kg   =   19,600

For a **USAGE** variance the quantity must be the quantity **USED**

$

AQSP

          5,200 kg   x $4/kg   =   20,800   }

AQAP $520 A Price

                                        =   21,320

As the price variance is calculated at the time of **PURCHASE** then the quantity must be the quantity **PURCHASED** and we had to use the more complicated format.

Labour variances

$

SHSR

    4 hrs/unit x 1,000 units   x $6/hr   =   24,000   }

AHSR   Efficiency $600 F

          3,900 hrs   x $6/hr   =   23,400

The efficiency variance looks at whether people **WORK** fast or slow and looks at hours **WORKED**.

$

AHSR

          4,100 units   x $6/hr   =   24,600   }

AHAR $2,460 A Rate

                                        =   27,060

The rate variance looks at the rate of **PAY** so it looks at the hours **PAID**.

Idle time variance

(4,100 – 3,900) × $6 per hour $1,200 A

Or the idle time variance is simply the difference between the $23,400 and the $24,600 above = $1,200 A.

Test your understanding 6

Material variances

$

SQSP

  3 kg/unit x 1,100 units x $5/kg = 16,500 } Usage

AQSP $500 A

    3,400 kg   x $5/kg = 17,000

For a **USAGE** variance the quantity must be the quantity **USED.**

$

AQSP

    3,600 kg   x $5/kg = 18,000

AQAP $720 A

                = 18,720 } Price

As the price variance is calculated at the time of **PURCHASE** then the quantity must be the quantity **PURCHASED** and we had to use the more complicated format.

Labour variances

$

SHSR

  5 hrs/unit x 1,100 units x $6/hr = 33,000

AHSR   Efficiency

    4,900 hrs   x $6/hr = 29,400 } $3,600 F

The efficiency variance looks at whether people **WORK** fast or slow and looks at hours **WORKED**.

$

AHSR

    5,200 hrs   x $6/hr = 31,200

AHAR $1,560 A

                = 32,760 } Rate

The rate variance looks at the rate of **PAY** so it looks at the hours **PAID**.

Idle time variance

$(5,200 - 4,900) \times 6 per hour $1,800 A

Or the idle time variance is simply the difference between the $29,400 and the $31,200 above = $1,800 A.

Test your understanding 7

Fixed overhead total variance

	$
Std cost of actual output	
$12/unit × 1,100 units	13,200
Actual cost	13,000
	——
	200 F
	——

Fixed overhead expenditure variance

	$
Budgeted Cost	12,000
Actual Cost	13,000
	——
	1,000 A
	——

Fixed overhead volume variance

	Units
Budgeted output	1,000
Actual output	1,100
	——
	100 F
× Std Fixed Overhead Cost per unit	x12
	——
	$1,200 F
	——

Under-/over-absorption

	$
Overheads incurred	13,000
Overheads absorbed	
$4/direct labour hour x (3 hours × 1,100 units)	13,200
	——
Over-absorption	200
	——

The overhead absorption rate is based on direct labour hours and =

$$\text{OAR} = \frac{\text{Budgeted overheads}}{\text{Budgeted level of activity}}$$

$$\text{OAR} = \frac{\$12,000}{1,000 \text{ units} \times 3 \text{ hrs}} \quad \$4/\text{direct labour hour}$$

It would now be very natural to calculate the overheads absorbed by multiplying the OAR by the actual number of hours, i.e. 3,080, but in a standard costing system, the overheads are absorbed on the standard hours, not the actual hours.

The standard hours are the standard hours of actual output, 3 hours × 1,100 units = 3,300 hours.

Test your understanding 8 – MALCOLM REYNOLDS LTD

(a) Standard product cost

		$	$
Standard selling price			1,250
Material X	12 kg @ $40/kg	480	
Material Y	8 kg @ $32/kg	256	
Direct labour	20 hrs @ $10/hr	200	
Production overhead (W1)		120	
		——	
			1,056
			——
Standard gross profit			194
			——

(b) Material X variances

					$	
SQSP						
12 kg/unit x 220 units	x	$40/kg	=	105,600		Usage
AQSP						$5,600 F
2,500 kg (W2)	x	$40/kg	=	100,000		
AQAP						$5,000 A
2,500 kg	x	$42/kg	=	105,000		Price

Material Y variances

					$	
SQSP						
8 kg/unit x 220 units	x	$32/kg	=	56,320		Usage
AQSP						$1,280 A
1,800 kg (W2)	x	$32/kg	=	57,600		
AQAP						$3,600 F
1,800kg	x	$30/kg	=	54,000		Price

Direct labour variances

					$	
SHSR						
20 hrs/unit x 220 units	x	$10/hr	=	44,000		Efficiency
AHSR						$2,000 A
4,600 hrs	x	$10/hr	=	46,000		
AHAR						$600 F
			=	45,400		Rate

Fixed Overhead Expenditure variance

	$
Budgeted Cost (W3)	24,000
Actual Cost	23,000
	1,000 F

Fixed overhead volume variance

	Units
Budgeted output (2,400 units p.a. ÷ 12 months)	200
Actual output	220
	20 F
x Std Fixed Overhead Cost per unit	×120
	$2,400 F

Sales price variance

	$
Std selling price	1,250
Actual selling price ($264,000/220 units)	1,200
	50 A
× Actual no of units sold	× 220
	$11,000 A

Selling volume profit variance

	Units
Budgeted sales	200
Actual sales	220
	20 F
× Std profit per unit	× 194
	$3,880 F

(c) **Operating statement**

	$	$	$
Budgeted gross profit (W4)			38,800
Sales volume profit variance			3,880 F
Standard profit on actual sales			42,680
Sales price variance			11,000 A
			31,680

		Favourable	Adverse
Cost variances			
Material X	Usage	5,600	
	Price		5,000
Material Y	Usage		1,280
	Price	3,600	
Direct labour	Efficiency		2,000
	Rate	600	
Fixed Prod overhead	Expenditure	1,000	
	Volume	2,400	
		13,200	8,280 4,920 F
Actual gross profit			36,600

Workings

(W1) Fixed over head per unit = $288,000/2,400 units = $120 per
unit

(W2)

	Material X	**Material Y**
	Kg	Kg
Op stock	680	450
+ Purchases	3,000	1,700
	3,680	2,150
− Cl stock	1,180	350
Materials issued/used	2,500	1,800

(W3) Budgeted fixed overhead per month = $288,000/12 = $24,000

(W4) Budgeted profit = 200 units × $194 = $38,800

Test your understanding 9 – GOOCH LTD

(a) This is a 'backwards' question. Rather than calculating the variances ourselves, we have been given some of them. We have to find some other information which is missing. We will use the variances to work backwards to find that missing information.

The starting point is usually to find a variance which mentions the missing information, i.e. for part (a) we are asked for the actual output. We need to find a variance which mentions the actual output somewhere along the line.

One set of variances which would work are the material variances. The first line of the format is SQSP, where SQ is the standard quantity of the **actual output**.

We plug in the information that we know, and we can then work backwards to find the missing information.

Material variances

				$		
SQSP						
2 kg/unit x ? units	x	$3/kg	=	?	}	Usage $1,380 A
AQSP						
? kg	x	$3/kg	=	?		
AQAP						}	$1,012 A
? kg	x	$?/kg	=	16,192		Price

We know that AQAP is 16,192 and we know that the price variance is 1,012 A, so we can work backwards to find AQSP.

AQSP = 16,192 - 1,012 = 15,180

Material variances

				$		
SQSP						
2 kg/unit x ? units	x	$3/kg	=	?	}	Usage $1,380 A
AQSP						
? kg	x	$3/kg	=	15,180 Bal 1		
AQAP						}	$1,012 A
? kg	x	$?/kg	=	16,192		Price

Now, we know AQSP is 15,180 and the usage variance is 1,380 A, so we can work backwards to find SQSP.

SQSP = 15,180 - 1380 A = 13,800

Material variances

						$		
SQSP								
2 kg/unit x ? units	x	$3/kg	=	13,800[Bal 2]			Usage	
AQSP							$1,380 A	
? kg	x	$3/kg	=	15,180[Bal 1]				
AQAP							$1,012 A	
? kg	x	$?/kg	=	16,192			Price	

Finally, for the first line, we know SQSP, i.e. we know 2 kg x something x $3/kg = 13,800. We can work backwards to find the actual output.

Actual output = 13,800 ÷ 2kg ÷ $3/kg = 2,300 units

Material variances

						$		
SQSP								
2 kg/unit x 2,300[Bal 3] units	x	$3/kg	=	13,800[Bal 2]			Usage	
AQSP							$1,380 A	
? kg	x	$3/kg	=	15,180[Bal 1]				
AQAP							$1,012 A	
? kg	x	$?/kg	=	16,192			Price	

(b) We have already worked out a lot of the figures that we need for the material variances. We can carry on from where we left off in part (a).

Material variances

						$		
SQSP								
2 kg/unit x 2,300 [Bal 3] units	x	$3/kg	=	13,800 [Bal 2]			Usage	
AQSP							$1,380 A	
? kg	x	$3/kg	=	15,180[Bal 1]				
AQAP							$1,012 A	
? kg	x	$?/kg	=	16,192			Price	

For the second line, we know AQSP = 15,180, i.e. we know that AQ x 3 = 15,180.

Actual quantity = 15,180 ÷ 3 = 5,060 kg

AQ appears on both the second line and the third line, so we can write 5,060 kg on both lines.

Material variances

						$		
SQSP								
2 kg/unit x 2,300 [Bal 3] units	x	$3/kg	=	13,800 [Bal 2]			Usage	
AQSP							$1,380 A	
5,060 [Bal 4] kg	x	$3/kg	=	15,180 [Bal 1]				
AQAP							$1,012 A	
5,060 [Bal 4] kg	x	$?/kg	=	16,192			Price	

Finally for the third line, AQAP = 5,060 Kg x something = 16,192

Actual price = 16,192 ÷ 5,060 = $3.20 per kg.

Material variances

						$		
SQSP								
2 kg/unit x 2,300 [Bal 3] units	x	$3/kg	=	13,800 [Bal 2]			Usage	
AQSP							$1,380 A	
5,060 [Bal 4] kg	x	$3/kg	=	15,180 [Bal 1]				
AQAP							$1,012 A	
5,060 [Bal 4] kg	x	$3.20/kg[Bal 5]	=	16,192			Price	

(c) Labour variances

			$	
SHSR				
3 hrs/unit x 2,300 units	x $8/hr	=	55,200	Efficiency $3,680 F
AHSR				
? hrs	x $8/hr	=	?	$920 A Rate
AHAR				
? hrs	x $?/hr	=	52,440	

To find out the labour hours we can use the labour variances format. We can find AHSR by subtracting the efficiency variance of 3,680 F from SHSR to get 51,520 or by adding the adverse rate variance of 920 to AHAR.

Once we know that AHSR is $51,520, we know that something x $8/hr = $51,520.

Actual hours = 51,520 ÷ 8 = 6,440 hours

Labour variances

			$	
SHSR				
3 hrs/unit x 2,300 units	x $8/hr	=	55,200	Efficiency $3,680 F
AHSR				
6,440 $^{Bal\ 2}$ hrs	x $8/hr	=	51,520 $^{Bal\ 1}$	$920 A rate
AHAR				
? hrs	x $?/hr	=	52,440	

(d) Fixed overhead volume variance

	Units
Budgeted output	2,000
Actual output	2,300
	300F
× Std Fixed Overhead Cost per unit	× 12
	$3,600F

(e) Fixed overhead expenditure variance

	$
Budgeted Cost	24,000
Actual Cost	23,500
	500 F

(f) **Selling volume profit variance**

	Units
Budgeted sales	1,900
Actual sales	2,300
	400 F
× Std profit per unit	x 12
=	$4,800 F

The profit margin is 20% of selling price. A profit margin of 20% is the same as a mark-up of 25%. Thus we know standard cost to be $48 per unit, standard profit must be 25% of that, must be $12 per unit.

(g) **Selling price variance**

	$
Std selling price	60
Actual selling price	57
	3 A
× Actual no of units sold	× 2,300
=	6,900 A

We know that standard cost is $48 per unit and we the standard profit (from part (f)) is $12. Therefore standard selling price = $48 + $12 = $60.

(h) Budgeted profit = 1,900 units × $12 per unit = $22,800.

(i)

		$	$
Sales	2,300 units × $57		131,100
Direct material		16,192	
Direct labour		52,440	
Variable overhead		14,168	
Fixed overhead		23,500	
			106,300
Actual profit			24,800

Test your understanding 10 – RBF TRANSPORT

Key answer tips

This is a very good test of the depth of your knowledge of variances. The basic technique is to set out your normal computations of the variances, putting in the figures you know and working back to those you don't. Often the results from one will be needed in another, so do all the related variances together.

(a)

(i) Budgeted fixed overhead cost/mile =

$$= \frac{(\$15,600 + \$400)}{200,000} = \$0.08/\text{mile}$$

Volume variance	= $1,760 (A)
Volume difference	= $1,760 ÷ $0.08
	= 22,000 miles(A)
Actual miles	= 200,000 – 22,000
	178,000

(ii)

$$\text{Standard rate/hr} = \frac{\$0.08}{0.02}$$

$$= \$4/\text{hour}$$

Rate variance = $1,086 (F)

= $1,086

$$\frac{\$1,086}{3,260} = \$0.30/\text{hr (F)}$$

Actual rate $4.00 − $0.30 = $3.70/hr

(iii)

$$\text{Standard price/litre} = \frac{\$0.04}{0.1}$$

= $0.40/litre

Actual price/litre = $0.42/litre

Price variance/litre = $0.02 (A)

Total price variance = $420 (A)

Actual number of litres

$$= \frac{\$420}{\$0.02} = 21,00$$

(iv) **Variable overhead variances**

$

SHSR
  0.02 hrs × 178,000 delivery miles × $3/hr = 10,680   Efficiency
AHSR $180 A
                         × $3/hr = ?
AHAR $280 F
                              = ?   Expenditure

We know all the above infor mation, but are trying to find the missing information represented by question marks. In particular we are trying to find the bottom question mark, the actual hours at the actual rate, i.e. the actual variable overhead expenditure. We can do this in one step or two. Taking it in two steps, we can find the middle question mark:

SHSR
  0.02 hrs × 178,000 delivery miles × $3/hr = 10,680   Efficiency
AHSR   Bal 1 $180 A
                       × $3/hr = 10,860
AHAR $280 F
                              =   ?   Expenditure

And then, the bottom question mark:

SHSR
  0.02 hrs × 178,000 delivery miles × $3/h = 10,680   Efficiency
AHSR   Bal 1 $ 180 A
                       × $3/hr = 10,860
AHAR $280 F
                            Bal 2
                            = 10,580   Expenditure

The actual variable overhead expenditure is $10,580

(b) Two possible causes of an adverse fuel usage variance are:

    (i)   Spillage of fuel occurred on filling vehicle fuel tanks.

    (ii) Vehicles are in need of servicing and as a result fuel usage is excessive.

(c) **To:**   Transport Operations Manager

From: Management Accountant

Date: XX – XX – XX

Subject: Standard costs

Introduction

This report explains the type of standard cost which may be set and importance of keeping standards meaningful and relevant.

Types of standard

A standard cost is a prediction of the cost per unit expected in a future period. It is dependent on estimates of resource requirements per output unit and the price to be paid per resource unit.

There are three types of standard which may be set and these are often referred to as:

— current standard;

— attainable standard; and

— ideal standard.

The current standard uses existing efficiency and achievement levels as the standard for the future period. This does not encourage improvement and may also allow existing inefficiencies to continue unnoticed.

The attainable standard sets a target which requires improvements in performance if it is to be achieved, but these are small and are considered to be achievable (or attainable). This form of standard is believed to be the best motivator to a manager.

The ideal standard assumes a perfect working environment (which never exists for a prolonged period). This is impossible to achieve.

Keeping standards useful

Standards are useful as a basis for performance evaluation. If such comparisons are to be valid the standard must reflect the current method of working AND resource prices which are realistic. If standards are not kept up to date they are no longer meaningful and thus their usefulness is reduced.

Conclusion

I recommend that attainable standards should be used, and that they should be reviewed regularly. Please contact me if you wish to discuss this further.

Test your understanding 11

B

$$\text{Contribution margin} = \frac{429{,}200 - 410{,}000}{94\% - 82\%}$$

$$= \$1{,}600 \text{ for every 1\% change}$$

$$\text{Budget for 87\% occupancy} = \$429{,}200 - (7 \times 1600)$$

$$= \$418{,}000$$

$$\text{Medical expenditure variance} = 418{,}000 - 430{,}000$$

$$= \$12{,}000 \text{ Adverse}$$

Variance analysis: discussion elements

Chapter learning objectives

Lead	Component
A1. discuss costing methods and their results.	(e) Explain why and how standards are set in manufacturing and in service industries with particular reference to the maximisation of efficiency and minimisation of waste.
	(f) Interpret material, labour, variable overhead, fixed overhead and sales variances, distinguishing between planning and operational variances.
	(g) Prepare reports using a range of internal and external benchmarks and interpret the results.

1 Chapter overview diagram

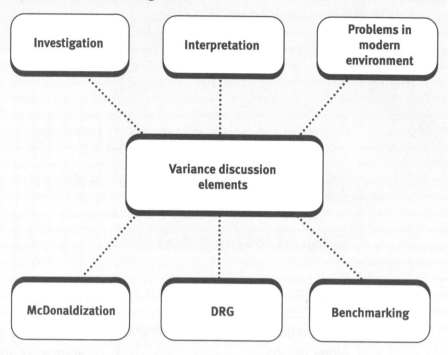

2 Variance investigation

Variances arise naturally in standard costing because a standard cost is a long term average cost. In any period actual costs may be higher or lower than standard but in the long run these should cancel out if the process is under control.

Variances may also arise because of:

- poor budgeting
- poor recording of cost
- operational reasons (the key emphasis in exam questions)
- random factors.

It is important to identify the reason for a variance so that appropriate action can be taken, but time and effort will be wasted if all variances are investigated as many will arise as a normal part of the process.

When should a variance be investigated?

Factors to consider include the following:

- the size of the variance
- the likelihood of the variance being controllable or its cause already known
- the likely cost of an investigation
- the interrelationship of variances
- the type of standard that was set

Investigating variances

Factors to consider

- The size of the variance. Costs tend to fluctuate around a norm and therefore 'normal' variances may be expected on most costs. The problem is to decide how large a variance must be before it is considered 'abnormal' and worthy of investigation.
  A rule of thumb may be established that any variance which exceeds, say, 5 per cent of its standard cost may be worthy of investigation. Alternatively control limits may be set statistically and if a cost fluctuates outside these limits it should be investigated.

- he likelihood of the variance being controllable or its cause already known. Managers may know from experience that certain variances may not be controllable even if a lengthy investigation is undertaken to determine their causes. They may also be immediately aware of the cause of a variance. For example, it may be argued that a material price variance is less easily controlled than a material usage variance because it is heavily influenced by external factors. The counter-argument to the latter is that a materials price variance may be caused by external market factors (uncontrollable) or the quality of procurement management – and one doesn't know which is the cause until it is investigated.

- The likely cost of an investigation. This cost would have to be weighed against the cost which would be incurred if the variance were allowed to continue in future periods.

- The interrelationship of variances. Adverse variances in one area of the organisation may be interrelated with favourable variances elsewhere. For example, if cheaper material is purchased this may produce a favourable material price variance. However, if the cheaper material is of lower quality and difficult to process, this could result in adverse variances for material usage and labour efficiency.

- The type of standard that was set. You have already seen that an ideal standard will almost always result in some adverse variances, because of unavoidable waste and so on. Managers must decide on the 'normal' level of adverse variance which they would expect to see.

  Another example is where a standard price is set at an average rate for the year. Assuming that inflation or a known upward trend exist, favourable price variances might be expected at the beginning of the year, to be offset by adverse price variances towards the end of the year as actual prices begin to rise.

Variance investigation techniques

Reporting by exception

Variance reports might identify significant variances. This is a form of reporting by exception, in which particular attention is given to the aspects of performance that appear to be exceptionally good or bad.

Alternatively, a rule might be applied generally that any adverse variance or favourable variance should be investigated if it exceeds more than a given percentage amount of the standard cost. For example, a rule might be applied that all adverse variances exceeding 5% of standard cost should be investigated and all favourable variances exceeding 10% of the standard should also be investigated.

Cumulative variances and control charts

An alternative method of identifying significant variances is to investigate the cause or causes of a variance only if the cumulative total for the variance over several control periods exceeds a certain limit.

The reason for this approach is that variances each month might fluctuate, with adverse variances in some months and favourable variances in the next. Provided that over time, actual results remain close to the standard, monthly variances might be acceptable.

For example, actual fixed overhead expenditure will not be exactly the same every month. Budgeted monthly expenditure, on the other hand, might be calculated by dividing the budgeted annual expenditure by 12. Consequently, there will inevitably be favourable or adverse expenditure variances from one month to the next, although over the course of the financial year, actual and budgeted expenditure should be the same.

This approach to identifying significant variances can be illustrated by the concept of a variance control chart. Variances should only be investigated when the cumulative total of variances exceeds predetermined control limits.

Setting the control limits

The control limits used as a basis for determining whether a variance should be investigated may be set statistically based on the normal distribution.

Using historical data a standard can be set as an expected average cost and a standard deviation can also be established. By assuming that a cost conforms to the normal distribution a variance will be investigated if it is statistically significant and has not arisen according to chance.

- If a company has a policy to investigate variances that fall outside the range that includes 95% of outcomes, then variances which exceed 1.96 standard deviations from the standard would be investigated.

- If a company has a policy to investigate variances that fall outside the range that includes 99% of outcomes, then variances which exceed 2.58 standard deviations from the standard would be investigated.

For control purposes, management might need to establish why a particular variance has occurred. Once the reason for the variance has been established, a decision can then be taken as to what control measures, if any, might be appropriate:

- to prevent the adverse variance continuing in the future, or

- to repeat a favourable variance in the future, or

- to bring actual results back on course to achieve the budgeted targets.

3 Interpretation of variances

Possible operational causes of variances are as follows:

Material price

(1) Using a different supplier, who is either cheaper or more expensive.

(2) Buying in larger-sized orders, and getting larger bulk purchase discounts. Buying in smaller-sized orders and losing planned bulk purchase discounts.

(3) An unexpected increase in the prices charged by a supplier.

(4) Unexpected buying costs, such as high delivery charges.

(5) Efficient or inefficient buying procedures.

(6) A change in material quality, resulting in either higher or lower purchase prices

Material usage

(1) A higher-than-expected or lower-than-expected rate of scrap or wastage.

(2) Using a different quality of material (higher or lower quality) could affect the wastage rate.

(3) Defective materials.

(4) Better quality control.

(5) More efficient work procedures, resulting in better material usage rates.

(6) Changing the materials mix to obtain a more expensive or less expensive mix than the standard.

Labour rate

(1) An unexpected increase in basic rates of pay.

(2) Payments of bonuses, where these are recorded as direct labour costs.

(3) Using labour that is more or less experienced (and so more or less expensive) than the 'standard'.

(4) A change in the composition of the work force, and so a change in average rates of pay.

Labour efficiency

(1) Taking more or less time than expected to complete work, due to efficient or inefficient working.

(2) Using labour that is more or less experienced (and so more or less efficient) than the 'standard'.

(3) A change in the composition or mix of the work force, and so a change in the level of efficiency.

(4) Improved working methods.

(5) Industrial action by the work force: 'working to rule'.

(6) Poor supervision.

(7) Improvements in efficiency due to a 'learning effect' amongst the work force.

(8) Unexpected lost time due to production bottlenecks and resource shortages.

Overhead variances

(1) Fixed overhead expenditure adverse variances are caused by spending in excess of the budget. A more detailed analysis of the expenditure variance would be needed to establish why actual expenditure has been higher or lower than budget.

(2) Variable production overhead efficiency variances: the causes are similar to those for a direct labour efficiency variance.

Sales price

(1) Higher-than-expected discounts offered to customers to persuade them to buy, or due to purchasing in bulk.

(2) Lower-than-expected discounts, perhaps due to strength of sales demand.

(3) The effect of low-price offers during a marketing campaign.

(4) Market conditions forcing an industry-wide price change.

Sales volume

(1) Successful or unsuccessful direct selling efforts.

(2) Successful or unsuccessful marketing efforts (for example, the effects of an advertising campaign).

(3) Unexpected changes in customer needs and buying habits.

(4) Failure to satisfy demand due to production difficulties.

(5) Higher demand due to a cut in selling prices, or lower demand due to an increase in sales prices.

4 Possible interdependence between variances

In many cases, the explanation for one variance might also explain one or more other variances in which case the variances are inter-related.

For control purposes, it might therefore be necessary to look at several variances together and not in isolation.

Some examples of interdependence between variances are listed below.

- Using cheaper materials will result in a favourable material price variance, but using the cheaper material in production might increase the wastage rate (adverse material usage) and cause a fall in labour productivity (adverse labour and variable overhead efficiency).

  A more expensive mix of materials (adverse mix variance) might result in higher output yields (favourable yield variance). Mix and yield variances are covered in the next chapter.

- Using more experienced labour to do the work will result in an adverse labour rate variance, but productivity might be higher as a result (favourable labour and variable overhead efficiency).

- Changing the composition of a team might result in a cheaper labour mix (favourable mix variance) but lower productivity (adverse yield variance).

- Workers trying to improve productivity (favourable efficiency variance) in order to win a bonus (adverse rate variance) might use materials wastefully in order to save time (adverse materials usage).

- Cutting sales prices (adverse sales price variance) might result in higher sales demand from customers (favourable sales volume variance).

5 The controllability principle

Controllability means the extent to which a specific manager can control costs or revenues or any other item (such as output quality). The controllability principle is that a manager should only be made accountable and responsible for costs and revenues that he or she can control directly.

In variance reporting, this means that variances should be reported to the managers who are in a position to control the costs or revenues to which the variances relate.

Composite variances

Sometimes a variance might be caused by a combination of two factors. The variance is a composite variance, because it is the result of the two factors combined. To apply the controllability principle, the variance should be reported to each of the managers who are in a position to control one of the factors.

6 Standard costing in the modern manufacturing environment

Standard costing may be inappropriate in the modern production environment because:

- products in these environments tend not to be standardised

- standard costs become outdated quickly

- production is highly automated

- modern environments often use ideal standards rather than current standards

- the emphasis is on continuous improvement so preset standards become less useful
- variance analysis may not give enough detail
- variance reports may arrive too late to solve problems

Further explanation

Non-standard products

Standard product costs apply to manufacturing environments in which quantities of an identical product are output from the production process. They are not suitable for manufacturing environments where products are non-standard or are customised to customer specifications.

Standard costs become outdated quickly

Shorter product life cycles in the modern business environment mean that standard costs will need to be reviewed and updated frequently. This will increase the cost of operating a standard cost system but, if the standards are not updated regularly, they will be of limited use for planning and control purposes. The extra work involved in maintaining up-to-date standards might limit the usefulness and relevance of a standard costing system.

Production is highly automated

It is doubtful whether standard costing is of much value for performance setting and control in automated manufacturing environments. There is an underlying assumption in standard costing that control can be exercised by concentrating on the efficiency of the workforce. Direct labour efficiency standards are seen as a key to management control. However, in practice, where manufacturing systems are highly automated, the rates of production output and materials consumption, are controlled by the machinery rather than the workforce.

Ideal standard used

Variances are the difference between actual performance and standard, measured in cost terms. The significance of variances for management control purposes depends on the type of standard cost used. JIT and TQM businesses often implement an ideal standard due to the emphasis on continuous improvement and high quality. Therefore, adverse variances with an ideal standard have a different meaning from adverse variances calculated with a current standard.

Emphasis on continuous improvement

Standard costing and adherence to a preset standard is inconsistent with the concept of continuous improvement, which is applied within TQM and JIT environments.

Detailed information is required

Variance analysis is often carried out on an aggregate basis (total material usage variance, total labour efficiency variance and so on) but in a complex and constantly changing business environment more detailed information is required for effective management control.

Monitoring performance is important

Variance analysis control reports tend to be made available to managers at the end of a reporting period. In the modern business environment managers need more 'real time' information about events as they occur.

Addressing the criticisms

An organisation's decision to use standard costing depends on its effectiveness in helping managers to make the correct planning and control decisions. Many of the above criticisms can be addressed by adaptations to traditional standard costing systems.

- Standard costs must be updated regularly if they are to remain useful for control purposes.

- The use of demanding performance standards can help to encourage continuous improvement.

- The standard costing system can be adapted to produce a broader analysis of variances that are less aggregated.

- It is possible to place less emphasis on labour cost variances and focus more on variances for quality costs, variable overhead costs, and so on.

- Real time information systems have been developed which allow for corrective action to be taken sooner in response to reported variances.

- Standard costing may still be useful even where the final product or service is not standardised. It may be possible to identify a number of standard components and activities for which standards may be set and used effectively for planning and control purposes.

7 McDonaldization

An area where standard costing becomes very useful is in industries where McDonaldization might apply. (The concept of McDonaldization comes from the successes of the fast food company).

In essence, McDonaldization is the **process of rationalisation**, albeit taken to extreme levels. One of the fundamental aspects of McDonaldization is that almost any task can (and should) be rationalised.

The process of McDonaldization takes a task and breaks it down into smaller tasks. This is repeated until all tasks have been broken down to the smallest possible level. The resulting tasks are then rationalised to find the single most efficient method for completing each task. All other methods are then deemed inefficient and discarded.

The impact of McDonaldization is that **standards can be more accurately set and assessed**. Managers know, with a high degree of accuracy, how much time and cost should go into each activity.

Although the principles are perhaps best understood by applying them to the way McDonalds has operated, it is important to remember that they can be applied to many other services, such as hairdressing, dentistry, or opticians' services.

More details

The term was defined by George Ritzer (1996) as 'the process by which the principles of the fast-food restaurant are coming to dominate more and more sectors of American society, as well as the rest of the world'.

Ritzer identified four dimensions to McDonaldization which are critical to the success of the model.

(1) **Efficiency**. This means choosing the optimum means to achieve a given end. Consumers should be able to get what they need more quickly and with less effort. Workers should perform tasks more quickly and with less effort. In McDonalds, for example, drinks dispensers, automatic coffee brewers, microwave ovens, automatic potato peelers, dishwashers and pre-programmed cash registers have saved time, reduced the need for human input and reduced the scope for error.

(2) **Calculability**. This means the ability to produce and obtain large quantities of something very quickly. A problem with fast high-volume production is that quality might suffer consequently non-human technologies should be used as much as possible to perform tasks. Quantity has become equivalent to quality, a lot of something, or the quick delivery of it, means that it must be good.

(3) **Control**. There should be effective controls over both employees and customers. In McDonalds restaurants, for example, customers are expected to clear their own tables after eating.

(4) **Predictability**. Customers (and employees) should know exactly what they are going to get at any service point anywhere in the world. In the case of McDonalds, for example, the predictability of what customers get in any outlet has been a significant factor in expansion through franchising.

Other principles on which McDonaldization is based are that:

- When goods and services are more uniform in quality, quality will be better.

- Standardisation of services is less expensive than customisation.

- Customers like familiarity, and feel that it is safer to do things within a controlled regime.

- People like to be treated in the same way as everyone else.

Features of the McDonalds service, which are probably familiar to you, are automation, speed, the use of disposable paper products and plastic wraps, pre-sliced cheese and packs of tomato ketchup, getting customers to do the work and having a limited menu of items with a short preparation time. Customers feel they are getting a good deal in terms of generous portions for a reasonable price and in a short time.

The relevance of standard costing to services of this nature should be apparent. Management should be able to set accurate standards for what is takes, in terms of materials and time, to provide standard items to customers. This in turn means that costs are both minimised and predictable, and with predictable costs, it becomes possible to set prices that customers see as fair (or even better) and still make a large profit.

8 Diagnostic related groups

One specific area where standard costing currently appears to be flourishing is in healthcare management. For the purposes of remunerating healthcare providers and evaluating the performance of those providers, it is often deemed necessary to determine the standard cost of providing healthcare to persons suffering from specific medical conditions.

One response to this is the use of the diagnostic reference (or related) group (DRG) otherwise known as the healthcare resource group or case mix group. The medical conditions from which patients admitted to hospital are suffering can be classified into DRGs.

Patients within a given DRG all suffer from broadly the same medical condition and will receive broadly the same treatment. Diagnostic reference groups are another application of standards in a service industry.

Hospitals will get paid a 'standard cost' for each treatment they provide and their efficiency and performance can be measured against standard treatment times etc.

More details

DRGs have been defined as 'systems for classifying patient care by relating common characteristics such as diagnosis, treatment and age to an expected consumption of hospital resources and length of stay. Its aim is to provide a framework for specifying care mix and to reduce hospital costs' (www.online-medical-dictionary.org).

The concept was developed in US healthcare in the early 1980s as a means of controlling the costs of the Medicare health service. In broad terms, patients are placed into one of several standard categories of condition and treatment, and the amount that Medicare will pay the hospitals providing the treatment is based on a standard price for that category.

Most practical applications of this approach involve the adoption of between 600 and 800 DRGs. Healthcare funders (insurance companies or the NHS) may undertake to pay a given amount per day to a hospital for the treatment of patients within a particular DRG. That per day rate will be determined with reference to the standard cost of treating a patient within the DRG – having regard to the resources required and the amount that the hospital has to pay for those resources. At the same time, the performance of a hospital may be evaluated by comparing its actual per day costs for given DRGs with the relevant standards. If a hospital incurs a cost of $5,000 per day for treating a patient requiring a liver transplant and the standard cost (or benchmark cost) is $4,000 per day, then this comparison offers a comment on the efficiency of the hospital concerned. Similarly, if a hospital takes 23 days to treat a particular DRG and the standard is 19 days, then this also is a comment on its efficiency.

However, the DRG approach is not without its critics. The clinical treatments available for any illness are varied. In the case of heart disease they range from a heart transplant at one extreme to merely counselling on lifestyle and diet at the other extreme. Each patient is different having regard to the detailed nature of the disease, its degree of progression and their own strength and state of general health. The clinician should evaluate each patient individually and decide on the programme of surgery, drugs and lifestyle counselling that is appropriate in each case. However, if a hospital is paid a fixed daily rate for treating a patient in a given DRG, then the clinician will be most reluctant to provide treatment above or below the standard package for that DRG. If treatment is provided above standard, then the hospital will not be paid any additional fee, and treatment below standard may result in unpleasant accusations of malpractice being levelled by both patients and funding providers.

The logic of the DRG approach is that each patient who presents with a given set of symptoms is offered a standard package of treatments – which may not always be entirely appropriate. A clinician may be tempted simply to offer the standard package to each patient in a DRG even though he or she may suspect that package to be inadequate in some cases and excessive in others. In effect, the approach may induce a degree of McDonaldisation with all patients served the medical equivalent of a Big-Mac. Unless great sensitivity is exercised in its application, the use of DRGs may result in clinical practice being distorted by what is essentially a financial control system.

9 Benchmarking

In addition to monitoring performance through variance analysis, or as an alternative to variance reporting, organisations might use benchmarking to:

- monitor their performance, and
- set targets for improved performance.

The basic idea of benchmarking is that performance should be assessed through a comparison of the organisation's own products or services, performance and practices with 'best practice' elsewhere. It is particularly relevant, for example, in TQM environments where measurement against pre-determined standards is less relevant due to the focus on continuous improvement.

 Definition of benchmarking

'Benchmarking is 'the establishment, through data gathering, of targets and comparators, that permit relative levels of performance (and particularly areas of under-performance) to be identified. Adoption of identified best practices should improve performance.' (CIMA *Official Terminology*).

Alternative definitions

'Benchmarking is simply about making comparisons with other organisations and then learning the lessons that those comparisons throw up' (The European Benchmarking Code of Conduct).

'Benchmarking is the continuous process of measuring products, services and practices against the toughest competitors ... recognised as industry leaders (best in class)' (The Xerox Corporation).

Benchmarking was pioneered by Xerox Business Systems in the late 1970s as a tactical planning tool, in response to the challenge from rival Japanese producers of photocopier machines.

The reasons for benchmarking might be summarised as:

- to receive an alarm call about the need for change
- learning from others in order to improve performance
- gaining a competitive edge (in the private sector)
- improving services (in the public sector).

Different types of benchmarking

Benchmarking can be categorised according to what is being benchmarked and whose performance is being used for comparison (as 'best in class').

- Internal benchmarking
- Competitive benchmarking
- Functional benchmarking
- Strategic benchmarking

Further details

It is important to remember that in order to use benchmarking, it is necessary to gather information about best practice. This leads on to the problem of how much information is available and where it can be obtained.

Benchmarking can be categorised according to what is being benchmarked and whose performance is being used for comparison (as 'best in class').

Internal benchmarking. With internal benchmarking, other units or departments in the same organisation are used as the benchmark. This might be possible if the organisation is large and divided into a number of similar regional divisions. Internal benchmarking is also widely used within government. In the UK for example, there is a Public Sector Benchmarking Service that maintains a database of performance measures. Public sector organisations, such as fire stations and hospitals, can compare their own performance with the best in the country.

Competitive benchmarking. With competitive benchmarking, the most successful competitors are used as the benchmark. Competitors are unlikely to provide willingly any information for comparison, but it might be possible to observe competitor performance (for example, how quickly a competitor processes customer orders). A competitor's product might be dismantled in order to learn about its internal design and its performance: this technique of benchmarking is called **reverse engineering**.

Functional benchmarking. In functional benchmarking, comparisons are made with a similar function (for example selling, order handling, despatch) in other organisations that are not direct competitors. For example, a fast food restaurant operator might compare its buying function with buying in a supermarket chain.

Strategic benchmarking. Strategic benchmarking is a form of competitive benchmarking aimed at reaching decisions for strategic action and organisational change.

Companies in the same industry might agree to join a **collaborative benchmarking process**, managed by an independent third party such as a trade organisation. With this type of benchmarking, each company in the scheme submits data about their performance to the scheme organiser. The organiser calculates average performance figures for the industry as a whole from the data supplied. Each participant in the scheme is then supplied with the industry average data, which it can use to assess its own performance.

The benchmarking process

The benchmarking process can be summarised as follows:

- Identify gaps in performance through comparisons with other organisations.
- Seek a fresh approach to achieve an improvement in performance where significant gaps are found. This does not necessarily mean copying what the other organisation does.
- Implement the improvements.
- Monitor progress.
- Repeat the process.

Benchmarking should be a continual process, not a 'one-off' exercise.

Performance measures

Gaps in performance are identified by comparing an organisation's own performance with the performance of the organisation acting as the benchmark.

- Several measures of performance will be used. Each measure should be a key performance measure, critical to the success of the organisation.
- Performance measures can be financial or non-financial.
- Ideally performance should be quantifiable and measurable, although qualitative assessments and comparisons might be necessary.
- The information available for comparison will depend on whether it has been provided voluntarily by the benchmark. Co-operative benchmarking should provide more extensive information.

Some writers identify three distinct approaches to benchmarking:

(1) *Metric benchmarking*. The practice of comparing appropriate metrics to identify possible areas for improvement;

(2) *Process benchmarking*. The practice of comparing processes with a partner as part of an improvement process;

(3) *Diagnostic benchmarking*. The practice of reviewing the processes of a business to identify those which indicate a problem and offer a potential for improvement.

Some clear reference point is needed in order to give such metrics clear meaning. That reference point should be a benchmark, derived from some internal or external source. An internal benchmark might be a standard cost calculated using work study methods or it might be an external benchmark provided by a benchmarking partner or through some consortium run by a third party.

However, caution should always be exercised in the interpretation of benchmarking reports. For example, let us say that Town A reports a sewage disposal cost of $250 per tonne whereas Town B reports a cost of $400 per tonne. Should stakeholders conclude from this that Town A is more efficient than Town B? Not necessarily. Town A might be pumping raw sewage direct into the sea while Town B is processing the sewage before its disposal. Also Towns A and B may have subtly different accounting policies which mean that the two do not classify costs in the same way and hence the two figures compared in the benchmarking report are not strictly comparable.

Great caution should also be taken in the selection of appropriate benchmarks as a guide to action. For example, a given objective (e.g. 'containment of youth crime') can be achieved in a variety of different ways – through spending on police, education, social services and recreation. Town A may appear to run a very efficient police service (using a benchmarked measure such as 'arrests per police officer') but if the spending balance of police relative to social services is not right then Town A may not be containing youth crime in the most effective way. A small increase in spending on vocational education might allow a big cut in spending on police without an associated increase in youth crime.

The performance measures used will vary. For your examination, you might be required to:

- Suggest suitable performance measures. Performance measures should allow for direct comparisons. For example, a profit/sales ratio might provide a useful comparison, but earnings per share would not. Remember that both financial and non-financial data might be significant.

- Comment on a benchmarking report, by comparing the performance of an organisation with a benchmark such as a leading competitor or another region in the same organisation.

Benefits and problems with benchmarking

Benefits	Problems
• Encourages continuous improvement	• Difficult to find suitable benchmark
• Can quantify improvements	• Comparison may not be suitable
• Can be used in marketing	• Doesn't explain how to close the gap
• Commonly used/popular	• Targets can be arbitrary
• More appropriate than standard costing	• Often not linked to rewards
• Internal benchmarks can identify best practice	• Can be time consuming and expensive

Further explanation

Benefits

- Because activities are constantly assessed and targets are constantly being updated, it encourages managers to seek out continuous improvements in performance in order to stay ahead of their targets and their rivals.

- Managers can quantify their improvements by examining the change in the gap between their performance and the next nearest benchmark.

- Benchmark 'leaders' can promote this in their marketing. For example, motor breakdown services often quote their reaction times and repair times against rivals to show how they are quicker and/or better.

- Benchmarking has become so widespread that it is easily understood by managers. They will find it more useful, understandable and relevant than standard costing variances.

- As already discussed in this chapter, standard costing suffers from problems in modern environments that benchmarking does not suffer from.

- If best practice can be identified internally then these systems and processes can be replicated and applied in other parts of the business to improve overall business performance. Internal champions can be appointed to manage and control this project.

Problems

- The most difficult element of benchmarking is in choosing an appropriate and relevant benchmark. This is more difficult when choosing external benchmarks where less data is available and systems and processes may not match up exactly.

- Comparisons may not be suitable if, for example, business units are at different stages of their life cycle, have different goals, different constraints etc.

- Benchmarking simply identifies a gap in performance between a business unit and its benchmark. It does not explain how to close this gap.

- Closing the gap may be possible all at once or on a step-by-step basis. It may not be known which is best until some progress is made towards the benchmark. This means that any target set is likely to be arbitrary until this process begins.

- Managers may not like a benchmarking process if their rewards are not linked to performance against the benchmark. However, attempting to do this can suffer from the arbitrary targets already stated.

- Benchmarking can be a difficult and time consuming exercise. Many authors believe that organisations spend too much time working out what the gap is and not enough time on closing the gap with the benchmark.

Internal benchmarking

Using internal benchmarks can overcome many of the problems associated with benchmarking. For example, it is easier to take action on results, it is easier to gather data, comparisons are more relevant and targets are likely to be more useful and meaningful.

The factors most ripe for internal benchmarking are productivity ratios, efficiency response time, cost ratios and pricing performance. Many of the numerators for such ratios come from a company's finance department, while the denominators often come from information kept by the business units. For example, in many organisations, finance keeps overhead cost data and sales keeps account data, so if you want to benchmark overhead per account, you must combine data sources. You may have to do some digging. Usually, however, there are just one to four high-level metrics that make the most sense for a company to track, with a larger set of measures underlying them. Internal benchmarking is most valuable when a company has multiple comparable units. These may be business units, branches, plants, sales offices, countries, even products. For example, how does widget plant A's reject rate compare with widget plant B's? Or what is the Asia/Pacific region's unit cost per account vis-à-vis that of Europe?

10 Chapter summary

Variance investigation

Consider
- size
- adv/fav
- cost v benefit
- ability to correct
- patterns
- reliability

Interpretation

Consider
- controllability
- interdependence
- changes in each part of the standard cost card

Variance discussion elements

Problems with standard costing

- Non-standard products
- quickly outdated
- High automation
- Ideal is unuseful
- Ignores continuous improvement
- Lacks detail

Developments

- McDonaldization
- DRG
- Benchmarking

11 Practice questions

Test your understanding 1

Describe whether standard costing applies in both manufacturing and service businesses and how it may be affected by modern initiatives of continuous performance improvement and cost reduction.

(5 marks)

Test your understanding 2

Explain the factors that should be considered before deciding to investigate a variance.

(5 marks)

Test your understanding 3 – BUSINESS EQUIPMENT SOLUTIONS

CM Limited was formed 10 years ago to provide business equipment solutions to local businesses. It has separate divisions for research, marketing, product design, technology and communication services, and now manufactures and supplies a wide range of business equipment (copiers, scanners, printers, fax machines and similar items).

To date it has evaluated its performance using monthly financial reports that analyse profitability by type of equipment.

While on a course, the Managing Director of CM Limited overheard someone mention how the performance of their company had improved after they introduced 'Benchmarking'.

Required:

Explain 'Benchmarking' and how it could be used to improve the performance of CM Limited.

(12 marks)

Test your understanding 4

Contrast the concepts of McDonaldization and benchmarking and illustrate how they might be best for dental practice offering standard treatments to patients. The practice has around 40 dentists in operation across 8 sites spread around a major city.

(5 marks)

Test your understanding answers

Test your understanding 1

Standard costing is most suited to organisations whose activities consist of a series of common or repetitive operations. Typically, mass production manufacturing operations are indicative of its area of application. It is also possible to envisage operations within the service sector to which standard costing may apply, though this may not be with the same degree of accuracy of standards which apply in manufacturing. For example, hotels and restaurants often use standard recipes for preparing food, so dealing with conference attendance can be like a mass production environment. Similarly, banks will have common processes for dealing with customer transactions, processing cheques, etc. It is possible therefore that the principles of standard costing may be extended to service industries.

In modern manufacturing and service businesses, continuous improvement and cost reduction are topical. In order to remain competitive it is essential that businesses address the cost levels of their various operations. To do this they have to deal with the costing of operations. But the drive to 'cost down' may mean in some cases that standards do not apply for long before a redesign or improvement renders them out of date. In such a setting an alternative to the use of standard costs is to compare actual costs with those of the previous operating period. We have seen above that a standard costing system has a variety of purposes. It is for management to judge their various reasons for employing standard costing and, consequently, whether their aims of continuous improvement and cost reduction render the system redundant.

Test your understanding 2

The factors that should be considered before deciding to investigate a variance include the following:

- The size of the variance, both in absolute terms and as a percentage of the standard cost.

- The trend in the variance. If the variance fluctuates from adverse to favourable and back again then over a period of time the trend in the variance might be insignificant and the cause is thus not worthy of investigation.

- The cost of conducting an investigation should be balanced against the likely benefit to be derived from the investigation.

- The likelihood of the variance being controllable. For example, certain price variances may be due to movements in external market prices which are outside the control of the organisation's management.

- The interrelationship of variances. An adverse material usage variance might be directly related to a favourable materials price variance due to lower quality material being purchased, leading to high wastage.

- The type of standard that was set. For example an ideal standard is likely to result in adverse efficiency variances and a price standard that was set as an average for a period might produce favourable variances early in the period, followed by adverse variances later in the period.

Test your understanding 3 – BUSINESS EQUIPMENT SOLUTIONS

Benchmarking is the continuous process of comparing products, services and activities against best practice. The best practice information could be taken from internal sources, e.g. other divisions or from external organisations which may be competitors or may even be companies in completely different industries, but with some similar processes.

By comparing the performance against best practice elsewhere, where company performance falls short of the target, questions can be asked as to why this is so and efforts directed at improving.

CM Ltd should determine what performance measures are important, which ones are critical to the company's success. It should be the divisional managers who choose the measures which are important for their divisions. Then, the source of the benchmark should be established. Some of the benchmarks will be internal, e.g. other divisions within the group and there will not be any problem obtaining the information, but some of the benchmarks will be external and this could cause more problems. Where the external benchmark is based upon performance by a non-competing company then there are no commercial confidence considerations to take into account, but even competing companies do sometimes agree to share information with the aim that both companies improve their performance. Sometimes various companies in the same industry agree to pool information to a trade association or other body which will collect information in confidence and then publish various statistics which the individual companies can then use for benchmarking. It is also possible to benchmark against an unwilling competitor but this relies on the information being publicly available.

For the manufacturing arm of CM Ltd, information about competing companies could be obtained by 'reverse engineering', i.e. literally taking a competitor's product apart to see what components and materials are used and what processes must have been involved.

CM Ltd could agree to benchmark with similar companies in the same industry, but operating in a different geographical area, hence not competing.

Test your understanding 4

McDonaldization aims at finding the quickest and cheapest ways to produce a product or provide a service. Once this aim is achieved then all other alternative methods are ignored. The method becomes the standard and allows management to set accurate standards for the provision of this product or service. In a dental practice different ways of providing treatment could be considered. Once the quickest and cheapest method is determined then codes of conduct and a universal standard could be applied to ensure that the treatment is provided in exactly the same way to all patients. Any deviations from this would lead to a variance that would have to be explained by the individual dentist.

Benchmarking is used to find best practice techniques – either by making comparisons between internal service provisions or using external benchmarks to examine the standards achieved by rivals. Once determined, the benchmark becomes the target for performance. In this way it encourages continuous improvement of the service and can therefore often play a role in quality management. If the dental practice is concerned more with quality than cost or efficiency (which are often the focus of McDonaldization), then they could examine how treatments are provided at rival dental practices. Benchmarks could be sought for areas such as the number of reworks and the percentage of repeat business. These could then be used as targets for each individual dentist or location and rewards could be based on their achievement.

Advanced variances

Chapter learning objectives

Lead	Component
A1. Discuss costing methods and their results.	(f) Interpret material, labour, variable overhead, fixed overhead and sales variances, distinguishing between planning and operational variances.

1 Chapter overview diagram

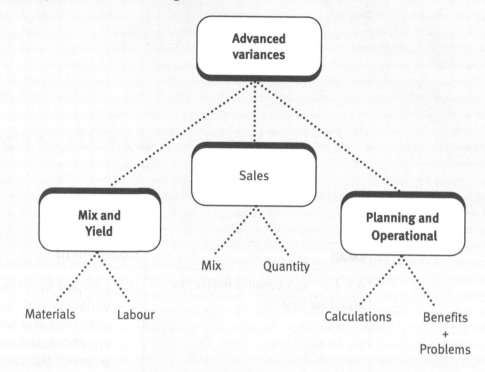

2 Advanced material variances – mix and yield

In many industries, particularly process industries, input consists of more than one type of material and it is possible to vary the mix. In many cases this would then affect the quantity of output produced. To analyse this the usage variance can be broken down into mix and yield variances.

Material mix variance

The material mix variance arises when the mix of materials used differs from the predetermined mix included in the calculation of the standard cost of an operation.

Material yield variance

The material yield variance arises when there is a difference between the standard output for a given level of input and the actual output attained.

Further details

The meaning of the mix variance

For materials and labour variances, a mix variance measures whether the actual mix that occurred was more or less expensive than the standard mix. If the mixture is varied so that a larger than expected proportion of a more *expensive* material is used there will be an *adverse* variance. When a larger than expected proportion of a *cheaper* material is included in the mix, then a *favourable* variance occurs.

For example, suppose that a product consists of two materials, X and Y, the standard mix of the two items is 50:50, and material X is much more expensive than material Y.

- If the actual mix used to make the product contains more than 50% of X and less than 50% of Y, the actual mix will be more expensive than the standard mix, because it includes a bigger-than-standard proportion of the expensive material. The mix variance will be adverse.

- Similarly, if the actual mix used to make the product contains less than 50% of X and more than 50% of Y, the actual mix will be less expensive than the standard mix, and the mix variance will be favourable.

The meaning of the yield variance

A materials yield variance is similar to a materials usage variance. However, instead of calculating a usage variance for each material separately, a single yield variance is calculated for all the materials as a whole. The yield variance is calculated first of all in terms of units of material, and is converted into a money value at the weighted average standard cost per unit of material.

When a mix variance is calculated, it is assumed that the mix of materials or labour can be controlled.

- The material yield should therefore be assessed for all the materials combined, not for each item of material separately.

- Similarly, the labour yield variance should be assessed for the labour team as a whole, not for each grade of labour separately.

The yield variance then tells us the effect of varying the total input of a factor of production (e.g. materials or labour) while holding constant the input mix (the proportions of the types of materials or labour used) and the weighted average unit price of the factor of production.

3 Calculating mix and yield variances

There are two different methods for calculating the mix variance mentioned in the syllabus – the individual units method and the weighted average method.

The individual units method is easier to calculate and understand (so you should use this in the exam if you have a choice), but the weighted average is technically superior.

Both methods produce exactly the same total figure for the mix variance.

Both methods compare the actual mix of materials with the standard mix.

- The actual mix = the actual quantities of materials used (for each material individually and in total).

- The standard mix = the actual total quantity of materials used, with the total divided between the individual materials in the standard proportions.

- The mix variance in units of material is the difference between the actual mix and the standard mix. A mix variance is calculated for each individual material in the mix.

Materials mix – individual units method

(1) Write down the actual input. (This is the **actual mix**.)

(2) Take the actual input in total and push it down one line and then work it back in the standard proportions. (This is the **standard mix**.)

(3) Calculate the difference between the standard mix (line 2) and the actual mix (line 1). This is the mix variance in terms of physical quantities and must add up to zero in total. (If you use a higher than expected proportion of one material, you must use a lower than expected proportion of something else!)

(4) Multiply by the standard price per kg

(5) This gives the mix variance in financial terms.

	Material A	Material B	Total
	Kg	Kg	Kg
1 Actual input	N	N	NN
			⇓
2 Actual input in std proportions	N	N	⇐ NN
	—	—	—
3 Difference in quantity	N	N	
4 × Std Price	× $N	× $N	
5 Mix variance	$N	$N	$N
	—	—	—

Materials mix – weighted average method

The format is similar to that used for the individual units method, except that once the difference in quantity has been calculated, instead of multiplying by the individual material price, we multiply by the difference between the individual price and the weighted average price.

Calculate the weighted average std cost of the materials. (This is needed for step 4). *You have to be very careful here. This weighted average is the weighted average cost per kg of input as we are just about to compare inputs.*

Further details on the weighted average method

The individual units method is easier to understand, but is slightly flawed. The weighted average method is theoretically superior, is recommended by CIMA and is much more likely to be asked for by the examiner. The superiority of the weighted average method will be seen in the a Test Your Understanding – Hordru – at the end of this chapter.

The detail stages in the calculation are as follows:

(1) Write down the actual usage. (This is the **actual mix**.)

(2) Take the actual usage in total and push it down one line and then work it back in the standard proportions. (This is the **standard mix**.)

(3) Calculate the difference between the standard mix (line 2) and the actual mix (line 1). This is the mix variance in terms of kgs or litres and must add up to zero in total. (If you use a higher proportion of one type of material, you must use a lower proportion of another type!)

Remember what a mix variance means – using a higher proportion of an expensive type of material is adverse, but using a higher proportion of a cheaper type of material would actually be regarded as a good thing.

We have just found out for each type of material whether we have used a higher or lower proportion of that material. In order to decide whether the variance is favourable or adverse we need to know whether that type of material is cheap or expensive. We determine this by comparing the individual costs of material with the weighted average rate.

(4) Determine for each type of material whether it is cheap or expensive compared to a weighted average price.

(5) Multiply the results from line 3 and line 4.

(6) This gives the mix variance in financial terms.

	Material A	Material B	Total
	Kgs	Kgs	Kgs
1 Actual usage	N	N	NN
			⇓
2 Actual usage in std proportions	N	N	← NN
	—	—	—
3 Difference in quantity	N	N	
4 × Difference in rate			
(weighted average std cost – individual material cost)			
× ($X – $X)	× $N		
× ($X – $X)		× $X	
	—	—	—
5 Mix variance	$N	$N	$N
	—	—	—

Yield variance

The yield variance only happens in total (CIMA and the examiner do not consider individual yield variances to be meaningful). The yield variance is calculated in the **same way under both methods**.

(1) Calculate the **standard yield**. This is the expected output from the actual input

(2) Compare this to **actual yield**.

(3) The difference is the yield variance in physical terms.

(4) To express the variance in financial terms we multiply by the standard cost. One thing to be careful of however is that the yield variance considers outputs and so the standard cost is the standard cost per kg **of output.**

(5) This gives the yield variance in financial terms.

		Kg
1	Standard yield of actual input	N
2	Actual yield	N
		—
3		N
4	× std cost per kg of output	× $N
		—
		$N
		—

Alternative yield valuation method

There are two approaches to calculating and valuing the yield variance. Both give the same answer and both are acceptable in the exam. You will see different TYU's in this chapter using different approaches, but it is probably best for the exam to learn one method and stick to using that method.

Here is an illustration of both methods:

Illustration

A company produces a product with the following inputs in each batch:

Material	Input (kg)	Cost per kg	Total Cost ($)
X	0.90	$0.05	0.0450
Y	0.10	$0.21	0.0210
Z	0.05	$0.29	0.0145
	—		—
Total	1.05		0.0805
	—		—

These inputs will provide 1 kg of output.

The actual results show:

Input = 22,880 kgs

Output = 21,500 kgs.

Use this information to calculate the materials yield variance.

Solution

There are possible approaches to the calculation:

(i)   value materials at the **cost per output**

The yield variance is based on an **output** measure.

Therefore the cost is $0.0805/1 kg = $0.0805

Now adjust the input to **calculate the expected output** (i.e. 22,880 kgs input should have produced (22,880/1.05) 21,790.5 kgs)

The yield variance =

(actual yield – standard yield) × standard cost per output
(21,500 – 21,790.5) × 0.0805

= $23.38 A

(ii)   value materials at the **cost per input**

The yield variance is based on an **input** measure.

Therefore the cost is $0.0805/1.05 kg = $0.0766

Now adjust the output to **calculate the expected input** (i.e. to get 21,500 kgs out, we should have put in (21,500 × 1.05) 22,575 kgs)

The yield variance =

(actual yield – standard yield) × standard cost per input
(22,880 – 22,575) × 0.0766

= $23.38 A

Both techniques give the same answer, so either approach is acceptable.

Example 1

Hordru Ltd operates a standard costing system.

The standard direct material mix to produce 1,000 kilos of output is as follows:

Material grade	Input quantity (kilos)	Standard price per kilo input $
A	600	1.10
B	240	2.40
C	360	1.50

During April the actual output of the product was 21,000 kilos.

The actual materials issued to production were:

Material grade	Quantity (kilos) (kilos)
A	14,000
B	5,500
C	5,500

Required:

(a) Calculate material mix variances for each material grade and in total, using individual material prices per kilo as the variance valuation base.

(b) Calculate material mix variances for each material grade and in total, using the budgeted weighted average material price per kilo as the variance valuation base.

(c) Calculate the materials yield variance.

Using mix and yield variances

Mix variances might be calculated when there is a mix of two or more items, and the mix is regarded as **controllable** by management.

- Two or more materials might be used in making a product or providing a service. If standard costing is used and the mix of the materials is seen as controllable, a materials mix variance and a materials yield variance can be calculated. These provide a further analysis of the materials usage variance.

- Two or more different types of labour might be used to make a product or provide a service. If standard costing is used and the labour mix in the team is seen as controllable, a labour mix variance and a labour yield variance can be calculated. These provide a further analysis of the labour efficiency variance.

If the mix cannot be controlled, it is inappropriate to calculate a mix and yield variance. Instead, a usage variance should be calculated for each individual material or an efficiency variance should be calculated for each individual type or grade of labour. *In other words, if the mix cannot be controlled, the usage or efficiency variance should not be analysed into a mix and yield variance.*

4 Advanced labour variances – mix and yield

Labour mix variance

The labour mix variance arises when the mix of labour used differs from the predetermined mix included in the calculation of the standard cost of an operation. If the mixture is varied so that a larger than expected proportion of a higher grade of labour is used there will be an *adverse* variance. When a larger than expected proportion of a *lower grade of labour* is included in the mix, then a *favourable* variance occurs.

Labour yield variance

The labour yield variance arises when there is a difference between the standard output for a given level of input (measured in terms of hours) and the actual output attained.

Calculations

These are **calculated in exactly the same way as the material mix and yield variances** except that the situation will involve different grades of labour instead of different types of material.

Calculations

Labour mix variance – individual units method

A labour mix variance is sometimes called a team composition variance. It measures whether the actual composition of the labour team was more or less expensive than the standard mix.

(1) Write down the actual hours. (This is the **actual mix**.)

(2) Take the actual hours in total and push it down one line and then work it back in the standard proportions. (This is the **standard mix**.)

(3) Calculate the difference between the standard mix (line 2) and the actual mix (line 1). This is the mix variance in terms of hours and must add up to zero in total. (If you use a higher proportion of one type of labour, you must use a lower proportion of another type!)

(4) Multiply by the standard rate per hour

(5) This gives the mix variance in financial terms.

	Skilled Labour	Unskilled Labour	Total
	Hrs	Hrs	Hrs
1 Actual hours	N	N	NN ⇓
2 Actual hours in std proportions	N —	N —	⇐ NN —
3 Difference in quantity	N	N	
4 × Std Rate	× $N	× $N	
5 Mix variance	$N —	$N —	$N —

Labour mix variance – weighted average method

The format is similar to that used for the individual units method, except that once the difference in quantity has been calculated, instead of multiplying by the individual labour rate, we multiply by the difference between the individual standard rate and the weighted average standard rate.

Calculate the weighted average standard cost of the labour. (This is needed for step 4). *You have to be very careful here. This weighted average is the weighted average cost per hour as we are just about to compare* **inputs***.*

(1) Write down the actual hours. (This is the **actual mix**.)

(2) Take the actual hours in total and push it down one line and then work it back in the standard proportions. (This is the **standard mix**.)

(3) Calculate the difference between the standard mix (line 2) and the actual mix (line 1). This is the mix variance in terms of hours and must add up to zero in total. (If you use a higher proportion of one type of labour, you must use a lower proportion of another type!)

Remember what a mix variance means – using a higher proportion of an expensive grade of labour is adverse, but using a higher proportion of a cheap grade would actually be regarded as a good thing.

We have just found out for each grade of labour whether we have used a higher or lower proportion of that grade. In order to decide whether the variance is favourable or adverse we need to know whether that grade of labour is cheap or expensive. We determine this by comparing the individual labour rate with the weighted average rate.

(4) Determine for each grade of labour whether it is cheap or expensive compared to a weighted average price.

(5) Multiply the results from line 3 and line 4.

(6) This gives the mix variance in financial terms.

	Skilled Labour	Unskilled Labour	Total
	Hrs	*Hrs*	*Hrs*
1 Actual hours	N	N	NN ⇓
2 Actual hours in std proportions	N —	N —	⇐ NN —
3 Difference in quantity	N	N	
4 × Difference in rate (weighted average std rate – individual labour std rate)			
× (X – X)	× $N		
× (X – X)		× $N	
	—	—	—
5 Mix variance	$N —	$N —	$N —

Labour yield variance

A labour yield variance is sometimes called a team productivity variance. It measures the efficiency of the team as a whole, rather than the efficiency of each grade of labour separately.

The yield variance is calculated in the same way under both methods. Again it only happens in total (CIMA and the examiner do not consider individual yield variances to be meaningful) and is calculated in the same way as the materials yield variance.

(1) Calculate the **standard yield**. This is the expected output from the actual input

(2) Compare this to **actual yield**.

(3) The difference is the yield variance in hours.

(4) To express the variance in financial terms we multiply by the standard cost. One thing to be careful of however is that the yield variance considers outputs and so the standard cost is the standard cost per hour **of output.**

(5) This gives the yield variance in financial terms.

		hrs
1	Standard yield of actual hours	N
2	Actual yield	N
		–
3		N
4	× std cost per hour of output	× N
		—
		N
		—

Limitations of mix variances

Mix and yield variances can provide useful control information, but only where the mix of materials or labour is controllable, and where the information about total yield is more useful than usage/efficiency variances for the individual materials or labour grades separately.

Using mix variances also has some other limitations.

- It is often found that the mix and yield variances are interdependent, and one variance cannot be assessed without also considering the other. For example, the inefficiency of a team (adverse labour yield variance) could be explained by the fact that the team has a larger-than-expected proportion of inexperienced, cheaper employees (favourable labour mix variance).

- If management is able to achieve a cheaper mix of materials or labour, without affecting yield, the standard becomes obsolete. The cheaper mix should become the new standard mix.

- Control measures to improve the mix by making it cheaper are likely to affect the quality of the output or the work done. Analysing mix and yield variances for control purposes does not take quality issues into consideration.

- Mix and yield variances are based on standard prices for material and standard rates for labour. Actual prices/rates may differ from standard and this will be measured using the material price/labour rate variances. For an overall assessment of performance these will also have to be taken into consideration.

Sales mix and quantity

The sales volume variance can be analysed into mix and quantity components using the same logic encountered in regard to materials usage and labour efficiency variances.

Illustration on sales mix and quantity

A business sells two products, X and Y, details for the current period as follows:

	Standard mix (units)	Standard profit ($ per unit)	Average profit ($ per unit)
X	2	5	
Y	3	6	
Total	5	((2×5)+(3×6))/5	5.60

Budget sales – 200 units X and 300 units Y
Actual sales – 180 units X and 310 units Y

Required:

(a) calculate the sales quantity profit variance

(b) calculate the sales mix profit variance using the individual method

(c) calculate the sales mix profit variance using the weighted average method

Solution

(a) Sales quantity profit variance

It is apparent that the overall sales volume profit variance for the period is $40 adverse (that is (20 units adverse of X times $5) plus (10 units favourable of Y times $6).

We can split this into a sales quantity profit variance (effectively a yield variance) and a sales mix profit variance. The sales quantity profit variance is calculated as follows:

(Actual units − budgeted units) × weighted average profit per unit

(500 units budget − 490 units actual) × $5.60 average profit = $56 A

(b) Sales mix profit variance (using the individual units method)

	Standard mix	Actual mix	Variance (units)	Profit per unit ($)	Variance ($)
X	196	180	16 (A)	5	80 (A)
Y	294	310	16 (F)	6	96 (F)
Total	490	490			16 (F)

The standard mix is the total unit sales (490) multiplied by 2/5 to give X and 3/5 to give Y.

(c) Sales mix profit variance (using the weighted average method)

	Standard mix	Actual mix	Variance (units)	Profit per unit ($)	Weighted average profit ($)	Difference ($)	Variance ($)
X	196	180	16 (A)	5	5.60	0.60 (A)	9.60 (F)
Y	294	310	16 (F)	6	5.60	0.40 (F)	6.40 (F)
Total	490	490					16.00 (F)

The product X variance is favourable overall because, although the company sold less of the product than the standard mix, this is the less profitable product.

This perhaps explains the superiority of the weighted average method overall. Overall we have sold more of the more profitable product and less of the least profitable product so that it can be argued that both variances are in the company's favour and should be favourable.

Note:

The example used relates to the sales volume profit variance, but exactly the same procedure can be used for its contribution and revenue variance alternatives.

Benefits and problems of mix and quantity variances

Benefits

- The sales mix variance can allow an organisation identify trends in sales of individual elements of its total product sales. For example, they may find that although overall sales are improving (as suggested by the sale quantity or sales volume variance being favourable, that one individual product has shown a period-on-period decline in volume).

- The sales quantity variance can be used to indicate changes in the size of the market and/or the change in the market share for an organisation.

- The sales mix variance may indicate future directions for sales strategies - organisations would aim to repeat any favourable variances by identifying and exploiting their causes.

- The sales mix variance can be used to gauge the success or failure of new marketing campaigns. For example, if an organisation were to launch a special edition of its product, it might be able to determine the impact that this has on its profits as well as any adverse impact it might have had on sales of its regular product.

- Responsibility accounting is improved when the sales volume variance is split between the sales mix and quantity variance as different managers might be responsible for different elements of sales. The sales quantity variance, for example, will indicate whether the sales team have performed well overall, whereas the mix variance will then provide information on the success of those responsible for applying the mix of sales.

Problems

- Like any variance, it will be important for the user to consider the controllability of the variance before making performance review decisions based on the output. For example, an adverse sales quantity variance might have been caused by an uncontrollable change in government restrictions on sales of the product, rather than having being caused by the actions of the sales team/manager.

- Likewise, variances should be considered as a whole rather than on an individual basis due to their interdependnce. Managers would have to be aware, for example, that sales volume variances might be affected by decisions taken in production (such as a change in materials or labour used).

- The sales mix variance is only relevant if the products have some sort of relationship between them. Examples of this are:
    - the products are of the same type but of a different variety (for example, where there are 'normal' and 'special' editions of a product
    - the products are complementary (for example, where a company sells both ebooks and ereaders)
    - the products can be substituted for each other (for example, a company might sell European and Asian holidays).

- It can sometimes be difficult to apply these techniques in organisations which have very broad product ranges. It can be difficult to determine which products are complementary, which are substitutes etc. and often computer based techniques are needed to perform the detailed calculations.

Overall, these can be complex calculations that might only apply for certain organisations. But for managers who can interpret these well, sales mix and quantity variance analysis can provide vital information on sales trends, marketing effects, marketing position and variance responsibility.

5 Planning and operational variances

One reason that a variance may arise may be that the original plan has subsequently been found to be inappropriate. This might arise, for example, if suppliers have increased the cost of raw materials and this has not been accounted for in the original standard cost card. In that case the total variance must be split into two constituent parts:

- the **planning variance** – this is the part of the variance caused by an inappropriate original (ex-ante) standard, and

- the **operational variance** – this is the part of the variance attributable to decisions taken within the business that has caused a change between the revised (ex-post) standard and the actual results.

Further explanation

Forecasts by their nature are unreliable, and yet most standards are set on a forecast basis, i.e. *ex ante* or before the event. A planning variance arises from an inability to make exact predictions of future costs and revenues at the budgeting stage.

If it were possible to set standards with the benefit of hindsight, i.e. *ex post* or after the event managers would be able to see more clearly what amount of variances was genuinely attributable to operating performance (*operational variances*) and what amount to difficulties or errors in setting the original standard (*planning variances*). Such information should improve operational control and may also provide guidance for the improvement of planning procedures.

The planning variance is usually regarded as uncontrollable and has arisen because the original standard was not reflective of the attainable standard. The operational variance is controllable.

Operational variances

Operational variances are variances that are assumed to have occurred due to operational factors. These are materials price and usage variances, labour rate and efficiency variances, variable overhead expenditure and efficiency variances, fixed overhead expenditure variances, and sales variances.

Operational variances are calculated with the 'realistic' ex post standard. They are calculated in exactly the same way as described in earlier chapters, the only difference being that the ex post standard is used, not the original standard.

Planning variances

A planning variance measures the difference between the budgeted and actual profit that has been caused by errors in the original standard cost. It is the difference between the ex ante and the ex post standards.

- A planning variance is **favourable** when the ex post standard cost is lower than the original ex ante standard cost.

- A planning variance is **adverse** when the ex post standard cost is higher than the original ex ante standard cost.

Controllability and responsibility

Management will wish to draw a distinction between these two variances in order to gain a realistic measure of operational efficiency. As planning variances are self-evidently not under the control of operational management, it cannot be held responsible for them, and there is thus no benefit to be gained in spending time investigating such variances at an operational level. Planning variances may arise from faulty standard-setting, but the responsibility for this lies with senior, rather than operational management.

Example 2

ABC Ltd produces Units and incurs labour costs. Details of actual and budget for period 9 are:

	Budget	Actual	Standard per unit
Units	500	550	
Labour hours	1,000	1,200	2
Labour cost ($)	5,000	5,100	10

A change in technology subsequent to the preparation of the budget resulted in a 25% increase in standard labour efficiency, such that it is now possible to produce 5 Units instead of 4 Units using 8 hours of labour – giving a revised standard labour requirement of 1.6 hours (thus $8 labour cost) per Unit.

Required:

Calculate all relevant labour variances for the period.

Example 3

Big plc set up a factory to manufacture and sell 'Advance', a new consumer product. The first year's budgeted production and sales were 1,000 units. The budgeted sales price and standard costs for 'Advance' were as follows:

	$	$
Standard sales price per unit		200
Standard costs per unit		
Raw materials (10 kg at $10)	100	
Labour (6 hours at $8)	48	
		(148)
Standard contribution per unit		52

Actual results for the first year were as follows:

	$000	$000
Sales (1,000 units)		316
Production costs (1,000 units)		
Raw materials (10,800 kg)	194.4	
Labour (5,800 hours)	69.6	
		(264)
Actual contribution (1,000 units)		52

The managing director made the following observations on the actual results:

In total, the performance agreed with budget; nevertheless, in every aspect other than volume, there were large differences.

Sales were made at what was felt to be the highest feasible price, but we now feel that we could have sold for $330 with no adverse effect on volume. Labour costs rose dramatically with increased demand for the specialist skills required to produce the product, and the general market rate was $12.50 per hour – although we always paid below the general market rate whenever possible.

The raw material cost that was expected at the time the budget was prepared was $10 per kilogram. However, the market price relating to efficient purchases of the material during the year was $17 per kilogram.

It is not proposed to request a variance analysis for the first year's results. In any event, the final contribution was equal to that originally budgeted, so operations must have been fully efficient.

Required:

Despite the managing director's reluctance to calculate it, produce an operating statement for the period ignoring the impact of any planning variances.

Calculate the impact of the planning variances for the business.

6 Causes of planning variances

There must be a good reason for deciding that the original standard cost is unrealistic. Deciding in retrospect that expected costs should be different from the standard should not be an arbitrary decision, aimed perhaps at shifting the blame for poor results from poor operational management to poor cost estimation.

A good reason for a change in the standard might be:

- a change in one of the main materials used to make a product or provide a service
- an unexpected increase in the price of materials due to a rapid increase in world market prices (for example, the price of oil or other commodities)
- a change in working methods and procedures that alters the expected direct labour time for a product or service
- an unexpected change in the rate of pay to the work force.

More than one planning error

A situation might occur where the difference between the standards is in two (or more) items.

In these circumstances, the rules for calculating planning and operational variances are as follows:

- Operational variances are calculated against the most up-to-date revision

- The total planning variance will be the difference between the original standard or budget and the most up-to-date revision. This can then be further divided between each individual planning error.

For example, the original standard cost for a product was $4 per kg and the actual cost was $6 per kg. Two planning variances were discovered. Firstly, the accountant had assumed that a bulk discount on purchases would arise but this was never likely, and it meant that the standard should have been set at $4.60 per kg,. Secondly, a worldwide shortage of materials led to an industry wide increase of $1 per kg to the cost of materials. This means that the most up-to-date standard cost would have been $5.60 per kg. The operational variance would therefore be $0.60 ($6 – $5.60)per kg adverse and the total planning variance would be $1.60 ($5.60 – $4) per kg. The planning variance could then be split between the two effects: there is a $0.60 per kg adverse variance caused by the failure to gain the bulk discount, and a $1 per kg adverse variance caused by the market conditions.

7 Benefits and problems of planning variances

Benefits	Problems
• More useful	• Subjective
• Up-to-date	• Time consuming
• Better for motivation	• Can be manipulated
• Assesses planning	• Can cause conflict

More details

Benefits of Planning and Operational Variances

(1) In volatile and changing environments, standard costing and variance analysis are more useful using this approach.

(2) Operational variances provide up to date information about current levels of efficiency.

(3) Operational variances are likely to make the standard costing system more acceptable and to have a positive effect on motivation.

(4) It emphasises the importance of the planning function in the preparation of standards and helps to identify planning deficiencies.

Problems of Planning and Operational Variances

(1) There is an element of subjectivity in determining the ex-post standards as to what is 'realistic'.

(2) There is a large amount of labour time involved in continually establishing up to date standards and calculating additional variances.

(3) There is a great temptation to put as much as possible of the total variances down to outside, uncontrollable factors, i.e. planning variances.

(4) There can then be a conflict between operating and planning staff. Each laying the blame at each other's door.

On the face of it, the calculation of operational and planning variances is an improvement over the traditional analysis. However, you should not overlook the considerable problem of data collection for the revised analysis: where does this information come from, and how can we say with certainty what should have been known at a particular point in time?

8 Chapter summary

Advanced variances

Mix and Yield

- Mix is adverse if we use more of the expensive material/labour
- Yield is adverse if we use more materials/labour overall

Planning and Operational

- Planning variance
  = original − revised
    standard   standard
- Operational variance
  = revised − actual
    standard   results

Sales mix and quantity

- analyses the sales volume variance
- mix is adverse if we sell less of the more profitable product

9 Practice questions

Test your understanding 1

A company manufactures a chemical using two components, A and B. The standard information for one unit of the chemical are as follows:

		$
Material A	10 kg at $4 per kg	40
Material B	20 kg at $6 per kg	120
		160

In a particular period, 160 units of the chemical were produced, using 1,000 kgs of material A and 1,460 kgs of material B.

Required:

Calculate the material usage, mix and yield variances for each material.

(8 marks)

Test your understanding 2

Buzz Lightyear Ltd makes a single product, of which the standard labour input per unit is:

Skilled labour	6 hrs @ $12/hr
Unskilled labour	4 hrs @ $7/hr

During Period 1:
1,000 units were produced

5,250 hours of skilled labour were used and

5,250 hours of unskilled labour were used

Calculate the labour mix variances for each grade of labour and the labour yield variance in total.

Use both the weighted average method and the individual units method.

(10 marks)

Test your understanding 3

Leopard Airlines has estimated that on any flight, the free drinks consumed by passengers will be *(for every 10 passengers)*:

	Number of drinks	Cost per drink	Total cost $
Low cost	5	$0.25	1.25
Medium cost	8	$0.50	4.00
High cost	12	$1.00	12.00
	25		17.25

On a flight to Bermuda with 300 passengers on board, the actual number of free drinks consumed was as follows:

	Number of drinks
Low cost	215
Medium cost	280
High cost	355
	850

Calculate the materials mix and yield variances for this flight.

(5 marks)

Test your understanding 4

Product XYZ is made by mixing three materials (X, Y and Z). There is an expected loss of 20% of the total input.

The budgeted and actual results for Period 1 are shown below. There were no opening or closing inventories of any materials or of the finished product.

	Budget	**Actual**
Output of XYZ	**800 kg**	**960 kg**
	___	___
Material		
X	500 kg @ $5.00 per kg	600 kg @ $4.70 per kg
Y	300 kg @ $6.00 per kg	380 kg @ $6.50 per kg
Z	200 kg @ $7.00 per kg	300 kg @ $7.10 per kg
	___	___
Total input	**1,000 kg**	**1,280 kg**

Calculate for Period 1:

(i)   the total materials mix variance;

(2 marks)

(ii) the total materials yield variance

(2 marks)

Test your understanding 5

Pan-Ocean Chemicals has one product, which requires inputs from three types of material to produce batches of Synthon. Standard cost details for a single batch are shown below:

Material type	Standard quantity (kgs)	Standard price per kg ($)
S1	8	0.30
S2	5	0.50
S3	3	0.40

A standard loss of 10% of input is expected. Actual output was 15,408 kgs for the previous week. Details of the material used were:

Material type	Quantity (kgs)
S1	8,284
S2	7,535
S3	3,334

Required:

Calculate the individual material mix and yield and the total usage variance.

(5 marks)

Test your understanding 6

The following data relates to Skilled Labour Grade ST1

Standard labour hours per unit	5 hours
Standard labour rate	$10 per hour
Actual production	250 units
Actual labour hours	1,450 hours
Actual labour cost	$13,050

During the month there was an unforeseen shortage of the Skilled Labour Grade ST1. Semi skilled workers (Grade ST2) were hired. As a consequence of this, the standard time was revised to 6 hours per unit.

Required:

Calculate labour rate and efficiency variances using a planning and operational approach.

(5 marks)

Test your understanding 7

Holmes Ltd uses one raw material for one of their products. The standard cost per unit at the beginning of the year was $28, made up as follows:

Standard material cost per unit = 7 kg per unit at $4 per kg = $28.

In the middle of the year the supplier had changed the specification of the material slightly due to problems experienced in the country of origin, so that the standard had to be revised as follows:

Standard material cost per unit = 8 kg per unit at $3.80 per kg = $30.40.

The actual output for November was 1,400 units. 11,000 kg of material was purchased and used at a cost of $41,500.

Calculate

(a) material price and usage variances using the traditional method

(b) all planning and operational material variances.

(5 marks)

Test your understanding 8

WC is a company that installs kitchens and bathrooms for customers who are renovating their houses. The installations are either pre-designed 'off-the-shelf' packages or highly customised designs for specific jobs.

The company operates with three divisions: Kitchens, Bathrooms and Central Services. The Kitchens and Bathrooms divisions are profit centres but the Central Services division is a cost centre. The costs of the Central Services division, which are thought to be predominantly fixed, include those incurred by the design, administration and finance departments. The Central Services costs are charged to the other divisions based on the budgeted Central Services costs and the budgeted number of jobs to be undertaken by the other two divisions.

The budgeting and reporting system of WC is not very sophisticated and does not provide much detail for the Directors of the company. The budgeted details for last year were:

	Kitchens	Bathrooms
Number of jobs	4,000	2,000
	$	$
Average price per job	10,000	7,000
Average direct costs per job	5,500	3,000
Central services recharge per job	2,500	2,500
Average profit per job	2,000	1,500

The actual results were as follows:

	Kitchens	Bathrooms
Number of jobs	2,600	2,500
	$	$
Average price per job	13,000	6,100
Average direct costs per job	8,000	2,700
Central services recharge per job	2,500	2,500
Average profit per job	2,500	900

The actual costs for the Central Services division were $17.5 million.

Required:

(a) Calculate the budgeted and actual profits for each of the profit centres and for the whole company for the year.

(4 marks)

(b) Calculate the sales price variances and the sales mix profit and sales quantity profit variances.

(6 marks)

(c) Prepare a statement that reconciles the budgeted and actual profits and shows appropriate variances in as much detail as possible.

(10 marks)

(d) Using the statement that you prepared in part (c) above, discuss the performance of the company for the year.

(5 marks)

(Total: 25 marks)

Test your understanding 9 – ATS LTD

The expected contribution per unit of the product manufactured by ATS Ltd is $26, ascertained as below:

		$	$
Selling price			110
Material	8 kg × $3/kg	24	
Labour	6 hours × $10/hour	60	
		—	
			84
			—
Contribution/unit			26
			—

The expected contribution was $31,200. The actual contribution was $38,800 as shown below:

		$	$
Actual sales revenue	1,000 units @ $135		135,000
Actual material cost	7,800 kg × $4/kg	31,200	
Actual labour cost	6,250 hours × $10.40/hour	65,000	
		——	
			96,200
			——
Actual contribution			38,800
			——

The Sales Director made the policy decision to sell at $5 above the prevailing market price of $125, suggesting that if they did suffer a decrease in volume, ATS Ltd would still be better off. It was also accepted that an efficient purchasing officer could have purchased at around $4.50 per kg.

There was no stock movement of either materials or finished goods in the period.

Required:

Prepare a variance statement which would be most helpful to the management of ATS Ltd, which clearly takes planning and operational variances into consideration.

(15 marks)

Test your understanding 10

A company budgeted to make and sell 2,000 units of its only product, for which the standard marginal cost is:

		$
Direct materials	4 kilos at $2 per kilo	8
Direct labour	3 hours at $6 per hour	18
		26

The standard sales price is $50 per unit and the standard contribution $24 per unit. Budgeted fixed costs were $30,000, giving a budgeted profit of $18,000.

Due to severe material shortages, the company had to switch to a less efficient and more expensive material, and it was decided in retrospect that the realistic (ex post) standard direct material cost should have been 5 kilos at $3 per kilo = $15 per unit.

Actual results were as follows:

Actual production and sales: 2,400 units

		$	$
Sales revenue			115,000
Direct materials	12,300 kilos at $3 per kilo	36,900	
Direct labour	7,500 hours at $6.10 per hour	45,750	
Total variable costs			82,650
Actual contribution			32.350
Actual fixed costs			32,000
Actual profit			350

Required:

Prepare an operating statement with planning and operational variances that reconciles the budgeted and actual profit figures.

(15 marks)

Test your understanding 11

It might be argued that only operational variances have significance for performance measurement. Planning variances cannot be controlled and so have little or no value for performance reporting.

Required:

State briefly, with your reason(s), whether you agree with this point of view.

(5 marks)

Test your understanding 12 – FB

FB makes and sells a single product. The standard cost and revenue per unit are as follows:

		$
Selling price		400
Direct material A	5 kg at $25 per kg	125
Direct material B	3 kg at $22 per kg	66
Direct labour	3 hours at $10 per hour	30
Variable overheads	3 hours at $7 per hour	21
Standard contribution		158

The budgeted production and sales for the period in question were 10,000 units.

The mix of materials can be varied and therefore the material usage variance can be sub-divided into mix and yield variances.

For the period under review, the actual results were as follows:

Production and sales		9,000 units
		$
Sales revenue		4,455,000
Material cost	A – 35,000 kg	910,000
	B – 50,000 kg	1,050,000
Labour cost	30,000 hours	385,000
Variable overhead		230,000

The general market prices at the time of purchase for material A and material B were $21 per kg and $19 per kg respectively.

There were no opening or closing inventories during the period.

Required:

(a) Prepare a statement detailing the variances (including planning and operational, and mix and yield variances) which reconciles the budgeted contribution and the actual contribution.

(17 marks)

(b) Explain the results and usefulness to FB of the planning and operational, and mix and yield variances that you have calculated in your answer to part (a).

(8 marks)

(Total: 25 marks)

Test your understanding answers

Example 1

(a) Mix variance (Individual units method)

		Material A	Material B	Material C	Total
		Kg	Kg	Kg	Kg
1	Actual input	14,000	5,500	5,500	25,000
2	Actual input in std proportions				⇓
	50%:20%:30%	12,500	5,000	7,500	⇐ 5,000
3	Difference in quantity	1,500 A	500 A	2,000 F	
4	× Std Price	× 1.10	× 2.40	× 1.50	
5	Mix variance	$1,650 A	$1,200 A	$3,000F	$150 F

(b) Mix variance (Weighted average method)

$$\text{Weighted average std cost} = \frac{600 \times 1.10 + 240 + 2.40 + 360 + 1.50}{1{,}200 \text{ kg}} = \$1.48/\text{kg}$$

	Material A	Material B	Material C	Total
	Kg	Kg	Kg	Kg
1 Actual input	14,000	5,500	5,500	25,000
2 Actual input in std proportions 50%:20%:30%	12,500	5,000	7,500	⇐25,000
3 Difference in quantity	1,500	500	– 2,000	
4 x Difference in price (weighted av. std price – Ind. material std price) × (1.48 – 1.10) × (1.48 – 2.40) × (1.48 – 1.50)	× 0.38	× – 0.92	– 0.02	
5 Mix variance	$570 F	$460 A	$40 F	$150 F

(c) **Yield variance**

This is calculated in exactly the same way under both methods.

$$\text{Std cost per kg of output} \;=\; \frac{600 \times 1.10 + 240 + 2.40 + 360 + 1.50}{1{,}000 \text{ kg}} \;=\; \$1.776/\text{kg}$$

		Kg
1	Std yield $25{,}000 \times \dfrac{1{,}000}{1{,}200}$	20,833.33
2	Actual yield	21,000
3		166.67 F
4	× Std price/cost per kg of output	× 1.776
	Yield variance	296 F

Example 2

The total labour cost variance for period 9 is $400 favourable (i.e. $5,500 standard cost less $5,100 actual cost). This may be analysed as follows:

Planning variance:

Original (ex-ante) standard less the revised (ex-post) labour cost
(550 Units × $10) – (550 Units × $8) = $1,100 favourable

Operational variances:

Labour efficiency:

(standard (ex-post) hours less actual hours) x standard hourly rate
((550 Units × 1.6 hours) – 1,200 hours) × $5 = $1,600 adverse

Labour rate:

(standard rate - actual rate) x actual hours
($5 – $4.25) × 1,200 = $900 favourable

Note that the three component variances add up to $400 favourable.

In this case, the separation of the labour cost variance into operational and planning components indicates a larger problem in the area of labour efficiency than might otherwise have been indicated. The operational variances are based on the revised (ex-post) standard and this gives a more meaningful performance benchmark than the original (ex-ante) standard

Example 3

Operating Statement

	$	$
Budgeted contribution		52,000
Sales volume contribution variance		–
Sales price variance		116,000 F
		168,000

		Adverse	Favourable
Cost variances			
Direct material price	($10 × 10,800) − $194,000		86,400
Direct material usage	(10,000 − 10,800) × $10		8,000
Direct labour rate	($8 × 5,800) − $69,600)		23,200
Direct labour efficiency	(6,000 − 5,800) × $8	1,600	
		1,600	117,600 116,000 A
Actual contribution			52,000

As the managing director states, and the above analysis shows, the overall variance for the company was zero: the adverse cost variances exactly offset the favourable sales price variance.

However, this analysis does not clearly indicate the efficiency with which the company operated during the period, as it is impossible to tell whether some of the variances arose from the use of inappropriate standards, or whether they were due to efficient or inefficient implementation of those standards. In order to determine this, a revised ex post plan should be constructed, setting out the standards that, with hindsight, should have been in operation during the period. These revised ex post standards are shown under (B) below.

	(A) Original plan	$	(B) Revised ex ante plan	$	(C) Actual result	$
Sales	(1,000 × $200)	200,000	(1,000 × $330)	330,000	(1,000 × $316)	316,000
Materials	(10,000 × $10)	100,000	(10,000 × $17)	170,000	(10,800 × $18)	194,400
Labour	(6,000 × $8)	48,000	(6,000 × $12.50)	75,000	(5,800 × $12)	69,600

	$	$
Planning variances (A – B)		
Sales price	130,000 F	
Materials price	70,000 A	
Labour rate	27,000 A	
	———	
		33,000 F
Operational variances		
Sales price (B – C)	14,000 A	
Materials price (10,800 × $1)	10,800 A	
Materials usage (800 × $17)	13,600 A	
Labour rate (5,800 × $0.50)	2,900 F	
Labour efficiency (200 hrs × $12.50)	2,500 F	
	———	
		33,000 A

A comparison of (B) and (C) produces operational variances, which show the difference between the results that were actually achieved and those that might legitimately have been achievable during the period in question. This gives a very different view of the period's operations. For example, on the cost side, the labour rate variance has changed from adverse to favourable, and the material price variance, while remaining adverse, is significantly reduced in comparison to that calculated under the traditional analysis; on the sales side, the sales price variance, which was particularly large and favourable in the traditional analysis, is transformed into an adverse variance in the revised approach, reflecting the fact that the company failed to sell at prices that were actually available in the market.

A comparison of the original plan (A) with the revised plan (B) allows the planning variances to be identified. As noted at the beginning of this section, these variances are uncontrollable by operating, staff, and may or may not have been controllable by the original standard-setters at the start of the budget period. Where a revision of standards is required due to environmental changes that were not foreseeable at the time the budget was prepared, the planning variances are truly uncontrollable. However, standards that failed to anticipate known market trends when they were set will reflect faulty standard-setting: it could be argued that these variances were controllable (avoidable) at the planning stage.

Test your understanding 1

Material A usage variance

AQ SP = 1,000 × $4 = $4,000

Variance = $2,400 F

SQ SP = (160 units × 10 kg/unit) × $4 = $6,400

Material B usage variance

AQ SP = 1,460 × $6 = $8,760

Variance = $10,440 F

SQ SP = (160 units × 20 kg/unit) × $6 = $19,200
Total usage variance = $2,400 + $10,440 = $12,840

Material mix variance

Material	Std mix	Actual material usage (kgs)	Actual usage @ std mix (kgs)	Mix variance (kgs)	Std cost per kg ($)	Mix variance ($)
A	10/30	1,000	820	180 A	4	720 A
B	20/30	1,460	1,640	180 F	6	1,080 F
		2,460	2,460	0	–	360 F

Material yield variance

Material	Std usage for actual output (kgs)	Actual usage @ std mix (kgs)	Yield variance (kgs)	Std cost per kg ($)	Yield variance ($)
A	160 × 10 kg = 1,600	820	780 F	4	3,120 F
B	160 × 20 kg = 3,200	1,640	1,560 F	6	9,360 F
	4,800	2,460	2,340 F	–	12,480 F

Alternatively, the material yield variance can be calculated in total using the following method:

(1) Total input = 1,000 kgs + 1,460 kgs = 2,460 kgs.	
This should produce (÷ 30 kgs)	82 units of output
(2) 2,460 kgs did produce	160 units of output
	———————
(3) Difference = yield variance in units	78 units F
	———————
(4) Value at the standard cost of	$160 per unit
(5) Yield variance	$12,480 F

Total mix and yield variance = $12,480 F + $360 F = $12,840 F (as per the usage variance)

Test your understanding 2

Individual units mix variance

	Skilled Labour	Unskilled Labour	Total
	Hrs	Hrs	Hrs
1 Actual input	5,250	5,250	10,500 ⇓
2 Actual input in std proportions 6:4	6,300	4,200 ⇐	10,500
	——	——	——
3 Difference in quantity	1,050 F	1,050 A	
4 × Std Price	× 12	× 7	
	——	——	
5 Mix variance	$12,600 F	$7,350 A	$5,250F

Weighted average method

$$\text{Weighted average std rate} \quad = \quad \frac{6 \times \$12 + 4 \times \$7}{6 \text{ hours} + 4 \text{ hours}} \quad = \$10 \text{ per hour}$$

Weighted average mix variance

	Skilled Labour	Unskilled Labour	Total
	Hrs	Hrs	Hrs
1 Actual input	5,250	5,250	10,500 ⇓
2 Actual input in std proportions 6:4	6,300	4,200	⇐ 10,500
3 Difference in hours	−1,050	1,050	
4 x Difference in rate (weighted average std rate − individual labour std rate) × (10 − 12) × (10 − 7)	× −2	× 3	
5 Mix variance	$2,100 F	$3,150 F	$5,250 F

Yield variance (same answer for both methods)

$$\text{Std cost per unit of output} \quad = \quad \frac{6 \times \$12 + 4 \times \$7}{1 \text{ unit}} \quad = \$100 \text{ per unit}$$

	Hrs
1 Std yield $10{,}500 \text{ hours} \times \dfrac{1 \text{ unit}}{10 \text{ hours}}$	1,050
2 Actual yield	1,000
3	50 A
4 × Std price/cost per kg of output	× 100
Yield variance	$5,000 A

Test your understanding 3

Average number of drinks per passenger = 25 / 10 = 2.5

Weighted standard average cost per drink = $17.25 / 25 = $0.69

	Drinks
300 passengers should consume (× 2.5 drinks)	750
They did consume	850
Yield variance in number of drinks	100 (A)
× weighted standard average cost per drink	$0.69
Yield variance	$69 (A)

	Actual usage	Standard mix	Mix variance	Standard cost per drink	Mix variance
	Drinks	Drinks	Drinks		$
Low cost	215 (5)	170	45 (A)	$0.25	11.25 (A)
Medium cost	280 (8)	272	8 (A)	$0.50	4.00 (A)
High cost	355 (12)	408	53 (F)	$1.00	53.00 (F)
	850	850			**37.75 (F)**

Mix and yield variances

Actual output was 960; therefore the standard input material quantity (with an expected loss of 20%) is 960/0.8 = 1,200 kg (to be mixed 50% X, 30% Y and 20% Z).

The standard cost per litre of input was

Material	Input	Standard price	Total cost
	kg	$	$
X	500	5.00	2,500
Y	300	6.00	1,800
Z	200	7.00	1,400
	1,000		5,700

Standard price per kg = $5.70

(i) *Yield variance*

Standard input	1,200
Actual input	1,280
Variance	80kg Adverse
Standard price per kg of input	$5.70
Yield variance	$456.00 Adverse

(ii) *Mix variance*

Material	Standard mix	Actual mix	Mix variance	Standard price	Mix Variance
	kg			$	$
X	640	600	40 F	5.00	200 F
Y	384	380	4 F	6.00	24 F
Z	256	300	44 A	7.00	308 A
	1,280 kg	1,280 kg			84 A

Test your understanding 5

Material mix variance

The material mix variance is not affected by the material wastage and should be calculated in the normal way:

Material	Std mix	Actual material usage (kgs)	Actual usage @ std mix (kgs)	Mix variance (kgs)	Std cost per kg ($)	Mix variance ($)
S1	8/16	8,284	9,576.5	1,292.5 F	0.30	387.75 F
S2	5/16	7,535	5,985.3	1,549.7 A	0.50	774.85 A
S3	3/16	3,334	3,591.2	257.2 F	0.40	102.88 F
		19,153	19,153	0	–	284.22 A

Material yield variance

The yield variance will take account of the material wastage of 10%:

Material	Std usage for actual output (kgs)	Actual usage @ std mix (kgs)	Yield variance (kgs)	Std cost per kg ($)	Yield variance ($)
S1	8/16 = 8,560	9,576.5	1,016.5 A	0.30	304.95 A
S2	5/16 = 5,350	5,985.3	635.3 A	0.50	317.65 A
S3	3/16 = 3,210	3,591.2	381.2 A	0.40	152.48 A
	15,408 × 100/90 = 17,120	19,153	2,033 A	–	775. 08 A

Material usage variance

Total = $775.08 A + $284.22 A = $1,059.3 A

Test your understanding 6

Conventional approach

				$	
SHSR					
5 hrs/unit x 250 units	x	$10/hr	=	12,500	Efficiency
AHSR					$2,000 A
1,450 hrs	x	$10/hr	=	14,500	
AHAR					$1,450 F
			=	13,050	Rate

Planning and operational approach

Planning variance

Efficiency (5 hrs/unit − 6 hrs/unit) x 250 units x $10/hr $2,500 A

Operational variances

				$	
SHSR					
6 hrs/unit x 250 units	x	$10/hr	=	15,000	Efficiency
AHSR					$500 F
1,450 hrs	x	$10/hr	=	14,500	
AHAR					$1,450 F
			=	13,050	Rate

Test your understanding 7

(a) **Traditional variances**

AQAP =		$41,500
		Price variance $2,500 F
AQSP =	11,000 × $4 =	$44,000
		Usage variance $4,800 A
SQSP =	1400 × 7 × $4 =	$39,200

(b) **Planning variances**

RSQ × RSP =	1,400 × 8 × $3.80=	$42,560
		Price variance $2,240 F
RSQ × SP =	1,400 × 8 × $4 =	$44,800
		Usage variance $5,600 A
SQ × SP =	1,400 × 7 × $4 =	$39,200

(c) **Operational variances**

AQ × AP =		$41,500	$300 F
		Price variance	
AQ × RSP =	11,000 × $3.80 =	$41,800	
		Usage variance	$760 F
RSQ × RSP =	1,400 × 8 × $3.80=	$42,560	

Test your understanding 8

(a) Budgeted and actual profits

Budget	Kitchens	Bathrooms	Total
	$m	$m	$m
Sales	40	14	54
Direct costs	(22)	(6)	(28)
Central services	(10)	(5)	(15)
Budgeted profit	8	3	11

Actual	Kitchens	Bathrooms	Total
	$m	$m	$m
Sales	33.8	15.25	49.05
Direct costs	(20.8)	(6.75)	(27.55)
Central services	(6.5)	(6.25)	(17.50)
Budgeted profit	6.5	2.25	4.00

(b) Sales variances

Sales price variance	Kitchens	Bathrooms	Total
	$	$	$
Standard sales price	10,000	7,000	
Actual sales price	13,000	6,100	
Variance	3,000 F	900 A	
Actual sales quantity	× 2,600	× 2,500	
Sales price variance	7,800,000 F	2,250,000 A	5,550,000 F

Sales mix profit variances

	Standard mix	Actual mix	Variance (units)	Profit per unit ($)	Variance ($m)
Kitchens	3,400	2,600	800 (A)	$2,000	1.60 (A)
Bathrooms	1,700	2,500	800 (F)	$1,500	1.20 (F)
Total	5,100	5,100			0.40 (F)

Sales quantity profit variances

	Standard mix	Budgeted sales	Variance (units)	Profit per unit ($)	Variance ($m)
Kitchens	3,400	4,000	600 (A)	$2,000	1.20 (A)
Bathrooms	1,700	2,000	300 (A)	$1,500	0.45 (A)
Total	5,100	6,000			1.65 (A)

Check

Sales volume variances

Kitchens   (4,000 – 2,600) × $2,000 = $2.8m A

Bathrooms   (2,000 – 2,500) × $1,500 = $0.75m F

Total $2.05m

Sales volume variance   = mix variance + quantity variance
                          = $0.4m A + $1.65m A = $2.05 m

(c) **Reconciliation of profits**

	Favourable ($m)	Adverse ($m)	$m
Budgeted profit (from part a)			11.00
Sales mix variance (from part b)			
– kitchens		1.60	
– bathrooms	1.20		
Sales quantity variance (from part b)			
– kitchens		1.20	
– bathrooms			
Sales price variances (from part b)			
– kitchens	7.80		
– bathrooms		2.25	
Direct costs (W1)			
– kitchens		6.50	
– bathrooms	0.75		
Central services (W2)			
– volume (kitchens)		3.50	
– volume (bathrooms)	1.25		
– expenditure		2.50	
	11.00	18.00	7 A
Actual profit (from part a)			4

Workings

(W1) **Direct cost variances:**

Kitchens   2,600 × (5,500 – 8,000) = \$6.5m A
Bathrooms 2,500 × (3,000 – 2,700) = \$0.75m F

(W2) **Central services volume variances:**

Kitchens (4,000 – 2,600) × \$2,500 = \$3.5m A
Bathrooms (2,500 – 2,000) × \$2,500 = \$1.25m F
Central services expenditure variance = \$15m – \$17.5m = \$2.5m A

(d) **Performance of the company for the year**

(Actual profit at $4m is $7m below budgeted profit, a shortfall of 64%). The main causes are as follows:

- an overall fall in the total volume of sales resulting in a sales quantity variance of $1.65m A. The lower than expected volume has also resulted in central services costs being under absorbed as shown by the volume variances (net impact $2.25A).

- the sales mix has also switched from more profitable kitchens to less profitable bathrooms and this is reflected in the sales mix variance of $0.4m A.

- the impact of the lower volume of kitchen sales has been partially offset by the favourable price variance for kitchens. It is possible that a higher proportion of jobs are of the highly customised category rather than the 'off the shelf' packages. This has led to higher average prices being charged but also higher direct costs being incurred. The opposite seems to have occurred with bathrooms.

- Central services costs have exceeded budget by $2.5m. This may be due to higher costs incurred designing customised jobs.

It would be worth investigating whether the extra price charged for customised designs is covering all of the additional costs incurred. Higher prices may be necessary or better control of costs.

Tutorial note

For part (a): The information given in the question suggests that an OAR of $2,500 per job is used to absorb central services costs. This means that there is under absorbed central services cost of $17.5 - 6.5 - 6.25 = $4.75m$. There is no indication that this is charged to profit centres but total costs must be shown to arrive at total profit.

Test your understanding 9 – ATS LTD

Operating Statement for ATS Ltd

		$	$
Original budgeted contribution	1,200 × $26		31,200
Sales volume contribution variance	(1,000 – 1,200) × $26		5,200 A
Budgeted contribution on actual sales			26,000

Planning variances

		$	$
Sales price	($110 – $130) × 1,000	20,000 F	
Material price	($3 – $4.50) × 8 × 1,000	12,000 A	
			8,000 F
Revised contribution on actual sales			34,000

Operational variances

		$	$
Sales price	($130 – $135) × 1,000	5,000 F	
Material price	($4.50 – $4) × 7,800	3,900 F	
Material usage	(8,000 – 7,800) × $4.50	900 F	
Labour rate	($10 – $10.40) × 6,250	2,500 A	
Labour efficiency	(6,000 – 6,250) × $10	2,500 A	
			4,800 F
Actual contribution			38,800

Test your understanding 10

In this example, since the change in both the material usage and material price are inter-related, the total planning variance only is reported in the operating statement below.

	$
Budgeted profit	18,000
Budgeted fixed costs	30,000
Budgeted contribution	48,000
Planning variance	16,800 (A)
Revised budgeted contribution	31,200
Sales volume contribution variance	9,600 (F)
Budgeted contribution on actual sales	40,800
Operational variances	
Sales price	5,000 (A)
Materials usage	900 (A)
Direct labour rate	750 (A)
Direct labour efficiency	1,800 (A)
Actual contribution	32,350
Budgeted fixed costs	30,000
Fixed cost expenditure variance	2,000 (A)
Actual profit	350

Operational variances

Materials price	$
12,300 kilos should cost (× $3)	36,900
They did cost	36,900
Direct materials price variance	0

Materials usage	Kilos
2,400 units of product should use (× 5 kilos)	12,000
They did use	12,300
Direct materials usage variance (in kilos)	300 (A)
Standard price per kilo (ex post)	$3
Direct materials usage variance	$900

Labour rate	$
7,500 hours should cost (× $6)	45,000
They did cost	45,750
Direct labour rate variance	750 (A)

Labour efficiency	*Hours*
2,400 units of product should take (× 3 hours)	7,200
They did take	7,500
Direct labour efficiency variance (in hours)	300 (A)
Standard rate per hour	$6
Direct labour efficiency variance	$1,800 (A)

Sales price	$
2,400 units should sell for (× $50)	120,000
They did sell for	115,000
Sales price variance	5,000 (A)

Fixed overhead expenditure	$
Budgeted fixed costs	30,000
Actual fixed costs	32,000
Fixed cost expenditure variance	2,000 (A)

Sales volume	*Units*
Budgeted sales	2,000
Actual sales	2,400
Sales volume variance (in units)	400 (F)
Standard contribution per unit	$24
Sales volume contribution variance	$9,600 (F)

Planning variances

Material costs	$ / unit
Ex ante standard per unit (4 kilos × $2)	8.0
Ex post standard per unit (5 kilos × $3)	15.0
Planning variance per unit	7.0 (A)
Actual units produced	× 2,400
Total planning variance	**$16,800** (A)

Test your understanding 11

A performance reporting and management control system depends on both reliable planning as well as control over operating activities.

Some planning variances might be caused by factors that could not have been foreseen in advance. However, some planning variances might be caused by weaknesses in the planning process. If so, they can be significant and indicate the need for better planning procedures in the future.

Test your understanding 12 – FB

Key answer tips

The planning variances may be based upon budget or actual level of activity, depending upon at what point the sales volume variance was calculated. It is most common in the exam to base the planning variance on the actual units produced.

The mix variance may be calculated using either the individual units method or the weighted average price method. The total result, which is the important figure in this question, will be the same.

	$000	$000
Original budgeted contribution (10,000 × $158)		1,580
Planning variances		
Material A price ($25 – $21) × 5 kg × 9,000	180 F	
Material B price ($22 – $19) × 3 kg × 9,000	81 F	
	—	
		261 F
Sales volume variance (9,000 – 10,000) × $158		158 A
		—
Revised contribution on actual sales		1,683
		—

NOTE

If the planning variances were calculated based on actual sales (this method is not commonly used in exam questions but is shown here for completeness), the first part of the answer would appear as follows:

	$000	$000
Original budgeted contribution (10,000 × $158)		1,580
Planning variances		
Material A price ($25 – $21) × 5 kg × 10,000	200 F	
Material B price ($22 – $19) × 3 kg × 10,000	90 F	
	—	
		290 F
Sales volume variance (9,000 – 10,000) × $187 (W1)		187 A
		—
Revised contribution		1,683
		—

Operational variances

Selling price ($400 – $495) × 9,000	855 F
Material A price (35,000 × $21) – $910,000	175 A
Material B price (50,000 × $19) – $1,050,000	100 A
Mix variance (W2)	36 F
Yield variance (W3)	263 A
Direct labour rate (30,000 hr × $10) – $385,000	85 A
Direct labour efficiency (9,000 × 3 – 30,000) × $10	30 A
Variable overhead expenditure (30,000 hr × $7) – $230,000	20 A
Variable overhead efficiency (9,000 × 3 – 30,000) × $7	21 A
	───
Total operational variances	197 F
	───
	1,880
	───

The above variances can also be calculated as follows:

Material A variance

$

AQSP

35,000 kg × $21 / kg = 735,000 ⎤
                                    ⎬ $175,000 A
AQAP   ⎥ Price
= 910,000 ⎦

Material B variance

$

AQSP

50,000kg × $19 / kg = 950,000 ⎤
                                  ⎬ $100,000 A
AQAP   ⎥ Price
= 1,050,000 ⎦

Labour variances

$

SHSR

3 hrs / unit × 9,000 units × $10 / hr = 270,000 ⎤ Efficiency
                                                  ⎬ $30,000 A
AHSR   ⎥
30,000 hrs × $10 / hr = 300,000 ⎬
                                                  ⎥ $85,000 A
AHAR   ⎦ Rate
= 385,000

Variable overhead variances

					$	
SHSR						
3 hrs / unit	× 9,000 units	×	$7 / hr	=	189,000	Efficiency
AHSR						$21,000 A
	30,000 hrs	×	$7 / hr	=	210,000	
AHAR						$20,000 A
				=	230,000	Rate

Sales price variance

	$
Std selling price	400
Actual selling price $4,455,000/9,000 units	495
	95 F
× Actual no of units sold	× 9,000
	$855,000 F

Workings

(W1) **Revised contribution per unit**

	$
Selling price	400
Material A 5 kg × $21	(105)
Material B 3 kg × $19	(57)
Direct labour 3 hr × $10	(30)
Variable overhead 3 hr × $7	(21)
Contribution	187

(W2) Mix variance

Note: A method is not specified. Use individual units method if given a choice as it is quicker and easier than the weighted average price method.

Material	Standard mix	Actual mix	Difference		@ Standard price	Variance
	000s	000s	000s			$000
A	53.125	35	18.125 F		$21	380.625 F
	31.875	50	18.125 A		$19	344.375 A
B	85	85	Nil			36.25 F

Standard mix of A : B is 5 kg : 3 kg

Hence, standard mix of actual input is:

$$A = 85 \times \frac{5}{8} = 53.125$$

$$A = 85 \times \frac{3}{8} = 31.875$$

(W3) Yield variance

Standard yield from actual input 85,000 kg ÷ 8 kg pu	10,625	units
Actual yield (output)	9,000	units
	1,625	units
@ Average price per unit of **output** (5 kg × $21) + (3 kg × $19)	$162	
Variance	$263,250	A

(W4)

	$000
Sales revenue	4,455
Less: Material A	(910)
Material B	(1,050)
Labour cost	(385)
Variable overhead	(230)
	1,880

(b) **Planning and operational variances**

The actual contribution is $300,000 higher than budget, despite sales volume falling from 10,000 units to 9,000 units. At first this appears to be an extraordinarily strong result. However, by calculating planning variances a new perspective emerges.

Both materials A and B were originally budgeted at prices that were quite substantially higher than the general market prices that emerged during the period. Material A could be bought at $4 less per kg than originally planned. This reduction in general market price immediately leads to a saving of $180,000 on the original budgeted cost. This is a significant saving. Similarly, material B's reduction in market price lead to a saving in the budget of $81,000. Planning variances indicate this large uncontrollable saving experienced by FB.

Once the budget is amended to reflect the new standard costs of the materials, actual results can be compared to the new budget. This exercise involves calculating operational variances. The operational variances for FB are quite revealing. There was a selling price variance of $855,000 favourable. However, virtually all the other variances were adverse. This would seem to indicate that FB did not perform particularly well in the latest period.

Planning and operational variances are useful for several reasons:

(1) They permit actual results to be compared to realistic up-to-date standards.

(2) The system is likely to provide more useful information for management.

(3) Operational staff may be more motivated by the feedback information, as their performance is judged against realistic standards.

(4) The importance of the planning function is emphasised – poor forecasting may be highlighted.

Mix and yield variances

The mix variance was $36,250 favourable. This was due to a far smaller proportion of the more expensive material A being used than was standard. The standard stated that 62.5% of material input should be material A. During the period, however, only 41% of input was material A. This is a significant difference. In each case the balance of material was material B (cheaper than A).

It is possible for FB to vary the input mix of raw materials. As this is the case, it would seem to be a useful exercise to examine how a deviation of the actual material mix from the expected mix has had an impact on costs.

Perhaps because of this mix variance there has been a massive drop in expected output. 85,000 kg of input should have produced 10,625 units of output. During the period only 9,000 units of output were produced. This is 15% below expectations. This has given rise to an adverse variance of $263,250 adverse. FB should investigate this significant variance and discover whether this variance was partly caused by the unusual mix in the period. It is probably important that FB correct the problems behind the yield variance and avoid it recurring in the future.

The budgeting framework

Chapter learning objectives

Lead	Component
B1. Explain the purposes of forecasts, plans and budgets.	(a) Explain why organisations prepare forecasts and plans. (b) Explain the purposes of budgets, including planning, communication, co-ordination, motivation, authorisation, control and evaluation, and how these may conflict.
B2. Prepare forecasts of financial results.	(b) Calculate projected revenues and costs based on product/service volumes, pricing strategies and cost structures.
B3. Prepare budgets based on forecasts.	(a) Prepare a budget for any account in the master budget, based on projections/forecasts and managerial targets. (b) Apply alternative approaches to budgeting.

1 Chapter overview diagram

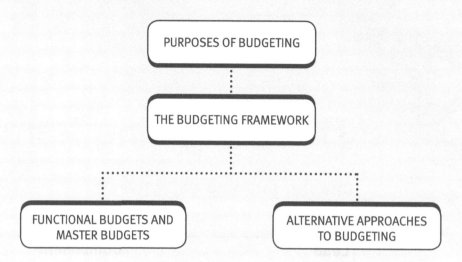

2 Budget

A quantitative or financial plan relating to the future. It can be for the company as a whole or for departments or functions or products or for resources such as cash, materials, labour, etc. It is usually for one year or less.

3 Purposes of budgeting

Budgets have several different purposes:

(1) Planning

(2) Control and evaluation

(3) Co-ordination

(4) Communication

(5) Motivation

(6) Authorisation

Purposes of budgets explained

Budgets have several different purposes:

(1) Planning

Budgets **compel** planning. The budgeting process forces management to look ahead, set targets, anticipate problems and give the organisation purpose and direction. Without the annual budgeting process the pressures of day-to-day operational problems may tempt managers not to plan for future operations. The budgeting process encourages managers to anticipate problems before they arise, and hasty decisions that are made on the spur of the moment, based on expediency rather than reasoned judgements, will be minimised. Corporate planners would regard budgeting as an important technique whereby long-term strategies are converted into shorter-term action plans.

(2) Control and evaluation

The budget provides the plan against which actual results can be compared. Those results which are out-of-line with the budget can be further investigated and corrected. The performance of a manager is often evaluated by measuring his success in achieving his budgets. The budget might quite possibly be the only quantitative reference point available

(3) Co-ordination

The budget serves as a vehicle through which the actions of the different parts of an organisation can be brought together and reconciled into a common plan. Without any guidance managers may each make their own decisions believing that they are working in the best interests of the organisation. A sound budgeting system helps to co-ordinate the different activities of the business and to ensure that they are in harmony with each other.

(4) Communication

Budgets communicate targets to managers. Through the budget, top management communicates its expectations to lower-level management so that all members of the organisation may understand these expectations and can co-ordinate their activities to attain them.

(5) Motivation

The budget can be a useful device for influencing managerial behaviour and motivating managers to perform in line with the organisational objectives..

(6) Authorisation

A budget may act as formal authorisation to a manager for expenditure, the hiring of staff and the pursuit of the plans contained in the budget.

The **budget period** is the time for which the budget is prepared. This is typically 1 year which reflects the fact that the financial reports for most organisations cover 1 year periods. But a budget can be for any length of time that suits management purposes.

Each budget period is normally split into control periods known as **budget intervals**. The budget interval is normally 3 months or 1 month. The 1 year budget is split into component parts for each budget interval and a budgetary control report is prepared at the end of each interval in which the budget and actual results are compared.

Senior managers will often get less junior managers and other members of staff involved in creating budgets. This helps satisfy one of the purposes of budgeting in that it can aid motivation. But it can have a detrimental impact on the other purposes such as distorting the evaluation of actual performance if managers incorporate 'slack' into the budget in order to make it easier to achieve.

Behavioural aspects of budgeting

Involving managers in the completion of a budget can help achieve some of the purposes of budgets but may distort others.

Some of the purposes that are **enhanced** by manager involvement are:

- **Planning.** Planning is taking place at many levels, and should be more accurate than if it simply takes place at a high level, by individuals who are not familiar with the day to day needs of the business. More junior managers will have better information as they are 'closer to the action' and this should improve the quality of budgets overall.

- **Communication.** There should be more communication across all levels of management. It might also make it possible to communicate overall strategic goals to managers by explaining to them the purpose of the budget being prepared and how it fits in to overall budgets and organisational goals.

- **Motivation.** Managers often want to take on extra responsibilities and get further involved in the decision making process. Giving them the power to set budgets might achieve this goal. Managers might also take more personal ownership of achieving budget goals which they have set and be more motivated to achieve what they have promised in the budget.

Whilst the following purposes might be **distorted**:

- **Co-ordination.** This may become more complicated and slower. This is because, not only does there need to be co-ordination between departments but there also has to be co-ordination between the different levels of management within each department. Managers will have to co-ordinate with each other and it may be that inaccuracies occur in budgets if individual manager cannot see the overall ('big') picture or do not understand fully the organisation's goals for the budget period.

- **Evaluation.** In some instances managers might build 'slack' into a budget that they control. This means that they will make it more easily achievable by overstating target costs and/or understating target revenues (if these are included in their budget). This will make it easier for them to achieve the budget targets and associated rewards. But it will make the evaluation of budget performance less useful for senior managers. For example, the variance system might only generate favourable variances because the original plan or standard was understated.

- **Authorisation.** It may be harder to control the authorisation of budget items if there are no checks on the manager. It may also be that managers disagree over budget responsibility and try to allocate costs to other managers rather than take responsibility for themselves.

But there this will not always be the case. Every manager and every company will react differently to a budgetary control system. For example, involvement of managers in one firm might lead to better motivation, but other managers may be reluctant to get involved and therefore become dissatisfied if they are asked to get involved in the process.

Conflicts between the goals of budgeting

These behavioural aspects help explain that many of the goals of budgeting are contradictory. One the one side we want to be able to fairly evaluate the performance of managers. But we also want to motivate managers and therefore, even if managers are not involved in the process, managers may find the budget too challenging and therefore reduce their effort. That in turn would distort any evaluation.

Likewise, we want budgets to act as a way of communicating organisational goals. But the budget themselves may distort the goals as they will be very short-term, be focused on cost reduction rather than, say, quality aspects, and they will solely focus on financial aspects of the organisation's goals. There is therefore a conflict between aiming to achieve financial control and communicating the organisation's goals.

Furthermore, the budget is designed to act as a plan for a manager or department. The manager may therefore follow this plan at the expense of other critical success factors that arise in the internal or external environment of the firm. For example, a production manager may continue to use the planned materials mix even if the sales department are indicating that customers would prefer a different product design and the purchasing department have adjusted their purchases accordingly. The production manager then has to choose between the plan and inter-departmental co-ordination.

Many of the conflicts arise due to the human nature of a budgetary control system. Managers do not always follow organisational goals, they do not always think long term, they may be wary of moving away from the plan etc. This provides a conflict between many of the goals of a budgetary control system which needs to be considered at a strategic level when implementing such a system.

Note: these ideas are explored in more detail in Paper P2.

4 Functional budgets and the master budget

A **master budget** for the entire organisation brings together the departmental or activity budgets for all the departments or responsibility centres within the organisation.

The structure of a budget depends on the nature of the organisation and its operations. In a manufacturing organisation, the budgeting process will probably consist of preparing several **functional budgets**, beginning with a sales budget (see 'principal budget factor' at the end of this section).

These stages in budgeting are illustrated in the following diagram.

Budget preparation

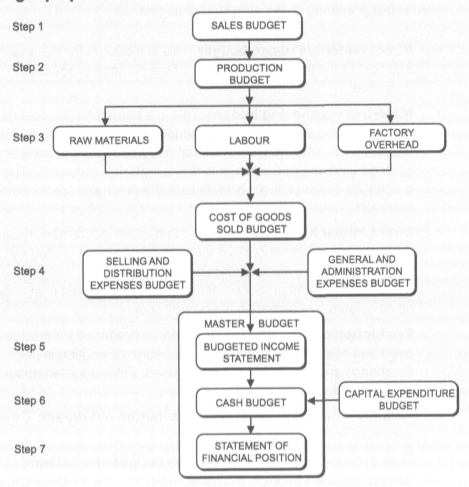

Step 1 — SALES BUDGET

Step 2 — PRODUCTION BUDGET

Step 3 — RAW MATERIALS | LABOUR | FACTORY OVERHEAD

COST OF GOODS SOLD BUDGET

Step 4 — SELLING AND DISTRIBUTION EXPENSES BUDGET | GENERAL AND ADMINISTRATION EXPENSES BUDGET

MASTER BUDGET

Step 5 — BUDGETED INCOME STATEMENT

Step 6 — CASH BUDGET | CAPITAL EXPENDITURE BUDGET

Step 7 — STATEMENT OF FINANCIAL POSITION

Explanation of each budget

- **Sales budget**. Budget for future sales, expressed in revenue terms and possibly also in units of sale. The budget for the organisation as a whole might combine the sales budgets of several sales regions.

- **Production budget**. A production budget follows on from the sales budget, since production quantities are determined by sales volume. The production volume will differ from sales volume by the amount of any planned increase or decrease in inventories of finished goods (and work-in-progress).

In order to express the production budget in financial terms (production cost), subsidiary budgets must be prepared for materials, labour and production overheads. Several departmental managers could be involved in preparing these subsidiary budgets.

- **Direct materials usage budget**. This is a budget for the quantities and cost of the materials required for the planned production quantities.

- **Materials purchasing budget**. This is a budget for the cost of the materials to be purchased in the period. The purchase cost of direct materials will differ from the material usage budget if there is a planned increase or decrease in direct materials inventory. The purchases budget should also include the purchase costs of indirect materials.

- **Direct labour budget**. This is a budget of the direct labour costs of production. If direct labour is a variable cost, it is calculated by multiplying the production quantities (in units) by the budgeted direct labour cost per unit produced. If direct labour is a fixed cost, it can be calculated by estimating the payroll cost.

- **Production overheads**. Budgets can be produced for production overhead costs. Where a system of absorption costing is used, overheads are allocated and apportioned, and budgeted absorption rates are determined.

- **Administration and sales and distribution overheads**. Other overhead costs should be budgeted.

- **Budgeted income statement, cash budget and balance sheet**. Having prepared budgets for sales and costs, the master budget can be summarised as an income statement for the period, a cash budget (or cash flow forecast) and a balance sheet (or statement of financial position) as at the end of the budget period.

If the budgeted profit, cash position or balance sheet are unsatisfactory, the budgets should be revised until a satisfactory planned outcome is achieved.

Example 1 – NEWTON LTD

Newton Ltd manufactures three products; the expected sales for each product are shown below.

	Product 1	Product 2	Product 3
Sales in units	3,000	4,500	3,000

Opening stock is expected to be:

Product 1	500 units
Product 2	700 units
Product 3	500 units

Management have stated their desire to reduce stock levels and closing stocks are budgeted as:

Product 1	200 units
Product 2	300 units
Product 3	300 units

Three types of material are used in varying amounts in the manufacture of the three products. Material requirements per unit are shown below:

	Product 1	Product 2	Product 3
Material M1	2 kg	3 kg	4 kg
Material M2	3 kg	3 kg	4 kg
Material M3	6 kg	2 kg	4 kg

The opening stock of material is expected to be:

Material M1	4,300 kg
Material M2	3,700 kg
Material M3	4,400 kg

Management are keen to reduce stock levels for materials as well and closing stocks are to be much lower. Expected levels are shown below:

Material M1	2,200 kg
Material M2	1,300 kg
Material M3	2,000 kg

Material prices are expected to be 10% higher than this year and current prices are $1.10/kg for material M1, $3.00/kg for material M2 and $2.50/kg for material M3.

Two types of labour are used in producing the three products. Standard hours per unit are shown below:

	Product 1	Product 2	Product 3
Skilled labour	3	1	3
Semi-skilled labour	3	3	4

Skilled labour are to be paid at the rate of $6/hour and semi-skilled labour at the rate of $4/hour.

Required:

Prepare budgets for:

(a) production (in quantity);

(b) materials usage (in quantity);

(c) materials purchases (in quantity and value);

(d) labour (in hours and value).

(25 marks)

Principal budget factor

When a key resource is in short supply and affects the planning decisions, it is known as the **principal budget factor** or **limiting budget factor**.

It is usually assumed in budgeting that sales demand will be the key factor setting a limit to what the organisation can expect to achieve in the budget period.

When the principal budget factor has been determined this should be the starting point for all other budgets.

Other limiting factors

In most organisations the principal budget factor is sales demand: a company is usually restricted from making and selling more of its products because there would be no sales demand for the increased output at a price which would be acceptable and/or profitable to the company.

Occasionally, however, there might be a shortage of a key resource, such as cash, raw material supplies, skilled labour or equipment. If a resource is in restricted supply, and the shortage cannot be overcome, the budget for the period should be determined by how to make the best use of this key budget resource, rather than by sales demand.

Principles such as linear programming, key factor analysis (neither of these first two techniques is examinable in this paper), throughput accounting and capital rationing (covered later in the text) could then be used to determine production plans.

5 Sensitivity analysis

There is always a significant degree of uncertainty concerning many of the elements incorporated within a business plan or budget. The budget officer is often required to report on such uncertainty in some way. There are various approaches to this issue and one of the most widely used is 'sensitivity analysis'.

A sensitivity analysis exercise involves revising the budget on the basis of a series of varied assumptions. **One assumption can be changed at a time** to determine the impact on the budget overall. For example, if sales quantities were to be changed the impact on profits, cash flow etc. could be observed.

When changing more than one variable at a time it may be better to use spreadsheets to simplify and speed up the process.

Example of sensitivity analysis

An organisation has a budget for the first quarter of the year as follows:

	$
Sales: 100 units @ $40 per unit	4,000
Variable costs: 100 units @ $20 per unit	(2,000)
Fixed costs	(1,500)
Profit	500

There is some uncertainty over the variable cost per unit and that cost could be anywhere between $10 and $30, with $20 as the 'expected' outcome. We are required to carry out a sensitivity analysis on this.

One approach to this would be to present the budget shown above as an 'expected' case but with two other cases as 'worst' and 'best' possible outcomes.

Worst-case budget ($30 unit variable cost)

	$
Sales: 100 units @ $40 per unit	4,000
Variable costs: 100 units @ $30 per unit	(3,000)
Fixed costs	(1,500)
Profit	(500)

Best-case budget ($10 unit variable cost)

	$
Sales: 100 units @ $40 per unit	4,000
Variable costs: 100 units @ $10 per unit	(1,000)
Fixed costs	(1,500)
Profit	1,500

This gives managers a range of possible outcomes and allows them to make decisions accordingly. In practice they may build in targets and monitoring points during the period to determine which budget is appearing most likely. This would allow them to take further action during the period rather than wait until the end of the quarter when it may be too late.

The effect of the change in variable costs on the statement of financial position can also be determined.

Let's assume that the opening position at the start of the quarter was as follows:

	$
Non-current assets	5,000
Receivables	1,500
Cash/ (overdraft)	500
Net assets	7,000
Equity	5,000
Profit and loss reserve	2,000
Capital	7,000

Sales are all on 6 weeks credit and all expenses are paid for immediately they are incurred. Three alternative budgeted statements of financial position at the end of quarter 1 can be produced as follows:

	Expected	Worst	Best
Non-current assets	5,000	5,000	5,000
Receivables	2,000	2,000	2,000
Cash/ (overdraft)	500	(500)	1,500
Net assets	7,500	6,500	8,500
Equity	5,000	5,000	5,000
Profit and loss reserve	2,500	1,500	3,500
Capital	7,500	6,500	8,500

Calculation of the individual figures should be fairly obvious. But, let us consider *the worst case* cash balance as an example:

	$
Cash inflow from sales	2,000 (being 50% of sales)
Cash outflow for expenses	(4,500)
Cash inflow from opening debtors	1,500
Opening cash balance	500
Closing cash balance	(500)

In practical budgeting, there may be uncertainty concerning a large number of factors within the budget, and sensitivity analysis may consist of a series of complex 'what if?' enquiries – reworking the budget, on the basis of a range of different scenarios. In large organisations with complicated budgets, such exercises may be very demanding. In the pre-computer era, the relevant calculations were all carried out manually. This could be a time-consuming and error-prone exercise.

Computer spreadsheets have made the task much easier. However, the spreadsheet has to be designed carefully in order to facilitate sensitivity analysis exercises. A well-designed spreadsheet allows a single correction (on a unit price or an hourly wage rate) to update the whole budget. Spreadsheet modelling is one of the most critical of the practical skills required by management accountants.

6 Fixed and flexible budgets

A **fixed** budget contains information on costs and revenues for one level of activity.

A **flexible** budget shows the same information, but for a number of different levels of activity. Flexible budgets are useful for both planning purposes and control purposes.

(1) When preparing a flexible budget, managers are forced to consider the different scenarios and their responses to them. Thus for a number of different situations, managers will have calculated their costs and revenues. If an unexpected event does occur, changing the level of activity, management will be better prepared.

(2) Budgetary control is the comparison of actual results against budget. Where the actual level of activity is different to that expected, comparisons of actual results against a fixed budget can give misleading results.

Illustration – Fixed & flexible budgets

The principle of a flexible budget

A company, which uses a just in time inventory control system, expects to use 4 kg of material to manufacture one unit of its product. However, the price per kg is uncertain – the supplier will offer discounts based on the amount of materials purchased as follows:

- for orders of 10,000 kgs or fewer the price will be $20 per kg

- for orders exceeding 10,000 kgs, the price will be $18 per kg

- for orders of 20,000 kgs or more, the price will be $15 per kg

The company has used this information to produce a range of flexible budgets:

Production	2,000 units	3,000 units	4,000 units	5,000 units
Materials usage	8,000 kgs	12,000 kgs	16,000 kgs	20,000 kgs
Cost per kg	$20	$18	$18	$15
Materials purchases budget	$160,000	$216,000	$288,000	$300,000

These budgets can then be used to calculate variances and compare actual performance at the end of the period when actual production levels are known.

If, for example, actual production and sales were 3,250 units with $220,000 spent on materials. A meaningful variance could only be calculated if the actual results were compared to a budget for 3,250 units. A revised, end-of-period budget for variance calculations would be produced – this is known as a flexed budget. A manager could then assess performance against this budget as follows:

	Original budget	Flexed budget	Actual results	Variance
Production	3,000 units	3,250 units	3,250 units	–
Cost per unit	$72*	$72*		
Materials purchases	$216,000	$234,000	$220,000	$14,000 F**

* the budgeted cost per unit at this volume is $18 per kg multiplied by 4 kgs per unit = $72 per unit

** the variance is calculated as the difference between the flexed budget and the actual results.

Further illustration on a flexed budget

A software company has the following annual budget:

	$	$
Sales revenue		480,000
Material costs	48,000	
Labour costs	200,000	
Other expenses	180,000	
		428,000
Budgeted profit		52,000

Sales are expected to be 120,000 units for the year, with a constant amount sold each month.

- Material costs vary with sales.

- 30% of labour costs are variable with sales, and the rest are fixed costs.

- Other expenses are part-fixed and part-variable. Variable expenses are 10% of sales.

At the end of month 6, the company had expected to sell 60,000 units at $4.00 each. Although it did manage to achieve the $4.00 selling price, it only managed to sell 50,000 units. The following report is prepared for the six months to date:

Budgeted and actual results for the first six months

	Original budget	Actual results	Difference
Sales volume	60,000	50,000	10,000 (A)
	$	$	$
Sales revenue	240,000	200,000	40,000 (A)
Material costs	24,000	16,000	8,000 (F)
Labour costs	100,000	94,000	6,000 (F)
Other expenses	90,000	89,000	1,000 (F)
	214,000	199,000	15,000 (F)
Profit	26,000	1,000	25,000 (A)

This comparison of actual results with a fixed budget does not provide useful control information. It does not account for the fact that sales were 10,000 units below the level expected (and there should therefore have been an lower 'target' for expenditure on materials, labour etc.).

A more useful control report would be prepared by comparing actual results with a flexed budget.

	Original budget	Flexed budget	Actual results	Difference
Sales volume	60,000	50,000	50,000	–
	$	$	$	$
Sales	240,000	200,000	200,000	–
Materials	24,000	20,000	16,000	4,000 (F)
Labour costs (see W1)	100,000	95,000	94,000	1,000 (F)
Other expenses (see W2)	90,000	86,000	89,000	3,000 (A)
	214,000	201,000	199,000	2,000 (F)
Profit	26,000	(1,000)	1,000	2,000 (F)

Workings for the flexed budget:

(W1) **Labour costs:**

	$
Budgeted labour costs, original budget	200,000
Budgeted variable costs (30%)	60,000
Budgeted fixed costs	140,000

	$
Fixed cost budget for the first six months (× 6/12)	70,000
Flexible budget variable costs (50,000/60,000 × $30,000)	25,000
Total labour costs in the flexed budget	95,000

(W2) **Other expenses:**

	$
Budgeted other expenses, original budget	180,000
Budgeted variable costs (10% of $480,000)	48,000
Budgeted fixed costs	132,000

	$
Fixed cost budget for the first six months (× 6/12)	66,000
Flexed budget variable costs (50,000/60,000 × $24,000)	20,000
	———
Total labour costs in the flexed budget	86,000
	———

Reconciling budgeted and actual profit: sales variance

In order to reconcile the budgeted profit for a period with the actual profit or loss, a sales volume variance has to be calculated. If the flexed budget is prepared using marginal costing, the sales volume variance should be a contribution variance.

In the example above, the budgeted contribution margin should be calculated as a budgeted contribution/sales ratio:

	$	$
Sales revenue (for the year)		480,000
Material costs (all variable)	48,000	
Variable labour costs	60,000	
Variable other expenses	48,000	
	———	
Budgeted variable costs		156,000
		———
Budgeted contribution		324,000
		———

Budgeted contribution per unit would therefore be ($324,000/120,000) = $2.70 per unit.

The **sales volume contribution variance** is calculated in the same way as a sales volume variance in standard costing:

Budgeted sales for the 6 months	60,000	units
Actual sales for the 6 months	50,000	units
	———	
Sales Volume variance (in units)	10,000 (A)	units
	———	
Standard contribution per unit	$2.70	
Sales Volume contribution variance	$27,000 (A)	
	———	

Note: There is no sales price variance, because actual and standard sales price were the same.

7 Alternative approaches to budgeting

Incremental budgeting

The traditional approach to budgeting is to take the previous year's budget and to add on a percentage to allow for inflation and other cost increases. In addition there may be other adjustments for specific items such as an extra worker or extra machine.

> **Further explanation**
>
> - Fairly small changes are made to the current year's budget. For example, adjustments might be made to allow for a planned increase or decline in sales volume, and for inflationary increases in sales prices and costs.
>
> - A check is then made to ensure that the budget produced in this way meets the performance targets of the organisation. For example, the company might have a target of keeping the operating costs to sales ratio at less than, say, 60%.
>
> In a static business environment, incremental budgets are little more than 'last year's budget plus a percentage amount for inflation'.

Advantages and disadvantages of incremental budgeting

Advantages	Disadvantages
- simple	- backward looking
- cheap	- builds on previous inefficiencies
- suitable in stable environments	- doesn't remove waste / inefficiencies
- most practical	- unsuited to changing environments
	- targets are too easy
	- activities are not justified
	- encourages over-spending

Further explanation

The advantage of incremental budgeting is that it is an easy, quick and cheap method of preparing budgets for what may be many cost centres in a large organisation. However, the traditional approach has severe disadvantages.

Advantages

(1) It is a simple, low-cost budgeting system.

(2) If the business is fairly stable, the budgets produced by this method might be sufficient for management needs.

(3) There are some items of cost where an incremental budgeting approach is probably the most practical. For example, the easiest way of budgeting telephone expenses for the next year might be to base the planned cost on the previous year's budget (or possibly actual costs in the current year).

Disadvantages

(1) The main disadvantage is that it assumes that all current activities should be continued at the current level of operations and with the same allocation of resources.

(2) It is backward-looking in nature, since next year's budget is based on what has happened in the past. In a dynamic and rapidly-changing business environment, this approach to planning is inappropriate.

(3) It is often seen as a desk-bound planning process, driven by the accounts department.

(4) The performance targets in the budget are often unchallenging, based on past performance. Incremental budgeting does not encourage managers to look for ways of improving the business.

(5) When there are excessive costs in the budget for the current year, these will be continued in the future. Incremental budgeting is not a planning system for cutting out waste and overspending.

(6) Consideration will not be given to the justification for each activity. They will be undertaken merely because they were undertaken the previous year.

(7) Different ways of achieving the objective will not be examined.

(8) Past inefficiencies will be continued.

(9) Managers know that if they fail to spend their budget, it is likely to be reduced next period. They therefore try to spend the whole budget, regardless of whether or not the expenditure is justified.

ZBB is one method which may be used to overcome these problems.

Zero-based budgeting

ZBB may be defined as:

'A method of budgeting whereby all activities are re-evaluated each time a budget is formulated. Each functional budget starts with the assumptions that the function does not exist, and is at zero cost. Increments of costs are compared with increments of benefits, culminating in the planned maximum benefit for a given budgeted cost.'

Zero-based budgeting (ZBB) is a radical alternative to incremental budgeting. In ZBB, all activities and costs are budgeted from scratch (a zero base). For every activity, managers look at its costs and its purpose, and consider whether there are alternative ways of doing it. Inessential activities and costs are identified and eliminated, by removing them from next year's budget.

ZBB in practice

Implementing ZBB

All activities are subjected to the most basic scrutiny, and answers sought to such fundamental question as:

(a) Should the activity be undertaken at all?

(b) If the company undertakes the activity, how much should be done and how well should it be done (e.g. should an economy or a deluxe service level be provided)?

(c) How should the activity be performed – in-house or subcontracted?

(d) How much would the various alternative levels of service and provision cost?

In order to answer these questions, all existing and potential organisational activities must be described and evaluated in a series of 'decision packages', giving the following four-step process to a ZBB exercise:

(1) Determine the activities that are to be used as the object of decision packages – the provision of home support for the elderly or provision of catering facilities for the workforce, for example – and identify the manager responsible for each activity.

(2) Request the managers identified in (1) above to prepare a number of alternative decision packages for those individual activities for which they are responsible. (At least three packages are normally requested: one that sets out what could be delivered with funding maintained at the current level; one for a reduced level of funding, e.g. 80% of the current level; and one for an enhanced level of funding, e.g. 120% of the current level.)

(3) Rank the decision packages in order of their contribution towards the organisation's objectives.

(4) Fund the decision packages according to the ranking established under (3) above until the available funds are exhausted.

Adoption of ZBB

ZBB has been adopted more widely in the public sector than the private, although examples of organisations regularly adopting a full ZBB approach are rare. Full-scale ZBB is so resource-intensive that critics claim that its advantages are outweighed by its implementation costs. However, it is not necessary to apply ZBB to the whole of an organisation; benefits can be gained from its application to specific areas. For example, in the public sector, a decision could be made regarding the overall size of the childcare budget, and ZBB could be applied to allocate resources within that particular field; similarly, in a business organisation, ZBB could be applied to individual divisions on a rotational basis. This selective application ensures that a thorough reappraisal of activities is undertaken regularly, but not so regularly that the process itself is a major drain on organisational resources.

Notwithstanding the criticisms, the main plank of the ZBB approach – the rejection of past budgets as a planning baseline – is being increasingly accepted.

Illustration 1

A company is conducting a ZBB exercise, and a decision package is being prepared for its materials handling operations.

- The manager responsible has identified a base package for the minimum resources needed to perform the materials handling function. This is to have a team of five workers and a supervisor, operating without any labour-saving machinery. The estimated annual cost of wages and salaries, with overtime, would be $375,000.

- In addition to the base package, the manager has identified an incremental package. The company could lease two fork lift trucks at a cost of $20,000 each year. This would provide a better system because materials could be stacked higher and moved more quickly. Health and safety risks for the workers would be reduced, and there would be savings of $5,000 each year in overtime payments.

- Another incremental package has been prepared, in which the company introduces new computer software to plan materials handling schedules. The cost of buying and implementing the system would be $60,000, but the benefits are expected to be improvements in efficiency that reduce production downtime and result in savings of $10,000 each year in overtime payments.

The base package would be considered essential, and so given a high priority. The two incremental packages should be evaluated and ranked. Here, the fork lift trucks option might be ranked more highly than the computer software.

In the budget that is eventually decided by senior management, the fork lift truck package might be approved, but the computer software package rejected on the grounds that there are other demands for resources with a higher priority.

Advantages and disadvantages of ZBB

Advantages	Disadvantages
• creates an environment that accepts change	• time-consuming
• better focus on goals	• expensive
• forward looking	• encourages short-termism
• improves resource utilisation	• management may lose focus on the true cost drivers
• better performance measures	• managers require new budgeting skills
• focuses managers to examine activities	• can result in arbitrary decisions

Further explanation

Advantages

- It helps to create an organisational environment where change is accepted.

- It helps management to focus on company objectives and goals. It moves budgeting away from number-crunching, towards analysis and decision-making.

- It focuses on the future rather than on the past.

- It helps to identify inefficient operations and wasteful spending, which can be eliminated.

- Establishing priorities for activities provides a framework for the optimum utilisation of resources. This assists decision-makers when some expenditures are discretionary.

- It establishes a measure of performance for each decision package. This measure can be used to monitor actual performance and compare actual with budget.

- It involves managers in the budgeting process. Unlike incremental budgeting, it is not a desk-bound exercise driven by the accounting department. Preparation of the decision packages will normally require the involvement of many employees, and thus provides an opportunity for their view to be considered. This involvement may produce useful ideas, and promote job satisfaction among the wider staff.

Disadvantages

- It is a time-consuming exercise. It is unlikely that an organisation will have the time to carry out a ZBB exercise every year.

- There is a temptation to concentrate on short-term cost savings at the expense of longer-term benefits.

- It might not be useful for budgeting for production activities or service provision, where costs and efficiency levels should be well-controlled, so that budgets can be prepared from forecasts of activity volume and unit costs.

- In applying ZBB, 'activities' may continue to be identified with traditional functional departments, rather than cross-functional activities, and thus distract the attention of management from the real cost-reduction issues. For example, it could be argued that the costs incurred in a warranty department are largely a function of the reliability of products, which itself is a function of actions and decisions taken elsewhere. If the warranty department is treated as an activity under ZBB, the focus of the decision packages is likely to be on providing the same level of customer service at reduced cost, or enhancing the level of customer service for the same cost. The main driver behind the department's cost – product reliability – may remain unaddressed in ZBB, as it is with the blanket cut approach.

- It might require skills from management that the management team does not possess.

- The ranking process can be difficult, since widely-differing activities cannot be compared on quantitative measures alone. For example, it might be difficult to rank proposals for spending on better service quality, improvements in safety in the work place or more spending on new product development.

Activity-based budgeting

Introduction

In a manufacturing business, budgeting for direct costs is relatively straightforward. The costs of direct materials and direct labour are assumed to vary with production, and once production levels have been estimated, budgeting the direct costs of production is a matter of simple arithmetic.

Budgeting for overhead costs is not so simple. Traditionally, there has been a tendency to take an incremental approach in budgeting for overhead costs, and prepare next year's budget by simply adding a percentage to the current year budget, to allow for inflation. Zero-based budgeting is one method of bringing greater discipline to the process of budgeting for overhead activities and costs. Another method is activity-based budgeting.

As its name should suggest, activity-based budgeting (ABB) takes a similar approach to activity-based costing. ABB is defined as: 'a method of budgeting based on an activity framework and utilising cost driver data in the budget-setting and variance feedback processes' (CIMA *Official Terminology*).

Whereas ZBB is based on budgets (decision packages) prepared by responsibility centre managers, ABB is based on budgeting for activities.

In its simplest form, ABB is simply about using costs determined via ABC to prepare budgets for each activity. The basic approach of ABB is to budget the costs for each cost pool or activity as follows:

(1) The cost driver for each activity is identified. A forecast is made of the number of units of the cost driver that will occur in the budget period.

(2) Given the estimate of the activity level for the cost driver, the activity cost is estimated. Where appropriate, a cost per unit of activity, known as the **cost driver rate**, is calculated.

(There will also be some general overhead costs that are not activity-related, such as factory rental costs and the salary cost of the factory manager. General overhead costs are budgeted separately.)

Illustration 2

Consider the following example:

Septran operates two rail services. The Northern line operated for 20,000 hours last year. It had 200 full time staff. The Southern line operated for 39,000 hours last year. It had 300 full time staff. Eight train staff are needed for each journey on both lines. The total overhead for indirect wages was $39m.

Next year the government want to promote greater use of train services in the north of the country. Septran expect this to result in approximately 10,000 more journey hours for the Northern line. Because of transfers between services and other knock on effects, this is also likely to result in an extra 5,000 journey hours for the Southern line.

The company want to used an ABB approach to budget for the indirect wages cost next year.

Step 1

Firstly, the company need to determine how costs should be allocated to each service (each service effectively becomes a 'cost pool'). This might be the number of journeys or the number of full time employees. For indirect wages Septran believe that the number of full time staff would be the most appropriate way to allocate costs to each cost pool.

Step 2

The total overheads are then allocated to each cost pool on this basis.

	Northern line	Southern line	Total
	$m	$m	$m
Indirect wage cost – split 200:300	15.6	23.4	39.0

Step 3

The company then need to determine the cost driver. Semptrap believe that the cost is driven by the number of journey hours in operation.

	Northern line	Southern line
Indirect wage cost – split 20:30	$15.6m	$23.4m
Number of journey hours	20,000	39,000
Cost driver rate	$780 per journey hour	$600 per journey hour

Step 4

These established cost drivers will then be used to prepare the budget for next year:

	Northern line	Southern line
Cost driver rate	$780 per journey hour	$600 per journey hour
Budgeted level of activity	30,000 hours	44,000 hours
Budgeted indirect wage cost	$23.4m	$26.4m

The total budgeted indirect wage cost for next year will be $49.8m.

Advantages and disadvantages of ABB

Advantages	Disadvantages
• useful when overheads are significant	• expensive to implement
• better cost control	• only suited to ABC users
• better information for management	
• useful for TQM environments	

Further explanation

The advantages of ABB are similar to those provided by activity-based costing.

- It draws attention to the costs of 'overhead activities'. This can be important where overhead costs are a large proportion of total operating costs.

- It provides information for the control of activity costs, by assuming that they are variable, at least in the longer term.

- It provides a useful basis for monitoring and controlling overhead costs, by drawing management attention to the actual costs of activities and comparing actual costs with what the activities were expected to cost.

- It also provides useful control information by emphasising that activity costs might be controllable if the activity volume can be controlled.

- ABB can provide useful information for a total quality management (TQM) programme, by relating the cost of an activity to the level of service provided (for example, stores requisitions processed) – Do the user departments feel they are getting a cost-effective service?

The system however does have some disadvantages:

- It is an expensive system to implement. New information systems are required and managers need to be trained in its use.

- It will also rely on the use of activity based costing (ABC) as the standard costing system.

8 Chapter summary

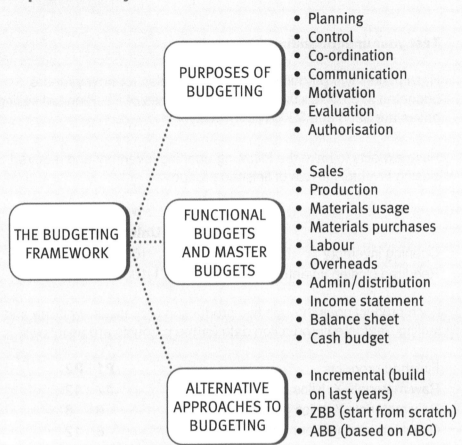

PURPOSES OF BUDGETING
- Planning
- Control
- Co-ordination
- Communication
- Motivation
- Evaluation
- Authorisation

THE BUDGETING FRAMEWORK

FUNCTIONAL BUDGETS AND MASTER BUDGETS
- Sales
- Production
- Materials usage
- Materials purchases
- Labour
- Overheads
- Admin/distribution
- Income statement
- Balance sheet
- Cash budget

ALTERNATIVE APPROACHES TO BUDGETING
- Incremental (build on last years)
- ZBB (start from scratch)
- ABB (based on ABC)

9 Practice questions

Test your understanding 1

Hash makes two products – P1 and P2. Sales for next year are budgeted at 5,000 units of P1 and 1,000 units of P2. Planned selling prices are $230 and $300 respectively.

Hash expects to have the following opening inventory and required closing inventory levels of finished products:

	P1 Units	P2 Units
Opening inventory	100	50
Required closing inventory	1,100	50

Each product goes through two production processes, whittling and fettling. Budgeted production data for the products are as follows:

Finished products:	P1	P2
Raw materials X: Kilos per unit	12	12
Raw materials Y: Kilos per unit	6	8
Direct labour hours per unit	8	12
Machine hours per unit: whittling	5	8
Machine hours per unit: fettling	3	4

Raw material inventories	Raw material	
	X	Y
Opening inventory (kilos)	5,000	5,000
Planned closing inventory (kilos)	6,000	1,000

Standard rates and prices:

Direct labour rate per hour	$7
Material X purchase price per kilo	$2
Material Y purchase price per kilo	$5

You should assume that the following production overhead absorption rates have already been established:

Production overhead absorption rates

Variable	$1 per direct labour hour
Fixed	$8 per direct labour hour

Budgeted administration and marketing overheads are $225,000.

The opening statement of financial position is expected to be as follows:

	$	$
Non current assets		950,000
Inventory	66,000	
Trade receivables	260,000	
Cash	25,000	
	351,000	
Trade payables	86,000	
Other short-term liabilities	24,000	
	110,000	
Net current assets		241,000
Net assets		1,191,000

Non-current assets in the statement of financial position are expected to increase by $40,000, but no change is expected in trade receivables, trade payables and other short-term liabilities.

There are no plans at this stage to raise extra capital by issuing new shares or obtaining new loans. The company currently has an overdraft facility of $300,000 with its bank.

Required:

For the budget period, prepare:

(a) a sales budget

(b) a production budget in units

(c) materials usage and purchases budgets

(d) a direct labour cost budget

(e) a machine utilisation budget

(f) a production cost budget

(g) a budgeted income statement

(h) a budgeted statement of financial position (or balance sheet) as at the end of the period.

(20 marks)

Test your understanding 2 – FLEMING PLC

Fleming plc has established a new subsidiary company on 1 November specifically for the manufacture and selling of a new product. The holding company will inject, for working capital purposes, $30,000 cash on 1 December. Fixed capital assets are being transferred from another company in the group.

Using the data given you are required to prepare a cash budget for each of the months of December, January, February and March. Calculations are to be made to the nearest $1.

Data

The variable production cost per unit is expected to be:

	$
Direct materials	4.0
Direct wages	3.0
Variable production overhead	1.5
Variable production cost	8.5

Fixed overhead estimated at $48,000 per annum is expected to be incurred in equal amounts each month from 1 December.

Production will commence in December and sales on 1 January. The estimated sales for the first four months are:

20X7	Units	Sales Value
		$
January	6,200	65,100
February	6,800	70,720
March	5,400	59,400
April	6,000	63,000

The following information is to be taken into consideration:

(1) Stocks, finished goods: 75% of each month's invoiced sales units to be produced in the month of sale and 25% of each month's invoiced sales units to be produced in the previous month.

(2) Stocks, direct materials: 50% of direct materials required for each month's production to be purchased in the previous month. Direct materials to be paid for in the month following purchase.

(3) Direct wages to be paid 75% in the month used and 25% in the following month.

(4) Variable production overhead: 40% to be paid in the month of use and the balance in the following month.

(5) Fixed overhead: 30% to be paid in the month in which it is incurred and 40% in the following month, the balance represents depreciation of fixed assets.

(6) Payments to be received from customers as follows:

January	$12,369
February	$45,987
March	$59,666

Prepare a cash budget

(25 marks)

Test your understanding 3 – RESEARCH DIVISION

For a number of years, the research division of Z plc has produced its annual budget (for new and continuing projects) using incremental budgeting techniques. The company is now under new management and the annual budget for 2004 is to be prepared using zero based budgeting techniques.

Required:

(a) Explain the differences between incremental and zero based budgeting techniques.

(5 marks)

(b) Explain how Z plc could operate a zero based budgeting system for its research projects.

(8 marks)

The operating divisions of Z plc have in the past always used a traditional approach to analysing costs into their fixed and variable components. A single measure of activity was used which, for simplicity, was the number of units produced. The new management does not accept that such a simplistic approach is appropriate for budgeting in the modern environment and has requested that the managers adopt an activity-based approach to their budgets for 2004.

Required:

(c) (i) Briefly explain activity-based budgeting (ABB)

(3 marks)

(ii) Explain how activity-based budgeting would be implemented by the operating divisions of Z plc.

(9 marks)

(Total: 25 marks)

Test your understanding 4

AW Inc produces two products, A and C. In the last year (20X4) it produced 640 units of A and 350 units of C incurring costs of $672,000. Analysis of the costs has shown that 75% of the total costs are variable. 60% of these variable costs vary in line with the number of A produced and the remainder with the number of C.

The budget for the year 20X5 is now being prepared using an incremental budgeting approach. The following additional information is available for 20X5:

- All costs will be 4% higher than the average paid in 20X4.
- Efficiency levels will remain unchanged.
- Expected output of A is 750 units and of C is 340 units.

Calculate the budgeted total variable cost of products A and C for the full year 20X5?

(4 marks)

Test your understanding 5

Identify which of the following statements is correct regarding the benefits to be gained from using ABB?

A   If there is much inefficiency within the operations of a business then ABB will identify and remove these areas of inefficiency

B   In a highly direct labour intensive manufacturing process, an ABB approach will assist management in budgeting for the majority of the production costs

C   In an organisation currently operating efficiently, where the next period will be relatively unchanged from the current one, then ABB will make the budgeting process simpler and quicker

D   If an organisation produces many different types of output using different combinations of activities then ABB can provide more meaningful information for budgetary control

(2 marks)

Test your understanding answers

Example 1 – NEWTON LTD

(a) **Production budget**

	Product 1	Product 2	Product 3
	units	units	units
Sales	3,000	4,500	3,000
+ Cl. inventory	200	300	300
	3,200	4,800	3,300
– Op. inventory	500	700	500
Production Qty	2,700	4,100	2,800

(b) **Material usage budget**

	Material M1	Material M2	Material M3
	Kg	Kg	Kg
Production Requirement			
2,700 Product 1	5,400	8,100	16,200
4,100 Product 2	12,300	12,300	8,200
2,800 Product 3	11,200	11,200	11,200
Usage Qty	28,900	31,600	35,600

(c) **Material purchases budget**

	Material M1	Material M2	Material M3
	Kg	Kg	Kg
Usage Qty	28,900	31,600	35,600
+ Cl. inventory	2,200	1,300	2,000
	31,100	32,900	37,600
– Op. inventory	4,300	3,700	4,400
Purchase Qty	26,800	29,200	33,200
	× $1.21	× $3.30	× $2.75
	$32,428	$96,360	$91,300

(d) Labour budget

	Skilled	Semi-skilled
	hrs	hrs
Production Requirement		
2,700 Product 1	8,100	8,100
4,100 Product 2	4,100	12,300
2,800 Product 3	8,400	11,200
Usage Qty	20,600	31,600
	× $6/hr	× $4/hr
	$123,600	$126,400

Test your understanding 1

(a) The sales budget

The sales budget is the plan for the volume of sales, in quantities and sales revenue. Unless there is a production limiting factor, the sales budget is the starting point for preparing the master budget.

Here, the sales budget is:

	Product P1		Product P2		Total
	Units	$	Units	$	$
Sales	5,000	1,150,000	1,000	300,000	1,450,000

In practice, organisations prepare their sales budget in more detail, with planned sales analysed by region and area as well as by product.

Comparative figures for the previous year will also usually be shown, to indicate whether planned sales are higher or lower than in the previous period, and by how much.

(b) The production budget

The production budget can be calculated by taking the sales budget in units and adjusting the figures for planned changes in inventories of finished goods (and work in progress). If there is a planned increase in inventory levels, production volume will exceed the planned sales volume. If inventory levels are planned to fall, production will be lower than sales.

	Product P1	Product P2
	Units	Units
Sales budget	5,000	1,000
planned closing inventory (finished goods)	1,100	50
	6,100	1,050
Trade payables	(100)	(50)
	6,000	1,000

Having established the production budget in quantity terms, the various elements of production cost can be budgeted.

(c) The raw materials usage and purchases budget

The raw materials usage budget is calculated from production quantities, in both units of raw material and direct material production cost.

The raw materials purchases budget is the usage budget adjusted for any planned increase or decrease in raw materials inventories.

In this example, raw materials are assumed to be direct materials only. In practice, a purchases budget is also required for indirect materials, where these are significant in volume and cost.

	Material X		Material Y		Total
To produce	Kilos	$	Kilos	$	$
6,000 units of P1	72,000	144,000	36,000	180,000	324,000
1,000 units of P2	12,000	24,000	8,000	40,000	64,000
Materials usage budget	84,000	168,000	44,000	220,000	388,000
Planned closing inventory	6,000	12,000	1,000	5,000	17,000
	90,000	180,000	45,000	225,000	405,000
Opening inventory	(5,000)	(10,000)	(5,000)	(25,000)	(35,000)
Materials purchases budget	85,000	170,000	40,000	200,000	370,000

(d) The direct labour cost and production overhead budgets

The cost budget for direct labour is also derived from the budgeted production volumes.

Since production overhead costs are being absorbed on a direct labour hour basis, the production overhead costs for each product can also be calculated.

	Product P1 6,000 units		Product P2 1,000 units		Total
	Hours	$	Hours	$	$
Direct labour cost	48,000	336,000	12,000	84,000	420,000
Variable production o/h	48,000	48,000	12,000	12,000	60,000
Fixed production o/h	48,000	384,000	12,000	96,000	480,000

(e) The machine utilisation budget

This is a budget for the number of machine hours required for production. A separate budget is required for each different group of machines. Once again, the starting point for preparing the budget is the production volume for each product. Since machine hours are not specifically costed, the budget is in hours only.

To produce:	Whittling Machine hours	Fettling Machine hours
6,000 units of P1	30,000	18,000
1,000 units of P2	8,000	4,000
Machine utilisation budget	38,000	22,000

(f) Production cost budget

The production budget has already been prepared in units. A production cost budget can now be prepared, for each product and in total.

	Product P1 6,000 $	Product P2 1,000 $	Total $
Direct materials:			
Material X	144,000	24,000	168,000
Material Y	180,000	40,000	220,000
	324,000	64,000	388,000
Direct labour	336,000	84,000	420,000
Variable production overhead	48,000	12,000	60,000
Fixed production overhead	384,000	96,000	480,000
Total production cost	1,092,000	256,000	1,348,000
Production cost per unit	$182	$256	

(g) Budgeted income statement

A budgeted income statement can now be prepared. The production cost of sales is calculated by adjusting the production cost budget to allow for changes in inventories of finished goods. Here, it is assumed that opening units of inventory have the same production cost per unit as units produced in the budget period.

	Product P1		Product P2	
Cost per unit	$182		$256	
	Units	$	Units	$
Opening inventory	100	18,200	50	12,800
Closing inventory	1,100	200,200	50	12,800

Administration and marketing overheads are deducted as a period charge from the gross profit.

	Product P1	Product P2	Total
	$	$	$
Sales	1,150,000	300,000	1,450,000
Opening inventory	18,200	12,800	31.000
Cost of production	1,092,000	256,000	1,348,000
	1,110,200	268,800	1,379,000
Closing inventory	(200,200)	(12,800)	(213,000)
Production cost of sales	910,000	256,000	1,166,000
Gross profit	240,000	44,000	284,000
Administration/marketing costs			(225,000)
Net profit			59,000

(h) Budgeted closing statement of financial position

A closing statement of financial position can be constructed from the information provided.

The net assets of the business will increase by the amount of the net profit, minus any drawings or dividends paid to the owners. If we assume that drawings/dividends will be nil, the net assets at the year end will be:

	$
Opening net assets	1,191,000
Budgeted net profit	59,000
Closing net assets	1,250,000

The non-current assets will increase by $40,000, closing inventory has been calculated in the budget, and budgeted assumptions are available for receivables and payables. We can calculate the total closing inventory as follows:

	$
Finished goods	213,000
Raw materials	17,000
	230,000

The last figure that we need for the statement of financial position is the cash balance. We could deduce this as a balancing figure but it can be proved as follows:

	$
Opening cash balance	25,000
Profit	59,000
Purchase of non-current assets	(40,000)
Cash effect of inventory increase	(164,000)
(Closing inventory – opening inventory)	
Closing cash balance (overdraft)	(120,000)

The closing statement of financial position is as follows (assuming no dividend payments):

	$	$
Non current assets		990,000
Inventory	230,000	
Trade receivables	260,000	
	490,000	
Bank overdraft	120,000	
Trade payables	86,000	
Other short-term liabilities	24,000	
	230,000	
Net current assets		260,000
Net assets		1,250,000

This budget is for the entire year. For control purposes, the budget should be analysed in much greater detail. A sales and production budget will be prepared for each control period (typically each month or each quarter).

Test your understanding 2 – FLEMING PLC

Cash budget

	December $	January $	February $	March $
Receipts –		12,369	45,987	59,666
Payments				
Materials	3,100	15,800	25,600	24,000
Wages	3,488	15,450	19,275	17,325
Variable overheads	930	5,205	9,585	9,135
Fixed overheads	1,200	2,800	2,800	2,800
	8,718	39,255	57,260	53,260
Net cash flow for month	(8,718)	(26,886)	(11,273)	6,406
Balance b/d	30,000	21,282	(5,604)	(16,877)
Balance c/d	21,282	(5,604)	(16,877)	(10,471)

Workings

	Nov	Dec	Jan	Feb	March	April
1 Production budget						
Sales			6,200	6,800	5,400	6,000
75% current			4,650	5,100	4,050	4,500
25% previous		1,550	1,700	1,350	1,500	?
		1,550	6,350	6,450	5,550	

	Nov	Dec	Jan	Feb	March	April
2 Materials budget						
Production (units)		1,550	6,350	6,450	5,550	
×$/unit		× 4	× 4	× 4	× 4	
Production required ($)		6,200	25,400	25,800	22,200	
50% previous	3,100	12,700	12,900	11,100	?	
50% current		3,100	12,700	12,900	11,100	
	3,100	15,800	25,600	24,000		
Payment 1 month delay		3,100	15,800	25,600	24,000	
3 Wages budget						
Production (units)		1,550	6,350	6,450	5,550	
× $/unit		× 3	× 3	× 3	× 3	
Production required ($)		4,650	19,050	19,350	16,650	
75% current		3,488	14,288	14,513	12,488	
25% following			1,162	4,762	4,837	
		3,488	15,450	19,275	17,325	
4 Variable overhead budget						
Production (units)		1,550	6,350	6,450	5,550	
× $/unit		× 1.50	× 1.50	× 1.50	1.50	
Production required ($)		2,325	9,525	9,675	8,325	
40% current		930	3,810	3,870	3,330	
60% following		–	1,395	5,715	5,805	
		930	5,205	9,585	9,135	

	Nov	Dec	Jan	Feb	March	April
5 Fixed overhead budget						
Cost per month ($)		4,000	4,000	4,000	4,000	4,000
30% current		1,200	1,200	1,200	1,200	1,200
40% following		–	1,600	1,600	1,600	1,600
		1,200	2,800	2,800	2,800	2,800

Test your understanding 3 – RESEARCH DIVISION

(a) An incremental budget starts off with last year's budget or last year's actual results and adds on a certain percentage to take account of expected inflation and/or any expected changes in the level of activity. It is a very simple, quick and cheap budget to produce, but it does not promote a questioning attitude. Activities are undertaken without thought. They are simply incorporated into the next budget because they were in the last budget and nobody has given any thought as to whether the activity is still really worthwhile.

With ZBB, each manager sets out what he or she wishes to accomplish over the forthcoming period. For each activity they want to undertake, they look at different ways of achieving the objective and they look at providing the service at different levels. They estimate the costs and benefits and the activity only takes place if the benefits exceed the costs. Also once all the activities have been evaluated, they can be ranked against each other and the company's resources directed to the best activities.

(b) The managers/researchers responsible for each project should decide which projects they wish to undertake in the forthcoming period. These projects will be a mixture of continued projects and new projects. For the projects which have already been started and which the managers want to continue in the next period, we should ignore any cash flows already incurred (they are sunk costs), and we should only look at future costs and benefits. Similarly, for the new projects we should only look at the future costs and benefits. Different ways of achieving the same research goals should also be investigated and the projects should only go ahead if the benefit exceeds the cost. Once all the potential projects have been evaluated if there are insufficient funds to undertake all the worthwhile projects, then the funds should be allocated to the best projects on the basis of a cost-benefit analysis.

ZBB is usually of a highly subjective nature. (The costs are often reasonably certain, but usually a lot of uncertainty is attached to the estimated benefits.) This will be even truer of a research division where the researchers may have their own pet projects which they are unable to view in an objective light.

(c) (i) Activity based budgeting is where the budget is based upon a number of different levels of activity, i.e. on a number of different cost drivers, rather than being based on just one level of activity such as machine hours or output in units.

The activity based budget will be based upon the number of units of the cost driver multiplied by the cost per unit of cost driver. The cost driver is that factor which actually causes the cost and therefore should lead to a more accurate budget as the budgeted cost will be based on the thing that should influence that cost. The alternative is to use absorption costing and assume that all overheads vary with output or machine hours or labour hours or that they are fixed.

(ii) Z plc may employ an outside specialist such as a management consultant who will investigate the business and determine what activities the business undertakes during the course of its operations.

The consultant will discuss matters with the staff and the process will normally be time consuming. For each activity, efforts will be made to determine the factor which is most closely related to the costs of that activity, i.e. the cost driver. The investigation may bring to light non-value-added activities which can then be eliminated. It should improve the understanding of all those involved as to the true relationship between cost and level of activity.

Managers would then estimate the expected incidence of their cost drivers and multiply by the budgeted cost driver rate to get the budget for the forthcoming period. ABB would be more complicated than a traditional budget and the overheads would be broken down into many activities such as set-up costs, materials, handling costs, etc rather than expenses such as rent, heating, depreciation, etc.

With ABB the majority of the overhead costs would be perceived as variable rather than fixed. Of course it is not necessary to employ an outside consultant. The company may feel that they have their own managers with sufficient skills and time to undertake the exercise.

Test your understanding 4

	Total variable cost	Variable cost per unit
20X4:		
Product A	$672,000 × 75% × 60% = $302,000	$302,000 ÷ 640 units = $472.50
Product C	$672,000 × 75% × 40% = $201,600	$201,600 ÷ 350 units = $576
20X5:		
Product A	$472.50 × 1.04 × 750 units = $368,550	n/a
Product C	$576 × 1.04 × 340 units = $203,674	n/a

Test your understanding 5

D is the correct answer.

Situation A would be best suited by implementing Zero Base Budgeting.

Situation B does not require ABB since it has relatively low overheads.

Situation C would be suitable for incremental budgeting. ABB will certainly not be quicker.

Forecasting techniques

Chapter learning objectives

Lead	Component
B2. Prepare forecasts of financial results.	(a) Calculate projected product/service volumes employing appropriate forecasting techniques.
	(b) Calculate projected revenues and costs based on product/service volumes, pricing strategies and cost structures.

1 Chapter overview diagram

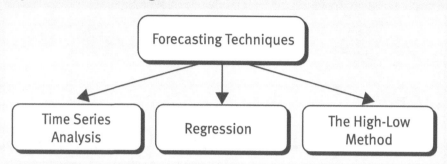

Forecasts in budgeting

Budgets are based on forecasts. Forecasts might be prepared for:

*   the volume of output and sales

*   sales revenue (sales volume and sales prices)

*   costs.

The purpose of forecasting in the budgeting process is to establish realistic assumptions for planning. Forecasts might also be prepared on a regular basis for the purpose of feed-forward control reporting.

A forecast might be based on simple assumptions, such as a prediction of a 5% growth in sales volume or sales revenue. Similarly, budgeted expenditure might be forecast using a simple incremental budgeting approach, and adding a percentage amount for inflation on top of the previous year's budget.

On the other hand, forecasts might be prepared using a number of forecasting models, methods or techniques. The reason for using these models and techniques is that they might provide more reliable forecasts.

This chapter describes:

*   the high-low method

*   the uses of linear regression analysis

*   techniques of time series analysis.

Forecasting can also be carried out using a diagram (known as a scatter diagram). The data is plotted on a graph. The y-axis represents the *dependent* variable, i.e. that variable that depends on the other. The x-axis shows the *independent* variable, i.e. that variable which is not affected by the other variable. From the scatter diagram, the line of best fit can be estimated. The aim is to use our *judgement* to draw a line through the middle of data with the same slope as the data. Because it is based on judgement it is potentially less accurate than some of the more mathematical approaches used in this chapter.

More complex models might be used in practice, but these are outside the scope of the syllabus.

2 The high-low method

This is a method of breaking semi-variable costs into their two components. A semi-variable cost being a cost which is partly fixed and partly variable.

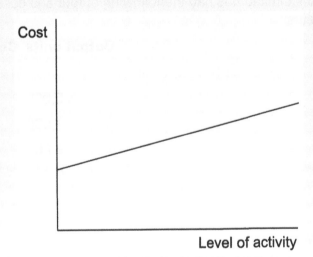

In the exam in computational questions, semi-variable costs must be broken down into their 2 components using the *high-low method*.

Step 1 Determine the variable costs

It is important that we start with the **highest and lowest output** (activity) and their associated costs.

$$\text{Variable cost per unit} = \frac{\text{Increase in cost}}{\text{Increase in activity}}$$

Choose either the highest or lowest output and multiply it by the variable cost per unit just calculated. This will tell us the total variable costs at that output.

Step 2 Find the fixed cost

A semi-variable cost consists of two components. We have found the variable component. What is left must be the fixed component. If we take the total cost and deduct the variable costs (just calculated) then we are left with the fixed costs.

Step 3 Calculate the expected cost

Once the variable cost per unit and the total fixed costs are known, these can be used to predict future cost levels. The total expected future costs will be:

= total fixed costs (from step 2) + [forecast production (in units) x variable cost per unit (from step 1)]

Example 1

Great Auk Limited has had the following output and cost results for the last 4 years:

	Output units	Cost
		$
Year 1	5,000	26,000
Year 2	7,000	34,000
Year 3	9,000	42,000
Year 4	10,000	46,000

In year 5 the output is expected to be 13,000 units. Calculate the expected costs?

Inflation may be ignored.

3 Regression analysis

The high-low method only takes account of two observations – the highest and the lowest. To take account of all observations a more advanced calculation is used known as **linear regression** which uses a formula to estimate the linear relationship between the variables as follows:

The equation of a straight line is:

$$y = a + bx$$

where y = dependent variable
        a = intercept (on y-axis)
        b = gradient
        x = independent variable

and $b = \dfrac{n\Sigma xy - \Sigma x \Sigma y}{n\Sigma x^2 - (\Sigma x)^2}$

where n = number of pairs of data

and $a = \bar{y} - b\bar{x}$

Example 2

Marcus Aurelius Ltd is a small supermarket chain, that has 6 shops. Each shop advertises in their local newspapers and the marketing director is interested in the relationship between the amount that they spend on advertising and the sales revenue that they achieve. She has collated the following information for the 6 shops for the previous year:

Shop	Advertising expenditure $000	Sales revenue $000
1	80	730
2	60	610
3	120	880
4	90	750
5	70	650
6	30	430

She has further performed some calculations for a linear regression calculation as follows:

- the sum of the advertising expenditure (x) column is 450

- the sum of the sales revenue (y) column is 4,050

- when the two columns are multiplied together and summed (xy) the total is 326,500

- when the advertising expenditure is squared (x^2) and summed, the total is 38,300, and

- when the sales revenue is squared (y^2) and summed, the total is 2,849,300

Calculate the line of best fit using regression analysis.

Detailed proof of totals in example 2

Advertising Expenditure $000	Sales $000			
x	y	xy	x^2	y^2
80	730	58,400	6,400	532,900
60	610	36,600	3,600	372,100
120	880	105,600	14,400	774,400
90	750	67,500	8,100	562,500
70	650	45,500	4,900	422,500
30	430	12,900	900	184,900
450	4,050	326,500	38,300	2,849,300

Interpretation of the line

Mathematical interpretation (No good! No marks!)

If x = 0, then y = 300 and then each time x increases by 1 y increases by 5

Business interpretation (This is what the examiner wants.)

If no money is spent on advertising then sales would still be $300,000. Then for every additional $1 increase in advertising sales revenue would increase by $5.

Linear regression in budgeting

Linear regression analysis can be used to make forecasts or estimates whenever a linear relationship is assumed between two variables, and historical data is available for analysis.

Two such relationships are:

- **A time series and trend line.** Linear regression analysis is an alternative to calculating moving averages to establish a trend line from a time series. (Time series is explained later in this chapter)
  - The independent variable (x) in a time series is time.
  - The dependent variable (y) is sales, production volume or cost etc.

- **Total costs, where costs consist of a combination of fixed costs and variable costs** (for example, total overheads, or a semi-variable cost item). Linear regression analysis is an alternative to using the high-low method of cost behaviour analysis. It should be more accurate than the high-low method, because it is based on more items of historical data, not just a 'high' and a 'low' value.
    - The independent variable (x) in total cost analysis is the volume of activity.
    - The dependent variable (y) is total cost.
    - The value of a is the amount of fixed costs.
    - The value of b is the variable cost per unit of activity.

Regression analysis is concerned with establishing the relationship between a number of variables. We are only concerned here with linear relationships between 2 variables.

When a linear relationship is identified and quantified using linear regression analysis, values for a and b are obtained, and these can be used to make a forecast for the budget. For example:

- a sales budget or forecast can be prepared, or
- total costs (or total overhead costs) can be estimated, for the budgeted level of activity.

Forecasting

The regression equation can be used for predicting values of y from a given x value.

Example 2 – CONTINUED

Marcus Aurelius Ltd has just taken on 2 new stores in the same area and the predicted advertising expenditure is expected to be $150,000 for one store and $50,000 for the other.

(a) Calculate the predicted sales revenues?
(b) Explain the reliability of the forecasts.

Limitations of simple linear regression

(1) Assumes a linear relationship between the variables.

(2) Only measures the relationship between two variables. In reality the dependent variable is affected by many independent variables.

(3) Only interpolated forecasts tend to be reliable. The equation should not be used for extrapolation.

(4) Regression assumes that the historical behaviour of the data continues into the foreseeable future.

(5) Interpolated predictions are only reliable if there is a significant correlation between the data.

Interpolation and extrapolation

(1) If the value of x is within the range of our original data, the prediction is known as *Interpolation*.

(2) If the value of x is outside the range of our original data, the prediction is known as *Extrapolation*.

In general, interpolation is much safer than extrapolation.

4 Adjusting forecasts for inflation

The accuracy of forecasting is affected by the need to adjust historical data and future forecasts to allow for price or cost inflation.

- When historical data is used to calculate a trend line or line of best fit, it should ideally be adjusted to the same index level for prices or costs. If the actual cost or revenue data is used, without adjustments for inflation, the resulting line of best fit will include the inflationary differences.

- When a forecast is made from a line of best fit, an adjustment to the forecast should be made for anticipated inflation in the forecast period.

Example 3

Production overhead costs at company BW are assumed to vary with the number of machine hours worked. A line of best fit will be calculated from the following historical data, with costs adjusted to allow for cost inflation over time.

Year	Total production overheads $	Number of machine hours	Cost index
20X1	143,040	3,000	192
20X2	156,000	3,200	200
20X3	152,320	2,700	224
20X4	172,000	3,000	235

Required:

(a) Reconcile the cost data to a common price level, to remove differences caused by inflation.

(b) If the line of best fit, based on current (20X4) prices, is calculated as:

y = 33,000 + 47x

where y = total production overhead costs in $ and x = the number of machine hours:

calculate the expected total overhead costs in 20X5 if expected production activity is 3,100 machine hours and the expected cost index is 250.

5 Time series analysis

A time series is a series of figures recorded over time, e.g. unemployment over the last 5 years, output over the last 12 months, etc.

A graph of a time series is called a *historigram*.

Examples of a time series

Examples of time series might include the following:

- quarterly sales revenue totals over a number of years

- annual overhead costs over a number of years

- daily production output over a month.

Where the item being measured is subject to 'seasonal' variations, time series measurements are usually taken for each season. For example, if sales volume varies in each quarter of the year, a time series should be for quarterly sales. Similarly, if the sales in a retail store vary according to the day of the week, a time series might measure daily sales

A time series has 4 components:

(1) The trend (T)

(2) Seasonal variations (S)

(3) Cyclical variations (C)

(4) Residual variations (R)

We are primarily interested in the first two – the trend and the seasonal variation.

Time series analysis is a term used to describe techniques for analysing a time series, in order to:

- identify whether there is any **underlying historical trend** and if there is, measure it

- use this analysis of the historical trend to forecast the trend into the future

- identify whether there are any **seasonal variations** around the trend, and if there is measure them

- apply estimated seasonal variations to a trend line forecast in order to prepare a forecast season by season.

In other words, a trend over time, established from historical data, and adjusted for seasonal variations, can then be used to make predictions for the future.

The trend

Most series follow some sort of long term movement - upwards, downwards or sideways. In time series analysis the trend is measured.

Seasonal variations

Seasonal variations are short-term fluctuations in value due to different circumstances which occur at different times of the year, on different days of the week, different times of day, etc e.g.:

- Ice cream sales are highest in summer
- Sales of groceries are highest on Saturdays
- Traffic is greatest in the morning and evening rush hours.

Illustration 1

A business might have a flat trend in sales, of $1 million each six months, but with sales $150,000 below trend in the first six months of the year and $150,000 above trend in the second six months. In this example, the sales would be $850,000 in the first six months of the year and $1,150,000 in the second six months.

- If there is a straight-line trend in the time series, seasonal variations must cancel each other out. The total of the seasonal variations over each cycle should be zero.
- Seasonal variations can be measured:
    - in units or in money values, or
    - as a percentage value or index value in relation to the underlying trend.

Cyclical and residual factors

Cyclical variations

Cyclical variations are medium-term to long term influences usually associated with the economy. These cycles are rarely of consistent length. A further problem is that we would need 6 or 7 full cycles of data to be sure that the cycle was there.

Residual or random factors

The residual is the difference between the actual value and the figure predicted using the trend, the cyclical variation and the seasonal variation, i.e. it is caused by irregular items, which could not be predicted.

Calculation of the trend

There are three main methods of finding the underlying trend of the data:

(1) *Inspection.* The trend line can be drawn by eye with the aim of plotting the line so that it lies in the middle of the data.

(2) *Least squares regression analysis.* The *x* axis represents time and the periods of time are numbers, e.g. January is 1, February is 2, March is 3, etc.

(3) *Moving averages.* This method attempts to remove seasonal or cyclical variations by a process of averaging.

Calculating a moving average

A moving average is in fact a series of averages, calculated from time series historical data.

- The first moving average value in the series is the average of the values for time period 1 to time period n. (So, if n = 4, the first moving average in the series would be the average of the historical values for time period 1 to time period 4.)

- The second moving average value in the series is the average of the values for time period 2 to time period (n + 1). (So, if n = 4, the second moving average in the series would be the average of the historical values for time period 2 to time period 5.)

- The third moving average value in the series is the average of the values for time period 3 to time period (n + 2). (So, if n = 4, the third moving average in the series would be the average of the historical values for time period 3 to time period 6.)

The moving average value is associated with the mid-point of the time periods used to calculate the average.

The moving average time period

When moving averages are used to estimate a trend line, an important issue is the choice of the number of time periods to use to calculate the moving average. How many time periods should a moving average be based on?

There is no definite or correct answer to this question. However, where there is a regular cycle of time periods, it would make sense to calculate the moving averages over a full cycle.

- When you are calculating a moving average of daily figures, it is probably appropriate to calculate a seven-day moving average.

- When you are calculating a moving average of quarterly figures, it is probably appropriate to calculate a four-quarter moving average.

- When you are calculating a moving average of monthly figures, it might be appropriate to calculate a 12-month moving average, although a shorter-period moving average might be preferred.

The seasonal variation

Once the trend has been found, the seasonal variation can be determined. A seasonal variation means that some periods are better than average (the trend) and some worse. Then the model can be used to predict future values.

Measuring seasonal variations

The technique for measuring seasonal variations differs between an additive model and a multiplicative model. The additive model method is described here.

- Seasonal variations can be estimated by comparing an actual time series with the trend line values calculated from the time series.

- For each 'season' (quarter, month, day etcetera), the seasonal variation is the difference between the trend line value and the actual historical value for the same period.

- A seasonal variation can be calculated for each period in the trend line. When the actual value is higher than the trend line value, the seasonal variation is positive. When the actual value is lower than the trend line value, the seasonal variation is negative.

- An average variation for each season is calculated.

- The sum of the seasonal variations has to be zero in the additive model. If they do not add up to zero, the seasonal variations should be adjusted so that they do add up to zero.

- The seasonal variations calculated in this way can be used in forecasting, by adding the seasonal variation to the trend line forecast if the seasonal variation is positive, or subtracting it from the trend line if it is negative.

When a multiplicative model is used to estimate seasonal variations, the seasonal variation for each period is calculated by expressing the actual sales for the period as a percentage value of the moving average figure for the same period.

The additive model

The additive model. Here the seasonal variation is expressed as an absolute amount to be added on to the trend to find the actual result, e.g. ice-cream sales in summer are good and in general we would expect sales to be $200,000 above the trend.

Actual/Prediction = T + S + C + R

In exam questions we would not be required to calculate the cyclical variation, and the random variations are by nature random and cannot be predicted and also ignored. The equation simplifies to:

Prediction = T + S

Example of the calculation

A small business operating holiday homes in Scotland wishes to forecast next year's sales for the budget, using moving averages to establish a straight-line trend and seasonal variations. Next year is 20Y0. The accountant has assumed that sales are seasonal, with a summer season and a winter season each year.

Seasonal sales for the past seven years have been as follows:

	Sales	
	Summer	Winter
	$000	$000
20X4	124	70
20X5	230	180
20X6	310	270
20X7	440	360
20X8	520	470
20X9	650	

Required:

(a) Calculate a trend line based on a two-season moving average.

(b) Use the trend line to calculate the average increase in sales each season.

(c) Calculate the adjusted seasonal variations in sales.

(d) Use this data to prepare a sales forecast for each season in 20Y0.

Solution

(a)

Season and year	Actual sales	Two-season moving total	Seasonal moving average	Centred moving average (Trend)	Seasonal variation
	(A)			(B)	= (A) – (B)
	$000	$000	$000	$000	$000
Summer 20X4	124				
		194	97		
Winter 20X4	70			123.5	– 53.5
		300	150		
Summer 20X5	230			177.5	+ 52.5
		410	205		
Winter 20X5	180			225.0	– 45.0
		490	245		
Summer 20X6	310			267.5	+ 42.5
		580	290		
Winter 20X6	270			322.5	– 52.5
		710	355		
Summer 20X7	440			377.5	+ 62.5
		800	400		
Winter 20X7	360			420.0	– 60.0
		880	440		
Summer 20X8	520			467.5	+ 52.5
		990	495		
Winter 20X8	470			527.5	– 57.5
		1,120	560		
Summer 20X9	650				

The trend line is shown by the centred moving averages.

(b) The average increase in sales each season in the trend line is:

($527,500 – $123,500) / 8 seasons = $50, 500 each season

(c) Seasonal variations need to add up to zero in the additive model. The seasonal variations calculated so far are:

Year	Summer	Winter
	$000	$000
20X4		– 53.5
20X5	+ 52.5	– 45.0
20X6	+ 42.5	– 52.5
20X7	+ 62.5	– 60.0
20X8	+ 52.5	– 57.5
Total variations	+ 210.0	– 268.5

	Summer	Winter	Total
Number of measurements	4	5	
Average seasonal variation	+ 52.5	– 53.7	– 1.2
Reduce to 0 (share equally)	+ 0.6	+ 0.6	+ 1.2
Adjusted seasonal variation	+ 53.1	– 53.1	0.0

The seasonal variations could be rounded to + $53,000 in summer and – $53,000 in winter.

(d) To predict the sales in 20Y0 we first need to extrapolate the trend line into 20Y0 and then adjust it for the expected seasonal variation.

	Expected trend (W1)	Adjusted seasonal variation	Forecast sales
Summer 20X9	578.0		
Winter 20X9	628.5		
Summer 20Y0	679.0	+ 53.0	732.0
Winter 20Y0	729.5	– 53.0	676.5

(W1)

If the actual trend in Winter 20X8 was 527.5, then we can expect the next trend figure to be 578 (527.5 plus the average increase in trend calculated in part (b) of 50.5). We can continue this process for each trend figure over the next few periods.

The multiplicative model

Here the seasonal variation is expressed as a ratio/proportion/ percentage to be multiplied by the trend to arrive at the actual figure, e.g. ice-cream sales in summer are good and in general we would expect sales to be 50% more than the trend

Actual/Prediction = T × S × C × R

Again this simplifies to:

Prediction = T × S

Illustration 2

Consider a business with the following actual results in a year:

Year	Quarter	Units sold
20X1	1	65
20X1	2	80
20X1	3	70
20X1	4	85

The trend is expected to increase by 10 units per month and has been calculated as 60 units for the first quarter. This provides the following table:

Year	Quarter	Units sold	Trend
20X1	1	65	60
20X1	2	80	70
20X1	3	70	80
20X1	4	85	90

Required:

How might these figures be used to develop a time series model in order to forecast unit sales in each quarter of year 2, using

(a) an additive modelling approach, and

(b) a multiplicative modelling approach?

Solution

The point of departure is to take the actual unit sales and compare the trend figures with the actual figures for year 1 in order to determine the seasonal variation for each quarter. This variation can be expressed as (a) a lump sum for each quarter (the additive model) or (b) an index representing the percentage of trend (the multiplicative, or proportional, model).

Year	Quarter	Units sold	Trend	(a) Variation	(b) var %
20X1	1	65	60	5	+8.33
20X1	2	80	70	10	+14.29
20X1	3	70	80	−10	−12.50
20X1	4	85	90	−5	−5.56

Notes:

(1) The multiplicative model season variations may be expressed in several different ways. For example, the quarter 3 factor may be expressed as an indexation 87.5% or 0.875.

(2) In the multiplicative model the total seasonal variations should add to zero (or 0%). In this scenario we are looking only at an abstract of a longer trend and therefore it does not add to 0% here.

One may then apply these variation figures to trend projections in order to produce a quarterly forecast for unit sales in Year 2. The two modelling approaches produce two alternative forecasts under headings (a) and (b).

Year	Quarter	Trend	Additive (forecast)	Multiplicative (forecast)
20X2	5	100	105	108
20X2	6	110	120	126
20X2	7	120	110	105
20X2	8	130	125	123

Note that this is the simplest possible example. In particular, we are basing our analysis on only one set of observations (those for this particular year). In practice, one would prefer to calculate the seasonal variations on the basis of the average of two or three sets of observations. Thus, if one observed quarter 1 variations from trend (additive model) of 6 (year A), 5 (year B) and 7 (year C) then one would adopt the average of the three (6) as the quarter 1 seasonal variation. The averaging process has the effect of 'ironing out' the impact of random variations over the past period you are considering.

Advantages and disadvantages

The advantages of forecasting using time series analysis are that:

- forecasts are based on clearly-understood assumptions
- trend lines can be reviewed after each successive time period, when the most recent historical data is added to the analysis; consequently, the reliability of the forecasts can be assessed
- forecasting accuracy can possibly be improved with experience.

The disadvantages of forecasting with time series analysis are that:

- there is an assumption that what has happened in the past is a reliable guide to the future
- there is an assumption that a straight-line trend exists
- there is an assumption that seasonal variations are constant, either in actual values using the additive model (such as dollars of sales) or as a proportion of the trend line value using the multiplicative model.

None of these assumptions might be valid.

However, the reliability of a forecasting method can be established over time. If forecasts turn out to be inaccurate, management might decide that they are not worth producing, and that different methods of forecasting should be tried. On the other hand, if forecasts prove to be reasonably accurate, management are likely to continue with the same forecasting method.

6 Chapter summary

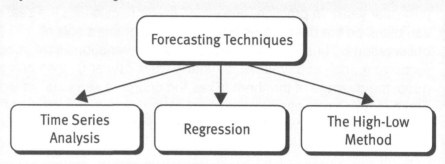

Forecasting Techniques

Time Series Analysis | Regression | The High-Low Method

7 Practice questions

Test your understanding 1

The following extract is taken from the production cost budget of S Limited:

Production (units)	2,000	3,000
Production cost ($)	11,100	12,900

Identify the budget cost allowance for an activity level of 4,000 units:

A $7,200

B $14,700

C $17,200

D $22,200

Test your understanding 2

The following data have been extracted from the budget working papers of BL Limited

Production volume	1,000	2,000
	$/unit	$/unit
Direct materials	4.00	4.00
Direct labour	3.50	3.50
Production overhead – department 1	6.00	4.20
Production overhead – department 2	4.00	2.00

Identify the total fixed cost and variable cost per unit

	Total fixed cost	Variable cost per unit
A	3,600	7.50
B	3,600	9.90
C	7,600	7.50
D	7,600	9.90

Test your understanding 3

A company will forecast its quarterly sales units for a new product by using a formula to predict the base sales units and then adjusting the figure by a seasonal index.

The formula is BU = 4,000 + 80Q

Where BU = Base sales units and Q is the quarterly period number.

The seasonal index values are:

Quarter 1	105%
Quarter 2	80%
Quarter 3	95%
Quarter 4	120%

Identify the forecast increase in sales units from Quarter 3 to Quarter 4:

A   25%

B   80 units

C   100 units

D   1,156 units

(2 marks)

Test your understanding 4

W plc is preparing its budgets for next year.

The following regression equation has been found to be a reliable estimate of W plc's deseasonalised sales in units:

y = 10x + 420

Where y is the total sales units and x refers to the accountancy period. Quarterly seasonal variations have been found to be:

Q1	Q2	Q3	Q4
+10%	+25%	−5%	−30%

In accounting period 33 (which is quarter 4) identify the seasonally adjusted sales units:

A 525

B 589

C 750

D 975

(3 marks)

Test your understanding 5

A company has achieved the following sales levels of its key product, article B, over the last four years:

Sales of article B ('000 units)

	Q1	Q2	Q3	Q4
20X3	24.8	36.3	38.1	47.5
20X4	31.2	42.0	43.4	55.9
20X5	40.0	48.8	54.0	69.1
20X6	54.7	57.8	60.3	68.9

(a) Explain what sort of trend and seasonal pattern would be expected to emerge from the analysis of this data?

(2 marks)

(b) Numbering 20X3 Q1 as $t = 1$, through to 20X6 Q4 as $t = 16$, calculate the equation of the trend (T) as a linear regression line.

(5 marks)

(c) Forecast the trend in sales for the four quarters of 20X7.

(2 marks)

(d) Calculate the seasonal component (S) using the multiplicative model. Adjust your average seasonal variations so that they add to 4.

(10 marks)

(e) Forecast the sales of B for the four quarters of 20X7.

(2 marks)

(f) If actual sales for this company in a particular year were 60,000 units, seasonally adjust this figure to estimate the underlying trend line.

(2 marks)

The calculations so far have been based on the use of linear regression in order to determine the trend line. Let's look at this same question but this time using time series analysis.

(g) Calculate the trend for the sales of article B as a centred four-point moving average.

(10 marks)

(h) Evaluate the seasonal component for each quarter based on the moving average trend;

(5 marks)

(i) Forecast the sales of B for the four quarters of 20X7 using trend forecasts of 66.7, 68.8, 70.9 and 73.

(4 marks)

Note: This question totals more than 25 marks, but an exam question is unlikely to involve all of these components. Some information or calculations would be provided so that not all of the above calculations would be necessary in one exam question.

Test your understanding answers

Example 1

Step 1 Calculate the variable cost per unit

$$\text{Variable cost per unit} = \frac{\text{Increase in cost}}{\text{Increase in level of activity}}$$

$$= \frac{\$46,000 - \$26,000}{10,000 \text{ units} - 5,000 \text{ units}}$$

$$= \$4 \text{ per unit}$$

Step 2 Find the fixed cost

The fixed cost can be determined either at the high level or the low level.

	High Level	Low Level
	$	$
Semi-variable cost	46,000	26,000
Variable costs		
$4 per unit × 10,000 units	40,000	
$4 per unit × 5,000 units		20,000
Fixed cost	6,000	6,000

Step 3 Calculate the expected cost

Therefore cost for 13,000 units = (13,000 units × $4 per unit) + $6,000 = $58,000

Example 2

$$b = \frac{n\Sigma xy - \Sigma x\Sigma y}{n\Sigma x^2 - (\Sigma x)^2}$$

$$= \frac{6 \times 326,500 - 450 \times 4,050}{6 \times 38,300 - 450^2}$$

$$= \frac{136,500}{27,300} \qquad = \quad 5$$

$$a = \bar{y} - b\bar{x}$$

$$a = \frac{4,050}{6} - 5 \times \frac{450}{6} \qquad = \quad 300$$

The regression equation is $\qquad y = 300 + 5x$

Example 2 – CONTINUED

(a)

			$000
Sales revenue	= $300k + (5 × $150k)	=	1,050
Sales revenue	= $300k + (5 × $50k)	=	550

(b) The second prediction is the more reliable as it involves interpolation. The first prediction goes beyond the original data upon which the regression line was based and thus assumes that the relationship will continue on in the same way, which may not be true.

Example 3

(a) As the line of best fit is based on 20X4 prices, use this as the common price level. Costs should therefore be adjusted by a factor:

$$\frac{\text{Index level to which costs will be adjusted}}{\text{Actual index level of costs}}$$

Year	Actual overheads $	Cost index	Adjustment factor	Costs at 20X4 price level $
20X1	143,040	192	× 235/192	175,075
20X2	156,000	200	× 235/200	183,300
20X3	152,320	224	× 235/224	159,800
20X4	172,000	235	× 235/235	172,000

(b) If the forecast number of machine hours is 3,100 and the cost index is 250:

Forecast overhead costs = [$33,000 + ($47 × 3,100 hours)] × (250/235)

= $178,700 × (250/235)

= $190,106

Test your understanding 1

B

The high-low method

Step 1 Calculate the variable cost per unit

Variable cost per unit $= \dfrac{\text{Increase in cost}}{\text{Increase in level of activity}}$

$= \dfrac{\$12{,}900 - \$11{,}100}{3{,}000 \text{ units} - 2{,}000 \text{ units}}$

$= \$1.80 \text{ per unit}$

Step 2 Find the fixed cost

A semi-variable cost has only got 2 components – a fixed bit and a variable bit. We now know the variable part. The bit that's left must be the fixed cost. It can be determined either at the high level or the low level.

	High Level	Low Level
	$	$
Semi-variable cost	12,900	11,100
Variable part		
$1.80/unit × 3,000 units	5,400	
$1.80/unit × 2,000 units		3,600
Fixed cost	7,500	7,500

Therefore cost for 4,000 units = 4,000 units × $1.80 per unit + $7,500 = $14,700.

Test your understanding 2

D

We know the cost per unit. We need to multiply by the number of units so that we can find the total cost for 1,000 units and 2,000 units. Then we can apply the high-low method.

Production volume	1,000	2,000
	$/unit	$/unit
Direct materials	4.00	4.00
Direct labour	3.50	3.50
Production overhead – department 1	6.00	4.20
Production overhead – department 2	4.00	2.00
	17.50	13.70
× No of units	× 1,000	× 2,000
Total cost	17,500	27,400

Now we can do the high-low method.

The high-low method

Step 1 Calculate the variable cost per unit

$$\text{Variable cost per unit} = \frac{\text{Increase in cost}}{\text{Increase in level of activity}}$$

$$= \frac{\$27,400 - \$17,500}{2,000 \text{ units} - 1,000 \text{ units}}$$

$$= \$9.90 \text{ per unit}$$

Step 2 Find the fixed cost

A semi-variable cost has only got 2 components – a fixed bit and a variable bit. We now know the variable part. The bit that's left must be the fixed cost. It can be determined either at the high level or the low level.

	High Level	Low Level
	$	$
Semi-variable cost	27,400	17,500
Variable part		
$9.90/unit × 2,000 units	19,800	
$9.90/unit × 1,000 units		9,900
Fixed cost	7,600	7,600

Test your understanding 3

D

Sales in quarter 3 (Q=3)

Base = 4000 + (80 × 3)   =   4,240

Seasonal adjustment   95%

Actual sales   =   4,028

Sales in quarter 4 (Q=4)

Base = 4000 + (80 × 4)   =   4,320

Seasonal adjustment   120%

Actual sales   =   5,184

Overall increase in sales   =   5,184 – 4,028   = 1,156 units

Test your understanding 4

A

y = 10x + 420

We are told that x refers to the accountancy period, which is 33, therefore:

y = 420 + (33 × 10) = 750

This is the trend, however and we need to consider the seasonal variation too. Accounting period 33 is quarter 4. Quarter 4 is a bad quarter and the seasonal variation is -30%, therefore the expected results for period 33 are 30% less than the trend.

Expected sales = 750 × 70% = 525 units

Test your understanding 5

(a) For every quarter, each year shows an increase in sales, so an increasing trend is expected. Also, there is a regular seasonal pattern with a steady increase in sales from Q1 to Q4.

(b) Letting $x = t$ and $y = T$, the necessary summations are n = 16; Σx = 136; Σy = 772.8; Σxy = 7,359.1; Σx^2 = 1,496.

$$b = \frac{n\Sigma xy - \Sigma x \Sigma y}{n\Sigma x^2 - (\Sigma x)^2} = \frac{(16 \times 7,359.1) - (136 \times 772.8)}{(16 \times 1,496) - 136^2} = 2.3244 \text{ (to 4 dp)}$$

$$a = \bar{y} - b\bar{x} = \frac{772.8}{16} - 2.324411765 \times \frac{136}{16} = 28.54 \text{ (to 2dp)}$$

The trend equation is thus:

$$T = 28.54 + 2.3244t$$

(c) In 20X7, t takes values 17 to 20, giving trend forecasts as follows:

Q1 $t = 17$ $T = 28.54 + 2.3244 \times 17 = 68.0548$

Q2 $t = 18$ $T = 70.3792$

Q3 $t = 19$ $T = 72.7036$

Q4 $t = 20$ $T = 75.028$

(d)

Year	Quarter	t	T	Sales, Y	Y/T
20X3	1	1	30.8669	24.8	0.8034
	2	2	33.1913	36.3	1.0937
	3	3	35.5157	38.1	1.0728
	4	4	37.8401	47.5	1.2553
20X4	1	5	40.1646	31.2	0.7768
	2	6	42.4890	42.0	0.9885
	3	7	44.8134	43.4	0.9685
	4	8	47.1378	55.9	1.1859
20X5	1	9	49.4622	40.0	0.8087
	2	10	51.7866	48.8	0.9423
	3	11	54.1110	54.0	0.9979
	4	12	56.4354	69.1	1.2244
20X6	1	13	58.7599	54.7	0.9309
	2	14	61.0843	57.8	0.9462
	3	15	63.4087	60.3	0.9510
	4	16	65.7331	68.9	1.0482

Year	Q1	Q2	Q3	Q4	
20X3	0.8034	1.0937	1.0728	1.2553	
20X4	0.7768	0.9885	0.9685	1.1859	
20X5	0.8087	0.9423	0.9979	1.2244	
20X6	0.9309	0.9462	0.9510	1.0482	
Total	3.3198	3.9707	3.9902	4.7138	Total
Average	0.8300	0.9927	0.9976	1.1785	3.9988
+	0.0003	0.0003	0.0003	0.0003	0.0012
Comp.	0.8303	0.9930	0.9979	1.1788	4.0000

Quite a few rounding errors will have built up by now, so do not worry if your results differ a little from these. *Note: to improve accuracy and minimise the presence of rounding errors, in calculating T you should use all the decimal places in your regression line equation from part b, i.e. $T = 28.5425 + 2.324411765 \times t$.*

To two decimal places, the seasonal components are

0.83	0.99	1.00	1.18

(e) The model is $Y = T \times S$ so the forecast sales *(Y)* in '000 units are given by multiplying the trend forecasts *(T)* by the seasonal factors *(S)*.

Using a regression equation and seasonal components to create the forecast:

Forecast trend	68.0548	70.3792	72.7036	75.028
Seasonal	0.8303	0.993	0.9979	1.1788
Forecast sales	56.5	69.9	72.6	88.4

(f) The seasonally adjusted figure is an estimate of the trend and so is given by $Y/S = 60,000/0.8303 = 72,263$ units.

(g)

Year	Quarter	Sales (Y)	Four-point moving total	Eight-point moving total	Four-point moving ave. trend (T)
20X3	1	24.8			
	2	36.3			
			146.7		
	3	38.1		299.8	37.4750
			153.1		
	4	47.5		311.9	38.9875
			158.8		
20X4	1	31.2		322.9	40.3625
			164.1		
	2	42.0		336.6	42.0750
			172.5		
	3	43.4		353.8	44.2250
			181.3		
	4	55.9		369.4	46.1750
			188.1		
20X5	1	40.0		386.8	48.3500
			198.7		
	2	48.8		410.6	51.3250
			211.9		
	3	54.0		438.5	54.8125
			226.6		
	4	69.1		462.2	57.7750
			235.6		
20X6	1	54.7		477.5	59.6875
			241.9		
	2	57.8		483.6	60.4500
			241.7		
	3	60.3			
	4	68.9			

(h) Calculating Y/T and arranging the values according to their quarters gives:

	Q1	Q2	Q3	Q4	
20X3			1.017	1.218	
20X4	0.773	0.998	0.981	1.211	
20X5	0.827	0.951	0.985	1.196	
20X6	0.916	0.956			
Total	2.516	2.905	2.983	3.625	**Total**
Average	0.839	0.968	0.994	1.208	4.009
–	0.002	0.002	0.002	0.002	0.008
Comp.	0.837	0.966	0.992	1.206	4.001

Rounding to two decimal places gives seasonal components of:

0.84	0.97	0.99	1.21

(i) Forecast for 20X7

	Q1	Q2	Q3	Q4
Trend	66.70	68.80	70.90	73.00
Comp.	0.84	0.97	0.99	1.21
Sales	56.028	66.736	70.191	88.33

Hence the sales forecasts for the four quarters of 20X7 are (in '000 units):

56	67	70	88

The treatment of uncertainty and risk in decision making

Chapter learning objectives

Lead	Component
D1. Analyse information to assess the impact on decisions of variables with uncertain values.	(a) Analyse the impact of uncertainty and risk on decision models that may be based on relevant cash flows, learning curves, discounting techniques etc.
	(b) Apply sensitivity analysis to both short and long-run decision models to identify variables that might have significant impacts on project outcomes.
	(c) Analyse risk and uncertainty by calculating expected values and standard deviations together with probability tables and histograms.
	(d) Prepare expected value tables.
	(e) Calculate the value of information.
	(f) Apply decision trees.

1 Chapter overview diagram

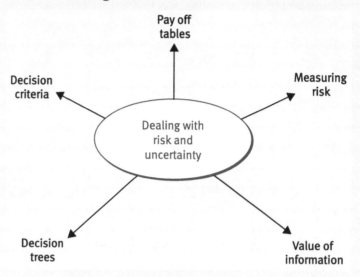

Pay off tables

Decision criteria

Measuring risk

Dealing with risk and uncertainty

Decision trees

Value of information

Topic overview

Over the next few chapters we explore some decision making problems such as whether to launch new products, whether to buy machines, choosing between products etc.

All of these decisions will involve an element of risk and uncertainty. This chapter looks at how risk and uncertainty can be built into the decision making process. This is often achieve by building in probabilities for expected outcomes and using expected values and decision trees to assess the problem.

Forecasting and decision making often include an element of risk or uncertainty. Because they look to the future they often involve estimates of future costs and benefits. In this chapter we look at how these risks and uncertainty can be built into the decision making process.

Decision making involves making decisions now about what will happen in the future. Events in the future can be predicted, but managers can rarely be 100% confident that these predicted future events will actually arise. As actual results emerge managers are likely to discover that they have achieved better or worse results than those predicted originally.

There are several ways of dealing with this variability of outcomes. In this session we will consider several different possible outcomes that may arise. It is common in practice to consider three possible outcomes; the most likely outcome, the pessimistic (worst possible) outcome and the optimistic (best possible) outcome. Analysts may consider more than these three possibilities, but more information will become more complicated and cumbersome to analyse and understand.

Examination questions will generally provide all the different possible outcomes that may arise, together with the associated chance (probability) of the outcome occurring. It is our task to analyse the information given, recommend an appropriate strategy for management to follow and finally to highlight the potential risk involved in the various choices.

2 Risk and uncertainty

The difference between risk and uncertainty

Investment appraisal faces the following problems:

- all decisions are based on forecasts
- all forecasts are subject to uncertainty
- this uncertainty needs to be reflected in the financial evaluation.

The decision maker must distinguish between:

- **risk** – quantifiable – possible outcomes have associated probabilities, thus allowing the use of mathematical techniques
- **uncertainty** – unquantifiable – outcomes cannot be mathematically modelled.

Illustration on risk and uncertainty

Risk: there are a number of possible outcomes and the probability of each outcome is known.

For example, based on past experience of digging for oil in a particular area, an oil company may estimate that they have a 60% chance of finding oil and a 40% chance of not finding oil.

Uncertainty: there are a number of possible outcomes but the probability of each outcome is not known.

For example, the same oil company may dig for oil in a previously unexplored area. The company knows that it is possible for them to either find or not find oil but it does not know the probabilities of each of these outcomes.

One possible approach to dealing with risk is to deploy sophisticated modelling techniques in an attempt to improve the reliability of business forecasts. The use of trend analysis, encountered earlier in this text, is one possibility. The key point is to develop a mathematical model to predict how future costs will behave having regard to labour becoming more adept at tasks (and hence unit resource requirements falling) the more times they are repeated.

3 Probabilities and expected values

An expected value summarises all the different possible outcomes by calculating a single weighted average. It is the long run average (mean).

The expected value is not the most likely result. It may not even be a possible result, but instead it finds the average outcome if the same event was to take place thousands of times.

Expected value formula

$$EV = \Sigma px$$ **LEARN**

where   x represents the future outcome

and   p represents the probability of the outcome occurring

Illustration 1

An organisation is considering launching a new product. It will do so if the expected value of the total revenue is in excess of $1,000. It is decided to set the selling price at $10. After some investigation a number of probabilities for different levels of sales revenue are predicted; these are shown in the following table:

Units sold	Revenue $	Probability	Pay-off $
80	800	0.15	120
100	1,000	0.50	500
120	1,200	0.35	420
		1.00	EV = 1,040

The expected sales revenue at a selling price of $10 per unit is $1,040, that is [800 × 0.15] + [1,000 × 0.50] + [1,200 × 0.35]. In preparing forecasts and making decisions management may proceed on the assumption that it can expect sales revenue of $1,040 if it sets a selling price of $10 per unit. The actual outcome of adopting this selling price may be sales revenue that is higher or lower than $1,040. And $1,040 is not even the most likely outcome; the most likely outcome is $1,000, since this has the highest probability.

Histograms

Probability data may be presented diagrammatically in the form of a histogram. The information given in the illustration immediately above might be presented as follows:

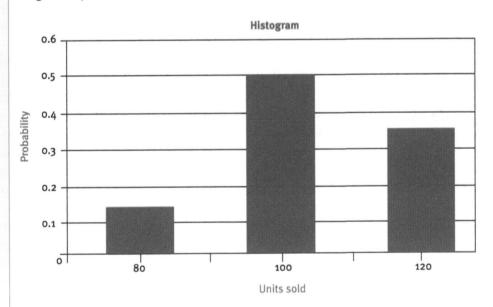

The single figure of the expected value of revenue can hide a wide range of possible actual results.

Example 1 – Calculating an expected value

A company has identified four possible outcomes from a new marketing strategy as follows:

Outcome	Profit ($)	Probability
A	100,000	0.10
B	70,000	0.40
C	50,000	0.30
D	−20,000	0.20

Calculate the expected outcome of this strategy.

Furthermore, not all decision-makers will have the same attitude towards risk. There are three main types of decision-maker.

- **Risk neutral** decision-makers consider all possible outcomes and will select the strategy that maximises the expected value or benefit.

- **Risk seekers** are likely to select the strategy with the best possible outcomes, regardless of the likelihood that they will occur. They will apply the maximax criteria (covered later).

- **Risk averse** decision-makers try to avoid risk. They would rather select a lower, but certain, outcome than risk going for a higher pay-off which is less certain to occur. They will apply the maximin criterion or the minimax regret approach (both covered later).

Illustration 2

For instance, after investigation in the previous illustration the predicted revenues might have been different. They might have been as follows:

Units sold	Revenue $	Probability	Pay-off $
40	400	0.15	60.00
100	1,000	0.50	500.00
137	1,370	0.35	479.50
		1.00	EV= 1039.50

Both situations give rise to the same expected sales revenue of $1,040 (to the nearest $), but the two situations are not the same. The second involves a wider dispersal of possible outcomes; hence it involves higher risk. If the decision-makers are risk averse they will judge the range of possible outcomes described in the second situation to be worse than the first. If the decision-makers are risk seekers they may prefer the second situation, because of the higher outcome in the best possible situation. However, in this case, the dire downside of $400 may put them off. Whatever the case it can be seen that the evaluation of the options solely on the basis of their expected value may not always be appropriate.

Utility theory

Utility is another important aspect of risk and uncertainty. The basis of the theory is that an individual's attitude to certain risk profiles will depend on the amount of money involved. For example, most people would accept a bet on the toss of a coin, if the outcome were that they would win $6 if it came down heads and if it came down tails they would pay $4. The average person would be happy to play secure in the knowledge that they would win if the game were repeated over a long enough period; if not it would still be a good bet. But if the stakes were raised so that the win was $6,000 on a single toss coming down heads and a loss of $4,000 if it came down tails, the average person might think twice and reject the bet as being too risky. Utility theory attaches weights to the sums of money involved; these are tailor-made to the individual's attitude towards winning and losing certain sums of money.

Therefore, considering a proposed option solely on the basis of its expected value ignores the range of possible outcomes.

Further expected value examples

Situation 1

A company buys in sub-assemblies in order to manufacture a product. It is reviewing its policy of putting each sub-assembly through a detailed inspection process on delivery, and is considering not inspecting at all. Experience has shown that the quality of the sub-assembly is of acceptable standard 90 per cent of the time. It costs $10 to inspect a sub-assembly and another $10 to put right any defect found at that stage. If the sub-assembly is not inspected and is then found to be faulty at the finished goods stage the cost of rework is $40.

Required:

Advise the company whether or not they should change their policy.

Solution

Four outcomes are possible:

(i)   Inspect and find no problems – cost $10.

(ii) Inspect and find problems – cost $20.

(iii) Do not inspect and no problems exist – no cost.

(iv) Do not inspect and problems do exist – cost $40.

If sub-assemblies achieve the required standard 90 per cent of the time then there is a 10 per cent chance that they will be faulty.

The expected value of the cost of each policy is as follows:

Inspect $[0.9 \times \$10] + [0.1 \times \$20] = \$11$
Do not inspect $[0.9 \times \$0] + [0.1 \times \$40] = \$4$

Taken over a long enough period of time, a policy of not carrying out an inspection would lead to a saving in cost of $7 per sub-assembly. On a purely quantitative analysis, therefore, this is the correct policy to adopt.

However, in the real world such a high level of failures is incompatible with a requirement for a 'quality product', and the concept of continuous improvement. It would be more useful to ask the supplier some basic questions regarding his quality management, in order to bring about a fundamental shift towards outcome (iii), rather than simply implementing a policy on the basis of such an uncritical analysis of the situation.

Situation 2

An individual is considering backing the production of a new musical in the West End. It would cost $100,000 to stage for the first month. If it is well received by the critics, it will be kept open at the end of the first month for a further 6 months, during which time further net income of $350,000 would be earned. If the critics dislike it, it will close at the end of the first month. There is a 50:50 chance of a favourable review.

Required:

Should the individual invest in the musical?

Solution

The expected value of backing the musical is:

$[0.5 \times \$250,000] - [0.5 \times \$100,000] = \$75,000$

As this provides a positive return it would be accepted on the basis of expected values as the alternative yields zero. However, the expected value can be misleading here as it is a one-off situation and the expected profit of $75,000 is not a feasible outcome. The only feasible outcomes of this project are a profit of $250,000 or a loss of $100,000.

While almost everybody would welcome a profit of $250,000, not many individuals could afford to sustain a loss of $100,000 and they would place a high utility on such a loss. Many investors would be risk averse in such a situation because they would not consider that a 50 per cent chance of making $250,000 was worth an equal 50 per cent risk of losing $100,000; the loss might bankrupt them. On the other hand, if the individual were a multi-millionaire the return of 250 per cent would be very appealing and the loss of a mere $100,000 would have a low utility attached to it.

The two exercises have only had single-point outcomes, that is conformity or otherwise with a pre-set quality standard and a successful show or a flop. It is obvious that the two outcomes of the first exercise represent the only possible alternatives and so quantification of the related pay-offs along the lines of the example appears reasonable. It is also obvious that the profit of $250,000 predicted for a successful show in the case of the second exercise is far too precise a figure. It would be more realistic to assume a range of possible successful pay-offs, which will vary, according to the number of seats sold and the price of the seats. If probabilities are attached to each estimate, the expected value of a successful outcome will take account of the range of possible outcomes, by weighting each of them by its associated probability. The range of possible outcomes might be as follows:

Profit ($)	Probability	Expected Value ($)
(100,000)	0.5000	(50,000)
200,000	0.1750	35,000
250,000	0.2000	50,000
300,000	0.0075	22,500
350,000	0.0500	17,500
	1.0000	75,000

The statement of a range of possible outcomes and their associated probabilities is known as a probability distribution. Presenting the distribution to management allows two further useful inferences to be drawn:

- *The most likely successful outcome.* That is the successful outcome with the highest probability (a profit of $250,000).

- *The probability of an outcome being above or below a particular figure.* The particular figure will either be the expected value or a figure of consequence, such as zero profit, where a lesser outcome might have dire consequences. By summing the probabilities for pay-offs of $200,000 and $250,000, it can be concluded that there is a 37.5 per cent probability that profits will be $250,000 or less if the musical is successful. By summing those for $300,000 and $350,000 it can be determined that the probability of a profit of $300,000 or more in the event of success is only 12.5 per cent.

Standard deviations

In order to measure the risk associated with a particular project, it is helpful to find out how wide ranging the possible outcomes are. The conventional measure is the standard deviation. The standard deviation compares all the actual outcomes with the expected value (or mean outcome). It then calculates how far on average the outcomes deviate from the mean. It is calculated using a formula.

The basic idea is that the standard deviation is a measure of volatility: the more that actual outcomes vary from the average outcome, the more volatile the returns and therefore the more risk involved in the investment/decision.

Further details on standard deviations

The standard deviation is calculated using the following formula:

$$\sigma = \sqrt{\frac{\sum (x - \bar{x})^2}{n}}$$

σ = standard deviation
$\sum$ = sum of
x = each value in the data set
$\bar{x}$ = mean of all values in the data set
n = number of value in the data set

Let's examine how standard deviations are calculated and used by considering the following illustration.

Illustration

A company is considering whether to make product X or product Y. They cannot make both products. The estimated sales demand for each product is uncertain and the following probability distribution of the NPVs for each product has been identified.

Product X

NPV ($)	Probability	Expected Value ($)
3,000	0.10	300
3,500	0.20	700
4,000	0.40	1,600
4,500	0.20	900
5,000	0.10	500
	1.00	4,000

Product Y

NPV ($)	Probability	Expected Value ($)
2,000	0.05	100
3,000	0.10	300
4,000	0.40	1,600
5,000	0.25	1,250
6,000	0.20	1,200
	1.00	4,450

Using an expected value approach the company's decision would be to produce product Y. However, let's consider the standard deviation calculations for each product:

Product X

NPV Deviation from Expected value	Squared deviation	Probability	Weighted amount ($)
3,000 − 4,000 = −1,000	1,000,000	0.10	100,000
3,500 − 4,000 = −500	250,000	0.20	50,000
4,000 − 4,000 = 0	0	0.40	0
4,500 − 4,000 = 500	250,000	0.20	50,000
5,000 − 4,000 = 1,000	1,000,000	0.10	100,000
			300,000

Sum of weighted squared deviation	300,000
Standard deviation	547.72
Expected value	4,000

Product Y

NPV Deviation from Expected value	Squared deviation	Probability	Weighted amount ($)
2,000 – 4,450 = –2,450	6,002,500	0.05	300,125
3,000 – 4,450 = –1,450	2,102,500	0.10	210,250
4,000 – 4,450 = –450	202,500	0.40	81,000
5,000 – 4,450 = 550	302,500	0.25	75,625
6,000 – 4,450 = 1,550	2,402,500	0.20	480,500
		Sum of weighted squared deviation	1,147,500
		Standard deviation	1,071.21
		Expected value	4,450

The expected net present value for each product gives us an average value based upon the probability associated with each possible profit outcome. If net present value is used for decision-making, then on that basis Product Y would be produced as it yields the highest return.

However, the net present value for each product does not indicate the range of profits that may result. By calculating the standard deviation, this allows us to identify a range of values that could occur for the profit for each product. Product Y has a higher standard deviation than Product X and is therefore more risky. There is not a significant difference in net present value for each of the products. However, Product X is less risky than Product Y and therefore the final selection will depend on the risk attitude of the company.

The coefficient of variation

If we have two probability distributions with different expected values their standard deviations are not directly comparable. We can overcome this problem by using the coefficient of variation (the standard deviation divided by the expected value) which measures the relative size of the risk.

For example, the standard deviation of the numbers 2, 7 and 9 is 2.94. The mean is 6 {(2 + 7 +9)/ 3}. The standard deviation is calculated by taking the squares of the three deviations from the mean (16 + 1 + 9 = 26) and then calculating the square root of their average ($\sqrt{(26/3)}$ = 2.94). In this case, equal weighting is given to the three figures. The coefficient of variation is the standard deviation of the series divided by its mean which is 0.49 in this case (2.94/6).

The standard deviation of a range of numbers gives a measure of the associated level of uncertainty. The measure is an absolute one and in order to allow comparison of two different series where the mean values of the two differ significantly, then the coefficient of variation is used.

Expected values, standard deviations or coefficient of variations are used to summarise the outcomes from alternative courses of action however it must be remembered that they do not provide all the relevant information to the decision maker. The probability distribution will provide the decision maker with all of the information they require. It would be appropriate to use expected values, standard deviations or coefficient of variations for decision making when there are a large number of alternatives to consider i.e. where it is not practical to consider the probability distributions for each alternative.

Advantages and disadvantages of EVs

Advantages	Disadvantages
• takes account of risk	• subjective
• easy decision rule	• not useful for one-offs
• simple	• ignores attitudes to risk
	• answer may not be possible

Further explanation

Advantages:

- Takes risk into account by considering the probability of each possible outcome and using this information to calculate an expected value.

- The information is reduced to a single number resulting in easier decisions.

- Calculations are relatively simple.

Disadvantages:

- The probabilities used are usually very subjective.

- The EV is merely a weighted average and therefore has little meaning for a one-off project.

- The EV gives no indication of the dispersion of possible outcomes about the EV, i.e. the risk.

- The EV may not correspond to any of the actual possible outcomes.

4 Pay off tables and decision criteria

When evaluating alternative courses of action, management's decision will often depend upon their attitude towards the risk. To consider the risk borne by each alternative it is necessary to consider ALL the different possible profits/losses that may arise. A pay off table is simply a table that illustrates all possible profits/losses.

Two way data tables

Two way data tables are used to represent inter-related data in an easy to understand manner.

For example, consider a company who are unsure about both selling price and variable cost. They believe that selling price may be either $40 or $50 depending on differing market conditions, and that variable production cost will be either $20 or $30 depending on wage negotiations currently taking place. The company has therefore got a number of potential contributions per unit that could be represented in a two way table as follows:

	Selling price	
	$40	$50
Variable production cost		
$20	$20	$30
$30	$10	$20

A user can interpret the table quickly and easy. It can be seen, for example, that if selling price is $40 and variable production costs are $30, then the contribution per unit will be $10.

Two way data tables can be expanded to calculate expected contribution from different volume levels. This will be explored further in the following illustration.

Illustration 3

Geoffrey Ramsbottom runs a kitchen that provides food for various canteens throughout a large organisation. A particular salad is sold to the canteen for $10 and costs $8 to prepare. Therefore, the contribution per salad is $2.

Based upon past demands, it is expected that, during the 250-day working year, the canteens will require the following daily quantities:

On 25 days of the year	40 salads
On 50 days of the year	50 salads
On 100 days of the year	60 salads
On 75 days	70 salads

Total 250 days

The kitchen must prepare the salad in batches of 10 meals and it has to decide how many it will supply for each day of the forthcoming year.

Constructing a pay-off table:

- If 40 salads will be required on 25 days of a 250-day year, the probability that demand = 40 salads is:

P(Demand of 40) = 25 days ÷ 250 days

P(Demand Of 40) = 0.1

- Likewise, P(Demand of 50) = 0 .20; P(Demand of 60 = 0.4) and P (Demand of 70 = 0.30).

- Now let's look at the different values of profit or losses depending on how many salads are supplied and sold. For example, if we supply 40 salads and all are sold, our profits amount to 40 × $2 = 80.

- If however we supply 50 salads but only 40 are sold, our profits will amount to 40 × $2 – (10 unsold salads x $8 unit cost) = 0.

- Note too that there is an upper limit to the potential profit in some instances. If, for example, we supply 60 salads then the maximum we can sell is 60 salads with a profit of $2 per unit (and $120 overall). If demand reaches 70 salads we can still only sell 60 salads and therefore the maximum profit we can make from supplying 60 salads is $120.

Solution

The pay off table would appear as follows:

		Probability	Daily Supply			
			40 salads	50 salads	60 salads	70 salads
Daily demand	40 salads	0.10	$80	$0	($80)	($160)
	50 salads	0.20	$80	$100	$20	($60)
	60 salads	0.40	$80	$100	$120	$40
	70 salads	0.30	$80	$100	$120	$140

This could then be used to determine the expected value from each daily supply level:

EV (of supplying 40 salads) = 0.10(80) + 0.20(80) + 0.40(80) + 0.30(80) = 80

EV (of supplying 50 salads) = 0.10(0) + 0.20(100) + 0.40(100) + 0.30(100) = 90

EV (of supplying 60 salads) = 0.10(–80) + 0.20(20) + 0.40(120) + 0.30(120) = 80

EV (of supplying 70 salads) = 0.10(–160) + 0.20(–60) + 0.40(40) + 0.30(140) = 30

On the basis of expected values, the best strategy would be to supply 50 salads and gain an EV of 90.

Example 2

- Hofgarten Newsagents stocks a weekly magazine which advertises local second-hand goods. Marie, the owner, can:
  - buy the magazines for 15c each
  - sell them at the retail price of 25c

- At the end of each week unsold magazines are obsolete and have no value.

- Marie estimates a probability distribution for weekly demand which looks like this:

Weekly demand in units	Probability
10	0.20
15	0.55
20	0.25
	————
	1.00
	————

Required:

(i) Calculate the expected value of demand?

(ii) If Marie is to order a fixed quantity of magazines per week, calculate how many should that be. Assume no seasonal variations in demand.

5 Maximax, maximin and minimax regret

When probabilities are not available, there are still tools available for incorporating uncertainty into decision making.

Maximax

The maximax rule involves selecting the alternative that maximises the maximum pay-off achievable.

This approach would be suitable for an optimist who seeks to achieve the best results if the best happens.

Illustration 4 – The 'Maximax' rule

Let's apply the maximax rule to the previous illustration on Geoffrey Ramsbottom

Geoffrey Ramsbottom's table looks as follows:

		Probability	Daily Supply			
			40 salads	50 salads	60 salads	70 salads
Daily demand	40 salads	0.10	$80	$0	($80)	($160)
	50 salads	0.20	$80	$100	$20	($60)
	60 salads	0.40	$80	$100	$120	$40
	70 salads	0.30	$80	$100	$120	$140

The manager who employs the maximax criterion is assuming that whatever action is taken, the best will happen; he/she is a risk-taker.

Here, the highest maximum possible pay-off is $140. We should therefore decide to supply 70 salads a day.

Example 3

A company is choosing which of three new products to make (A, B or C) and has calculated likely pay-offs under three possible scenarios (I, II or III), giving the following pay-off table.

Profit (loss)	Product chosen		
Scenario	A	B	C
I	20	80	10
II	40	70	100
III	50	(10)	40

Required:

Using maximax, which product would be chosen?

Maximin

The maximin rule involves selecting the alternative that maximises the minimum pay-off achievable.

This approach would be appropriate for a pessimist who seeks to achieve the best results if the worst happens.

Illustration 5 – The 'Maximin' rule

Geoffrey Ramsbottom's table looks as follows:

		Probability	Daily Supply			
			40 salads	50 salads	60 salads	70 salads
Daily demand	40 salads	0.10	$80	$0	($80)	($160)
	50 salads	0.20	$80	$100	$20	($60)
	60 salads	0.40	$80	$100	$120	$40
	70 salads	0.30	$80	$100	$120	$140

If we decide to supply 40 salads, the minimum pay-off is $80.

If we decide to supply 50 salads, the minimum pay-off is $0.

If we decide to supply 60 salads, the minimum pay-off is ($80).

If we decide to supply 70 salads, the minimum pay-off is ($160).

The highest minimum payoff arises from supplying 40 salads.

Example 3 continued

Required:

Using the information from Example 3, apply the maximin rule to decide which product should be made.

The minimax regret rule

The minimax regret strategy is the one that minimises the maximum regret. It is useful when probabilities for outcomes are not available or where the investor is risk averse and wants to avoid making a bad decision. Essentially, this is the technique for a 'sore loser' who does not wish to make the wrong decision.

'Regret' in this context is defined as the opportunity loss through having made the wrong decision.

Illustration 6 – The 'Minimax Regret' rule

Following up from the pay-off table example, Geoffrey Ramsbottom's table looks as follows:

				Daily Supply	
		Probability	40 salads	50 salads	60 salads	70 salads
Daily demand	40 salads	0.10	$80	$0	($80)	($160)
	50 salads	0.20	$80	$100	$20	($60)
	60 salads	0.40	$80	$100	$120	$40
	70 salads	0.30	$80	$100	$120	$140

If the minimax regret rule is applied to decide how many salads should be made each day, we need to calculate the 'regrets'. This means we need to find the biggest pay-off for each demand row, then subtract all other numbers in this row from the largest number.

For example, if the demand is 40 salads, we will make a maximum profit of $80 if they all sell. If we had decided to supply 50 salads, we would achieve a nil profit. The difference, or 'regret' between that nil profit and the maximum of $80 achievable for that row is $80.

Regrets can be tabulated as follows:

		Daily Supply			
		40 salads	**50 salads**	**60 salads**	**70 salads**
Daily demand	40 salads	$0	$80	$160	$240
	50 salads	$20	$0	$80	$160
	60 salads	$40	$20	$0	$80
	70 salads	$60	$40	$20	$0

Conclusion

If we decide to supply 40 salads, the maximum regret is $60. If we decide to supply 50 salads, the maximum regret is $80. For 60 salads, the maximum regret is $160, and $240 for 70 salads. A manager employing the minimax regret criterion would want to minimise that maximum regret, and therefore supply 40 salads only.

Example 3 continued

Required:

Using the information from Example 3, apply the minimax regret rule to decide which product should be made.

Perfect and imperfect information

In many questions the decision makers receive a forecast of a future outcome (for example a market research group may predict the forthcoming demand for a product). This forecast may turn out to be correct or incorrect. The question often requires the candidate to calculate the value of the forecast.

Perfect information — The forecast of the future outcome is always a correct prediction. If a firm can obtain a 100% accurate prediction they will always be able to undertake the most beneficial course of action for that prediction.

Imperfect information — The forecast is usually correct, but can be incorrect. Imperfect information is not as valuable as perfect information. Imperfect information may be examined in conjunction with Decision Trees (see later in this chapter).

The value of information (either perfect or imperfect) may be calculated as follows:

Expected profit (outcome) WITH the information

minus

Expected profit (outcome) WITHOUT the information

Illustration 7 – The value of information

A new ordering system is being considered, whereby customers must order their salad online the day before. With this new system Mr Ramsbottom will know for certain the daily demand 24 hours in advance. He can adjust production levels on a daily basis. How much is this new system worth to Mr Ramsbottom?

Supply = demand	X Pay off	P Probability	px
40	$80	0.1	8
50	$100	0.2	20
60	$120	0.4	48
70	$140	0.3	42
			118

E.V. with perfect information	= $118
E.V. without perfect information (from the original EV calculation)	= $90
Value of perfect information	$28 per day

Example 3 continued

Following on from the data provided in Example 3, the company has made an estimate of the probability of each scenario occurring as follows:

Scenario	Probability
I	20%
II	50%
III	30%

However, an external consultant has some information about each likely scenario and can say with certainty which scenario will arise.

Calculate the value of the external consultants information.

6 Decision trees and multi-stage decision problems

A decision tree is a diagrammatic representation of a decision problem, where all possible courses of action are represented, and every possible outcome of each course of action is shown. Decision trees should be used where a problem involves a series of decisions being made and several outcomes arise during the decision-making process. In some instances it may involve the use of joint probabilities – where the outcome of one event depends of the outcome of a preceding event.

Joint probabilities

So far only a very small number of alternatives have been considered in the examples. In practice a greater number of alternative courses of action may exist, uncertainty may be associated with more than one variable and the values of variables may be interdependent, giving rise to many different outcomes.

The following exercise looks at the expected value of a manufacturing decision, where there are three alternative sales volumes, two alternative contributions, and three alternative levels of fixed cost. The number of possible outcomes will be 3 × 2 × 3 = 18.

Example

A company is assessing the desirability of producing a souvenir to celebrate a royal jubilee. The marketing life of the souvenir will be 6 months only. Uncertainty surrounds the likely sales volume and contribution, as well as the fixed costs of the venture. Estimated outcomes and probabilities are:

Units sold	Probability	Cont'n per unit $	Probability	Fixed cost $	Probability
100,000	0.3	7	0.5	400,000	0.2
80,000	0.6	5	0.5	450,000	0.5
60,000	0.1			500,000	0.3
	1.0		1.0		1.0

The next table shows the expected value of the net contribution to be $49,000. Totalling up the joint probabilities for each set of sales shows the project has a 56.5 per cent chance of making a net contribution, a 33 per cent chance of making a loss, and a 10.5 per cent chance of making neither a net contribution nor a loss. (For example, to calculate the probability of making a loss: we can see from the next table that a loss will arise in 7 situations. So if we add the overall probability of this happening we add up the joint probabilities associated with each of these outcomes – 0.150 + 0.090 + 0.025 + 0.015 + 0.010 + 0.025 + 0.015 = 0.33).

Units sold	Cont'n per unit $	Total Cont'n $ a	Fixed Cost $ b	Probability	Joint Prob. c	EV of net cont. $ (a-b) x c
100,000	7	700,000	400,000	0.3×0.5×0.2=	0.030	9,000
	7	700,000	450,000	0.3×0.5×0.5=	0.075	18,750
	7	700,000	500,000	0.3×0.5×0.3=	0.045	9,000
	5	500,000	400,000	0.3×0.5×0.2=	0.030	3,000
	5	500,000	450,000	0.3×0.5×0.5=	0.075	3,750
	5	500,000	500,000	0.3×0.5×0.3=	0.045	0
80,000	7	560,000	400,000	0.6×0.5×0.2=	0.060	9,600
	7	560,000	450,000	0.6×0.5×0.5=	0.150	16,500
	7	560,000	500,000	0.6×0.5×0.3=	0.090	5,400
	5	400,000	400,000	0.6×0.5×0.2=	0.060	0
	5	400,000	450,000	0.6×0.5×0.5=	0.150	−7,500
	5	400,000	500,000	0.6×0.5×0.3=	0.090	−9,000
60,000	7	420,000	400,000	0.1×0.5×0.2=	0.010	200
	7	420,000	450,000	0.1×0.5×0.5=	0.025	−750
	7	420,000	500,000	0.1×0.5×0.3=	0.015	−1,200
	5	300,000	400,000	0.1×0.5×0.2=	0.010	−1,000
	5	300,000	450,000	0.1×0.5×0.5=	0.025	−3,750
	5	300,000	500,000	0.1×0.5×0.3=	0.015	−3,000
			1.0		1.0	49,000

Decisions like this can be quite hard to visualise and it may be more useful to use a decision tree to express the situation.

Three-step method

Step 1: Draw the tree from left to right showing appropriate decisions and events/outcomes.

Symbols to use:

☐ A square is used to represent a decision point. At a decision point the decision maker has a choice of which course of action he wishes to undertake.

◯ A circle is used at a chance outcome point. The branches from here are always subject to probabilities.

> Label the tree and relevant cash inflows/outflows
> (discounted to present values if necessary) and probabilities
> associated with outcomes.

Step 2: Evaluate the tree from right to left carrying out
these two actions:

> Calculate an EV at each outcome point.
>
> Choose the best option at each decision point.

Step 3: Recommend a course of action to management.

Example 4 – Decision trees

An oil company has recently acquired rights in a certain area to conduct
surveys and geological test drillings that may lead to extracting oil where
it is found in commercially exploitable quantities.

The area is already considered to have good potential for finding oil in
commercial quantities. At the outset the company has the choice to
conduct further geological tests or to carry out a drilling programme
immediately. On the known conditions, the company estimates that there
is a 70% chance of further tests indicating that a significant amount of oil
is present.

Whether the tests show the possibility of oil or not, or even if no tests are
undertaken at all, the company could still pursue its drilling programme
or alternatively consider selling its rights to drill in the area.

Thereafter, however, if it carries out the drilling programme, the
likelihood of final success or failure in the search for oil is considered
dependent on the foregoing stages. Thus:

(i)   If the tests indicated that oil was present, the expectation of success
in drilling is given as 80%.

(ii) If the tests indicated that there was insufficient oil present, then the
expectation of success in drilling is given as 20%.

(iii) If no tests have been carried out at all, the expectation of finding
commercially viable quantities of oil is given as 55%.

Costs and revenues have been estimated for all possible outcomes and
the net present value of each is given below:

Outcome	Net present value
	$ millions
Geological testing	(10)
Drilling cost	(50)
Success in finding oil	150

Sale of exploitation rights:

Tests indicate oil is present	65
Tests indicate 'no oil'	15
Without geological tests	40

Required:

(a) Prepare a decision tree diagram to represent the above information.

(8 marks)

(b) For the management of the company, calculate its best course of action.

(7 marks)

(c) Explain the value of decision trees in providing management with guidance for decision making. Illustrate examples of any situations where you consider their use would be of benefit.

(5 marks)

(Total: 20 marks)

More on decision trees

Decision trees force the decision maker to consider the logical sequence of events. A complex problem is broken down into smaller, easier-to-handle sections. The financial outcomes and probabilities are shown separately, and the decision tree is 'rolled back' by calculating expected values and making decisions. In the examination ensure that only relevant costs and revenues are considered, and that all cash is expressed in present value terms.

A number of other factors should be taken into account when considering decision tree-type problems:

- *Time value of money.* The time value of money should be incorporated in the calculations if the project is to last for more than one year. The time value of money is discussed in detail later in this text.

- *Assumes risk neutrality.* As mentioned under probability, some decision-makers do not choose options which give the greatest expected value, because they are either risk seekers or risk averse.

- *Sensitivity analysis.* The analysis depends very much on the values of the probabilities in the tree. The values are usually the subjective estimates of the decision-makers, and, no matter how experienced the people involved are, the values must be open to question. Sensitivity analysis can be used to consider 'break-even' positions for each variable – i.e. the value for a variable (such as probability) at which the decision would change. Sensitivity analysis is covered later in this chapter.

- *Oversimplification.* In order to make the tree manageable, the situation has often to be greatly simplified. This makes it appear far more discrete than it really is. In practice, it is much more likely that the outcomes would form a near continuous range of inflows and outflows. This cannot be shown on a decision tree, and so any decision tree usually represents a simplified situation.

7 Sensitivity analysis

Sensitivity analysis takes each uncertain factor in turn, and calculates the change that would be necessary in that factor before the original decision is reversed.

By using this technique it is possible to establish which estimates (variables) are more critical than others in affecting a decision.

The process in calculating sensitivities

The process is as follows:

- Best estimates for variables are made and a decision arrived at. For example, a NPV calculation may indicate accepting a project.

- Each of the variables is analysed in turn to see how much the original estimate can change before the original decision is reversed. For example, it may be that the estimated selling price can fall by 5% before the NPV becomes negative and the project would be rejected.

- Estimates for each variable can then be reconsidered to assess the likelihood of the decision being wrong. For example, what is the chance of the selling price falling by more than 5%?

Illustration 8

A manager is considering a make v buy decision based on the following estimates:

	If made in-house	If buy in and re-badge
	$	$
Variable production costs	10	2
External purchase costs	–	6
Ultimate selling price	15	14

Identify the sensitivity of the decision to the external purchase price.

Step 1: What is the original decision?

Comparing contribution figures, the product should be bought in and re-badged:

	If made in-house	If buy in and re-badge
	$	$
Contribution	5	6

Step 2: Calculate the sensitivity (to the external purchase price)

For indifference, the contribution from outsourcing needs to fall to $5 per unit. Thus the external purchase price only needs to increase by $1 per unit (or $1/ $6 = 17%).

If the external purchase price rose by more than 17% the original decision would be reversed.

Example 5 – Sensitivity analysis

A manager has identified the following two possible outcomes for a process

Outcome	Probability	Financial implications ($000s)
Poor	0.4	Loss of 20
Good	0.6	Profit of 40

The expected value has been calculated as EV = (0.4 × -20) + (0.6 × 40) = +16. This would suggest that the opportunity should be accepted.

Required:

(a) Suppose the likely loss if results are poor has been underestimated. What level of loss would change the decision? In effect we want a break-even estimate.

(b) Suppose the probability of a loss has been underestimated. What is the break-even probability?

Strengths and weaknesses

Strengths of sensitivity analysis

- There is no complicated theory to understand.

- Information will be presented to management in a form which facilitates subjective judgement to decide the likelihood of the various possible outcomes considered.

- It identifies areas which are crucial to the success of the project. If the project is chosen, those areas can be carefully monitored.

Weaknesses of sensitivity analysis

- It assumes that changes to variables can be made independently, e.g. material prices will change independently of other variables. Simulation allows us to change more than one variable at a time.

- It only identifies how far a variable needs to change; it does not look at the probability of such a change.

- It provides information on the basis of which decisions can be made but it does not point to the correct decision directly.

8 Chapter summary

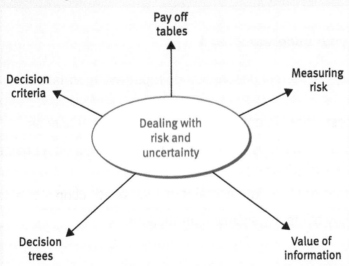

9 Practice questions

Test your understanding 1

Identify the correct description of imperfect information:

A   costs more to collect than its value to the business

B   is available only after preliminary decisions on a business venture
     have been taken

C   does not take into account all factors affecting a business

D   may contain inaccurate predictions

(2 marks)

Test your understanding 2

A company is considering investing in one of the following projects.

Project	Expected value $000	Standard deviation $000
A	850	500
B	1,200	480
C	150	200
D	660	640

It wishes to select the project with the lowest risk factor (coefficient of
variation). Identify which project should it select:

A   Project A

B   Project B

C   Project C

D   Project D

(2 marks)

Test your understanding 3

Three investors are considering the same investments. The net returns from the investments depend on the state of the economy and are illustrated as follows:

State of the economy	Returns from investment			Probability of economic state
	A $	B $	C $	
Good	6,000	14,000	3,000	0.1
Fair	5,000	3,000	5,000	0.4
Poor	4,000	500	8,000	0.5

Details on the attitudes to risk of the three investors is as follows:

- Micah is risk neutral

- Zhang is a risk seeker

- Jill is risk averse and typically follows a minimax regret strategy with her investments

Calculate which investment would be best suited to each investor's risk attitude.

(5 marks)

Test your understanding 4 – CHARITY ORGANISATION

For the past 20 years a charity organisation has held an annual dinner and dance with the primary intention of raising funds.

This year there is concern that an economic recession may adversely affect both the number of persons attending the function and the advertising space that will be sold in the programme published for the occasion.

Based on past experience and current prices and quotations, it is expected that the following costs and revenues will apply for the function:

			$
Cost:	Dinner and dance:	Hire of premises	700
		Band and entertainers	2,800
		Raffle prizes	800
		Photographer	200
		Food at $12 per person (with a guarantee of 400 persons minimum)	
	Programme:	A fixed cost of $2,000 plus $5 per page	
Revenues:	Dinner and dance:	Price of tickets	$20 per person
		Average revenue from:	
		Raffle	$5 per person
		Photographs	$1 per person
	Programme:	Average revenue from advertising	$70 per page

A sub-committee, formed to examine more closely the likely outcome of the function, discovered the following from previous records and accounts:

Number of tickets sold	Number of past occasions
250 to 349	4
350 to 449	6
450 to 549	8
550 to 649	2

Number of programme pages sold	Number of past occasions
24	4
32	8
40	6
48	2

Required:

Calculate the expected value of the profit to be earned from the dinner and dance this year.

(10 marks)

Test your understanding 5 – RS GROUP

The RS Group owns a large store in Ludborough. The store is old-fashioned and profits are declining. Management is considering what to do – there appear to be three possibilities:

(1) Shut down and sell the site for $15m.

(2) Continue as before with profits declining.

(3) Upgrade the store.

The Group has had problems in the past and experience suggests that when stores are upgraded, 60% achieve good results and 40% poor results.

Because of the doubts, management is considering whether to contact a leading market research company to carry out consumer research in Ludborough for $1m. It has been fortunate in obtaining details of the track record of the research company, as follows:

		Actual outcome	
		Good	Poor
Attitude predicted by research	Positive	0.85 *	0.10
	Negative	0.15	0.90

* This means that when the actual results were good the research had predicted this 85% of the time.

If the research indicates a positive attitude, management will consider deluxe upgrading which will generate more profit but will cost $12m, as compared with standard upgrading costing $6m.

If the research indicates a negative attitude, then management will consider standard upgrading compared with shutting down and selling the site.

The time scale for the analysis is 10 years and the following estimates of returns have been made:

With Deluxe upgrading: Good results $40m total present value

Poor results $20m total present value

With Standard upgrading: Good results $25m total present value

Poor results $10m total present value

If operations continue as before, returns over the next 10 years will be $13.03m in present value terms.

Required:

(a) prepare a decision tree to represent the above information;

(19 marks)

Note: No discounting is necessary for this question as the values are already expressed in present value terms.

(b) calculate what decisions should be taken;

(3 marks)

(c) explain the basis of your analysis.

(3 marks)
(Total: 25 marks)

Test your understanding 6

A company can make either of two new products, X and Y, but not both. The profitability of each product depends on the state of the market, as follows:

Market state	Profit from product		Probability of market state
	X $	Y $	
Good	20,000	17,000	0.2
Fair	15,000	16,000	0.5
Poor	6,000	7,000	0.3

Calculate the expected value of perfect information as to the state of the market

A $0

B $600

C $800

D $1,000

(2 marks)

Test your understanding 7

The Venus Department Store operates a customer loan facility. If one of its new customers requests a loan then Venus either refuses it, gives a high loan limit, or gives a low loan limit. From a number of years past experience the probability that a new customer makes a full repayment of a loan is known to be 0.95, whilst the probability of non-repayment is 0.05 (these probabilities being independent of the size of loan limit). The average profit in $, per customer made by Venus is given by the following table.

	Loan Limit	
	High	Low
Full-repayment	50	20
Non-repayment	–200	–30

Required:

(a) In the past the company has used a selection criterion that is totally arbitrary (i.e. it is not influenced by the customer's ability to repay).

Prepare a decision tree to represent the information. Calculate the expected value and explain what the management of Venus should do if a new customer requests a loan?

(6 marks)

(b) Venus can apply to an agency to evaluate the credit-rating of a customer. This agency would provide a rating for the customer as either a good risk or as a bad risk, this credit-rating being independent of the size of the loan being considered. Analysis of the last 1,000 customer ratings by this agency revealed the following information.

Agency	Type of customer		
Credit Rating	Full-repayment	Non-repayment	Total
Good risk	790	10	800
Bad risk	160	40	200
Total	950	50	1,000

Determine the value of this credit rating to Venus

(9 marks)

(c) The Venus management believe that this first agency is not very good at selecting full-payers and non-payers. It considers contacting a second agency which guarantees perfect information concerning the credit rating of the customers.

Explain the meaning of the term 'perfect information' in the context of this question.

Calculate the value of this perfect information.

(5 marks)

(Total: 20 marks)

Test your understanding 8 – SITERAZE LTD

Siteraze Ltd is a company which engages in site clearance and site preparation work. Information concerning its operations is as follows:

(a) It is company policy to hire all plant and machinery required for the implementation of all orders obtained, rather than to purchase its own plant and machinery.

(b) Siteraze Ltd will enter into an advance hire agreement contract for the coming year at one of three levels – high, medium or low, which correspond to the requirements of a high, medium or low level of orders obtained.

(c) The level of orders obtained will not be known when the advance hire agreement contract is entered into. A set of probabilities have been estimated by management as to the likelihood of the orders being at high, medium or low level.

(d) Where the advance hire agreement entered into is lower than that required for the level of orders actually obtained, a premium rate must be paid to obtain additional plant and machinery required.

(e) No refund is obtainable where the advance hire agreement for plant and machinery is at a level in excess of that required to satisfy the site clearance and preparation orders actually obtained.

A summary of the information relating to the above points is as follows:

Level of orders	Revenue $000	Probability	Plant and machinery hire costs Advance hire $000	Conversion premium $000
High	15,000	0.25	2,300	
Medium	8,500	0.45	1,500	
Low	4,000	0.30	1,000	
Low to medium				850
Medium to high				1,300
Low to high				2,150
Variable cost (as a percentage of turnover)			70%	

Required:

(a) Prepare a summary which shows the forecast net margin earned by Siteraze Ltd for the coming year for each possible outcome.

(8 marks)

(b) On the basis of maximising expected value, calculate for Siteraze whether the advance contract for the hire of plant and machinery should be at the low, medium or high level.

(6 marks)

(c) Explain how the risk preferences of the management members responsible for the choice of advance plant and machinery hire contract may alter the decision reached in (b) above.

(6 marks)

(d) Siteraze Ltd are considering employing a market research consultant who will be able to say with certainty in advance of the placing of the plant and machinery hire contract, which level of site clearance and preparation orders will be obtained. On the basis of expected value, calculate the maximum sum which Siteraze Ltd should be willing to pay the consultant for this information.

(5 marks)

(Total: 25 marks)

Test your understanding answers

Example 1 – Calculating an expected value

Expected value calculation

Outcome	Profit ($)	Probability	Profit x Probability ($)
A	100,000	0.10	10,000
B	70,000	0.40	28,000
C	50,000	0.30	15,000
D	–20,000	0.20	–4,000
Expected value			49,000

Expected profit is $49,000.

Example 2

(i) EV of demand = $(10 \times 0.20) + (15 \times 0.55) + (20 \times 0.25) = 15.25$ units per week.

(ii) The first step is to set up a decision matrix of possible strategies (numbers bought) and possible demand, as follows:

Outcome (number demanded)	Strategy (number bought)		
	10	15	20
10			
15			
20			

The 'pay-off' from each combination of action and outcome is then computed:

No sale: cost of 15c per magazine.

Sale: profit of 25c – 15c = 10c per magazine

Pay-offs are shown for each combination of strategy and outcome.

Probability	Outcome (number demanded)	Decision (number bought)		
		10	15	20
0.20	10	100	25	(50)
0.55	15	100	150	75
0.25	20	100	150	200
────	────	────	────	────
1.00	EV	100c	125c	81.25c
────	────	────	────	────

Conclusion: The strategy which gives the highest expected value is to stock 15 magazines each week.

Workings

(i) If 10 magazines are bought, then 10 are sold no matter how many are demanded and the payoff is always 10 × 10c = 100c.

(ii) If 15 magazines are bought and 10 are demanded, then 10 are sold at a profit of 10 × 10c = 100c, and 5 are scrapped at a loss of 5 × 15c = 75c, making a net profit of 25c

(iii) The other contributions are similarly calculated.

Example 3

Using maximax, an optimist would consider the best possible outcome for each product and pick the product with the greatest potential.

Here C would be chosen with a maximum possible gain of 100.

Example 3 continued

- Using maximin, a pessimist would consider the poorest possible outcome for each product and would ensure that the maximum pay-off is achieved if the worst result were to happen.

- Therefore, product A would be chosen resulting in a minimum pay-off of 20 compared to a minimum pay-off of (10) for product B and 10 for product C.

Example 3 continued

In the pay-off matrix above, if the market state had been scenario I:

The correct decision would have been:	B (net income $80)
If A had been chosen instead:	The company would have been out of pocket by $60 (i.e. 80 – 20)
If C had been chosen:	It would have been out of pocket by $70 (i.e. 80 – 10)

- The opportunity loss associated with each product is: A = $60, B =$0, C = $70.

Scenario II and III can be considered in the same way and the results can be summarised in a regret table.

The completed opportunity loss ('regret') table is thus as follows.

State	Decision		
	A	B	C
I	60	0	70
II	60	30	0
III	0	60	10
Maximum regret	60	60	70

The maximum regret value for:

A = $60

B = $60

C = $70

The minimum value of these is $60, hence the minimax regret strategy would be either A or B.

B would probably be adopted because its second-highest regret outcome ($30) is lower than the second-highest for A ($60).

Example 3 continued

Firstly, we have to calculate the expected value without the information.

EV (A) = 0.2(20) + 0.5(40) + 0.3(50) = 39

EV (B) = 0.2(80) + 0.5(70) + 0.3(−10) = 48

EV (C) = 0.2(10) + 0.5(100) + 0.3(40) = 64

So the company would choose project C, with an expected pay-off of 64.

If the company had perfect information it would act as follows:

Scenario indicated by perfect information	Company's decision*	Pay-off
I	Invest in product B	80
II	Invest in product C	100
III	Invest in product A	50

* this will be based on the highest expected pay-off in that scenario. For example, if scenario I is predicted the company will face a pay-off of 20 from product A, 80 from product B, and 10 from product C. It will therefore decide to invest in product B.

The expected value from these decisions would be:

EV (C) = 0.2(80) + 0.5(100) + 0.3(50) = 81

This is 17 higher than the expected value (64) when the company had no information. Therefore the information has a value of 17.

Example 4 – Decision trees

(a) and (b)

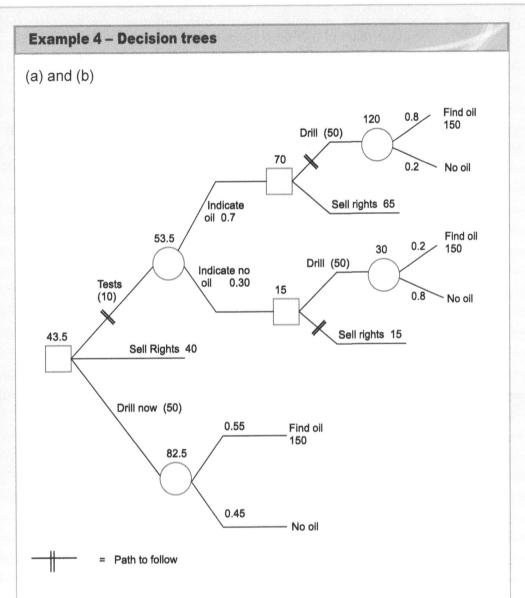

= Path to follow

Advice:

The company should undertake geological tests. If the tests indicate that oil is present then a drilling programme should be carried out. However, if the tests indicate that there is no oil then the company should sell the drilling rights.

This strategy will maximise expected returns at $43.5m.

(c) The main value of a decision tree is that it maps out clearly all the decisions and uncertain events and exactly how they are interrelated. They are especially beneficial where the outcome of one decision affects another decision. For example in the above, the probability of eventual success changes depending on the test outcomes. The analysis is made clearer by annotating the tree with probabilities, cash flows, and expected values so that the optimum decisions (based on expected values) can be clearly seen.

However, drawing a tree diagram is only one way of undertaking a decision. It is based on the concept of expected value and as such suffers from the limitations of this technique. For example, in this example, if the test drilling proves positive, the tree indicated the company should drill, as opposed to selling the rights. But if it does there is a 20% chance of it losing $50 million. A risk-averse company may well decide to accept the safer option and sell the rights and settle for $65 million.

Example 5 – Sensitivity analysis

(a) The EV would have to decrease by $16,000 before the original decision is reversed, i.e. this is the break-even point.

- Let the loss be L

    Currently, $EV = (0.4 \times L) + (0.6 \times 40)$

    If EV falls to zero:

    EV of $0 = (0.4 \times L) + (0.6 \times 40)$

    $0 = 0.4L + 24$

    $-24 = 0.4L$

    $-24/0.4 = L$

    $L = -60$

- The loss would have to increase from $20,000 to $60,000 before the decision is reversed. This is a 200% increase in the loss.

(b) The EV would have to decrease by $16,000 before the original decision is reversed, i.e. this is the break-even point.

- Let the probability of a loss be P and the probability of a profit be 1 – P.

  Currently, EV = (P × –20) + (1–p × 40)

  If EV falls to zero:

  EV of 0 = (P × –20) + (1–p × 40)

  0 = –20P + 40 –40P

  60P = 40

  P = 40/60

  P = 0.67

- The probability of a loss would have to increase to 0.67 from 0.4 before the decision is reversed.

Test your understanding 1

D

Perfect information is certain to be right about the future. Imperfect information may predict wrongly.

Test your understanding 2

B

Project	Expected value $000	Standard deviation $000	Coefficient of variation
A	850	500	0.59
B	1,200	480	0.40
C	150	200	1.33
D	660	640	0.97

Test your understanding 3

Micah

As a risk neutral investor Micah will base his decision on the expected value of each investment. These are calculated as follows:

Investment A = ($6,000 × 0.1) + ($5,000 × 0.4) + ($4,000 × 0.5) = $4,600

Investment B = ($14,000 × 0.1) + ($3,000 × 0.4) + ($500 × 0.5) = $2,850

Investment C = ($3,000 × 0.1) + ($5,000 × 0.4) + ($8,000 × 0.5) = $6,300

Micah will therefore choose to invest in Investment C as it has the highest overall expected value.

Zhang

As a risk seeker Zhang will ignore the expected values and probabilities, and she will focus solely on the payouts. She will apply the maximax criteria and consider where the highest payout might arise. The highest possible return is the $14,000 that arises in a good market state for Investment B. Zhang will therefore choose to invest in Investment B.

Jill

To apply the minimax regret criteria Jill will have to create a regret table as follows:

State of the economy	Regret		
	A $	B $	C $
Good	8,000	0	11,000
Fair	0	2,000	0
Poor	4,000	7,500	0
Maximum regret	8,000	7,500	11,000

Jill will therefore choose to invest in Investment B as it has the lowest maximum regret ($7,500) of the three investments.

Test your understanding 4 – CHARITY ORGANISATION

Revenue per person = $20 + $5 + $1

Number of tickets	Probability	Revenue	Food cost	Net benefit	Prob. × benefit
		$	$	$	$
300	0.2	7,800	(4,800)	3,000	600
400	0.3	10,400	(4,800)	5,600	1,680
500	0.4	13,000	(6,000)	7,000	2,800
600	0.1	15,600	(7,200)	8,400	840
	1.0			Expected value =	5,920

Number of pages	Probability	Contribution $65 per page	Prob. × contribution
		$	$
24	0.2	1,560	312
32	0.4	2,080	832
40	0.3	2,600	780
48	0.1	3,120	312
	1.0	Expected value =	2,236

Total contribution	$5,920 + $2,236	=	$8,156
Less fixed costs		=	($6,500)
Expected profit			$1,656

Test your understanding 5 – RS GROUP

(a)

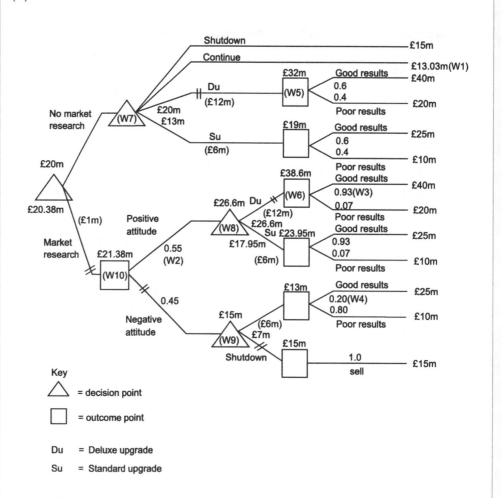

Key

△ = decision point

☐ = outcome point

Du = Deluxe upgrade

Su = Standard upgrade

Workings 2, 3 and 4

A probability tree is the best way of understanding the dependent probabilities given in the question.

The probability of the prediction depends upon whether the results are good or poor.

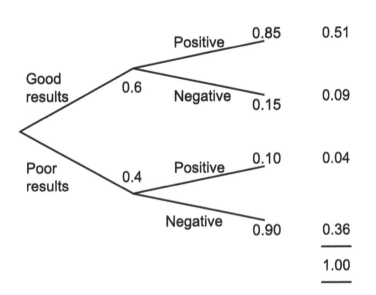

Joint probabilities

Good results — 0.6
- Positive 0.85 — 0.51
- Negative 0.15 — 0.09

Poor results — 0.4
- Positive 0.10 — 0.04
- Negative 0.90 — 0.36

1.00

(W2)   p(positive attitude) = 0.51 + .04 = 0.55

(W3)   p(good results/positive attitude) =

$$\frac{p\,(\text{good results and positive attitude})}{p\,(\text{positive attitude})}$$

$$= \frac{0.51}{0.55} = 0.93$$

(W4)   p(good results/negative attitude) = $\dfrac{p\,(\text{good results and negative attitude})}{p\,(\text{negative attitude})}$

$$= \frac{0.09}{0.45} = 0.20$$

(W5)   Expected profit = \$40m × 0.6 + \$20m × 0.4 = \$32m

(W6)   Expected profit = \$40m × 0.93 + \$20m × 0.07 = \$38.6m

(W7)   The deluxe upgrade provides an expected profit of (\$32m − \$12m) \$20m

(W8)   Deluxe upgrade profit = \$38.6m − \$12m = \$26.6m

Standard upgrade profit = \$23.95 − \$6m = \$17.95m

∴ Deluxe upgrade is recommended.

(W9)   Standard upgrade profit = \$7m

Shutdown and sell site = \$15m

∴ Shutdown and sell is recommended

(W10) Expected profit = \$26.6m × 0.55 + \$15m × 0.45 = \$21.38m

(b) In order to maximise expected profit:

Undertake the market research.

If the attitude is positive upgrade deluxe.

If the attitude is negative shutdown and sell the site.

(c) Comment

(i) This assumes that all estimates are correct; sensitivity analysis could be carried out on each estimate.

(ii) It is assumed that the RS Group are risk neutral since expected values have been used – although the highest ENPV has a lower risk than the next highest.

(iii) Ten years is a long time period over which to predict profits – a reasonable period for the life of the store but this makes estimation difficult.

(iv) Comments on the courses of action open to the RS Group have been made in (a).

Test your understanding 6

B

Without information, the expected profits are:

Product X: $20,000 × 0.2 + $15,000 × 0.5 + $6,000 × 0.3 = $13,300
Product Y: $17,000 × 0.2 + $16,000 × 0.5 + $7,000 × 0.3 = $13,500

So without information, product Y would be selected.

With perfect information, product X would be selected if the market was good, and product Y in the other two cases. The expected value would then be:

$20,000 × 0.2 + $16,000 × 0.5 + $7,000 × 0.3 = $14,100

The expected value of perfect information is therefore
$14,100 – $13,500 = $600

Test your understanding 7

(a)

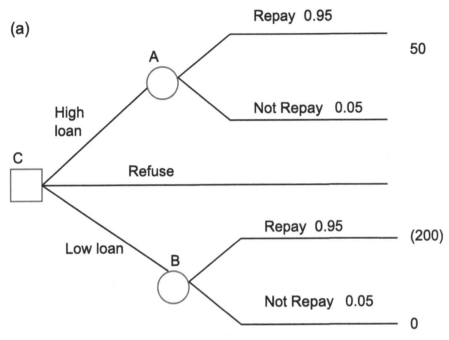

At points A and B calculate Expected Values;

At A   EV = (0.95 × 50) + (0.05 × (200))   **= 37.5**

At B   EV = (0.95 × 20) + (0.05 × (30))   **= 17.5**

At C   compare the EVs of $37.5 and $17.5.

Recommendation; if a customer requests a loan give him/her a high loan limit.

(b)

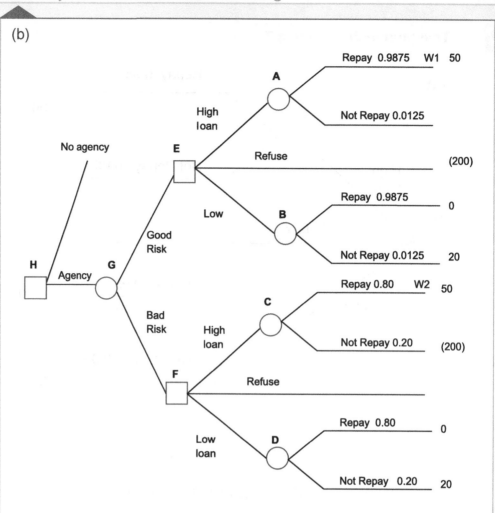

Workings

(W1) 800 customers have been assessed as being a good risk. Of these 790 did repay the loan. This represents 98.75% (790 ÷ 800) of the good risk customers.

Hence, the remaining 1.25% of the good risk customers did not repay the loan. (10 ÷ 800).

(W2) In a similar way to (W1), 160 out of the 200 bad risk customers did repay the loan, i.e. 80%.

40 out of the 200 bad risk customers did not repay the loan, i.e. 20%.

Expected Values

At A	$(0.9875 \times 50) + (0.0125 \times (200))$	=	$46.875
At B	$(0.9875 \times 20) + (0.0125 \times (30))$	=	$19.375
At C	$(0.8 \times 50) + (0.2 \times (200))$	=	0
At D	$(0.8 \times 20) + (0.2 \times (30))$	=	$10.00

Decisions

At E compare A and B. Choose A, i.e. give customers a high loan

At F compare C and D. Choose D, i.e. give customers a low loan.

Expected Values

At G $(0.8 \times 46.875) + (0.2 \times 10.00)$ = $39.5

Decision

At H compare "No agency" (return = $37.50) with the "agency" (return = $39.50)

The information from the agency is expected to increase profits by $2 per rating. This is the value of the information.

(c) Perfect information is a forecast that is 100% accurate. In the context of this problem it would be the credit rating agency providing an accurate forecast of the customer's ability to repay the loan.

If the new agency is approached;

Forecast	Decision	Outcome	Profit	Probability	Expected Value
Good risk	High loan	Repay	$50	0.95	47.50
Bad risk	Refuse loan	Nothing	$0	0.05	0
					$47.50

The expected return with perfect information	=	$47.50
The expected return with no information	=	($37.50)
		————
Therefore the value of the information is	=	$10.00

Test your understanding 8 – SITERAZE LTD

(a) Calculate the contribution for each turnover figure.

There is a 30% C/S ratio

Turnover $000	Contribution $000
15,000	4,500
8,500	2,550
4,000	1,200

Calculate the net margin for each of the different possible outcomes.

Advance hire level	Demand level	Contribution $000	Advance hire costs $000	Extra hire costs $000	Net margin $000
High	High	4,500	2,300	–	2,200
	Medium	2,550	2,300	–	250
	Low	1,200	2,300	–	(1,100)
Medium	High	4,500	1,500	1,300	1,700
	Medium	2,550	1,500	–	1,050
	Low	1,200	1,500	–	(300)
Low	High	4,500	1,000	2,150	1,350
	Medium	2,550	1,000	850	700
	Low	1,200	1,000	–	200

(b) High hire level

EV = (2,200 × 0.25) + (250 × 0.45) + (−1,100 × 0.30) = $332,500

Medium hire level

EV = (1,700 × 0.25) + (1,050 × 0.45) + (−300 × 0.30) = $807,500

Low hire level

EV = (1,350 × 0.25) + (700 × 0.45) + (200 × 0.30) = $712,500

The expected net gain is maximised at the medium hire level.

(c) Managers could either seek risk or avoid it. While the calculations of expected values seem to indicate that the medium-usage advance hire contract was the best option, this is only the result when using the weighted average and probabilities. A risk-averse manager will examine the options to see which of the demand levels is providing the worst net gains. He/she will then select the best from these worst outcomes. In the case of Siteraze this would mean selecting the low hire level. With a low hire level a net gain of $200,000 or higher is guaranteed. However, if the manager was a risk seeker, he would select the high hire level in the hope that demand would subsequently be high. This combination would yield a net gain of $2,200,000.

(d)

Demand level	Hire decision	Net gain $000	Probability	px
High	High	2,200	0.25	550.00
Medium	Medium	1,050	0.45	472.50
Low	Low	200	0.30	60.00
				1,082.50

EV with perfect information $1,082,500

EV without perfect information $807,500

Value of the information $275,000

Siteraze should not pay more than $275,000 to the consultant.

Investment appraisal techniques

Chapter learning objectives

Lead	Component
C1. Prepare information to support project appraisal.	(a) Explain the processes involved in making long-term decisions.
	(e) Explain the financial consequences of dealing with long-run projects, in particular the importance of accounting for the 'time value of money'.
C2. Evaluate project proposals.	(a) Evaluate project proposals using the techniques of investment appraisal.
	(b) Compare and contrast the alternative techniques of investment appraisal.
	(c) Prioritise projects that are mutually exclusive, involve unequal lives and/or are subject to capital rationing.

1 Chapter overview diagram

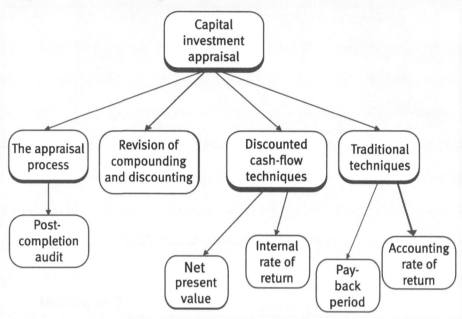

Introduction

Capital investment decisions normally represent the most important decisions that an organisation makes, since they commit a substantial proportion of a firm's resources to actions that are likely to be irreversible. Many different investment projects exist including; replacement of assets, cost-reduction schemes, new product/service developments, product/service expansions, statutory, environmental and welfare proposals, etc.

One characteristic of all capital expenditure projects is that the cash flows arise over the long term (a period usually greater than 12 months). Under this situation it becomes necessary to carefully consider the time value of money.

2 The time value of money

Money received today is worth more than the same sum received in the future, i.e. it has a **time value.**

Discounted cash flow (DCF) techniques take account of this time value of money when appraising investments.

The time value of money

There are three main reasons for the time value of money:

Consumption Preferences

There is a strong preference for the immediate rather than delayed consumption. Investors would typically prefer to receive returns sooner rather than later. they may even be willing to receive smaller returns now. Money like any other desirable commodity has a price. Given the choice of $100 now or the same amount in one year, it is always preferable to take the $ 100 now because it could be invested over the next year at say 10% interest rate to produce $110 at the end of the year.

Impact of inflation

In most countries, in most years prices rise as a result of inflation. Therefore funds received today will buy more than the same amount a year later, as prices will have risen in the meantime. The funds are subject to a loss of purchasing power over time.

Risk

The earlier cash flows are due to be received, the more certain they are – there is less chance that events will prevent payment. Earlier cash flows are therefore considered to be less risky.

3 Compound interest

A sum invested today will earn interest. Compounding calculates the future (or **terminal value**) of a given sum invested today for a number of years.

To compound a sum, the figure is increased by the amount of interest it would earn over the period.

FORMULA FOR COMPOUNDING

$$V = X(1 + r)^n$$

Where | V | = | Future value

X = Initial investment (present value)

r = Interest rate (expressed as a decimal)

n = Number of time periods

Example 1

$100 is invested in an account for five years. The interest rate is 10% per annum. Calculate the value of the account after five years.

Example 2

$450 is invested in an account earning 6.25% interest p.a. Calculate the fund value after 12 years.

Example 3

$5000 is required in 10 years. $x is invested in an account earning 5% interest p.a. Calculate the value of $x.

4 Discounting

Discounting performs the opposite function to compounding. Compounding finds the future value of a sum invested now, whereas discounting considers a sum receivable in the future and establishes its equivalent value today. This value in today's terms is known as the **Present Value (PV).**

In potential investment projects, cash flows will arise at many different points in time. Calculating the present value of future flows is a key technique in investment appraisal decisions.

FORMULAE FOR DISCOUNTING

Present value = Future value x discount factor **LEARN**

Where: Discount factor = $\dfrac{1}{(1+r)^n}$ or $(1+r)^{-n}$ **GIVEN**

where: r is the interest rate expressed as decimal

     n is the number of time periods

$(1 + r)^{-n}$ can be looked up in discounting tables. It is known as the discount factor.

Example 4

Calculate the present value of $25,000 receivable in six years' time, if the interest rate is 10% p.a.

Example 5

Calculate how much should be invested now in order to have $250 in eight years' time? The account pays 12% interest per annum.

The cost of capital

In the above discussions we referred to the rate of interest. There are a number of alternative terms used to refer to the rate a firm should use to take account of the time value of money:

- cost of capital
- discount rate
- required rate of return.

Whatever term is used, the rate of interest used for discounting reflects the cost of the finance that will be tied up in the investment.

5 Capital investment appraisal

Initial assumptions

(1) All cash inflows and outflows are known with certainty.

(2) Sufficient funds are available to undertake all profitable investments.

(3) There is zero inflation.

(4) There is zero taxation.

These assumptions are all considered in the next session.

Appraisal methods

There are four widely used appraisal methods:

(1) Net present value (NPV).

(2) Internal rate of return (IRR).

(3) The payback period.

(4) Accounting rate of return (ARR).

The NPV and IRR both consider the time value of money. They are discounted cash flow (DCF) techniques.

6 Net present value (NPV)

The net benefit or loss of benefit in present value terms from an investment opportunity.

NPV is the 'difference between the sum of the projected discounted cash inflows and outflows attributable to a capital investment or other long-term project' (Official CIMA Terminology).

The NPV represents the surplus funds (after funding the investment) earned on the project. This means that it tells us the impact on shareholder wealth. Therefore:

Decision criteria

- Any project with a positive NPV is viable.

- Projects with a negative NPV are not viable.

- Faced with mutually-exclusive projects, choose the project with the highest NPV.

What does the NPV actually mean?

NPV is defined as the:

> *difference between the sum of the projected discounted cash inflows and outflows attributable to a capital investment or other long-term project.*
>
> *(CIMA Official Terminology)*

However, it is often easier to understand it as the surplus of funds available to the investor.

Suppose, in an investment problem, we calculate the NPV of certain cash flows at 12% to be − $97, and at 10% to be zero, and yet at 8% the NPV of the same cash flows is + $108. Another way of expressing this is as follows.

- If the company's cost of capital is 12% the investor would be $97 out of pocket – i.e. the investment earns a yield below the cost of capital.

- If the company's cost of capital is 10% the investor would break even – i.e. the investment yields a return equal to the cost of capital.

- If the company's cost of capital is 8% the investor would be $108 in pocket – i.e. the investment earns a return in excess of the cost of capital.

In other words, a positive NPV is an indication of the surplus funds available to the investor as a result of accepting the project.

Assumptions used in NPV & IRR

- All cash flows occur at the start or end of a year.

Although in practice many cash flows accrue throughout the year, for discounting purposes they are all treated as occurring at the start or end of a year. Note also that if today (T_0) is 01/01/20X0, the dates 31/12/20X1 and 01/01/20X2, although technically separate days, can be treated for discounting as occurring at the same point in time, i.e. at T_1.

- Initial investments occur at once (T_0), other cash flows start in one year's time (T_1).

In project appraisal, the investment needs to be made before the cash flows can accrue. Therefore, unless the examiner specifies otherwise, it is assumed that investments (including any working capital requirement) occur in advance. The first cash flows associated with running the project are therefore assumed to occur one year after the project begins, i.e. at T_1.

Example 6 – PROJECT APPRAISAL

Mickey Ltd is considering two mutually-exclusive projects with the following details:

Project A

Initial investment	$450,000
Scrap value at the end of year 5	$20,000

Year:	1	2	3	4	5
Annual cash flows ($000)	200	150	100	100	100

Project B

Initial investment	$100,000
Scrap value at the end of year 5	$10,000

Year:	1	2	3	4	5
Annual cash flows ($000)	50	40	30	20	20

Assume that the initial investment is at the start of the project and the annual cash flows are at the **end** of each year.

Required:

Calculate the Net Present Value for Projects A and B if the relevant cost of capital is 10%.

		Project A		Project B	
Year	Discount factor 10%	Net cash flow $000	PV $000	Net cash flow $000	PV $000
0					
1					
2					
3					
4					
5					

Calculate which project has the highest NPV.

Advantages	Disadvantages
• Does consider the time value of money	• Fairly complex
• It is a measure of absolute profitability	• Not well understood by non-financial managers
• Considers cash flows	• It may be difficult to determine the cost of capital
• It considers the whole life of the project	
• A company selecting projects on the basis of NPV maximisation should maximise shareholders wealth	

Advantages and disadvantages of NPV

When appraising projects or investments, NPV is considered to be superior (in theory) to most other methods. This is because it:

- considers the time value of money – discounting cash flows to PV takes account of the impact of interest, inflation and risk over time. (See later sessions for more on inflation and risk.) These significant issues are ignored by the basic methods of payback and accounting rate of return (ARR)

- is an absolute measure of return – the NPV of an investment represents the actual surplus raised by the project. This allows a business to plan more effectively. Neither ARR nor payback is an absolute measure

- is based on cash flows not profits – the subjectivity of profits makes them less reliable than cash flows and therefore less appropriate for decision making.

- considers the whole life of the project – methods such as payback only consider the cash flows prior to the payback. NPV takes account of all relevant cash flows

- should lead to maximisation of shareholder wealth. If the cost of capital reflects the investors' (i.e. shareholders') required return, then the NPV reflects the theoretical increase in their wealth. For a company, this is considered to be the primary objective of the business.

However, there are some potential drawbacks:

- It is difficult to explain to managers. To understand the meaning of the NPV calculated requires an understanding of discounting. The method is not as intuitive as techniques such as payback.

- It requires knowledge of the cost of capital. The calculation of the cost of capital is, in practice, more complex than identifying interest rates. It involves gathering data and making a number of calculations based on that data and some estimates. The process may be deemed too protracted for the appraisal to be carried out.

- It is relatively complex. For the reasons explained above, NPV may be rejected in favour of simpler techniques.

Note: some of the advantages and disadvantages refer to the ARR and payback techniques which are covered later in the chapter. These issues may therefore need to be reviewed after studying those techniques.

7 Internal rate of return (IRR)

This is the rate of return at which the project has a NPV of zero.

Decision criteria

- If the IRR is greater than the cost of capital the project should be accepted. If the IRR is less than the cost of capital the project should be rejected.

Further explanation of IRR

Using the NPV method, PVs are calculated by discounting cash flows at a given cost of capital, and the difference between the PV of costs and the PV of benefits is the NPV. In contrast, the IRR method of analysis is to calculate the exact rate of return that the project is expected to achieve.

If an investment has a positive NPV, it means it is earning more than the cost of capital. If the NPV is negative, it is earning less than the cost of capital. This means that if the NPV is zero, it will be earning exactly the cost of capital.

Conversely, the percentage return on the investment must be the rate of discount or cost of capital at which the NPV equals zero. This rate of return is called the IRR and if it is higher than the target rate of return then the project is financially worth undertaking.

Calculating the IRR (using linear interpolation)

The steps in linear interpolation are:

(1) Calculate two NPVs for the project at two different costs of capital

(2) Use the following formula to find the IRR:

FORMULA FOR IRR

$$IRR = L + \frac{N_L}{N_L - N_H} \times (H - L)$$

where:

L = Lower rate of interest

H = Higher rate of interest

N_L = NPV at lower rate of interest

N_H = NPV at higher rate of interest.

Accuracy of the formula

The formula makes an approximation of the IRR by assuming that the NPV will move downward in a straight line. In reality the NPV line is curved and therefore there will be an element of error in the IRR estimation. The choice of rates to estimate the IRR can effect the answer provided by the formula.

Ideally you should aim to satisfy two criteria:

- do not use rates which are too far apart. A 5% difference should be sufficient. The further the rates are away from each other then the greater the amount of error in the IRR calculation.

- try to have one discount rate which gives a positive NPV, and another which gives a negative NPV. If we use two positive NPV's then we are likely to under-estimate the IRR, whilst the use of two negatives is likely to over-estimate the IRR. So having one positive and one negative is likely to give a slightly more accurate estimate.

Example 6 – CONTINUED 1

(a) Calculate the internal rate of return of Project A.

		Project A	
Year	Discount factors at ?%	Net cash flow $000	PV $000
0		(450)	
1		200	
2		150	
3		100	
4		100	
5		120	

(b) Calculate the internal rate of return of Project B.

You are given the following:

At 10% the NPV was $33,310
At 20% the NPV is $8,510
At 30% the NPV is – $9,150

Calculating the IRR using a graph

The IRR may be calculated by a linear interpolation, i.e. by assuming a linear relationship between the NPV and the discount rate. Plotting a graph would give an approximate IRR, but the same point can also be found using a formula.

Step 1   Calculate two NPVs for the project at two different costs of capital. You can choose any costs of capital and get a fair result. However, it helps to find two costs of capital for which the NPV is close to 0, because the IRR will be a value close to them. Ideally, you should use one cost of capital where the NPV is positive and the other cost of capital where the NPV is negative, although this is not essential. You should not waste time in the exam.

Step 2 Once the two NPVs have been calculated, they and their associated costs of capital can be used to calculate the IRR. In other words, we can estimate the IRR by finding the point where a line joining these points would cross the x-axis (the point where the NPV is zero) in a graph plotting the project NPV against various discount rates.

To calculate the exact IRR requires a more complex technique, best carried out using an Excel spreadsheet. This will not be expected in the exam.

IRR where there are annuities/perpetuities

(**Note:** This section should only be reviewed after annuities and perpetuities have been studied later in this chapter)

Calculating the IRR of a project with even cash flows

There is a simpler technique available, using annuity tables, if the project cash flows are annuities i.e. where it equal annual cash flows from year 1 onwards.

(1) Find the cumulative discount factor, Initial investment ÷ Annual inflow

(2) Find the life of the project, n.

(3) Look along the n year row of the cumulative discount factor until the closest value is found.

(4) The column in which this figure is found is the IRR.

Illustration – Calculating IRR of a project with even cash flows

Find the IRR of a project with an initial investment of $1.5 million and three years of inflows of $700,000 starting in one year.

Solution

NPV calculation:

		Cash flow $000	DF (c) %	PV $000
Time				
0	Investment	(1,500)	1	(1,500)
1–3	Inflow	700	(b)	(a)
				_____
NPV				Nil
				_____

- The aim is to find the discount rate (c) that produces an NPV of nil.

- Therefore the PV of inflows (a) must equal the PV of outflows, $1,500,000.

- If the PV of inflows (a) is to be $1,500,000 and the size of each inflow is $700,000, the DF required (b) must be 1,500,000 ÷ 700,000 = 2.143.

- The discount rate (c) for which this is the 3-year factor can be found by looking along the 3-year row of the cumulative discount factors shown in the annuity table.

- The figure of 2.140 appears under the 19% column suggesting an IRR of 19% is the closest.

Calculating the IRR of a project where the cash flows are perpetuities

$$\text{IRR of a perpetuity} = \frac{\text{Annual inflow}}{\text{Initial investment}} \times 100$$

Illustration – Calculating IRR where cash flows are perpetuities

Find the IRR of an investment that costs $20,000 and generates $1,600 for an indefinitely long period.

Solution

$$\text{IRR} = \frac{\text{Annual inflow}}{\text{Initial investment}} \times 100 = \frac{\$1,600}{\$20,000} \times 100 = 8\%$$

Advantages	Disadvantages
• Does consider the time value of money	• It is not a measure of absolute profitability
• As a percentage return it is easily understood by non-financial managers	• Interpolation only provides an estimate of the true IRR
• Considers cash flows	• Fairly complicated to calculate – although spreadsheets now have built-in programs
• It considers the whole life of the project	• The IRR of projects may conflict with the NPV. If this occurs the NPV must take precedence
• It can be calculated without reference to the cost of capital (but the cost of capital is necessary in applying the decision criteria)	
• A company selecting projects where the IRR exceeds the cost of capital will normally increase shareholders' wealth	

Advantages and disadvantages of IRR

Advantages:

- IRR considers the time value of money. The current value earned from an investment project is therefore more accurately measured. As discussed above this is a significant improvement over the basic methods.

- IRR is a percentage and therefore easily understood. Although managers may not completely understand the detail of the IRR, the concept of a return earned is familiar and the IRR can be simply compared with the required return of the organisation.

- IRR uses cash flows not profits. These are less subjective as discussed above.

- IRR considers the whole life of the project rather than ignoring later flows (which would occur with payback).

- The IRR can be calculated when the cost of capital is unknown (say, if finance for a project has yet to be determined). It therefore may provide a useful benchmark for appraising potential sources of capital.

- IRR a firm selecting projects where the IRR exceeds the cost of capital would normally increase shareholders' wealth. This holds true provided the project cash flows follow the typical pattern of an outflow followed by a series of inflows, as in the investment examples above.

However there are a number of difficulties with the IRR approach:

- It is not a measure of absolute profitability. A project of $1,000 invested now and paying back $1,100 in a year's time has an IRR of 10%. If a company's required return is 6%, then the project is viable according to the IRR rule but most businesses would consider the absolute return too small to be worth the investment.

- Interpolation only provides an estimate (and an accurate estimate requires the use of a spreadsheet programme). The cost of capital calculation itself is also only an estimate and if the margin between required return and the IRR is small, this lack of accuracy could actually mean the wrong decision is taken.

  For example if the cost of capital is found to be 8% (but is actually 8.7%) and the project IRR is calculated as 9.2% (but is actually 8.5%) the project would be wrongly accepted. Note that where such a small margin exists, the project's success would be considered to be sensitive to the discount rate (see session 12 on risk).

- Non-conventional cash flows may give rise to no IRR or multiple IRRs. For example a project with an outflow at T0 and T2 but income at T1 could, depending on the size of the cash flows, have a number of different profiles on a graph (see below). Even where the project does have one IRR, it can be seen from the graph that the decision rule would lead to the wrong result as the project does not earn a positive NPV at any cost of capital.

For example, a project with an immediate outflow of $10m, followed by an inflow of $90m in one year's time and a final outflow of $100m would have the following NPVs:

Discount rate	NPV ($m)
10%	−10.8
29.85%	0
60%	7.2
670.5%	0
1000%	−2.64

The NPV starts off negative, then at rates above 30% will become positive, before becoming negative again at rates above 670.5%. This could be represented by the dark line in the diagram/graph below

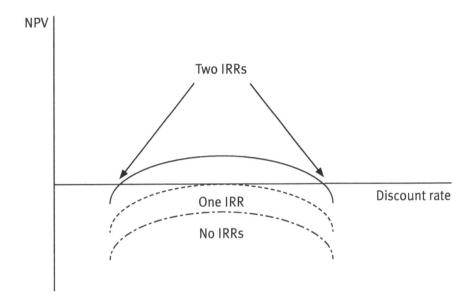

As the size of the project flows reduce the NPV would likewise reduce and the NPV line fall (as in the lower dashed lines). It can therefore be seen that there might only be one NPV (if the line just touches the zero NPV point) or no IRR's at all if the project has negative NPVs at all discount rates.

8 NPV versus IRR

Both NPV and IRR are investment appraisal techniques which discount cash flows and are superior to the basic techniques discussed in the previous session. However only NPV can be used to distinguish between two mutually-exclusive projects, as the diagram on the next page demonstrates.

Explanation of the principle

NPV and IRR may sometimes give conflicting advice and recommend different projects.

Consider the following two projects:

	Initial investment ($m)	Year 1 flow ($m)	Year 2 flow ($m)	NPV ($m) @ **10%**	IRR
Project A	(10)	0	25	10.7	58.1%
Project B	(10)	10	12	9.0	70.4%

Project A has the higher NPV but the lower IRR. The choice of project appraisal method would therefore affect the choice of project.

The NPV of these projects could be represented diagrammatically as follows:

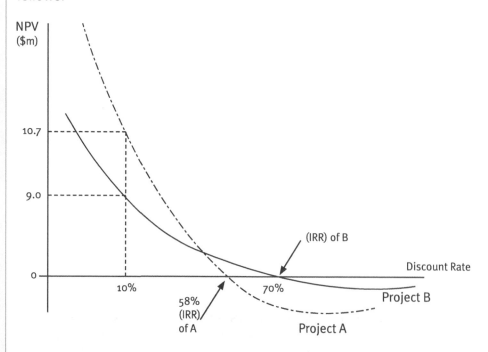

It can be seen that the NPV curves cross. But the vital piece of information is the firm's cost of capital. This is the actual cost of financing the project (i.e. it is the cost that the company will have to pay for financing the initial $10m investment). Once this cost is met, the remaining project surplus (the NPV) can be returned to shareholders. It is therefore the NPV information which will be of more concern to investors or shareholders..

The IRR is not an actual cost of capital. It instead tells us the cost of capital at which the project will break even. This cost of capital might never arise.

Another problem with the IRR is that it assumes that the project flows will be re-invested at the IRR. But again, because it is not an actual cost of capital it will also not be an actual rate at which capital can be invested. It is unlikely, for example, that Project A could re-invest funds at over 58% per annum.

The IRR is a useful piece of information when we are examining one project. It allows us to determine the highest acceptable cost of capital. But when comparing one project to another, the NPV figure is based on a more appropriate cost of capital. Therefore the NPV of projects should be used when deciding which project in which to invest.

The advantage of NPV is that it tells us the absolute increase in shareholder wealth as a result of accepting the project, at the current cost of capital. The IRR simply tells us how far the cost of capital could increase before the project would not be worth accepting.

Attitudes to risk

The general decision rule in DCF analysis is that where mutually exclusive projects are being considered, the one with the highest NPV is preferred. However, some caution should be exercised in the use of this rule. Our earlier exploration of attitude to risk indicated that a low-risk project with a lower expected NPV may be preferred to a high risk project with a higher NPV.

IRR is normally reported as part of a project appraisal. However, since it is a relative measure which lacks an element of scale it should not be used to select between alternatives. A large project with a high NPV will normally be preferred to a small project with a lower NPV but a higher IRR. A tiny project can have a very high IRR. But IRR can still be informative since it offers insights into the return that alternative uses for capital offer and this can be a guide to future strategy and decision-making.

9 The payback period

The payback period is the time a project will take to pay back the money spent on it. It is based on expected cash flows and provides a measure of liquidity and risk (the quicker that an investor can recover the initial investment the quicker they can reinvest it elsewhere and the lower the risk of this particular investment).

This is the time which elapses until the invested capital is recovered. It considers cash flows only. Unlike DCF techniques, it is assumed that the **cash flows** occur evenly during the year.

Decision criteria

- Compare the payback period to the company's maximum return time allowed and if the payback is quicker the project should be accepted.

- Faced with a choice between mutually-exclusive projects, choose the project with the quickest payback (provided it meets the company's target payback period).

Calculation – Constant annual flows

$$\text{Payback period} = \frac{\text{Initial investment}}{\text{Annual cash inflow}}$$

A payback period may not be for an exact number of years. To calculate the payback in years and months you should multiply the decimal fraction of a year by 12 to the number of months.

Example 7
An expenditure of $2 million is expected to generate net cash inflows of $500,000 each year for the next seven years.   Calculate the payback period for the project?

Calculations – Uneven annual flows

However, if cash inflows are uneven (a more likely state of affairs), the payback has to be calculated by working out the cumulative cash flow over the life of a project

Example 6 – CONTINUED 2
Calculate which project should the company select if the objective is to minimise the payback period?

Discounted payback

One of the major criticisms of using the payback period is that it does not take into account the time value of money. The discounted payback technique attempts to overcome this criticism by measuring the time required for the **present values** of the cash inflows from a project to equal the present values of the cash outflows.

The techniques are identical but the present value of the cash flows is used to calculate the cumulative cash flow and to determine the payback period.

Advantages	Disadvantages
• Simple to understand	• Is not a measure of absolute profitability
• A project with a long payback period tends to be riskier than one with a short payback period. Payback is a simple measure of risk	• Ignores the time value of money. **Note:** A discounted payback period may be calculated to overcome this problem
• Uses cash flows, not subjective accounting profits	• Does not take into account cash flows beyond the payback period
• Emphasises the cash flows in the earlier years	
• Firms selecting projects on the basis of payback periods may avoid liquidity problems	

Advantages and disadvantages of payback

Advantages

- Simplicity

As a concept, it is easily understood and is easily calculated.

- Rapidly changing technology

If new plant is likely to be scrapped in a short period because of obsolescence, a quick payback is essential.

- Improving investment conditions

When investment conditions are expected to improve in the near future, attention is directed to those projects that will release funds soonest, to take advantage of the improving climate.

- Payback favours projects with a quick return

It is often argued that these are to be preferred for three reasons.

- Rapid project payback leads to rapid company growth – but in fact such a policy will lead to many profitable investment opportunities being overlooked because their payback period does not happen to be particularly swift.
- Rapid payback minimises risk (the logic being that the shorter the payback period, the less there is that can go wrong). Not all risks are related to time, but payback is able to provide a useful means of assessing time risk (and only time risk). It is likely that earlier cash flows can be estimated with greater certainty.
- Rapid payback maximises liquidity – but liquidity problems are best dealt with separately, through cash forecasting.

- Cash flows

Cash flows are much more objective than accounting figures such as profit. Profit figures are easily manipulated using accounting policies, whereas this is not possible for cash flows.

Disadvantages

- Project returns may be ignored – In particular, cash flows arising after the payback period are totally ignored.

- Timing ignored – Cash flows are effectively categorised as pre-payback or post-payback, but no more accurate measure is made. In particular, the time value of money is ignored. This problem can be overcome if the discounted payback method is used.

- Lack of objectivity – There is no objective measure as to what length of time should be set as the minimum payback period. Investment decisions are therefore subjective.

- Project profitability is ignored – Payback takes no account of the effects on business profits and periodic performance of the project, as evidenced in the financial statements. This is critical if the business is to be reasonably viewed by users of the accounts.

10 Accounting rate of return (ARR)

The ARR method calculates a percentage return provided by the *accounting* profits of the project.

The most common formula is:

$$\text{ARR} = \frac{\text{Average annual profit}}{\text{Average value of investment}} \qquad \textbf{LEARN}$$

Important notes to the formula:

- The 'average annual profit' is after depreciation.
- Net cash flow is normally equivalent to 'profit before depreciation'.

Average annual profit = Net cash flow less depreciation

- The average value of the investment represents the average capital employed over the life of the project.

$$\text{Average value of investment} = \frac{\text{Initial investment plus residual value}}{2} \qquad \textbf{LEARN}$$

Decision criteria

- The ARR for a project may be compared with the company's target return and if higher the project should be accepted.

- Faced with a choice of mutually-exclusive investments, the project with the highest ARR should be chosen (provided it meets the company's target return).

Example 6 – CONTINUED 3

Project A

Initial investment					$450,000
Scrap value in year 5					$20,000

Year:	1	2	3	4	5
Annual cash flows ($000)	200	150	100	100	100

Project B

Initial investment					$100,000
Scrap value in year 5					$10,000

Year:	1	2	3	4	5
Annual cash flows ($000)	50	40	30	20	20

Required:

Calculate the ARR for each project, and indicate which project should be chosen.

Advantages	Disadvantages
• Simple to understand	• Ignores the time value of money
• Widely used and accepted	• Is not a measure of absolute profitability
• It considers the whole life of the project	• Does not consider cash flows. Uses subjective accounting profits, which include depreciation

Advantages and disadvantages of ARR

Advantages

- Simplicity – As with the payback period, it is easily understood and easily calculated.

- Link with other accounting measures – Return on capital employed, calculated annually to assess a business or sector of a business (and therefore the investment decisions made by that business), is widely used and its use for investment appraisal is consistent with that. The ARR is expressed in percentage terms with which managers are familiar. However, neither this nor the preceding point necessarily justify the use of ARR.

Disadvantages

There are a number of specific criticisms of the ARR.

- It fails to take account of either the project life or the timing of cash flows (and time value of money) within that life. For example, a project with a very long life which has a high ARR might be accepted before a project with a shorter life and marginally lower ARR. The NPV of the shorter project may actually be higher. In example 6, it can be seen that Project B has a much higher ARR but that Project A has a much higher NPV. Project A is the project that should be accepted by management on a financial basis.

- It will vary with specific accounting policies, and the extent to which project costs are capitalised. Profit measurement is thus 'subjective', and ARR figures for identical projects could vary from business to business depending on the accounting policies used.

- Like all rate of return measures, it is not a measurement of absolute gain in wealth for the business owners.

- There is no definite investment signal. The decision to invest or not remains subjective in view of the lack of an objectively set target ARR.

- It is concluded that the ARR does not provide a reliable basis for project evaluation.

11 NPV and IRR with equal cash flows

Discounting annuities

 An annuity is a constant annual cash flow for a number of years.

When a project has equal annual cash flows the annuity factor may be used to calculate the NPV (and hence the IRR).

 The **annuity factor** (AF) is the name given to the sum of the individual DF.

The PV of an annuity can therefore be quickly found using the formula:

PV = Annual cash flow × AF

As when calculating a discount factor, the annuity factors (AF) can be found using an annuity formula or annuity tables (cumulative present value tables).

Annuity factor formula

The formula is:

$$AF = \frac{1 - (1+r)^{-n}}{r}$$

Where

r = cost of capital

n = the number of periods

For example, for a six-year annuity at 10%:

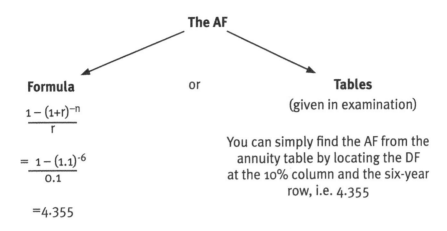

The AF

Formula   or   **Tables**
(given in examination)

$$\frac{1-(1+r)^{-n}}{r}$$

You can simply find the AF from the annuity table by locating the DF at the 10% column and the six-year row, i.e. 4.355

$$= \frac{1-(1.1)^{-6}}{0.1}$$

$$=4.355$$

Note: there is a small difference due to roundings.

Note: annuity tables are titled cumulative present value tables in the exam.

Example 8 – ANNUITIES

(a) Pluto Ltd has been offered a project costing $50,000. The returns are expected to be $10,000 each year for seven years. Cost of capital is 10%. Calculate whether the project be accepted.

(b) Calculate the IRR of the project?

Discounting perpetuities

A perpetuity is an annual cash flow that occurs forever.

It is often described by examiners as a cash flow continuing 'for the foreseeable future'.

The PV of a perpetuity is found using the formula:

$$PV = \frac{\text{cashflow}}{r}$$

'r' in the formula is the company's required rate of return (or cost of capital).

or

$$PV = \text{cashflow} \times \frac{1}{r}$$

$\dfrac{1}{r}$ is known as the perpetuity factor.

Example 9 – PERPETUITIES

An investment of $50,000 is expected to yield $5,670 per annum in perpetuity. Calculate the net present value of the investment opportunity if the cost of capital is 9%.

Annuities/perpetuities in advance

The use of annuity factors and perpetuity factors both assume that the first cash flow will be occurring in one year's time. If this is not the case, you will need to adjust your calculation.

Advanced annuities and perpetuities

Some regular cash flows may start now (at T_0) rather than in one years time (T_1).

Calculate the PV by ignoring the payment at T_0 when considering the number of cash flows and then adding one to the annuity or perpetuity factor.

Illustration – Advanced annuities and perpetuities

A 5-year $600 annuity is starting today. Interest rates are 10%. Find the PV of the annuity.

Solution

This is essentially a standard 4-year annuity with an additional payment at T_0. The PV could be calculated as follows:

	T_0	T_1	T_2	T_3	T_4
CF	600	600	600	600	600
PV	600 +		$600 \times$ 4-year 10% AF		

PV = 600 + 600 × 3.17 = 600 + 1902 = $2,502

The same answer can be found more quickly by adding 1 to the AF:

PV = 600 × (1 + 3.17) = 600 × 4.17 = $2,502.

Illustration – Advanced perpetuities

A perpetuity of $2,000 is due to commence immediately. The interest rate is 9%. What is the PV?

Solution

This is essentially a standard perpetuity with an additional payment at T_0. The PV could be calculated as follows:

T_0		T_1	T_2	T_3		T_4 ....
2,000		$2,000 \to \infty$				

PV (2000) + (2000 × 9% perpetuity formula)

Again, the same answer can be found more quickly by adding 1 to the perpetuity factor.

$$2000 \times \left(1 + \frac{1}{0.09}\right) = 2000 \times 12.11 = \$24,222$$

Annuities/perpetuities in arrears

Delayed annuities and perpetuities

Some regular cash flows may start later than T_1.

These are dealt with by:

(1) applying the appropriate factor to the cash flow as normal

(2) discounting your answer back to T_0.

Illustration – Delayed annuities and perpetuities

What is the PV of $200 incurred each year for four years, starting in three year's time, if the discount rate is 5%?

Solution

Method: A four-year annuity starting at T_3
                                           (1 – 4)

T_0	T_1	T_2	T_3	T_4	T_5	T_6
			200	200	200	200

PV   **2.**

1.

Step 1.   Discount the annuity as usual

200 × 4yr 5% AF = 200 × 3.546 = 709.2

Note that this gives the value of the annuity at T_2

Step 2.   Discount the answer back to T_0

709.2 × 2yr 5% DF = 709.2 × 0.907 = $643

Annuity or perpetuity factors will discount the cash flows back to give the value one year before the first cash flow arose. For standard annuities and perpetuities this gives the present (T_0) value since the first cash flow started at T_1.

However for delayed cash flows, applying the factor will find the value of the cash flows one year before they began, which in this example is T_2. To find the PV, an additional calculation is required – the value must be discounted back to T_0.

Care must be taken to discount back the appropriate number of years. The figure here was discounted back two years because the first step gave the value at T_2. It can help to draw a timeline as above and mark on the effect of the first step (as shown with a 1. here) to help you remember.

12 Changing discount rates

Throughout this chapter we have assumed that a company will have a constant discount rate. This allows us to use the tables of discount rates that are provided in the exam. However, in reality discount rates might change from year to year. For example, in the next chapter we will see that inflation affects discount rates, and because inflation is not constant discount rates will not be constant.

Therefore in these instances we cannot use the tables that we are provided with and instead must calculate each year's discount factor individually using the discounting formula from the start of this chapter.

Illustration

A company is considering a four year investment. Its cost of capital during this period is expected to rise each year as interest rates and inflation rates rise in the economy. It expects its cost of capital to be as follows:

Year 1	10%
Year 2	12%
Year 3	15%
Year 4	16%

Calculate the discount rate that should be used for each year.

Answer

Because the cost of capital is changing each year we cannot use the tables that we are provided with. Instead we have to calculate the discount rate for each year individually.

The best way to do this is to divide the discount factor for the previous year by (1 + the cost of capital for the year in question). This can be shown as follows:

	Calculation	Discount factor
Year 0		1.000
Year 1	1.000 / 1.10	0.909
Year 2	0.909 / 1.12	0.812
Year 3	0.812 / 1.15	0.706
Year 4	0.706 / 1.16	0.608

These are the discount factors that would be used in any NPV calculation employed by the company.

This technique can be very important when dealing with inflation in the next chapter.

13 Dealing with non annual periods

In some instances we may have to deal with cash flows which are not in annual terms – for example, costs might be paid in 6 monthly blocks. In these cases we need to pro-rate the discount rate to match the period of the cash flows.

Illustration

If, say, we are given an annual discount rate of 10% but cashflows are received in non-annual instalments, in order to calculate the appropriate cost of capital to use for calculations we would need to pro-rate the 10% as follows:

Cashflows are in...	Pro-rata formula	Calculation	Appropriate discount rate
Quarters	$(1+i)^{1/4} - 1$	$(1.10)^{1/4} - 1$	2.41% per quarter
6 monthly periods	$(1+i)^{1/2} - 1$	$(1.10)^{1/2} - 1$	4.88% per 6 months
Months	$(1+i)^{1/12} - 1$	$(1.10)^{1/12} - 1$	0.8% per month
2 yearly instalments	$(1+i)^2 - 1$	$(1.10)^2 - 1$	21% per two years

This technique will be particularly useful in calculating the cost of receivables and payables later in the syllabus.

14 The capital investment process

A decision making model for capital expenditure decisions is shown below:

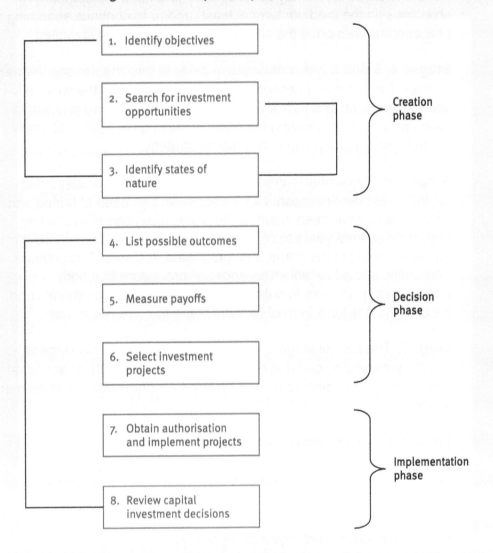

Notes to the diagram

Stage 1 indicates the objectives or goals of the organisation. Most organisations pursue a variety of goals, for example maximisation of profits, maximisation of sales, survival of the firm, achieving satisfactory profits and obtaining the largest share of the market. Achieving profit maximisation in the long term will ensure maximisation of the market value of the shareholders' wealth. The capital investment process seeks to achieve maximisation of wealth by maximising the net present value of future net cash inflows.

Stage 2 involves the search for investment opportunities. Without a proactive, deliberate search for creative projects and opportunities, even the most sophisticated evaluation techniques are worthless. A firm's prosperity is dependent upon its ability to create investment opportunities.

Stage 3 requires data to be gathered about possible future environments that may affect the outcomes of the project. Examples of states of nature include economic booms/recessions, high inflation, world shortages etc. It may be necessary to amend the company objectives (in the medium term at least) and/or to continue searching for new opportunities once the states of nature have been identified.

Stages 4, 5 and 6 are considered in detail in this chapter and the next chapter. Examination questions typically involve listing the various alternatives open to a firm, identifying cash flows that are relevant to each opportunity, evaluating the value of these cash flows and finally recommending an optimum investment strategy.

Stage 7. It is essential to implement a sound system for approving capital investment proposals. Once approval has been obtained and initial outlays have been incurred the firm is often committed to the project for several years to come. Approval should not merely be a rubberstamping of the managers' proposals. A Capital Expenditure Committee should establish an approval procedure that both encourages managers to submit realistic, achievable proposals and ensures that the long-term objectives of the firm are being met.

Stage 8. The review stage is an important final step. This stage is usually achieved by carrying out a post-completion audit or appraisal. The audit is often initiated approximately 12 months into the investment project.

The capital expenditure committee

The Committee is usually responsible for overseeing the capital investment process. The functions of such a committee are to:

- co-ordinate capital expenditure policy;
- appraise and authorise capital expenditure on specific projects;
- review actual expenditure on capital projects against the budget (see next section).

In many organisations, multidisciplinary teams, or working parties, are set up to investigate individual proposals and report back to top management on their findings.

Such a team might comprise:

- project engineer;

- production engineer;

- management accountant;

- relevant specialist, e.g. personnel officer, for a project involving sports facilities or canteens, safety officers, etc.

15 Post-completion audit

The post-completion appraisal of projects provides a mechanism whereby experience gained from current and past projects can be fed into the organisation's decision-making process to aid decisions on future projects. In other words, it aids organisational learning. A post-completion appraisal reviews all aspects of an ongoing project in order to assess whether it has fulfilled its initial expectations. It is a forward-looking rather than a backward-looking technique. The task is often carried out by the Capital Expenditure Committee, or an appointed sub-committee.

Further discussion on post-completion audits

Benefits of post-completion audit

(1) If managers know in advance that projects are going to be subject to a post-completion appraisal they ensure that assumptions and plans for the project are more accurate and realistic.

(2) If an appraisal is carried out before the project life ends, and it is found that the benefits have been less than expected because of management inefficiency, then steps can be taken to improve efficiency.

(3) It might identify weaknesses in the forecasting techniques and the estimating techniques used to evaluate the project. The discipline and quality of forecasting for future investments can be improved.

(4) Managers may be motivated to achieve the forecast results if they are aware of a pending post-completion appraisal.

(5) The appraisal reveals the reliability and quality of contractors and suppliers involved in the project.

(6) The appraisal may highlight the reasons for success or failure in previous projects – thereby providing a learning experience for managers to aid better decision making in the future.

Problems with post-completion audits

(1) It may not be possible to identify separately the costs and benefits of any particular project.

(2) It can be a time-consuming and costly exercise.

(3) Applied punitively, post-completion appraisal may lead managers to becoming over-cautious and risk averse.

(4) The strategic effects of a capital investment project may take years to materialise and it may never be possible to identify and quantify them correctly.

(5) There are many uncontrollable factors in long-term investments. A post-completion appraisal will not help managers change these factors in the future.

Role of post-appraisal in project abandonment

Those intimately involved with a project may be reluctant to admit, even to themselves, that early problems with a project are likely to continue. When problems are being experienced in project implementation, those involved may be tempted to try to resolve the situation in one of two ways. They can make a change in the original plans and/or incur further expenditure in order to meet the original objective.

Whether either of these responses is appropriate will depend on the particular circumstances of the project but any significant changes or deviations should not be undertaken without the formal approval of higher management. The control systems in place will normally require changes of scope to be documented and approved before they are undertaken. It is usually the responsibility of the engineers associated with the project to ensure that this is done.

Expected project cost overruns should be highlighted by the routine monitoring of project expenditure by accounting staff, and formal approval should be obtained for the anticipated overspend. A prerequisite of approval by top management will often be the provision of the same level of detailed justification as was required when the initial funds were sanctioned. These controls ensure that significant changes to the character of a project cannot be made without top management's approval. However, they do not, of themselves, ensure that the option to terminate a project is considered, although it would be unlikely that management would fail to consider this possibility.

Some companies require an audit on all projects that need additional funds. The request for further funding would then be considered alongside the audit report. Routine monitoring of projects tends to focus almost exclusively on costs. An audit will review both costs and revenues, and, most importantly, focuses on the future. By checking the continuing validity of both forecast costs and revenues, the post-audit team is in a position to prepare a report to advise management on the wisdom of continuing with the project.

16 Project abandonment

During a post-completion appraisal it may be realised that the project is not likely to be so profitable as first thought and the possibility of abandoning it or terminating it early should be considered. Past cash flows are, of course, irrelevant to the decision – only future cash flows need to be considered. Abandoning the project is only necessary when the net discounted expected future cash flow of the project becomes negative.

Example project abandonment decisions

Case I

A project, P, has expected cash flows as follows:

Year	Cash flow	DF @ 10%	PV
$			$
0	(3,500)	1.000	(3,500)
1	2,000	0.909	1,818
2	2,000	0.826	1,652
3	2,000	0.751	1,502
NPV			+ 1,472

The initial investment of $3,500 in project P represents the purchase of a customised machine, the price of which is known with certainty. Because it is a customised machine its resale value is low; it can only be sold for $1,000 immediately after purchase. Once the machine is bought, therefore, the expected value of abandoning the project would be $1,000 (1.0 × $1,000). This must be compared with the expected value of continuing with the project, which is $4,972 ($1,818 + $1,652 + $1,502). In this case the expected benefits of continuing with the project far outweigh the returns from abandoning it immediately.

Case II

The decision to abandon a project will usually be made as a result of revised expectations of future revenues and costs. These revisions may be consistent with the data on which the original investment decision was based, or represent an alteration to earlier expectations. If the decision is consistent with the original data, the possibility, but not the certainty, that the project might have to be abandoned would have been known when the project was accepted. In these circumstances, project abandonment is one of a known range of possible outcomes arising from accepting the project.

In Case I, the cashflows for the project were based on expected value techniques. The expected cash flows and probabilities were as follows:

Year 0	Year 1		Year 2		Year 3	
$	p	$	p	$	p	$
3,500	0.33	3,000	0.33	3,000	0.33	3,000
	0.33	2,000	0.33	2,000	0.33	2,000
	0.33	1,000	0.33	1,000	0.33	1,000
Expected value		2,000		2,000		2,000

In year 0, the expected net cash inflow in each year of project P's 3-year life is $2,000. The actual outcome of any of the 3 years is unknown at this point, and each of the three possible outcomes is equally likely. The factors that will cause any one of these results to occur may differ each year, or they may be the same each year. In some instances, a particular outcome in the first year may determine the outcome of years 2 and 3 with certainty. For example, the outcome of $3,000 in year 1 may mean that this same outcome will follow with certainty in years 2 and 3. Similarly outcomes of $2,000 and $1,000 in year 1 may be certain to be repeated in years 2 and 3. In year 0, the investor can only calculate the expected net cash flow in years 2 and 3, but with perfect correlation of flows between years these future flows are known with certainty at the end of year 1. If the year 1 inflow is either $3,000 or $2,000, perfect correlation between years will ensure that the actual NPV of the project will be positive. But if the first year's outcome is $1,000, the investment will have a negative NPV of $1,014, that is ($[3,500] + $1,000 × 2.486).

Should the project be abandoned? The information is now certain and so the decision on whether to abandon should be made using a risk-free interest rate and not the company's normal cost of capital. If we assume that the risk-free rate is 5 per cent, the present value of *continuing* at the end of year 1 will be:

Year	Cash flow	DF @ 5%	PV
$			$
0	(1,000)	1.000	(1,000)
1	1,000	0.952	952
2	1,000	0.907	907
PV of continuing after 1 year			+ 859

Clearly the project should not be abandoned.

Case III

Consider another project, Project X with the following expected cash flows:

Year	Discounted cash flow
	$m
1	(8)
2	(16)
3	(24)
4	55
NPV	+ 7

The company experienced great difficulty in implementing the project in year 1, and the actual costs incurred during that year were $16 m. The company must then ask itself whether the actual outcome in year 1 necessitates any revision in the expected outcomes of later years. If no revision is required, further costs of $40 m (year 0 values) must be incurred to secure inflows of $55 m (year 0 values). The expected net present value of continuing with project X beyond year 1 will thus be $15 m (year 0 values). (Note that adjusting the figures to year 1 values would increase the expected NPV slightly, strengthening the case for continuation.)

The overall result of the investment would, of course, be negative by $1 m, if years 2–4 costs and revenues are as forecast. The excess spend of $8 m in year 1 is greater than the $7 m net present value originally predicted. However, at the end of year 1 the $16 m is a sunk cost and does not influence a decision on termination made at that time.

17 Chapter summary

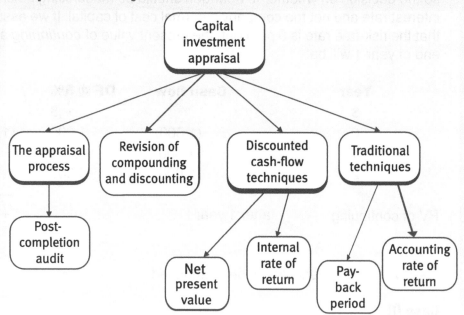

18 Practice questions

Test your understanding 1

An organisation is considering a capital investment in new equipment. The estimated cash flows are as follows.

Year	Cash flow
	$
0	(240,000)
1	80,000
2	120,000
3	70,000
4	40,000
5	20,000

The company's cost of capital is 9%.

Calculate the NPV of the project to assess whether it should be undertaken.

(2 marks)

Test your understanding 2

A company is considering a project with a three-year life producing the following costs and revenues:

	$
Cost of machine	100,000
Depreciation of machine (for three years)	20,000 p.a.
Residual value of machine	40,000
Annual cost of direct labour	20,000
Annual charge for foreman (10% apportionment)	5,000
Annual cost of components required	18,000
Annual net revenues from machine	80,000
Cost of capital	20%

Identify which of the following is closest to the net present value of the machine:

A   ($13,000)

B   ($11,380)

C $11,610

D $22,370

(2 marks)

Test your understanding 3

A potential project's predicted cash flows give a NPV of $50,000 at a discount rate of 10% and –$10,000 at a rate of 15%.

Calculate the internal rate of return (IRR).

(2 marks)

Test your understanding 4

Identify the correct explanation of the internal rate of return – it is the interest rate that equates the present value of expected future net cash flows to:

A   the initial cost of the investment outlay

B   the depreciation value of the investment

C   the terminal (compounded) value of future cash receipts

D   the firm's cost of capital

(2 marks)

Test your understanding 5

A business undertakes high-risk investments and requires a minimum expected rate of return of 17% pa on its investments. A proposed capital investment has the following expected cash flows:

Year	$
0	(50,000)
1	18,000
2	25,000
3	20,000
4	10,000

State, on financial grounds alone, whether this project should go ahead.

(4 marks)

Note: you should calculate the NPV of the project at a cost of capital of 15% and 20%.

Test your understanding 6

$50,000 is to be spent on a machine having a life of five years and a residual value of $5,000. Operating cash inflows will be the same each year, except for year 1 when the figure will be $6,000. The accounting rate of return (ARR) is measured as average annual profit as a percentage of the initial investment. If the ARR is 30% then identify the payback period:

A 2.75 years

B 2.15 years

C 1.85 years

D 2.54 years

(4 marks)

Test your understanding 7

A project has a normal pattern of cash flows (i.e. an initial outflow followed by several years of inflows).

Identify what would be the effects of an increase in the company's cost of capital on the internal rate of return (IRR) of the project and its discounted payback period (DPP)?

	IRR	DPP
A	Decrease	Decrease
B	Decrease	Increase
C	No change	Increase
D	No change	Decrease

(2 marks)

Test your understanding 8

A business is considering a project which would last 5 years and have an initial investment of $40,000 in machinery. At the end of the project the machinery would have a scrap value of $4,000. The project would provide annual net cash inflows as follows:

Year	Net cashflow ($000)
1	16
2	20
3	12
4	12
5	10

The company has a target payback period of 2.5 years and new projects must also provide and average accounting rate of return of at least 15% p.a.

Advise the company on whether this project meets the company's targets.

(4 marks)

Test your understanding 9

Calculate the present value of the following cash flows:

(1) A fifteen year annuity of $300 starting at once. Interest rates are 6%.

(2 marks)

(2) A perpetuity of $33,000 commencing immediately. Interest rates are 22%.

(2 marks)

Test your understanding 10

$100,000 is deposited in a bank account paying 8% interest each year. Calculate the maximum sum that can be withdrawn from the account at the end of each year in perpetuity.

(2 marks)

Test your understanding 11

In order to earn a perpetuity of $2,000 per annum calculate how much would need to be invested today. The account will pay 10% interest.

(2 marks)

Test your understanding 12

Goofy Ltd is considering a project, the estimated costs of which are $90,000. The returns are expected to be $20,000 p.a. for the first five years and $10,000 each year for the next five years. The assets may be sold at the end of the tenth year for $8,000. Cost of capital is 10%. Calculate whether the project be accepted.

(2 marks)

Test your understanding 13

Calculate the IRR of an investment of $50,000 if the inflows are:

(a) $5,000 in perpetuity

(2 marks)

(b) $8,060 for eight years.

(2 marks)

Test your understanding 14

MN plc has a rolling programme of investment decisions. One of these investment decisions is to consider mutually-exclusive investments A, B and C. The following information has been produced by the investment manager.

	Investment decision A $	Investment decision B $	Investment decision C $
Initial investment	105,000	187,000	245,000
Cash inflow for A: years 1 to 3	48,000		
Cash inflow for B: years 1 to 6		48,000	
Cash inflow for C: years 1 to 9			48,000
Net present value (NPV) at 10% each year	14,376	22,040	31,432
Ranking	3rd	2nd	1st
Internal rate of return (IRR)	17.5%	14%	13%
Ranking	1st	2nd	3rd

Required:

(a) Prepare a report for the management of MN plc which includes:

- a graph showing the sensitivity of the three investments to changes in the cost of capital;

- a statement of the reasons for differences between NPV and IRR rankings – use investment A to illustrate the points you make;

- a brief summary which gives MN plc's management advice on which project should be selected.

(18 marks)

(b) One of the directors has suggested using payback to assess the investments. Explain to him the advantages and disadvantages of using payback methods over IRR and NPV. Use the figures above to illustrate your answer.

(7 marks)

(Total: 25 marks)

Test your understanding 15

The financial director of A Co has prepared the following schedule to enable her to appraise a new project. Interest rates are 10%. She wants to calculate the PV of the cash flows using two different assumptions regarding the project duration.

The assumptions are as follows:

A   That the real annual cash flow will be $250,000 from Year 4 for the foreseeable future.

B   That the real annual cash flow will be $250,000 from Year 4 to Year 18.

Year	T_0	T_1	T_2	T_3	Assumption (a) T_4 onwards	Assumption (b) T_4-T_{18}
	$000	$000	$000	$000	$000	$000
Net cash flow	(2,000)	(440)	363	399	250	250

Required:

Calculate the NPV from the project under both assumptions.

(4 marks)

Test your understanding answers

Example 1

$V = 100 (1.10)^5 = \$161.05$

Example 2

$V = 450(1.0625)^{12} = \$931.45$

Example 3

$$x \quad = \quad \frac{5{,}000}{1.05^{10}} \quad = \quad \$3{,}070$$

Example 4

$PV = 25{,}000 \times 0.564 = \$14{,}100$

Example 5

$x = 250 \times 0.404 = \$101$

Example 6 – PROJECT APPRAISAL

Year	Discount factor	Project A		Project B	
		Cash flow $000	Present value $000	Cash flow $000	Present value $000
0		(450)	(450)	(100)	(100)
1	0.909	200	181.8	50	45.45
2	0.826	150	123.9	40	33.04
3	0.751	100	75.1	30	22.53
4	0.683	100	68.3	20	13.66
5	0.621	120	74.52	30	18.63
		NPV =	73.62	NPV =	33.31

Example 6 – CONTINUED 1

(a)

Year	Discount factors at 20%	Project A	
		Net cash flow $000	PV $000
0	1.000	(450)	(450)
1	0.833	200	167
2	0.694	150	104
3	0.579	100	58
4	0.482	100	48
5	0.402	120	48
		NPV @ 20% =	(25)

$$IRR = L + \cfrac{N_L}{N_L - N_H} \times (H - L)$$

$$IRR = 10 + \cfrac{74}{74 - (-25)} \times (20 - 10)$$

$$IRR = 10 + \cfrac{74}{99} \times (10)$$

$$IRR = 10 + (0.747 \times 10)$$

IRR = 17.5%

(b) **Project B**

At 10% the NPV was $33,310
At 20% the NPV is $8,510
At 30% the NPV is − $9,150

$$IRR = 20 + \cfrac{8,510}{8,510 - (-9,150)} \times (30 - 20)$$

$$IRR = 20 + \cfrac{8,510}{17,660} \times (10)$$

$$IRR = 20 + (0.482 \times 10)$$

IRR = 24.8%

Example 7

Calculation – constant annual flows

$$\text{Payback Period} = \frac{\$2m}{\$500{,}000}$$

Payback Period = 4 years

Example 6 – CONTINUED 2

Project A	Cashflow	Cumulative cash flow
Year 0	(450)	(450)
Year 1	200	(250)
Year 2	150	(100)
Year 3	100	0

Payback period = 3 years

Project B		
Year 0	(100)	(100)
Year 1	50	(50)
Year 2	40	(10)
Year 3	30	20

Payback period = 3 years

Note:

The question states that cashflows only arise at year ends. If they were to arise evenly throughout the year then a more accurate payback period would be 2 years and 4 months.

Example 6 – CONTINUED 3

	Project A	Project B
	$000	$000
Total profit before depreciation (total operating cash)	650	160
Less total depreciation	(430)	(90)
Total profit after depreciation	220	70
÷ number of years	5	5
Average annual profit	44	14
Average value of investment	235	55
Accounting rate of return	18.7%	25.5%

Conclusion: the firm should select project B

Overall summary for the projects:

Project A
NPV:	$73,620
IRR:	17.5%
Payback period:	3 years
Discounted payback period:	just over 4 years
ARR:	18.7%

Project B
NPV:	$33,310
IRR:	24.8%
Payback period:	2 years and 4 months
Discounted payback period:	just under 3 years
ARR:	25.5%

It can be seen that different methods recommend different projects. All of the methods except NPV would recommend Project B. Yet the NPV method should prevail and Project A is the project which will provide the most wealth for shareholders and most closely achieve the organisation's goals. More on the conflict between NPV and IRR is covered later in the chapter.

Example 8 – ANNUITIES

(a)

Year	Cash flow $	Discount factor	Present value $
0	(50,000)	1.000	(50,000)
1–7	10,000	4.868	48,680
			(1,320)

The project should therefore be rejected.

(b) $10,000 × annuity factor = $50,000

Annuity factor = 5

Using tables and a life of seven years, the closest annuity factor to 5 is 5.033. This means the IRR is approximately 9%

Example 9 – PERPETUITIES

NPV = ($50,000) + $5,670 ÷ 0.09 = $13,000

Test your understanding 1

Year	Cash flow	DF at 9%	PV
	$		$
0	(240,000)	1.000	(240,000)
1	80,000	0.917	73,360
2	120,000	0.842	101,040
3	70,000	0.772	54,040
4	40,000	0.708	28,320
5	20,000	0.650	13,000
NPV			+ 29,760

The PV of cash inflows exceeds the PV of cash outflows by $29,760, which means that the project will earn a DCF return in excess of 9%, i.e. it will earn a surplus of $29,760 after paying the cost of financing. It should therefore be undertaken.

Test your understanding 2

Revenue – components – labour = $80,000 – $18,000 – $20,000 = $42,000

Year	Cash flow $000		Discount factor	Present value
0	Initial cost	(100)		(100)
1 – 3	Annual cash	42	2.106	88.452
3	Residual	40	0.579	23.16
				11.612

Net present value = $11,612

Answer C

Test your understanding 3

$$IRR = 10\% + \frac{50,000}{50,000 - (-10,000)} \times (15\% - 10\%) = 14.17\%$$

Test your understanding 4

At the IRR, PV of future net cash flows = initial capital outlay.

Answer A

Test your understanding 5

Year	Cash flow	DF @ 15%	PV @ 15%	DF @ 20%	PV @ 20%
	$		$		$
0	(50,000)	1.000	(50,000)	1.000	(50,000)
1	18,000	0.870	15,660	0.833	14,994
2	25,000	0.756	18,900	0.694	17,350
3	20,000	0.658	13,160	0.579	11,580
4	10,000	0.572	5,720	0.482	4,820
NPV			+ 3,440		(1,256)

The IRR is above 15% but below 20%.

Using the interpolation method:

(1)   The NPV is + 3,440 at 15%.

(2)   The NPV is – 1,256 at 20%.

(3)   The estimated IRR is therefore:

$$IRR = 15\% + \frac{3,440}{(440 - (-1,256)} \times (20 - 15)\%$$

$$= 15\% \quad + 3.7\%$$

$$= 18.7\%$$

The project is expected to earn a DCF return in excess of the target rate of 17%, so on financial grounds (ignoring risk) it is a worthwhile investment.

Test your understanding 6

Average annual profit = $50,000 × 30%	$15,000
	× 5 yrs
Total profit	$75,000
Add back depreciation	$45,000
	————
Total cash	$120,000
Less year 1 cash flow	(6,000)
	————
	$114,000
Cash per annum (yrs 2–5) 114 / 4	$28,500
Outlay	$50,000
Cash inflow after 2 years 6,000 + 28,500	$34,500
Still required	$15,500
Proportion of year 3 to gain balance of cash =	15,500 ÷ 28,500 = 0.54
Hence payback period =	2.54 years

Answer D

Test your understanding 7

The IRR will be unaffected by the cost of capital. As the discount rate increases future cash flow reduce in present value terms, therefore the discounted payback period will increase.

Answer C

Test your understanding 8

Payback period

After two years $36,000 of the initial $40,000 of the investment has been recovered. It will take one third of year 3 ($4,000 required/ $12,000 received in year 3) to recover the remaining investment.

So the payback period is 2.33 years, which satisfies the target of 2.5 years.

Accounting rate of return

$$\text{Average annual profit} = \frac{\text{Total net cashflows} - \text{Total depreciation}}{\text{Life of the project}}$$

$$= \frac{\$70,000 - \$36,000}{5 \text{ years}}$$

$$= \$6,800$$

$$\text{Average investment} = \frac{\text{Initial investment} + \text{Scrap value}}{2}$$

$$= \frac{\$40,000 + \$4,000}{2}$$

$$= \$22,000$$

$$\text{ARR} = \frac{\$6,800}{\$22,000}$$

ARR = 30.9% p.a.

This is above the target return of 15%.

Overall

The investment satisfies both target measures and should therefore be accepted.

Test your understanding 9

(1) This is a standard 14-year annuity with one additional payment at T_0.

Step 1: Look up the 14-year AF ⇨

AF = 9.295

Step 2: Add 1 ⇨ 9.295 + 1 = 10.295

Step 3: Calculate the PV ⇨300 × 10.295 = \$3,088.50

(2) This is simply a standard perpetuity with one additional payment at T_0.

Step 1: Calculate the perpetuity factor ⇨ 1/0.22 = 4.545

Step 2: Add 1 ⇨ 4.545 + 1 = 5.545

Step 3: Calculate the PV ⇨ 33,000 × 5.545 = \$182,982

Test your understanding 10

Maximum withdrawal = \$100,000 × 0.08 = \$8,000 per annum in perpetuity.

Test your understanding 11

Initial investment required = \$2,000 ÷ 0.10 = \$20,000.

Test your understanding 12

Year	Cash flow $	Discount factor	Present value $
0	(90,000)		(90,000)
1 – 5	20,000 p.a	3.791	75,820
6 – 10	10,000 p.a.	2.354	23,540
10	8,000	0.386	3,088
			12,448

Test your understanding 13

(a) IRR = $\dfrac{\text{Annual inflow}}{\text{Initial investment}} \times 100 = \dfrac{\$5,000}{\$50,000} \times 100 = 10\%$

(b) NPV calculation

Time		Cash flow $	DF(c) %	PV $
0	Investment	(50,000)	1	(50,000)
1–8	Inflow	8,060	(b)	(a)
			NPV	Nil

- The aim is to find the discount rate (c) that produces an NPV of nil.
- Therefore the PV of inflows (a) must equal the PV of outflows, $50,000.
- If the PV of inflows (a) is to be $50,000 and the size of each inflow is $8,060, the DF required must be 50,000 ÷ 8,060 = 6.20.
- The discount rate (c) for which this is the 8-year factor can be found by looking along the 8-year row of the cumulative DFS shown in the annuity table.
- The figure of $6.210 appears under the 6% column suggesting an IRR of 6% is the closest.

Test your understanding 14

(a)

To:	The Management
From:	The Management Accountant
Subject:	Investment projects A, B and C
Date:	1 July 2006

The investment manager has analysed three mutually-exclusive investment opportunities A, B and C. The financial benefits from these opportunities are illustrated below in diagrammatical form.

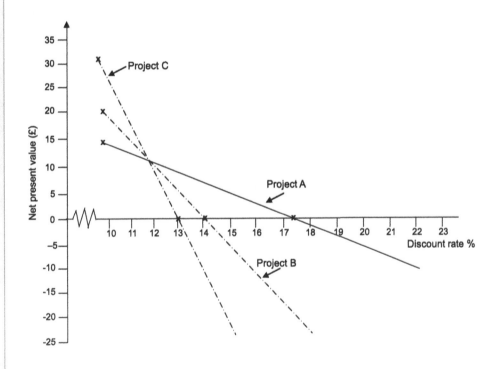

Reasons for differences between NPV and IRR rankings

There are two main reasons that NPV and IRR rankings differ:

(1) The magnitude of the cash flows.

(2) The timing of the cash flows.

Magnitude of cash flows

Imagine we were faced with a choice between the following two projects:

Project A$_1$	Year	Cash flow $
	0	(105,000)
	1	48,000
	2	48,000
	3	48,000

Project A$_2$	Year	Cash flow $
	0	(105)
	1	49
	2	49
	3	49

The cash flows in Project A$_1$ are approximately 1,000 times bigger than those in Project A$_2$. Hence the NPV of Project A$_1$ will be approximately 1,000 times bigger than the NPV of Project A$_2$. The NPV of Project A$_1$ is $14,376, but the NPV of A$_2$ will be just over $16.86. NPV would therefore suggest that Project A$_1$ should be preferred.

Consider the IRRs of A$_1$ and A$_2$. In project A$_2$ the return is $48,000 p.a., whereas project A$_2$ yields $49 p.a. The relative percentage return from Project A$_2$ is thus higher than that of Project A$_1$. Hence A$_2$ has a greater IRR than A$_1$.

The inconsistency in ranking has been caused by the magnitude of the figures.

Timing of cash flows

The actual time periods when the cash is generated can produce conflicting results.

Again consider two projects.

Project A$_1$	Year	Cash flow $
	0	(105,000)
	1	48,000
	2	48,000
	3	48,000

Project A$_2$	Year	Cash flow $
	0	(105,000)
	1	130,000
	2	0
	3	0

The NPV of Project A$_2$ is $13,170 (130 × 0.909 – 105).

This NPV is lower than the NPV of Project A$_1$.

The magnitude of the cash sums is very similar in both projects.

If we consider how the NPVs of the two projects reduce as the discount rate rises.

The NPV of A$_1$ will fall rapidly as the cash flows in the years 2 and 3 very quickly reduce in present value terms. The NPV of this project becomes zero at a 17.5% discount rate.

The cash in Project A$_2$ is all received in the first year. This cash sum is only $130,000, compared to cash in flows of $144,000 in Project A$_1$. However the value of the year 1 cash flow remains strong even as the discount rate rises.

Indeed, at a discount rate of 17.5% the NPV of A$_2$ is still positive at $5,630 (130 × 1/1.175 – 105).

Hence the IRR of Project A$_2$ MUST be greater than 17.5%.

Again there has been a conflict in the rankings, this time because of the timing of the cash flows.

These examples should illustrate that it is just as important to consider WHEN the cash flows arise as to consider HOW MUCH the cash flows are. It is very important to obtain cash in the early years of a project whilst it holds a high present value.

Comparison of opportunities A, B and C

The capital outlay in Project C is much greater than the other two projects. Cash inflows are generated for 9 years.

At a low cost of capital this project is worth the most to the company. The cash in years 6-9 maintains a high value when discount rates are low.

However, this project is very sensitive to increases in discount rates. As the cost of capital rises the NPV of Project C declines rapidly. This is illustrated in the graph at the beginning of the report.

Project A is less sensitive to increases in discount rates. All its cash is received in years 1 to 3. These maintain a strong value as the discount rate increases. Project A could be said to be the least risky of the three choices if interest rates are volatile.

Which project should be selected?

The company has a cost of capital of 10%. At this rate Project C produces an NPV of $31,432. This is of higher benefit to MN plc than either projects A or B. Hence this project should be selected.

Assumptions: cash flows are known and certain. The cost of capital is known. Taxation and inflationary aspects have been ignored.

If MN plc is very risk averse, Project A may be considered as its NPV is more robust to increases in the cost of capital than projects B or C.

If you require any further information on this matter, please do not hesitate to contact me.

Signed: Management Accountant

(b) The payback period is the time that elapses before the initial cash outlay is recovered.

The paybacks in the example are:

	Assuming even cash flows	Assuming year end cash flows
Project A:	2 years 2 months	3 years
Project B:	3 years 10 months	4 years
Project C:	5 years 1 month	6 years

Advantages of payback

(1) *Exposure to risk*. It is widely recognised that long-term forecasting is less reliable than short-term forecasts. Projects with short paybacks tend to be less risky than projects with long paybacks. A project with a one-year payback is less risky than a project with a 10-year payback. Management can have very little confidence in forecasts of events ten years from now.

(2) *Liquidity*. Investment opportunities often require significant capital outlay. It may be important to recover this capital expenditure quickly for the company to maintain a strong position. Payback illustrates how quickly the capital can be recovered.

(3) *Simple measure*. The payback period is not a complicated measure. Technical expertise is not required to understand the meaning of payback.

(4) *Not subjective*. Payback period uses cash flows. Some investment appraisal methods use the rather more subjective measure of accounting profit (the accounting rate of return).

Disadvantages of payback

(1) The time value of money is ignored. Each of the projects being considered by MN plc generates $48,000. Payback period fails to recognise that as time elapses the present value of this cash diminishes. It would be possible to overcome this problem by calculating a discounted payback period.

(2) Cash flows after the payback are ignored. Option C has a payback of a little over five years. This information does not reveal that Project C continues to generate cash for four further years.

(3) Not a measure of absolute profitability. Payback fails to indicate HOW MUCH each project is worth. It seems naïve to select a project on the basis of payback without considering the amount of benefit received.

In the example Project A has a payback of just over two years, however its NPV is only $14,376.

Project C yields an NPV of $31,432 – more than double A's NPV. Payback period ignores this fact.

Test your understanding 15

Year	T_0	T_1	T_2	T_3	Assumption (a) T_4onwards	Assumption (b) $T_4 - T_{18}$
	$000	$000	$000	$000	$000	$000
Net cash flow	(2,000)	(440)	363	399	250	250
Perpetuity factor (here discounts the cash flow to T_3)					$1 \div 0.1 = 10$	
AF (here discounts the cash flow to T_3)						15-yr 10% AF =7.606
DFs @ 10%	1.000	0.909	0.826	0.751	0.751	0.751
PV	(2,000)	(400)	300	300	1,878	1,428
NPV (a)						
					78	
NPV (b)						(372)

Further aspects of investment appraisal

Chapter learning objectives

Lead	Component
C1. Prepare information to support project appraisal.	(b) Apply the principles of relevant cash flow analysis to long-run projects that continue for several years.
	(c) Calculate project cash flows, accounting for tax and inflation, and apply perpetuities to derive 'end of project' value where appropriate.
	(d) Apply activity-based costing techniques to derive approximate 'long-run' product or service costs appropriate for use in strategic decision making.
	(f) Apply sensitivity analysis to cash flow parameters to identify those to which net present value is particularly sensitive.
	(g) Prepare decision support information for management, integrating financial and non-financial considerations.

1 Chapter overview diagram

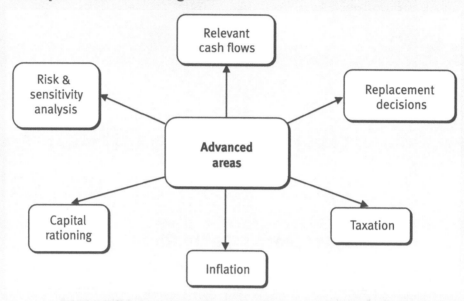

2 Dealing with risk in investment appriasal decisions

Investment appraisal often involves a degree of uncertainty and risk, this may be dealt with in a number of ways:

- Adding a risk premium to the discount rate in order to compensate for risk

- Calculating the payback period to give an indication of risk

- Sensitivity analysis – explored further here

- Using probability distributions to give an indication of risk

- Monte Carlo Simulation – a computerised system that extends sensitivity analysis

Further details

- **Adding a risk premium to the discount rate**

  A premium may be added to the usual discount rate to provide a safety margin. The premium may vary from project to project to reflect the different levels of risk.

- **Payback period**

  Estimates of cash flows several years ahead are quite likely to be inaccurate and unreliable. It may be difficult to control capital projects over a long period of time. Risk may be limited by selecting projects with short payback periods (though this might also induce short-termism into the decision making process and longer-term value-adding projects may be rejected unnecessarily).

- **Sensitivity charts**

  These diagrams illustrate how the NPV is affected by changes in one of the input parameters. The charts have been examined frequently in the management accounting examinations. Typical charts may show:

  NPV vs. discount rate,

  NPV vs. level of activity,

  NPV vs. change in variable cost per unit,

  NPV vs. change in selling price.

  The NPV should be plotted on the y-axis and the other parameter on the x-axis. Calculate two NPVs at two different levels (e.g. low demand and high demand) and then plot the two points. Draw the relationship assuming linearity.

- **Probability distribution**

  A probability distribution of expected cash flows may be determined and hence the expected NPV (EV) may be found together with risk analysis, e.g. best possible outcome, worst possible outcome, probability of a negative NPV, etc. A more sophisticated measure of risk is to calculate the standard deviation. This considers the degree of dispersion of the different possible NPVs around the expected NPV. The greater the spread of outcomes around the expected NPV, the higher the potential risk. The coefficient of variation should be calculated to compare projects. This was considered in an earlier Lesson.

- **Monte Carlo Simulation**

  Actual possible cash flows are considered together with the predicted probability. The simulation run will generate various combinations of actual possible cash flows and calculate the associated NPV. The computer generation of the events will reflect the probability of the event occurring. This may be done with the help of random numbers. The simulation package will usually be run several times to illustrate to managers the full range of actual possible outcomes. Simulations should reveal potential problem areas and areas of risk.

NPV and standard deviation

In order to measure the risk associated with a particular project, it is helpful to find out how wide ranging the possible outcomes are. The conventional measure is the standard deviation explained in a previous chapter. The standard deviation compares all the actual outcomes with the expected value (or mean outcome). It then calculates how far on average the outcomes deviate from the mean. It is calculated using a formula.

If we have two probability distributions with different expected values their standard deviations are not directly comparable. We can overcome this problem by using the coefficient of variation (the standard deviation divided by the expected value) which measures the relative size of the risk.

Expected values, standard deviations or coefficient of variations are used to summarise the outcomes from alternative courses of action however it must be remembered that they do not provide all the relevant information to the decision maker. The probability distribution will provide the decision maker with all of the information they require. It would be appropriate to use expected values, standard deviations or coefficient of variations for decision making when there are a large number of alternatives to consider i.e. where it is not practical to consider the probability distributions for each alternative.

Sensitivity Analysis

Sensitivity analysis in NPV questions typically involves posing 'what if' questions. The NPV is recalculated under different conditions, e.g. what would happen if demand fell by 10%, how would the result be affected if variable costs are 5% higher, etc.

Alternatively, we may wish to discover the maximum possible change in one of the parameters before the opportunity becomes non-viable.

This maximum possible change is often expressed as a percentage:

$$\text{Sensitivity margin} = \frac{\text{NPV}}{\text{PV of flow under consideration}}$$

LEARN

This formula works for total cash flows. It cannot be used for individual units, selling prices, variable cost per unit, etc. Have a go at the following example.

Example 1 – SENSITIVITY ANALYSIS

BJS Ltd is considering investing $120,000 in equipment that has a life of 15 years. Its final scrap value is $25,000.

The equipment will be used to produce 15,000 deluxe pairs of rugby boots per annum, generating a contribution of $2.75 per pair. Specific fixed costs are estimated at $18,000 per annum. The firm has a 15 % cost of capital.

Required:

(a) Calculate the NPV of the project.
(b) Calculate the sensitivity of your NPV to the:
    (i) initial investment;

(ii)   annual contribution;

(iii)   annual fixed costs.

(c)   Identify the minimum annual sales required to ensure that the project at least breaks even.

Advantages and disadvantages of sensitivity analysis

Strengths of sensitivity analysis

- No complicated theory to understand.

- Information will be presented to management in a form which facilitates subjective judgement to decide the likelihood of the various possible outcomes considered.

- Identifies areas which are crucial to the success of the project. If the project is chosen, those areas can be carefully monitored.

- Indicates just how critical are some of the forecasts which are considered to be uncertain.

Weaknesses of sensitivity analysis

- It assumes that changes to variables can be made independently, e.g. material prices will change independently of other variables. This is unlikely. If material prices went up the firm may be able to increase selling price at the same time and there would be little effect on NPV. A technique called simulation (discussed earlier) allows us to change more than one variable at a time.

- It only identifies how far a variable needs to change. It does not look at the probability of such a change. In the above analysis, sales volume appears to be the most crucial variable, but if the firm were facing volatile raw material markets a 65% change in raw material prices would be far more likely than a 29% change in sales volume.

- It is not an optimising technique. It provides information on the basis of which decisions can be made. It does not point directly to the correct decision.

3 Relevant cash flows

Investment decisions, like all other decisions, should be analysed in terms of cash flows that can be directly attributable to them. This has many implications:

Sunk costs

A sunk cost has already been incurred and therefore will not be relevant to the investment decision.

Opportunity cost

As in all decision making, opportunity costs are relevant, and should be included in investment decisions.

Fixed costs

Should be treated as a whole, and only where relevant. This means that fixed overheads that are "absorbed"/ "charged"/ "allocated"/ "apportioned" to a project should be ignored. Only extra/incremental changes in fixed overheads should be included in discounted cash flow calculations.

Depreciation

Depreciation is not a cash flow, and so should **never** be included in a discounted cash-flow calculation. The only investment appraisal technique that will include depreciation is ARR.

Example 2

As part of a new product development a company has employed a building consultant to perform an initial survey. This initial survey has cost $40,000. But there will be an ongoing need for her services if the company decides to proceed with the project. This work will be charged at a fixed rate of $20,000 per annum.

What relevant cost should be included for the building consultants services in the first year when considering whether the project should proceed?

A $0

B $20,000

C $40,000

D $60,000

Further details

Relevant costs are those which will be affected by the decision being taken. All relevant costs should be considered in management decision-making. If a cost will remain unaltered regardless of the decision being taken, then it is called a non-relevant cost or irrelevant cost.

Non-relevant costs

Costs that are not usually relevant in management decisions include the following:

(a) Sunk or past costs. This is a 'cost that has been irreversibly incurred or committed and cannot therefore be considered relevant to a decision. Sunk costs may also be termed irrecoverable costs' *(CIMA Official Terminology).* An example of a sunk cost is expenditure that has been incurred in developing a new product. The money cannot be recovered even if a decision is taken to abandon further development of the new product. The cost is therefore not relevant to future decisions concerning the product.

(b) Absorbed fixed overheads that will not increase or decrease as a result of the decision being taken. The amount of overhead to be absorbed by a particular cost unit might alter because of the decision; however, this is a result of the company's cost accounting procedures for overheads. If the actual amount of overhead incurred by the company will not alter, then the overhead is not a relevant cost.

(c) Expenditure that will be incurred in the future, but as a result of decisions taken in the past that cannot now be changed. These are known as committed costs. They can sometimes cause confusion because they are future costs. However, a committed cost will be incurred regardless of the decision being taken and therefore it is not relevant. An example of this type of cost could be expenditure on special packaging for a new product, where the packaging has been ordered and delivered but not yet paid for. The company is obliged to pay for the packaging even if they decide not to proceed with the product; therefore it is not a relevant cost.

(d) Historical cost depreciation. Depreciation is an accounting adjustment but does not result in any future cash flows. They are merely the book entries that are designed to spread the original cost of an asset over its useful life.

(e) Notional costs such as notional rent and notional interest. These are only relevant if they represent an identified lost opportunity to use the premises or the finance for some alternative purpose.
In these circumstances, the notional costs would be opportunity costs. This explanation will become clearer when you learn more about opportunity costs later in this chapter.

Conclusion

It is essential to look to the future when deciding which costs are relevant to a decision. Costs that have already been incurred or that will not be altered in the future as a result of the decision being taken are not relevant costs.

Opportunity costs

An opportunity cost is a special type of relevant cost. An opportunity cost can be defined as 'the value of the benefit sacrificed when one course of action is chosen in preference to an alternative. The opportunity cost is represented by the foregone potential benefit from the best rejected course of action' *(CIMA Official Terminology)*.

With opportunity costs we are concerned with identifying the value of any benefit forgone as the result of choosing one course of action in preference to another

Examples of opportunity costs

The best way to demonstrate opportunity costs is to consider some examples.

(a) A company has some obsolete material in stock that it is considering to use for a special contract. If the material is not used on the contract it can either be sold back to the supplier for $2 per tonne or it can be used on another contract in place of a different material that would usually cost $2.20 per tonne.

    The opportunity cost of using the material on the special contract is $2.20 per tonne. This is the value of the next best alternative use for the material, or the benefit forgone by not using it for the other contract.

(b) Chris is deciding whether or not to take a skiing holiday this year. The travel agent is quoting an all-inclusive holiday cost of $675 for a week. Chris will lose the chance to earn $200 for a part-time job during the week that the holiday would be taken.

    The relevant cost of taking the holiday is $875. This is made up of the out-of-pocket cost of $675, plus the $200 opportunity cost, that is the part-time wages forgone.

Notional costs and opportunity costs

Notional costs and opportunity costs are often similar. This is particularly noticeable in the case of notional rent. The notional rent could be the rental that the company is forgoing by occupying the premises itself, that is it could be an opportunity cost. However, it is only a true opportunity cost if the company can actually identify a forgone opportunity to rent the premises. If nobody is willing to pay the rent, then it is not an opportunity cost.

If an examination question on relevant costs includes information about notional costs, read the question carefully and state your assumptions concerning the relevance of the notional cost.

Avoidable, differential and incremental costs

There are two other types of relevant cost that you will need to know about: avoidable costs and differential/incremental costs.

Avoidable costs

CIMA defines avoidable costs as 'the specific costs of an activity or sector of a business which would be avoided if that activity or sector did not exist'.

For example, if a company is considering shutting down a department, then the avoidable costs are those that would be saved as a result of the shutdown. Such costs might include the labour costs of those employed in the department and the rental cost of the space occupied by the department. The latter is an example of an attributable or specific fixed cost. Costs such as apportioned head office costs that would not be saved as a result of the shutdown are unavoidable costs. They are not relevant to the decision.

Differential/incremental costs

CIMA defines a differential/incremental cost as 'the difference in total cost between alternatives. This is calculated to assist decision making'.

For example, if the relevant cost of contract X is $5,700 and the relevant cost of contract Y is $6,200, we would say that the differential or incremental cost is $500, that is the extra cost of contract Y is $500.

Using incremental costs

Incremental costs can be useful if the cost accountant wishes to highlight the consequences of taking sequential steps in a decision. For example, the accountant might be providing cost information for a decision about whether to increase the number of employees in a department.

Instead of quoting several different total-cost figures, it might be more useful to say 'the incremental cost per five employees will be $5,800 per month'.

Remember that only relevant costs should be used in the calculations.

Incremental revenues

Just as incremental costs are the differences in cost between alternatives, so incremental revenues are the differences in revenues between the alternatives. Matching the incremental costs against the incremental revenue will produce a figure for the incremental gain or loss between the alternatives.

Cash flows to include

The cash flows that should be included are those which are specifically incurred as a result of the acceptance or non-acceptance of the project. In some cases, these may be opportunity costs.

When deciding what figure should be included in any DCF calculation it sometimes helps to tabulate for a particular element of cost.

| Cash flow if project accepted | − | Cash flow if project rejected | = Relevant cash flow |

Example 3

A mining operation uses skilled labour costing $4 per hour, which generates a contribution, after deducting these labour costs, of $3 per hour.

A new project is now being considered that requires 5,000 hours of skilled labour. There is a shortage of the required labour. Any used on the new project must be transferred from normal working. Calculate the relevant cost of using the skilled labour on the project. Calculate the contribution cash flow that is lost if the labour is transferred from normal working

Activity 2

Suppose the facts about labour are as above, but there is a surplus of skilled labour already employed (and paid) by the business which is sufficient to cope with the new project. The presently idle men are being paid full wages.

Calculate the contribution cash flow that is lost if the labour is transferred to the project from doing nothing.

More on opportunity costs

If there are scarcities of resources to be used on projects (e.g. labour, materials, machines), then consideration must be given to revenues that could have been earned from alternative uses of the resources.

For example, the skilled labour that is needed on the new project might have to be withdrawn from normal production causing a loss in contribution. This is obviously relevant to the project appraisal. The cash flows of a single department or division cannot be looked at in isolation. It is always the effects on cash flows of the whole organisation that must be considered.

Example

A new contract requires the use of 50 tons of metal ZX81. This metal is used regularly on all the firm's projects. There are 100 tons of ZX81 in stock at the moment that were bought for $200 per ton. The current purchase price is $210 per ton, and the metal could be disposed of for net scrap proceeds of $150 per ton. With what cost should the new contract be charged for the ZX81?

Solution

The use of the material in stock for the new contract means that more ZX81 must be bought for normal workings. The cost to the organisation is therefore the money spent on purchase, no matter whether existing stock or new stock is used on the contract. Assuming that the additional purchases are made in the near future, the relevant cost to the organisation is current purchase price, i.e.:

$$50 \text{ tons} * \$210 = \$10,500$$

Example

Suppose the organisation has no use for the ZX81 in stock. What is the relevant cost of using it on the new contract?

Solution

Now the only alternative use for the material is to sell it for scrap. To use 50 tons on the contract is to give up the opportunity of selling it for:

$$50 * \$150 = \$7,500$$

The contract should therefore be charged with this amount.

Example

Suppose that there is no alternative use for the ZX81 other than a scrap sale, but that there is only 25 tons in stock.

Solution

The relevant cost of the 25 tons in stock is $150 per ton. The organisation must then purchase a further 25 tons, and assuming this is in the near future, it will cost $210 per ton.

The contract must be charged with:

	$
25 tons @ $150	3,750
25 tons @ $210	5,250
	9,000

Relevant costs and the decision to abandon

During our initial consideration of project appraisals, it was noted that past costs were irrelevant to any decision regarding the future of a project. This remains true for those occasions when the company has already started a project and wishes to establish whether it should continue with it, or whether it should abandon the project part way through its life.

The only relevant costs are future costs: these will be compared with future revenues to decide the viability of abandonment. Management is often reluctant to take a decision to abandon a project half-way through, as it is often considered to reflect a poor past decision; however true this may be, it would be even worse to compound the error by making another poor decision. Projects must, therefore, be kept constantly under review.

Factors in the decision to abandon

The following considerations must be taken into account in deciding whether to continue or abandon a project:

- future cash outflows associated with the project
- future cash inflows associated with the project
- revenues/costs that would arise if the project were abandoned
  - other projects, which may be:
    alternatives to the project under consideration
    more profitable uses of funds tied up in the project under review.

Each of these factors must be consciously assessed at each stage of the project's life and, if it is seen that abandoning the project would be more beneficial than proceeding with it, then an abandonment decision must be made.

4 Dealing with taxation

There are tax effects that we need to deal with:

(1) corporation tax;

(2) tax depreciation , also known as capital allowances.

Corporation tax

Typical assumptions are:

(1) The taxable profits will be the net cash flows from the project less any tax depreciation (explored later).

(2) Timing of the payments: in exam questions corporation tax is usually paid in two instalments, in that, half the tax is payable in the year in which it arises, the balance is paid in the following year.

The corporation tax rate will be given in the question.

The impact of taxation on cash flows

Taxation may have a significant impact on the viability of a capital investment project. Taxation payments and savings in tax payments are clearly cash flows associated with the project. They are relevant, and should be considered in a DCF analysis.

Taxation has the following effects on an investment appraisal problem:

- Project cash flows will give rise to taxation which itself has an impact on project appraisal. Normally we assume that tax is paid in two installments, where half the tax is payable in the year in which it arises, and the balance is paid in the following year. However, it is possible for alternative assumptions to be made and so you should read any examination question carefully to ascertain precisely what assumptions are made in the question.

- Organisations benefit from being able to claim tax depreciation (also known as capital allowances) – a tax deductible alternative to depreciation. The effect of these is to reduce the amount of tax that organisations are required to pay. Again it is important to read any examination question carefully in order to identify what treatment is expected by the examiner. A common assumption is that tax depreciation is available on a 25% reducing balance basis.

Note that the **tax depreciation is not a cash flow** and to calculate the tax impact we have to multiply each year's tax depreciation by the corporation tax rate. The effect of tax depreciation is on the amount of tax payable, which is the relevant cash flow.

In dealing with these tax effects it is always assumed that:

- where a tax loss arises from the project, there are sufficient taxable profits elsewhere in the organisation to allow the loss to reduce any relevant (subsequent) tax payment (and it may therefore be treated as a cash inflow) and that the company has sufficient taxable profits to obtain full benefit from tax depreciation.

In practice, the effects of taxation are more complex, and are influenced by a number of factors including the following:

- the taxable profits and tax rate

- the company's accounting period and tax payment dates

- whether assets qualify for tax depreciation

- losses available for set-off

A detailed knowledge of tax is not required for this paper. Assumptions and simplifications will be made. These will usually be set out clearly in each examination question. It is important to follow the instructions for the treatment of tax in the question being attempted. Any assumptions that you make must also be clearly stated.

Tax depreciation

Tax depreciation is used to reduce taxable profits, and the consequent reduction in a tax payment should be treated as a cash saving arising from the acceptance of the project. In this examination tax depreciation is generally allowed on the cost of plant and machinery at the rate of 25% on a reducing balance basis. It may also be possible to claim tax depreciation on the costs of installation, such as labour and overhead costs of removing an old machine and levelling the area for the new machine.

Balancing allowance (or charge)

When the plant is eventually sold, there may be a difference between the reducing balance amount and the selling price of the asset. An appropriate adjustment must be made to ensure that the company receives allowances equal to the total allowance allowed (i.e. purchase price less final value).

Balancing allowances/charges

If a business buys a capital asset in one year and sells it several years later, the total tax relief it will receive is the tax on the cost of the asset less its eventual disposal value.

For example, if a business buys equipment for $100,000 in Year 0 and disposes of it in Year 5 for $20,000, it will receive tax relief on the net cost of $80,000. If the rate of corporation tax is 30%, the reduction in tax payments over the five years would be 30% × $80,000 = $24,000.

Balancing allowances are given as a final deduction to ensure the full fall in value has been allowed. Balancing charges occur where the total tax depreciation claimed exceeds the fall in value of the asset. The excess claimed is treated as a taxable amount in the year of disposal.

Timing of the tax savings associated with tax depreciation

It is likely that the corporation tax will be paid in four quarterly instalments. Hence, the benefit of tax saved because of tax depreciation is received when the corporation tax should have been paid. Thus, half the tax is saved in the current year, and half is saved in the year following.

Example 4 – Balancing allowance

An asset is purchased for $50,000. At the end of the fourth year it will be sold for $10,000. Tax depreciation is available at 25 per cent reducing balance and corporation tax is payable at 30 per cent per annum.

Corporation tax is paid in two instalments, with half the tax payable in the year in which it arises, and the balance paid in the following year.

Required:

(a) Calculate the tax depreciation each year and the associated corporation tax saving.

(b) Illustrate the timing of the tax savings calculated in part (a).

For tax purposes care must be taken to identify the exact time of asset purchase.

- Assets are assumed to be bought at T_0.

- It should be assumed that the asset is bought at the start of the accounting period and therefore the first tax depreciation is offset against the year 1 net cash flows.

5 Working capital

The next example has an investment of working capital included in it.

The treatment of working capital is as follows:

- It is treated as an investment at the start of the project, like any other investment. Any additional working capital requirements are invested when required. **Only *the change* in working capital is treated as a cash flow**.

- Working capital does not qualify for tax relief – so is ignored in the taxation and tax depreciation calculations.

- At the end of the project the working capital is 'released'. This is treated as a cash inflow at the end of the project, equal to the total investment in working capital (unless told otherwise).

Example 5

Camp plc has produced and marketed sleeping bags for several years. The sleeping bags are much heavier than some of the modern sleeping bags being introduced to the market. The company is concerned about the effect this will have on its sales.

Camp plc are considering investing in new technology that would enable them to produce a much lighter and more compact sleeping bag. The new machine will cost $250,000 and is expected to have a life of four years with a scrap value of $10,000. In addition an investment of $35,000 in working capital will be required initially.

The following forecast annual trading account has been prepared for the project:

	$
Sales	200,000
Material	(40,000)
Labour	(30,000)
Variable overheads	(10,000)
Depreciation	(20,000)
Annual profit	**100,000**

The company's cost of capital is 10%. Corporation tax is charged at 30% and is paid in two instalments, with half the tax payable in the year in which it arises, and the balance paid in the following year. Tax depreciation of 25% on reducing balance is available on capital expenditure.

Required:

Calculate whether Camp plc should invest in the new technology.

6 Proforma layout for calculations

NPV with tax – Example pro forma

(assuming a two Year Project)

	Year 0	Year 1	Year 2	Year 3
	$	$	$	$
Cash inflows		X	X	
Cash outflows		(X)	(X)	
		—	—	
Net cash flow		X	X	
Tax on net cash flow		(X)	(X)	(X)
Investment	(X)			
Scrap value			X	
Tax depreciation savings (which would need a separate working)		X	X	X
Working capital	(X)		X	
Net cash flows	(X)	X	X	X
Discount factor	1.00	x	x	x
Present value	PV	PV	PV	PV

In the examination, for a short life project, with cash flows inflating at different rates, it is best to set the NPV calculation out with the cash flows down the side and the time across the top.

7 The impact of inflation on cash flows

If an exam question involves inflation then we normally have to either:

- adjust the cash flows, or

- adjust the cost of capital.

Where cash flows have not been increased for expected inflation they are known as **current cash flows**, or **real cash flows**.

Where cash flows have been increased to take account of expected inflation they are known as **money cash flows**, or **nominal cash flows**. Remember, if they do take inflation into account, they represent expected flows of money, hence the term 'money cash flows'.

You can assume that cash flows you are given in the exam are the money cash flows unless told otherwise.

If the examiner specifies that the **cash flows are in current terms** you will generally need to put these in money terms before you can discount them. For example if the question tells you that sales for the next 3 years are $100 in current terms but are expected to inflate by 10%, then what he actually means is that the sales will be:

Year 1: $110

Year 2: $121   } i.e. these are the cash flows in money terms

Year 3: $133.10

Make sure you read the question carefully. Sometimes you will be given the **cash flows in Year 1 terms** with subsequent inflation.

- For example if the question says "Sales will be $100 in the first year, but are then going to inflate by 10% for the next two years", then the sales will be:

Year 1: $100

Year 2: $110 } compare these to the previous example – make sure

Year 3: $121   you understand why they are different!

8 Methods of dealing with inflation

The impact of inflation can be dealt with in two different ways – both methods give the same NPV.

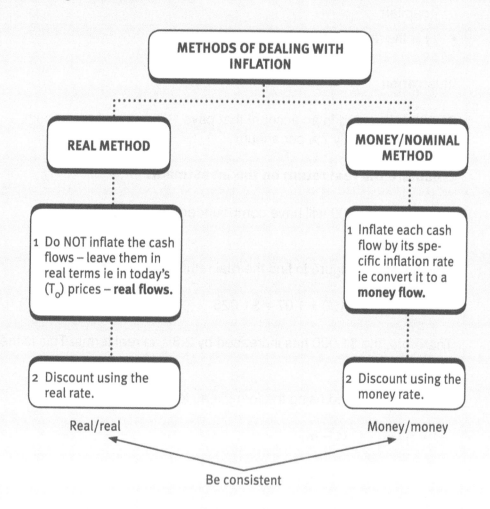

The real rate of return

If money is invested in an account, it will earn interest. However, inflation will have the effect of reducing the value of the return. By deflating the future cash (money) we can find the real return from the investment, i.e. the return at today's prices.

Formula

To find the real rate of return we can use the following formula:

$$(1+r) = \frac{(1+m)}{(1+i)}$$

LEARN

This is where:

- **r** is the real rate of return
- **m** is the money cost of capital (this is the company's normal cost of capital)
- **i** is the rate of inflation

Illustration

$1,000 is invested in an account that pays 10% interest per annum. Inflation is currently 7% per annum.

Calculate the real return on the investment.

After 1 year $1,000 will have compounded up to $1,000 × 1.10 = $1,100.

Now deflate this figure to find the real return on the investment:

$$\$1,100 \div 1.07 = \$1,028$$

Therefore, the $1,000 has increased by 2.8% in real terms. This is the real rate.

It can be calculated using the formula as follows:

$$(1 + r) = \frac{(1 + m)}{(1 + i)}$$

$$(1 + r) = \frac{(1 + 0.10)}{(1 + 0.07)}$$

$$(1 + r) = 1.028$$
$$r = 1.028 - 1$$
$$r = 0.028 = 2.8\%$$

Using the real rate of return in questions

If there is one rate of inflation in the question both the real and money method will give the same answer. However it is easier to adjust one discount rate, rather than all the cash flows over a number of years. This is particularly true where the cash flows are annuities. The real method is the only possible method where they are perpetuities.

Although it is theoretically possible to use the real method in questions incorporating tax, it is extremely complex. It is therefore much safer (and easier) to use the money/nominal method in all questions where tax is taken into account.

Example 6 – NPV AND INFLATION

Storm Ltd is evaluating project X which requires an initial investment of $50,000. Expected net cash flows are $20,000 per annum for 4 years at today's prices. However these are expected to rise by 5.5% per annum because of inflation. The firm's cost of capital is 15%. Calculate the NPV by:

(a) discounting money cash flows;

(b) discounting real cash flows.

9 Specific and general inflation rates

The examples given above had all cash flows inflating at the general rate of inflation. In practice, inflation does not affect all costs to the same extent. In some investment appraisal questions you may be given information on more than one inflation rate. In these situations you will have information on both specific inflation rates and general inflation rates.

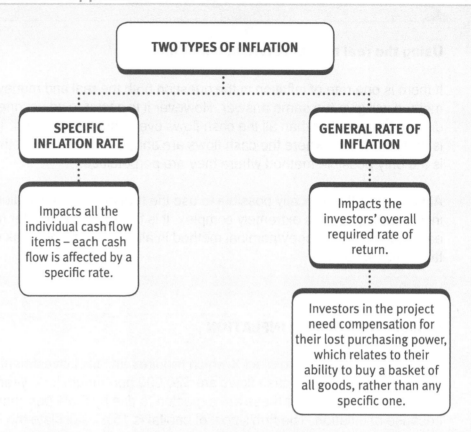

In situations where you are given a number of specific inflation rates, the real method outlined above cannot be used.

The following gives a useful summary of how to approach examination questions.

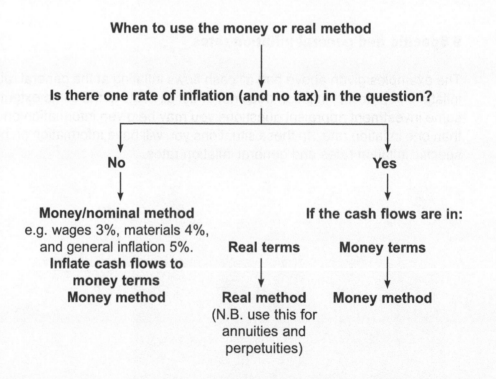

If a question contains both tax and inflation, it is advisable to use the money method.

The money method

To use the real method when cash flows inflate at different rates (specific rates) is extremely complex and would involve a lot of calculations. It is therefore advisable to always use the money method in these situations. This involves:

- inflating the cash flows at their specific inflation rates

- discounting using the money rate

Very often the money rate will not be given in the question but will need to be calculated. This should be done using the real rate and the general inflation rate.

Example 7

Thunder plc has just developed a new product to be called the Lightening and is now considering whether to put it into production. The following information is available:

(i) Costs incurred to date in the development of Lightening amount to $480,000.

(ii) Production of Lightening will require the purchase of new machinery at a cost of $2,400,000 payable immediately. This machinery is specific to the production of Lightening and will be obsolete and valueless when production ceases. The machinery has a production life of four years and a production capacity of 30,000 units per annum.

(iii) Production costs of Lightening (at year 1 prices) are estimated as follows:

	$
Direct material	8.00
Direct labour	12.00
Variable overheads	12.00

In addition, fixed production costs (at year 1 prices), including straight-line depreciation on plant and machinery specific to this project, will amount to $800,000 per annum.

(iv) The selling price of Lightening will be $80.00 per unit (at year 1 prices). Demand is expected to be 25,000 units per annum for the next four years.

(v) The retail price index is expected to be at 5% per annum for the next four years and the selling price of Lightening is expected to increase at the same rate. Annual inflation rates for production costs are expected to be as follows:

	%
Direct material	4
Direct labour	10
Variable overheads	4
Fixed costs	5

(vi) The company's cost of capital in money terms is expected to be 15%.

You may ignore the effects of taxation.

Unless otherwise specified all costs and revenues should be assumed to arise at the end of each year.

Required:

Calculate whether Thunder plc should produce Lightening on the basis of the information above.

(15 marks)

Deflation

Many western economies have very low rates of inflation at present and some are even experiencing deflation. Deflation may also apply to certain hi-tech materials which get considerably cheaper when they go into mass production.

Deflation may affect business decision making in several ways:

• Investing in projects that have long payback periods may require some courage.

• Borrowing to finance the purchase of assets that are going to fall in value may also require some courage: money rates will be low, but real rates are higher.

• It may be difficult to reduce some costs – especially wages – in line with deflation.

• Consumers may defer purchasing decisions if they anticipate that prices will fall.

10 Dealing with questions with both tax and inflation

Combining tax and inflation in the same question does not make it any more difficult than keeping them separate.

Questions with both tax and inflation are best tackled using the money method.

- Inflate costs and revenues, where necessary, before determining their tax implications.

- Ensure that the cost and disposal values have been inflated (if necessary) before calculating tax depreciation.

- Always calculate working capital on these inflated figures, unless given.

- Use a post-tax money discount rate.

Example 8

Ackbono Co is considering a potential project with the following forecasts:

	Now	T₁	T₂	T₃
Initial investment ($million)	(1,000)			
Disposal proceeds ($million)				200
Demand (millions of units)		5	10	6

The initial investment will be made on the first day of the new accounting period.

The selling price per unit is expected to be $100 and the variable cost $30 per unit. Both of these figures are given in today's terms.

Tax depreciation is available at 25 per cent reducing balance and corporation tax is payable at 30 per cent per annum.

Corporation tax is paid in two instalments, with half the tax payable in the year in which it arises, and the balance paid in the following year.

The company has a real required rate of return of 6.8%.

General inflation is predicted to be 3% pa but the selling price is expected to inflate at 4% and variable costs by 5% pa

Calculate the NPV of the project.

N.B. work in $ millions.

11 Capital asset replacement decisions

As the title suggests, this section considers the need to replace old, worn out capital assets within a firm.

There are two distinct types of decisions to consider:

(1) Considering mutually-exclusive options with unequal lives.

(2) Calculating an optimum replacement cycle.

We shall consider each in turn.

Mutually-exclusive options with unequal lives

Companies considering the replacement of an asset may be faced with alternatives where the life spans of the various machines differ, but the asset is required for the foreseeable future. The options must be evaluated over a comparable number of years.

In order to compare like with like we will calculate an **equivalent annual cost**. This is similar to an average annual cash flow. Once both machines' costs have been annualised the cheapest machine can be chosen by comparing annual costs.

FORMULA

$$\text{Equivalent annual cost} = \frac{\text{PV of costs}}{\text{Annuity factor for year n}}$$

LEARN

where n is the machine life time.

This is best explained by working through an example (the solution at the end of the chapter includes an explanation of the technique):

Example 9 – REPLACEMENT DECISION

Donald Ltd is considering replacing an asset with one of two possible machines:

Machine X	Initial cost	$120,000
	Life	3 years
	Running costs	$20,000 p.a.
	Residual value	nil
Machine Y	Initial cost	$60,000
	Life	2 years
	Running costs	Year 1 : $40,000
		Year 2 : $35,000
	Residual value	nil

The machines will be required into the foreseeable future. The company's cost of capital is 10%.

Required:

Calculate which machine should be purchased.

Lowest common multiple method

There is an alternative method for comparing machines with different lives known as the lowest common multiple method.

This is where we find the smallest number, which we can divide into by each of a set of numbers and evaluate the NPV cost over this period.

Example

If we look again at the decision faced in Example 9 and apply the lowest common multiple method, we have two projects, one with a life of 2 years and one with a life of 3 years. The common multiple is 6 years. We then calculate the NPV of the two options over 6 years and compare the results as follows:

Machine X

Year	Description	Cash flow $	Discount rate 15%	Present value $
0	Outlay	120,000	1.000	120,000
1 – 3	Running cost	20,000	2.487	49,740
3	Replace	120,000	0.751	90,120
4 – 6	Running cost	20,000	1.868	37,360
			NPV =	297,220

Machine Y

Year	Description	Cash flow $	Discount rate 15%	Present value $
0	Outlay	60,000	1.000	60,000
1 – 2	Running cost	35,000	1.736	60,760
2	Replace	60,000	0.826	49,560
3 – 4	Running cost	35,000	1.434	50,190
4	Replace	60,000	0.683	40,980
5 – 6	Running cost	35,000	1.185	41,475
			NPV =	302,965

Machine X should be purchased as it has the least cost option (lowest NPV cost).

Optimum replacement cycles

Companies purchasing new plant and machinery must decide how often to replace them. Generally, as machinery ages its residual value decreases and the annual running costs increase. However, companies are unlikely to want to replace assets too frequently because of the capital outlay associated with the purchase.

In the next section we shall calculate the optimum replacement cycle in order to minimise long-term costs.

Factors in replacement decisions

The factors to be considered include the following:

- Capital cost of new equipment – the higher cost of equipment will have to be balanced against known or possible technical improvements.
- Operating costs – operating costs will be expected to increase as the machinery deteriorates over time. This may be the result of:
  - increased repair and maintenance costs
  - loss of production due to 'down-time' resulting from increased repair and maintenance time
  - lower quality and quantity of output.
- Resale value – the extent to which old equipment can be traded in for new.
- Taxation and investment incentives.
- Inflation – both the general price level change, and relative movements in the prices of inputs and outputs.

Example 10 – REPLACEMENT CYCLE

A supermarket is trying to determine the optimal replacement policy for its fleet of delivery vehicles. The total purchase price of the fleet is $220,000.

The running costs and scrap values of the fleet at the end of each year are:

	Year 1	Year 2	Year 3	Year 4	Year 5
Running costs	$110,000	$132,000	$154,000	$165,000	$176,000
Scrap value	$121,000	$88,000	$66,000	$55,000	$25,000

The supermarket's cost of capital is 12% per annum.

Ignore taxation and inflation.

Identify at the end of which year the supermarket should replace its fleet of delivery vehicles.

Method of solution

(1) Consider each possible replacement cycle in turn: 1 year, 2 year, 3 year etc.

(2) Calculate the PV of costs for each cycle.

(3) Divide this PV by the annuity factor to find the equivalent annual cost.

(4) Select the replacement cycle with the lowest equivalent annual cost.

Limitations of replacement analysis

The replacement analysis model assumes that the firm replaces like with like each time it needs to replace an existing asset.

However this assumption ignores

- changing technology – machines fast become obsolete and can only be replaced with a more up-to-date model which will be more efficient and perhaps perform different functions

- inflation – the increase in price over time increases the cost structure of the different assets, meaning that the optimal replacement cycle can vary over time

- change in production plans – firms cannot predict with accuracy the market environment they will be facing in the future and whether they will even need to make use of the asset at that time.

12 Capital rationing

If investment funds are unlimited then all projects with a positive NPV should be undertaken. Capital rationing occurs when insufficient funds are available to undertake all beneficial projects.

Hard and soft capital rationing

The term soft capital rationing is often used to refer to situations where for various reasons the firm internally imposes a budget ceiling on the amount of capital expenditure. If the capital is restricted because of external constraints such as the inability to obtain funds from the financial markets, the term hard capital rationing is used. The type of rationing imposed on a firm will not, however, affect our analysis.

The objective of all capital rationing exercises is the maximisation of the total NPV of the chosen projects' cash flows at the cost of capital. Thus it becomes necessary to rank projects to enable the optimum combination to be undertaken.

Underlying assumptions:

- Individual projects are divisible. The resulting NPV will be pro-rated. For example, if only 25% of the capital is available for a project only 25% of its NPV will be earned.

- Annual cash flows cannot be delayed or brought forward.

- Capital funds are restricted in just one period (year 0).

Technique

The decision aims to maximise NPV given a single limiting factor. As with other decisions with one scarce resource, the opportunities should be ranked according to NPV per $1 invested. This measure is called the profitability index (PI).

$$\text{Profitability index} = \frac{\text{NPV}}{\text{Initial Investment}}$$

LEARN

The optimal investment plan is determined by:

(1) calculating a PI for each project

(2) ranking the projects according to their PI

(3) allocating funds according to the projects' rankings until they are used up.

Example 11 – CAPITAL RATIONING

A company may undertake any of the following investment projects.

Project	Investment required	Net present value
	$000	$000
A	3,400	850
B	2,750	825
C	2,000	720
D	3,400	680
E	860	430
F	950	400
G	1,250	350

In the next budget period there is only $9 million available for capital expenditure projects. Each project is divisible.

Required:

(a) If the company ranks the projects according to highest NPVs, which projects will be undertaken? Calculate the total NPV.

(b) If the company selects projects according to their profitability index, calculate which projects will be undertaken. Calculate the total NPV now.

Dealing with indivisible projects

There may be scenarios where 'common sense' has to come into play and this general rule has to be ignored. Consider the following example:

Example

A company has an investment limit of $800,000 and has to choose between the following three projects:

Project	Investment	Inflow PV	NPV	PI	Rank
A	600,000	700,000	100,000	1.17	1
B	500,000	560,000	60,000	1.12	3
C	300,000	345,000	45,000	1.15	2

On the basis of the general rule, Project A only would be selected since it has the highest PI. But this precludes any other projects, generating an NPV of $800,000 and leaving $200,000 of the capital limit uncommitted. Consequently, NPV is maximised by adopting two projects (B and C) both of which have lower PIs than A. By adopting these two projects we raise total NPV to $105,000.

In these circumstances, the objective can only be achieved by selecting from amongst the available projects on a trial and error basis. Because of the problem of indivisibility this may leave some funds unutilised. Consider another example:

Example

PQ has $50,000 available to invest. Its cost of capital is 10%. The following indivisible projects are available:

Project	Initial outlay $	Return p.a. to perpetuity $
1	20,000	1,500
2	10,000	1,500
3	15,000	3,000
4	30,000	5,400
5	25,000	4,800

Solution

The first stage is to calculate the NPV of the projects.

Project	Initial outlay $	PV of cash flows $	NPV $
1	20,000	15,000	(5,000)
2	10,000	15,000	5,000
3	15,000	30,000	15,000
4	30,000	54,000	24,000
5	25,000	48,000	23,000

The approach is then one of considering all possible combinations of projects under the investment limit of $50,000.

The optimum selection of projects is as follows:

Project	Initial outlay $	NPV $
2	10,000	5,000
3	15,000	15,000
5	25,000	23,000
	50,000	43,000
Unused funds	Nil	
Funds available		
	50,000	

13 ABC in longer term decisions

The role of ABC

Activity-based costing (ABC) has been discussed in an earlier chapter. In this section we briefly discuss the role of ABC in longer-term decision making.

ABC systems are primarily designed to furnish management with cost information relating to an organisation's products. However, the production of this information is not an end in itself. Indeed it is the use to which such activity-based information is put that represents its real purpose and its value should be assessed against this end-result.

An ABC system produces historic information relating to its products or service provision which is of much assistance to management in analysing and explaining an organisation's profitability. However, many commentators including Robert Kaplan and Robin Cooper have viewed ABC as supporting major areas of strategic decision making with organisations, these being:

- decisions concerning product pricing strategy

- changes to the range and mix of products via the promotion and discontinuance of current lines, and

- new product development.

When ABC information is used in the above ways then it will underpin policy decisions of senior management and will therefore have a significant influence upon the longer-term prosperity of an organisation. Advocates of the use of ABC for strategic decision making maintain that its value lies in greater accuracy attaching to product costing which in turn increases the degree of reliability of cost information used for the above purposes. They further maintain that the use of ABC may give an indication of the long-term variable cost of products which arguably is the most relevant cost information for use in decisions of the above type. Given the inherent uncertainty involved in strategic decision making, management may use ABC information in decision-modelling and sensitivity analysis to assist in the making of such decisions.

The end product of an ABC system is an estimate of the historic cost of each of an organisation's products. However, strategic decision making involves future time periods and thus it is future outlay costs that need to be taken into consideration as opposed to historic costs. Therefore, it is arguable that the results obtained from an ABC system should only be used as a starting point in the determination of cost information that is aimed at assisting in the making of longer-term decisions. This is especially the case if ABC based product costs are viewed as estimates of longer term product costs as 'nothing is forever' and historic costs are susceptible to substantial change since all factors of production become variable in the longer term.

Any cost information which has been produced based on past activities must be used with caution with regard to longer-term decisions. Even so, ABC information may provide a sound starting point for the preparation of cost information to be used in strategic decision making. It has been argued that a significant advantage of ABC over conventional costing systems lies in its suitability for strategic decision making. Kaplan has argued that for decisions of a strategic nature a long-term perspective is usual and maintains that an ABC system gives product cost information which matches this requirement particularly well. This is evidenced by his assertion that 'conventional notions of fixed and variable costs are ignored because, for the purposes of product cost analysis, the time period is long enough to warrant treatment of virtually all costs as variable'.

14 Qualitative factors

The emphasis in this chapter has been on investment appraisal as a computational exercise: known numbers are inserted into formulae and a numerical result is produced. But, in reality, investment decisions are also influenced by many qualitative factors that must also be borne in mind in the investment appraisal exercise.

Qualitative factors

Consider the typical example of the proposed purchase of a new machine in a manufacturing plant. The machine offers both quantitative and qualitative costs and benefits, as below.

Quantitative costs include:

- the purchase price of the machine
- installation and training costs.

Quantitative benefits include:

- lower direct labour costs
- lower scrap costs and items requiring rework
- lower stock costs.

Qualitative costs include:

- increased noise level
- lower morale if existing staff have to be made redundant.

Qualitative benefits include:

- reduction in product development time
- improved product quality and service
- increase in manufacturing flexibility.

Because the qualitative factors are difficult to state in numerical terms, they are conventionally ignored in the investment appraisal exercise. However such an approach is flawed. If a question asks you to carry out a DCF analysis and then comment on what you have done, be certain to point out the qualitative factors that could additionally be brought into the decision.

15 Chapter summary

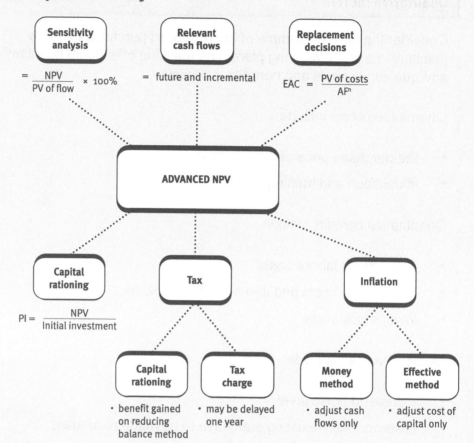

Sensitivity analysis

$= \dfrac{NPV}{PV \text{ of flow}} \times 100\%$

Relevant cash flows

$=$ future and incremental

Replacement decisions

$EAC = \dfrac{PV \text{ of costs}}{AF^n}$

ADVANCED NPV

Capital rationing

$PI = \dfrac{NPV}{\text{Initial investment}}$

Tax

Inflation

Capital rationing
- benefit gained on reducing balance method

Tax charge
- may be delayed one year

Money method
- adjust cash flows only

Effective method
- adjust cost of capital only

16 Practice questions

Test your understanding 1

Bacher Co is considering investing $500,000 in equipment to produce a new type of ball. Sales of the product are expected to continue for three years, at the end of which the equipment will have a scrap value of $80,000. Sales revenue of $600,000 pa will be generated at a variable cost of $350,000. Annual fixed costs will increase by $40,000.

(a) **Calculate whether, on the basis of the estimates given, the project should be undertaken, assuming that all cash flows occur at annual intervals and that Bacher Co has a cost of capital of 15%.**

(3 marks)

(a) **Calculate the percentage changes required in the following estimates for the investment decision to change:**

    (i)   initial investment

    (ii) scrap value

    (iii) selling price

    (iv) unit variable cost

    (v) annual fixed cost

    (vi) sales volume

    (vii) cost of capital.

(7 marks)

Test your understanding 2

A company is considering investing $1,000,000 in launching a new product. The project will incur annual fixed costs of $60,000. The investment capital will be sold at the end of the project life, seven years from now, for $50,000. The product is expected to generate a unit contribution of $12.50. The company has a cost of capital of 8%.

Identify the minimum annual sales required to make the project viable:

A   19,720 units

B   101,824 units

C   87,467 units

D   22,143 units

(3 marks)

Test your understanding 3

Which of the following costs for a proposed project are relevant:

(i)   The salary to be paid to a market researcher who will oversee the development of a new product. This is a new post to be created specially for the new product but the $12,000 salary will be a fixed cost. Is this cost relevant to the decision to proceed with the development of the product?

(ii)   The $2,500 additional monthly running costs of a new machine to be purchased to manufacture an established product. Since the new machine will save on labour time, the fixed overhead to be absorbed by the product will reduce by $100 per month. Are these costs relevant to the decision to purchase the new machine?

(iii) Office cleaning expenses of $125 for next month. The office is cleaned by contractors and the contract can be cancelled by giving 1 month's notice. Is this cost relevant to a decision to close the office?

(iv)   Expenses of $75 paid to the marketing manager. This was to reimburse the manager for the cost of travelling to meet a client with whom the company is currently negotiating a major contract. Is this cost relevant to the decision to continue negotiations?

(4 marks)

Test your understanding 4

ABC Ltd is deciding whether or not to proceed with a special order. Use the details below to determine the relevant cost of the order.

(a) Materials P and Q will be used for the contract. 100 tonnes of material P will be needed and sufficient material is in stock because the material is in common use in the company. The original cost of the material in stock is $1 per tonne but it would cost $1.20 per tonne to replace if it is used for this contract. The material Q required is in stock as a result of previous over-purchasing. This material originally cost $500 but it has no other use. The material is toxic and if it is not used on this contract, then ABC must pay $280 to have it disposed of.

(b) The contract requires 200 hours of labour at $5 per hour. Employees possessing the necessary skills are currently employed by the company but they are idle at present due to a lull in the company's normal business.

(c) Overhead will be absorbed by the contract at a rate of $10 per labour hour, which consists of $7 for fixed overhead and $3 for variable.

(d) The contract will require the use of a storage unit for 3 months. ABC is committed to rent the unit for 1 year at a rental of $50 per month. The unit is not in use at present. A neighbouring business has recently approached ABC offering to rent the unit from them for $70 per month.

(e) Total fixed overheads are not expected to increase as a result of the contract.

(10 marks)

Test your understanding 5

The management of a company are making a decision on whether or not to purchase a new piece of plant and machinery which costs $100,000. The new machine will generate a net cash flow of $30,000 each year for four years. At the end of the fourth year it will be sold for $20,000. The company's cost of capital is 5%. Tax depreciation is at 25% reducing balance and corporation tax is 30%. Corporation tax is payable in two instalments, with half paid in the current year and half paid in the following year.

Required:

Calculate the net present value of the project and advise management.

(5 marks)

Test your understanding 6

Dralin Co is considering an investment of $460,000 in a non-current asset expected to generate substantial cash inflows over the next five years. Unfortunately the annual cash flows from this investment are uncertain, but the following probability distribution has been established:

Annual cash flow ($)	Probability
50,000	0.3
100,000	0.5
150,000	0.2

At the end of its five-year life, the asset is expected to sell for $40,000. The cost of capital is 5%.

Calculate whether the investment should be undertaken.

(4 marks)

Test your understanding 7

Smith has decided to increase its productive capacity to meet an anticipated increase in demand for its products. The extent of this increase in capacity has still to be determined, and a management meeting has been called to decide which of the following two mutually exclusive proposals – A or B – should be undertaken.

The following information is available:

	Proposal A $	Proposal B $
Capital expenditure		
Buildings	50,000	100,000
Plant	200,000	300,000
Installation	100,000	15,000
Net Income		
Annual pre-depreciation profits (note (1))	70,000	95,000
Other relevant income and expenditure		
Sales promotion (note (2))	–	15,000
Plant scrap value	10,000	15,000
Buildings disposable value (note (3))	30,000	60,000
Working capital required over the project life	50,000	65,000

Notes:

(1) The investment life is ten years.

(2) An exceptional amount of expenditure on sales promotion of $15,000 will have to be spent in year 2 of proposal B. This has not been taken into account in calculating pre-depreciation profits.

(3) It is the intention to dispose of the buildings in ten years' time.

Using an 8% discount rate, calculate which of the two alternatives should be chosen.

(10 marks)

Test your understanding 8

A company has a money cost of capital of 21% per annum. The inflation rate is currently estimated at 9% per annum.

Identify the real cost of capital:

A   9%

B   11%

C   12%

D   14%

(2 marks)

Test your understanding 9

W is considering investing in a new machine which has a capital cost of $25,000. It has an estimated life of four years and a residual value of $5,000 at the end of four years. The machine qualifies for tax depreciation at the rate of 25% per year on a reducing balance basis.

An existing machine would be sold immediately for $8,000 if the new machine were to be bought. The existing machine has a tax written down value of $3,000.

The existing machine generates annual net contribution of $30,000. This is expected to increase by 40% if the new machine is purchased.

W pays corporation tax on its profits at the rate of 30%, with half of the tax being payable in the year that the profit is earned and half in the following year. The company's after tax cost of capital is 15% per year.

Calculate whether the investment is worthwhile.

(5 marks)

Test your understanding 10

A company is considering a cost-saving project. This involves purchasing a machine costing $7,000, which will result in annual savings (in real terms) on wage costs of $1,000 and on material costs of $400.

The following forecasts are made of the rates of inflation each year for the next five years:

Wage costs	10%
Material costs	5%
General prices	6%

The cost of capital of the company, in real terms, is 8.5%.

Calculate the NPV of the project, assuming that the machine has a life of five years and no scrap value.

(5 marks)

Test your understanding 11

Leo is contemplating spending $400,000 on new machinery. This will be used to produce a revolutionary type of lock, for which demand is expected to last three years. Equipment will be bought on 31 December 20X5 and revenue from the sale of locks will be receivable on the 31 December 20X6, 20X7 and 20X8. Labour costs for the three years, payable in arrears, are estimated at $500,000 per annum in current terms. These figures are expected to rise at the rate of 10% per annum.

Materials required for the three years are currently in stock. They originally cost $300,000; they would cost $500,000 at current prices although Leo had planned to sell them for $350,000. The sales revenue from locks in the first year is projected at $900,000. This figure will rise by 5% per annum over the product's life.

If Leo has a money cost of capital of 13%, identify the net present value of the project (to the nearest $000)

A   ($130,000)

B   ($23,000)

C $52,000

D $126,000

(4 marks)

Test your understanding 12

A contract is due to be commenced immediately. In one year's time it will require material XG. Price data relating to XG are as follows:

	$
Cost now	7,800
Cost in one year's time	8,800

The cost of storing XG for one year is $110, payable in one year's time.

If the cost of capital were 10% per annum, identify the present value of the cost of using material XG, assuming the contractor wished to maximise net present value:

A $7,800

B $7,900

C $7910

D $8,000

(2 marks)

Test your understanding 13

November 2007

In early November 20X7, R Ltd considered manufacturing a new product called Sparkle. Up to that time $750,000 had been spent on researching the product. The company estimated that it would take two further years to develop Sparkle to the point of production and by that time it would probably have a lead of 18 months over its chief competitor. R Ltd expected to launch Sparkle on 1 November 20X9 and to produce and sell 100,000 units in the first year if $1.5 million was spent on pre-launch advertising. During the first year of production, R Ltd planned to spend $750,000 on advertising; this level of expenditure would be maintained each year.

From the second year onwards, the market was expected to increase to between 160,000 and 200,000 units. Once the competitor entered the market, it was thought that the competitor would win 50% market share very quickly because of its reputation.

The development and engineering costs of Sparkle were estimated to be $6 million, $2 million of which would be incurred in the first year of development, 20X7/X8. A special piece of equipment costing $500,000 would be required for production and this was to be installed in the month prior to the commencement of manufacture.

R Ltd planned to set a selling price of $249 a unit on the basis that variable manufacturing and distribution costs were expected to be $122 per unit. The company normally sets selling prices so that the contribution/sales ratio is 50% or slightly more. The fixed administrative and space costs that relate to the product, and which would be incurred from the commencement of production, were estimated to be $7.5 million per annum. It was also estimated that working capital of $2.5 million would be needed at the start of production in November 20X9.

The product was expected to have a life span of about five years, at which time the equipment would be scrapped as having no value. The company estimated its cost of capital to be 12% per annum.

November 20Y0

Development of Sparkle took six months longer than planned. This was largely because it proved necessary to employ two extra members of staff in the engineering department for the technical aspects of the product development.

The engineering department did not have a budget for this in year 1 (20X7/X8) and so employment was delayed until the start of the second year, November 20X8, when the budget for the extra funds had been approved. This caused the planned expenditure on development for year 2 to be spread over the 18 month period from the start of year 2 to the middle of year 3. The two new members of staff were employed at salaries of $45,000 each and employment costs were estimated to be 100% of the first year's salary. As a result, production started six months late in May 20Y0, the pre-launch costs were delayed accordingly and only 55,000 units were sold in the year November 20X9 to October 20Y0.

As expected, the competitor has decided to enter the market and is launching its rival product Glitter this month, November 20Y0.

R Ltd now predicts the market for 20Y0/Y1 to be 150,000 units and its share of this to be 50%. Thereafter the market size will be as forecast previously, i.e. between 160,000 and 200,000 units each year, and the product life cycle will stop at the same date as planned previously. The monetary value of all expenditures and revenues to date has been very close to the estimates and there is no reason to revise future forecasts in this respect.

Required:

Using the case of Sparkle in the scenario:

(a) Calculate the net present value of the project as perceived at the beginning of November 20X7, when R Ltd decided to manufacture Sparkle. State clearly any assumptions you make.

(11 marks)

(b) Calculate the revised net present value of the whole project as perceived at the beginning of November 20Y0.

(8 marks)

(c) Describe the position revealed by the figures you have calculated in (a) and (b) and on the events which have taken place. Identify what the company should do now?

(6 marks)

(Total: 25 marks)

Test your understanding 14

A landowner in Scotland proposes to develop a number of ski runs down the side of a mountain. The runs will be approximately 5 km long, dropping 1,000 metres from the mountain's summit to a car park. Two alternative strategies (each giving the same capacity) are being considered for the development.

- *Low investment*, involving the construction of a series of tows to haul skiers from the car park to the summit: the initial cost of constructing the tows will be $250,000 and tow motors will have to be replaced after five years at a cost of $50,000; operating costs will be $90,000 per year (fixed) and $3.50 per skier (variable).

- *High investment*, involving the construction of a cable-car system giving a non-stop ride to the summit: the initial cost of constructing the lift will be $1,200,000; operating costs will be $30,000 per year (fixed) and $1 per skier (variable).

The Regional Tourist Board will subsidise the initial construction cost of the development (using either strategy) by providing a loan for half the value of the initial construction cost. The loan is at an interest rate of 4% repayable over six years on an annuity basis. The Tourist Board requires (as a condition of the loan) that a flat fee of $8 is charged for each skier towed/ lifted to the summit.

The number of skiers using the runs will be dependent on the quality of snow cover. The better the snow cover, then the more runs it will be possible to open and the longer the runs will be able to stay open. The landowner forecasts that in any 10-year period, and assuming an $8 fee, the seasons will be as follows:

Quality of snow cover	Number of seasons	Number of skiers
Good	3	60,000
Moderate	4	40,000
Poor	3	5,000

The landowner has stated:

'Although the quality of snow cover is unpredictable for any one year, we can determine the expected outcome for an average year using probabilities and base our investment appraisal and business plan on that.'

A business adviser has commented on this statement as follows:

'The whole problem about winter sports in Scotland is the variability and unpredictability of snow cover. On average conditions are as good as any in Europe. However, if your first three seasons are poor then this could have a devastating effect on project viability.'

The landowner's cost of money is 12% per annum and in appraising investments he considers cash flows over a 10-year period only.

Required:

Identify for the landowner which strategy he should adopt (low or high investment) on the basis of the expected value methodology he advocates, and assuming an $8 fee.

(10 marks)

Test your understanding answers

Example 1 – SENSITIVITY ANALYSIS

(a)

Year		Cash flow $	15% discount rate	Present Value
0	Investment	(120,000)		(120,000)
1–15	Contribution	41,250	5.847	241,189
1–15	Fixed costs	(18,000)	5.847	(105,246)
15	Scrap value	25,000	0.123	3,075
				19,018

Net Present Value = $19,018

(b)

    (i)   If the capital outlay were to rise by more than $19,018 the project would cease to be viable. As a percentage increase this is:

$$\text{Sensitivity margin} = \frac{\$19,018}{\$120,000} \times 100\% = 15.85\%$$

    (ii)   If the PV of contribution were to fall by more than $19,018 the project would cease to be viable. As a percentage change this is:

$$\text{Sensitivity margin} = \frac{\$19,018}{\$241,189} \times 100\% = 7.89\%$$

    (iii)   If the PV of fixed costs were to rise by more than $19,018 the project would cease to be viable. As a percentage increase this is:

$$\text{Sensitivity margin} = \frac{\$19,018}{\$105,246} \times 100\% = 18.07\%$$

(c)   The break-even point can be calculated as follows:

    To remove the current NPV of $19,018, the PV of contribution would have to fall to $222,171 ($241,189 – $19,018). Calculating this as an annual amount can be done using the relevant annuity factor:

Annual cash amount	= $222,171 ÷ 5.847 = $37,997
Let 'x' be minimum sales level	
Annual contribution	= $2.75 × = $37,997
Therefore	× = 13,817 units

Example 2

The correct answer is **B**.

The initial $40,000 fee will be deemed to be a sunk cost - it has already been committed and won't be affected by any decision to proceed from this point.

The $20,000 is a future cost. Despite the fact that it is called a fixed cost it will only be incurred if the project proceeds. It is therefore and extra or incremental cost of the project and should be included in any future decision making.

Example 3

	$
Contribution per hour lost from normal working	3
Add back: labour cost per hour that is not saved	4
	7

The contract should be charged with 5,000 × $7 = $35,000

Activity 2

Nothing. The relevant cost is zero.

Example 4 – Balancing allowance

(a) Tax depreciation and the associated savings can be calculated as follows:

Year	$	Tax depreciation $	Tax saved at 30% $
0 – Investment	50,000		
1 – Tax depreciation (@25%)	12,500	12,500	3,750
	37,500		
2 – Tax depreciation (@25%)	9,375	9,375	2,813
	28,125		
3 – Tax depreciation (@25%)	7,031	7,031	2,109
	21,094		
4 – Disposal	10,000		
	11,094		
4 – Balancing allowance	11,094	11,094	3,328
Total tax depreciation / tax saved		40,000	12,000

The total tax depreciation will equal the difference between the initial cost ($50,000) and the residual value ($10,000). The total tax saving will be 30% of the tax depreciation (30% × $40,000).

(b)

Year	Cash benefit received	Total
1	$1,875	**$1,875**
2	$1,875 + $1,407	**$3,282**
3	$1,406 + $1,055	**$2,461**
4	$1,054 + $1,664	**$2,718**
5	$1,664	**$1,664**

Example 5

Corporation tax

Depreciation is not an allowable expense.

Therefore, taxable profit = $100,000 + $20,000 = $120,000 p.a.

Corporation tax at 30% = $36,000 p.a.

Half payable in current year, half payable in year following.

Tax depreciation

Capital cost:	$250,000
Scrap value:	$10,000
Total tax depreciation:	$240,000

Year	Reducing balance	Tax depreciation	Tax saved (30%)	Benefit received	Total cash benefit
1	$187,500	$62,500	$18,750	$9,375	$9,375
2	$140,625	$46,875	$14,063	$9,375 + $7,032	$16,407
3	$105,469	$35,156	$10,547	$7,031 + $5,274	$12,305
4	$10,000	$95,469	$28,641	$5,273 + $14,321	$19,594
5				$14,320	$14,320

Net present value

Year	0	1	2	3	4	5
	$	$	$	$	$	$
Net inflows		120,000	120,000	120,000	120,000	
Corporation tax		(18,000)	(36,000)	(36,000)	(36,000)	(18,000)
Tax depreciation		9,375	16,407	12,305	19,594	14,320
Investment	(250,000)				10,000	
Working capital	(35,000)				35,000	
Total net flows	(285,000)	111,375	100,407	96,305	148594	(3,680)
Discount factors	1.000	0.909	0.826	0.751	0.683	0.621
Present value	(285,000)	101,240	82,936	72,325	101,490	(2,285)

Net present value = $70,706

* working capital of $35,000 is injected in Year 0 and then released in Year 4.

Example 6 – NPV AND INFLATION

(a) **Discounting money cash flow at the money rate**

Year	Money cash flow $	Discount rate 15%	Present value $
0	(50,000)		(50,000)
1	21,100	0.870	18,357
2	22,261	0.756	16,829
3	23,485	0.658	15,453
4	24,776	0.572	14,172
		NPV =	14,811

(b) **Discounting the real cash flows at the real rate**

Calculate the real rate.

$$(1+r) = \frac{(1+m)}{(1+i)}$$

$$(1+r) = \frac{(1+0.15)}{(1+0.055)}$$

$$(1+r) = 1.0900$$

$$\therefore r = 0.09, \text{ i.e. } 9\%$$

Year	Real cash flow $	Discount rate 9%	Present value $
0	(50,000)		(50,000)
1–4	20,000 p.a.	3.240	64,800
		NPV =	14,800

Example 7

Notes:

$480,000 development cost is a sunk cost.

Depreciation is not a cash flow and should be excluded from the fixed costs.

Depreciation = $2,400,000 + 4 years = $600,000 p.a.

Therefore relevant fixed cost = $800,000 – $600,000 = $200,000.

Year 1 cash flows are:

		$000
Revenue	25,000 × $80	2,000 – rises at 5%
Direct material	25,000 × $8	200 – rises at 4%
Direct labour	25,000 × $12	300 – rises at 10%
Variable overheads	25,000 × $12	300 – rises at 4%
Fixed costs		200 – rises at 5%

Year	0	1	2	3	4
			$000		
Capital	(2,400)				
Revenue		2,000	2100	2205	2315
Direct material		(200)	(208)	(216)	(225)
Direct labour		(300)	(330)	(363)	(399)
Variable OH		(300)	(312)	(324)	(337)
Fixed cost		(200)	(210)	(221)	(232)
Net cash flow	(2,400)	1000	1040	1081	1122
15% disc. factor		0.870	0.756	0.658	0.572
Present value	**(2,400)**	**870**	**786**	**711**	**642**

The net present value is $609,000.

Therefore the company should invest in the project.

Example 8

$ millions	T_0	T_1	T_2	T_3	T_4
Sales (W1)		520	1082	675	
Variable costs (W2)		(158)	(331)	(208)	
		――	――	――	
Net trading inflows		362	751	467	
Taxation (30%) – in year		(54)	(112)	(70)	
Taxation – in year (30%)			(55)	(113)	(70)
Initial investment	(1,000)				
Scrap proceeds				200	
Tax depreciation benefit (W3)		37	66	82	55
		――	――	――	――
Net cash flows	(1,000)	345	650	566	(15)
DF @ 10% (W3)	1	0.909	0.826	0.751	0.683
		――	――	――	――
PV	(1,000)	314	537	425	(10)
				NPV	266

(W1) Revenue

Revenue needs to be expressed in money terms.

Revenue at T_1 = 5m × $100 × (1.04) = $520m.

Revenue at T_2 = 10m × $100 × $(1.04)^2$ = $1,082m.

Revenue at T_3 = 6m × $100 × $(1.04)^3$ = $675m.

(W2) Costs

Costs need to be expressed in money terms.

Costs at T_1 = 5m × $30 × (1.05) = $158m.

Costs at T_2 = 10m × $30 × $(1.05)^2$ = $331m.

Costs at T_3 = 6m × $30 × $(1.05)^3$ = $208m.

(W3) Tax depreciation ($m)

Year	Bal b/f	Tax depr (25%)	Tax relief (30%)	Year relief received			
				1	2	3	4
1	1,000	250	75	37	38		
2	750	188	56		28	28	
3	562	362 *	109			54	55
				37	66	82	55

*Disposal = $200m when the TWDV was $562m. Therefore the balancing allowance = $362.

(W3) Discount rate

$(1+m) = (1+r) \times (1+i) = 1.068 \times 1.03 = 1.10$, giving a money rate (m) = 10%.

Example 9 – REPLACEMENT DECISION

Method and answer guide

Firstly calculate the NPV of costs:

Year	Discount factor	Machine X		Machine Y	
		Cash flow $000	Present value $000	Cash flow $000	Present value $000
0		120	120	60	60
1	0.909	20	18	40	36
2	0.826	20	17	35	29
3	0.751	20	15		
Net present value			170		125

It is not appropriate to compare these two NPVs. Machine X shows three years of costs whereas Machine Y only has two years worth of costs. Remember that the machines are needed into the foreseeable future, so do not pick the cheapest single purchase. The machine will be replaced many times over the next few years. Because of this we need to find a way of comparing the costs over an equal time period (not unequal years).

Machine X:

NPV of one life cycle	= $170k
EAC	= $170k ÷ 2.487
	= $68k p.a.

Machine Y:

NPV of one life cycle	= $125k
EAC	= $125k ÷ 1.736
	= $72k p.a.

Machine X is the cheapest.

Example 10 – REPLACEMENT CYCLE

		Replacement Cycle									
	Discount	1 year		2 year		3 year		4 year		5 year	
Year	Factor	Cash	PV	Cash	PV	Cash	PV	Cash	PV	Cash	PV
0		(220)	(220)	(220)	(220)	(220)	(220)	(220)	(220)	(220)	(220)
1	0.893	11	9.8	(110)	(98.2)	(110)	(98.2)	(110)	(98.2)	(110)	(98.2)
2	0.797			(44)	(35.1)	(132)	(105.2)	(132)	(105.2)	(132)	(105.2)
3	0.712					(88)	(62.6)	(154)	(109.6)	(154)	(109.6)
4	0.636							(110)	(70.0)	(165)	(104.9)
5	0.567									(151)	(85.6)
Net present value			(210.2)		(353.3)		(486.0)		(603.0)		(723.5)
÷ Annuity factor			÷ 0.893		÷ 1.690		÷ 2.402		÷ 3.037		÷ 3.605
			—		—		—		—		—
Equivalent annual cost			(235.4)		(209.1)		(202.3)		(198.6)		(200.7)
			—		—		—		—		—

Notes:

- In year 0 the cost of the machine is shown

- In each year after that the cash column shows the running costs of the machine

- In the year of sale, net cash flow is scrap less running cost

- The PV (present value) column represents the cash column multiplied by the discount factor for that year.

- The net present value is then the sum of the present values

- In order to compare net present values an equivalent annual cost is calculated by dividing the NPV by the annuity factor for the length of the investment. So, for example, the 4 year NPV of $603.0 is divided by the 4 year 12% annuity factor of 3.037 to give an annual equivalent cost of $198.6

- These equivalent annual costs are compared and the lowest one is the optimal replacement cycle.

Therefore, the most economical replacement cycle is four years.

Example 11 – CAPITAL RATIONING

Project	Investment Required $000	Net Present Value $000	NPV ranking	Profitability Index	Index ranking
A	3,400	850	1	0.25	6
B	2,750	825	2	0.30	4
C	2,000	720	3	0.36	3
D	3,400	680	4	0.20	7
E	860	430	5	0.50	1
F	950	400	6	0.42	2
G	1,250	350	7	0.28	5

(a)

Project	Investment $000	NPV $000
A	3,400	850
B	2,750	825
C	2,000	720
D	850	170 *
TOTAL	9,000	2,565

* NPV has been pro-rated: (850/3,400) × 680

(b)

Project	Investment $000	NPV $000
E	860	430
F	950	400
C	2,000	720
B	2,750	825
G	1,250	350
A	1,190	297.50*
TOTAL	9,000	3,022.50

* (1,190/3,400) × 850

Test your understanding 1

Although part (a) could be completed most efficiently by finding the PV of net annual inflows ($600,000 − $350,000 − $40,000), i.e. of $210,000, part (b) would be most effectively negotiated if the separate PVs were found.

NPV calculation

Time		Cash flow	15% DF	PV
		$000		$000
0	Equipment	(500)	1.000	(500)
1–3	Revenue	600	2.283	1,370
1–3	Variable costs	(350)	2.283	(799)
1–3	Fixed costs	(40)	2.283	(91)
3	Scrap value	80	0.658	53
NPV ($000)				33

The project should, on the basis of these estimates, be accepted.

(a) **Sensitivity analysis**

   (i) **Initial investment**

      For the decision to change, the NPV must fall by $33,000. For this to occur, the cost of the equipment must rise by $33,000.

      This is a rise of: $\dfrac{33}{500} \times 100 = 6.6\%$

  (ii) **Scrap value**

      If the NPV is to fall by $33,000, the PV of scrap proceeds must fall by $33,000. The PV of scrap proceeds is currently $53,000. It must fall by: $33 \div 53 \times 100 = 62.26\%$, say 62.

(iii) **Selling price**

If sales price varies, sales revenue will vary (assuming no effect on demand). If the NPV of the project is to fall by $33,000, the selling price must fall by:

$$\frac{33}{1,370} \times 100 \qquad = 2.4\%$$

(iv) **Unit variable cost**

The project's NPV must fall by $33,000 therefore the PV of the variable costs must rise by $33,000. Since the PV of variable costs is $799,000, a rise of $33,000 is an increase of:

$$\frac{33}{799} \times 100 \qquad = 4.1\%$$

(v) **Annual fixed costs**

Since the PV of fixed costs is $91,000, a rise of $33,000 is an increase of:

$$\frac{33}{91} \times 100 \qquad = 36\%$$

(vi) **Sales volume**

If sales volume falls, revenue and variable costs fall (contribution falls). If the NPV is to fall by $33,000, volume must fall by:

$$\frac{33}{1,370 - 799} \times 100 \qquad = 5.8\%$$

(vii) Cost of capital

If NPV is to fall, cost of capital must rise. The figure which the cost of capital must rise to, that gives an NPV of zero, is the project's IRR.

NPV ($000) = − 500 + [210 × 2.210] + [80 × 0.624] = 14 The IRR is a little more than 17%, possibly 18%, but the formula can be used.

$$\text{IRR} \approx 15 + \frac{33}{33 - 14} \times (17 - 15)$$

≈ 18.47%, say 18.50%

To find the IRR, which is probably not much above 15%, the NPV at 17% can be found using the summarised cash flows.

The cost of capital would have to increase from 15% to 18½% before the investment decision changes

---

Test your understanding 2

Year	Cash flow $000		Discount factor	Present Value $000
0	Initial cost	(1,000)		(1,000)
1–7	Fixed costs	(60)	5.206	(312.36)
7	Residual	50	0.583	29.15
				(1,283.21)

PV of annual contribution required:	$1,283,210
Annuity factor years 1 − 7	÷ 5.206
Annual contribution required	$246,486.75
Contribution per unit	÷ $12.50
Minimum number of units	19,719 units

Answer A

Test your understanding 3

(i) The salary is a relevant cost of $12,000. Do not be fooled by the fact that it is a fixed cost. The cost may be fixed in total but it is definitely a cost that is relevant to the decision to proceed with the future development of the new product. This is an example of a directly attributable fixed cost. A directly attributable fixed cost may also be called product-specific fixed cost.

(ii) The $2,500 additional running costs are relevant to the decision to purchase the new machine. The saving in overhead absorption is not relevant since we are not told that the total overhead expenditure will be altered. The saving in labour cost would be relevant but we shall assume that this has been accounted for in determining the additional monthly running costs.

(iii) This is not a relevant cost for next month since it will be incurred even if the contract is cancelled today. If a decision is being made to close the office, this cost cannot be included as a saving to be made next month. However, it will be saved in the months after that so it will become a relevant cost saving from month 2 onwards.

(iv) This is not a relevant cost of the decision to continue with the contract. The $75 is sunk and cannot be recovered even if the company does not proceed with the negotiations.

Test your understanding 4

(a) The relevant cost of a material that is used regularly is its replacement cost. This will ensure that the business profits are unaffected by the use of the material for this contract. The relevant cost of material P is therefore $1.20 per tonne.

Material Q has a 'negative' cost if used for the contract. This is the saving that will be made through not having to pay the disposal cost of $280.

(b) The relevant cost of labour is zero. The labour cost is being paid anyway and no extra cost will be incurred as a result of this contract.

(c) The fixed overhead is not relevant because we are told that fixed overheads are not expected to increase. The relevant variable overhead cost is $3 per hour × 200 hours = $600.

Even if you are not specifically told that fixed overheads will remain unaltered, it is usual to assume that they will not increase, stating the assumption clearly.

(d) The rental cost $50 per month is not relevant because it will not be affected by the contract. The relevant cost of using the storage unit is the forgone rental income of $70 per month.

Summary of relevant costs

		$
(a)	Material P	120
	Material Q	(280)
(b)	Labour	–
(c)	Variable overhead	600
(d)	Rent foregone	210
(e)	Fixed overheads	–
		650

Test your understanding 5

Before you start a table of cash flows sort out corporation tax and tax depreciation benefits.

Corporation tax

30% of net cash flows (profits), i.e. 30% of $30,000 = $9,000.

Half is payable in the year of the profit, and half in the year following, i.e.:

Year	Corporation tax
1	$4,500
2	$9,000
3	$9,000
4	$9,000
5	$4,500

Tax depreciation

Capital cost: $100,000

Scrap value: $20,000

Total tax depreciation: $80,000

Year	Reducing balance	Tax depreciation	Tax saved (30%)	Benefit received	Total cash benefit
1	$75,000	$25,000	$7,500	$3,750	**$3,750**
2	$56,250	$18,750	$5,625	$3,750 + $2,813	**$6,563**
3	$42,188	$14,062	$4,219	$2,813 + $2,110	**$4,922**
4	$20,000	$22,188	$6,656	$2,110 + $3,328	**$5,437**
5				$3,328	**$3,328**

Now you can calculate the net cash flow each year, and discount:

Yr	Asset $	Profits $	Corporation tax $	Tax dep'n benefit $	Total net cash $	Discount factor	Present value $
0	(100,000)				(100,000)		(100,000)
1		30,000	(4,500)	3,750	29,250	0.952	27,846
2		30,000	(9,000)	6,563	27,563	0.907	25,000
3		30,000	(9,000)	4,922	25,922	0.864	22,397
4	20,000	30,000	(9,000)	5,437	46,437	0.823	38,218
5			(4,500)	3,328	(1,172)	0.784	(919)
						NPV =	**12,542**

Test your understanding 6

Expected annual cash flows are:

Annual cash flow (x)	Probability (p)	PV
50,000	0.3	15,000
100,000	0.5	50,000
150,000	0.2	30,000
		95,000

NPV calculation:

Time	Cash flow $	DF 5%	PV $
0	(460,000)	1.000	(460,000)
1–5	95,000	4.329	411,255
5	40,000	0.784	31,360
		NPV =	(17,385)

As the ENPV is negative, the project should not be undertaken.

An alternative approach would be to calculate three separate NPVs and then combine them, giving the following figures:

Annual cash flow $	Probability	NPV $
50,000	0.3	(212,190)
100,000	0.5	4,260
150,000	0.2	220,710

$$ENPV = 0.3 \times (-212,190) + 0.5 \times 4,260 + 0.2 \times (220,710) = \quad (17,385)$$

Even though the ENPV is negative these figures show that there is a 70% chance of the project giving a positive NPV. Some investors may consider the project acceptable on this basis.

Test your understanding 7

Since the decision has been made to increase capacity (i.e. 'to do nothing' is not an alternative), the easiest approach is to discount the incremental cash flows.

The tabular approach of the previous chapter is still appropriate particularly as the project lasts for ten years (other forms of presentation will appear later).

Time		A $000	B $000	B – A $000	8% DF/AF	PV $000
0	Capital expenditure	(260)	(415)	(155)	1	(155)
0	Working capital	(50)	(65)	(15)	1	(15)
2	Promotion	–	(15)	(15)	0.857	(13)
1–10	Net income	70	95	25	6.710	168
10	Scrap proceeds	40	75	35	0.463	16
	Net present value					8

The present value of proposal B exceeds that of proposal A by $8,000 at 8% and therefore proposal B is preferred.

Assumptions

- The disposal value of buildings is realistic and all other figures have been realistically appraised.

- Expenditure on working capital is incurred at the beginning of the project life and recovered at the end.

- Adequate funds are available for either proposal.

- All cash flows occur annually in arrears.

Test your understanding 8

$1.21 \div 1.09 = 1.11$

Answer B

Test your understanding 9

(W1) The incremental increase in contribution earned as a result of using the new machine is $30,000 × 40% = $12,000 per year.

(W2) Tax due/paid on incremental contribution earned:

Year	Incr. Contribution	Tax due (30%)	Year tax paid				
			1	2	3	4	5
1	12,000	3,600	1,800	1,800			
2	12,000	3,600		1,800	1,800		
3	12,000	3,600			1,800	1,800	
4	12,000	3,600				1,800	1,800
5	12,000	3,600					
			1,800	3,600	3,600	3,600	1,800

(W3) Tax depreciation/ tax relief

Existing machine

The sale of the existing machine leads to a balancing charge of $8,000 – $3,000 = $5,000. Tax payable on this is $5,000 × 30% = $1,500. Assume this is paid half in year 0 and half in year 1.

New machine

Year	Bal b/f	Tax depr (25%)	Tax relief (30%)	Year relief received				
				1	2	3	4	5
1	25,000	6,250	1,875	937	938			
2	18,750	4,688	1,406		703	703		
3	14,063	3,515	1,055			528	527	
4	10,547	5,547*	1,664				832	832
				937	1,641	1,231	1,359	832

* Disposal = $5,000 when the TWDV was $10,547. Therefore the Balancing allowance = $5,547.

All figures $	Year 0	Year 1	Year 2	Year 3	Year 4	Year 5
Incremental contribution (W1)		12,000	12,000	12,000	12,000	
Capital	(25,000)				5,000	
Tax paid (W2)		(1,800)	(3,600)	(3,600)	(3,600)	(1,800)
Tax paid on existing machine (W3)	(750)	(750)				
Tax relief on new machine (W3)		937	1,641	1,231	1,359	832
Net cash flow	(25,750)	10,387	10,041	9,631	14,759	(968)
DCF @ 15%	1	0.870	0.756	0.658	0.572	0.497
Present values	(25,750)	9,037	7,591	6,337	8,442	(4.81)

Net present value = $5,176

The net present value is positive and therefore it is worthwhile purchasing the machine.

Test your understanding 10

Since the question contains both specific and general inflation rates, the money method should be used

Step 1

The money method needs to be calculated using the information provided on the real rate of return and the general rate of inflation

$(1 + i) = (1 + r)(1 + h)$

$(1 + i) = (1.085)(1.06)$

$i = 15\%$

Step 2

Inflate the cash flows using the specific inflation rates and discount using the money rate calculated above.

	T₀	T₁	T₂	T₃	T₄	T₅
	$	$	$	$	$	$
Investment	(7,000)					
Wages savings (inflating @ 10%)		1,100	1,210	1,331	1,464	1,610
Materials savings (inflating @ 5%)		420	441	463	486	510
Net cash flow	(7,000)	1,520	1,651	1,794	1,950	2,120
PV factor @ 15%	1.000	0.870	0.756	0.658	0.572	0.497
PV of cash flow	(7,000)	1,322	1,248	1,180	1,115	1,054

Therefore NPV = $(1,081) which suggests the project is not worthwhile.

Test your understanding 11

All cash flows shown are money cash ($000)

Year	Capital	Labour	Material	Revenue	Net cash	13% factors	Present value
0	(400)		(350)		(750)		(750)
1		(550)		900	350	0.885	310
2		(605)		945	340	0.783	266
3		(665.5)		992	326.5	0.693	226
						NPV =	52

Net Present Value = $52,000

Answer C

Test your understanding 12

If buy now PV of costs = $7,800 + $110 × 0.909 = $7,900

If buy in one year, PV of costs = $8,800 × 0.909 = $8,000

Therefore, buy XG now

Answer B

Test your understanding 13

(a) *Examination tip*: Set up a table of cash flows. Keep all workings separate from this table.

Year	Date	Advertising $000	Capital costs $000	Contribution $000	Working capital $000	Net cash flow $000	12% discount factor $000	Present value $000
0	1.11.07							
1	1.11.08		(2,000)			(2,000)	0.893	(1,786)
2	1.11.09	(1,500)	(4,500)		(2,500)	(8,500)	0.797	(6,775)
3	1.11.10	(750)		12,700		11,950	0.712	8,508
4	1.11.11	(750)		17,145		16,395	0.636	10,427
5	1.11.12	(750)		11,430		10,680	0.567	6,056
6	1.11.13	(750)		11,430		10,680	0.507	5,415
7	1.11.14	(750)		11,430	2,500	13,180	0.452	5,957
								27,803
				Less PV of fixed costs: 7,500 × (4.564 − 1.690)				(21,555)
								——
				Net present value				6,24
								——

Production:

Year

1	100,000 units
2	135,000 units*
3	90,000
4	90,000
5	90,000
*(160 + 200)/2	180
1st 6 months	90
2nd 6 months	45 (50% because of competitor)
Total for year	135

Contribution per unit: $249 – $122 = 4127

Examination tip: Stating assumptions is very important in this question.

Assumptions:

- The amount already spent is not relevant – it is a sunk cost.
- The sales figures are the average of the range and the competitor takes 50% of market share after 18 months of sales.
- The equipment has no scrap value after five years.
- Working capital is released immediately production ceases.
- Inflation has been ignored.

Conclusion: the NPV is $6,248,000. Hence the project should be accepted.

(b)

Year	Date	Fixed cost $000	Advertising $000	Capital costs $000	Contribution $000	Working capital $000	Net cash flow $000	12% discount factor $000	Present value $000
0	1.11.07								
1	1.11.08			(2,000)			(2,000)	0.893	(1,786)
2	1.11.09			(2,847)		(2,500)	(2,847)	0.797	(2,269)
3	1.11.10	(3,750)	(1,875)	(1,923)	6,985		(3,063)	0.712	(2,181)
4	1.11.11	(7,500)	(750)		9,525		1,275	0.636	811
5	1.11.12	(7,500)	(750)		11,430		3,180	0.567	1,803
6	1.11.13	(7,500)	(750)		11,430		3,180	0.507	1,612
7	1.11.14	(7,500)	(750)		11,430	2,500	5,680	0.452	2,567
									———
				Net present value					558
									———

Development costs:

Year

1		= $2m
2	2/3 of $4m = $2.667m + $0.180	= $2.847m
3	1/3 of $4m = $1.333m + $0.090 + $0.5m	= $1.923m

Salary costs
in Year 2: $180,000

Salary costs
in Year 3: $90,000

Advertising
in Year 3: $1.5m + $0.375 (50% of $750,000) =$1.875m

Production:

Year

3	55,000 units @ $127	= $6.985m
4	150,000 × 50% @ $127	= $9.525m
5	90,000 units @ $127	= $11.430m

(c) The project is extremely sensitive to the sales in early years of the life cycle. These have been severely reduced due to the delay in the project (55,000 v 100,000 in Year 3) and the reduced total sales in Year 4 (down 30,000 units). This second reduction may also be attributable to the delay in product launch.

This large loss in profits is due to a budget constraint which involves a very small increase in the total development budget. The need for and the effects of not spending this small increase should have been made clear early on to avoid this ludicrous situation. If the sales figures in the remaining years are at the lower bound of the forecast, the project may well make a loss.

As the major cash outflows have already taken place (development, operating equipment and pre-launch marketing) the project should continue to reap the positive cash flows forecast for the next four years. The company can attempt to improve the size of the future positive cash flows by:

–   finding ways to compete with its competitor that holds 50% of the market share;

–   further develop the product or market to extend the life cycle of the project;

–   an ongoing cost-reduction exercise.

Test your understanding 14

Low investment

Year		Cash flow $000	12% discount factor	Present value $000
0	Initial cost	(250)	1.000	(250)
5	Replacement of motors	(50)	0.567	(28.35)
1–10	Fixed costs	(90)	5.650	(508.50)
1–10	Contribution (W1)	159.75	5.650	902.6
0	Loan	125	1.000	125.0
1–6	Loan repayment (W2)	(23.8)	4.111	(97.8)
				―――
				142.9

High investment

Year		Cash flow $000	12% discount factor	Present value $000
0	Initial cost	(1,200)	1.000	(1,200)
1–10	Fixed costs	(30)	5.650	(169.5)
1–10	Contribution (W1)	248.5	5.650	1,404.0
0	Loan	600	1.000	600
1–6	Loan repayment (W2)	(114.5)	4.111	(470.7)
				———
				163.8

Workings:

(W1) **Expected values**

Expected demand = 0.3 × 60 + 0.4 × 40
+ 0.3 × 5 = 35,500 skiers

Low investment: Contribution
per annum = ($8 – $3.50) × 35,500   = $159,750

High investment: Contribution
per annum = ($8 – $1) × 35,500   = $248,500

(W2) **Annuity**

Initial loan = PV
of repayments

PV of repayments = $x per annum
× annuity factor

Low investment

$125,000 = $X × 5.242
(annuity factor, year 6, 4%)

∴ $X = $23,800

High investment

$600,000 = $X × 5.242

∴ $X = $114,500

Low investment: NPV   = $142,900

High investment: NPV   = $163,800

∴ Adopt high investment strategy.

Working capital management

Chapter learning objectives

Lead	Component
E1. Analyse the working capital position and identify areas for improvement.	(a) Explain the importance of cash flow and working capital management.
	(b) Interpret working capital ratios for business sectors.

1 Chapter overview diagram

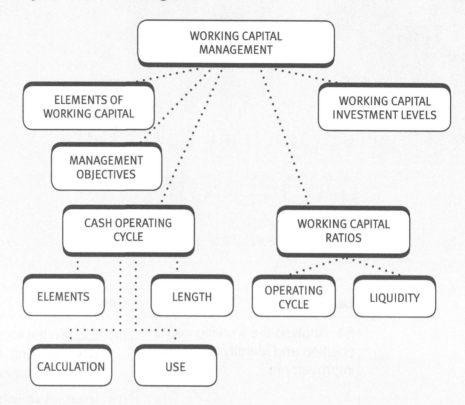

2 The elements of working capital

Working capital is the capital available for conducting the day-to-day operations of an organisation; normally the excess of current assets over current liabilities.

Working capital management is the management of all aspects of both current assets and current liabilities, to minimise the risk of insolvency while maximising the return on assets.

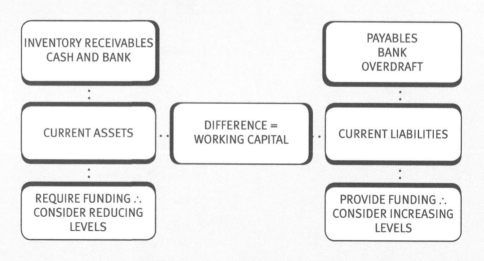

Investing in working capital has a cost, which can be expressed either as:

- the cost of funding it, or
- the opportunity cost of lost investment opportunities because cash is tied up and unavailable for other uses.

Working capital and cash flows

Working capital is an investment which affects cash flows.

- When inventory is purchased, cash is paid to acquire it.

- Receivables represent the cost of selling goods or services to customers, including the costs of the materials and the labour incurred.

- The cash tied up in working capital is reduced to the extent that inventory is financed by trade payables. If suppliers give a firm time to pay, the firm's cash flows are improved and working capital is reduced.

---

3 The objectives of working capital management

The main objective of working capital management is to get the balance of current assets and current liabilities right.

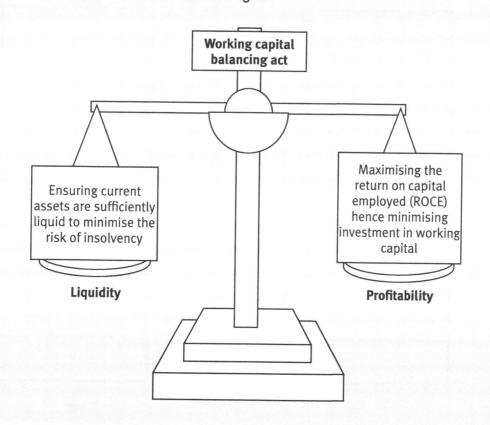

This can also be seen as the trade-off between cash flow versus profits.

Current assets are a major item on the statement of financial position and are especially significant to smaller firms. Mismanagement of working capital is therefore a common cause of business failure, e.g.:

- inability to meet bills as they fall due
- demands on cash during periods of growth being too great (overtrading)
- overstocking.

The trade-off between liquidity and profitability and its role in determining a business' overall investment in working capital is fundamental to your understanding of working capital management for the examination.

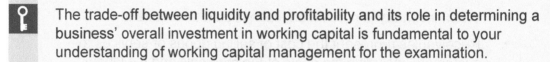

Example 1 – LIQUIDITY VERSUS PROFITABILITY

Fill in the blanks in the table to identify the advantages of having more or less working capital.

Advantages of keeping it high ⇧		Advantages of keeping it low ⇩
	INVENTORY	
	+	
	RECEIVABLES	
	+	
	CASH	
	=	
	CURRENT ASSETS	
	−	
	TRADE PAYABLES	
	=	
	WORKING CAPITAL	

Profitability v liquidity

The decision regarding the level of overall investment in working capital is a cost/benefit trade-off – **liquidity versus profitability**, or **cash flow versus profits**.

Cash flow versus profit

It is worth while stressing the difference between cash flow and profits. Cash flow is as important as profit. Unprofitable companies can survive if they have liquidity. Profitable companies can fail if they run out of cash to pay their liabilities (wages, amounts due to suppliers, overdraft interest, etc.).

Some examples of transactions that have this 'trade-off' effect on cash flows and on profits are as follows:

(a) Purchase of non-current assets for cash. The cash will be paid in full to the supplier when the asset is delivered; however profits will be charged gradually over the life of the asset in the form of depreciation.

(b) Sale of goods on credit. Profits will be credited in full once the sale has been confirmed; however the cash may not be received for some considerable period afterwards.

(c) With some payments such as tax there may be a significant timing difference between the impact on reported profit and the cash flow.

Clearly, cash balances and cash flows need to be monitored just as closely as trading profits. The need for adequate cash flow information is vital to enable management to fulfil this responsibility.

Profitability versus liquidity

Liquidity in the context of working capital management means having enough cash or ready access to cash to meet all payment obligations when these fall due. The main sources of liquidity are usually:

- cash in the bank

- short-term investments that can be cashed in easily and quickly

- cash inflows from normal trading operations (cash sales and payments by receivables for credit sales)

- an overdraft facility or other ready source of extra borrowing.

The basis of the trade off is where a company is able to improve its profitability but at the expense of tying up cash. For example:

- Receiving a bulk purchase discount (improved profitability) for buying more inventory than is currently required (reduced liquidity)

- Offering credit to customers (attracts more customers so improves profitability but reduces liquidity)

Sometimes, the opposite situation can be seen where a company can improve its liquidity position but at the expense of profitability. For example. offering an early settlement discount to customers.

Investing in and financing working capital

Working capital financing decisions involve the determination of the mix of long- versus short-term debt.

There is a basic difference between cash and inventories on the one hand and receivables on the other. In the case of cash and inventories, higher levels mean safety inventory, hence a more conservative position. There is no such thing as a 'safety level of receivables' and a higher level of receivables in relation to sales would generally mean that the firm was extending credit on more liberal terms. If we characterise aggressive as being risky, then lowering inventories and cash would be aggressive but raising receivables would also be aggressive.

The financing of working capital depends upon how current and non-current asset funding is divided between long-term and short-term sources of funding. Three possible policies exist.

(1) *Conservative.* A conservative policy is where all of the permanent assets, both non-current assets and the permanent part of the current assets (i.e. the core level of investment in inventory and receivables, etc.) as well as part of the fluctuating current assets, are financed by long-term funding, . Short-term financing is only used for part of the fluctuating current assets. The conservative policy is the least risky but also results in the lowest expected return.

(2) *Aggressive.* An aggressive policy for financing working capital uses short-term financing to fund all the fluctuating current assets as well as some of the permanent part of the current assets. This policy carries the greatest risk of illiquidity, as well as the greatest return (because short-term debt costs are typically less than long-term costs).

(3) *Moderate.* A moderate (or maturity matching) policy matches the short-term finance to the fluctuating current assets, and the long-term finance to the permanent part of current assets plus non-current assets. This policy falls between the two extremes.

Shortening the working capital cycle

A number of steps could be taken to shorten the working capital cycle:

- Reduce raw materials inventory holding. This may be done by reviewing slow-moving lines, reorder levels and reorder quantities. Inventory control models may be considered if not already in use. More efficient links with suppliers could also help. Reducing inventory may involve loss of discounts for bulk purchases, loss of cost savings from price rises, or could lead to production delays due to inventory shortages.

- Obtain more finance from suppliers by delaying payments, preferably through negotiation. This could result in a deterioration in commercial relationships or even loss of reliable sources of supply. Discounts may be lost by this policy.

- Reduce work in progress by improving production techniques and efficiency (with the human and practical problems of achieving such change).

- Reduce finished goods inventory perhaps by reorganising the production schedule and distribution methods. This may affect the efficiency with which customer demand can be satisfied and result ultimately in a reduction of sales.

- Reduce credit given to customers by invoicing and following up outstanding amounts more quickly, or possibly offering discount incentives. The main disadvantages would be the potential loss of customers as a result of chasing too hard and a loss of revenue as a result of discounts.

- Debt factoring, generating immediate cash flow by the sale of receivables to a third party on immediate cash terms.

The working capital cycle is the time span between incurring production costs and receiving cash returns; it says nothing in itself about the amount of working capital that will be needed over this period.

Overtrading

Healthy trading growth typically produces:

- increased profitability
- the need to increase investment in non-current assets and working capital.

If the business does not have access to sufficient capital to fund the increase, it is said to be "overtrading". This can cause serious trouble for the business as it is unable to pay its business creditors.

Typical indicators of overtrading

- A rapid increase in turnover
- A rapid increase in the volume of current assets
- Most of the increase in assets being financed by credit
- A dramatic drop in the liquidity ratios (see next section)

Solutions to overtrading

Overtrading can be a very serious risk, especially if there is a possibility that the bank will withdraw its overdraft facility. Potential solutions to the problem include:

- raising more long-term capital, in the form of new shares or loans;
- slowing down growth to reduce the increases in working capital requirements until sufficient cash has been built up to finance it;
- improving working capital management, so that there is a reduction in the inventory holding period or a reduction in the average time for customers to pay.

4 Working capital ratios – liquidity

Two key measures, the current ratio and the quick ratio, are used to assess short-term liquidity. Generally a higher ratio indicates better liquidity.

Current ratio

Measures how much of the total current assets are financed by current liabilities.

$$\text{Current ratio} = \frac{\text{Current assets}}{\text{Current liabilities}}$$

A measure of 2:1 means that current liabilities can be paid twice over out of existing current assets.

Quick (acid test) ratio

The quick or acid test ratio:

- measures how well current liabilities are covered by liquid assets
- is particularly useful where inventory holding periods are long.

$$\text{Quick ratio (acid test)} = \frac{\text{Current assets} - \text{Inventory}}{\text{Current liabilities}}$$

A measure of 1:1 means that the company is able to meet existing liabilities if they all fall due at once.

Typical targets

These liquidity ratios are a guide to the risk of cash flow problems and insolvency. If a company suddenly finds that it is unable to renew its short-term liabilities (for instance if the bank suspends its overdraft facilities) there will be a danger of insolvency unless the company is able to turn enough of its current assets into cash quickly.

In general, high current and quick ratios are considered 'good' in that they mean that an organisation has the resources to meet its commitments as they fall due. However, it may indicate that working capital is not being used efficiently, for example that there is too much idle cash that should be invested to earn a return.

The 'ideal' current ratio is commonly considered to be about 2.0 times (or 2:1), and the 'ideal' quick ratio is considered to be 1.0 times (1:1).

However, a 'safe' ratios vary widely between different types of business, because businesses in different industries have differing operating cash flow patterns. It is more useful to look at changes in the ratios over time, or for a company to compare its ratios with the ratios of other companies in the same industry.

When the current ratio is less than 1.0 (1:1), this means that the business has more current liabilities than it has current assets. This could be an indication of liquidity problems. However, companies in certain industries can operate successfully with low current ratios, without any liquidity problems. For example, a supermarket has no receivables because all its sales are for cash, and its inventory holding period is often much shorter than the time it takes to pay its suppliers. As a result, unless the supermarket holds on to its spare cash, its current liabilities will usually be larger than its current assets. A supermarket is likely to have both a low current ratio and a very low quick ratio.

Note on overdrafts

Some companies use an overdraft as part of their long-term finance, in which case the current and quick ratios may appear worryingly low. In such questions you could suggest that the firm reschedule the overdraft as a loan. Not only would this be cheaper but it would also improve liquidity ratios.

5 The working capital cycle

The elements of the working capital cycle

The working capital cycle is the length of time between the company's outlay on raw materials, wages and other expenditures and the inflow of cash from the sale of goods.

The faster a firm can 'push' items around the cycle the lower its investment in working capital will be.

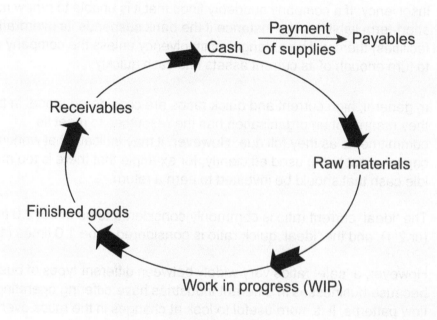

The working capital cycle

The working capital cycle reflects a firm's investment in working capital as it moves through the production process towards sales. The investment in working capital gradually increases, first being only in raw materials, but then in labour and overheads as production progresses. This investment must be maintained throughout the production process, the holding period for finished goods and up to the final collection of cash from trade receivables.

(**Note:** The net investment can be reduced by taking trade credit from suppliers.)

Calculation of the working capital cycle

For a manufacturing business, the working capital cycle is calculated as:

Raw materials holding period	X
Less: payables' payment period	(x)
WIP holding period	X
Finished goods holding period	X
Receivables' collection period	X
	——
	X
	——

For a wholesale or retail business, there will be no raw materials or WIP holding periods, and the cycle simplifies to:

Inventory holding period	X
Less: payables' payment period	(x)
Receivables' collection period	X
	——
	X
	——

The cycle may be measured in days, weeks or months and it is advisable, when answering an exam question, to use the measure used in the question.

Example 2 – WORKING CAPITAL CYCLE

A company has provided the following information:

Receivables collection period	56 days
Raw material inventory holding period	21 days
Production period (WIP)	14 days
Suppliers' payment period	42 days
Finished goods holding period	28 days

Calculate the length of the working capital cycle

Factors affecting the length of the operating cycle

Length of the cycle depends on:

* liquidity versus profitability decisions
* management efficiency
* industry norms, e.g. retail versus construction.

The optimum level of working capital is the amount that results in no idle cash or unused inventory, but that does not put a strain on liquid resources.

The length of the cycle

The length of the cycle depends on how the balancing act between liquidity and profitability is resolved, the efficiency of management and the nature of the industry.

Trying to shorten the cash cycle may have detrimental effects elsewhere, with the organisation lacking the cash to meet its commitments and losing sales since customers will generally prefer to buy from suppliers who are prepared to extend trade credit, and who have items available when required.

Additionally, any assessment of the acceptability or otherwise of the length of the cycle must take into account the nature of the business involved.

A supermarket chain will tend to have a very low or negative cycle – they have very few, if any, credit customers, they have a high inventory turnover and they can negotiate quite long credit periods with their suppliers.

A construction company will have a long cycle – their projects tend to be long-term, often extending over more than a year, and whilst progress payments may be made by the customer (if there is one), the bulk of the cash will be received towards the end of the project.

The amount of cash required to fund the working capital cycle will increase as either:

- the cycle gets longer
- the level of activity/sales increases.

This can be summed up as follows:

Activity/sales	Length of cycle	Funds needed increase proportionate to:
Stays constant =	Increases ↑	Days in cycle
Increase ↑	Stays constant =	Sales

Where level of activity (sales) is constant and the number of days of the working capital cycle increase the amount of funds required for working capital will increase in approximate proportion to the number of days.

Where the cycle remains constant but activity (sales) increase the funds required for working capital will increase in approximate proportion to sales.

By monitoring the working capital cycle the manager gains a macro view of the relative efficiency of the working capital utilisation. Further it may be a key target to reduce the operating cycle to improve the efficiency of the business.

6 Working capital ratios

The periods used to determine the working capital cycle are calculated by using a series of working capital ratios.

The ratios for the individual components (inventory, receivables and payables) are normally expressed as the number of days/weeks/months of the relevant income statement figure they represent.

Illustration – Working capital ratios

X plc has the following figures from its most recent accounts:

	$m
Average trade receivables	4
Average trade payables	2
Average raw material inventory	1
Average WIP inventory	1.3
Average finished goods inventory	2
Sales (80% on credit)	30
Materials usage	20
Materials purchases (all on credit)	18
Production cost	23
Cost of sales	25

Required:

Calculate the relevant working capital ratios. Round your answers to the nearest day.

Raw material inventory holding period

The length of time raw materials are held between purchase and being used in production.

Calculated as:

$$= \frac{\text{Average raw material inventory held}}{\text{Material usage}} \times 365$$

$$= \frac{(\text{Opening inventory} + \text{closing inventory}) \div 2}{\text{Material usage}} \times 365$$

NB. Where usage cannot be calculated, purchases gives a good approximation.

Solution 1 to Illustration

$$\frac{\$1m}{\$20m} \times 365 = 18 \text{ days}$$

WIP holding period

The length of time goods spend in production.

Calculated as:

$$= \frac{\text{Average WIP}}{\text{Production cost}} \times 365$$

NB. Where production cost cannot be calculated, cost of goods sold gives a good approximation.

Solution 2 to Illustration

$$\frac{\$1.3m}{\$23m} \times 365 = 21 \text{ days}$$

Finished goods inventory holding period

The length of time finished goods are held between completion or purchase and sale.

Calculated as:

$$= \frac{\text{Average finished goods inventory held}}{\text{Cost of goods sold}} \times 365$$

For all inventory period ratios, a low ratio is usually seen as a sign of good working capital management. It is very expensive to hold inventory and thus minimum inventory holding usually points to good practice.

Solution 3 to Illustration

$$\frac{\$2m}{\$25m} \times 365 = 29 \text{ days}$$

Inventory turnover

For each ratio, the corresponding turnover ratio can be calculated as:

$$\text{Inventory turnover (no of times)} = \frac{\text{Cost of goods sold}}{\text{Average inventory held}}$$

Generally this is less useful in the examination.

Using finished goods information from illustration 1:

$$\text{Inventory turnover} = \frac{\$25m}{\$2m} = 12.5 \text{ times}$$

Thus finished goods inventory turns round/is turned into sales 12.5 times in the year.

Trade receivables days

The length of time credit is extended to customers.

Calculated as:

$$= \frac{\text{Average receivables}}{\text{Credit sales}} \times 365$$

Generally shorter credit periods are seen as financially sensible but the length will also depend upon the nature of the business.

Solution 4 to Illustration

$$\frac{\$4m}{\$30m \times 80\%} \times 365 = 61 \text{ days}$$

Interpreting trade receivables collection periods

Businesses which sell goods on credit terms specify a credit period. Failure to send out invoices on time or to follow up late payers will have an adverse effect on the cash flow of the business. The receivables collection period measures the average period of credit allowed to customers.

In general, the shorter the collection period the better because receivables are effectively 'borrowing' from the company. Remember, however, that the level of receivables reflects not only the ability of the credit controllers but also the sales and marketing strategy adopted, and the nature of the business. Any change in the level of receivables must therefore be assessed in the light of the level of sales.

Trade payables days

The average period of credit extended by suppliers.

Calculated as:

$$= \frac{\text{Average payables}}{\text{Credit purchases}} \times 365$$

Solution 5 to Illustration

$$\frac{\$2m}{\$18m} \times 365 = 41 \text{ days}$$

Complications in calculations

There are differences in the way that the ratio might be calculated:

- Total purchases for the year should be used where possible. If the figure for purchases is not available, the cost of sales in the year should be used instead.

- The figure for purchases excludes any sales tax recoverable, whereas the carrying amount for payables includes sales tax. To make a like-for-like comparison, it might be appropriate to add recoverable sales tax back into purchases, or remove the sales tax element from trade payables. However, this is not usually done.

> • Where available, the average trade payables during the year should be used, normally calculated as the average of the trade payables at the beginning and the end of the year. However, if you wish to compare the average payment period in the most recent year and the previous year, and you only have figures for the two years, it will be necessary to use the end-of-year trade payables rather than an average value for the year. The same issue will arise when making receivables calculations.

Generally, increasing payables days suggests advantage is being taken of available credit but there are risks:

• losing supplier goodwill

• losing prompt payment discounts

• suppliers increasing the price to compensate.

The working capital cycle

The ratios can then be brought together to produce the working capital cycle.

	Days
Raw material inventory days	18
Trade payables days	(41)
WIP period	21
Finished goods inventory days	29
Receivables days	61
Length of working capital cycle	88

The working capital cycle tells us it takes X plc 88 days between paying out for material purchases and eventually receiving cash back from customers.

As always this must then be compared with prior periods or industry average for meaningful analysis.

Working capital turnover

One final ratio that relates to working capital is the working capital turnover ratio and is calculated as:

$$\frac{\text{Sales revenue}}{\text{Net working capital}}$$

This measures how efficiently management is utilising its investment in working capital to generate sales and can be useful when assessing whether a company is overtrading.

It must be interpreted in the light of the other ratios used.

Additional points for calculating ratios

The ratios may be needed to provide analysis of a company's performance or simply to calculate the length of the working capital cycle.

There are a few simple points to remember which will be of great use in the examination:

- Where the period is required in days, the multiple in the ratios is 365, for months the multiple is 12, or 52 for weeks.

- If you are required to compare ratios between two statements of financial position, it is acceptable to base each holding period on closing figures on the statement of financial position each year, rather than an average, in order to see whether the ratio has increased or decreased.

- For each ratio calculated above, the corresponding turnover ratio can be calculated by inverting the ratio given and removing the multiple.

- When using the ratios to appraise performance, it is essential to compare the figure with others in the industry or identify the trend over a number of periods.

- Ratios have their limitations and care must be taken because:
  - the statement of financial position values at a particular time may not be typical
  - balances used for a seasonal business may not represent average levels, e.g. a fireworks manufacturer
  - ratios can be subject to window dressing/manipulation
  - ratios concern the past (historic) not the future
  - figures may be distorted by inflation and/or rapid growth.

From an examination point of view, calculating the ratios is only the start – interpretation is the key to a good answer. Try to build a cumulative picture, e.g. the current ratio looks good until we find out from calculating the inventory holding period that there are high levels of illiquid inventory.

Do not be afraid to point out further information that may be required to provide a better interpretation of your calculations, e.g. the company credit policy, industry benchmarks, etc.

7 Working capital investment levels

The working capital ratios shown above can be used to predict the future levels of investment (the statement of financial position figure) required. This is done by re-arranging the formulas. For example:

$$\text{Trade receivables balance} = \frac{\text{Trade receivables days}}{365} \times \text{Credit sales}$$

Example 3 – WORKING CAPITAL INVESTMENT LEVELS

X plc has the following expectations for the forthcoming period.

	$m
Sales revenue	10
Cost of sales	(6)
Non-production costs	(2)
Net profit	2

The following working capital ratios are expected to apply.

Finished goods inventory days	30 days
Receivables days	60 days
Payables days	40 days

Required:

Calculate the working capital requirement.

Working capital investment levels

The level of working capital required is affected by the following factors:

(1) The nature of the business, e.g. manufacturing companies need more inventory than service companies.

(2) Uncertainty in supplier deliveries. Uncertainty would mean that extra inventory needs to be carried in order to cover fluctuations.

(3) The overall level of activity of the business. As output increases, receivables, inventory, etc. all tend to increase.

(4) The company's credit policy. The tighter the company's policy the lower the level of receivables.

(5) The length of the working capital cycle. The longer it takes to convert material into finished goods into cash the greater the investment in working capital

(6) The credit policy of suppliers. The less credit the company is allowed to take, the lower the level of payables and the higher the net investment in working capital.

8 Chapter summary

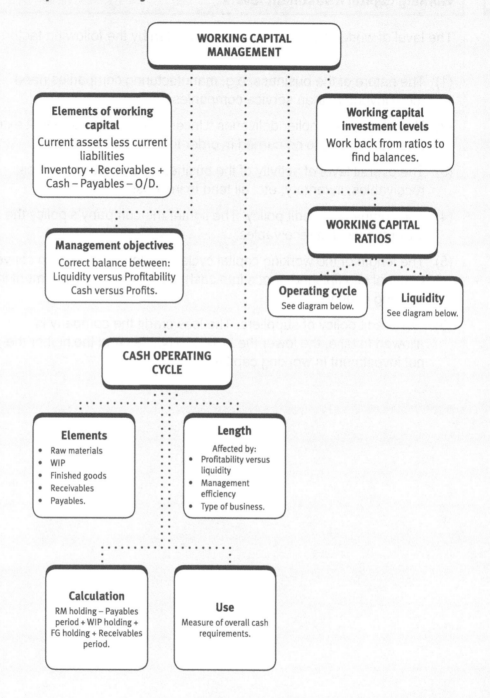

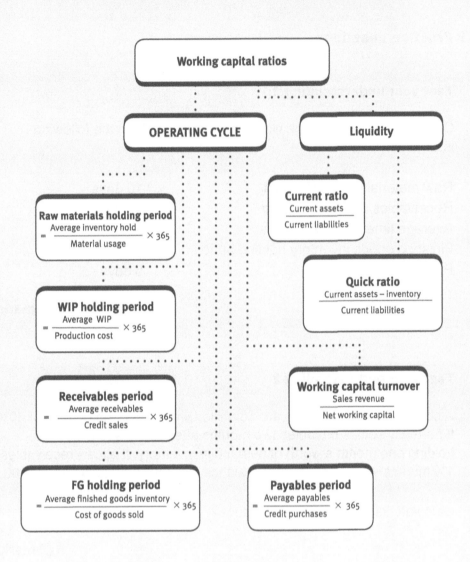

9 Practice questions

Test your understanding 1

Calculate the length of the working capital cycle from the following information:

Raw materials holding period	10 days
Receivables collection period	60 days
Average time to pay suppliers	45 days
Finished goods inventory holding period	20 days
Production cycle	5 days

(2 marks)

Test your understanding 2

A company's annual sales are $8 million with a mark-up on cost of 60%. It normally settles payables two months after purchases are made, holding one month's worth of demand in inventory. It allows receivables 1½ months' credit and its cash balance currently stands at $1,250,000.

Calculate its current and quick ratios?

(2 marks)

Test your understanding 3

A company has a quick (or acid test) ratio of 0.80:1. State whether the quick ratio would increase or decrease in each of the following situations.

(Take each situation individually, not together.)

(a) it receives payment of an amount owed by a trade customer.

(b) it sells an item of inventory at a loss

(c) it pays an invoice from a trade supplier.

(3 marks)

Test your understanding 4

Marlboro Co estimates the following figures for the coming year.

Sales – all on credit	$3,600,000
Average receivables	$306,000
Gross profit margin *	25% on sales
Finished goods	$200,000
Work in progress	$350,000
Raw materials (balance held)	$150,000
Trade payables	$130,000

Inventory levels are constant.

* Raw materials are 80% of cost of sales – all on credit.

Required:

Calculate the working capital cycle.

(5 marks)

Test your understanding 5

Identify which of the following transactions will result in an increase in working capital:

A   Writing off a debt as uncollectable

B   Paying the invoice of a trade supplier

C   Selling goods on credit at a profit

D   Buying inventory for cash

(2 marks)

Test your understanding 6

Appraisal of working capital management

You have been given the following information for a company:

Summarised balance sheets(statements of financial position) at 30 June

	20X7		20X6	
	$000	$000	$000	$000
Non-current assets (carrying value)		130		139
Current assets:				
Inventory	42		37	
Receivables	29		23	
Bank	3		5	
		74		65
Total assets		204		204
Equity and liabilities				
Ordinary share capital (50 cent shares)		35		35
Share premium account		17		17
Revaluation reserve		10		–
Profit and loss account		31		22
		93		74
Non-current liabilities				
5% secured loan notes		40		40
8% Preference shares ($1 shares)		25		25
Current liabilities				
Trade payables	36		55	
Taxation	10		10	
		46		65
Total equity and liabilities		204		204

Summarised income statements for the year ended 30 June

	20X7		20X6	
	$000	$000	$000	$000
Sales		209		196
Opening inventory	37		29	
Purchases	162		159	
	199		188	
Closing inventory	42		37	
		157		151
Gross profit		52		45
Finance costs	2		2	
Depreciation	9		9	
Sundry expenses	14		11	
		25		22
Operating profit		27		23
Taxation		10		10
Profit after taxation		17		13
Dividends:				
Ordinary shares	6		5	
Preference shares	2		2	
		8		7
Retained profit		9		6

Required:

(a) Calculate the liquidity ratios in 20X6 and 20X7

(5 marks)

(b) Calculate the length of the working capital cycle in 20X6 and 20X7

(10 marks)

(c) Evaluate whether the working capital is being managed effectively

(10 marks)

(Total: 25 marks)

Test your understanding 7

The following data relate to Mugwump Co, a manufacturing company.

Sales revenue for year:	$1,500,000
Costs as percentage of sales:	30%

Direct materials	
Direct labour	25%
Variable overheads	10%
Fixed overheads	15%
Selling and distribution	5%

Average statistics relating to working capital are as follows:

- receivables take 2½ months to pay
- raw materials are in inventory for three months
- WIP represents two months' half-produced goods
- finished goods represent one month's production
- credit is taken

– Materials	2 months
– Direct labour	1 week
– Variable overheads	1 month
– Fixed overheads	1 month
– Selling and distribution	½ month

WIP and finished goods are valued at the cost of material, labour and variable expenses.

Calculate the working capital requirement of Mugwump Co assuming that the labour force is paid for 50 working weeks in each year.

(10 marks)

Test your understanding 8

Brash is a medium-sized company producing a range of engineering products. Recently its sales have risen rapidly. It is now early in Year 3, and a summary of the company's performance and financial position in Years 1 and 2 are set out below:

Summary income statements for the year ended 31 December

	Year 1	Year 2
	$000	$000
Sales	12,000	16,000
Cost of sales	7,000	9,150
Operating profit	5,000	6,850
Interest	200	250
Profit before taxation	4,800	6,600
Taxation	1,000	1,600
Profit after taxation	3,800	5,000

	Year 1 $000	Year 2 $000
Non-current assets	9,000	12,000
Current assets		
Inventory	1,400	2,200
Receivables	1,600	2,600
Cash	1,500	100
	4,500	4,900
Total assets	13,500	16,900
Ordinary shares (50c each)	3,000	3,000
Accumulated profit	6,500	9,500
	9,500	12,500
Non-current liabilities (10% loan)	2,000	2,000
Current liabilities		
Trade payables	1,500	2,000
Other payables	500	200
Bank overdraft	0	200
	2,000	2,400
	13,500	16,900

Required:

Explain why Brash might be overtrading, by identifying how the company is showing four symptoms of overtrading.

(10 marks)

Test your understanding 9

Hottubes Co is a small company specialising in the supply of high quality amplifier do-it-yourself kits for sale to Hi-Fi enthusiasts. These include superior electronic components, circuit boards and detailed instructions. Promotion is carried out through adverts in electronics and Hi-Fi magazines. The company buys most of its components from a specialist supplier in Hong Kong and the remainder from a few local suppliers.

The CEO (and founder) is very proud of the company's performance and recently made the following comment.

'We have excellent products as seen in the recent rave reviews in a major consumer electronics magazine. Our business has grown rapidly over recent years and we have good profitability. We also have good liquidity with current assets easily covering current liabilities. This is partly due to improved credit control over receivables. However, our Hong Kong supplier demands payment at the end of each month for all items shipped in that month…'

As with many other small businesses, Hottubes uses its bank overdraft to finance working capital and has no other longer term funding. The current overdraft rate is 1.0% per month on the monthly outstanding balance.

Extracts from the management accounts for the last two years are as follows.

31 December

	20X2	**20X1**
	$000	$000
Sales	1,024	640
Cost of sales	640	400
Other expenses	132	81
Inventories		
Components	300	208
Finished kits	220	96
Trade receivables	320	204
Trade payables	135	104
Other payables	31	30
Corporation tax due	63	40
Purchases for the year	776	490
Bank overdraft	180	100

Required:

Prepare briefing notes for a meeting with the CEO calculating the company's working capital position and identify areas for improvement. Include in your answer a calculation of the working capital cycle and any other calculations you feel are appropriate.

(Total: 15 marks)

Test your understanding answers

Example 1 – LIQUIDITY VERSUS PROFITABILITY

Advantages of keeping it high ⬆		Advantages of keeping it low ⬇
Few stockouts Bulk purchase discounts Reduced ordering costs	**INVENTORY**	Less cash tied up in inventory Lower storage costs
	+	
Customers like credit – ∴ profitable as attracts more sales	**RECEIVABLES**	Less cash tied up Less chance of irrecoverable debts Reduced costs of credit control
	+	
Able to pay bills on time Take advantage of unexpected opportunities Avoid high borrowing costs	**CASH**	Can invest surplus to earn high returns Less vulnerable to takeover
	=	
	CURRENT ASSETS	
	–	
Preserves own cash – cheap source of finance	**TRADE PAYABLES**	Lose prompt payment discounts Loss of credit status Less favourable supplier treatment
	=	
	WORKING CAPITAL	

Example 2 – WORKING CAPITAL CYCLE

	Days
Raw materials inventory holding period	21
Less: suppliers' payment period	(42)
WIP holding period	14
Finished goods holding period	28
Receivables' collection period	56
Operating cycle (days)	77

Example 3 – WORKING CAPITAL INVESTMENT LEVELS

We need to use the ratios to calculate statement of financial position values in order to construct the projected working capital position.

				$m
Inventory	=	30 ÷ 365	× $6m	= 0.49
Receivables	=	60 ÷ 365	× $10m	1.64
Trade payables	=	40 ÷ 365	× $6m	= (0.66)
Working capital required				1.47

Test your understanding 1

	Days
Raw materials holding period	10
Production cycle	5
Finished goods inventory holding period	20
Receivables collection period	60
	95
Average time to pay suppliers	(45)
Working capital cycle	50

Test your understanding 2

Step 1 Calculate annual cost of sales, using the cost structure.

	%	$m
Sales	160	8
Cost of sales (COS)	100	5
Gross profit	60	3

Step 2 Calculate payables, receivables and inventory.

	20X6	**20X5**

$$\text{Payables} = \frac{2}{12} \times \text{annual COS} = \frac{2}{12} \times \$5m = \$0.833m$$

$$\text{Receivables} = \frac{1.5}{12} \times \text{annual sales} = \frac{1.5}{12} \times \$8m = \$1m$$

$$\text{Inventory} = \frac{1}{12} \times \text{annual COS} \quad \frac{1}{12} \times \$5m = \$0.417m$$

Step 3 Calculate the ratios.

$$\text{Current ratio} = \frac{\text{Inventory} + \text{receivables} + \text{cash}}{\text{Payables}} = \frac{0.417 + 1 + 1.25}{0.833} = 3.2$$

$$\text{Quick ratio} = \frac{\text{Receivables} + \text{cash}}{\text{Payables}} = \frac{1 + 1.25}{0.833} = 2.7$$

Test your understanding 3

(a) There is no change in the quick ratio. There is no change in current assets excluding inventory, and no change in current liabilities. The effect of the transaction is to reduce receivables and increase cash by the same amount.

(b) The quick ratio will rise higher than 0.80:1. The sale of the inventory, even at a loss, will result in an increase in either receivables or cash. Inventory is not included in the calculation of the quick ratio; therefore the reduction in inventory is irrelevant. Since current assets excluding inventory increase and current liabilities are unchanged, the quick ratio must increase.

(c) The quick ratio will fall. There will be an equal decrease in cash and trade payables.

It may be easier to understand by making up some numbers. Say the current assets (without inventories) were $80,000 and current liabilities were $100,000 to begin with. If a $30,000 supplier invoice was paid then the new balances would be $50,000 of current assets and $70,000 of current liabilities. The quick ratio would have lowered to ($50,000/$70000) 0.714:1.

Test your understanding 4

Income statement

	$	$
Turnover		3,600,000
Cost of sales		
Materials - 80% (given)	2,160,000	
Other (balancing figure)	540,000	
		2,700,000
Gross profit – 25% (given)		900,000

Working capital cycle

Raw materials holding period

$$\frac{\$150,000}{\$2,160,000} \times 365 = 25 \text{ days}$$

Trade payables days

$$\frac{\$130,000}{\$2,160,000} \times 365 = (22) \text{ days}$$

WIP holding days

$$\frac{\$350,000}{\$2,700,000} \times 365 = 48 \text{ days}$$

Finished goods holding period

$$\frac{\$200,000}{\$2,700,000} \times 365 = 27 \text{ days}$$

Receivables collection period

$$\frac{\$306,000}{\$3,600,000} \times 365 = 31 \text{ days}$$

$$109 \text{ days}$$

Test your understanding 5

The correct answer is **C**

Items B and D result in no change in working capital. Item B results in an equal reduction in both cash and trade payables. Item D results in an increase in inventory but an equal decrease in cash. Writing off a receivable (item A) reduces working capital, because there is a reduction in receivables but no reduction in current liabilities. Selling goods on credit reduces inventory but increases receivables by a larger amount (= the gross profit on the sale); therefore total working capital increases by the amount of the gross profit.

Test your understanding 6

(a) **Liquidity ratios**

The current ratio:

20X7		20X6	
$\frac{74}{46}$	= 1.6	$\frac{65}{65}$	= 1.0

The quick (or acid test) ratio:

20X7		20X6	
$\frac{32}{46}$	= 0.7	$\frac{28}{65}$	= 0.4

(b) **Working capital cycle**

To better understand the liquidity ratios we can then look at each individual component of working capital:

The inventory holding period:

20X7		20X6	
$\frac{(\frac{1}{2}(37 + 42) \times 365 \text{ days})}{157}$	= 92 days	$\frac{(\frac{1}{2}(29 + 37) \times 365 \text{ days})}{151}$	= 80 days

Receivables days:

	20X7	**20X6**
Average daily sales	$209,000	$196,000
	$\dfrac{209,000}{365} = \$573$	$\dfrac{196,000}{365} = \$537$
Closing trade receivables	$29,000	$23,000
Receivables days	$29,000	$23,000
	$\dfrac{29,000}{\$573} = 51\text{ days}$	$\dfrac{23,000}{\$537} = 43\text{ days}$

Or more quickly:

20X7	**20X6**
$\dfrac{29,000}{209,000} \times 365\text{ days} = 50.6\text{ days}$	$\dfrac{23,000}{196,000} \times 365 = 42.8\text{ days}$

Payables days:

	20X7	**20X6**
Average daily purchases	$162,000	$159,000
	$\dfrac{162,000}{365} = \$444$	$\dfrac{159,000}{365} = \$436$
Closing trade receivables	$36,000	$55,000
Payables' payment period	81 days	126 days

Or more quickly:

20X6	**20X6**
$\dfrac{36,000}{162,000} \times 365\text{ days} = 81.1\text{ days}$	$\dfrac{55,000}{159,000} \times 365 = 126.3\text{ days}$

Length of the working capital cycle:

	20X7 days	20X6 days
Inventory holding period	92	80
+		
Receivables' collection period	51	43
−		
Payables' payment period	(81)	(126)
=		
Working capital cycle	62 days	(3 days)

(c) **Commentary**

Assessment of liquidity ratios

Both of these ratios show an improvement. The extent of the change between the two years seems surprising and would require further investigation. It would also be useful to know how these ratios compare with those of a similar business, since typical liquidity ratios for supermarkets, say, are quite different from those for heavy engineering firms.

In 20X7 current liabilities were well covered by current assets. Liabilities payable in the near future are 70% covered by cash and receivables (a liquid asset, close to cash).

Assessment of the working capital cycle

Inventory

The inventory holding period has lengthened. In general, the shorter the stock holding period the better. It is very expensive to hold stock and thus minimum stock holding usually points to good management.

The current ratio calculation now seems less optimistic, considering the holding period for inventory of 92 days. Inventory that takes nearly four months to sell is not very liquid! It would be better to focus attention on the acid test ratio.

Receivables

Compared with 20X6, the receivables collection period has worsened in 20X7. It would be important to establish the company policy on credit allowed. If the average credit allowed to customers was, say, 30 days, then something is clearly wrong. Further investigation might reveal delays in sending out invoices or failure to 'screen' new customers.

This situation suggests yet a further review of the liquidity ratios. The acid test ratio ignores inventory but still assumes receivables are liquid. If debt collection is a problem then receivables too are illiquid and the company could struggle to pay its current liabilities were they all to fall due in a short space of time.

Payables

The payables' payment period has reduced substantially from last year. It is, however, in absolute terms still a high figure. Often, suppliers request payment within 30 days. The company is taking nearly three months. Trade creditors are thus financing much of the working capital requirements of the business, which is beneficial to the company.

A high level of creditor days may be good in that it means that all available credit is being taken, but there are three potential disadvantages of taking extended credit:

– Future supplies may be endangered.
– Availability of cash discounts is lost.
– Suppliers may quote a higher price for the goods knowing the company takes extended credit.

Additionally when viewed alongside the previous ratios calculated, this might suggest a cash flow problem causing suppliers to be left unpaid.

Overall

Our example shows that, in 20X7, there is approximately a 62-day gap between paying cash to suppliers for goods, and receiving the cash back from customers. However, in 20X6, there was the somewhat unusual situation where cash was received from the customers, on average, more than 3 days before the payment to suppliers was needed.

Test your understanding 7

(1) Costs incurred

	$
Direct materials 30% of $1,500,000	450,000
Direct labour 25% of $1,500,000	375,000
Variable overheads 10% of $1,500,000	150,000
Fixed overheads 15% of $1,500,000	225,000
Selling and distribution 5% of $1,500,000	75,000

(2) Average value of current assets

	$	$
Finished goods 1/12 × $975,000		81,250
Raw materials 3/12 × $450,000		112,500
WIP:		
(2 months @ half produced –		
1 month equivalent cost)		
Materials		
1/12 × $450,000	37,500	
Labour 1/12 × $375,000	31,250	
Variable overheads 1/12 × $150,000	12,500	
	———	
		81,250
Receivables 2 ½ /12 × $1,500,000		312,500
		———
		587,500

(3) Average value of current liabilities

	$	$
Materials 2/12 × $450,000	75,000	
Labour 1/50 × $375,000	7,500	
Variable overheads 1/12 × $150,000	12,500	
Fixed overheads 1/12 × $225,000	18,750	
Selling and distribution 1/24 × $75,000	3,125	
	———	
		(116,875)
		———

(4) Working capital required   470,625

Test your understanding 8

Sales increased by 33.3% between Year 1 and Year 2, but total working capital (= current assets minus current liabilities) remained the same, at $2,500,000. Companies that increase their sales without a sufficient increase in working capital might be at risk of overtrading (or 'under-capitalisation').

The liquidity position has deteriorated between Year 1 and Year 2. At the end of Year 1, the current ratio was 2.25:1 and at the end of Year 2 it was 2.04:1 (4,900:2,400). At the end of Year 2, the quick ratio was 1.55:1 and at the end of Year 2 it was 1.13:1 (2,700:2,400). A worsening liquidity position, in spite of being profitable, is also a sign of overtrading.

The worsening liquidity is also evident in the decline in the cash position, from a cash balance of $1,500,000 at the end of Year 1 to a negative net balance of $100,000 at the end of Year 2.

The average time for customers to pay was 49 days in Year 1 (365 days × 1,600/12,000). This had risen to about 59 days in Year 2 ((365 days × 2,600/16,000). Allowing customers a longer time to pay can also be a sign of overtrading, because a company might have to offer more generous credit terms in order to achieve growth in sales.

Test your understanding 9

Tutorial note: detailed discussions of receivables, payables and inventories policies are covered in later chapters. However, you should still be able to use some common sense to comment on the reasonableness of Hottubes' figures, especially given the description of its products, customers, suppliers and market.

Briefing Notes

(1) **Introduction – the profitability v liquidity trade-off**

    – Sales have grown 60% over the last year, reflecting increasing customer awareness of a quality product.

    – However, the overdraft has increased by $80,000 suggesting that there may be problems with working capital management.

    – Has growth been pursued at the expense of liquidity?

    – Over-trading is common in small companies with high growth.

(2) **Overview – Liquidity ratios**

- Current ratio is 2.05 and growing. This is >1 and, viewed in isolation, suggests that there are few short term liquidity problems (as indicated by the CEO).

- However, the quick ratio is only 0.78. This is <1 suggesting potential problems.

- In particular the company would struggle to repay its overdraft should the bank recall the facility for any reason.

- The current ratio appears healthy only because of the very high levels of inventory.

(3) **Overview – The working capital cycle**

- The working capital cycle has increased from 282 to 317 days and seems excessively high at over ten months.

- This means that more funds are tied up in working capital and is a concern, given the high growth rates of Hottubes.

- New business will result in increased cash outflows with resulting increased inflows delayed a further ten months. This is likely to result in the overdraft increasing in the short term.

(4) **Specific issues – Receivables**

- Credit control does appear to have improved as receivables days has fallen from 116 to 114 days.

- However, this still seems excessively high given that most customers are individual enthusiasts and not major corporations.

- Given the specialist nature of the product would it be possible to insist on payment up front before kits are despatched? It is unlikely that such a policy would lose sales. There is no reason for the firm to offer credit.

- Note: even halving receivables would free up $160,000 cash – this would reduce the overdraft significantly.

(5) **Specific issues – Inventories**

- Hottubes is holding over 4 months' worth of kits and the figure seems to be rising.

- It is difficult to justify why such high kit inventory levels are being held. Presumably the production period is quite short (components simply need to be placed in boxes) and, in any case, customers will probably be happy to wait for kits should there be production delays.

– The holding period of components has fallen but, as with kits, seems excessive. The time period could be justified if certain components are rare and difficult to source but there is no suggestion that the Hong Kong supplier could not send additional components at short notice if the need arose (e.g. by airmail?)

(6) **Specific issues – Payables**

– Hottubes is currently taking two months to pay suppliers. This seems high given the Hong Kong supplier's insistence that goods are paid for in the month they are shipped.

– While delaying payment is good for Hottubes' liquidity, there is a danger that the Hong Kong supplier will respond through some or all of the following:

– Price rises.

– Refusing to supply.

– Refusing to allow further credit.

– Sending Hottubes lower grade components.

– It appears that Hottubes is dependent on the supplier for its competitive advantage and would thus be advised to ensure this relationship does not deteriorate due to late payment.

(7) **Specific issues – Overdraft**

– Hottubes is dependent on its overdraft for financing. Unless working capital policies change, the overdraft looks set to increase.

– The firm should do detailed cash flow forecasts to identify how large it will grow, to ensure that any limits are not breached.

– The possibility of consolidating part of the overdraft into a loan should also be considered.

Appendix – Key Figures

	20X2	20X1
Receivables credit period	114	116
Components holding period	141	155
Finished kits holding period	125	88
Trade payables period	(63)	(77)
Length of working capital cycle	317	282
Current ratio(840/409 and 508/274)	2.05	1.85
Quick ratio(320/409 and 204/274)	0.78	0.74

Working capital management – inventory control

Chapter learning objectives

Lead	Component
E1. Analyse the working capital position and identify areas for improvement.	(g) Analyse the impacts of alternative policies for stock management.

1 Chapter overview diagram

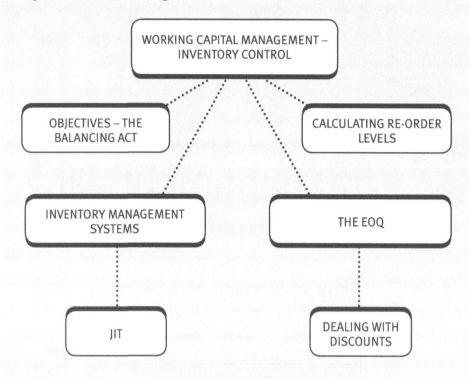

2 The objectives of inventory management

Inventory is a major investment for many companies. Manufacturing companies can potentially be carrying inventory equivalent to between 3 and 6 months worth of sales depending on where they source their inventory from and the relative power of suppliers. It is therefore essential to reduce the levels of inventory held to the necessary minimum.

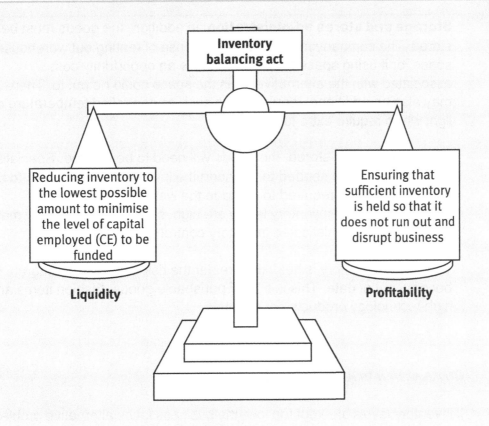

Costs of high inventory levels

Keeping inventory levels high is expensive owing to:

- the foregone interest that is lost from tying up capital in inventory
- holding costs:
  - storage
  - stores administration
  - risk of theft/damage/obsolescence.

Costs of high inventory levels

Carrying inventory involves a major working capital investment and therefore levels need to be very tightly controlled. The cost is not just that of purchasing the goods, but also storing, insuring, and managing them once they are in inventory.

Interest costs: once goods are purchased, capital is tied up in them and until sold on (in their current state or converted into a finished product), the capital earns no return. This lost return is an opportunity cost of holding the inventory.

Storage and stores administration: in addition, the goods must be stored. The company must incur the expense of renting out warehouse space, or if using space they own, there is an opportunity cost associated with the alternative uses the space could be put to. There may also be additional requirements such as controlled temperature or light which require extra funds.

Other risks: once stored, the goods will need to be insured. Specialist equipment may be needed to transport the inventory to where it is to be used. Staff will be required to manage the warehouse and protect against theft and if inventory levels are high, significant investment may be required in sophisticated inventory control systems.

The longer inventory is held, the greater the risk that it will deteriorate or become out of date. This is true of perishable goods, fashion items and high-technology products, for example.

Costs of low inventory levels

If inventory levels are kept too low, the business faces alternative problems:

- stockouts:
  - lost contribution
  - production stoppages
  - emergency orders
- high re-order/setup costs
- lost quantity discounts.

Costs of low inventory levels

Stockout: if a business runs out of a particular product used in manufacturing it may cause interruptions to the production process – causing idle time, stockpiling of work-in-progress (WIP) or possibly missed orders. Alternatively, running out of finished goods or inventory can result in dissatisfied customers and perhaps future lost orders if custom is switched to alternative suppliers. If a stockout looms, the business may attempt to avoid it by acquiring the goods needed at short notice. This may involve using a more expensive or poorer quality supplier.

Re-order/setup costs: each time inventory runs out, new supplies must be acquired. If the goods are bought in, the costs that arise are associated with administration – completion of a purchase requisition, authorisation of the order, placing the order with the supplier, taking and checking the delivery and final settlement of the invoice. If the goods are to be manufactured, the costs of setting up the machinery will be incurred each time a new batch is produced.

Lost quantity discounts: purchasing items in bulk will often attract a discount from the supplier. If only small amounts are bought at one time in order to keep inventory levels low, the quantity discounts will not be available.

The challenge

The objective of good inventory management is therefore to determine:

- the optimum re-order level – how many items are left in inventory when the next order is placed, and

- the optimum re-order quantity – how many items should be ordered when the order is placed

In practice, this means striking a balance between holding costs on the one hand and stockout and re-order costs on the other.

The balancing act between liquidity and profitability, which might also be considered to be a trade-off between holding costs and stockout/re-order costs, is key to any discussion on inventory management.

Terminology

Other key terms associated with inventory management include:

- lead time – the lag between when an order is placed and the item is delivered

- buffer inventory – the basic level of inventory kept for emergencies. A buffer is required because both demand and lead time will fluctuate and predictions can only be based on best estimates.

Ensure you can distinguish between the various terms used: re-order level, re-order quantity, lead time and buffer inventory.

3 Economic order quantity (EOQ)

For businesses that do not use just in time (JIT) inventory management systems (discussed in more detail below), there is an optimum order quantity for inventory items, known as the EOQ.

The challenge

The aim of the EOQ model is to minimise the total cost of holding and ordering inventory.

EOQ explanation

To minimise the total cost of holding and ordering inventory, it is necessary to balance the relevant costs. These are:

- the variable costs of holding the inventory
- the fixed costs of placing the order

Holding costs

The model assumes that it costs a certain amount to hold a unit of inventory for a year (referred to as C_H in the formula). Therefore, as the average level of inventory increases, so too will the total annual holding costs incurred.

Because of the assumption that demand per period is known and is constant (see below), conclusions can be drawn over the average inventory level in relationship to the order quantity.

When new batches or items of inventory are purchased or made at periodic intervals, the inventory levels are assumed to exhibit the following pattern over time.

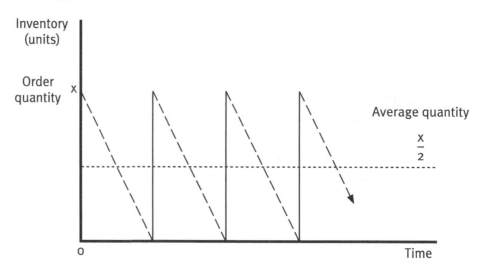

If x is the quantity ordered, the annual holding cost would be calculated as:

Holding cost per unit × Average inventory:

$$C_H \times \frac{x}{2}$$

We therefore see an upward sloping, linear relationship between the re-order quantity and total annual holding costs.

Ordering costs

The model assumes that a fixed cost is incurred every time an order is placed (referred to as C_O in the formula). Therefore, as the order quantity increases, there is a fall in the number of orders required, which reduces the total ordering cost.

If D is the annual expected sales demand, the annual order cost is calculated as:

Order cost per order × no. of orders per annum.

$$C_O \times \frac{D}{x}$$

However, the fixed nature of the cost results in a downward sloping, curved relationship.

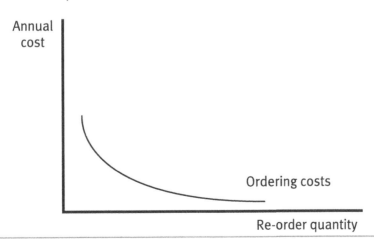

Total costs

Because we are trying to balance these two costs (one which increases as re-order quantity increases and one which falls), total costs will always be minimised at the point where the total holding costs equals the total ordering costs. This point will be the economic order quantity (when the re-order quantity chosen minimises the total cost of holding and ordering).

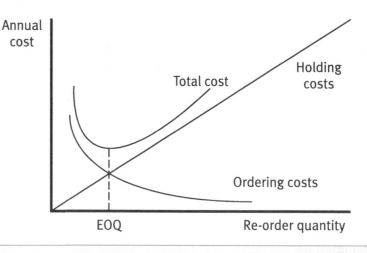

Assumptions

The following assumptions are made:

- demand and lead time are constant and known
- purchase price is constant
- no buffer inventory held as it is assumed that it is not needed since demand and lead times are known with certainty.

These assumptions are critical and should be discussed when considering the validity of the model and its conclusions, e.g. in practice, demand and/or lead time may vary.

The calculation

The EOQ can be found using a formula (given in the examination):

$$EOQ = \sqrt{\frac{2C_OD}{C_H}}$$

where:

C_O = cost per order

D = annual demand

C_H = cost of holding one unit for one year.

Example 1

A company requires 1,000 units of material X per month. The cost per order is $30 regardless of the size of the order. The annual holding costs are $2.88 per unit.

Required:

Investigate the total cost of buying the material in quantities of 400, 500, or 600 units at one time. Identify the cheapest option.

Apply the EOQ formula to prove your answer is correct.

Dealing with quantity discounts

Discounts may be offered for ordering in large quantities. If the EOQ is smaller than the order size needed for a discount, should the order size be increased above the EOQ?

To work out the answer you should carry out the following steps:

Step 1: Calculate EOQ, ignoring discounts.

Step 2: If the EOQ is below the quantity qualifying for a discount, calculate the total annual inventory cost arising from using the EOQ.

Step 3: Recalculate total annual inventory costs using the order size required to just obtain each discount.

Step 4: Compare the cost of Steps 2 and 3 with the saving from the discount, and select the minimum cost alternative.

Step 5: Repeat for all discount levels.

Example 2

W Co is a retailer of barrels. The company has an annual demand of 30,000 barrels. The barrels cost $12 each. Supplies can be obtained immediately, with ordering and transport costs amounting to $200 per order. The annual cost of holding one barrel in stock is estimated to be $1.20 per barrel.

A 2% discount is available on orders of at least 5,000 barrels and a 2.5% discount is available if the order quantity is 7,500 barrels or above.

Required:

Calculate the EOQ ignoring the discount and calculate if it would change once the discount is taken into account.

Criticisms of EOQ

The EOQ model can be criticised in several ways:

*   It is based on simplifying assumptions, such as constant and predictable material usage rates.
*   It will not indicate the optimal purchase quantity when there are price discounts for buying in larger quantities.
*   It ignores the problem of managing stock-outs.
*   It is inconsistent with the philosophy of just-in-time management and total quality management.

4 Inventory control systems

Three main systems are used to monitor and control inventory levels:

(1) reorder level system (whereby inventory is ordered at a particular, set order level)
(2) periodic review system (whereby inventory is checked and ordered at set periods in time)
(3) mixed systems, incorporating elements of both of the above.

Control systems explained

Reorder level system

With this system, whenever the current inventory level falls below a pre-set 'reorder level' (ROL), a replenishment (replacement) order is made. Since there is normally a gap (lead time) between the placing of an order and receipt of supplies this has to be allowed for. Buffer inventory is usually held as insurance against variations in demand and lead time.

This system used to be known as the 'two-bin' system. Inventory is kept in two bins, one with an amount equal to the ROL quantity, and the rest in the other. Inventory is drawn from the latter until it runs out, whence a replenishment order is triggered.

A reorder level system is simple enough to implement if the variables (such as average usage, supplier lead time, etc.) are known with certainty. In practice, this is rarely the case.

Periodic review system

This is also referred to as a 'constant cycle' system. Inventory levels are reviewed after a fixed interval, for example, on the first of the month. Replenishment orders are issued where necessary, to top up inventory levels to pre-set target levels. This means that order sizes are variable.

Mixed systems

In practice, mixtures of both systems are sometimes used, depending on the nature of the problem, the amount of computerisation and so on.

Calculating the re-order level (ROL)

Known demand and lead time

Having decided how much inventory to re-order, the next problem is when to re-order. The firm needs to identify a level of inventory which can be reached before an order needs to be placed.

The **ROL** is the quantity of inventory on hand when an order is placed.

When demand and lead time are known with certainty the ROL may be calculated exactly, i.e. ROL = demand in the lead time.

Example 3

Using the data for W Co, assume that the company adopts the EOQ as its order quantity and that it now takes two weeks for an order to be delivered.

Calculate how frequently the company will place an order? Calculate how much inventory it will have on hand when the order is placed?

ROL with variable demand or variable lead time

When there is uncertainty over demand or lead time are known then the **ROL will be calculated as = maximum demand x maximum lead time**. This will lead to the creation of **buffer stock**.

Buffer stock

Buffer stock is a quantity of inventory that should not usually be needed, but that might be needed if actual demand during the supply lead time exceeds the average demand or if lead times are longer than expected. Buffer stock has a cost. The annual cost of holding buffer stock is the amount of the buffer stock multiplied by the annual holding cost for one unit of the inventory item.

Calculating buffer stock:

	Units
Reorder level*	X
(Maximum demand per day, in units x maximum re-order lead time)	
Average usage	Y
(Average demand per day, in units x average re-order lead time)	
Buffer Stock	X – Y

* note that this is the ROL when demand or lead time are uncertain.

Where there is uncertainty, an optimum level of buffer stock (or inventory) must be found.

This depends on:

- variability of demand
- cost of holding inventory
- cost of stockouts.

You will not be required to perform this calculation in the examination.

Inventory warning levels

Two warning levels might also be used, to indicate when the quantity of an item in inventory is either:

- higher than should be expected, or
- below the buffer stock level.

If the quantity of inventory goes above the maximum level or below the minimum level, the inventory manager should monitor the position carefully, and where appropriate take control measures.

The **maximum inventory level** should be:

- Reorder level
- Plus reorder quantity
- Minus [Minimum demand per day/week, in units] × [Minimum re-order lead time].

The maximum inventory level will occur when a new order has just been delivered by the supplier, the order has been delivered within the minimum lead time, and demand has been at a minimum during the lead time.

The **minimum inventory level** should be the buffer stock level:

- Reorder level
- Minus [Average demand per day/week, in units] × [Average re-order lead time].

5 Centralised versus decentralised purchasing

An organisation might have several locations, departments or group companies that each use the same raw materials and components. These might all be located within the same country, or they might be scattered across the world and geographically remote from each other.

In such cases, a policy decision must be made about whether to have centralised or decentralised purchasing of materials.

Advantages and disadvantages

- With centralised purchasing, all materials are purchased by the same central purchasing department. Purchases prices and quantities are decided centrally and inventory levels are also monitored and controlled centrally.

- With decentralised purchasing, the authority to purchase materials is delegated to several operating units within the organisation, each with its own buying department or buying managers. Purchases prices and quantities are decided locally and the local management is also responsible for inventory management at a local level.

Advantages of centralised purchasing

- A centralised buyer is able to order in larger quantities, and might be able to negotiate lower prices for bulk purchase orders.

- A centralised buyer might have a wider network of suppliers than a local buyer would have, and should be able to ensure that the best available prices are identified.

- It is easier to enforce common quality standards for purchased materials.

- With centralised buying, it should also be easier to manage inventory levels efficiently. The buyer should have access to information about the current inventory quantities at all locations in the organisation, and where appropriate can arrange for inventory to be transferred from one location to another, without having to purchase additional quantities.

- In an organisation whose operating units are all within a fairly small geographical area, it should also be possible to operate with a single centralised stores department as well as a centralised purchasing department. It should be much easier to control inventory levels with a central store than with several localised stores.

- Decisions about taking early settlement discounts can be co-ordinated and taken on a global basis, taking due account of the cash flow position of the organisation as a whole.

Disadvantages of centralised purchasing

- Local buying managers should be able to develop stronger relationships with local suppliers, possibly ensuring greater reliability of supply.

- A local buying manager might be much more flexible, and able to take advantage of temporary low prices locally that a central buying manager might not notice.

- A local manager can respond to inventory shortages more quickly than a centralised buying team. New materials can often be ordered and delivered much more quickly when the buying is done locally: central buyers might be slow and bureaucratic.

- Buying and inventory control are important aspects of operational and financial management. If authority is delegated to operating units (investment centres) within an organisation, it is appropriate that the responsibility for buying and inventory management should also be delegated.

6 Chapter summary

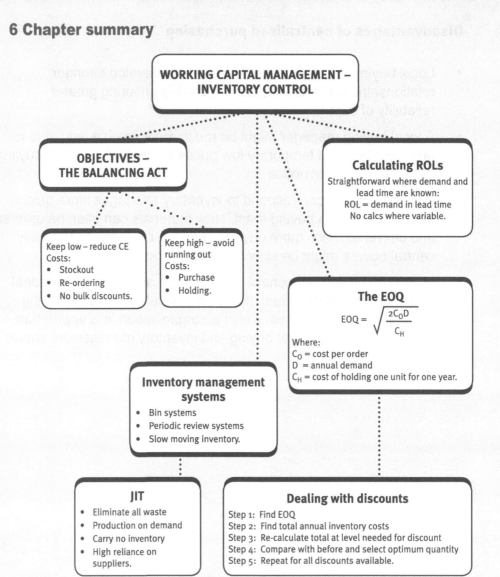

WORKING CAPITAL MANAGEMENT – INVENTORY CONTROL

OBJECTIVES – THE BALANCING ACT

Keep low – reduce CE
Costs:
- Stockout
- Re-ordering
- No bulk discounts.

Keep high – avoid running out
Costs:
- Purchase
- Holding.

Calculating ROLs
Straightforward where demand and lead time are known:
ROL = demand in lead time
No calcs where variable.

The EOQ

$$EOQ = \sqrt{\frac{2C_O D}{C_H}}$$

Where:
C_O = cost per order
D = annual demand
C_H = cost of holding one unit for one year.

Inventory management systems
- Bin systems
- Periodic review systems
- Slow moving inventory.

JIT
- Eliminate all waste
- Production on demand
- Carry no inventory
- High reliance on suppliers.

Dealing with discounts
Step 1: Find EOQ
Step 2: Find total annual inventory costs
Step 3: Re-calculate total at level needed for discount
Step 4: Compare with before and select optimum quantity
Step 5: Repeat for all discounts available.

7 Practice questions

Test your understanding 1

Identify which of the following is not a required assumption for the basic EOQ model?

A   The lead time is zero

B   There are no stock-outs

C   The demand is known and constant

D   The purchase price is constant regardless of order quantity

(2 marks)

Test your understanding 2

Monthly demand for a product is 10,000 units. The purchase price is $10/unit and the company's cost of finance is 15% pa. Warehouse storage costs per unit pa are $2/unit. The supplier charges $200 per order for delivery.

Calculate the EOQ.

(2 marks)

Test your understanding 3

D Co uses component V22 in its construction process. The company has a demand of 45,000 components pa. They cost $4.50 each. There is no lead time between order and delivery, and ordering costs amount to $100 per order. The annual cost of holding one component in inventory is estimated to be $0.65.

A 0.5% discount is available on orders of at least 3,000 components and a 0.75% discount is available if the order quantity is 6,000 components or above.

Calculate the optimal order quantity.

(5 marks)

Test your understanding 4

Using the data relating to D Co (previous question), and ignoring discounts, assume that the company adopts the EOQ as its order quantity and that it now takes three weeks for an order to be delivered.

(a) Calculate how frequently will the company place an order

(b) Calculate how much inventory will it have on hand when the order is placed

(4 marks)

Test your understanding 5

A company has estimated that for the coming season weekly demand for components will be 80 units. Suppliers take three weeks on average to deliver goods once they have been ordered and a buffer inventory of 35 units is held.

If the inventory levels are reviewed every six weeks, calculate how many units will be ordered at a review where the count shows 250 units in inventory.

(2 marks)

Test your understanding 6

(a) Explain why the net present value (NPV) method of investment appraisal is thought to be superior to other approaches.

(7 marks)

(b) Hexicon Inc manufactures and markets automatic washing machines. Among the many hundreds of components which it purchases each year from external suppliers for assembling into the finished article are drive belts, of which it uses 40,000 units pa. It is considering converting its purchasing, delivery and inventory control of this item to a just-in-time system. This will raise the number of orders placed but lower the administrative and other costs of placing and receiving orders. If successful, this will provide the model for switching most of its inwards supplies on to this system. Details of actual and expected ordering and carrying costs are given in the table below.

		Actual	Proposed
C_O =	Ordering cost per order	$100	$25
P =	Purchase cost per item	$2.50	$2.50
C_H =	Inventory holding cost	20%	20%
	(as a percentage of the purchase cost)		

To implement the new arrangements will require 'one-off' reorganisation costs estimated at $4,000 which will be treated as a revenue item for tax purposes. The rate of corporation tax is 33% and Hexicon can obtain finance at 12%. The effective life span of the new system can be assumed to be eight years.

Required:

(i) Calculate the effect of the new system on the economic order quantity (EOQ).

(ii) Calculate whether the new system is worthwhile in financial terms.

(12 marks)

(c) You are required to briefly explain the nature and objectives of JIT purchasing agreements concluded between components users and suppliers.

(6 marks)

(Total: 25 marks)

Test your understanding answers

Example 1

	Order quantity		
	400 units	**500 units**	**600 units**
Average inventory	200	250	300
No. of orders per annum	30	24	20
	$	$	$
Holding cost – average inventory × $2.88	576	720	864

	Order quantity		
	400 units	500 units	600 units
Ordering cost – no. of orders × $30	900	720	600
Total cost	1,476	1,440	1,464

Therefore the best option is to order 500 units each time.

Note that this is the point at which total cost is minimised and the holding costs and order costs are equal.

Solution using the formula:

$$EOQ = \sqrt{\frac{2C_0D}{C_H}}$$

$C_O = 30$

$D = 1,000 \times 12 = 12,000$

$C_H = 2.88$

$$EOQ = \sqrt{\frac{2 \times 30 \times 12,000}{2.88}} = 500$$

Example 2

Step 1 Calculate EOQ, ignoring discounts.

$$EOQ = \sqrt{\frac{2C_O D}{C_H}}$$

$C_O = \$200$

$D = 30,000$ units

$C_H = \$1.20$

$$EOQ = \sqrt{\frac{2 \times 200 \times 30,000}{1.2}} = 3,162$$

Step 2 As this is below the level for discounts, calculate total annual inventory costs.

Total annual costs for the company will comprise holding costs plus re-ordering costs.

$=$ (Average inventory $\times C_H$) $+$ (Number of re-orders pa $\times C_O$)

$= \dfrac{3,162}{2} \times \$1.20 + \dfrac{30,000}{3,162} \times \$200$

$= \$1,897.20 + \$1,897.53$

$= \$3,794.73$

$= \$3,795$

Step 3 Recalculate total annual inventory costs using the order size required to just obtain the discount.

At order quantity 5,000, total costs are as follows.

= (Average inventory + (Number of re-orders pa
  × C_H) × C_O)

= $\dfrac{5{,}000}{2}$ × 1.20 + $\dfrac{30{,}000}{5{,}000}$ × 200

= $3,000 + $1,200

= $4,200

	$
Extra costs of ordering in batches of 5,000 (4,200 – 3,795)	(405)
Saving on discount 2% × $12 × 30,000	7,200
Step 4 Net saving	6,795

Hence batches of 5,000 are worthwhile.

Step 3 (again)

At order quality 7,500, total costs are as follows:

= (Average inventory + (Number of re-orders pa
  × C_H) × C_O)

= $\dfrac{7{,}500}{2}$ × 1.20 + $\dfrac{30{,}000}{7{,}500}$ × 200

= $4,500 + $800

= $5,300

Extra costs of ordering in batches of 7,500 (5,300 – 4,200)	(1,100)
Saving on extra discount (2.5% – 2%) × 30,000	1,800
Step 4 Net saving (again)	700

So a further cost saving can be made on orders of 7,500 units.

Note: If Step 1 produces an EOQ at which a discount would have been available, and the holding cost would be reduced by taking the discount, i.e. where C_H is based on the purchase price × the cost of finance, the EOQ must be recalculated using the new C_H before the above steps are followed.

Alternative approach

An alternative approach is to compare the total costs at each level and choose the lowest total cost as the best order level. The total cost will be made up of the total purchasing costs, the holding costs and the order costs as follows:

Order size	3,162	5,000	7,500
	$	$	$
Total purchase costs (30,000 barrels x $12 each)	360,000	360,000	360,000
Discount	nil	(7,200)	(9,000)
Holding and order costs	3,795	4,200	5,300
	363,795	357,000	356,300

(Note that many of the same calculations would be needed in order to complete this table)

This confirms that the best order size would be 7,500 units.

Example 3

- Annual demand is 30,000. The original EOQ is 3,162. The company will therefore place an order once every

  3,162 ÷ 30,000 × 365 days = 38 days

- The company must be sure that there is sufficient inventory on hand when it places an order to last the two weeks' lead time. It must therefore place an order when there is two weeks' worth of demand in inventory:

  i.e. ROL is 2 ÷ 52 × 30,000 = 1,154 units

Test your understanding 1

The correct answer is **A**.

The EOQ model assumes a known and constant order lead time. The lead time does not have to be zero.

Test your understanding 2

$$EOQ = \sqrt{\frac{2C_oD}{C_H}}$$

$C_O = 200$

$D = 10{,}000 \times 12 = 120{,}000$

$C_H = (10 \times 0.15) + 2 = 3.5$

$$EOQ = \sqrt{\frac{2 \times 200 \times 120{,}000}{3.5}} = 3{,}703$$

Test your understanding 3

Step 1

$$EOQ = \sqrt{\frac{2C_OD}{C_H}}$$

$C_O = 100$

$D = 45{,}000$

$C_H = 0.65$

$$EOQ = \sqrt{\frac{2 \times 100 \times 45{,}000}{0.65}} = 3{,}721, \text{ which would qualify for a 0.5\% discount}$$

Step 2

Total annual costs for the company will comprise holding costs plus re-ordering costs.

= (Average inventory × C_H) + (Number of re-orders pa × C_O)

$$= \left(\frac{3,721}{2} \times \$0.65\right) + \left(\frac{45,000}{3,721} \times \$100\right)$$

= $2,419

Step 3

At order quantity 6,000, total costs are as follows.

(6,000 × $0.65/2) + (45,000 × $100 ÷ 6,000) = $2,700

	$
Extra costs of ordering in batches of 6,000 (2,700 − 2,419)	(281)
Less: Saving on extra discount (0.75% − 0.5%) × $4.5 × 45,000	506.25

Step 4

Net cost saving	225.25

So a saving can be made on orders of 6,000 units.

Test your understanding 4

(a) Annual demand is 45,000. The original EOQ is 3,721.

 The company will therefore place an order once every

 3,721 ÷ 45,000 × 365 days = 30 days

(b) The company must be sure that there is sufficient inventory on hand when it places an order to last the three weeks' lead time. It must therefore place an order when there is three weeks' worth of demand in inventory:

 3/52 × 45,000 = 2,596 units

Test your understanding 5

Demand per week is 80 units. The next review will be in six weeks by which time 80 × 6 = 480 units will have been used.

An order would then be placed and during the lead time – three weeks – another 80 × 3 = 240 units will be used.

The business therefore needs to have 480 + 240 = 720 units in inventory to ensure a stockout is avoided. Since buffer inventory of 35 units is required, the total number needed is 755 units.

Since the current inventory level is 250 units, an order must be placed for 755 – 250 = 505 units.

Test your understanding 6

(a) **Use of NPV**

The following reasons may be cited for using the net present value (NPV) method of investment appraisal:

– Compared to accounting rate of return (ARR), it discounts real cash flows as opposed to accounting profits which are affected by non-cash items.

– Compared to measuring internal rate of return (IRR), the NPV method only gives one solution. In some circumstances, (when there are a number of outflows occurring at different times), multiple IRR solutions are possible.

– Compared to the payback method, NPV considers all of the cash flows of a project.

– By using a discount rate it measures the opportunity cost of the money invested by a person in a project.

– The interest rate used can be increased/decreased depending upon the level of perceived risk in the investment.

– The NPV of a project can be shown to be equal to the increase in the value of shareholder's equity in the company. Thus the method is consistent with the objective of shareholder wealth maximisation.

(b) Economic order quantity:

(i)

The present EOQ is $\sqrt{\dfrac{2C_OD}{C_H}} = \sqrt{\dfrac{2 \times 100 \times 40{,}000}{20\% \times 2.50}} = 4{,}000$ units/order

The revised EOQ is $\sqrt{\dfrac{2C_OD}{C_H}} = \sqrt{\dfrac{2 \times 25 \times 40{,}000}{20\% \times 2.50}} = 2{,}000$ units/order

From this it can be seen that the EOQ is halved.

(ii) The number of orders has increased from (40,000 ÷ 4,000) 10 orders to (40,000 ÷ 2,000) 20 orders. However, ordering costs are reduced by:

(10 × $100) – (20 × $25) = $500 per annum

Average inventories have also reduced from 2,000 units (4,000 ÷ 2) to 1,000 units (2,000 ÷ 2). Consequently carrying costs have reduced by 20% × $2.50 × 1,000 = $500 per annum.

Total inventory costs are thereby reduced by $1,000 per annum (before tax).

Assuming that Hexicon Inc pays tax in the same year as it earns profits, the present value of the proposal is found by comparing the outflow cost with the discounted after-tax savings over the eight-year life of the proposal (using a 12% discount rate). The after-tax savings are $1,000 × 67% = $670.

Discounted savings:

Year	Narrative	Cash flow $	DF @ 12%	PV $
1 – 8	After tax savings	670	4.968	3,329
0	Cost of reorganisation	(4,000)	1.000	(4,000)
0	Tax saving (assume same year: 33% × $4,000)	1,320	1.000	1,320
	Net benefit			649

As the present value of the proposal is positive, it is worthwhile.

(c) **JIT**

The main objective of Just In Time (JIT) purchasing is to match the delivery of components from suppliers to their usage in production. If this is achieved there are significant benefits to be gained by both the supplier and the customer.

The customer is likely to use only one supplier for each component and to build up a relationship with the supplier which encourages communication thus enabling the supplier to benefit from advanced production planning and economies of scale. To enhance this relationship, the customer makes a long-term commitment to future orders.

The supplier guarantees to deliver goods of an appropriate quality in accordance with an agreed delivery schedule. The benefit to the customer is thereby a reduction (or elimination) of inventory holding and significant cost savings. These arise in both holding costs and also in materials handling, because goods are transferred directly from goods inwards to production.

Working capital management – cash control

Chapter learning objectives

Lead	Component
E1. Analyse the working capital position and identify areas for improvement.	(c) Analyse cash-flow forecasts over a twelve-month period. (d) Discuss measures to improve a cash forecast situation.

1 Chapter overview diagram

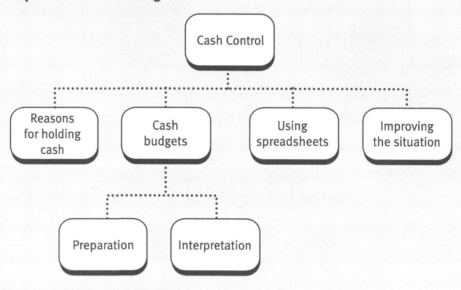

2 Reasons for holding cash

Although cash needs to be invested to earn returns, businesses need to keep a certain amount readily available. The reasons include:

- transactions motive
- precautionary motive
- investment/speculative motive.

Failure to carry sufficient cash levels can lead to:

- loss of settlement discounts
- loss of supplier goodwill
- poor industrial relations
- potential liquidation.

Reasons for holding cash

Cash is required for a number of reasons:

Transactions motive – cash required to meet day-to-day expenses, e.g. payroll, payment of suppliers, etc.

Precautionary motive – cash held to give a cushion against unplanned expenditure (the cash equivalent of buffer inventory).

Investment/speculative motive – cash kept available to take advantage of market investment opportunities.

The cost of running out of cash depends on the firm's particular circumstances but may include not being able to pay debts as they fall due which can have serious operational repercussions:

- settlement discounts for early payment are unavailable

- trade suppliers refuse to offer further credit, charge higher prices or downgrade the priority with which orders are processed

- if wages are not paid on time, industrial action may well result, damaging production in the short-term and relationships and motivation in the medium-term

- the court may be petitioned to wind up the company if it consistently fails to pay bills as they fall due.

3 Efficient cash management

The amount of cash available to an entity at any given time is largely dependent on the efficiency with which cash flows are managed. The key principles of cash management are:

- collect debts as quickly as possible

- pay suppliers as late as possible

- bank cash takings promptly

Once again the firm faces a balancing act:

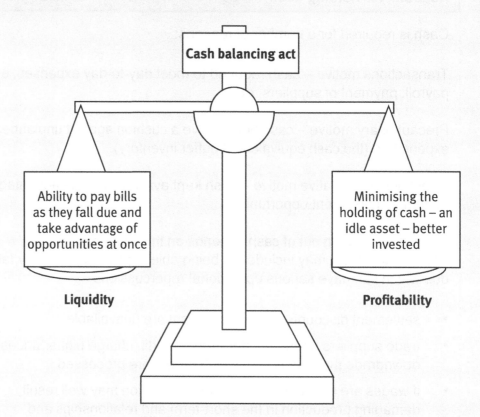

Cash balancing act

Ability to pay bills as they fall due and take advantage of opportunities at once

Liquidity

Minimising the holding of cash – an idle asset – better invested

Profitability

Remember to consider the motives for holding cash and the liquidity/profitability trade-off in a question that asks for a discussion of cash management.

4 Cash budgets and cash flow forecasts

A **cash forecast** is an estimate of cash receipts and payments for a future period under existing conditions.

A **cash budget** is a commitment to a plan for cash receipts and payments for a future period after taking any action necessary to bring the forecast into line with the overall business plan.

Cash budgets are used to:

- assess and integrate operating budgets
- plan for cash shortages and surpluses
- compare with actual spending.

There are two different techniques that can be used to create a cash budget:

- a receipts and payments forecast

- a balance sheet forecast

Receipts and payments forecast

This is a forecast of cash receipts and payments based on predictions of sales and cost of sales and the timings of the cash flows relating to these items.

Preparing forecasts from planned receipts and payments

Every type of cash inflow and receipt, along with their timings, must be forecast. Note that cash receipts and payments differ from sales and cost of sales in the income statement because:

- not all cash receipts or payments affect the income statement, e.g. the issue of new shares or the purchase of a non-current asset

- some income statement items are derived from accounting conventions and are not cash flows, e.g. depreciation or the profit/loss on the sale of a non-current asset

- the timing of cash receipts and payments does not coincide with the income statement accounting period, e.g. a sale is recognised in the income statement when the invoice is raised, yet the cash payment from the receivable may not be received until the following period or later.

- bad debts will never be received in cash and doubtful debts may not be received. When you are forecasting the cash receipts from debtors you must remember to adjust for these items.

The following approach should be adopted for examination questions.

Step 1 – Prepare a proforma

There is no definitive format that should be used for a cash budget. However, whichever format you decide to use, it should include the following:

(i) A clear distinction between the cash receipts and cash payments for each control period. Your budget should not consist of a jumble of cash flows. It should be logically arranged with a subtotal for receipts and a subtotal for payments.

(ii) A figure for the net cash flow for each period. It could be argued that this is not an essential feature of a cash budget. However, you will find it easier to prepare and use a cash budget in an examination if you include the net cash flow. Also, managers find in practice that a figure for the net cash flow helps to draw attention to the cash flow implications of their actions during the period.

(iii) The closing cash balance for each control period. The closing balance for each period will be the opening balance for the following period.

The following is a typical format:

Month:	1	2	3	4
	$	$	$	$
Receipts (few lines)				
Sub total				
Payments (Many lines)				
Sub total				
Net cash flow				
Opening balance				
Closing balance				

Step 2 – Fill in the simple figures

Some payments need only a small amount of work to identify the correct figure and timing and can be entered straight into the proforma. These would usually include:

- wages and salaries
- fixed overhead expenses
- dividend payments
- purchase of non-current assets.

Step 3 – Work out the more complex figures

The information on sales and purchases can be more time consuming to deal with, e.g.:

- timings for both sales and purchases must be found from credit periods
- variable overheads may require information about production levels
- purchases may require calculations based on production schedules and inventory balances.

Example 1 – FORECAST CASH RECEIPTS

The forecast sales for an organisation are as follows:

	January	February	March	April
	$	$	$	$
Sales	6,000	8,000	4,000	5,000

All sales are on credit and receivables tend to pay in the following pattern:

	%
In month of sale	10
In month after sale	40
Two months after sale	45

The organisation expects the rate of irrecoverable debts to be 5%.

Calculate the forecast cash receipts from receivables in April.

Example 2 – FORECAST CASH PAYMENTS

A manufacturing business makes and sells widgets. Each widget requires two units of raw materials, which cost $3 each. Production and sales quantities of widgets each month are as follows:

Month	Sales and production units
December (actual)	50,000
January (budget)	55,000
February (budget)	60,000
March (budget)	65,000

In the past, the business has maintained its inventories of raw materials at 100,000 units. However, it plans to increase raw material inventories to 110,000 units at the end of January and 120,000 units at the end of February. The business takes one month's credit from its suppliers.

Calculate the forecast payments to suppliers each month, for raw material purchases.

Example 3 – FULL CASH FLOW FORECAST

The following budgeted income statement has been prepared for Quest Company for the four months January to April Year 5:

	January $000	February $000	March $000	April $000
Sales	60.0	50.0	70.0	60.0
Cost of production	50.0	55.0	32.5	50.0
(Increase)/decrease in inventory	(5.0)	(17.5)	20.0	(5.0)
Cost of sales	45.0	37.5	52.5	45.0
Gross profit	15.0	12.5	17.5	15.0
Administration and selling overhead	(8.0)	(7.5)	(8.5)	(8.0)
Net profit before interest	7.0	5.0	9.0	7.0

The working papers provide the following additional information:

- 40% of the production cost relates to direct materials. Materials are bought in the month prior to the month in which they are used. 50% of purchases are paid for in the month of purchase. The remainder are paid for one month later.

- 30% of the production cost relates to direct labour which is paid for when it is used.

- The remainder of the production cost is production overhead. $5,000 per month is a fixed cost which includes $3,000 depreciation. Fixed production overhead costs are paid monthly in arrears. The remaining overhead is variable. The variable production overhead is paid 40% in the month of usage and the balance one month later.

- The administration and selling costs are paid quarterly in advance on 1 January, 1 April, 1 July and 1 October. The amount payable is $15,000 per quarter.

- Trade payables on 1 January Year 5 are expected to be:
  – Direct materials: $10,000
  – Production overheads: $11,000

- All sales are on credit. 20% of receivables are expected to be paid in the month of sale and 80% in the following month. Unpaid trade receivables at the beginning of January were $44,000.

- The company intends to purchase capital equipment costing $30,000 in February which will be payable in March.

- The bank balance on 1 January Year 5 is expected to be $5,000 overdrawn.

Required:

Prepare a cash budget for each of the months January to March Year 5 for Quest Company.

Preparing a cash budget from a statement of financial position

This is a forecast derived from predictions of future balance sheets. Predictions are made of all items except cash, which is then derived as a balancing figure.

Although you could be asked to do use this method in the exam – it is most likely that cash budgets would be required on the basis of a receipts and payments forecast.

Illustration

Used to predict the cash balance at the end of a given period, this method will typically require forecasts of:

- changes to non-current assets (acquisitions and disposals)
- future inventory levels
- future receivables levels
- future payables levels
- changes to share capital and other long-term funding (e.g. bank loans)
- changes to retained profits.

Examination questions in this area can require you to calculate profit forecasts from cash forecasts or cash flow forecasts from profit and statement of financial position forecasts.

Example

CBA is a manufacturing entity in the furniture trade. Its sales have risen sharply over the past six months as a result of an improvement in the economy and a strong housing market. The entity is now showing signs of 'overtrading' and the financial manager, Ms Smith, is concerned about its liquidity. The entity is 1 month from its year-end. Estimated figures for the full 12 months of the current year and forecasts for next year, on present cash management policies, are shown below.

	Next year $000	Current year $000
Income statement		
Turnover	5,200	4,200
Less:		
Cost of sales (Note 1)	3,224	2,520
Operating expenses	650	500
Operating profit	1,326	1,180
Interest paid	54	48
Tax payable	305	283
Profit after tax	967	849
Dividends declared	387	339

Current assets and liabilities at year end:

Inventory/work in progress	625	350
Trade receivables	750	520
Cash	0	25
Trade payables	(464)	(320)
Other payables (incl. dividends)	(692)	(622)
Overdraft	(11)	0
	————	————
Total equity and liabilities	208	(47)
	————	————

Note 1:

Cost of sales includes depreciation of	225	175

Ms Smith is considering methods of improving the cash position. A number of actions are being discussed:

Trade receivables

Offer a 2 per cent discount to customers who pay within 10 days of despatch of invoices. It is estimated that 50 per cent of customers will take advantage of the new discount scheme. The other 50 per cent will continue to take the average credit period for next year.

Trade payables and inventory

Reduce the number of suppliers currently being used and negotiate better terms with respect to flexibility of delivery and lower purchase prices. The aim for next year will be to reduce the end-of-year forecast cost of sales (excluding depreciation) by 5 per cent and inventory/work in progress levels by 10 per cent. However, the number of days' credit taken by the entity will have to fall to 30 days to help persuade suppliers to improve their prices.

Other information

- All sales are on credit. Official terms of sale at present require payment within 30 days. Interest is not charged on late payments.

- All purchases are made on credit.

- Operating expenses for next year will be $650,000 under either the existing or proposed policies.

- Tax and interest payments are paid in the year in which they arise.

- Dividends are paid in the year after they are declared.

- Capital expenditure of $550,000 is planned for next year.

Required:

(a) Provide a cash flow forecast for next year, assuming:

    (i)   the entity does not change its policies;

    (ii) the entity's proposals for managing trade receivables, trade payables and inventory are implemented.

In both cases, assume a full twelve-month period, i.e. the changes will be effective from day 1 of next year.

(b) As assistant to Ms Smith, write a short report to her evaluating the proposed actions. Include comments on the factors, financial and non-financial, that the entity should take into account before implementing the new policies.

Solution

(a)

All figures in $000s

	No change	With change
Profit from operations	1,326	1,424
+ depreciation	225	225
+/– change in trade receivables	–230	72
+/– change in trade payables	144	–86
Operating profit	1,465	1,635
Interest paid	–54	–48
Tax paid	–305	–283
Dividends declared	–339	–339
Investing activities		
Non-current assets	–550	–550
Inventory	–275	–212
Net cash flow	–36	206
Opening balance	25	25
Closing balance	–11	231

Changes implemented

(1) Profit from operations

Turnover	5200
Less discounts	–52
Cost of sales	–3,074
(3,224 – 225) × 95% + 225)	
Operating expenses (unchanged)	–650
Profit	1,424

(2) Change in current assets

Decrease in trade receivables

$$= 520 – [(2,600/365 × 53^*) + (2,600/365 × 10^*)] = 72$$

Decrease in trade payables

$$= [320 – (2,849^{**}/365 × 30)] = 86$$

Change in inventory

$$= 350 – (625 × 90\%) = 212$$

* Forecast receivables = 750/5,200 × 365 = 53, reduces to 10 days for 50% of turnover

** Forecast payables = 3,224 – 225 = 2,999, these reduce by 5% to 2,849.

(b) Report

To: Ms Smith

From: Assistant

Subject: Proposed working capital policy changes

The answer should be set out in report format and include the following key points:

– Comment that cash flow is improved by almost a quarter of a million pounds if the proposed changes are made.

– Problems appear to have arisen because trade receivables and inventory control have not been adequate for increased levels of turnover.

- Liquidity: current ratio was 0.95:1 (all current assets to trade and other payables), will be around 1.2:1 under both options. Perversely, ratio looks to improve even if the entity takes no action and causes an overdraft. This is because of high receivables and inventory levels. Moral: high current assets do not mean high cash. Cash ratio perhaps a better measure.

- Receivables' days last year was 45, forecast to rise to 53 on current policies despite 'official' terms being 30. Entity could perhaps look to improve its credit control before offering discounts.

- Trade payables' days were 46, forecast to rise to 52. Are discounts being ignored? Are relationships with suppliers being threatened?*

- Dramatic increase in inventory levels forecast: 50 days last year, 71 days forecast this year. If change implemented, inventory will still be 67 days.*

- Operating profit percentage forecast to fall to 25.5% from 28.1% if no changes made. Percentage will fall to 27.4% if changes implemented; a fall probably acceptable if cash flow improved and overdraft interest saved.

- Non-financial factors include relationships with customers and suppliers.

- Other financial factors, is increase in turnover sustainable?

*Using cost of sales figures including depreciation.

Interpretation of a cash budget

Examples of factors to consider when interpreting a cash budget include:

- Is the balance at the end of the period acceptable/matching expectations?

- Does the cash balance become a deficit at any time in the period?

- Is there sufficient finance (e.g. an overdraft) to cover any cash deficits? Should new sources of finance be sought in advance?

- What are the key causes of cash deficits?

- Can/should discretionary expenditure (such as asset purchases) be made in another period in order to stabilise the pattern of cash flows?

- Is there a plan for dealing with cash surpluses (such as reinvesting them elsewhere)?

- When is the best time to make discretionary expenditure?

Illustration

If we were to examine the cash budget in Example 3, the following issues might be brought to management's attention:

This cash budget forewarns the management of the business that their plans will lead to a cash deficit of $16,650 at the end of March. They can also see that it will be a short-term deficit and can take appropriate action.

They may decide to delay the purchase of the capital equipment for one month in order to allow the cash position to move to a positive one before the investment is made. Alternatively, an extension of the overdraft facilities may be arranged for the appropriate period.

If it is decided that overdraft facilities are to be arranged, it is important that due account is taken of the timing of the receipts and payments within each month.

For example, all of the payments in January may be made at the beginning of the month but receipts may not be expected until nearer the end of the month. The cash deficit could then be considerably greater than it appears from looking only at the month-end balance.

If the worst possible situation arose, the overdrawn balance during January could become as large as $5,000 (Opening balance) minus $66,000 (January payments) = $71,000 before the receipts begin to arise. If management had used the month-end balances as a guide to the overdraft requirement during the period then they would not have arranged a large enough overdraft facility with the bank. It is important, therefore, that they look in detail at the information revealed by the cash budget, and not simply at the closing cash balances.

5 Using spreadsheets in cash forecasting

Many businesses prepare cash budgets and cash forecasts using a computer and spreadsheet software such as Excel®.

Spreadsheets are useful for cash forecasting for several important reasons:

- They **save time** in preparing forecasts. When the basic 'model' has been constructed, it is a relatively simple task to insert figures into the model, and leave it to the model to produce the completed forecast. The model, once established, can then be used whenever a new forecast is required.

- They are extremely useful for **sensitivity analysis**. When there is uncertainty in the forecast, the assumptions for the forecast can be changed and an alternative forecast produced. This allows management to consider a range of different possible outcomes, without needing much time or effort.

- Cash flow forecasts **can be consolidated**. For example, if the same spreadsheet model is used to prepare cash forecasts for each division or region in the company, a spreadsheet model can also automatically produce a consolidated cash flow forecast for the company as a whole.

More details

Sensitivity analysis

When budgets are prepared, there are a very large number of assumptions and estimates, for example the estimated sales each month, the estimates of costs, assumptions about when receivables will pay and when suppliers will be paid, and so on. Any of these estimates and assumptions could turn out to be inaccurate.

One of the enormous benefits of using spreadsheets to prepare a cash budget is that it is very easy to carry out sensitivity analysis.

Sensitivity analysis involves asking 'What if…?' questions, and finding out by how much the expected results will change if some of the forecasts or assumptions are altered.

For example, what if sales are 10% less than predicted, or what if capital expenditure is double the amount forecast? Depending on what the results of the analysis show, management might decide to take action to reduce the potential risks.

Consolidation

As well as being of assistance in preparing cash flow forecasts for individual business units, a computerised spreadsheet package may also be used to consolidate individual forecasts into one overall forecast for the organisation as a whole.

Individual forecasts may be prepared by:

- the various group companies

- individual operating units, e.g. branches of a retail store

- individual cost centres, e.g. stores, purchasing, production, service centres

- individual budget holders, e.g. marketing.

If all the individual forecasts are prepared using the same spreadsheet software, it will be possible for these to be uploaded to a central computer, programmed to produce a consolidated forecast.

6 Measures to improve a cash forecast situation

Introduction

An initial cash forecast might predict an unsatisfactory cash flow situation. The forecast might indicate that the company will have a cash deficit that cannot be met by existing short-term borrowing arrangements, such as a bank overdraft facility.

When this situation occurs, action will need to be taken to manage future cash flows in order to improve the forecast position. The nature of this management action will depend upon the answers to the following questions:

- Does the forecast indicate a continuing trend of an increasing surplus or an increasing cash deficit, or do net monthly balances move between surplus and deficit on a seasonal basis?

- What size of cash surpluses are forecast (if any) and for how long will they be available?

- Are the forecast cash deficits within the current overdraft facility?

- Which cash flows are to some extent discretionary, either in size or timing?

Cash deficits can arise from:

- Basic trading factors underlying the business, such as falling sales or increasing costs. To correct these, normal business measures need to be taken. Sales may be improved by increased marketing activity or revised pricing policies. Cost cutting exercises may also be necessary.

- Short-term deficiencies in the working capital cycle, such as an exceptionally long average holding period for inventory or a long average time to pay by credit customers.

Possible decisions that could be taken to deal with forecast short-term cash deficits include:

- additional short-term borrowing

- negotiating a higher overdraft limit with the bank

- the sale of short-term investments, if the company has any

- using different forms of financing to reduce cash flows in the short term, such as leasing instead of buying outright

- changing the amount of discretionary cash flows, deferring expenditures or bringing forward revenues. For example:
  - reducing the dividend to shareholders

  - postponing non-essential capital expenditure

  - bringing forward the planned disposal of non-current assets

  - reducing inventory levels, perhaps incorporating 'just-in-time' techniques (although this will take time to implement)

  - shortening the operating cycle by reducing the time taken to collect receivables, perhaps by offering a discount or using a factor or invoice discounting. (The management of trade receivables is dealt with more fully in a later chapter.)

  - shortening the operating cycle by delaying payment to payables. The management of trade payables is dealt with in Chapter 17.

Dealing with surpluses

If the forecast shows cash surpluses, these will be dealt with according to their size and duration. Management should consider a policy for how surplus cash should be invested so as to achieve a return on the money, but without investing in items where the risk of a fall in value is considered too high. The interest or other return earned can be used to improve the overall cash position. Care must be taken to ensure these investments can be realised as needed, to fund forecast deficits.

Where long-term cash surpluses are forecast, management might consider other possible uses of the surpluses, such as paying a higher dividend or repaying loans and other debts.

Dealing with surpluses is dealt with in much more detail in a later chapter.

7 Chapter summary

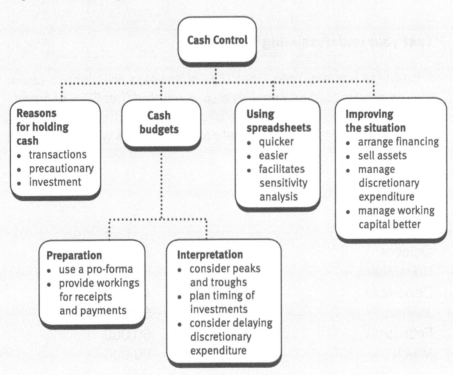

Cash Control

Reasons for holding cash
- transactions
- precautionary
- investment

Cash budgets

Using spreadsheets
- quicker
- easier
- facilitates sensitivity analysis

Improving the situation
- arrange financing
- sell assets
- manage discretionary expenditure
- manage working capital better

Preparation
- use a pro-forma
- provide workings for receipts and payments

Interpretation
- consider peaks and troughs
- plan timing of investments
- consider delaying discretionary expenditure

8 Practice questions

Test your understanding 1

A business has estimated that 10% of its sales will be cash sales, and the remainder credit sales. It is also estimated that 50% of credit customers will pay in the month following sale, 30% two months after sale, 15% three months after sale and bad debts will be 5% of credit sales.

Total sales figures are as follows:

Month	$
October	80,000
November	60,000
December	40,000
January	50,000
February	60,000
March	90,000

Required:

Prepare a month-by-month budget of cash receipts from sales for the months January to March.

(5 marks)

Test your understanding 2

Winters Company expects 75% of sales to be collected in the month of sale, 20% in the month following and 5% to be bad debts. At 31 December 20X4, $50,000 of December's sales are still outstanding receivables.

Identify receipts in January from sales in December:

A   10,000

B   20,000

C   37,500

D   40,000

Test your understanding 3

A company sells a range of services, all on credit. Customers on average pay as follows:

	%
In month after sale	30
Two months after sale	65

The organisation expects a bad debt rate of 5%.

At 1 January Year 2, opening trade receivables were $322,200, before deducting any allowance for doubtful debts. Sales in December Year 1 were $213,000.

Required:

Calculate the receipts from the opening trade receivables in January Year 2 and in February Year 2

(5 marks)

Test your understanding 4

You are given the following budgeted information about an organisation:

	January	February	March
Opening inventory in units	100	150	120
Closing inventory in units	150	120	180
Sales in units	400	450	420

The cost of materials is $2 per unit. 40% of purchases are paid for immediately in cash. 60% of purchases are on credit and are paid two months after the purchase.

Required:

Calculate the budgeted payments in March for purchases of materials.

(5 marks)

Test your understanding 5

In the near future a company will purchase a manufacturing business for $315,000, this price to include goodwill ($150,000), equipment and fittings ($120,000), and inventory of raw materials and finished goods ($45,000).

A delivery van will be purchased for $15,000 as soon as the business purchase is completed. The delivery van will be paid for in the second month of operations.

The following forecasts have been made for the business following purchase:

(i) Sales (before discounts) of the business's single product, at a mark-up of 60% on production cost will be:

Month	1	2	3	4	5	6
($000)	96	96	92	96	100	104

   25% of sales will be for cash; the remainder will be on credit, for settlement in the month following that of sale. A discount of 10% will be given to selected credit customers, who represent 25% of gross sales.

(ii) Production cost will be $5 per unit. The production cost will be made up of:

Raw materials	$2.50
Direct labour	$1.50
Fixed overhead	$1.00

(iii) Production will be arranged so that closing inventory at the end of any month is sufficient to meet sales requirements in the following month. A value of $30,000 is placed on the inventory of finished goods, which was acquired on purchase of the business. This valuation is based on the forecast of production cost per unit given in (ii) above.

(iv) The single raw material will be purchased so that inventory at the end of a month is sufficient to meet half of the following month's production requirements. Raw material inventory acquired on purchase of the business ($15,000) is valued at the cost per unit that is forecast as given in (ii) above. Raw materials will be purchased on one month's credit.

(v) Costs of direct labour will be met as they are incurred in production.

(vi) The fixed production overhead rate of $1.00 per unit is based upon a forecast of the first year's production of 150,000 units. This rate includes depreciation of equipment and fittings on a straight-line basis over the next five years. Fixed production overhead is paid in the month incurred.

(vii) Selling and administration overheads are all fixed, and will be $208,000 in the first year. These overheads include depreciation of the delivery van at 30% pa on a reducing balance basis. All fixed overheads will be incurred on a regular basis, and paid in the month incurred, with the exception of rent and rates. $25,000 is payable for the year ahead in month one for rent and rates.

Required:

(a) **Prepare a monthly cash flow forecast. You should include the business purchase and the first four months of operations following purchase.**

(15 marks)

(b) **Calculate the inventory, receivables, and payables balances at the end of the four-month period. Describe briefly the liquidity situation.**

(10 marks)

(Total: 25 marks)

Test your understanding 6

Thorne Co values, advertises and sells residential property on behalf of its customers. The company has been in business for only a short time and is preparing a cash budget for the first four months of 2006. Expected sales of residential properties are as follows.

	2005	2006	2006	2006	2006
Month	December	January	February	March	April
Units sold	10	10	15	25	30

The average price of each property is $180,000 and Thorne Co charges a fee of 3% of the value of each property sold. Thorne Co receives 1% in the month of sale and the remaining 2% in the month after sale. The company has nine employees who are paid on a monthly basis. The average salary per employee is $35,000 per year. If more than 20 properties are sold in a given month, each employee is paid in that month a bonus of $140 for each additional property sold.

Variable expenses are incurred at the rate of 0.5% of the value of each property sold and these expenses are paid in the month of sale. Fixed overheads of $4,300 per month are paid in the month in which they arise. Thorne Co pays interest every three months on a loan of $200,000 at a rate of 6% per year. The last interest payment in each year is paid in December.

An outstanding tax liability of $95,800 is due to be paid in April. In the same month Thorne Co intends to dispose of surplus vehicles, with a net book value of $15,000, for $20,000. The cash balance at the start of January 2006 is expected to be a deficit of $40,000.

Required:

Prepare a monthly cash budget for the period from January to April 2006. Your budget must clearly indicate each item of income and expenditure, and the opening and closing monthly cash balances.

(10 marks)

Test your understanding 7

Zed Co has the following balance sheet(Statement of financial position) at 30 June 20X3:

	$	$
Non-current assets:		
Plant and machinery		192,000
Current assets:		
Inventory	16,000	
Receivables	80,000	
Bank	2,000	
		98,000
Total assets		290,000
Equity and liabilities:		
Issued share capital		216,000
Retained profits		34,000
		250,000

Current liabilities	
Trade payables	10,000
Dividend payable	30,000
	40,000
Total equity and liabilities	290,000

(a) The company expects to acquire further plant and machinery costing $8,000 during the year to 30 June 20X4.

(b) The levels of inventories and receivables are expected to increase by 5% and 10% respectively by 30 June 20X4, due to business growth.

(c) Trade payables and dividend liabilities are expected to be the same at 30 June 20X4.

(d) No share issue is planned, and retained profits for the year to 30 June 20X4 are expected to be $42,000.

(e) Plant and machinery is depreciated on a reducing balance basis, at the rate of 20% pa, for all assets held at the balance sheet date.

Prepare a balance sheet (statement of financial position) forecast as at 30 June 20X4, and identify what the cash balance or bank overdraft will be at that date.

(10 marks)

Test your understanding 8

Identify which of the following is unsuitable as a cash flow to be deferred to avoid a temporary cash shortage:

A   Replacement of office furniture

B   Investment in a short-term cash deposit

C   Investment in a long-term strategic expansion

D   Dividend payment (deferral agreed by the shareholders)

Test your understanding answers

Example 1 – FORECAST CASH RECEIPTS

Cash from:		$
April sales:	10% × $5,000	500
March sales:	40% × $4,000	1,600
February sales:	45% × $8,000	3,600
		_____
		5,700

Example 2 – FORECAST CASH PAYMENTS

When inventories of raw materials are increased, the quantities purchased will exceed the quantities consumed in the period.

Figures for December are shown because December purchases will be paid for in January, which is in the budget period.

Quantity of raw material purchased in units:

		Material (@ 2 units per widget)			
	Units of widgets produced	December	January	February	March
	Units	Units	Units	Units	Units
December	50,000	100,000			
January	55,000		110,000		
February	60,000			120,000	
March	65,000				130,000
Increase in inventories		–	10,000	10,000	–
		_____	_____	_____	_____
Total purchase quantities		100,000	120,000	130,000	130,000
		_____	_____	_____	_____
At $3 per unit		300,000	360,000	390,000	390,000

Having established the purchases each month, we can go on to budget the amount of cash payments to suppliers each month. Here, the business will take one month's credit.

	January $	February $	March $
Payment to suppliers	300,000	360,000	390,000

At the end of March, there will be payables of $390,000 for raw materials purchased, which will be paid in April.

Example 3 – FULL CASH FLOW FORECAST

We can take each item of cash flow in turn, and use workings tables to calculate what the monthly cash flows are.

(W1) **Cash from sales**

	Total sales $	Cash receipts January $	Cash receipts February $	Cash Receipts March $
Opening receivables		44,000	–	–
January	60,000	12,000	48,000	–
February	50,000	–	10,000	40,000
March	70,000	–	–	14,000
		56,000	58,000	54,000

(W2) Payments for materials purchases

Material purchases are made in the month prior to the month in which they are used, so the starting point for working out materials purchases and payments for the purchases is the production costs in each month.

	January $	February $	March $	April $
Total cost of production	50,000	55,000	32,500	50,000
Material cost of production (40%)	20,000	22,000	13,000	20,000
Purchases in the month	22,000	13,000	20,000	unknown

Payments are made 50% in the month of purchase and 50% in the following month. The trade payables at 1 January will all be paid in January, since these represent 50% of material purchases in December.

	Purchases $	January $	February $	March $
Opening payables for materials		10,000		
January	22,000	11,000	11,000	–
February	13,000	–	6,500	6,500
March	20,000	–	–	10,000
Total payments		21,000	17,500	16,500

(W3) Payments for overheads

In this example, we have to separate fixed and variable overheads. Total overhead costs are 30% of production costs (100% – 40% direct materials – 30% direct labour).

	January $	February $	March $
Total cost of production	50,000	55,000	32,500
Overhead cost of production (30%)	15,000	16,500	9,750
Fixed costs	(5,000)	(5,000)	(5,000)
Variable overhead costs	10,000	11,500	4,750

Of the monthly fixed overhead costs of $5,000, $3,000 is depreciation which is not a cash expenditure. Monthly fixed cost cash expenditure is therefore $2,000.

The opening balance of unpaid overhead costs at the beginning of January must consist of $2,000 fixed overheads and $9,000 (the balance) variable overheads. All these costs should be paid for in January. Variable overheads are paid 40% in the month of expenditure and 60% the following month.

Fixed overheads	Cost $	January $	February $	March $
Opening payables for fixed overheads		2,000		
January	2,000	–	2,000	–
February	2,000	–	–	2,000
March	2,000	–	–	–
Total payments		2,000	2,000	2,000

Variable overheads	Cost $	January $	February $	March $
Opening payables for variable overheads		9,000		
January	10,000	4,000	6,000	–
February	11,500	–	4,600	6,900
March	4,750	–	–	1,900
Total payments		13,000	10,600	8,800

The other items of cash flow are straightforward, although it is important to notice that the payments for administration and selling overheads are paid quarterly, and the cash payment ($15,000) is not the same as the total overhead cost for the quarter. Presumably there are depreciation charges within the total costs given.

Payments for direct labour are 30% of direct labour costs (= 30% of production costs) in the month.

The cash budget can be prepared as follows:

	January $	February $	March $
Receipts			
From sales	56,000	58,000	54,000
Payments			
Capital expenditure	–	–	30,000
For direct materials	21,000	17,500	16,500
For direct labour (30% × prod'n cost)	15,000	16,500	9,750
For fixed production overheads	2,000	2,000	2,000
For variable production overheads	13,000	10,600	8,800
For admin/selling overhead	15,000	–	–
Total outflow	66,000	46,600	67,050
Net cash flow for month	(10,000)	11,400	(13,050)
Opening balance	(5,000)	(15,000)	(3,600)
Closing balance	(15,000)	(3,600)	(16,650)

Analysis

The company will be overdrawn throughout the three-month period, therefore it is essential that it should have access to borrowings to cover the shortfall. The bank might already have agreed an overdraft facility, but this should be at least $16,650 and ideally higher, to allow for the possibility that the actual cash flows will be even worse than budgeted.

Test your understanding 1

Sales month	Total sales $	Cash receipts January $	Cash receipts February $	Cash receipts March $
October	80,000	10,800	–	–
November	60,000	16,200	8,100	–
December	40,000	18,000	10,800	5,400
January	50,000	5,000	22,500	13,500
February	60,000	–	6,000	27,000
March	90,000	–	–	9,000
Total Receipts		50,000	47,400	54,900

Test your understanding 2

The correct answer is **D.**

$50,000 represents 25% of December sales (100% – 75%).

Total sales in December were therefore $5,000/25% = $200,000.

Expected amount to be received in January = 20% × $200,000 = $40,000.

Test your understanding 3

The trade receivables at the beginning of January Year 2 represent 100% of sales in December Year 1 and the unpaid receivables for sales in November Year 1. They can be analysed as follows:

	$
Total trade receivables	322,200
Consisting of:	
100% of sales for December Year 1	(213,000)
Unpaid amounts for sales in November Year 1	109,200

The unpaid amounts from November Year 1 represent 70% of total sales in that month, because 30% pay in the month following sale (December Year 1).

It therefore follows that total sales in November Year 1 were $109,200/70% = $156,000.

Sales month	Total sales		Cash receipts January		Cash receipts February
	$		$		$
November	156,000	65%	101,400	–	–
December	213,000	30%	63,900	65%	138,450
			165,300		138,450

Test your understanding 4

Purchases	January units	February units	March units
Sales quantity	400	450	420
Less: opening inventory	(100)	(150)	(120)
Add: closing inventory	150	120	180
Production in units = units purchased	450	420	480
Cost of purchase @ $2 per unit	$900	$840	$960

		$
Payments in March		
For January purchases	(60% of $900)	540
For March purchases	(40% of $960)	384
Total payments for materials		924

Test your understanding 5

(a) Monthly cash budget

	Month 1	Month 2	Month 3	Month 4
	$	$	$	$
Cash inflows:				
Cash sales	24,000	24,000	23,000	24,000
Credit sales		72,000	72,000	69,000
Less: Discounts		(2,400)	(2,400)	(2,300)
Total inflow	24,000	93,600	92,600	90,700
Cash outflows:				
Purchases (W1)	–	44,375	29,375	30,625
Labour (W1)	27,000	17,250	18,000	18,750
Production overhead (W2)	10,500	10,500	10,500	10,500
Selling and administration overhead (W3)	39,875	14,875	14,875	14,875
Purchase of business	315,000	–	–	–
Purchase of van	–	15,000	–	–
Total outflow	392,375	102,000	72,750	74,750
Net cash flow for month	(368,375)	(8,400)	19,850	15,950
Opening balance	0	(368,375)	(376,775)	(356,925)
Closing balance	(368,375)	(376,775)	(356,925)	(340,975)

Workings

(W1)

	Month 1	Month 2	Month 3	Month 4	Month 5	Month 6
Sales ($)	96,000	96,000	92,000	96,000	100,000	104,000
Sales units	12,000	12,000	11,500	12,000	12,500	13,000
+ Closing inventory	12,000	11,500	12,000	12,500	13,000	
− Opening inventory	6,000	12,000	11,500	12,000	12,500	13,000
Production (units)	18,000	11,500	12,000	12,500	13,000	
Raw material usage (Production × $2.50)	45,000	28,750	30,000	31,250	32,500	
+ Closing inventory	14,375	15,000	15,625	16,250		
− Opening inventory	15,000	14,375	15,000	15,625		
Purchases (one month delay)	44,375	29,375	30,625	31,875		
Labour cost (production × $1.50)	27,000	17,250	18,000	18,750		

(W2) **Production overheads**

	$
Annual overheads (150,000 × $1)	150,000
Depreciation (120,000/5)	(24,000)
	126,000
Monthly cash outflow (126,000/12)	10,500

(W3) **Selling and administration overheads**

	$
Annual overheads	208,000
Depreciation (15,000 × 0.3)	(4,500)
	203,500
Less: Rent and rates in month 1	25,000
	178,500
Monthly cash outflow – months 2, 3, 4 (178500/12)	
Month 1: 25,000 + 14,875	14,875
	39,875

(b) **Closing balances:**

	$
Inventory:	
Finished goods (12,500 × $5)	62,500
Raw materials	16,250
	78,750
Receivables:	
Month 4 credit sales (96,000 × 0.75)	72,000
Less: Discount (10% × 0.25 × 96,000)	(2,400)
	69,600
Payables	31,875

Apart from the purchase of the business, which will require separate long-term finance, the cash flow forecast suggests that there will be sufficient cash inflows to meet the cash outflows on an ongoing basis. The current assets and receivables provide sufficient funds to cover the payables.

Test your understanding 6

Cash budget for Thorne Co:

	January	February	March	April
Receipts	$	$	$	$
Cash fees	18,000	27,000	45,000	54,000
Credit fees	36,000	36,000	54,000	90,000
Sale of assets				20,000
Total receipts	54,000	63,000	99,000	164,000
Payments				
Salaries	26,250	26,250	26,250	26,250
Bonus			6,300	12,600
Expenses	9,000	13,500	22,500	27,000
Fixed overheads	4,300	4,300	4,300	4,300
Taxation				95,800
Interest			3,000	
Total payments	39,550	44,050	62,350	165,950
Net cash flow	14,450	18,950	36,650	(1,950)
Opening balance	(40,000)	(25,550)	(6,600)	30,050
Closing balance	(25,550)	(6,600)	30,050	28,100

Workings

Month	December	January	February	March	April
Units sold	10	10	15	25	30
Sales value ($000)	1,800	1,800	2,700	4,500	5,400
Cash fees at 1% ($)	18,000	18,000	27,000	45,000	54,000
Credit fees at 2% ($)	36,000	36,000	54,000	90,000	108,000
Variable costs at 0.5% ($)		9,000	13,500	22,500	27,000

Monthly salary cost = (35,000 × 9)/12 = $26,250

Bonus for March = (25 – 20) × 140 × 9 = $6,300 Bonus for April = (30 – 20) × 140 × 9 = $12,600.

Test your understanding 7

Zed Co – Balance sheet (Statement of financial position) at 30 June 20X4

	$	$	$
Non-current assets:			
Plant and machinery[(192,000 + 8,000) × 80%]			160,000
Current assets:			
Inventory (16,000 × 105%)		16,800	
Receivables (80,000 × 110%)		88,000	
Bank (balancing figure)		67,200	
		————	
			172,000
			————
Total assets			332,000
			————
Equity and liabilities			
Issued share capital			216,000
Retained profits (34,000 + 42,000)			76,000
			————
			292,000
Current liabilities:			
Trade payables		10,000	
Dividend payable		30,000	
		————	
			40,000
			————
Total equity and liabilities			332,000
			————

The forecast is that the bank balance will increase by $65,200 (i.e. $67,200 – $2,000). This can be reconciled as follows:

	$	$
Retained profit		42,000
Add: Depreciation (20% of ($192,000 + $8,000))		40,000
		82,000
Less: Non-current asset acquired		(8,000)
		74,000
Increase in inventory	800	
Increase in receivables	8,000	
		(8,800)
Increase in cash balance		65,200

Test your understanding 8

The correct answer is **B**.

A short-term deposit is a cash equivalent. Deferring the transfer of cash to a short-term deposit will not deal with the problem of a temporary cash shortage, because it will usually be possible to withdraw the cash from deposit on demand, for the loss of some or all of the interest.

Working capital management – accounts receivable and payable

Chapter learning objectives

Lead	Component
E1. Analyse the working capital position and identify areas for improvement.	(e) Analyse trade debtor and creditor information. (f) Analyse the impacts of alternative debtor and creditor policies.

1 Chapter overview diagram

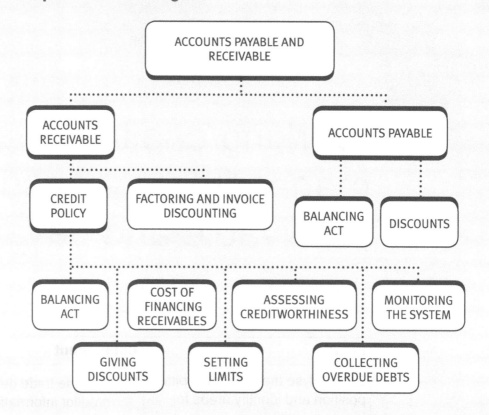

2 Accounts receivable – establishing a credit policy

The balancing act

Management must establish a credit policy. The optimum level of trade credit extended represents a balance between two factors:

- profit improvement from sales obtained by allowing credit
- the cost of credit allowed.

Why have a credit policy?

A firm must establish a policy for credit terms given to its customers. Ideally the firm would want to obtain cash with each order delivered, but that is impossible unless substantial settlement (or cash) discounts are offered as an inducement. It must be recognised that credit terms are part of the firm's marketing policy. If the trade or industry has adopted a common practice, then it is probably wise to keep in step with it.

A lenient credit policy may well attract additional customers, but at a disproportionate increase in cost.

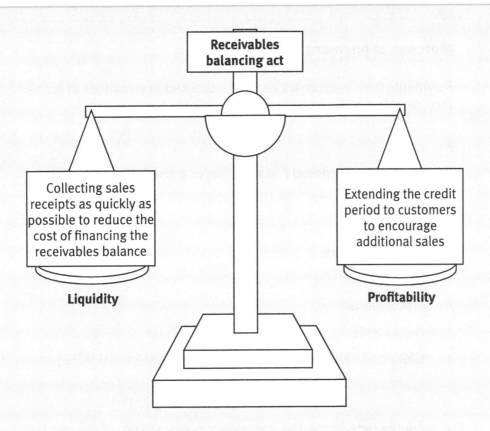

Remember this trade-off is a key factor in determining the company's working capital investment.

Different payment terms

The payment terms will need to consider the period of credit to be granted and how the payment will be made. The terms agreed will need to specify the price, the date of delivery, the payment date or dates, and any discounts to be allowed for early settlement.

Examples of payment terms may be:

- *Payment within a specified period.* For example, customers must pay within 30 days.

- *Payment within a specified period with discount.* For example, a 2 per cent discount would be given to customers who pay within 10 days, and others would be required to pay within 30 days.

- *Weekly credit.* This would require all supplies in a week to be paid by a specified day in the following week.

- *Related to delivery of goods.* For example, cash on delivery (COD).

Methods of payment

Payments from customers may be accepted in a number of forms, including:

- cash
- Bankers Automated Clearing Service (BACS)
- cheques
- banker's draft
- standing orders
- direct debit
- credit cards
- debit cards
- Clearing House Automated Payments System (CHAPS).

For accounts receivable, the company's policy will be influenced by:

- demand for products
- competitors' terms
- risk of irrecoverable debts
- financing costs
- costs of credit control.

Receivables management has four key aspects:

(1) Assessing creditworthiness.

(2) Setting credit limits.

(3) Invoicing promptly and collecting overdue debts.

(4) Monitoring the credit system.

This is a useful structure to adopt for examination questions that ask about the management of receivables.

3 Assessing creditworthiness

A firm should assess the creditworthiness of:

- all new customers immediately, before offering credit terms
- existing customers periodically.

Information may come from:

- bank references
- trade references
- visit to the customer's premises
- competitors
- published information
- credit reference agencies
- legal sources of credit information
- company's own sales records
- credit scoring
- credit rating (large corporate customers only).

Assessing creditworthiness

To minimise the risk of irrecoverable debts occurring, a company should investigate the creditworthiness of all new customers (credit risk), and should review that of existing customers from time to time, especially if they request that their credit limit should be raised. Information about a customer's credit rating can be obtained from a variety of sources.

These include:

- Bank references – A customer's permission must be sought. These tend to be fairly standardised in the UK, and so are not perhaps as helpful as they could be.

- Trade references – Suppliers already giving credit to the customer can give useful information about how good the customer is at paying bills on time. There is a danger that the customer will only nominate those suppliers that are being paid on time.

- Visit to the customer's premises – A sales representative might visit the business premises of the customer. A visit will provide information about the actual 'physical' operations and assets of the customer, and might provide some reassurance that the customer's business has substance.

- Competitors – in some industries such as insurance, competitors share information on customers, including creditworthiness.

- Published information – The customer's own annual accounts and reports will give some idea of the general financial position of the company and its liquidity.

- Credit reference agencies – Agencies such as Dunn & Bradstreet publish general financial details of many companies, together with a credit rating. They will also produce a special report on a company if requested. The information is provided for a fee.

- Legal sources of credit information – Instead of using a credit reference agency, a company might check available legal records itself to find out whether the customer has a history of insolvency or non-payment. For example, in the UK information can be obtained from the Register of County Court Judgements and from the Individual Insolvency Register.

- Company's own sales records – For an existing customer, the sales ledgers will show how prompt a payer the company is, although they cannot show the ability of the customer to pay.

- Credit scoring – Indicators such as family circumstances, home ownership, occupation and age can be used to predict likely creditworthiness. This is useful when extending credit to the public where little other information is available. A variety of software packages is available which can assist with credit scoring.

- Large corporate customers only: credit rating – Very large companies might have a credit rating from one of the major credit rating agencies, Moody's and Standard & Poors. A supplier might use a company's credit rating to decide how much credit to allow, without having to carry out a detailed credit check itself.

4 Setting credit limits

When setting credit limits there are two limits that need to be set:

- the amount of credit available

- the length of time allowed before payment is due.

Both of these limits might be adjusted in accordance to the risk profile of the customer.

Managing existing customers

The 'risk' associated with a customer's credit status should be based on:

- the customer's payment record and history of prompt or late payments, and

- any new information that is obtained about the customer, for example from its most recent annual financial statements or recent press reports.

The level of credit available and the length of settlement period offered to a customer (if across-the-board standard terms are not used) should then be based on the assessment of this risk.

Example

A company might group its existing customers into six categories, as follows:

Customer categories

	Financially strong	Financially stable	Financially weak
Prompt payer	Category A	Category B	Category C
Late payer	Category D	Category E	Category F

The amount of credit offered to the customer (and possibly also the length of the payment terms) would vary according to the category of the customer. If a customer moves from one category to a stronger category, a higher credit limit (or longer settlement period) would be allowed if required.

If the customer's credit status does not improve, a request for more credit from the customer should be refused.

The ledger account should be monitored to take account of orders in the pipeline as well as invoiced sales, before further credit is given.

5 Invoicing and collecting overdue debts

A credit period only begins once an invoice is received so prompt invoicing is essential. If debts go overdue, the risk of default increases, therefore a system of follow-up procedures is required:

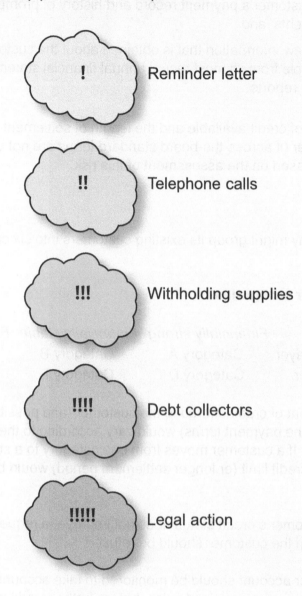

! Reminder letter

!! Telephone calls

!!! Withholding supplies

!!!! Debt collectors

!!!!! Legal action

Invoicing and collecting overdue debts

The longer a debt is allowed to run, the higher the probability of eventual default. A system of follow-up procedures is required, bearing in mind the risk of offending a valued customer to such an extent that their business is lost.

Techniques for 'chasing' overdue debts include the following:

- Reminder letters: these are often regarded as being a relatively poor way of obtaining payment, as many customers simply ignore them. Sending reminders by email have proven to be more productive than using the postal system as it is harder for customers to claim that they have not received them.

- Telephone calls: these can be an efficient way of speeding payment and identifying problems at an early stage.

- Withholding supplies: putting customers on the 'stop list' for further orders or spare parts can encourage rapid settlement of debts.

- Debt collection agencies and trade associations: these offer debt collection services on a fixed fee basis or on 'no collection no charge' terms. The quality of service provided varies considerably and care should be taken in selecting an agent.

- Legal action: this is often seen as a last resort. A solicitor's letter often prompts payment and many cases do not go to court. Court action is usually not cost effective but it can discourage other customers from delaying payment.

Motivating debt collection staff (credit control staff): collection targets

If employees in the payments collection team are to operate effectively, they need to be convinced of the value of their work and their contribution to the objectives of the organisation. One way of improving performance and increasing staff motivation might be to set collection targets. A collection target is a target for the amount of payments to collect for trade receivables within a given period of time. Targets can be set for:

- individual members of the collection team, and

- the credit control team as a whole.

Targets for collection will not be a motivator, however, unless performance is assessed and individuals are rewarded (with a bonus) on the basis of meeting or exceeding targets.

Illustration on collection targets

Consider the following example of a company aiming to set a collection target:

At the end of March, the trade receivables of M were as follows:

		$
From March sales	(100% of sales in the month)	1,200,000
From February sales	(70% of sales in the month)	700,000
From January sales	(30% of sales in the month)	270,000
		2,170,000

This represents an average of 60 days' sales outstanding, made up as follows:

		Days
From March sales	(100% × 31 days)	31
From February sales	(70% × 28 days)	20
From January sales	(30% × 31 days)	9
		60

The company wants to reduce its average days sales outstanding from 60 days to 50 days by the end of April. Sales in April are expected to be $1,100,000, all on credit. It intends to do this by aiming to collect payments of the oldest outstanding receivables.

Required:

Calculate the collection target that should be set for staff.

Solution

- If no money is collected at all during April, the days sales outstanding would increase from 60 days to 90 days (= 60 days + 30 days in April).

- If days sales outstanding is reduced to 50 days, representing the most recent sales, these will be the sales in April and 20 days of sales in March.

- To reach the target of 50 days by collecting the oldest unpaid receivables, the company must collect 40 days of sales, representing:

	Days	$
From March sales *	11	425,806
From February sales	20	700,000
From January sales	9	270,000
		1,395,806

* March amount calculated as (11/31 × $1,200,000)

The collection target for April should therefore be $1,395,806, probably rounded up to $1,400,000.

Note: In this example, the collection target focuses on the trade receivables that have been unpaid for the longest time. A different policy could be followed, such as chasing the customers who are most likely to pay early, or chasing customers who are overdue with their payment by only one or two weeks.

6 Monitoring the system

The position of receivables should be regularly reviewed as part of managing overall working capital and corrective action taken when needed. Methods include:

- age analysis
- ratios
- statistical data.

Monitoring the system

Management will require regular information to take corrective action and to measure the impact of giving credit on working capital investment. Typical management reports on the credit system will include the following points.

- Age analysis of outstanding debts.

  As an aid to effective credit control, an age analysis of outstanding debts may be produced. This is simply a list of the customers who currently owe money, showing the total amount owed and the period of time for which the money has been owed. The actual form of the age analysis report can vary widely, but a typical example is shown below for a sole trader called Robins.

Account number	Name	Balance	Up to 30 days	31–60 days	61–90 days	Over 90 days
B002	Brennan	294.35	220.15	65.40	8.80	0.00
G007	Goodridge	949.50	853.00	0.00	96.50	0.00
T005	Taylor	371.26	340.66	30.60	0.00	0.00
T010	Thorpe	1,438.93	0.00	0.00	567.98	870.95
T011	Tinnion	423.48	312.71	110.77	0.00	0.00
Totals		3,477.52	1,726.52	206.77	673.28	870.95
Percentage		100%	50%	6%	19%	25%

The age analysis of trade receivables can be used to help decide what action should be taken about debts that have been outstanding for longer than the specified credit period. It can be seen from the table above that 41% of Robins's outstanding trade receivable balance is due by Thorpe. It may be that Thorpe is experiencing financial difficulties. There may already have been some correspondence between the two entities about the outstanding debts.

As well as providing information about individual customer balances, the age analysis of trade receivables provides additional information about the efficiency of cash collection. The table above shows that over 50 per cent of debts have been outstanding for more than 30 days. If the normal credit period is 30 days, there may be a suggestion of weaknesses in credit control. It may also be useful to show the credit limit for each customer on the report, to identify those customers who are close to, or have exceeded, their credit limit.

The age analysis can also provide information to assist in setting and monitoring collection targets for the credit control section. A collection target could be expressed as a percentage of credit sales collected within a specified period or it could be expressed in terms of the average number of trade receivable days outstanding. When trying to achieve a collection target the age analysis can be very useful in identifying large balances that have been outstanding for long periods; these can be targeted for action to encourage payment.

– Ratios, compared with the previous period or target, to indicate trends in credit levels and the incidence of overdue and irrecoverable debts.

– Statistical data to identify causes of default and the incidence of irrecoverable debts among different classes of customer and types of trade.

Example 1

Explain the factors that might be considered when revising a credit limit for an existing customer, and list the tools that a credit controller can use to help in making a credit limit decision.

7 Accounts receivable – calculations

Costs of financing receivables

Key working:

$$\text{Finance cost} = \text{Receivable balance} \times \text{Interest (overdraft) rate}$$

$$\downarrow$$

$$\text{Receivable balance} = \text{Sales} \times \frac{\text{Receivable days}}{365}$$

Example 2 – COST OF FINANCING RECEIVABLES

Paisley Co has sales of $20 million for the previous year, receivables at the year end were $4 million, and the cost of financing receivables is covered by an overdraft at the interest rate of 12% pa.

Required:

(a) calculate the receivables days for Paisley

(b) calculate the annual cost of financing receivables.

Early settlement discounts

Cash discounts are given to encourage early payment by customers. The cost of the discount is balanced against the savings the company receives from having less capital tied up due to a lower receivables balance and a shorter average collection period. Discounts may also reduce the number of irrecoverable debts.

The calculation of the annual cost can be expressed as a formula:

$$\text{Annual cost of discount} = \left[1 + \frac{\text{discount}}{\text{amount left to pay}} \right]^{\text{no.of periods}} - 1$$

$$\text{where no. of periods} = \frac{365 / 52 / 12}{\text{no. of days / weeks / months earlier the money is received.}}$$

Notice that the annual cost calculation is always based on the amount left to pay, i.e. the amount net of discount.

If the cost of offering the discount exceeds the rate of overdraft interest then the discount should not be offered.

Example 3 – EARLY SETTLEMENT DISCOUNTS

Paisley Co has sales of $20 million for the previous year, receivables at the year end of $4 million and the cost of financing receivables is covered by an overdraft at the interest rate of 12% pa. It is now considering offering a cash discount of 2% for payment of debts within 10 days. Calculate whether the new policy should be introduced?

Evaluating a change in credit policy

In an examination, you may be required to evaluate whether a proposed change in credit policy is financially justified. The illustration below illustrates the approach required to carry out this evaluation.

Evaluating a change in credit policy

The table below gives information extracted from the annual accounts of Supergeordie.

	$
Raw materials	180,000
Work in progress	93,360
Finished goods	142,875
Purchases	720,000
Cost of goods sold	1,098,360
Sales	1,188,000
Trade receivables	297,000
Trade payables	126,000

The sales director of Supergeordie estimates that if the period of credit allowed to customers was reduced from its current level to 60 days, this would result in a 25 per cent reduction in sales but would probably eliminate about $30,000 per annum bad debts. It would be necessary to spend an additional $20,000 per annum on credit control. The entity at present relies heavily on overdraft finance costing 9 per cent per annum.

You are required to make calculations showing the effect of these changes, and to advise whether they would be financially justified. Assume that purchases and inventory holdings would be reduced proportionally to the reduction in sales value.

Solution

The first stage is to identify the reduction in the level of working capital investment as a result of the change in policy. Inventory and trade payables are assumed to fall by 25 per cent in line with sales, but the new level of trade receivables will need to be calculated using the trade receivable collection formula.

Reduction in working capital

	Existing level		**New level**	**Change**
	$		$	$
Raw materials	180,000	ß 75% =	135,000	45,000
Work in progress	93,360	× 75% =	70,020	23,340
Finished goods	142,875	× 75% =	107,156	35,719
Trade receivables	297,000	(W1)	146,466	150,534
Trade payables	(126,000)	× 75% =	(94,500)	(31,500)
Total	587,235		364,142	223,093

Working

(W1)

$$\text{Receivable collection period} = \frac{\text{trade receivables}}{\text{sales}} \times 365$$

$$60 = \frac{\text{trade receivables}}{1{,}188{,}000 \times 75\%} \times 365$$

$$\text{Trade receivables} = \frac{891{,}000 \times 60}{365}$$

$$= \$146{,}466$$

The second stage is to consider the annual costs and benefits of changing the credit policy. A key element here is to recognise the saving in finance costs as a result of the reduction in the level of working capital investment recognised above.

Annual costs and benefits

			$
Saving in finance costs (223,093 × 9%)	=		20,078
Reduction in gross profit (1,188,000 – 1,098,360)	= 89,640 × 25%		(22,410)
	=		
Reduction in bad debts	=		30,000
Credit control costs	=		(20,000)
Net saving per annum before tax			7,668

The change in credit policy appears to be justified financially, but it should be remembered that there are a number of assumptions built in that could invalidate the calculations.

8 Accounts receivable – factoring

Factoring is the 'sale of debts to a third party (the factor) at a discount in return for prompt cash' *(CIMA Official Terminology)*.

The debts of the company are effectively sold to a factor (normally owned by a bank). The factor takes on the responsibility of collecting the debt for a fee. The company can choose one or both of the following services offered by the factor:

(1) debt collection and administration – recourse or non-recourse

(2) credit insurance.

These are of particular value to:

- smaller firms
- fast growing firms.

Make sure you can discuss the various services offered and remember that non-recourse factoring is more expensive as the factor bears the costs of any irrecoverable debts.

More details

Debt collection and administration – the factor takes over the whole of the company's sales ledger, issuing invoices and collecting debts.

Credit insurance – the factor agrees to insure the irrecoverable debts of the client. The factor would then determine to whom the company was able to offer credit.

Some companies realise that, although it is necessary to extend trade credit to customers for competitive reasons, they need payment earlier than agreed in order to assist their own cash flow. Factors exist to help such companies.

Factoring is primarily designed to allow companies to accelerate cash flow, providing finance against outstanding trade receivables. This improves cash flow and liquidity. The factor will advance up to 80% of the value of a debt to the company; the remainder (minus finance costs) being paid when the debts are collected. The factor becomes a source of finance. Finance costs are usually 1.5% to 3% above bank base rate and charged on a daily basis.

Factoring is most suitable for:

- small and medium-sized firms which often cannot afford sophisticated credit and sales accounting systems, and

- firms that are expanding rapidly. These often have a substantial and growing investment in receivables, which can be turned into cash by factoring the debts. Factoring debts can be a more flexible source of financing working capital than an overdraft or bank loan.

Factoring can be arranged on either a 'without recourse' basis or a 'with recourse' basis.

- When factoring is without recourse or 'non-recourse', the factor provides protection for the client against irrecoverable debts. The factor has no 'comeback' or recourse to the client if a customer defaults. When a customer of the client fails to pay a debt, the factor bears the loss and the client receives the money from the debt.

- When the service is with recourse ('recourse factoring'), the client must bear the loss from any irrecoverable debt, and so has to reimburse the factor for any money it has already received for the debt.

Credit protection is provided only when the service is non-recourse and this is obviously more costly.

Typical factoring arrangements

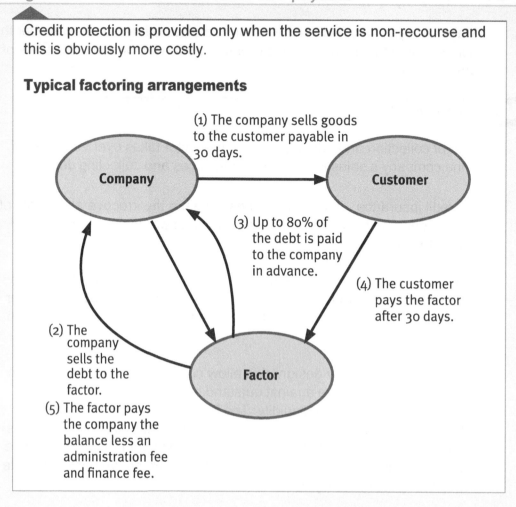

(1) The company sells goods to the customer payable in 30 days.

(3) Up to 80% of the debt is paid to the company in advance.

(4) The customer pays the factor after 30 days.

(2) The company sells the debt to the factor.

(5) The factor pays the company the balance less an administration fee and finance fee.

Advantages	Disadvantages
(1) Saving in administration costs.	(1) Likely to be more costly than an efficiently run internal credit control department.
(2) Reduction in the need for management control.	
(3) Particularly useful for small and fast growing businesses where the credit control department may not be able to keep pace with volume growth.	(2) Factoring has a bad reputation associated with failing companies; using a factor may suggest your company has money worries.
	(3) Customers may not wish to deal with a factor.
	(4) Once you start factoring it is difficult to revert easily to an internal credit control system.
	(5) The company may give up the opportunity to decide to whom credit may be given (non-recourse factoring).

Benefits and problems with factoring

The benefits of factoring are as follows.

- A business improves its cash flow, because the factor provides finance for up to 80% or more of debts within 24 hours of the invoices being issued. A bank providing an overdraft facility secured against a company's unpaid invoices will normally only lend up to 50% of the invoice value. (Factors will provide 80% or so because they set credit limits and are responsible for collecting the debts.)

- A factor can save the company the administration costs of keeping the sales ledger up to date and the costs of debt collection.

- If the business were to allow the factor to administer the sales ledger, it can use the factor's credit control system to assess the creditworthiness of both new and existing customers.

- Non-recourse factoring is a convenient way of obtaining insurance against irrecoverable debts.

Problems with factoring

- Although factors provide valuable services, companies are sometimes wary about using them. A possible problem with factoring is that the intervention of the factor between the factor's client and the debtor company could endanger trading relationships and damage goodwill. Customers might prefer to deal with the business, not a factor.

- When a non-recourse factoring service is used, the client loses control over decisions about granting credit to its customers.

- For this reason, some clients prefer to retain the risk of irrecoverable debts, and opt for a 'with recourse' factoring service. With this type of service, the client and not the factor decides whether extreme action (legal action) should be taken against a non-payer.

- On top of this, when suppliers and customers of the client find out that the client is using a factor to collect debts, it may arouse fears that the company is beset by cash flow problems, raising fears about its viability. If so, its suppliers may impose more stringent payment terms, thus negating the benefits provided by the factor.

Example 4 – FACTORING ARRANGEMENTS

Edden is a medium-sized company producing a range of engineering products, which it sells to wholesale distributors. Recently, its sales have begun to rise rapidly due to economic recovery. However, it is concerned about its liquidity position and is looking at ways of improving cash flow.

Its sales are $16 million pa, and average receivables are $3.3 million (representing about 75 days of sales).

One way of speeding up collection from receivables is to use a factor. It has considered an agreement from an interested factoring company.

The factor will pay 80% of the book value of invoices immediately, with finance costs charged on the advance at 10% pa.

The factor will charge 1% of sales as their fee for managing the sales ledger and there will be administrative savings of $100,000. It will be a non-recourse agreement – which means that the factor will bear the responsibility for any bad debts.

The company is currently paying 8% interest on its overdraft.

Required:

Calculate the relative costs and benefits of using the factor.

9 Accounts receivable – invoice discounting

Invoice discounting is a method of raising finance against the security of receivables without using the sales ledger administration services of a factor.

While specialist invoice discounting firms exist, this is a service also provided by a factoring company. Selected invoices are used as security against which the company may borrow funds. This is a temporary source of finance, repayable when the debt is cleared. The key advantage of invoice discounting is that it is a confidential service, and the customer need not know about it.

In some ways it is similar to the financing part of the factoring service without control of credit passing to the factor.

Ensure you can explain the difference between factoring and invoice discounting, and the situations where one may be more appropriate than the other.

Invoice discounting

Typical arrangement

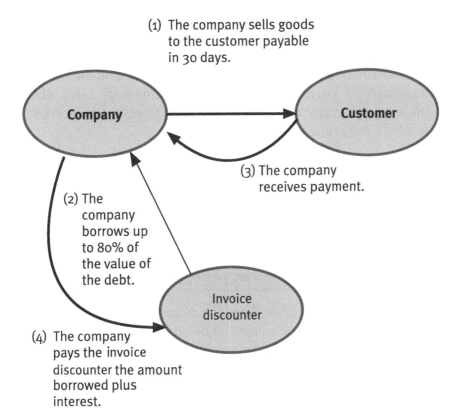

(1) The company sells goods to the customer payable in 30 days.

Company

Customer

(3) The company receives payment.

(2) The company borrows up to 80% of the value of the debt.

Invoice discounter

(4) The company pays the invoice discounter the amount borrowed plus interest.

Invoice discounting is a method of raising finance against the security of receivables without using the sales ledger administration services of a factor. With invoice discounting, the business retains control over its sales ledger, and confidentiality in its dealings with customers. Firms of factors will also provide invoice discounting to clients.

The method works as follows:

- The business sends out invoices, statements and reminders in the normal way, and collects the debts. With 'confidential invoice discounting', its customers are unaware that the business is using invoice discounting.

- The invoice discounter provides cash to the business for a proportion of the value of the invoice, as soon as it receives a copy of the invoice and agrees to discount it. The discounter will advance cash up to 80% of face value.

- When the business eventually collects the payment from its customer, the money must be paid into a bank account controlled by the invoice discounter. The invoice discounter then pays the business the remainder of the invoice, less interest and administration charges.

Invoice discounting can help a business that is trying to improve its cash flows, but does not want a factor to administer its sales ledger and collect its debts. It is therefore equivalent to the financing service provided by a factor.

Administration charges for this service are around 0.5–1% of a client's turnover. It is more risky than factoring since the client retains control over its credit policy. Consequently, such facilities are usually confined to established companies with high sales revenue, and the business must be profitable. Finance costs are usually in the range 3–4% above base rate, although larger companies and those which arrange credit insurance may receive better terms.

The invoice discounter will check the sales ledger of the client regularly, perhaps every three months, to check that its debt collection procedures are adequate.

Illustration of the invoice discounting process

At the beginning of August, Basildon plc sells goods for a total value of $300,000 to regular customers but decides that it requires payment earlier than the agreed 30-day credit period for these invoices.

A discounter agrees to finance 80% of their face value, i.e. $240,000, at an interest cost of 9% pa.

The invoices were due for payment in early September, but were subsequently settled in mid-September, exactly 45 days after the initial transactions. The invoice discounter's service charge is 1% of invoice value. A special account is set up with a bank, into which all payments are made.

The sequence of cash flows is:

August	Basildon receives cash advance of $240,000.	
Mid-September	Customers pay $300,000.	
	Invoice discounter receives the full $300,000	
	paid into the special bank account.	
	Basildon receives the balance payable, less charges, i.e.	
	Service fee = 1% × $300,000 =	$3,000
	Finance cost = 9% × $240,000 × 45/365 =	$2,663
	Total charges	$5,663
	Basildon receives:	
	Balance of payment from customer	$60,000
	Less charges	$5,663
		$54,337
Summary $300,000 invoiced	Total receipts by Basildon: $240,000 + $54,337	$294,337
	Invoice discounter's fee and interest charges	$5,663

10 Accounts payable – managing trade credit

Trade credit is the simplest and most important source of short-term finance for many companies.

Again it is a balancing act between liquidity and profitability.

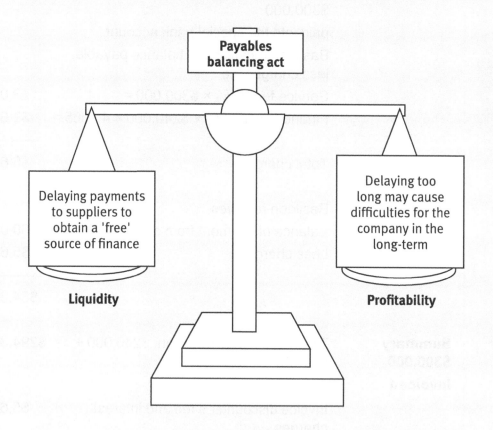

By delaying payment to suppliers companies face possible problems:

- supplier may refuse to supply in future
- supplier may only supply on a cash basis
- there may be loss of reputation
- supplier may increase price in future.

Trade credit is normally seen as a 'free' source of finance. Whilst this is normally true, it may be that the supplier offers a discount for early payment. In this case delaying payment is no longer free, since the cost will be the lost discount.

In the examination, you need to be able to calculate the cost of this discount foregone.

Trade payables

Using **trade credit** a firm is able to obtain goods (or services) from a supplier without immediate payment, the supplier accepting that the firm will pay at a later date.

Trade credit periods vary from industry to industry and each industry will have what is a generally accepted norm which would be from seven days upwards. A typical credit period might be 30 days, but it can range anywhere from 7 to 90 days dependent on the relative power of the supplier and buyer. Normally considerable scope for flexibility exists and longer credit periods are sometimes offered, particularly where the type of business activity requires a long period to convert materials into saleable products, e.g. farming.

Some of the firm's suppliers may offer **settlement discounts**. However, if the firm is short of funds, it might wish to make maximum use of the credit period allowed by suppliers regardless of the settlement discounts offered. Favourable credit terms are one of several factors which influence the choice of a supplier. Furthermore, the act of accepting settlement discounts has an opportunity cost, i.e. the cost of finance obtained from another source to replace that not obtained from creditors.

Whilst trade credit may be seen as a source of free credit , there will be **costs** associated with extending credit taken beyond the norm – lost discounts, loss of supplier goodwill, more stringent terms for future sales.

In order to compare the cost of different sources of finance, all costs are usually converted to a rate per annum basis. The cost of extended trade credit is usually measured by loss of discount, but the calculation of its cost is complicated by such variables as the number of alternative sources of supply, and the general economic conditions.

Certain assumptions have to be made concerning (a) the maximum delay in payment which can be achieved before the supply of goods is withdrawn by the supplier, and (b) the availability of alternative sources of supply.

Also, it is a mistake to reduce working capital by holding on to creditors' money for a longer period than is allowed as, in the long-term, this will affect the **supplier's willingness to supply** goods and raw materials, and cause further embarrassment to the firm.

Example 5 – ACC. PAYABLE: DISCOUNT FOR EARLY PAYMENT

One supplier has offered a discount to Box Co of 2% on an invoice for $7,500, if payment is made within one month, rather than the three months normally taken to pay. If Box's overdraft rate is 10% pa, calculate if it is financially worthwhile for them to accept the discount and pay early?

Age analysis of payables

The value of an age analysis of trade payables is probably less obvious than the value of an age analysis of trade receivables. However, management needs to be aware of:

- the total amount payable to suppliers

- when the money will be payable

- the amounts payable to each individual supplier, and how close this is to the credit limit available from the supplier

- whether the company is failing to pay its trade suppliers on time.

11 Chapter summary

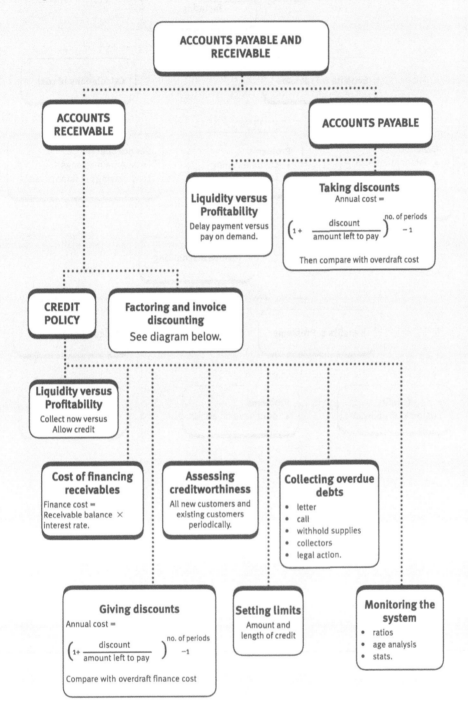

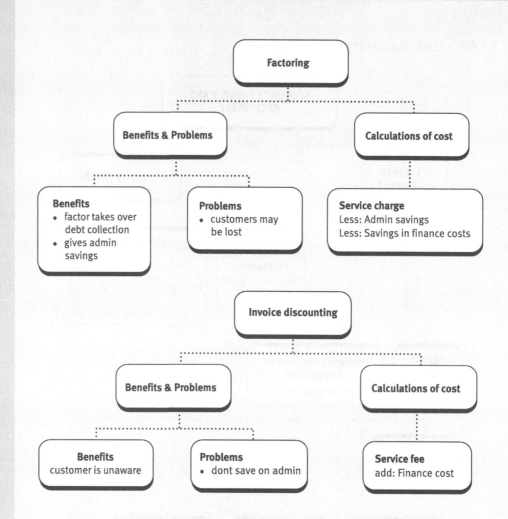

12 Practice questions

Test your understanding 1

Identify which of the following occurs first in the credit cycle:

A   Deliver goods

B   Accept order

C   Send invoice

D   Send statement

(2 marks)

Test your understanding 2

A company expects credit sales of $110,000 in July, rising by $10,000 each month for the next two months. Outstanding trade receivables at the beginning of July were $165,000, representing all of June sales and 22 days of May sales. Sales in June were $95,000.

The company wishes to reduce the average days sales outstanding to 45 days by the end of July and 40 days by the end of August.

On the assumption that the target should be to collect first the receivables that have been unpaid for the longest time, calculate the collection targets for:

(a)   July, and

(b)   August.

(5 marks)

Test your understanding 3

List five methods of carrying out a credit check on a potential new customer, before deciding whether to give credit and if so, what the credit limit should be.

(5 marks)

Test your understanding 4

A company is considering a change in its credit policy. It has estimated that if credit terms are extended from 30 days to 60 days, total annual sales will increase by 10% from the current level of $12 million. It has been estimated that as a consequence of the change in credit terms and the higher sales volume, bad debts would increase from 2% to 3% of sales. The company's cost of capital is 8%.

The increase in sales would not affect annual fixed costs. The contribution to sales ratio is 40%.

Required:

Calculate the effect of the change in credit policy on the annual profit before taxation. Assume a 360-day year of 30 days each month.

(5 marks)

Test your understanding 5

A company is offering a cash discount of 2.5% to receivables if they agree to pay debts within one month. The usual credit period taken is three months.

Calculate the effective annualised cost of offering the discount and should it be offered, if the bank would loan the company at 18% pa?

(3 marks)

Test your understanding 6

Calculate the equivalent annual cost of the following credit terms: 1.75% discount for payment within three weeks; alternatively, full payment must be made within eight weeks of the invoice date. Assume there are 50 weeks in a year.

(3 marks)

Test your understanding 7

Marton Co produces a range of specialised components, supplying a wide range of customers, all on credit terms. 20% of revenue is sold to one firm. Having used generous credit policies to encourage past growth, Marton Co now has to finance a substantial overdraft and is concerned about its liquidity.

Marton Co borrows from its bank at 13% pa interest. No further sales growth in volume or value terms is planned for the next year.

In order to speed up collection from customers, Marton Co is considering two alternative policies:

Option one

Factoring on a non-recourse basis, the factor administering and collecting payment from Marton Co's customers. This is expected to generate administrative savings of $200,000 pa and to lower the average receivable collection period by 15 days. The factor will make a service charge of 1% of Marton Co's revenue and also provide credit insurance facilities for an annual premium of $80,000.

Option two

Offering discounts to customers who settle their accounts early. The amount of the discount will depend on speed of payment as follows.

Payment within 10 days of despatch of invoices 3%

Payment within 20 days of despatch of invoices 1.5%

It is estimated that customers representing 20% and 30% of Marton Co's sales respectively will take up these offers, the remainder continuing to take their present credit period.

Extracts from Marton Co's most recent accounts are given below:

	($000)
Sales (all on credit)	20,000
Cost of sales	(17,000)
	————
Operating profit	3,000
	————
Current assets:	
inventory	2,500
receivables	4,500
cash	Nil
	————

Calculate the relative costs and benefits in terms of annual profit before tax of each of the two proposed methods of reducing receivables, and identify the most financially advantageous policy.

(10 marks)

Test your understanding answers

Example 1

There are a number of factors which a credit controller might consider, such as:

- the customers past payment history. If a customer has usually paid on time in the past then a higher credit limit might be approved.

- any new public information about the customer. For example, if recent press reports suggest that the customer might be in financial difficulty then it may be unwise to raise a customers credit limit.

- a change in the customers credit rating. For large customers especially, credit ratings are easily obtained and any change to a rating should have an impact on the amount of credit offered to the customer.

In making the decision the credit controller will be able to use a variety of tools, such as:

- past customer history
- an aged receivables report
- credit reference agencies
- ratio analysis

Example 2 – COST OF FINANCING RECEIVABLES

Solution

(a) Receivables days = $4m ÷ $20m × 365 = 73 days

(b) Cost of financing receivables = $4m × 12% = $480,000.

Example 3 – EARLY SETTLEMENT DISCOUNTS

Discount as a percentage of amount paid = 2 ÷ 98 = 2.04%

Receivables days are currently 73 ($4m/$20m × 365), so:

Saving is 63 days (dropping from 73 days to 10) and there are 365 ÷ 63 = 5.794 periods in a year

Annualised cost of discount % is

$(1 + 0.0204)^{5.794} - 1 = 0.1241 = 12.41\%$.

The overdraft rate is 12%.

It would be marginally cheaper to borrow the money from the bank rather than offer the discount.

Example 4 – FACTORING ARRANGEMENTS

	Costs of factoring	Savings
	$	$
Sales ledger administration 1% × $16m	160,000	
Administration cost savings		100,000
Cost of factor finance 10% × 80% × $3.3m	264,000	
Overdraft finance costs 8% × 80% × $3.3m saved		211,200
Total	424,000	311,200
Net cost of factoring	112,800	

The firm will have to balance this cost against the security offered by improved cash flows and greater liquidity.

Example 5 – ACC. PAYABLE: DISCOUNT FOR EARLY PAYMENT

Discount saves 2% of $7,500 = $150

Financed by overdraft for extra two months in order to pay early:

Cost = 10% × $\dfrac{2}{12}$ × $7,500 = ($125)

Net saving = $25

It is worth accepting the discount.

Alternatively:

Discount as a percentage of amount paid = $\dfrac{150}{7,350}$ = 2.04%

Saving is 2 months and there are $\dfrac{12}{2}$ = 6 periods in a year

Annualised cost of not taking the discount
(and therefore borrowing from the supplier) is:
$(1+0.0204)^6 - 1$
= 0.1288 = 12.88%

The overdraft rate is 10%.

It would be cheaper to borrow the money from the bank to pay early and accept the discount.

Test your understanding 1

The correct answer is **B**.

The supplier accepts an order before delivering the goods, sending an invoice and subsequently sending a statement.

Test your understanding 2

Target receivables

End of July	Days		$
July sales	31		110,000
June sales (balance)	14	(14/30 × $95,000)	44,333
	45		154,333

End of August	Days		$
August sales	31		120,000
July sales (balance)	9	(9/31 × $110,000)	31,935
	40		151,935

Target collections

	July $	August $
Receivables at the beginning of the month	165,000	154,533
Sales in the month	110,000	120,000
	275,000	274,333
Receivables at the end of the month	(154,333)	(151,935)
Target collections in the month	120,667	122,398

Test your understanding 3

Choose 5 from the following list:

- bank references
- trade references
- visit to the customer's premises
- competitors
- published information
- credit reference agencies
- legal sources of credit information
- company sales records
- credit scoring
- credit rating (large corporate customers only).

Test your understanding 4

	Without the new credit policy	With the new credit policy
Annual sales	$12,000,000	$13,200,000
Average trade receivables	$1,000,000 ($12m × 30/360)	$2,200,000 ($13.2m × 60/360)
Increase in trade receivables		$1,200,000
Bad debts	$240,000 (= 2%)	$396,000 (= 3%)
Increase in bad debts		$156,000
Increase in annual sales		$1,200,000

	$	$
Increase in annual contribution (40%)		480,000
Increase in bad debts	156,000	
Increase in interest cost of receivables (8% × $1,200,00)	96,000	
	———	(252,000)
Net increase in profit before tax		228,000

Test your understanding 5

Discount as a percentage of amount paid = 2.5/97.5 = 2.56%

Saving is 2 months and there are 12/2 = periods in a year.

Annualised cost of discount % is

$(1+0.0256)^6 - 1 = 0.1638 = 16.38\%$.

The loan rate is 18%.

It would therefore be worthwhile offering the discount.

Test your understanding 6

Step 1

Work out the discount available and the amount due if the discount were taken.

Discount available on a $100 invoice = 1.75% × $100 = $1.75.

Amount due after discount = $100 × $1.75 = $98.25

Step 2

The effective interest cost of not taking the discount is:

1.75 ÷ 98.25 = 0.0178

for an 8 − 3 = five-week period.

Step 3

Calculate the equivalent annual rate. There are ten five-week periods in a year.

The equivalent interest annual rate is $(1 + 0.018)^{10} − 1 = 0.195$ or 19.5%.

Test your understanding 7

The relative costs and benefits of each option are calculated as follows:

Option 1 – Factoring

Reduction in receivables days	= 15 days		
Reduction in receivables	= 15 ÷ 365 × $20m	=	$821,916
Effect on profit before tax:			
Finance cost saving	= (13% × $821,916)	=	$106,849
Administrative savings		=	$200,000
Service charge	= (1% × $20m)	=	($200,000)
Insurance premium		=	($80,000)
Net profit benefit		=	$26,849

Option 2 – The discount

With year-end receivables at $4.5 million, the receivables collection period was: $4.5m ÷ $20m × 365 = 82 days.

The scheme of discounts would change this as follows:

10 days for 20% of customers

20 days for 30% of customers

82 days for 50% of customers

Average receivables days become:

(20% × 10) + (30% × 20) + (50% × 82) = 49 days

Hence, average receivables would reduce from the present $4.5 million to:

49 × $20m ÷ 365 = $2,684,932

Finance cost saving = 13% × ($4.5m − $2.685m) = $235,950

The cost of the discount:

(3% × 20% × $20m) + (1.5% × 30% × $20m) = ($210,000)

The net benefit to profit before tax : $25,950

The figures imply that factoring is marginally the more attractive, but this result relies on the predicted proportions of customers actually taking up the discount and paying on time. It also neglects the possibility that some customers will insist on taking the discount without bringing forward their payments. Marton Co would have to consider a suitable response to this problem.

Conversely, the assessment of the value of using the factor depends on the factor lowering Marton Co's receivables days. If the factor retains these benefits for itself, rather than passing them on to Marton Co, this will raise the cost of the factoring option. The two parties should clearly specify their mutual requirements from the factoring arrangement on a contractual basis.

Short-term finance and investments

Chapter learning objectives

Lead	Component
E2. Identify short-term funding and investment opportunities.	(a) Identify sources of short-term funding.
	(b) Identify alternatives for investment of short-term cash surpluses.
	(c) Identify appropriate methods of finance for trading internationally.
	(d) illustrate numerically the financial impact of short-term funding and investment methods.

1 Chapter overview diagram

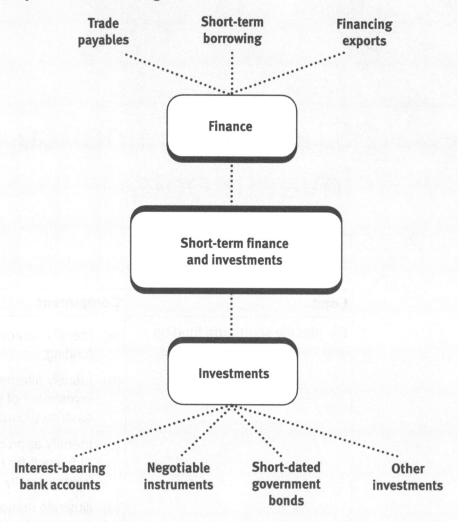

2 Short-term finance

Current liabilities should not be allowed to increase to a level where the cash position and liquidity of the company are at risk. This requires careful management of short-term finance.

The main sources of short-term funding are:

*   trade payables

*   bank overdrafts and short-term loans

*   possibly, using trade receivables to borrow from a factor or invoice discounter (covered in an earlier chapter).

Trade payables

Benefits of paying suppliers late	Potential problems when paying suppliers late
• alleviates cash flow difficulties	• loss of any settlement discount
• cash can earn a return whilst still in the paying company's account	• could obtain a poor credit rating
	• supplier may stop further supplies
	• supplier may increase future selling prices to compensate
	• could face legal action from the supplier

Trade payables as a source of short-term funds

Suppliers are a source of short-term finance because they provide goods (inventory) on credit. In some cases, suppliers might not be paid until after the goods they have supplied have been re-sold. This occurs, for example, in supermarkets. A supermarket might re-sell the goods provided by a supplier many days before the supplier is eventually paid.

It is a well-established business practice that trade credit should be agreed, which means that suppliers should finance the business of their customers to some extent.

The amount of trade credit varies from one industry to another, and can also vary with changes in economic conditions. However, if normal credit terms are 30 days, and a company purchases, say, $1,200,000 of goods on credit each year, it should be financed by $100,000 of trade credit on average.

A huge attraction of trade credit is that it has no interest cost. Unlike banks, trade suppliers do not charge interest on debts.

Short-term borrowing

Short-term cash requirements can also be funded by borrowing from the bank. There are two main sources of bank lending:

*   bank overdraft
*   bank loans.

Bank overdrafts are mainly provided by the clearing banks and are an important source of company finance.

Advantages	Disadvantages
• Flexibility	• Repayable on demand
• Only pay for what is used, so cheaper	• May require security
	• Variable finance costs

Bank loans are a contractual agreement for a specific sum, loaned for a fixed period, at an agreed rate of interest. They are less flexible and more expensive than overdrafts but provide greater security.

Short term borrowing

Finance costs on bank loans and overdrafts are normally variable, i.e. they alter in line with base rates. Fixed rate loans are available, but are less popular with firms (and providers of finance).

Bank overdrafts

A common source of short-term financing for many businesses is a bank overdraft. These are mainly provided by the clearing banks and represent permission by the bank to draw funds even though the firm has insufficient funds deposited in the account to meet the expected withdrawal amount.

An overdraft limit will be placed on this facility, but provided the limit is not exceeded, the firm is free to make as much or as little use of the overdraft as it desires. The bank charges interest on amounts outstanding at any one time, and the bank may also require repayment of an overdraft at any time.

The advantages of overdrafts are the following.

- Flexibility – they can be used as required.

- Cheapness – interest is only payable on the finance actually used, usually at 2–5% above base rate (and all loan interest is a tax deductible expense).

The disadvantages of overdrafts are as follows.

- Overdrafts are legally repayable on demand. Normally, however, the bank will give customers assurances that they can rely on the facility for a certain time period, say six months.

- Security is usually required by way of fixed or floating charges on assets or sometimes, in private companies and partnerships, by personal guarantees from owners.

- Interest costs vary with bank base rates. This makes it harder to forecast and exposes the business to future increases in interest rates.

Overall, bank overdrafts are one of the most important sources of short-term finance for industry.

Bank loans

A bank loan represents a formal agreement between the bank and the borrower, that the bank will lend a specific sum for a specific period (one to seven years being the most common). Interest must be paid on the whole of this sum for the duration of the loan.

This source is, therefore, liable to be more expensive than the overdraft and is less flexible but, on the other hand, there is no danger that the source will be withdrawn before the expiry of the loan period. Interest rates and requirements for security will be similar to overdraft lending.

Comparison of bank loans and overdrafts

Consider a company that requires a maximum of $600 over the next four months. However, it is only halfway through month four that it actually requires the full amount.

The difference can be shown as follows:

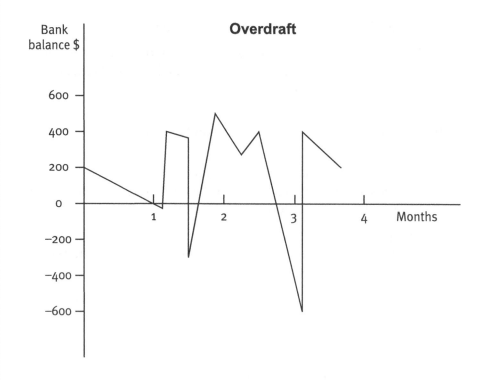

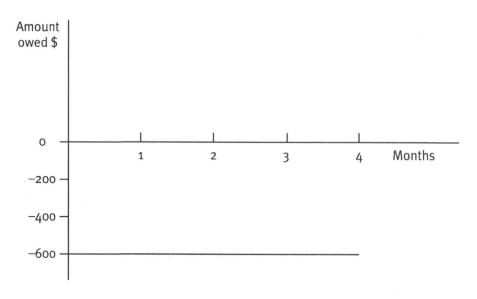

If an overdraft is used, the company will pay interest on the maximum amount part way through month 4. For the remainder of the period it will pay interest on an overdraft of substantially less than that, or it will pay no interest at all as it has a positive bank balance. If it borrows $600 by way of a bank loan at the beginning of the four months, it must pay interest for four months on the amount borrowed, despite the fact that it rarely requires the full sum.

3 Financing exports

Companies exporting goods to other countries often have much greater problems with credit and finance than companies selling goods and services to domestic markets.

Export risks

The particular problems of exporters can be:

- The credit risk. There might be inadequate credit information about foreign customers. If payment from a foreign customer is overdue, it might be difficult to try to collect the money due to the geographical distance, different time zones and lack of familiarity with the legal system in the customer's country.

- The long time that may elapse between supplying goods to a foreign buyer and receiving payment: this problem is particularly severe when goods are sent by ship to a distant country.

- Due to this long time period between supply and payment, an exporter might have cash flow difficulties, and could need short-term finance to support its export operations.

- There may be foreign exchange control restrictions in the buyer's country, and weak domestic currency in the buyer's country. It might be difficult to obtain payment from the buyer due to the weakness of the domestic currency in the buyer's country.

  - The government of the country might impose restrictions on payments by its nationals to foreign suppliers in a 'hard' currency such as US dollars. This makes it difficult for the exporter to invoice the buyer in a hard currency.

  - The exporter might be unwilling to invoice the customer in the customer's own currency, because it might lose much of its value even within the trade credit period.

  - The exporter may also be wary in dealing in 'soft' currencies. A soft currency is one who's value fluctuates as a result of the country's political or economic uncertainty. As a result of the of this currency's instability, foreign exchange dealers tend to avoid it as it is difficult to predict and 'price'. It may therefore be difficult for the exporter to sell this currency and convert it back to their own domestic currency.

Several methods are available for dealing with the problems of financing exports and controlling the credit risk. These include:

- documentary credits
- bills of exchange
- export factoring
- forfeiting.

Financial instruments

Documentary credits (irrevocable letters of credit)

A letter of credit is a document issued by a bank on behalf of a customer authorising a person to draw money to a specified amount from its branches or correspondents, usually in another country, when the conditions set out in the document have been met.

Business transactions between businesses in some countries are carried out on normal commercial terms. For example, trading between companies in the European Union is carried out mainly on normal credit terms, although a foreign currency might be involved for either the buyer or seller.

Trading between other countries, however, is more complex, particularly when it will take a considerable time to ship the goods from the exporter's country to the importer. The exporter might want payment as soon as possible, but the importer needs to be satisfied before paying that the exporter has complied with the terms of the sale agreement.

The problem of guaranteeing payment can be overcome by using an irrevocable letter of credit, also called an irrevocable documentary credit. A letter of credit is an undertaking given by its issuer that payment will be guaranteed for the exporter, provided that the exporter complies with certain specific requirements within a specified time limit.

The specific requirements relate mainly to the provision of satisfactory documentation for the exports, such as valid shipping documents and insurance documents, and valid import or export licences. The exporter must provide these as evidence that goods of the proper quantity and description are being shipped in the agreed manner, and are properly insured. This gives comfort to the buyer that the goods will be delivered as ordered.

The letter of credit is provided not by the importer, but by a bank on behalf of the importer. It might be issued by a bank in the importer's country, and confirmed by another bank in the exporter's country. A confirmed irrevocable letter of credit therefore provides payment guarantees to the exporter from two banks, thereby minimising the credit risk. Once issued, the irrevocable letter of credit cannot be revoked and cancelled. However, it ceases to apply if the exporter fails to comply with any of the specified terms and conditions.

An irrevocable letter of credit is arranged as follows:

- The importer asks a bank in its country to provide an irrevocable letter of credit for an import transaction. The exporter might require the letter of credit also to be confirmed by another bank in its own country.

- The letter of credit is issued, and a copy is given to the exporter.

- The cost of the letter of credit is usually paid by the importer.

- The exporter complies with the requirements of the letter of credit, and provides the specified documentation to a bank that will check to make sure that all the documentation is in order. This bank could be either the bank that issued the letter of credit or the confirming bank.

- If the documents are in order, the exporter will be paid under the terms of the letter of credit. In many cases, this involves a bill of exchange (see below).

The guarantee provided by the issuing bank in its letter of credit relates to compliance by the exporter with requirements relating to the documentation. The bank does not get involved in the details of the trading transaction itself.

- Even if the goods are shipped correctly, the bank will not guarantee payment if the documentation fails to meet the specifications in the letter of credit.

- If there is a dispute between the buyer and the importer about the actual shipment, the bank will honour its guarantee provided that the documentation was provided correctly and as specified in the letter of credit.

A bill of exchange

A bill of exchange is a negotiable instrument, drawn by one party on another, for example, by a supplier of goods on a customer, who by accepting (signing) the bill, acknowledges the debt, which may be payable immediately (a sight draft) or at some future date (a time draft). The holder of the bill can thereafter use an accepted time draft to pay a debt to a third party, or can discount it to raise cash.

A bill of exchange is a method of arranging a payment. There are three parties to a bill of exchange:

- the drawer, who is the person who issues the bill
- the drawee, who is the person to whom the bill is addressed, and
- the payee, who is the person to whom payment should be made.

The drawer and the payee are often the same person. A bill of exchange might be a sight bill, which is payable immediately, but bills used for export finance are term bills, which are payable at a specified future date.

Payment by means of a bill of exchange is arranged as follows:

- The drawer issues a bill of exchange (or 'draws the bill on the drawee'). It might help to think of the bill at this stage as a 'You Owe Me'. It specifies that a sum of money must be paid by the drawee to the payee on a specified date.
- The drawee acknowledges the obligation to make the payment by signing the bill. The drawee is said to 'accept' the bill by signing it. In effect, an accepted bill is no longer a 'You Owe Me' from the drawer, but an 'I promise to pay' by the drawee.
- The accepted bill is returned to the drawer, who might hold it until maturity.
- When the bill reaches its maturity (the payment date specified), the drawer presents the bill for payment through the banking system.

A significant characteristic of bills of exchange is that:

- the drawee is given a period of credit before having to pay a term bill, but
- the drawer or payee can obtain payment earlier than the bill's maturity date, by means of discounting the bill.

When a bill is discounted, it is sold in the financial markets at a discount to face value. The size of the discount reflects the rate of interest that the buyer of the bill requires from holding the bill to maturity.

Export factoring

Export factoring is similar to ordinary factoring, with the exception that the factoring organisation agrees to factor the client's trade receivables for exports. The factor's services include administration of the receivables ledger and collecting payment, and providing factor finance.

In view of the problems that can arise with collecting payments from customers in other countries, the expertise of an export factor can be very helpful, particularly for small and medium-sized businesses with little experience in collecting foreign payments.

Forfeiting

Forfeiting can be a source of medium-term trade finance. It is particularly suitable for the financing of export transactions for which, due to the nature of the goods involved or the size of the transactions, payments are made over a period of several years. It has been used fairly widely in Europe, particularly in Switzerland and Germany where forfeiting originated.

An importer might want to buy capital goods, such as machinery or equipment, but needs finance for the purchase. The capital goods will be used to earn profits in future years, and the importer might want to use these future profits to provide the cash to pay for the goods.

In order to set up a forfeiting arrangement, the importer must be prepared to:

- pay some of the purchase price on delivery, and
- make the remaining payments at regular intervals over a period of several years.

In a forfeiting arrangement:

- The importer issues a number of promissory notes with payment dates at regular intervals. A promissory note is a promise to make a specified payment, and by issuing a series of promissory notes the importer is promising to make a series of payments at future dates, over a period of several years. (Instead of using promissory notes, the importer might be required to accept a series of term bills of exchange drawn on it by the exporter.)

- The importer must then find a bank that is prepared to guarantee the promissory notes. Guaranteeing a promissory note is called avalising the note. The avalised notes can be sold, like bank bills of exchange, at 'fine' rates of discount.

- The exporter's bank finds another bank that is willing to act as forfaiter. Some banks specialise in this type of finance. Forfeiting involves buying the avalised promissory notes at a discount to face value (or buying bills of exchange at a discount). The rate of discount at which the forfeiting bank buys the notes is specified as a fixed rate in the forfaiting agreement.

- The exporter therefore receives immediate payment from the forfaiting bank for the notes that it has purchased.

- The forfaiting bank holds onto the notes, and at the appropriate payment dates presents them to the importer for payment.

The forfeiter buys the promissory notes without recourse to the exporter. The exporter has therefore obtained payment for the goods, without any risk of having to return the money if the importer fails to meet its payment obligations.

The forfeiter therefore accepts the risk of non-payment by the importer (failing to honour the promissory notes or bills of exchange).

The key features of forfaiting are therefore that:

- The importer obtains medium-term finance for much of the purchase cost of the goods.

- The exporter receives immediate payment.

- The credit risk is accepted by the forfeiting bank, although this risk is reduced by the avalisation of the promissory notes by the avalising bank.

> Forfeiting has been defined in CIMA's Official Terminology as follows:
> 'Forfeiting is the purchase of financial instruments such as bills of
> exchange ... on a non-recourse basis by a forfeiter, who deducts interest
> (in the form of a discount) at an agreed rate for the period covered by the
> notes. The forfeiter assumes the responsibility for collecting the debts
> from the importer (buyer) who initially accepted the financial instrument
> drawn by the seller of the goods. Traditionally, forfeiting is fixed rate
> medium-term (one-to-five year) finance.'

4 Short-term investments

A business might have surplus cash for a period of time. Surplus cash is
usually temporary and available for several weeks or months. Eventually it
will be used to pay suppliers or settle other liabilities, invest in new non-
current assets or pay a dividend.

Money in an operational bank account earns no income, because banks do
not pay interest to businesses for cash in their day-to-day accounts. If a
business wishes to maximise its profits, it should consider using the cash to
earn some return in the time when it is temporarily surplus to requirements.

Cash surpluses can be invested in a range of short-term interest-earning
investments such as:

- Interest-bearing bank accounts
- Negotiable instruments
- Short-dated government bonds
- Other short-term investments

Investment criteria

When a business has surplus cash to invest temporarily, it has to decide
which investments to select from the different choices available. There are
several criteria that should be considered when making these choices:

- maturity
- return
- risk
- liquidity
- diversification

More details

Maturity

A short-term investment might involve investing an amount of money for a specific period of time, and receiving interest and the payment of a principal amount at a specified future date (the 'maturity' of the investment). If the investment is cashed in or sold before maturity, there could be a risk of some loss of market value or some loss of interest.

The maturity of a short-term investment should ideally be no longer than the duration of the cash surplus. If the cash is needed before the investment reaches maturity, the investment will have to be 'cashed in' early, with some risk of loss of capital value or interest.

Return

With short-term investments, return is the interest yield on the investment. Some investments offer a higher yield than others. If the investment is 'redeemable' (i.e. where a capital amount will be repaid to the investor) then the capital repayment will also form part of the return.

Risk

Some investments are more risky than others. Risk refers to the possibility that the investment might fall in value, or that there might be some doubt about the eventual payment of interest or repayment of investment principal. As a general rule, higher-risk investments have to offer a higher return in order to attract investors.

For example, suppose that two banks offer high-interest savings accounts to businesses, for which there is a minimum notice period of two weeks for withdrawal of funds. Bank A might be a major bank with a 'triple-A' credit rating, and Bank B might be a regional bank in a developing country. To attract investors, Bank B would have to offer a higher interest rate on its savings accounts than Bank A, because the perceived risk for investors in an investment in Bank B would be higher.

Investing in equities is high risk. The value of equities depends on the profitability and future prospects of the company, and share prices also rise or fall more generally in line with broader movements in the stock market. Since share prices can fall by a large amount in a short period of time, equities are generally regarded as an unsuitable form of short-term investment.

Short-term investments should usually be preferred to longer-dated investments, because the risk of a fall in market value is less. Prudent companies should also avoid high-risk investments such as equities, and should look for short-term investments that will keep the value of the investment secure.

Liquidity

Liquidity refers to the ease with which an investment can be 'cashed in' quickly, without any significant loss of value or interest. All short-term investments are less liquid than cash in an operational bank account, but some are more liquid than others. For example, many savings accounts or deposit accounts are reasonably liquid, and a depositor can often withdraw cash immediately for the loss of only several days' interest.

In contrast, works of art such as paintings might be a profitable long-term investment, but they are very illiquid as short-term investments. Paintings cannot be sold quickly without a significant risk of having to sell at below true market value.

Diversification

There is a general rule that investors should not 'put all their eggs in one basket'. They should perhaps diversify by investing in a range of different investments. In this way, if some investments perform badly, the investor is not exposed to significant losses, because the other investments in the portfolio should perform better.
However, diversification is less essential for investing short-term cash surpluses than for investing long-term in equities and bonds.

Interest-bearing accounts

These can fall into two categories:

- bank deposit accounts
- money market deposits

Deposit accounts

- Some deposit accounts are 'instant access' accounts, which allow the investor to withdraw the money without notice and without loss of interest. The interest rate is usually low on these accounts, and they are used when the investor wants to earn some interest on surplus cash, but places great importance on instant liquidity.

- Some deposit accounts or savings accounts allow the investor to withdraw funds without notice, but the investor will suffer some loss of interest. For example, a deposit account might require a notice of withdrawal of at least seven days, but the investor might be permitted to withdraw the funds without notice with a penalty of seven days' lost interest.

- In some cases, an investor might be unable to withdraw funds from the account without giving a minimum notice period.

Money market deposits

Money market deposits are amounts of money deposited through a bank in the money markets. These are the financial markets for short-term borrowing and lending. The money markets are used largely by banks and other financial institutions, for depositing and lending funds. Banks can deposit short-term funds with other banks, or borrow short-term from other banks in the inter-bank market.

Interest yields in the inter-bank market are often reasonably attractive, and it is now quite common for companies with large temporary cash surpluses to arrange with their bank to have the money deposited in the money markets (interbank market) or at money market interest rates.

Money invested in a money market deposit cannot be withdrawn until the deposit matures. It is therefore important that money should not be invested for a period longer than the investor's expected cash surplus. Money market deposits can be for very short periods of time, as little as one day, or for as long as several months (and even up to one year). However, very short-term deposits should be large amounts of money, so that the interest earned justifies the effort of making the deposits.

Effective annual interest yield

Interest on bank deposits accumulates on the principal sum invested. Interest is added at specified regular intervals, such as every month, every three months, every six months or annually. The frequency of adding interest affects the actual interest yield on the investment.

Example 1

A company has $1,000,000 to invest for 12 months.

The choices available are:

- a deposit account offering interest at 10% per year, with interest calculated quarterly
- a deposit account offering interest at 10.25% per year, with interest added annually.

Calculate which deposit provides the best return.

Interest earned

You might be required to calculate the amount of interest earned on a deposit or savings account within a particular period of time. If you are given the effective annual yield (or if you are given an 'annual yield' with no further information), the interest calculation is simply:

$$\text{Interest} = \text{Amount deposited} \times \text{Interest rate} \times \frac{\text{Number of days' interest earned}}{\text{Annual day count}}$$

The annual day count is the number of days in the year, for interest calculation purposes. This might seem unusual, since a year has either 365 or 366 days. However, in the financial markets, there are special conventions for the number of days in a year. Whereas interest on sterling is calculated on the assumption of a 365-day year, interest on the US dollar in the money markets is calculated on the assumption of 360 days in the year

Negotiable instruments

Negotiable instruments are financial instruments that may be obtained as investments. A key feature of negotiable instruments is that title passes when the instrument is handed from one person to another. They are 'bearer instruments', and ownership does not have to be recorded in a register of owners. This means that a negotiable instrument can easily be sold by one person to another.

Examples of negotiable instruments are:

- banknotes
- bearer bonds
- Certificates of Deposit
- Bills of Exchange
- Treasury bills.

The most important negotiable instruments as short-term investments are Certificates of Deposit and Treasury bills, and possibly also bills of exchange (particularly bank bills of high quality banks).

More details

Certificate of Deposit

A Certificate of Deposit or CD is a negotiable instrument that provides evidence of a short-term deposit with a bank with a fixed term and earning a specified amount of interest. The maturity of the deposit is usually 90 days or less, but can be longer. The amount deposited is at least US$100,000 (or its equivalent in other currencies), but usually larger.

The holder of the CD at maturity has the right to take the deposit with interest. The CD holder presents the CD at maturity to a recognised bank, which will then present the instrument to the bank holding the deposit, and arrange for the withdrawal of the deposit with interest.

Until maturity, the money is 'locked up' with the bank, and cannot be withdrawn.

When an organisation has a temporary cash surplus, it might arrange with its bank to place the money in a fixed term deposit account, and for the bank to issue a CD. The CD will state the identity of the bank, the amount deposited, the maturity date of the deposit and the interest that will accumulate.

- The organisation can hold the CD until maturity and then claim the money.
- Alternatively, if it needs cash before the deposit matures, it can sell the CD. There is an active secondary market in Certificates of Deposit, and a company can arrange for its bank to sell a CD on its behalf.

Another company with a short-term cash surplus could either arrange its own Certificate of Deposit or purchase an existing CD in the secondary market.

Investment yield on CDs

Since Certificates of Deposit are negotiable instruments, they are more attractive investments than money market deposits from the point of view of liquidity. A CD holder can sell the CD to obtain funds quickly, whereas a money market deposit cannot be withdrawn until maturity. Yields on CDs are therefore slightly lower than interest yields on money market deposits.

Bills of exchange

Bills of exchange have been described earlier in the chapter, in the context of export finance, although they have a broader use and are not restricted to export finance arrangements.

The significance of bills of exchange as a short-term investment is that they are negotiable instruments. There is an active money market for bills of exchange (which is called the discount market) and investors can buy bills. The market is particularly active in bills of exchange that are payable by top-quality banks: in the UK these are sometimes called 'eligible bank bills'.

The buyer of a bill of exchange obtains the right to receive payment of the bill when it matures. A bill of exchange is usually an undertaking to pay a fixed sum of money at maturity, with no interest. An investor in a bill will therefore buy the bill at a discount to face value. Bills of exchange are therefore examples of discount paper.

Although it is possible to buy bills of exchange that have been accepted (and so are payable) by trading companies, investors place more value in bank bills. These are bills of exchange that have been accepted by a bank, and are payable by the bank. If the bank has a high credit status, the risk of investing in its bills is very low.

Yields on bills vary according to the credit risk associated with the bill, and an investor will be prepared to pay more for a top-quality bank bill than for a trade bill with much higher credit risk.

Treasury bills

Treasury bills are negotiable instruments issued by the government, with a maturity of less than one year. In practice, most Treasury bills have a maturity of three months (91 days). Treasury bills are used by a government to finance short-term cash requirements, and in countries such as the US and the UK, Treasury bills are issued at regular intervals when investors are invited to apply to buy bills in the new issue.

Since Treasury bills are debts of the government, they have a high credit quality, risk is low, and yields for investors are therefore also lower than for many other short-term investments. Treasury bills issued by a government and denominated in the domestic currency should be risk-free. For example, US Treasury bills are risk-free investments, because there is no doubt that the US government will redeem the debt at maturity.

Treasury bills are redeemable at face value. For example, the US government will redeem a 91-day $1,000 Treasury bill for $1,000 91 days after its issue. Since the bills are redeemable at par, investors pay less than face value to buy them. Like bills of exchange, Treasury bills are examples of discount paper.

Although yields on Treasury bills are relatively low, they can be attractive short-term investments because of their risk-free nature and their liquidity. There is a large and active secondary market in Treasury bills, such as US Treasury bills in the US and UK government Treasury bills in the UK.

Calculations

The amount of discount on a bill can be calculated as follows:

$D = R \times F \times T/Y$

where:

D = the amount of the discount

R = the rate of discount or discount yield, expressed as a proportion (for example, 6% = 0.06)

F = the face value of the bill: this will be paid to the bill holder at maturity

T = time, measured as the number of days in the interest period

Y = the days in a standard year (applying the appropriate 'day count convention' for the number of days in a year)

The issue price of a discount interest instrument such as a Treasury bill or bill of exchange is its face value less the discount:

Price = F – D

The discount explained

Whereas some investments such as bank deposit accounts and money market deposits earn interest on a capital sum invested, other instruments are issued at a discount to face value, and investors earn their return from the difference between the discount price on purchase and the par redemption value at maturity. The mathematics of discount paper returns are slightly different from the calculation of interest-yielding investments.

When a financial instrument is quoted on a discount interest basis, it is redeemed at maturity at its face value, and issued at a discount to face value. For example, a 91-day Treasury bill for $1,000 might be issued at $998.25 and redeemed at $1,000. The difference between the issue price and the redemption value is the discount which represents the return that the investor will make by holding the bill until maturity. The size of this return can be measured as a discount interest rate.

Example 2

A US Treasury bill with a face value of $1,000 is issued at a 5% discount yield for 91 days. Calculate its issue price?

(There are 360 days in a year for interest purposes.)

Short-dated government bonds

Companies can invest temporary surplus cash in government bonds. If they do so:

- they will receive interest on the due payment dates

- they can liquidate their investment at any time by selling the bonds in the secondary market

- if the bonds are short-dated when purchased, they can hold the bonds to maturity and have them redeemed at par.

However, there is some price risk with bonds, particularly longer-dated bonds. If interest rates change in the market, the market value of bonds will rise or fall. Bond prices rise when interest rates fall, but prices fall when interest rates go up. The movement in price is greater for longer-dated bonds.

Government bonds

Treasury bills are government debt instruments with a maturity of less than one year when they are issued. Government bonds are longer-dated government debt instruments, with a maturity of several years, sometimes 20 years or longer, when they are issued.

Government bonds are issued by governments in order to borrow long-term, and they can be purchased by any investors, including private individuals and companies. Investors can buy government bonds when they are first issued. Alternatively, they can be purchased in the secondary market at any time up to maturity of the bonds. There is a very large and active secondary market for the bonds of some governments, such as:

- the 'Treasuries' market in the US for US government Treasury bonds and notes (a note is similar to a bond, but with a shorter maturity on issue), and

- the 'gilts' market in the UK. 'Gilts' is short for gilt-edged securities, which is a term used to describe Treasury Stock and other bonds issued by the UK government.

An attractive feature of government bonds issued by a national government is that in many countries they can be considered to be almost risk-free when they are issued in the domestic bond market and denominated in the domestic currency. For example, UK gilt-edged securities denominated in sterling are risk-free, in the sense that there is no credit risk. It is absolutely certain that the UK government will pay the due interest on time and will redeem the bonds at maturity. It should be noted that this might not apply in all countries and the international financial crisis in 2009/2010 threw up many examples of countries who were unable to meet their payments.

Investors with a temporary cash surplus wishing to invest in government bonds should ideally invest in short-dated bonds. These are bonds with only a short time remaining to maturity. However, they can invest instead in longer-dated bonds, which can be sold easily in the secondary market when cash is needed.

Characteristics

Government bonds and corporate bonds (bonds issued by companies) have many features in common

- **Face value.** Bonds have a face value or nominal value.

- **Coupon.** Interest is payable on bonds at regular intervals, such as every six months or every year. Interest is usually a fixed rate, although some bonds (floating rate notes or FRNs) pay a variable rate of interest. For example, if bonds have an 8% 'coupon' on which interest is payable every six months, interest will be paid at the rate of 4% (8%/2) on the face value of the bonds every six months.

- **Redemption date and redemption value.** Bonds are redeemable at maturity (unless they are 'perpetual bonds' or unless they are 'convertible' into another financial instrument). Bonds are usually redeemable at their face value ('at par').

- **Market value.** Bonds are not necessarily issued at par, although they are usually issued at close to their par value. Their market value will vary over time, between their issue and their redemption. However, if they are redeemable at par, their value will move towards par value as the redemption date approaches. For comparative purposes, the market prices of bonds are quoted relative to their par value of $100. For example, if bonds are priced at $102.50, this means that their current market price is $102.50 for every $100 face value of the bonds.

Calculations

The yield on a bond investment is usually measured as a **redemption yield**. The redemption yield can be calculated as the discounted annual rate of return (internal rate of return) at which the present value of the future interest payments and the redemption value of the bond at maturity are equal to the current market value of the bond.

More details

Although interest on bonds is shown as a coupon rate, the actual investment yield earned by investors in bonds is a different amount. There are two reasons for this:

- The market value of a bond is not the same as its face value. For example, suppose that a bond with a 4% coupon has a market value of $95.00. The coupon is 4%, but the interest yield is 4.21% (4/95.00).

- The market price of a bond is not the same as its eventual redemption value, which is usually at par, and the yield for the investor should also take into account the gain or the loss for the investor from holding the bond to maturity. For example, if a bond has a market price of $95.00 and is redeemable in four years at $100.00, the investor will gain $5.00 on the investment of $95.00 by holding the bond for four more years.

The yield on a bond investment is usually measured as the yield to maturity. This is the yield that will be obtained from an investment in the bond at a price P, and holding the bond until maturity. The yield to maturity is a combination of:

- the interest yield on the bond (the coupon as a percentage of the market price),

- plus an annualised return to maturity from the capital gain on redemption of the bond at par,
  100 – P, where P is less than 100, or

- minus an annualised negative return from the capital loss at redemption, P – 100, where P is higher than 100.

The yield to maturity can be calculated as the discounted annual rate of return (internal rate of return) at which the present value of the future interest payments and the redemption value of the bond at maturity are equal to the current market value of the bond.

Investors are interested in the yield to maturity from a bond, not the coupon yield.

Example 3

A bond with a coupon rate of 7% is redeemable in eight years' time for $100. Its current purchase price is $82 ex-interest (this is a term used to explain that interest has just been paid and that the next interest payment will not be due for another year). Calculate the percentage yield to maturity?

Other short-term investments

This chapter has described the short-term investments that are most commonly purchased or used by companies. There are other short-term investments such as:

- corporate bonds, and
- commercial paper (CP).

These are more likely to be purchased by investment institutions rather than by companies with a short-term cash surplus.

More details

Corporate bonds

Corporate bonds are bonds issued by a company. They are long-term investments, and so unsuitable for investing a short-term cash surplus, and they can also be a high risk investment. Bond prices fluctuate with movements in the general level of interest rates, and corporate bond values are also affected by the perceived credit risk of the company issuing the bonds.

Commercial paper (CP)

Commercial paper consists of short-dated negotiable debt instruments issued by a company, and sold by a bank managing the company's commercial paper programme. In practice, although CP is negotiable, it is generally purchased by large investment institutions and held to maturity. It is not normally regarded as a suitable type of short-term investment of cash surpluses by a trading company.

Chapter summary

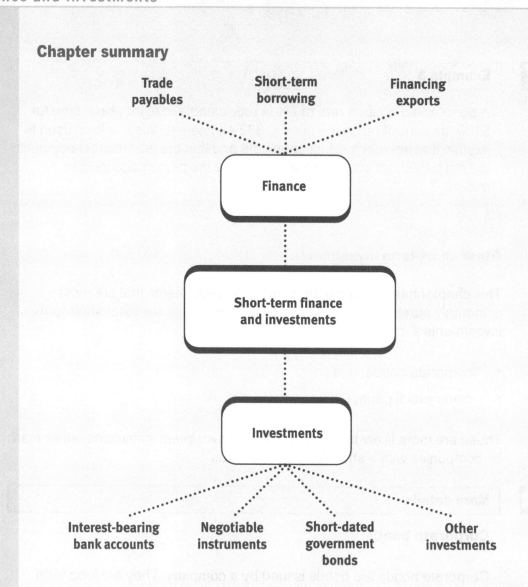

5 Practice questions

Test your understanding 1

Identify which of the following investments offers the highest effective annual interest yield:

A A deposit account paying interest at 5%, interest payable monthly

B A deposit account paying interest at 5.25%, interest payable every three months

C A deposit account paying interest at 5.4%, interest payable every six months

D A deposit account paying interest at 5.5%, interest payable annually

(2 marks)

Test your understanding 2

On 1 April 20X4 a company placed $5 million on deposit at an interest rate of 6.25%. The deposit has a maturity date of 30 June 20X4.

Calculate the amount of cash that the company will receive on maturity of the deposit.

(2 marks)

Test your understanding 3

Which of the following would not normally be used to deal with the credit risk associated with exporting:

A Documentary credits

B Forfeiting

C Bills of exchange

D Treasury bills

(2 marks)

Test your understanding 4

A Treasury bill with a face value of $100 is issued at a 8% discount yield for 30 days. Calculate its issue price.

(4 marks)

(There are 360 days in a year for interest purposes.)

Test your understanding 5

Which of the following would not normally be used when choosing between different sources of investment:

A   Risk

B   Liquidity

C   Currency

D   Maturity

(2 marks)

Test your understanding 6

A company treasurer has a short term surplus of funds. He believes that there may be around $50,000 to $80,000 surplus cash available for the next month. At the end of the month the cash will be needed again in the business. He is unsure where he should invest this cash but he is considering a choice between treasury bills and a fixed interest bank account with 30 days notice. He expects the base rate in the country to increase in the next month.

Evaluate which investment, if either, he should make.

(5 marks)

Test your understanding answers

Example 1

It might seem that the better investment is the deposit account offering 10.25%, but this is not the case.

When interest is quoted at 10% per year, payable quarterly, this means that the interest rate is 10%/4 = 2.5% each quarter. Interest is paid on the initial deposit plus the interest accumulated in previous quarters. In other words, interest is earned on the interest. The actual effective annual yield on an investment at 10% with interest paid quarterly is:

$[(1 + 2.5\%)^4 - 1] \times 100\%$

$= [(1.025)^4 - 1] \times 100\%$

$= [1.1038 - 1] \times 100\%$

$= 10.38\%.$

This is a higher effective annual yield than a deposit paying 10.25% annually.

Example 2

$D = R \times F \times T/Y$

where:

R = 5%
F = $1000
T = 91
Y = 360

D= 0.05 × 1000 × 91/360 = 12.64

P = F – D

  = 1000 – 12.64

  = $987.36

Example 3

To answer this question you will need to use the annuity factors and discount rates from the tables.

We need to assume two discount rates between which the required percentage is likely to fall. The yield to maturity will obviously be greater than 7% as the bond was purchased for less than its par value, so we will use rates of 10% and 12%:

t = 8; r = 10

PV = Pv of interest + PV of redemption return – Initial investment

    = (7 × 5.335) + (100 × 0.467)   –82.00 = 37.345 + 46.7 – 82.00 = \$2.045

t = 8; r = 12

    = (7 × 4.968) + (100 × 0.404)   –82.00 = 34.776 + 40.4 – 82.00 = \$–6.824

By interpolation:

10% +(((2.045)/(2.045 – (–6.824)) × 2) =

10% + (2.045/8.869 × 2) =

10% + 0.461 + 10.461% = **10.46%**

Test your understanding 1

The correct answer is **D.**

A

Interest at 5% per year, payable monthly means interest at 5%/12 = 0.4167% each month.

The effective annual yield is $[(1.004167)^{12} - 1] \times 100\% = 5.12\%$.

B

Interest at 5.25% per year, interest payable three-monthly means interest at 5.25%/4 = 1.3125% every three months.

The effective annual yield is $[(1.013125)^4 - 1] \times 100\% = 5.35\%$.

C

Interest at 5.4% per year, interest payable six-monthly means interest at 5.4%/2 = 2.7% every six months.

The effective annual yield is $[(1.027)^2 - 1] \times 100\% = 5.47\%$.

D

The effective annual yield on the deposit account paying interest annually is 5.5%.

Test your understanding 2

The interest on the deposit will be $5 million × 6.25% × 91/360 = $78,993.

At maturity the deposit will be $5 million + $78,993 = $5,078,993.

Test your understanding 3

The correct answer is **D.**

Treasury bills are used as a source of investment rather than a way for reducing export risks.

Test your understanding 4

$D = R \times F \times T/Y$

where:

$R = 8\%$
$F = \$100$
$T = 30$
$Y = 360$

$D = 0.08 \times 100 \times 30/360 = 0.67$

$P = F - D$

$= 100 - 0.67$

$= \$99.33$

Test your understanding 5

The correct answer is C.

Currency may influence areas such as risk and liquidity of the investment, but the currency itself would largely be irrelevant as long as the investment was within acceptable risk limits and sufficiently liquid.

Test your understanding 6

Treasury bills are government debt instruments with a maturity of less than one year when they are issued. The treasurer is likely to have to buy the bills on the market with a maturity of one month's time. The yield (or return) is likely to be low as treasury bills of this nature are likely to be seen to be very low risk. But treasury bills are very liquid and it would mean that if the company needed the money again urgently then it could quickly convert the bill to cash again. However, if interest rates in the country increase over the next month then the value of the bills is likely to fall. This means that the treasurer may not be able to fully recover the initial investment.

The fixed interest bank account may pay interest at a slightly higher rate. However this interest will not change if interest rates in the economy increase and therefore may become less attractive over the month. The notice of withdrawal is likely to be given almost immediately but it means that the account cannot be re-converted to cash until the end of the month which may make the investment a little more risky.

But of the treasury manager is confident that at least $50,000 of surplus cash is available during the next month then the best advice would to put this in the bank deposit account. Treasury bills may be seen as being too risky in the face of expected increases in interest rates.

Pillar P

P1 – Performance Operations

Specimen Examination Paper

Instructions to candidates

You are allowed three hours to answer this question paper.
You are allowed 20 minutes reading time **before the examination begins** during which you should read the question paper and, if you wish, highlight and/or make notes on the question paper. However, you will **not** be allowed, **under any circumstances**, to open the answer book and start writing or use your calculator during this reading time.
You are strongly advised to carefully read ALL the question requirements before attempting the question concerned (that is all parts and/or sub-questions). The requirements for questions 3 and 4 are contained in a dotted box.
ALL answers must be written in the answer book. Answers or notes written on the question paper will **not** be submitted for marking.
Answer the ONE compulsory question in Section A. This has seven sub-questions on pages 2 to 4.
Answer the SIX compulsory sub-questions in Section B on pages 5 to 7.
Answer the TWO compulsory questions in Section C on pages 8 to 10.
Maths Tables are provided on pages 11 to 14.
The list of verbs as published in the syllabus is given for reference on page 15.
Write your candidate number, the paper number and examination subject title in the spaces provided on the front of the answer book. Also write your contact ID and name in the space provided in the right hand margin and seal to close.
Tick the appropriate boxes on the front of the answer book to indicate which questions you have answered.

P1 – Performance Operations

TURN OVER

SECTION A – 20 MARKS

[Note: The indicative time for answering this section is 36 minutes]

ANSWER *ALL* SEVEN SUB-QUESTIONS IN THIS SECTION

Instructions for answering Section A:

The answers to the SEVEN sub-questions in Section A should ALL be written in your answer book.

Your answers should be clearly numbered with the sub-question number then ruled off, so that the markers know which sub-question you are answering. **For multiple choice questions, you need only write the sub-question number and the letter of the answer option you have chosen.** You do not need to start a new page for each sub-question.

For sub-questions **1.5** to **1.7** you should show your workings as marks are available for the method you use to answer these sub-questions.

Question One

1.1 The original budgeted profit statement for a product is as follows:

	$
Revenue	200,000
Variable costs	100,000
Fixed costs	36,000
Profit	64,000

It has now been realised that sales volume will be 10% higher than budgeted volume with no change in selling price. The product has also been redesigned to lower variable costs by 20% per unit.

The percentage increase in the budgeted profit as a result of the two changes will be:

A   2·0%

B   30·0%

C   50·0%

D   62·5%

(2 marks)

1.2 A project has the following present values when discounted at the company's cost of capital of 8% per annum:

	$
Initial investment	250,000
Cash inflows	500,000
Cash outflows	200,000

The sensitivity of the project to changes in the cash inflows is:

A   8%

B   10%

C   20%

D   50%

(2 marks)

The following data is for questions 1.3 and 1.4

D provides a motorist rescue service to its members. It has been proposed to change the annual membership fee to $120 for the next year. The impact of this on the number of members is uncertain but the following estimates have been made:

Number of members	Probability
20,000	0·1
30,000	0·6
40,000	0·3

It is thought that the variable operating costs vary in relation to the number of members but the cost per member is uncertain. The following estimates have been made:

Variable cost per member	Probability
$70	0·3
$60	0·5
$40	0·2

D expects to incur annual fixed costs of $1,100,000.

1.3 Calculate, based on expected values, the profit for the next year

(2 marks)

1.4 The Management Accountant of D has produced a two-way data table.

(i)   Calculate the value that would be shown in that table in the cell for the profit from 40,000 members with a variable cost per member of $40.

(2 marks)

(ii) Calculate the joint probability of having 20,000 members and a variable cost per member of $40.

(2 marks)

1.5 GF wants to sell an unquoted bond. The bond has a coupon rate of 5% and will repay its face value of $1,000 at the end of four years.

GF estimates that the market requires a yield to maturity of 11% from this type of bond. GF has asked you to recommend a selling price for the bond.

Calculate the selling price for the bond.

(4 marks)

1.6 A company has the following information:

	Actual 31 December 2009	Forecast 30 June 2010
Balances	*$'000*	*$'000*
Trade receivables	75	80
Trade payables	47	40
Inventory of raw materials	29	31

The production budget for the six month period to 30 June 2010 shows that the cost of raw materials to be used in that period will be $331,000.

Calculate the cash that will be paid to suppliers during the six month period to 30 June 2010.

(3 marks)

1.7 A company's trade payables days outstanding at 30 September 2009 were 45 days. Purchases for the year to 30 September 2009 were $324,444 occurring evenly throughout the year.

The company's budgeted purchases for the year ending 30 September 2010 are $356,900 occurring evenly throughout the year.

Calculate the budgeted trade payables days outstanding at 30 September 2010.

(Assume that the trade payables outstanding balance at 30 September 2010 will be the same amount as at 30 September 2009.)

(3 marks)

(Total for Section A = 20 marks)

Reminder

All answers to Section A must be written in your answer book.

Answers or notes to Section A written on the question paper will **not** be submitted for marking.

End of Section A

SECTION B – 30 MARKS

[Note: The indicative time for answering this section is 54 minutes]

ANSWER ALL SIX SUB-QUESTIONS IN THIS SECTION – 5 MARKS EACH.

Question Two

(a)   A company manufactures office equipment in England but sells it in the UK and to overseas customers.

Current situation

UK customers (£2·1m annual revenue)

The company offers a cash discount of 3% for payment within 10 days to UK customers. Approximately 40% of customers take advantage of the early payment discount whilst the remainder pay in 30 days.

Overseas customers (£0·9m annual revenue)

All sales are on credit but customers are required to pay a 20% deposit when they place their orders and the balance in 60 days.

Debt factoring

The company is thinking about debt factoring. Investigations have revealed that a non-recourse factor will accept 85% of the company's UK customers. It is assumed that the remaining 15% will not take advantage of the early settlement discount.

Required:

Calculate, based on a 365-day year, the total debtors' days if

   (i)   the current situation continues
   (ii)   debt factoring is introduced

(5 marks)

(b)   Discuss the non-financial factors that a company would need to consider before making a decision to factor its debts.

(5 marks)

(c)   The manager of a hotel is deciding if he should carry out repairs to the hotel immediately or postpone them for a year. He has made the following estimates for the coming year:

The cost of the repairs would be £90,000.

If the repairs are started immediately there is only a two-in-three chance of them being completed in time. If the repairs are completed in time the contribution for the hotel could be any one of the three levels below with equally probability. If the repairs are not completed on time some rooms will be unavailable and consequently demand could be either medium or low, with equal probability.

Contribution for the coming year if the repairs are undertaken could be:

> £200,000 if there is high demand
> £150,000 if there is medium demand
> £100,000 if demand is low

If the repairs are not undertaken the contribution for the coming year is estimated to be £37,500.

Required:

Demonstrate, using a decision tree, if the repairs should be started immediately or postponed for a year.

(5 marks)

(d)   A fast food outlet served the following number of burgers in the past 13 quarters:

	2007				2008				2009				2010
	Q1	Q2	Q3	Q4	Q1	Q2	Q3	Q4	Q1	Q2	Q3	Q4	Q1
Burgers '000	75	80	110	175	92	96	122	210	111	116	164	259	135

Regression analysis was used to determine the following equation for the trend of sales:

$S = 134 \cdot 23 + 7 \cdot 945Q$ where

S = quarterly sales ('000)
Q = quarter number. (The 13 quarters in the period Q1 2007 to Q1 2010 were coded from –6 through to +6).

Previous research has established that the sales follow a seasonal pattern:

Quarter	1	2	3	4
Seasonality	-25%	-25%	0	+50%

Required:

Calculate the number of burgers that are forecast to be sold in quarters 2, 3 and 4 of 2010.

(5 marks)

(e)   Explain how a budget can cause conflict between "motivation" and "control".

(5 marks)

(f)   Two classifications of environmental costs are "environmental internal failure costs" and "environmental external failure costs".

Explain each one of the two classifications of environmental costs mentioned above. Your answer should include, for each classification, an example of an activity that would cause such costs.

(5 marks)

(Total for Section B = 30 marks)

End of Section B

SECTION C – 50 MARKS

[Note: The indicative time for answering this section is 90 minutes]

ANSWER *BOTH* QUESTIONS IN THIS SECTION - 25 MARKS EACH.

Question Three

The Board of Directors of a company are considering two mutually exclusive projects. Both projects necessitate buying new machinery and both projects are expected to have a life of five years.

Project One
This project has already been evaluated. Details of the project are:

Initial investment needed	£500,000
Net present value	£41,000
Accounting rate of return	31%

Project Two
Details of Project Two are:

Year	1	2	3	4	5
Revenue (£000)	370	500	510	515	475
Operating costs (£000)	300	350	380	390	400
Depreciation (£000)	90	90	90	90	90

The figures for revenue and operating costs in the table above are cash flow estimates, have been stated at current values and are assumed to occur at the year end. However differential inflation is expected: 8% per annum for revenue and 6% per annum for operating costs.

The machinery will cost £500,000 and will be sold for £50,000 cash at the end of year 5.

Additional information
The company pays tax at 30%. Tax is paid and / or received one year in arrears.

The machines qualify for tax depreciation at the rate of 25% per annum on a reducing balance basis.

The company's cost of capital is 12% per annum. The current rate of return on investments in the money market is 7%.

The project chosen will be funded by internal funds.

The target accounting rate of return is 30%. The company defines "Accounting rate of return" as the average profit before tax divided by the average investment.

Required:

(a)

(i) Calculate the Net Present Value and the Accounting Rate of Return of Project Two.

(12 marks)

(ii) Prepare a report for the Board of Directors which

- recommends which of the projects, if any, they should invest in;
- identifies two non-financial factors that are relevant to the decision;
- explains the strengths and weaknesses of net present value and accounting rate of return.

(8 marks)

(b) A government organisation has a fixed interest ten-year loan. The interest rate on the loan is 8% per annum. The loan is being repaid in equal annual instalments at the end of each year. The amount borrowed was £250,000. The loan has just over 4 years to run.

Ignore taxation.

Required:

Calculate the present value of the amount outstanding on the loan.

(5 marks)

(Total for Question Three= 25 marks)

Question Four

A hospital specialises in the provision of a particular surgical procedure. The hospital seeks to provide a value-for-money service. In order to do this it hires teams of specialist staff on a sub-contract basis and pays them only for the hours that they have worked. The hospital uses a standard marginal costing system.

Overhead costs are attributed to the procedures based on direct labour cost.

Budget for November

Budgeted number of procedures to be performed: 20 procedures

Standard marginal cost per procedure:

		$
Team fee	2 hours @ $1,500 per hour	3,000
Variable overheads	65% of team fee	1,950
		4,950

The budgeted fixed overheads for November were $48,000

Actual results for November

Procedures performed: 22 procedures

Costs incurred:

Team fees: the team worked 47 hours and were paid a total of $75,400.
Variable overheads: $48,000
Fixed overheads: $46,000

Required:

(a) Prepare a statement which reconciles the original budget cost for November and the actual costs incurred, in as much detail as possible.

(14 marks)

(b) It has now been realised that the budgeted rate for the team should have been $1,625 per hour.

Calculate the planning variance and the operational rate and efficiency variances for the team fees for November.

(6 marks)

(c) Explain why budgetary control and standard costing are most effective when used together as a means of cost control in service-based organisations.

(5 marks)

(Total for Question Four = 25 marks)

MATHS TABLES AND FORMULAE

Present value table

Present value of $1, that is $(1+r)^{-n}$ where r = interest rate; n = number of periods until payment or receipt.

Periods	Interest rates (r)									
(n)	1%	2%	3%	4%	5%	6%	7%	8%	9%	10%
1	0.990	0.980	0.971	0.962	0.952	0.943	0.935	0.926	0.917	0.909
2	0.980	0.961	0.943	0.925	0.907	0.890	0.873	0.857	0.842	0.826
3	0.971	0.942	0.915	0.889	0.864	0.840	0.816	0.794	0.772	0.751
4	0.961	0.924	0.888	0.855	0.823	0.792	0.763	0.735	0.708	0.683
5	0.951	0.906	0.863	0.822	0.784	0.747	0.713	0.681	0.650	0.621
6	0.942	0.888	0.837	0.790	0.746	0705	0.666	0.630	0.596	0.564
7	0.933	0.871	0.813	0.760	0.711	0.665	0.623	0.583	0.547	0.513
8	0.923	0.853	0.789	0.731	0.677	0.627	0.582	0.540	0.502	0.467
9	0.914	0.837	0.766	0.703	0.645	0.592	0.544	0.500	0.460	0.424
10	0.905	0.820	0.744	0.676	0.614	0.558	0.508	0.463	0.422	0.386
11	0.896	0.804	0.722	0.650	0.585	0.527	0.475	0.429	0.388	0.350
12	0.887	0.788	0.701	0.625	0.557	0.497	0.444	0.397	0.356	0.319
13	0.879	0.773	0.681	0.601	0.530	0.469	0.415	0.368	0.326	0.290
14	0.870	0.758	0.661	0.577	0.505	0.442	0.388	0.340	0.299	0.263
15	0.861	0.743	0.642	0.555	0.481	0.417	0.362	0.315	0.275	0.239
16	0.853	0.728	0.623	0.534	0.458	0.394	0.339	0.292	0.252	0.218
17	0.844	0.714	0.605	0.513	0.436	0.371	0.317	0.270	0.231	0.198
18	0.836	0.700	0.587	0.494	0.416	0.350	0.296	0.250	0.212	0.180
19	0.828	0.686	0.570	0.475	0.396	0.331	0.277	0.232	0.194	0.164
20	0.820	0.673	0.554	0.456	0.377	0.312	0.258	0.215	0.178	0.149

Periods	Interest rates (r)									
(n)	11%	12%	13%	14%	15%	16%	17%	18%	19%	20%
1	0.901	0.893	0.885	0.877	0.870	0.862	0.855	0.847	0.840	0.833
2	0.812	0.797	0.783	0.769	0.756	0.743	0.731	0.718	0.706	0.694
3	0.731	0.712	0.693	0.675	0.658	0.641	0.624	0.609	0.593	0.579
4	0.659	0.636	0.613	0.592	0.572	0.552	0.534	0.516	0.499	0.482
5	0.593	0.567	0.543	0.519	0.497	0.476	0.456	0.437	0.419	0.402
6	0.535	0.507	0.480	0.456	0.432	0.410	0.390	0.370	0.352	0.335
7	0.482	0.452	0.425	0.400	0.376	0.354	0.333	0.314	0.296	0.279
8	0.434	0.404	0.376	0.351	0.327	0.305	0.285	0.266	0.249	0.233
9	0.391	0.361	0.333	0.308	0.284	0.263	0.243	0.225	0.209	0.194
10	0.352	0.322	0.295	0.270	0.247	0.227	0.208	0.191	0.176	0.162
11	0.317	0.287	0.261	0.237	0.215	0.195	0.178	0.162	0.148	0.135
12	0.286	0.257	0.231	0.208	0.187	0.168	0.152	0.137	0.124	0.112
13	0.258	0.229	0.204	0.182	0.163	0.145	0.130	0.116	0.104	0.093
14	0.232	0.205	0.181	0.160	0.141	0.125	0.111	0.099	0.088	0.078
15	0.209	0.183	0.160	0.140	0.123	0.108	0.095	0.084	0.079	0.065
16	0.188	0.163	0.141	0.123	0.107	0.093	0.081	0.071	0.062	0.054
17	0.170	0.146	0.125	0.108	0.093	0.080	0.069	0.060	0.052	0.045
18	0.153	0.130	0.111	0.095	0.081	0.069	0.059	0.051	0.044	0.038
19	0.138	0.116	0.098	0.083	0.070	0.060	0.051	0.043	0.037	0.031
20	0.124	0.104	0.087	0.073	0.061	0.051	0.043	0.037	0.031	0.026

Cumulative present value of $1 per annum, Receivable or Payable at the end of each year for n years $\frac{1-(1+r)^{-n}}{r}$

Periods	Interest rates (r)									
(n)	1%	2%	3%	4%	5%	6%	7%	8%	9%	10%
1	0.990	0.980	0.971	0.962	0.952	0.943	0.935	0.926	0.917	0.909
2	1.970	1.942	1.913	1.886	1.859	1.833	1.808	1.783	1.759	1.736
3	2.941	2.884	2.829	2.775	2.723	2.673	2.624	2.577	2.531	2.487
4	3.902	3.808	3.717	3.630	3.546	3.465	3.387	3.312	3.240	3.170
5	4.853	4.713	4.580	4.452	4.329	4.212	4.100	3.993	3.890	3.791
6	5.795	5.601	5.417	5.242	5.076	4.917	4.767	4.623	4.486	4.355
7	6.728	6.472	6.230	6.002	5.786	5.582	5.389	5.206	5.033	4.868
8	7.652	7.325	7.020	6.733	6.463	6.210	5.971	5.747	5.535	5.335
9	8.566	8.162	7.786	7.435	7.108	6.802	6.515	6.247	5.995	5.759
10	9.471	8.983	8.530	8.111	7.722	7.360	7.024	6.710	6.418	6.145
11	10.368	9.787	9.253	8.760	8.306	7.887	7.499	7.139	6.805	6.495
12	11.255	10.575	9.954	9.385	8.863	8.384	7.943	7.536	7.161	6.814
13	12.134	11.348	10.635	9.986	9.394	8.853	8.358	7.904	7.487	7.103
14	13.004	12.106	11.296	10.563	9.899	9.295	8.745	8.244	7.786	7.367
15	13.865	12.849	11.938	11.118	10.380	9.712	9.108	8.559	8.061	7.606
16	14.718	13.578	12.561	11.652	10.838	10.106	9.447	8.851	8.313	7.824
17	15.562	14.292	13.166	12.166	11.274	10.477	9.763	9.122	8.544	8.022
18	16.398	14.992	13.754	12.659	11.690	10.828	10.059	9.372	8.756	8.201
19	17.226	15.679	14.324	13.134	12.085	11.158	10.336	9.604	8.950	8.365
20	18.046	16.351	14.878	13.590	12.462	11.470	10.594	9.818	9.129	8.514

Periods	Interest rates (r)									
(n)	11%	12%	13%	14%	15%	16%	17%	18%	19%	20%
1	0.901	0.893	0.885	0.877	0.870	0.862	0.855	0.847	0.840	0.833
2	1.713	1.690	1.668	1.647	1.626	1.605	1.585	1.566	1.547	1.528
3	2.444	2.402	2.361	2.322	2.283	2.246	2.210	2.174	2.140	2.106
4	3.102	3.037	2.974	2.914	2.855	2.798	2.743	2.690	2.639	2.589
5	3.696	3.605	3.517	3.433	3.352	3.274	3.199	3.127	3.058	2.991
6	4.231	4.111	3.998	3.889	3.784	3.685	3.589	3.498	3.410	3.326
7	4.712	4.564	4.423	4.288	4.160	4.039	3.922	3.812	3.706	3.605
8	5.146	4.968	4.799	4.639	4.487	4.344	4.207	4.078	3.954	3.837
9	5.537	5.328	5.132	4.946	4.772	4.607	4.451	4.303	4.163	4.031
10	5.889	5.650	5.426	5.216	5.019	4.833	4.659	4.494	4.339	4.192
11	6.207	5.938	5.687	5.453	5.234	5.029	4.836	4.656	4.486	4.327
12	6.492	6.194	5.918	5.660	5.421	5.197	4.988	7.793	4.611	4.439
13	6.750	6.424	6.122	5.842	5.583	5.342	5.118	4.910	4.715	4.533
14	6.982	6.628	6.302	6.002	5.724	5.468	5.229	5.008	4.802	4.611
15	7.191	6.811	6.462	6.142	5.847	5.575	5.324	5.092	4.876	4.675
16	7.379	6.974	6.604	6.265	5.954	5.668	5.405	5.162	4.938	4.730
17	7.549	7.120	6.729	6.373	6.047	5.749	5.475	5.222	4.990	4.775
18	7.702	7.250	6.840	6.467	6.128	5.818	5.534	5.273	5.033	4.812
19	7.839	7.366	6.938	6.550	6.198	5.877	5.584	5.316	5.070	4.843
20	7.963	7.469	7.025	6.623	6.259	5.929	5.628	5.353	5.101	4.870

Formulae

PROBABILITY

$A \cup B = A$ **or** B. $\qquad A \cap B = A$ **and** B (overlap).

$P(B \mid A)$ = probability of B, **given** A.

Rules of Addition

If A and B are mutually exclusive: $\quad P(A \cup B) = P(A) + P(B)$

If A and B are **not** mutually exclusive: $P(A \cup B) = P(A) + P(B) - P(A \cap B)$

Rules of Multiplication

If A and B are *independent*: $P(A \cap B) = P(A) * P(B)$

If A and B are **not** *independent*: $\quad P(A \cap B) = P(A) * P(B \mid A)$

$E(X) = \sum$ (probability * payoff)

Quadratic Equations

If $aX^2 + bX + c = 0$ is the general quadratic equation, the two solutions (roots) are given by:

$$X = \frac{-b \pm \sqrt{b^2 - 4ac}}{2a}$$

DESCRIPTIVE STATISTICS

Arithmetic Mean

$$\overline{x} = \frac{\sum x}{n} \qquad \overline{x} = \frac{\sum fx}{\sum f} \quad \text{(frequency distribution)}$$

Standard Deviation

$$SD = \sqrt{\frac{\sum (x - \overline{x})^2}{n}} \qquad SD = \sqrt{\frac{\sum fx^2}{\sum f} - \overline{x^2}} \quad \text{(frequency distribution)}$$

INDEX NUMBERS

Price relative = $100 * P_1/P_0 \qquad$ Quantity relative = $100 * Q_1/Q_0$

Price: $\qquad \dfrac{\sum w * \left(\dfrac{P_1}{P_0}\right)}{\sum w} \times 100$

Quantity: $\qquad \dfrac{\sum w * \left(\dfrac{Q_1}{Q_0}\right)}{\sum w} \times 100$

TIME SERIES

Additive Model

$$\text{Series} = \text{Trend} + \text{Seasonal} + \text{Random}$$

Multiplicative Model

$$\text{Series} = \text{Trend} * \text{Seasonal} * \text{Random}$$

LINEAR REGRESSION AND CORRELATION

The linear regression equation of Y on X is given by:

$$Y = a + bX \quad or \quad Y - \bar{Y} = b(X - \bar{X})$$

where

$$b = \frac{\text{Covariance}(XY)}{\text{Variance}(X)} = \frac{n\sum XY - (\sum X)(\sum Y)}{n\sum X^2 - (\sum X)^2}$$

and

$$a = \bar{Y} - b\bar{X}$$

or solve

$$\sum Y = na + b\sum X$$
$$\sum XY = a\sum X + b\sum X^2$$

Coefficient of correlation

$$r = \frac{\text{Covariance}(XY)}{\sqrt{\text{Var}(X).\text{Var}(Y)}} = \frac{n\sum XY - (\sum X)(\sum Y)}{\sqrt{\{n\sum X^2 - (\sum X)^2\}\{n\sum Y^2 - (\sum Y)^2\}}}$$

$$R(\text{rank}) = 1 - \frac{6\sum d^2}{n(n^2 - 1)}$$

FINANCIAL MATHEMATICS

Compound Interest (Values and Sums)

Future Value S, of a sum of X, invested for n periods, compounded at $r\%$ interest

$$S = X[1 + r]^n$$

Annuity

Present value of an annuity of £1 per annum receivable or payable for n years, commencing in one year, discounted at $r\%$ per annum:

$$PV = \frac{1}{r}\left[1 - \frac{1}{[1+r]^n}\right]$$

Perpetuity

Present value of £1 per annum, payable or receivable in perpetuity, commencing in one year, discounted at $r\%$ per annum:

$$PV = \frac{1}{r}$$

LIST OF VERBS USED IN THE QUESTION REQUIREMENTS

A list of the learning objectives and verbs that appear in the syllabus and in the question requirements for each question in this paper.

It is important that you answer the question according to the definition of the verb.

LEARNING OBJECTIVE	VERBS USED	DEFINITION
Level 1 - KNOWLEDGE What you are expected to know.	List	Make a list of
	State	Express, fully or clearly, the details/facts of
	Define	Give the exact meaning of
Level 2 - COMPREHENSION What you are expected to understand.	Describe	Communicate the key features
	Distinguish	Highlight the differences between
	Explain	Make clear or intelligible/State the meaning or purpose of
	Identify	Recognise, establish or select after consideration
	Illustrate	Use an example to describe or explain something
Level 3 - APPLICATION How you are expected to apply your knowledge.	Apply	To put to practical use
	Calculate/compute	Ascertain or reckon mathematically
	Demonstrate	To prove with certainty or to exhibit by practical means
	Prepare	Make or get ready for use
	Reconcile	Make or prove consistent/compatible
	Solve	Find an answer to
	Tabulate	Arrange in a table
Level 4 - ANALYSIS How you are expected to analyse the detail of what you have learned.	Analyse	Examine in detail the structure of
	Categorise	Place into a defined class or division
	Compare and contrast	Show the similarities and/or differences between
	Construct	Build up or compile
	Discuss	Examine in detail by argument
	Interpret	Translate into intelligible or familiar terms
	Prioritise	Place in order of priority or sequence for action
	Produce	Create or bring into existence
Level 5 - EVALUATION How you are expected to use your learning to evaluate, make decisions or recommendations.	Advise	Counsel, inform or notify
	Evaluate	Appraise or assess the value of
	Recommend	Propose a course of action

Performance Pillar

Operational Level Paper

P1 – Performance Operations

Specimen Paper

Wednesday Morning Session

The Examiner's Answers – Specimen Paper

P1 - Performance Operations

SECTION A

Answer to Question One

1.1   **C**

Contribution after reduction in variable cost = $120,000
Contribution following volume increase = $132,000
Increase in contribution = increase in profit = $32,000
Original profit was $64,000 therefore increase = 50%

1.2   **B**

Net present value = $50,000
Present value of cash in flows = $500,000
Sensitivity = 50,000/500,000 = 10%

1.3   EV of variable cost = $(70 *0·3)+(60*0·5)+(40*0·2) = $59
Therefore the expected contribution is $61 per member

EV of number of members = (20,000*0.1)+ (30,000*0·6)+ (40,000*0·3)=32,000

Expected total contribution = $61 * 32,000 = $1,952,000

Expected profit = $1,952,000 – 1,100,000 = **$852,000**

1.4   (i)   If VC = $40 then the contribution per member will be $80
Total contribution = 40,000 * $80 = $3,200,000
Profit = $2,100,000

(ii)   Joint probability of 20,000 members and $40 variable cost = 0.1 * 0.2 = 0.02

1.5   Selling price= ($50 x (annuity factor t = 4, r = 11)+ ($1,000 x (disc factor t = 4, r =11)

From tables:

Selling price = $(50 x 3·102) + (1,000 x 0·659) = 155·1 + 659 = $814·10

GF should sell the bond for $814·10

1.6

	$000
Inventory used in production	331
Adjustment for increase in inventory	2
	333
Add reduction in trade payables	7
Forecast cash required	340

1.7 The outstanding balance of trade payables in 2008 is $40,000. This is calculated as shown below:

$$\frac{x}{324,444} \times 365 = 45$$

$$x = 45 \times \frac{324,444}{365}$$

$$x = 40,000$$

2009 forecast average payment period:

$$x = \frac{40,000}{356,900} \times 365$$

$$x = 40 \cdot 91$$

Days outstanding = 41 days

SECTION B

Answer to Question Two

Requirement (a)

(i)

		£
UK non-discount	60%*£2·1m*30/365	103,561
UK discount	40%*£2·1m*10/365	23,014
Overseas	80%*£0·9m*60/365	118,356
Total debtors		**244,931**

Debtors days = £244,931 * 365/£3m = **29·8 days**

(ii)

		£
UK non factored	15%*£2·1m*30/365	25,890
Overseas	80%*£0·9mm*60/365	118,356
Total debtors		**144,246**

Debtors days = £144,246 * 365/£3m = **17·5 days**

Requirement (b)

Flexibility - it offers a flexible source of finance, as sales increases with a corresponding demand for finance, so finance from this source increases.

Security - it allows the firm to pledge other assets as security for the finance.

Last resort – it may be the most cost effective lender to a firm that has no assets to offer as security.

Administration – it relieves management of the responsibility for the sales ledger and the factor can probably perform credit checking better than the firm.

Risk of future changes - Management must balance the disruption from cutting back its administrative function with the financial and other advantages of factoring. However, the financial advantage may change and it may be costly to re-establish a sales ledger function.

Reputation – factoring is associated in many people's mind with financial difficulties or at best with small businesses, which may have an impact on the image of the business in the eyes of its suppliers.

Customer relationship - The use of factoring may create a barrier between the firm and its customers.

Requirement (c)

EV with repairs = £51,670
Earnings without repairs = £37,500

Therefore do the repairs.

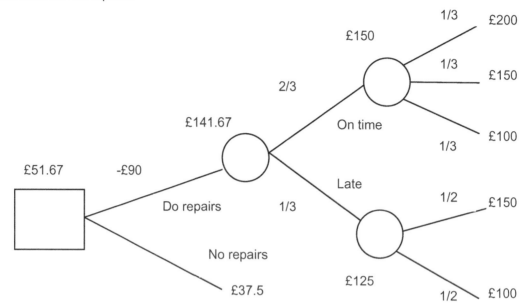

Requirement (d)

	Trend values	Seasonal adjustment	Forecast
2009 Q2	134·23 + (7·945 * 7)	0·75	142
2009 Q2	134·23 + (7·945 * 8)	1·00	198
2009 Q2	134.23 + (7·945 * 9)	1·50	309

Requirement (e)

When preparing the whole company's budget it is important to have a realistic forecast of what is likely to happen, particularly for cash, purchases, labour and capital budgets. However, for a budget to be effective for motivation, targets must be set that are challenging. It is also argued that for control purposes the budget must be a realistic benchmark against which actual performance can be compared, that is, it must be close to a forecast.

The difficulty is that both of these objectives are valid and beneficial. Thus the issue becomes whether one budget can do both tasks or whether companies need to choose which task the budget will be used for.

Requirement (f)

Environmental internal failure costs are costs that are incurred after hazardous materials, waste and / or contaminants have been produced. The costs are incurred in an attempt to comply with expected or enforced standards. Examples include treating and disposing of toxic materials and recycling scrap.

Environmental external failure costs are the most significant costs: they are incurred after the hazardous materials have been introduced into the environment. Examples of costs that an organisation has to pay include decontaminating land and clearing a river after leakage. These costs can give rise to adverse publicity. Some external failure costs may be caused by the organisation but 'paid' by society.

SECTION C

Answer to Question Three

Requirement (a)

Workings £000

Year	0	1	2	3	4	5	6
Money Sales		399.600	583.200	642.453	700.652	697.931	
Money costs		318.000	393.260	452.586	492.366	535.290	
Tax profit		81.600	189.940	189.867	208.286	162.641	
Tax		24.480	56.982	56.960	62.486	48.792	
tax offset			24.480	56.982	56.960	62.486	48.792
Capital value		500	375	281.25	210.9375	158.2031	
Allowance		125	93.75	70.3125	52.73438	108.2031	
C/f		375	281.25	210.9375	158.2031		
Tax		37.5	28.125	21.09375	15.82031	32.46094	
offset			37.5	28.125	21.09375	15.82031	32.46094

Cash flows

	0	1	2	3	4	5	6
Investment	-500					50	
Sales-costs		81.600	189.940	189.867	208.286	162.641	
Tax			-24.480	-56.982	-56.960	-62.486	-48.792
Tax allow			37.5	28.125	21.09375	15.82031	32.46094
net cash flow	-500	81.6	202.96	161.01	172.4194	165.9752	-16.3312
Discount factor	1.00	0.893	0.797	0.712	0.636	0.567	0.507
Present Value	-500	72.87	161.76	114.64	109.66	94.11	-8.28

Net present value = £44,760

	1	2	3	4	5
Sales Revenue	399.600	583.200	642.453	700.652	697.931
Operating Costs	318.000	393.260	452.586	492.366	535.290
Depreciation	90.00	90.00	90.00	90.00	90.00
Profit	(8.40)	99.94	99.867	118.286	72.641

Total profit = £382,334.

Average profit = £382,334/5 = £76,467
Average investment = (500,000+50,000)/2 = £275,000
Accounting Rate of Return = £76,467 /£275,000 = 0.278
Accounting Rate of Return = 28%

To: Board of Directors
From: Management Accountant
Date: July 2009
Subject: Investment projects

From a financial perspective based on the information given and that the projects are mutually exclusive the company should invest in Project 2. Investment decisions should be based on Net Present Values as this methodology is consistent with maximising company wealth. However, the company will also need to consider non-financial factors that could affect the decision.

Examples include:

- Consistency with the company's strategy
- Impact on other areas of the business
- Technical compatibility and obsolescence

Accounting rate of return is a simple method of investment appraisal but has many disadvantages. In particular it is based on accounting profit rather than cash flow. Accounting profit is a subjective and dependant on the choice of accounting methods used. Accounting rate of return also ignores the time value of money.

The Net Present Value method is preferable as it ensures that shareholders wealth is maximised and recognises that cash received in the future is less valuable than cash received today. Net present value does suffer from a number of disadvantages as follows:-

- The speed of the repayment of the original investment is not highlighted
- Non-financial managers may have difficulty in understanding the concept
- Determination of the correct discount rate can be difficult

Requirement (b)

Annual repayments   = £250,000/(10 year 8% annuity factor)
                       = £250,000/6·71
                       = £37,258

There are just over years remaining therefore the company will be about to make a payment and then will have four more annual payments to make. The value of these five payments is:

£37,258 + (37,258 * 3·312) = **£160,656**

Answer to Question Four

Requirement (a)

Surgical procedure – November reconciliation

	$	$	$
Original budget (20 procedures)			
Team			60,000
Variable overheads			39,000
Fixed overheads			48,000
Total cost			147,000
Flexed budget (22 procedures)			
Additional variable costs			9,900
Expected total cost of 22 procedures			**156,900**
Variances	F	A	
Team fee rate (47 x 1,500) – 75,400		4,900	
Team efficiency ((22 x 2) – 47) x 1,500		4,500	
Variable overhead expenditure (47 x 975) – 48,000		2,175	
Variable overhead efficiency ((22 x 2) – 47) x 975		2,925	
Fixed overhead expenditure (48,000 – 46,000)	2,000	......	
	2,000	14,500	12,500
Actual cost			**169,400**

Requirement (b)

Revised standard cost = $1,625 per hour
Original standard cost = $1,500 per hour

Original total team cost for 22 procedures (22 * 2 * $1,500)	66,000	
Actual cost	75,400	
Total variance	**9,400**	adverse
Planning variance (22 * 2 * (1,500 – 1,625))	5,500	adverse
Operational team rate variance (75,400 – (47*1,625))	975	favourable
Operational team efficiency variance (3 * 1,625)	4,875	adverse
	9,400	

Requirement (c)

Budgets are projected cost (and/or revenue) aggregates which quantify expectations about future performance. They are used as comparators against which current performance can be measured and as "authority to spend" within which expenditure will be allowed. A budget is an effective planning and control tool for service based organisation.

Standards measure performance at a lower, operational, level. Standard costing is extensively used in manufacturing industries but can equally be applied to service based organisations e.g. in the insurance industry, a standard may be the time to process an insurance claim or key in a document.

Standard costing and budgetary control can be used effectively in both manufacturing and service organisation. They should however be used in combination because together they are more powerful and embrace the organisation more completely than either can do in isolation. It makes little sense to control, or plan, at operational level, without considering impacts at higher levels. Similarly, overall budgets cannot be realistically set without looking at the feasibility of setting operational standards.

Index

A

Absorption costing.....13 – 18
    absorption rates.....14
    advantages.....17
    limitations.....17, 123
    over/under absorption.....16
    profit statement.....20
    modern problems.....123
Accounting rate of return (ARR).....497
Accounts payable
    age analysis.....756
    management.....754
    ratio.....635
    source of funds.....773
Accounts receivable
    age analysis.....741
    assessing creditworthiness.....735
    balancing act.....732
    collecting overdue debts.....738
    cost of financing receivables.....742
    early settlement discounts.....743
    factoring.....746
    invoice discounting.....737
    motivating staff.....739
    payment terms.....733
    ratio.....634
    setting credit limits.....736
Acid test ratio.....627
Activity based budgeting (ABB).....357
Activity based costing (ABC).....122 – 134
    benefits/problems.....132
    calculations.....128
    comparison to absorption.....125
    cost driver.....124
    cost pool.....124
    environmental costs.....142
    identifying activities.....126
    identifying drivers.....127
    implications.....133
    long term decision making.....577
    variances.....195
    when relevant.....130
Additive model.....394
Advanced manufacturing technology (AMT).....62
Advanced variances.....271
Age analysis of outstanding debts.....741
Annual equivalent cost.....568
Annuities.....500
Appraisal costs.....69, 140
Assessing creditworthiness.....735
Avoidable costs.....560

B

Backflush accounting.....79 – 84
    advantages/disadvantages.....82
    comparison with traditional systems.....80
    trigger points.....83
    variants.....83
Balancing allowance / charge.....556
Bank loans.....775
Bank overdrafts.....774
Behavioural aspects of budgeting.....336
Benchmarking
    benefits/problems.....261
    definitions.....256, 259
    process.....259
    types.....257
Bill of exchange.....780, 789
Bills of materials (BOM).....76
Break even analysis.....28
Budgeting.....333 – 360
    activity based.....357
    behavioural aspects.....336
    flexible budgets.....346
    forecasts.....382
    functional budgets.....338
    incremental.....351
    master budget.....338
    principal budget factor.....342
    purposes.....334
    sensitivity analysis.....343
    zero based.....353
Buffer stock.....667, 674

C

Calculability.....253
Capital asset replacement decisions.....568
Capital investment appraisal.....479
Capital investment process.....507
Capital rationing.....572
Cash control
    budget..... 694
    forecasts.....694
    from a statement of financial position....700
    interpretation of budgets.....704
    management.....693, 707
    using spreadsheets.....705
Centralised purchasing.....676
Certificate of Deposit (CD).....788
Changing discount rates.....505
Coefficient of variation.....428
Collecting overdue debts.....738
Commercial paper.....795

Index

Composite variances.....250
Compound interest.....477
Computer aided design (CAD).....66
Computer aided manufacturing (CAM).....66
Computer integrated manufacturing (CIM).....66
Constraints on throughput.....104
Consumption preferences.....477
Contribution sales ratio.....27
Controllability of variances.....250
Corporate bonds.....795
Corporation tax.....554
Cost behavior.....11
Cost driver.....124
Cost pool.....124
Costing.....10
Cost of capital.....479
Cost of financing receivables.....742
Cost reduction.....63, 65
Cost-volume-profit (CVP) analysis.....27
Coupon rate.....793
Current ratio.....626
Cyclical factors.....390,391

D

Decentralised purchasing.....676
Decision trees.....439
Deficits.....707
Deflation.....566
Depletion of natural resources.....136
Deposit accounts.....786
Diagnostic related groups (DRG).....254
Discounted payback.....495
Discounting.....478
   annuities.....500
   changing rates.....505
   non-annual periods.....506
   perpetuities.....501
Documentary credits.....778

E

Early settlement discounts.....743
Economic order quantity (EOQ).....668 - 672
   assumptions.....670
   calculations.....670
   criticisms.....672
   explained.....668
   holding costs.....668
   order costs.....669
   quantity discounts.....671
Effective annual interest yield.....786
Efficient cash management....693

Efficiency.....253
Electronic data interchange (EDI).....66
Enterprise resource planning (ERP).....79
Environmental costing.....134 – 145
   advantages/disadvantages.....144
   classification of costs.....140
   impact on financial statements.....137
   input/output analysis.....145
   link to ABC.....142
Environmental management.....134
Environmental management accounting
   (EMA).....134
   link to TQM.....139
Environmental appraisal costs.....140
Environmental prevention costs.....140
Equivalent annual cost.....568
Expected idle time.....183
Expected values.....420
   advantages/disadvantages.....429
Export factoring.....781
Export risks.....777
External failure costs.....69, 141

F

Factoring.....746, 781
Financing exports.....777
Finished goods holding period.....633
Fixed budget.....346
Fixed cost.....11
Fixed overhead variances
   calculations.....189
   causes.....249
   expenditure.....190
   marginal costing.....192
   total.....189
   volume.....191
Flexed budget.....348
Flexible budgets.....346
Flexible manufacturing system (FMS).....66
Forecasting.....381
   in budgets.....382
   high low method.....383
   with inflation.....388
   regression analysis.....384
   time series analysis.....389
Forfaiting.....781
Functional budgets.....338

G

General inflation....563
Government bonds.....792

Index

H

Hard capital rationing.....572
High low method.....383
Histograms.....421

I

Identifying cost drivers.....127
Idle time variances.....181
    definition.....182
    expected idle time.....183
    explanation.....181
    and variable overheads.....188
Imperfect information.....437
Importance of environmental management.....134
Incremental budgeting.....351
Incremental costs.....550
Indivisible projects.....575
Inflation
    in forecasting.....388
    in project appraisal.....559 – 566
Input/output analysis.....145
Interdependence of variances.....247
Internal failure costs.....69, 141
Internal rate of return (IRR).....484
    annuities/perpetuities.....487
    basic principles.....485
    benefits/problems.....487
    using a graph.....486
    versus NPV.....491
Interpretation of variances.....247
Inventories
    buffer stock.....674
    control systems.....672
    costs.....665
    EOQ.....668 - 672
    file.....77
    holding period ratio.....632
    management.....664
    reorder levels.....673
    turnover.....634
    warning levels.....675
Investigating variances.....245
Investment appraisal.....475
Investment criteria.....783
Invoice discounting.....750

J

Joint probabilities.....439
Just in time (JIT).....71 – 74
    benefits/problems.....74
    prerequisites.....73

L

Labour budget.....340
Labour variances
    calculations.....178 – 184
    causes.....248
    CIMA definitions.....179
    efficiency.....180
    idle time.....185
    mix and yield.....280
    rate.....179
    total.....178
Lead time.....667
Limiting factor analysis.....101
Liquidity ratios.....626
Lowest common multiple method.....569

M

Managing existing customers.....737
Manufacturing resources planning (MRP II).....77
Margin of safety.....28
Marginal costing.....18 – 19
    limitations.....19
    modern problems.....124
    profit statement.....21
Master budget.....338
Master production schedule (MPS).....76
Materials budget.....340
Material requirements planning (MRP).....75 – 77
Materials variances
    calculations.....174 – 177
    causes.....247
    CIMA definitions.....175
    mix and yield.....272
    price.....176
    total.....174
    usage.....176
Maximax.....433
Maximin.....435
Maximising throughput.....99
McDonaldization.....253
Methods of payment.....734
Minimax regret.....436
Mix and yield variances.....272

Index

Modern manufacturing environment.....60
    background.....61
    characteristics.....62
    impact on production costs.....122
    standard costing.....250
Money market deposits.....786
Monte Carlo simulation.....544
Motivating debt collection staff.....739
Moving average.....392
Multiplicative model.....397

N

Natural resources.....136
Negotiable instruments.....787
Net present value.....480, 542 – 576
    assumptions.....481
    basic principles.....480
    benefits/problems.....483
    inflation.....559
    meaning.....480
    pro-forma.....559
    sensitivity analysis.....542
    standard deviation.....544
    taxation.....554
    versus IRR.....491
    working capital.....557
Nominal method.....561
Non-annual discounting.....506
Non-relevant costs.....548
Notional costs.....550

O

Operating statement.....192
Operational variances.....287
Opportunity cost.....547, 549, 552
Optimised production technology (OPT).....66
Optimum replacement cycle.....570
Overdrafts.....774
Overhead allocation.....15
Overhead apportionment.....15
Overhead budget.....340
Overtrading.....625

P

Payables (see accounts payable)
Payback period.....493
Payment terms.....733
Pay off tables.....430
Perfect information.....437
Performance measures.....105, 259

Periodic review system.....673
Perpetuities.....501
Planned receipts and payments.....695
Planning and operational variances.....287
    benefits/problems.....292
    causes.....291
Post completion audit.....509
Predetermined absorption rates.....16
Predictability.....254
Prevention costs.....69, 140
Principal budget factor.....342
Probabilities.....420
Probability distribution.....544
Problems with traditional costing.....123
Production budget.....339
Profitability index.....573
Profit reconciliation.....22
Profit statements.....20
Project abandonment.....511
Purposes of budgeting.....334
Purpose of costing.....10

Q

Qualitative factors in decision making.....578
Quality related costs.....69
Quantity discounts.....671
Quick ratio.....627

R

Raw material inventory holding period.....632
Real rate of return.....561
Reasons for holding cash.....692
Receivables (see accounts receivable)
Reconciling profits.....22
Redemption value.....793
Redemption yield.....794
Regression analysis.....384
Relevant cash flows.....547
Reorder levels.....673
Replacement decisions.....568 – 572
Reporting by exception.....246
Risk and uncertainty.....419
Risk attitudes (averse, neutral, seeker).....422

S

Sales budget.....339
Sales variances
    calculations.....172 – 173
    causes.....249
    mix and quantity.....284 – 287

Index

price variance.....172
volume variance.....172 – 173
Seasonal variation.....391, 393
Semi-variable cost.....12
Sensitivity analysis
benefits/problems.....546
budgeting.....343
decision making.....444
NPV.....542
spreadsheets.....706
Setting credit limits.....736
Short dated government bond.....792
Short-term borrowing.....774
Short-term investments.....783
Soft capital rationing.....572
Specific inflation.....563
Spreadsheets.....705
Standard costing.....170
explained.....170 – 171
in modern environments.....250
Standard deviation
in decision making.....426
NPV.....544
Sunk cost.....547
Super variable costing.....98
Supply chain management (SCM).....66
Surplus cash.....708

T

Taxation.....554
Tax depreciation.....556
Theory of constraints.....104
Throughput accounting.....95 – 107
accounting measures.....105
criticisms.....106
decision making.....100
inventory valuation.....98
investment.....97
operating expenses.....97
origins.....97
profit reporting.....98
throughput.....96
Time series analysis.....389
additive model.....394
advantages/disadvantages.....399
multiplicative model.....397
Time value of money.....476
Total quality management (TQM).....67
and standard costing.....68
Trade payables (see accounts payable)
Trade receivables (see accounts receivable)

Treasury Bill.....790
Trend.....391
Trigger points.....83
Two way data tables.....430

U

Uncertainty.....419
Utility theory.....423

V

Value analysis.....65
Value of information.....438
Variable cost.....12
Variable overhead variances
causes.....249
CIMA definitions.....186
expenditure.....186
efficiency.....186
idle time.....188
total.....185
Variance investigation.....244
Variances.....169
ABC.....195
advanced.....271
calculations 169 – 198
causes.....247 – 249
discussion elements.....243 – 263
fixed overhead variances.....189
groups.....170
idle time variances.....181
interdependence.....249
interpretation.....247
investigation.....244
labour variances.....178
materials variances.....174
mix and quantity.....284
mix and yield.....272
operating statement.....196
planning and operating.....287
reporting.....193
sales variances.....172
standard costing.....170
variable overhead variances.....185
working backwards.....197
Variants of backflush accounting.....83
Verb hierarchy.....1

Index

W

Waste.....72
WIP holding period.....633
Working capital
    aggressive.....624
    conservative.....624
    cycle.....636
    elements.....620
    in project appraisal.....557
    investment levels.....638
    moderate.....624
    overtrading.....625
    ratios.....626
    trade-off.....621

Y

Yield variance.....276, 280

Z

Zero based budgeting.....353